BRAZIL AND BEYOND

LONG DISTANCE VOYAGING WITH
ANNIE HILL

Thomas Reed Publications
United Kingdom

St. Michaels, MD

Published 2000 in the United States by Tiller Publishing, P.O. Box 447, St. Michaels, MD, USA.

Published 2000 in the United Kingdom by Thomas Reed Publications (a division of The ABR Company, Ltd.)

ISBN 1-888671-21-1 (USA)
USBN 0-901281-86-7 (UK)

Watercolor map of *Badger's* voyage © 1998 Janette Watson.

Photographs by Annie and Pete Hill.

Sketch charts by Pete Hill, reproduced from *Cruising Notes on the South Atlantic Coast of South America* and *Supplement to Falkland Islands Shores*, both published by the Royal Cruising Club Pilotage Foundation. All soundings are in metres.

Cover design by Waterline.

Graphic production by Words & Pictures, Inc.

Printed in the USA by Victor Graphics, 1211 Bernard Drive, Baltimore, MD 21223

Questions regarding the contents of this book should be addressed to:

Tiller Publishing
P.O. Box 447
St. Michaels, MD 21663 USA
410-745-3750 • 410-745-9743 fax

Thomas Reed Publications
The Barn, Ford Farm, Bradford Leigh
Bradford-on-Avon, Wiltshire BA15 2RP, UK
01225 868821 • 01225 868831 fax

To the people of the
Falkland Islands
who only
Desire the Right
to live as they choose.

Jarette Watson

Chapter One

We were about twelve hours out when my fuzzy brain suddenly buzzed: `My God! This is it, mate. We've set off on our voyage towards the Falkland Islands.' As it sunk in, I lay there, rather numb, wondering how on earth I was going to cope with it. `Well, we've got to get to Portugal first,' I told myself, `Let's get that out of the way and then worry about what's going to happen when it arrives.' Sound advice, which I often give to myself and almost as often ignore.

We have sailed south from Britain enough times now to take it in many ways for granted, yet the more I sail, the more superstitious I become, a good thing, because I feel that underrating what lies ahead is tempting Fate. When people said to us, `I hear that you're off to South America, then,' I always found myself having to placate the gods: `That's the plan,' I would admit and add, `but we've got to get out of the Channel first!' I would rather people feel that I was falsely modest than say, `Oh yes, it'll be a holiday at first: a piece of cake to Portugal and the Canaries.' When first you sail, a guardian angel stands by you, extricating you from situations that, with experience, you would never have got into. Or should never. After a while he leaves you, to look after some other tyro and there you are, all on your own. Once you really get some experience and self-confidence, the gods demand your respect and any complacency or arrogance will soon get its just rewards. Until `They' can predict the weather to a hundred percent accuracy, together with tides, currents and the rest of the natural world, we will be forced to be humble whenever we set out to sea. And a good thing, too.

We had left on a good forecast, in spite of the fact that I was laid up with a cold severe enough almost to be classified as 'flu. On the other hand, easterly winds are not a common phenomenon in England in the month of September and I was at least capable of keeping watch so we left while we could. In fact the wind soon shifted, but as it stayed between north and north-west, we could still lay our course without difficulty.

As it happened, our passage down to Portugal was largely uneventful, although at one time we altered course for Brest, the weatherman having warned of a hurricane in the Azores which was heading for sea area Finisterre. It seemed prudent to try to avoid it and, of course, it then headed up north. Had we chosen to continue on our way, it would undoubtedly have come straight for us. As I mentioned, I am superstitious. Weather forecasts are a mixed blessing. I suppose that we lost about twelve hours due to that one and we actually felt a sense of relief once we could no longer pick them up.

We then had a mixed bag of winds, but eventually found the `Portuguese Trades' which blew to such good effect that we averaged six knots for the last two days down to Cape São Vincent. It was rather rough going for a while, with a nasty cross swell that set the contents of the lockers a-rattling and me to hunting round with a torch, trying to track down and eliminate the more annoying ones.

Cape São Vincent looks as a cape ought to look, and Browning's words ran through my mind as we romped past:

Nobly, nobly Cape Saint Vincent to the North-west died away:

Another ten miles and we were in the lee of the land. The wind shut off and the scent of the Algarve, heat and pine, was heavy in our noses. The breeze rose and fell, backed and shifted, and we made our way along gently, enjoying the feel of the sunshine and the sights ashore. In the small hours of the morning, we arrived at the entrance to Faro, just as the wind died. The sea was calm and gentle, and the tides were at neaps, so we reckoned that whether it was flooding or ebbing, we could have a try. With a spring ebb and an onshore swell, this entrance can be very frightening, as I know from personal experience.

We dropped the mainsail and, using its halliards, hauled our trusty Seagull out of the lazarette, secured it to its bracket and then fitted it on to the slide at the stern. A tug on the starter cord and it roared into life, shattering the stillness of the night, before settling down to its quieter, purposeful, working rhythm as it pushed us on towards the entrance. The tide was ebbing, we discovered, but still young and we had enough power to make against it, so that soon we were through and into the widening waters behind the island of Culatra. Turning towards Faro, we sought safe anchorage for the night and found water just out of the channel, where we dropped the hook. Pete put up the riding light, while I had a quick tidy-up below and then we turned in. I lay for a while, savouring the perfect peace and tranquillity after ten days at sea. There was not a sound. Not even a fishing-boat engine broke the silence but occasionally the call of a curlew rippled through the night, enhancing the restfulness of our secure berth.

The alarm dragged us back to life; we wanted to take the tide up to Faro. Once on deck, our previous night's estimate of the time of high water seemed to be fairly accurate and in a flat calm, we got underway at once, the Seagull pushing us busily along. The sun came up into a peerless sky, Pete made breakfast and we ate in the cockpit, removing first jacket and then sweater as the sun made his presence felt.

After anchoring, we got together bags and a shopping list, our passports and the ship's papers. Then we dug out some *escudos* from our last visit in Portuguese waters and rowed ashore. The pantiles and stucco, the cobbled streets, the differences between here and anywhere else on earth all struck me.

`How much more interesting a town like Faro is, then most English towns,' I said, `I suppose it's because so much of it is original — just grown up. It's not been really developed yet.'

We talked of the great joys of travelling: the simple pleasure of just experiencing the variety. Of course, town centres all over the world are becoming depressingly homogeneous, but here the traffic-free streets, so carefully paved in white and black stones, laid in symmetrical patterns, take one's eyes from the plate glass and concrete of the generally ugly modern buildings.

We walked around the harbour, savouring the park to the right, the workmen planting trees along the new harbour wall, the sight of the brightly painted boats and the warm sunshine. We visited the Port Captain and the Customs, filling in forms, embarrassed by our almost total lack of Portuguese, but hoping that our attempts at their language at least showed willing. In spite of the large number of yachts that visit Portugal and the fact that the country is a member of the EC, the entry procedure is still cumbersome and complicated. We reflected how often it is that although dictatorships may lose their dictators, the system that allowed for complete control of a population's movements seems to be much harder to remove.

Paperwork completed, we went and found a `magic money machine' and sauntered off, buying bread at the padaria before making our way to the market.

I love markets, probably because I love food, but I also find them pleasing to the eye, with their still-lifes of fruit and vegetables and with the activity of the people walking around and making their purchases. Those who work at the stalls always seem to be more lively than their equivalents in shops and I enjoy seeing the little old ladies, usually so demure and anonymous, suddenly come into their own as they dispute the quality or weight of something that they are hoping to buy.

Pete and I did our usual tour comparing prices, and then selected from the cheapest stalls those items that we wanted. We were pleased with our tomatoes: much cheaper than on several other stalls, but nearly as good; the lady had chosen them for us with care. We were less pleased with the peaches to whose temptation we had succumbed. They were rather dry and flavourless and I recalled, too late, buying disappointing peaches on the Algarve during an earlier visit.

From the market, we went to a supermarket, buying in some litres of cheap plonk, happy to be able to afford wine again. I needed to make one or two telephone calls, but we were feeling hungry, so we bought some rolls and choriço and made our way back to the park near the harbour, where we enjoyed bread and sausage, washed down with white wine from glasses that we had, with great foresight, brought from *Badger*. This seemed to amuse some of the passers-by and one gentleman indicated to us that the bottle was in the sun and should be moved, which I promptly did.

The telephone calls were important, so I resisted the temptation to help Pete finish the litre of wine and left him sitting abstemiously in the sun, while I went back to the Post Office.

`Fala inglês?' I asked, expecting an affirmative in this tourist oriented town.

`Não' came the reply and the assistant turned away leaving me, mouth ajar, thinking `Oh no!' I had to reverse the charges and so it was essential to make her understand. After several minutes, I managed to attract her attention.

`Quero telefoner al Estados Unidos - call collect,' I said, desperately.

`Ah! call collect! Sim! Que es o número?' That was the easy bit. I then had to get through and the line was engaged. I also wanted to contact my brother in England, but only got the answerphone. Fortunately, the telephones were on a meter and I realized that it was an answering machine and put the receiver back in its cradle before the meter started. After a quarter of an hour, I gave the lady the USA number and we tried again. Engaged. Brother Mike. Answerphone. A quarter of an hour later, we tried again. And again. Eventually, I successfully made both calls and returned to Pete, waiting patiently, half asleep, in the park and contemplating the falling tide. So often people suggest that we telephone them while we are cruising, but they have no idea of what is involved.

We rowed back to *Badger* and eventually concluded that conditions were too crowded for sailing out, so we gave the Seagull another short run. With a fair wind and a fair tide, we had a delightful sail down the river and then on to the anchorage, where we hoped to find our friends, Joni and Frank, the reason that we were visiting Culatra. At first we could see no sign of them, but found them at last, in the lagoon, in a tiny *Tramontana*-sized pool, which allowed them to float even at low water. It was good to see them again and the next day we moved together to another pool through whose tricky entrance they led us so that we could anchor side by side.

We spent several days with them, catching up on news, discussing our plans, the state of the world and the price of food, as cruising people always do when they get together. We could not stay long, time was short: a combination of circumstances had already made us well behind our original schedule and our plan was to get to the Canaries, we hoped in short order, stay a few days and then go directly to Montevideo. There is always a sadness in departure, it is part of the price we pay for our way of life. We meet so many people who quickly become good friends, friends with whom we keep in touch by letter, year after year, looking forward eagerly to our infrequent reunions, but suffering real pain on separation, after the all too brief time we spend together.

Leaving on this occasion was worse than most. Frank and Joni have made their home on the Algarve for several years now and we have been able to visit them fairly regularly on our way south from the UK and in and out of the Mediterranean. This time, though we knew that it would probably be several years before we saw them again and our regrets were increased by the knowledge that Joni would have given her right arm to get the anchor and come with us. Sadly Frank, no longer young, suffers from ill-health and is more or less an invalid. His sailing days are over. But Joni is like a pinioned petrel: her spirit responds to the music of the wind and the waves, her heart yearns to rove the oceans and know the sea in all its moods. Instead she waits in Portugal, seeing yachts come and go, cruising vicariously from letters received, her adventurous soul pining, her loyalty preventing her from uttering a word of complaint. I know that when we leave, she will stand and watch us until our sails disappear over the horizon.

Entering and leaving Culatra, most people use the dredged channel over the bar, going out through a narrow passage between two breakwaters. I hate bars and ever since leaving here on one occasion, with a brisk onshore wind and a spring ebb, I hate this bar in particular. We were completely swept. No harm was done, except to my nerves, which jangle with apprehension each time we come to leave the place. Anchored as we were, at `Seldom Seen', we were several miles from this entrance, but close to another passage that the local fishermen use, through the sand banks and over a far less daunting bar. With only four and a half feet of draught, we can often consider such an alternative and Pete felt that he would like to give it a try. At low water, from up the mast, he examined the route and, after a final lunch with our friends, we got our anchor and sailed out through the shallows. Although at one point we only had six inches under the keel, we found the route fairly straight forward and within half an hour, had cleared the bar and close hauled the sails on a southerly course towards the Canary Islands.

All offshore passages are the same. All offshore passages are totally different. The sameness is in the ordered routine we follow, the repetition of watches, of turning in and rising again, three hours later. Dinner follows breakfast and we each have our own pattern that we follow on watch. A look around every ten minutes or so, a certain time at which we brew up or eat our supper. Sails need to be reefed or reefs shaken out, the self-steering may need adjustment, the white light is switched on at dark and off as dawn comes. Occasionally it is changed for the tri-colour lantern, when a ship hoves into view. A morning sight is taken, one at noon and another later on.

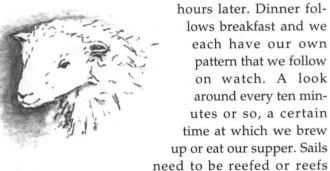

The differences are endless. Different weather, different lengths of day and night. The temperature, the swell, the wildlife, the clarity of the air, the colour of the sea all vary, not only from one passage to another, one season to another, but from day to day. Looking back at an old log book, it is interesting to compare what conditions were like the last time you were in the area. It is interesting too, to note how often memory plays you false: a passage remembered with affection as a `good' one, on re-reading the log turns out to have been slow, be-devilled by calms or containing a two-day gale that has mysteriously been expunged from one's conscious memory.

Normally, sailing in October from the Algarve to the Canaries, we would expect a gentle start until we leave the lee of Portugal, followed by a brisk passage on the back of the `Portuguese Trades'. Although not a pukka Trade Wind, anyone who has ever tried to sail directly from Gibraltar to the UK will tell you that, in

their season, they are completely dependable. These winds also explain the oft-repeated assertion that once a would-be, transatlantic voyager has reached the Canaries, he is committed. It is easier to go on than it is to turn back.

On this passage, though, they let us down. We were wanting to press on, the Falkland Islands were many thousands of miles distant and already, their spring was well under way. That malicious little spirit who visits yachtsmen realized this and arranged for head winds, near calms, and squalls to hinder us as far as possible. We sailed one hundred and fifty miles further than the Great Circle course, which was only just over seven hundred miles!

We had a gentle start, a light, fair breeze and sunshine. Then the wind died almost to a calm and we sighted two yachts, apparently under power. We guessed that they were heading towards Madeira and saw their masthead lanterns in the gloaming. After dark, their lights suddenly vanished. Had they switched them off? I wondered. Odd, with another vessel in sight.

The next morning brought a breeze from east by north and for a while, we pottered along happily, but it gradually backed, cloud came in and the wind, little by little, increased. Twenty-four hours later, we were taking in reefs with the wind right on the nose. The small hours of the morning saw a list of complaints in the log: the line from the towing generator had got caught around the servo paddle, one of the tiller lines had worked slack and caught in the vane mechanism, causing it to jam and make *Badger* wander off course. We beat, we tacked, our progress was slow, but at least the sun came out.

Saturday, made more bearable anyway by a pre-prandial snorter and wine with dinner, brought an improvement, as the wind freed us, but soon it died away to nothing. By next morning, we were being hit by nasty little squalls out of the south-west and the sails were going up and down like pantomime scenery. A lumpy sea built up; *Badger*, pile-driving, made `poor progress', the log notes, but by midnight we were back to full sail, under a cloudless sky. We even laid the course for a couple of hours! And so it continued: `horribly rough and uncomfortable' followed by `Wind WNW 1. Sunny, but no progress'.

As the days went by, we came to realize that we were going to make a slow passage of it to the Canaries. Perhaps foolishly, I looked at Tilman's accounts of the voyages that he had made from the Canary Isles to Montevideo and Punta Arenas, similar to our proposed route to the Falkland Islands, and was aghast at how long both passages had taken. I said to Pete that we would be spending about eighty days at sea for about forty in the Falklands and that if we made a slow passage, we would be leaving the Falkland Islands before we had had a chance to see anything. Added to that was the fact that our plan to sail from the Falkland Islands to Argentina, Uruguay and Brazil was against the prevailing winds, which, with *Badger*, tends to mean a short distance in a long time. To my amazement, my arguments seemed to bear weight, and Pete thought it over and suggested that maybe we ought to revise our plan.

In retrospect, I suspect that my most powerful argument had been the brevity of our stay in the Falkland Islands. Be that as it may, Pete pondered for a while and then came up with a new idea. Why not turn the whole voyage on its head? Start in Brazil, cruise south and then leave for the Falkland Islands at an appropriate moment, and from much closer. Although this would add to the length of the ultimate voyage (the plan included South Africa, Australia, New Zealand and the Pacific North-West) it would have the added advantage of giving us more time in Brazil, a country that had long fascinated us. And so it was decided.

The night before we reached La Palma, I bodged reefing the foresail, allowing it to gybe in a vicious squall, with the result that the sail was torn and the batten broken. I was not popular. We picked up the lights of Santa Cruz de la Palma just before dawn and anchored that afternoon after a weary ten day passage.

Chapter Two

La Palma, our landfall at the Canaries, is our favourite of the group. This truly is one of the 'Fortunate Islands' as the archipelago is sometimes known. Its many high mountains encourage the passing clouds to give up their burden of moisture and the island is lush, green and, in places, thickly forested. In conjunction with the inherent beauty of any small, mountainous island, this verdure makes for an exceptionally lovely landscape. Admittedly, one's first impression from a yacht, the commercial harbour of Santa Cruz, is not prepossessing and it is not until you have walked the length of the docks and crossed the large, dualled road that you enter the town itself and can begin to realize that you have actually arrived at a place worth visiting. The view from the anchorage shows the usual concrete high-rise, but once into the

streets, if you raise your eyes from their cobbled surface, above the ground floors to the unchanged facades overhead, you begin to find a delightful small city, a town really. Santa Cruz de la Palma is the capital of the island and is blessed with some truly lovely architecture, a plethora of splendid balconies, fascinating streets and, of course, an excellent market.

Although the attraction of unknown places, of a whole world waiting to be seen, is undeniable, there is for me, a feeling of inner warmth generated by returning to a place that I like. I like Santa Cruz. It holds good memories from previous visits, it reminds me of old friends, and I enjoy finding somewhere that is familiar. To walk the streets and to notice changes; to know where to find the bread shop, to recognize faces, all bring a pleasure that is gentle and mellow. But nothing stays the same and it soon became apparent that Santa Cruz, with its unspoilt ways and its pleasant memories would soon be lost to us as sailors, perhaps forever.

This was because the tiny corner of the harbour available for visiting yachts, was about to be filled in, to make way for a container park. Moreover, the public beach, used for decades by the townspeople from infant to grandparent, was also to be destroyed. A new beach has been created, complete with a delightful, wide pavement on which to promenade, but it is a poor substitute. Even in calm conditions, a swell breaks on it. It is inconceivable that anyone

The harbour at Santa Cruz de la Palma, before it was filled in.

could teach a baby to swim there, or that an elderly lady could take her lunchtime dip and preserve both dignity and coiffure, as at the old beach. Besides, it is a good walk from the town: a reflection, no doubt, of the motor-car owning authorities who never stop to ask themselves if everyone enjoys the same privileges as they do.

Even while we lay at anchor, the bulldozers and the tip-up wagons arrived. Too late, the townspeople woke up to what was happening. Some youths swam to the end of the infill and, not unaware that many young women were watching, made heroic gestures to stop the lorries and bulldozers. The police came, three different types in fact — it is astonishing how they manage to keep on, even when a 'police state' is supposedly a thing of the past. In an earlier time and not too many years ago, men with shovels and donkey carts would have been doing the job and they would have taken a lot longer to have filled in the harbour. There might have been time for reconsideration, but now, within a week, the wagons and bulldozers went on their way. The little beach and yacht harbour were filled, ruined. The crew of a French boat, anchored behind us, had hastily to retrieve their stern lines before they were buried. Unable to find any other spot to anchor, they left.

As to the local boats: well, The Authorities have built a new harbour for fishing boats, but it is very small, very shallow. It cannot hold any more boats than are already there and one or two of the local sailing yachts have too much draught or are simply too big to go there. A friend of ours, Sergio, looks after one of these, a thirty-five foot Vindö. Even when we left, he still had no idea as to where the boat could be moored. He had put her alongside the wall, where the large fishing boats loaded and unloaded. It is no place for a yacht. Even the little bight in which we anchored is now filled in. Where will yachts go in the future? Who cares? After all, empty containers have to be parked somewhere and no doubt the people enjoying Sunday lunch in the Yacht Club would as soon look at them as at visiting yachts, with their gay flags and the happy to-ing and fro-ing of their crews.

We stayed longer in Santa Cruz than we had originally intended, waiting for mail which we were expecting and knew would have to be dealt with before we set off. Fortunately, having changed our plans, instead of rushing off, we could relax and enjoy ourselves, the boats around us and the island.

The pleasure to be had from getting to know other cruising people is, to my mind, one of the best things about our way of life. An advantage of Santa Cruz over other anchorages in the Canaries, is that it was so small that the boats at anchor there were sufficiently few that we could get to meet most of them. They also got to know one another, so that the feeling of community that we have come to expect, was able to grow up. In larger, more crowded anchorages, this is no longer possible, not in the least because there are simply so many yachts on the 'Milk Run' these days. We were particularly fortunate in our company on this occasion. Looking back, I appreciate this even more, because once we left the Canaries, it was a surprisingly rare event to come across another cruising boat.

One of our first encounters was with an English couple on a Nicholson 38, *Seacale*, who anchored alongside us not long after we had arrived. I rowed over and introduced myself on some pretext or other and soon we came to know them. They had both taken early retirement and were now hoping to fulfil Bill's long-held ambition of sailing to New Zealand. Lyn, who had worked in hospital administration, had had to think long and hard about giving up a good job, that she obviously did well, as she was by no means convinced that she would enjoy ocean sailing. A shy person, at first she seemed rather abrupt, even perhaps a little hostile, but she relaxed after knowing us a while, and we much enjoyed her company and conversation. Bill, with elegant silver hair and beard, became rather a favourite of mine, I confess, possessing a puckish sense of humour that brought a twinkle to his eye and a sly glance to be sure that you had caught the joke. He shared my penchant for puns and I thoroughly enjoyed an evening in his company. He loved his boat and never tired of pottering about on her, washing down, tidying up, finding odd jobs to do. He too had worked for the public, as a surveyor in the Inland Revenue: the same job, in fact, that I had been working at before I went a-cruising. Their tales of life for the Public Weal did nothing to convince us that we have missed out in not having 'careers.'

Lyn and Bill had an unusually healthy attitude towards their children. They had brought them up, enjoyed them and seen them begin their adult lives. As parents, their job was finished and they felt that it was time for them to get on with their own lives. We sensed that the 'children' felt a little outraged at their parents' cavalier attitude: taking off into the blue without so much as a by-your-leave.

Several months after meeting *Seacale*, we received a post-card from Antigua. They had enjoyed the crossing and Lyn was looking forward to going on. We were pleased for them. Unfortunately they wrote no address in the visitors' book and so I could never write back. I hope that we meet them again along the way.

The boat that anchored on the other side of us was Swedish; one of the typical fibreglass, double-ended boats of about thirty-two feet that so many Swedes seem to sail. We later discovered that there is a company in Sweden that will hire out the moulds and supply the materials for these yachts, so that you can lay up your own hull and decks, in their factory. Of course, plenty of people have taken advantage of this cut-price way of getting a good hull and decks, hence the preponderance of these spitsgatters, all the same and all so different.

The couple aboard our neighbour were both stunningly attractive and Betúlia's peals of laughter rang around the anchorage. They had met aboard a cruise ship, on which Anders was an officer and Betúlia a travel courier. She was Brazilian, dark and slender, and he was Swedish, with the blonde hair and blue eyes of that country. Betúlia had spent a lot of her youth in the USA and spoke perfect 'English.' As did Anders, which was just as well because he had no Brazilian and she had no Swedish, so that they talked to one another in English, proving that it too, can be the language of love! Before meeting Anders, Betúlia had never been on a small boat and, although she got seasick and frightened, she was determined to learn all about sailing. Her present project was to teach herself to row and her awe at my competence was extremely flattering, and not at all deserved. The boats being anchored so close together, we could talk to one another in normal conversational tones, without difficulty, sitting on deck, but to get to know them better, we invited them over one evening and spent an interesting and amusing few hours together.

Anders, we discovered, had already made a circumnavigation aboard *Kami*. When he ran out of money, he would find a safe place to leave his boat and go off to work in the merchant navy. The ships he sailed on sounded friendly and he told us a wonderful story of a tanker on which he had recently served.

The trouble with tankers, is that they can be very boring. Often you never see the land, let alone set foot ashore, because the pipelines are led offshore to remote places and it is here that the tankers load or discharge their cargo. Then, of course, there is not a lot to do on watch, out in the ocean, so any diversion is welcome. Well, on this ship we were sailing back towards Sweden and a homing pigeon came aboard. He was obviously nearly exhausted and we manoeuvred him into a sheltered spot and the cook gave him a fine meal. Then he went to sleep. The next day, he was still with us, walking round the decks, quite ready to make friends, and very happy when the cook gave him another good meal. By the following day he seemed quite at home.

Jan, the second officer was worried that he would forget how to fly and so once a day, he picked up our pigeon, who we had christened "Sven" and threw him into the air to have a fly around. We all gathered round to watch him make his flight, hoping that he would not decide to go away, because he was part of the crew by now, but after a few minutes, Sven would return and settle down on board again. However, one day when he was given his start, Jan had not realized that the wind was really quite strong and right on the bow. Sven went off as usual, but when he finished his downwind run and turned to come back, he found that he could not fly fast enough to catch us up. The poor bird was struggling, but slowly losing ground. We were hundreds of miles from land! What could we do? Sven would certainly drown. Then Jan ran onto the bridge and rang down for neutral. The ship started to slow down. A moment later, the Captain rushed up from below.

"What's going on?" he demanded.

"Sven flew off and can't make it back," we told him, "so we've slowed down so that he can catch up with us. Look!" We all stared astern. A little dark spot grew bigger and bigger and then suddenly there was Sven. He landed with a sigh of relief and the cook gave him a big feed.

"Oh, that's all right then," said the Captain. "Poor old Sven, he's had a hard struggle. Well, maybe we can start making progress again, now."

While they were on board, we took the opportunity of finding out about Betúlia's native country. In fact she knew it surprisingly little, so much so that she had bought the *Lonely Planet* guide to Brazil and lent it to us so that we could read the relevant sections. Of course, when we considered the size of Brazil and the fact that Betúlia had spent a lot of time in the USA, we should not have been surprised that it was a new experience for her, too. Her family came from Brasilia and she and Anders were looking for somewhere in the Canary Islands, to leave *Kami* so that they could fly out there and get married. Betúlia was going to have the whole works and was looking forward to it. Afterwards, there would be sailing on *Kami*, of course, but they had bought a small house and a little land, just north of Goteborg and would be spending time there. They were talking about babies. We wondered how Anders would get on with such ties after so many years of roaming the oceans, a free agent, with only himself to please.

In a time where so many people are cruising large and expensive yachts, it made a pleasant change at Santa Cruz, to be among a fleet composed mainly of yachts under forty feet. One exception was a Swiss aluminium boat, built by Ovni, that stayed for a few days, but the couple aboard were so busy `doing' the island, that noone got a chance to meet them. They came and then they went. Another unusually reticent crew was a middle-aged couple aboard a British yacht. Pete went to help them with their lines when they arrived and we rowed over and spoke with them on another occasion, but were never invited aboard. Betúlia nearly had hysterics when I explained that the boat's name was a pun of their combined ones.

`But that's so *tacky*!' she cried.

Twenty years ago, any popular anchorage would have contained at least one Rival 32, and many a skipper on his twenty-eight foot wooden sloop `of a certain age' would have been heard to say: `Now there's a real cruising boat. When I'm rich ...' Nowadays, Rivals are built in a range of sizes and the larger ones are opulently fitted out and a far cry from the sturdy simplicity that the home-completed Rival 32 seemed to personify. However, our little fleet of unfashionably small yachts contained one of these Rival 32s, doing precisely what it was designed for and loved and cherished by the two men aboard: Derek, the owner and Ron, who was his mate, both nautically and socially. They came from Merseyside, these two, and it was a great delight for me to hear once again the accents of my native country. Indeed, I almost forgot what it was that I rowed over for, not that it mattered. Ron and Derek were always happy to meet a fellow sailor and had me seated in the cockpit with a glass in my hand before they had even worked out which boat I came from.

Derek, a big, burly man, with a handsome beard, had an old-fashioned gallantry towards 'the ladies' that no doubt many a 'liberated' woman would dislike. But that would be a mistake. As far as sailing was concerned, he was quite happy to ask for and listen to my opinion equally with a man's; he respected women but he enjoyed treating them differently. Ron was smaller and slimmer than Derek, with a shiny, red face and a permanent twinkle in his eye. This bachelor ménage, we were to discover, went back a long way and was strictly a water-based situation. In fact Derek was married and Ron a widower, but they had sailed together for many years. Derek's wife was not very fond of sailing, but had been happy to let him go off to fulfil his lifetime's ambition, on condition that she could fly out

and have a holiday with him on occasion. Then she would join the boat and live quite happily aboard.

Unlike many all-male crew, Derek and Ron kept a very smart ship. A place for everything and neatly put away at that.

`Are you ex RN?' I asked Derek, on one occasion, looking for an explanation of this unusual behaviour and having noticed that he flew the RNSA burgee.

`Not at all,' he said, `I've always liked things to be done properly.'

The reason that I had rowed over, was to swop books.

`I'm afraid that we don't have any,' Ron apologized.

`Oh,' said I, 'I've been pipped at the post, have I?'

`Oh, no,' he replied, `we don't read, that's all.'

I was stunned; I dare say my mouth hung agape for a few moments. `You don't read?' I asked incredulously, `Well, what do you do on watch?' After all, the self-steering gear obviously was not for ornament.

`Oh, on watch?' replied Ron rather vaguely, `We, er, well I anyway, listen to the radio.'

`You mean the World Service?' I queried, `But surely that gets boring — it's the same thing over and over if you listen for long.'

`Oh no,' said Ron, `that's not it. What I do is listen on short wave, just moving the dial a tiny amount at a time. It's fascinating.'

`Yes, I do the same,' said Derek, `it's really interesting. You hear some music that you like and then move on when that ends. Then you hear a voice telling the news in English. It sounds a bit funny and then you realize it's Radio Moscow and their idea of the news is quite different from, say, Voice of America and that's different from the BBC. Then sometimes you can pick up part of a conversation. There are all sorts of things to listen to. The watch is over in moments!'

`Oh yes,' said Ron, `it's very interesting.' And then, with a typical Liverpool glint in his eye, `but don't think that I'm not a reader. I did read a book once!'

Ron and Derek went out for a drink every night and had found a bar where English people gathered. These turned out to be employees at the Observatory, set up in La Palma, to take advantage of the clear air. Our two sailors had got to know the staff very well and had been taken on a visit to the Observatory, which had clearly impressed them. One of the people to whom they had spoken had been something of a radio buff and on hearing of Derek and Ron's hobby had offered them a second-hand ham set, so that they could listen to a lot more things and probably hear them more clearly, too. In fact, Derek bought the set just before they left. They would have gained a lot of pleasure from it and Derek is probably a fully-fledged ham by now.

Before Derek's, wife, Pat, arrived, we had invited them over for supper and a rum tasting. This rum tasting is part of a continuing study, initiated by Nick-on-*Wylo II* for the benefit of the cruising fraternity. The idea is that any new rum should be given a formal tasting by a quorum of four rum drinkers. We did this with a rather pleasant rum that Pete and I had discovered. Subsequently, when we came across several good rums in Brazil, we could never gather together a quorum for tasting, but this night's results were noted and sent off to Nick, who duly added them to the collection. These notes are of great value, as they can save one from wasting good money on bad rum.

When Pat did arrive, we spent a very enjoyable evening on *Dee Rival*. She was as friendly and convivial as her husband and had pulled out the stops and provided a veritable buffet. While we were on board, Ron showed me some of the marquetry that he had made. I particularly admired one of a Thames barge sailing past a lighthouse and I was very touched when he made a present of the picture to me when we came to leave.

I asked Pat how she was finding life aboard, especially with their cabin being small and the nights hot and still. She told me that in fact their friend at the Observatory had offered Derek and her the use of his bedroom, while he used a spare one. His wife had been ill and had had to go back to England for treatment and he was obviously very lonely. It was soft living for a while, but it was not home and when their friend's wife returned, Pat moved back to *Dee Rival*'s forepeak with no sign of regret.

Another boat that we got to know well was the French yacht, *Steradenn*, who subsequently had to leave when the filling in of the harbour commenced. The owners, Christian and Maria, had a tiny baby, the joy of their lives. At first we were puzzled by his name, Pablo, but all was explained when we found out that Maria was Mexican. She was a doctor and met Christian when they were both at medical school. Following a motor accident in which he lost the sight of one eye and suffered brain damage, he went cruising in a twenty-six foot boat that he bought with the compensation that he had received after the accident. He spent a year or so away and then went back to University, but due to his accident found that he could no longer cope with medical studies, although he took a degree in another subject. He and Maria met again and came to

know one another better. In due course they bought *Steredenn*, a Trismus design. There were two crew aboard, Anne and Jacques, and we were invited aboard for apéritifs, one afternoon. They were good company and in fact, we were invited to stay on for lunch. As is regrettably often the case on French boats, the cuisine was not quite up to Escoffier's standards. We find it strange that a nation renowned for its cuisine should produce so many bad cooks. Or maybe the good ones stay in France. Of course, like all generalisations, there are exceptions, but of all the French with whom we have dined, I can only think of two or three who cooked well. It must be said that they certainly redressed the balance.

Christian, tall and fair, was very French, quite anarchic and great fun. I remember time spent with the crew of *Steradenn* as full of laughter. Maria spoke excellent English, (as well as French, and, of course, Spanish). Christian and Anne spoke good English, and Jacques and I spoke each other's language rather badly. Pete is a total monoglot, so it was pleasant for him that the others spoke English. We were sorry to see them leave, but as they also were going to Brazil, we hoped to meet them later.

In fact, both yachts benefited from meeting in La Palma. We had acquired and borrowed a veritable hotch-potch of charts of much of the coast of Brazil, but with notable gaps. Christian, on the other hand, had a more ordered collection, but it was limited in its extent. So we put them all together and then borrowed each other's charts to complete our folios. Due to the bureaucracy that still hangs heavily over Spain (as in all ex-dictatorships we have ever visited), there is a great demand for photocopying. One wonders what people used to do before the machine was invented. In any Spanish town, you will come across a plethora of businesses offering photocopying services and with the price of charts at around £15 each, yachtsmen are very keen to take advantage of these. Indeed the islands of Gran Canaria and Tenerife, both extremely popular with yachts, have many places with machines that will copy a full-sized Admiralty chart onto one piece of paper for about £2. In Santa Cruz, the only business with one of these large copiers charged a lot more, and so Christian shopped around until he found the best place.

`It is very cheap,' he told us `and they let you do it yourself so you can check you have all the bits you need.' If this seems a little incomprehensible, perhaps I should explain that the largest paper that this outfit could use was A4, that is about twelve inches by eight. Nevertheless, the copies were clear and certainly cheap at fourpence a page, for at this time the average price in England was about tenpence a page.

When we photocopied Christian's charts, we found that several of them were of fairly small scale, showing the coastline as a strip from the top to the bottom of the chart. Pete reckoned that the rest of the information was unnecessary (apart from checking that there was at least one indication of magnetic variation and a latitude scale) and just photocopied the relevant parts. This led to some rather odd-shaped charts. I later stuck more pieces of scrap paper to them in order to square them up a little and make them less likely to get torn.

Although photocopying charts is a cheap way of acquiring them, it is of course, anything but legal and also not entirely satisfactory, because photocopies can be less than permanent. If the surface is chafed, the finish may wear off, and over-enthusiastic use of a rubber can have the same effect. They also need to be used with caution, as distortions might occur during the copying, so that scales are inaccurate. Needless to say, those compiled from numerous sheets of A4 paper, are far from accurate, and I was interested to note that it was often impossible to align a sheet perfectly with the one above and the one to the side. On the other hand, most of us do not navigate to the sort of accuracy implied by all this and any chart is better than none. Knowing it to be unreliable keeps you on your toes and suspicious of anything dubious in the water ahead.

One morning we heard the usual bustle that announces a new arrival in the anchorage and Pete stood up to see what was happening.

'Well, would you believe it?' he said, 'It's *Darsi*!'

'You're joking!' I exclaimed leaping to my feet to look out, but sure enough there was a large trimaran trying to manoeuvre her way into the fleet, to the hole left by a boat that had sailed the previous day. There didn't seem to be enough room, but an hour or so later, the boat was securely tied into position with warps and anchors and when we were sure that they were settled, we climbed into Skip and rowed over.

'What are you doing here?' we asked, 'You're the last people we expected to see!'

'Come aboard and have a glass of wine,' said Carole, 'and we can catch up with each other's news.'

Nothing loth, we scrambled aboard and settled ourselves comfortably in the wheelhouse. We had met Carole and John the previous June when we were both at anchor together at São Jorge in the Azores. They had left the following day, but we had caught up with them again on Terceira and had spent some time together, enjoying one another's company. Carole is an American from Seattle and John an Englishman. When they met, they had each been sailing their own boat, both single-handed, as Carole's crew, her son, had gone back to America and John's partner had realized that he didn't want to sail any more. At the time, John had an eight-metre Catalac in which he had been down to Brazil, but he was feeling a bit lost, not being fond of either sailing or living, single-handed. He and Carole had found that they had a lot in common and in due course, John concluded that three hulls might be an improvement on two and they had thrown in their lot together. The arrangement should have been fraught with difficulties; they were both experienced, both used to being skipper and *Darsi* was Carole's yacht and had remained hers. In spite of this, they seemed to be an excellent team, each aware of the other's strengths and obviously quite capable of running the boat as a partnership, rather than Skipper and Mate: a quite extraordinary feat of co-operation.

When we had met them they had been on their way to the UK, where John wanted to see family and so forth. They had been planning to spend some time there, maybe even to overwinter, which is why we were so taken aback to see them in Santa Cruz.

'Oh, but the weather was so awful!' explained Carole, 'I just couldn't stand it any more!'

'We've decided to go down to the Gambia,' said John, 'and then on to the Cape Verde Islands and from there to Brazil.'

'Well, I'm still not quite sure about Brazil,' interrupted Carole, 'I know you tell me that it's OK and that all the tales of crime and violence are exaggerated, but it's a long way and I still think I'd like to go back to the States for a visit.'

As with many cruising people, John and Carole did not bother planning too far ahead; we tend to be the other extreme.

It was fun to be with them again and we showed them where to shop and had one or two joint 'stocking-up' expeditions ashore. We asked John about wine in Brazil: 'Oh yes, it's just like here,' he said. 'It costs about the same and you can buy it in any shop or supermarket.'

'In that case we may as well buy it there,' we said, 'and stock up on the things here that we probably won't be able to buy in Brazil.'

John also told us about Brian Stevens at Jacaré. He is an Englishman who sailed to Brazil in the early seventies and stayed. In the fulness of time he set up a boatyard in the village of Jacaré and he is always delighted to see any cruising yacht and makes them very welcome. We had heard something about him already, from another friend who went to Brazil several years ago, and were pleased when John was able to give us more information, agreeing that this seemed a good place to enter Brazil.

We spent one particularly memorable evening aboard *Darsi*. Carole and John had a video player and after dinner, suggested that we `go to the movies'. Carole made us comfortable on one of the wing berths, `in the circle', and kept us supplied with wine and popcorn while we watched the film. I can't remember its name now, but we thoroughly enjoyed it and the novelty of the experience made it good fun.

John and Carole left before we did, having arranged to meet friends in the Gambia. We anticipated that we would meet again in Brazil, but have never heard anything of them since. There was a rumour that, in a tit-for-tat move, the Brazilians were telling American citizens that they could only acquire a visa to visit Brazil if they applied for it in their own country, and we wonder if Carole was unable to obtain her visa at the Cape Verde Islands, as they had planned. I dare say that we will cross tacks again, one day.

As well as our fellow sailors, we also saw quite a lot of our friend Sergio, and his beautiful girlfriend, Ana. We first met Sergio in 1983, when he was a lad of sixteen, looking forward with less than enthusiasm to doing his National Service. It turned out to be even worse than he had anticipated, when the poor young man was sent to the mountains of Spain, in the middle of winter, straight from the Canaries. His overwhelming memory of this unhappy time was of being cold, a state of affairs he has no wish ever to experience again.

Back in '83, Sergio had got to know some of our friends, Keith and Viv, on *Calidris of Lune*. They had become very fond of him and treated him as another son. He remembered them with warm feelings and told us with real regret that he had never answered Viv's letter because his written English was so poor. He asked us for news of them and we brought him up to date, as far as we could, and gave him their forwarding address. He said that he would write to them and perhaps see if he could visit them. I wonder if he did.

During the intervening years, Sergio had seen many cruising yachts come and go and had managed to find a position as crew on a yacht to Brazil. She had been fitted out on La Palma and Sergio had helped with this work. He then sailed across to Fernando do Noronha and Fortaleza, in Brazil, but by that time he was running short of money and upset by the tensions among the rest of the crew. He found another place on a Brazilian saveiro and sailed on it to the Cape Verde Islands, where he left the ship and flew home with the last of his money.

The time spent on these yachts had convinced him that he, too, wanted to go cruising. He did not earn much money, but this was more of a drawback than it should have been, because Sergio wanted to do it `properly'. He felt that the thirty-five foot *Vindô* that he looked after was the right sort of yacht, and of course she was an excellent vessel; but not on Sergio's budget. Sadly, he did not realize that to get a twenty-five foot wooden boat of uncertain age and to go next year, was infinitely more satisfying, than to sit in Santa Cruz, watching cruising boats come and go while dreaming of how he was going to sail off `one day'. Ana seemed keen on the idea, which was quite amazing considering that both times the poor girl came aboard *Badger*, she was miserably seasick. And Santa Cruz is not an uncomfortable harbour. Sergio was not convinced: `Ana wants to get married and to have children,' he told us, `but I'm not ready to do that yet.' Maybe they should go their separate ways, he thought, but she obviously adored him, and I suspect that such a beautiful woman would be difficult for any young man to resist.

Sergio lived in a bedsit outside town and took us back once a week to shower and wash clothes. We had supper there once or twice and he obviously enjoyed talking boats, in a vague sort of way. One beautiful day, he and Ana drove down to take us on a tour of the island. He showed us a place, where people launched their Parapents, those lovely half parachute, half hangliders that one sees drifting around. They flew overhead from where we stood and called down to us as they passed. They stayed aloft for ages, slowly descending to a beach, several miles away. Sergio and Ana had also done a bit of parapenting and he was thinking of buying one. It was a popular pastime in Santa Cruz, too, where people leapt off the cliff and landed on the new beach. We watched them several times and concluded that we'd like to have a go.

`The landing looks a lot less heavy than with a parachute,' I commented.

`Yes,' said Pete, `and a parapent is supposed to be more controllable than a hanglider.'

One day I hope to get the chance. How wonderful, to fly like a bird, the only sound being the air whistling through the cords.

Sergio had also bought a jetski, to our horror, but admitted to having become quickly bored with it. We felt that because what he wanted to achieve, that is, a *Vindô* or a similar boat, was in reality so far beyond his capabilities, that there was no real reason for him to save money for The Boat. It was a shame. We like Sergio and would love to meet him one day in some distant anchorage, undoubtedly somewhere warm, on his own yacht, but I feel it is unlikely.

Eventually our errant parcel arrived and was duly dealt with and we could leave La Palma. We wanted to visit El Hierro, the only major island in the Canaries that we had never seen and invited Sergio to come with us and to catch the ferry back. Unfortunately, the ferries did not tie in the with the time he could be away from work and so he could not come with us. He was almost in tears and I had a lump in my throat as I kissed him and Ana `Adios'. Then we rowed out to *Badger*, got our various anchors and headed out of the harbour towards El Hierro.

We had planned on an overnight sail and it was already going dark when we left. The lights in Santa Cruz came on, one by one and from the offing, the sparkling town looked beautiful, ringing the harbour. A light, offshore wind pushed us gently on our way, bringing the warm scents of the land. Although glad to be underway again, I was sorry to leave this lovely island, especially with the feeling that we might never be able to anchor in Santa Cruz harbour again.

We had a pleasant sail, averaging about four knots until we came into the lee of El Hierro and lost the wind. It was, therefore, nearly noon, before we brought up in Estaca Harbour and dropped anchor in thirty-two feet. To our surprise, the anchorage was uncomfortable: the swell obviously hooked around and came into the harbour, in spite of the fact that it was in about the middle of the island. We put the dinghy over and rowed ashore for a look round and then decided to walk up to Valverde, the island's capital. The distance was further than we had anticipated and we had to trudge up a long hill in hot sunshine. When a car stopped to offer us a lift we accepted

gratefully. Valverde was a pleasant enough town, with a delightful square behind its large central church, but I don't think it was really worth the walk. It seemed a long way back to Estaca, and at times we were quite cold, once the sun had sunk behind the mountain, but at least it was all downhill.

Back aboard, we had a good supper, washed down with wine and turned in, thoroughly tired from our long walk, but the anchorage was so rolly that we slept badly and woke disenchanted with Estaca. We had intended to spend another day there and leave on the morrow, the 23rd November, the date on which we had so often left to cross the Atlantic. We discussed whether we should move down to an anchorage on the southern end of the island, to see if we could get a better night's sleep and agreed to give it a try. We had brought the Seagull aboard, thinking that we probably would not be needing it in these fairly large and uncrowded harbours, but the wind in Estaca was erratic and vagrant and in the end, Pete put *Skip* over and tried to tow us out that way. He was having remarkably little success, when a local speedboat came by and offered us a tow, which we accepted. Five minutes later, the sails were drawing and we slowly pulled away from the shore. Still in the island's lee, the wind was very light and in the end, we decided to scrap the idea of going to the other harbour and to head off towards Brazil instead.

Town square, Valverde, Hierro

Estaca Harbour, El Hierro

Chapter Three

I do not know whether it was because our departure was almost accidental, or whether it was because we had left from an empty harbour without the usual good -byes and wishes for a fair passage, or even whether it was the knowledge that for the first time, *Badger*'s bows were directed south of the Equator; but whatever the reason, the start of this passage felt different from the other occasions that we had left the Canaries to cross the Atlantic.

We drifted along slowly all night, with the lightest of winds dead astern and the foresail reefed and sheeted hard in, because it was unable to stay asleep in these conditions. Just after one in the morning, Punta Restinga, the end of El Hierro, was abeam and a few hours later the breeze seemed to gain confidence and gradually filled in. By breakfast time the wind had shifted onto the quarter and we had the full foresail set and drawing. The log entry for nine o'clock tells of sunny conditions with *Badger* `bowling along'.

This happy start was somewhat marred, not long after. Firstly, the line from the towing generator got caught over the self-steering gear. This was something that happened all too often when we were reaching fast in a big swell: the boat yawed and if the wave height was just right, it lifted the towing generator line high enough up to catch over one of the blocks through which the line to the servo pendulum passed. These lines were not bar taut, of course, and the result was that the heavily loaded generator line pressed down on the self-steering line and could not come off again when *Badger* yawed the other way. It was an extremely annoying event because either rope could chafe through very rapidly and the only solution to the problem was to more or less stop the boat so that the towing

generator stopped spinning and the load on the line became light enough that one could lift it off. (A year or so later, we replaced the servo blade with a trim tab on the rudder, which eliminated this problem.) I duly hove to and dealt with the matter and then, judging that we had too much foresail up and were rather over-pressed, which was causing the yawing, I dropped a couple of reefs. While I did this, we were beam on to the waves and the top of one slopped over the foredeck. I heard a horrible sound, as I stood in the companionway and my worst fears were realized when I went back below. Pete had opened the forehatch at some time during the previous night and had forgotten to mention it to me. Unaware of it, I had failed to dog it when the wind got up and the result was a couple of gallons of salt water over the double bunk. I grabbed towels and mopped most of it up; the duvet had taken its share, but if anything, this was a relief, as with the nights getting warmer, we should not be wanting it for quite some time and I could wash the salt out of it a lot more easily than out of the mattresses and on passage, we generally sleep in the saloon unless conditions are very gentle, and use a sleeping bag to cover us, rather than the quilt. It did not seem to be an auspicious start to a passage.

These rather blustery conditions, however, had only been a little reminder that we were back at sea, because by mid afternoon things had quietened down and we set a little more foresail after lunch. The sunny day was followed by a clear, starry night and, when I came on watch at half past one, I made myself a cup of tea and stood in the hatchway for a time enjoying the beauty of it all and the sensation of *Badger* sailing contentedly through the darkness. After a while I began to get a little cool and I went back down into the cosy, dimly-lit cabin and, settling down on the lee settee, picked up my book.

The following morning Pete woke me up to another fine, sunny day. The breeze was out of the east, Force 4, perfect conditions, as borne out by the log entry: `lovely sailing.' We felt that we had picked up the Trade Winds, in spite of the fact that the little, puffy clouds that one associates with them had not yet made an appearance. The wind was just far enough on the quarter for the foresail to draw and now and then we would put in, or shake out a reef as it rose and fell, never below Force 3, never above a brisk Force 4 and giving us a run of a hundred and forty-one miles, which boded well for the rest of the passage. It was the sort of sailing that people dream about while they are struggling with all the problems of getting a boat and a crew and enough money to take off for the West Indies and other exotic destinations.

The third morning out saw us enjoying the same conditions of perfect Trade Wind weather, even though the cloudless sky seemed out of character. Another good day's run, this time of a hundred and forty-three miles, made us start making calculations of how soon we would arrive, if we carried on at this rate. It is a temptation that is almost impossible to resist; the only consolation is that with the passage of time, it simply becomes a game and one grows inured to the disappointment of an expected fast passage being spoilt by two days of calms or contrary winds. It is a paradox of human behaviour that even those of us who thoroughly enjoy passage-making have the desire to make them in record time.

It occurred to me, when I woke up the next morning, that it was less than a month to Christmas and that I had still to make a cake and pudding for the event. The weather still being kind I reckoned that I had better get on with it and so that morning and part of the afternoon saw me surrounded by containers of flour, dried fruit, treacle and nuts, happily spooning and mixing ingredients and even more happily pouring in generous measures of brandy, made possible by the civilized prices reigning in the Canaries. The cake was steamed in the pressure cooker and, when cool, put away to mature.

That afternoon the foresail had to be lowered for a short while because one of the eyes in the leech, to which a batten is attached, had pulled out. Pete repaired it. With the wind so far astern, the sail had been reefed and sheeted hard in and we missed its steadying influence, once it was lowered. *Badger* does not have the sort of hull shape that picks up a rhythmic roll, but even so she rolled much more without the foresail. In spite of this, the repair was soon made and the sail hoisted once more with two panels up. Later in the afternoon the wind shifted more onto the quarter and it was let draw with another reef shaken out.

On watch that night, I heard the unmistakeable sounds of dolphins: their squeaks and chirrups, transmitted through the water and thence to *Badger*'s hull. Although it was dark by now, I went out in the hope of seeing them, but all I could make out were trails of phosphorescence as they danced and weaved around the boat. The `chuff' of their breathing made me jump, always coming unexpectedly. That they choose to accompany us invariably makes me feel privileged and their *joie de vivre* is completely infectious.

As we approached the vicinity of the Cape Verde Islands, the clear skies were replaced by haze. Our course took us very close to the group and we were considering sailing through them, just to see what they looked like, although we did not intend to stop there. On 28th November we were in the same latitude as the islands, but the haze had become so thick that we agreed not to bother with them. We reckoned that we would probably not reach the nearest island until nightfall and in such poor visibility and with reputedly unreliable lights on the islands, it did not seem worth the risk and so we sailed outside them. The haze was caused by dust, a clinging, red film that covered the boat; it had probably come on the offshore winds from the Sahara.

For most of the time that we have been sailing, we have never really bothered with fishing, but in the last year or so have become quite keen on the idea and had invested in some spinners while back in the UK. We had good success this day, pulling in two, beautiful, yellow-tailed tuna, which made a fine dinner for us. There were many about, but we hauled in the line, not wanting to catch more than we could eat and knowing that fish would not keep well in prevailing weather conditions. Those that we caught were sufficient for two full meals and I cooked one fish in the pressure cooker for the following day. With the weight left on, food will keep perfectly well for a day or so, even in a hot climate, and we enjoyed it immensely, eaten cold with mayonnaise and a potato salad. In fact I had a busy day in the galley, because I had already made up my mind to make my Christmas puddings — I usually make a couple, because we can then have one for some celebration at a later date. By the time these were cooked and the second fish had been dealt with, my watch off was so abbreviated that it hardly seemed worthwhile to turn in; but that was no hardship because I was very well rested with our sailing being so comfortable up to now.

By Sunday we had reached one of those invisible spots on the surface of the ocean where we had to alter course. We were following the directions for Sailing Vessels given in *Ocean Passages for the World*. From the Cape Verde Archipelago, the instructions were to: *stand S between the meridians of 26° and 29°, being nearer . . . 29°W in November. The equator should be crossed at points varying according to the season as follows: . . . In October, November and December, the S'ly winds will be met between the parallels of 8° and 6°N. On meeting them, steer so as to cross 5°N between 20° and 23°W, then take the tack which gives most southing, and cross the equator between 29° and 24° W.*

Although a modern sailing yacht is probably more weatherly than an old square rigger, it makes sense to follow this advice because it will still reduce your time close-hauled to a minimum and most people prefer not to sail to windward. I also find a certain aesthetic satisfaction in the idea of sailing the old routes of the wind ships and in contemplating all those *splendid ships, each with her grace, her glory* and feeling, too, that *Earth will not see such ships as those agen.* Perhaps, in our own way, we are helping to preserve the memories of a life *Under all sail, running free, in all beauty, all swiftness.* That a small yacht is a very different vessel from a full-rigged ship is undeniable, but the winds, the ocean and the currents all affect her in the same way and the relationship is unaltered: she will look after you if you look after her, an interdependence that brings immense, if intangible rewards.

This interdependence rarely makes itself felt in romantic mood, more usually in the form of mild irritation, such as happened on Pete's watch the following morning. *Badger* suddenly luffed up into the wind and on putting his head out, Pete saw that one of the lines leading from the self-steering gear to the tiller had parted. We always had a few spare ones cut to length and handy, but fitting them was an unpleasant task, with the tiller sweeping from side to side, and great acrobatics were required on the extreme end of the boat. If it was at all rough, as it usually was when this happens, the rope having snapped from being subject to heavy loads, it was common sense to wear a safety harness, but by the time you had wriggled around the tiller, the horse and the sheets, the wretched thing had usually snagged on something and prevented you from leaning out far enough to tie on the necessary fisherman's bend to the head of the servo rudder. This was no mean task in itself, as you needed one hand to hang on while you stretched out well beyond the stern. Fortunately it is a knot that can be tied single-handed.

More or less. On this occasion, Pete took the hint and replaced both lines. We got through a reasonable number of these lengths of rope as we usually used condemned sheets or halliards because the lines were subject to so much chafe that even new rope would soon have worn out. As good rope is expensive, it seemed to make more sense to use old stuff, which we no longer trusted, and replace it more often. Of course, we should have rove new tiller lines before every passage, or every thousand miles, or something sensible like that, to avoid the circus performance that usually accompanied changing them, but human nature being what it is, we tended to hope that they'd get us there.

For a couple of days, our noon to noon run became less impressive, because we were sailing pretty much close-hauled, and yet our worst was still a hundred and ten miles, which we felt was very creditable. The sunny weather made for pleasant sailing, but the heat that accompanied the sun and increased every day was less welcome. In fact life became decidedly uncomfortable once we were hard on the wind, due to the fact that we had to close the saloon hatch, forehatch and scuttles, in order to avoid spray getting below. I contemplated the advances made in modern yacht accommodation and began to wonder if our forebears perhaps did not know better. Had our forecabin been purely a storage area, rather than containing a double berth, we should have been able to keep the hatch open a little in the knowledge that the odd dash of spray was unlikely to do real harm and thus ventilate the boat much more effectively. If we had had a conventional wooden hatch, preferably of the Maurice Griffiths, double-coaming type with side flaps, we should have been able to leave it open with a fair degree of confidence that very few drops of water would even find their way down. As it was, the two forward hatches were both sealed tight and we came to bless our pram hood more than ever. Although this is designed to be turned with its back to the wind, it is possible to alter it to whatever direction you wish and we adjusted it so that it scooped in the maximum of air, with the minimum of spray. There was not that much spray around anyway, at the after end of the cabin, and any that comes down is unlikely to do any harm in the companionway. The worst time of the day was after our main meal, when the cooker had been on for an hour. I usually turn in after dinner, but I found little sleep in the overheated cabin, with the sun blazing in through various hatches and scuttles. Nevertheless, *Badger* made rapid progress and we only had to suffer near suffocation for a few days. The heat and humidity are enough to put me off the Tropics for life.

By the first of December, we were undeniably in the Trade Winds, with lots of cotton-wool clouds and flying fish skittering across the surface of the water, flushed out by our bow or, in the distance, by the doradoes that pursue them so voraciously. Flying fish make good eating, although they tend to be rather bony, and are often sufficiently obliging as to catch themselves. *Badger* is not ideal for this because the centre deck has no rail around it and the fish tend to work their way off. We occasionally find them on the foredeck and around the cockpit and have even had the odd one come below. We would probably get to eat more but that I am too soft-hearted to let them die, if I hear one come aboard and will go on deck and return it whence it came. If the wind is Force 5 or so, there is often too much noise to hear their feeble flapping and in such conditions we get flying fish for breakfast. They are a lovely sight to watch and we get endless pleasure, sitting on the foredeck, backs to the warm teak of the cabin, watching them dart and swoop over the surface of the sea, sparkling and scintillating in the sun. Blue and silver, with delicate fan-shaped wings, they are beautiful creatures and almost compensate for the lack of other visible animal life in the tropical oceans.

The following day was Half-Way Day. Only ten days out we felt that we were making excellent progress and had even more to celebrate when the noon sight gave us a day's run of a hundred and sixty-eight miles. The wind, which had been blowing at Force 5, kindly reduced to a Force 4, which enabled us to enjoy our mandatory feast all the more. To add to our felicity, that morning we caught a fine bonito. I am a great believer in Occasions, which give me an excuse to raid the treats locker and to enjoy feasting and jollifications. For Half-Way Day, the menu was:

Pernod and Bombay mix
chorizo and crackers, red wine
sweet and sour bonito, fried rice, cabbage,
prawn crackers, red wine
apricots and raisins au rhum

We ate in the cockpit, taking our time and savouring it all, and feeling pretty mellow at the end.

The next day was overcast and humid, with the wind dropping down to Force 3-4. Our position indicated that we might be approaching the Doldrums and the conditions seemed to back this up. We had read many accounts of passages through this area and were anticipating it with a mixture of apprehension and interest. We did not look forward to the torrid heat, for which the Doldrums are infamous, nor for the sail drill, which even with our junk rig, we would rather avoid.

On the other hand, we were delighted at the idea of being able to catch gallons of fresh, sweet water, to wash ourselves and our hair and to refill our containers. We were also looking forward to the experience as a whole, feeling that as long-distance sailors we really ought to have crossed the Doldrums and to be able to know them from having encountered them ourselves, rather than from merely reading about them.

Just before dawn on the morning of the 4th, Pete noticed lightning away to the east and, an hour later, he altered course to avoid thunderheads, feeling that they might contain strong winds and would at least disturb the gentle north-east wind that we were then enjoying. Thunderstorms and squalls typify the conditions that we had read about in the Doldrums and when Pete woke me up, he said that he reckoned that we had reached them. When I looked out at nine o'clock, there was the most enormous thunderhead to port. It grumbled and growled away, but kept its distance. By lunchtime, the breeze had died away, there were showers about and we had had enough rain to clean off most of the dust that had gathered on the boat as we passed the Cape Verde Islands.

'One more shower and we'll be able to start collecting water,' I said to Pete.

'Once we've topped up the containers, we'll be able to have some for a shower,' he responded, 'or even put the bungs in the cockpit and have a bath. How would you like that?' The thought was very appealing in the prevailing heat and humidity.

Another shower came over, a light one, and after it had passed, the wind shifted to the south-east, Force 2 to 3. The light conditions that had predominated since mid-morning gave us our worst day's run of the passage — a hundred and eight miles.

'We'll be lucky to achieve that tomorrow,' Pete remarked, as he laid off the position on the chart. 'With calms and variable winds, I suppose we'll be lucky to do forty or fifty miles a day.'

'I wonder how many miles they stretch, this year,' I said.

`Oh, I should expect at least a couple of hundred, but with any luck we'll be able to work through them in a few days.' To celebrate our arrival in the Doldrums, we treated ourselves to an extra drink at lunchtime.

All afternoon we sailed quietly along on a light south-easterly breeze.

`We've picked up the South-East Trades already,' I joked as Pete turned in and I settled down to my first watch of the night, but when I filled in the log at three o'clock, I recorded: `This day we entered the Doldrums and left them!!' And so we had. Indeed, we could hardly believe it and when I took over the following morning, Pete said in tones of incredulity: `The wind is still in the south-east!' and when I looked out of the hatch the sky was filled with neat rows of castellated, Trade Wind clouds, and the breeze was undeniably from the south-east at a steady Force 4. Astonishingly, we had crossed the Doldrums, purely under sail, between dawn and dusk on the same day. While we felt rather pleased with the achievement (as though it had anything to do with our abilities!), we also felt rather let down; it was an anticlimax after all the anticipation, and we really felt almost cheated of our experience. In truth, should anyone ask us: `What is it like to sail through the Doldrums?' we still can't really tell them. Our experience of a couple of rain squalls and a thunderstorm hardly even counts.

Sunday was a fine, sunny day and a hundred and thirty-six miles on the log had the skipper predicting that we would cross the Equator the next day. The wind continued to blow a steady Force 4 all through the night and the following morning I studied the log and the chart.

`It's bound to be Equator Day today,' I concluded, `I'd better get going on another feastex!'

After taking the morning sight, Pete worked out that we would probably actually cross the Line while we were eating our dinner, which seemed most appropriate.

`With any luck', I said, `Neptune will also be dining then and will leave me alone!' I had no ambition to be tarred and feathered, to have my mouth washed out with soap or indeed, to partake in any other of the quaint customs that pertain to `Crossing the Line'.

I started my preparations for celebrating the event in a more appropriate way and, burrowing under the port settee, produced a bottle of champagne, which I then wrapped in a damp cloth and put in the breeze, on the principal that the evaporating water would cool it. It certainly would have been warmer had I not done this, but not even the wildest optimist could have

described it as chilled. Not that this bothered us. I adore bubbly and the fact that it is usually reserved for Occasions adds to the feeling of festivity. The bottle that we had was one of several that we had bought in the Canaries. We had first come across Spanish champagne one Christmas that we spent in Mallorca and had been very impressed with the *brut* that we had tried. It is not always easy to come by, but we had found a supply in Santa Cruz. Under the impression that it would be readily available in Brazil, we did not buy much, an omission that we were to live to regret.

For a pre-prandial snorter we had a `Limey.' This is one of our favoured ways of drinking rum and is particularly to be recommended in hot climates because it is very refreshing. It is, quite simply, rum, water and fresh lime-juice. You may feel that this sounds too sour and be tempted to add sugar, but I would recommend that you try it without first. Its astringency is very welcome when you feel hot and jaded at the end of the day, or at lunchtime, for that matter. With the drink we had the inevitable popcorn, one of those marvellous treats of which we never tire. The meal was ushered in with asparagus vinaigrette which was followed by tuna and potato salad. For dessert I had reconstituted dried apricots and sultanas, aided by a generous slug of brandy, and we were happy and replete by the end. Having cunningly chosen a cold meal, I too, enjoyed the celebration from not having got overheated from cooking. It turned out that Pete's prediction was correct; we crossed the Equator at 1420, the day's run having been a hundred and forty miles. My ruse also worked: Neptune must have been dining because he failed to welcome me to his kingdom.

The following day we seemed to come across a stray patch of Doldrums, with the wind reducing to Force 3 and rain showers about. Our day's run was a mere a hundred and thirteen miles, but the following day was sunny again with the wind once more blowing a steady Force 4. Fernando de Noronha, we felt, was almost in sight and *Badger* seemed to sense our excitement, bustling along eagerly on her way.

That night there was a full moon and part of the way through my watch, when I looked out, I did a double-take. Instead of being full, the moon was well into its last quarter. I stared at it puzzled. Surely it was full? I distinctly remembered admiring it, earlier. I went back below and looked at a set of tide tables that we had on board. Yes, there it was: a full moon on the 9th of December. Once more I stood in the hatch and looked at it. If anything it looked smaller. Suddenly I understood. What I was seeing was an eclipse of the moon! I continued to watch this amazing sight and, at 2015, the moon disappeared completely in the shadow cast by the earth. This was the first time that I had ever seen an eclipse and to experience a total eclipse of the full moon, was, I felt, a fitting climax to a wonderful passage. I got Pete up to look at it, thinking that it would be over in a few moments, but in fact, the whole process took several hours and it was not until after midnight that the moon returned in all her glory, by which time, I was sound asleep.

When Pete came on watch he started to fiddle with our RDF set. This is always something of a challenge because the LCD display has gone and in order for it to be repaired, the set has to be returned to the manufacturers, something that is not easy to do when one is constantly on the move and might require the instrument. As it is, Pete has marked the knob to show when it is at the hundred kHz mark and can usually interpolate fairly easily. With the proliferation of GPS, a lot of RDF beacons have now been turned off and it is only the more powerful signals that are generally available. These are easy to pick up without tuning to decimal places.

We had been steering 275° and the bearing of the signal seemed to be at around 280°, so Pete altered course accordingly. At three in the morning, I picked up a flashing light bearing 290° and altered course again. Pete sighted land at around six o'clock and we seemed to be right on top of it when he called me. In the early morning light we gazed at our new island and looked in wonder at the astonishing finger of rock pointing high into the sky. Turning into the Baía de São Antonio we saw the breakwater and another yacht at anchor in the shelter of the reef. As we drew closer, we recognized *Steradenn* and a sleepy Anne, just got up, suddenly started in amazement and leapt for the companionway as she spotted us. Moments later she was back on deck, waving vigorously and trying to take our photograph at the same time. At 0820, we dropped the hook in thirty-seven feet of clear water and, after carrying us 2,306 miles, *Badger* folded her wings, seventeen days and twenty hours out from El Hierro. At last, we had arrived in Brazil.

Chapter Four

In spite of the breakwater and other signs of Man's presence, there is a wild and remote feeling to the anchorage at Baía de São Antonio. Even at low water, the surface breathes gently in subdued mimicry of the swell beyond the reef. Usually, the boats lie comfortably, wind-rode by the incessant trade wind blowing from the south east and bearing aloft countless birds: tropicbirds, noddies, frigatebirds, boobies and the exquisite fairy terns. Their sharp cries and shrill screams fill the air, stridulating against the background roar of surf against coral. At high water springs, there is a more forcible reminder that the anchorage is, in fact, well out into the Atlantic Ocean with only a thin band of coral to break the force of the waves that have travelled across thousands of miles. Come the big tides and the surge temporarily vanquishes the reef, unsettling the lagoon and catching the boats abeam to set them rolling for an hour or so, before the seas retreat once more behind the reef. The brooding presence of Morro do Pico, a weird, Gothic, three hundred and twenty-three metre tall finger of rock, is almost tangible. It appears to watch over the bay and has a decidedly sinister emanation, quite at variance with the bright, tropical scene.

While we tidied up on deck, we took in as much as we could of our surroundings, before going below to eat breakfast and to absorb the satisfaction of being once more at anchor in a totally new place. The meal was soon despatched and, changing into relatively tidy clothes, as we would be meeting with officialdom, we got together our papers and went on deck to launch *Skip*. Needless to say, we could hardly row past *Steradenn* without stopping and were invited on board.

'How was your crossing?' we each asked, the invariable question of sailors at the end of a passage. *Steradenn* had also had a good and quick crossing, but it had taken them over twenty-four hours to traverse the Doldrums, which they had thought very fast until we told them our tale. After a cup of coffee, we climbed back into *Skip* and rowed around the breakwater on the high swell, from whose hollows we could see only the masts of *Badger*.

Before the breakwater was built, landing on the beach was precarious indeed. As Pete put it: 'Landing has always been a

Fernando de Noronha, with the brooding finger of Morro do Pico in the background.

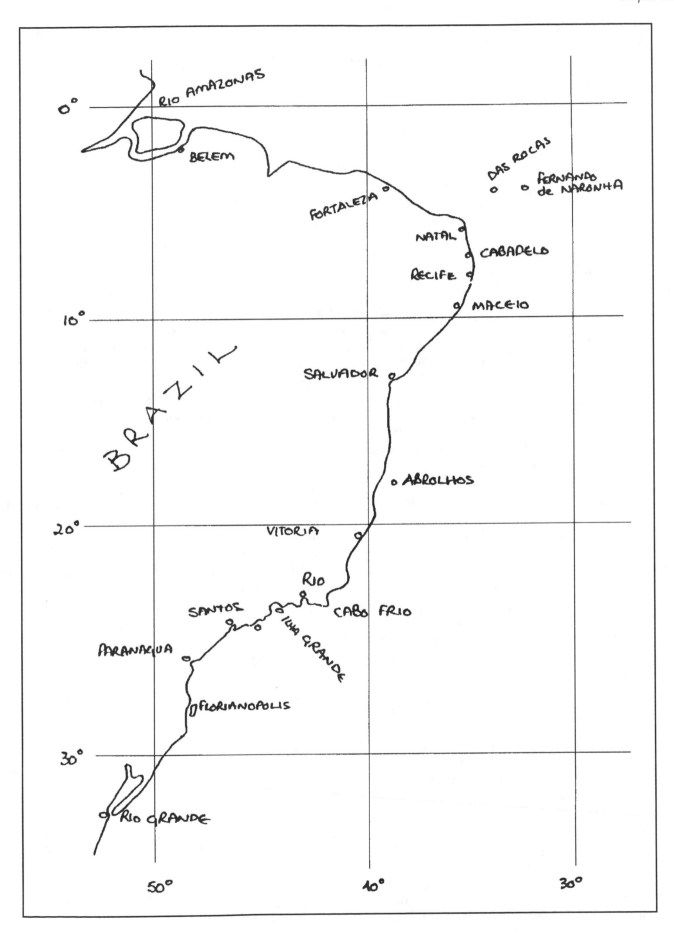

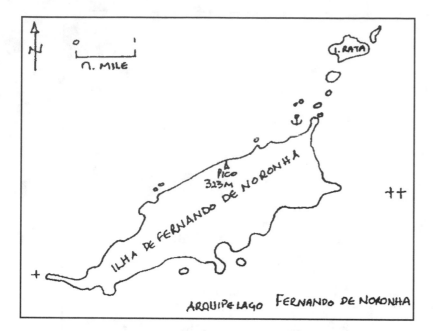

problem as a continual surf on the beach meant you either had to anchor the dinghy off the line of breakers and swim ashore or take it through the surf, capsize and swim ashore.' With the new breakwater, it is considerably easier, but even so you need to move pretty quickly if you want to get ashore without swamping the dinghy. With Pete having to wear his long trousers, our first landing was a little fraught, but I was in 'respectable' shorts and so could jump out first and pull *Skip* up with me on the same wave, so that Pete could hop out into the shallows. The amount of swell on the beach varied from day to day and depended on the state of the tide, but it was truly astonishing how it could hook around the reef, the offshore island and then the breakwater itself and still have so much vigour left in it to enliven our landings ashore.

The Capitão de Porto dwelt in a little white building up from the beach, next to a tank farm. His office was dark and sparsely furnished with a desk, a couple of metal-and-plastic chairs, an old filing cabinet and a calendar on the wall. He welcomed us with a friendly smile and then gave us a sheaf of papers, most of which turned out to be information about the island. We had to fill in a few details about *Badger* and ourselves, but the process was fairly painless. All the time he spoke to us in rapid-fire Portuguese. I speak very poor Spanish and had studied a Portuguese phrase book in anticipation of Brazil, but was lost in this flow of words. Eventually, we managed to make out, largely because we had been forewarned, that the Port Captain wished to know how long we were staying in order that he could make the appropriate charge. It turned out that there was a tax for visiting Fernando, because it is a National Park. The sum was US $10 a day. There

was also a fee for anchoring, which we felt was a bit thick, although we were allowed the first day gratis. *Badger* suddenly shrank a little in length and we were charged another $10 for our ten-metre boat. As the $30 represented all our cash, we were instantly cleaned out. Any money that we needed would have to be via VISA card, and it goes without saying that a bank accepting such things did not exist on Fernando. Brazil is not a wealthy country and National Parks are a 'Good Thing,' so apart from looking shocked and horrified at such piracy, we stumped up with pretty good grace. In two days, we ought to be able to see quite a lot. The Port Captain also indicated that there were a shower, toilets and wash basins available to us, but a quick glance inside convinced us that we were better off using our own facilities.

Around the back of the little white building there was a shed in which we saw a small boat. Curious, we went in to look at it and there discovered a young man at work, who greeted us with a smile. In broken Spanish/Portuguese, which I won't attempt to write down, I asked him about the boat. In return, he asked me if I spoke French, to which I responded with a grateful, `Oui, un peu.' The boat, he told us, was originally a large, sixteen-foot dinghy of French design, and indeed we recognized the hull. He was trying to convert it to a cruising boat and hoped to sail it to the mainland. We were interested in the project and I asked him a few more questions. He told me that he had found it difficult to work out exactly what he should do and how to design a suitable rig for his boat, but that several months ago a Swedish yacht had visited and the owner had given him a lot of help and ideas.

`What was the boat called?' I asked.

`*Peter Pan*', he replied. We were astonished.

`Is she very small?' I asked, `with two masts?'

`Yes, that's right,' he answered, `you know him then?'

`Why yes, we met him in Madeira a couple of years ago,' I replied. `Did he stay here long?'

`Oh yes, for quite a while. When he arrived he had damaged one of his masts and his self-steering gear and he needed to make repairs. In fact we lifted his boat out here and that's when I got to know him. He had many good ideas and knows a lot about building small boats. It was wonderful for me to meet someone like him. I now know what to do with my boat and I also know that my idea is not crazy. Some people thought it was, as perhaps you can imagine.'

We could indeed. Even in England, a country with a very high proportion of yachtsmen, a young man putting a cabin on a sixteen-foot dinghy in order to turn it into a cruising boat would meet with a lot of scepticism. In a country like Brazil, where sailing is not particularly popular, I imagine that there would be even less sympathy. We chatted on for some time and I asked him how he came to speak such good French. He told me that he had lived there for a year. His family paid for him to go there so that he would not be conscripted. A pleasant alternative, we agreed.

Anchorage at Fernando de Noronha

Letting him get back to his work, we walked on up the road to see what the island had to show us. Before arriving, we had read Bernard Moitessier's account of Fernando de Noronha in *Sailing to the Reefs*, but obviously civilisation had come since those days. The road that he described was now surfaced with tarmac and we walked past a garage selling petrol, diesel and alcohol on the way. There were obviously plenty of motor cars here, now.

After several weeks at sea, many people talk about the difficulties they encounter with walking when they go ashore again, but this is not something that we have ever noticed. What we did notice, however, was the heat. All the similes of furnaces, ovens, infernos and so on came immediately to my mind as we toiled up the hill and I wondered at the lack of shade trees along the long, straight road, but before we had gone very far, a lorry pulled up and offered us a lift. It turned out that the driver was a diver, who ran a shop at the only hotel. He took parties of visitors out in a boat and hired out equipment so that they could explore the reefs. He spoke very good American English and offered to change dollars for us. As the Port Captain had just relieved us of them all, we could not take him up on the offer and were at that time still ignorant of whom we could and could not trust to change money at a fair rate, although we felt that someone attached to a hotel was hardly likely to cheat us. In due course we discovered that many people running small businesses are keen to change their cruzeiros for dollars. When inflation is running at one percent a day, it makes sense to change your local currency for dollars whenever you can, because they do not dwindle away in value day by day.

Our driver took us up to a supermarket where he was buying provisions and we stayed in the back of the truck and watched the world go by as he attended to his business. When he returned he drove on and dropped us off in a *praçá* from where we commenced walking again.

Bernard Moitessier caught some little lizards, when he was ashore, to take back aboard so that they could wax fat on his cockroaches. How he managed to

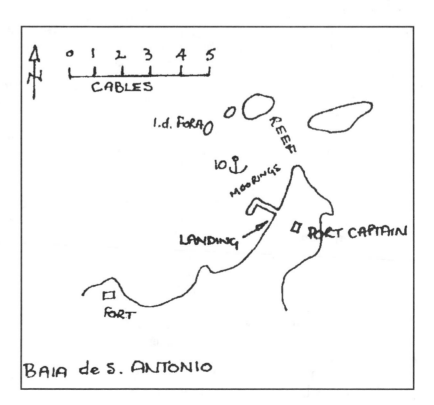

catch them I do not know, because they moved like lightning. I was even more fascinated by some enormous lizards that we caught sight of on the bank at the side of the road. Although not obviously scared of us, they were cautious and wary and did not let you approach within ten feet of them. I would have loved to be able to observe them more closely; they must have been at least four feet long from nose tip to tail tip. I later read that they are called *teju* and were introduced to eat the rats which had escaped onto the island from ships. Not surprisingly, they prefer to eat small birds and crabs and so probably do as much damage as the rats they were supposed to eradicate.

We were walking without real intention, but following the odd sign that appeared to indicate that we were heading in the direction of the beaches. Fernando is famous for its beautiful, palm-fringed beaches that are virtually deserted and made dramatic with surf. Sure enough, we eventually found ourselves at the top of a steep little trail that led us down a cliff onto just the sort of beach for which we were looking. We walked along it, watching the birds flitting in and out of the trees and then came to some rock pools, which seemed inviting in the hot sun. We did not have bathing costumes, but we stripped to our pants and sat in the pools. Topless bathing is considered quite acceptable on the beaches of Cococabana in Rio, but I was not quite sure of the position here, and when a local youth came jogging down the beach I felt that the best thing was merely to keep my back turned to him in order to avoid causing offence. Pete said that he barely glanced at us.

Lying in the pools was delightful, the water warm and just deep enough to cover us, the breeze evaporating that which lapped onto exposed portions and cooling us down. On the other hand, it was a little disconcerting to find that the fishy inhabitants of the pools were wondering if we were some sort of enormous feast laid on for their delectation and we withdrew when we discovered that some of them could nip quite hard. Back where we had left our clothes, we found little black lizards thoroughly exploring them and we came to discover that they could give quite a nip, too. They were extremely curious little animals and, as long as we moved slowly, quite unafraid of us. We dressed again and walked back up the track and along to the road. Even now, in the late afternoon, it was very hot and the walk down the long, straight road seemed to take an age, but we were soon back aboard and with the breeze blowing through the open hatches, life was comfortable once more.

The archipelago of Fernando de Noronha was first discovered in 1500 by the Spanish explorer Juan de la Costa, but was awarded by King Dom Manoel to Fernando de Noronha, after he had sighted it in 1504, on another expedition of discovery. The English, the French and the Dutch have also aspired to own the islands and squabbled over them, but the Portuguese finally got control in 1557 and the well-preserved ruins of a substantial fort that they built are within easy walking distance of the anchorage. The main island has been used for a variety of purposes over the years. For a long time, as with many other Brazilian islands, it was a prison and it was during those years that the trees with which it was originally covered, were cut down, the idea being that the prisoners would otherwise use them in order to escape. Apparently several did, in fact, manage to get back to the mainland and, if they managed to survive the voyage, no one pursued the matter any further, so long as they kept out of trouble. At the time, the enlightened constitution of Brazil said that no one could be executed or given a life sentence. In order to circumvent this, the less liberal judges would sentence someone they considered to have committed a particularly heinous offence to a hundred years on Fernando de Noronha. Apart from being separated from family and friends and the chronic shortage of women, the prisoners did not have too bad an existence. They were allowed to wander at will during the day and to fish or grow fruit and vegetables if they wished to.

During the Second World War, Fernando was used as a base by the USA. It has been a missile tracking station and at one time Air France, of all people, used it as an airport. Now, of course it is a national park, perhaps the happiest phase of its existence since it was discovered. There is a limited amount of tourism, an hotel (the ex-barracks) and several *pousadas*, a sort of guest house that is found all over Brazil. The tourist who comes to Fernando is in search of peace, quiet and the beauties of nature, which he will find in abundance on this delightful island, with its many deserted beaches, walks in the national park, and bird life.

The next morning, we agreed to go and visit the fort that lurks on the edge of the island's town, Vila dos Remedios. There was more surf on the beach and Pete was glad that he was wearing shorts rather than his long trousers as we raced the waves, pulling *Skip*. Our legs were powdered with golden sand to above the knee.

It was a pleasant walk once we had left the main road and the fort was very interesting and surprisingly well preserved. Tropic birds flew around and were nesting in some of the masonry. We strolled around the wall and into the guard towers and felt that the soldiers who had been stationed there had at least had a superb view, even if their jobs had been dull. There were still quite a few cannon lying around, fallen on their sides, the trunnions long since rotted away. We were amused to see the Broad Arrow and the coat of arms of King George cast into them. We spent some time in fruitless speculation as to which King George was represented but had no real idea of when the cannon would have been purchased. It was enlightening, if disheartening, to realize that our country has been dealing in arms for so many centuries, but there was a certain perverse satisfaction in comparing these cannon with others lying

Vila dos Remedios, with the remains of the old fort in the foreground.

around, presumably of the same era. These had suffered much more from the passage of time and were very badly rusted; where the coat of arms might have been, there was merely a raised bump on the corroded iron.

After having a good look round, we wandered onwards into the town itself, a curious collection of architecture. There were many stone, barrack-type buildings probably dating from the time of the fort, together with a hotchpotch variety of dwellings varying from shacks to properly built houses. There were large trees throughout the town, which in fact was only the size of a small village, and a very grand, if dilapidated square in the centre. There were one or two indications of tourism, many bars and some rather handsome roads, apparently leading to nowhere and with no buildings along them. The whole place had the appearance of being long past its prime, although the people seemed friendly and happy enough and not one passed us without a smile and a word of greeting. We walked along what might have been the front, had the town ever been a resort, and ended up in a terraced area with a well-built wall running along the top of a low cliff. We sat down on this to enjoy a picnic lunch, shaded by beautiful, vast trees and soon visited by the ubiquitous, charcoal-grey lizards. We felt that Vila dos Remedios had some way to go before it could be a tourist mecca.

While we were there, we discovered a bank, which needless to say did not take VISA cards, and also went into the supermarket that we had visited the previous day and had a look round. There was not much for sale and even fewer items were priced, but they seemed expensive, by any standards. On the other hand, we might well have been doing our sums wrong.

There were 10,000 cruzeiros to the dollar at the time, but the punctuation and the noughts on the hand-written labels were confusing and in the end we gave up.

`We've no money anyway,' I said, `and we'll find out soon enough how far our money goes. Even if we've worked out the prices correctly, they are bound to be distorted here, with it being so isolated and also a bit of a tourist place.'

Rowing back to *Badger* we made a detour to *Steradenn*, where we were made welcome, as always. We had seen Maria and Christian the previous day at the little bar on the beach, where they had kindly bought us each an ice-cold beer. We told them of our trip to the fort and asked them what they had been up to.

`Ah!' said Christian, `it is too hot to do much. Pablo is finding it hot, but we try to make a breeze for him somehow. Today I lie in bed for a long time and sleep.'

`You can't spend all day in bed!' we expostulated, with true British puritanism.

`I like to sleep,' replied Christian with irrefutable logic. `I enjoy it.'

For all that, he was now very much awake and in a mood to enjoy himself. He made a request to Jacques and a moment later was unfastening an accordion.

`I have sometimes made money playing this,' he explained, `but to be honest I don't know how to play that many tunes.' For all that, we enjoyed listening to his repertoire and if he sometimes hit the wrong note, who were we to criticize when neither of us can play any musical instrument even passably?

`I wonder why it is that the accordion is so French,' I mused. `I'm sure there's more to it than simply the cliché of the accordion player on the street corner, or the Maigret series.'

Maria and Christian were surprised.

`You think it a very French instrument?' they asked. `We don't regard it as such.'

`Oh, yes. In England we always associate it with France and, it suits French songs so well: they are quite different from English ones which have a much stronger rhythm.'

`Like this you mean?' said Christian, changing over to a vigorous sea shanty, a real foot tapper.

`Yes' I said, `just that sort. Do you know any more?'

`No, I'm afraid not. I don't even know many French sailors' songs. I really ought to learn some new songs, but,' smiling disarmingly, `I never get round to it.'

`How much longer are you staying here?' asked Maria.

`We thought of leaving tomorrow,' Pete replied. `We only paid for the one day and this is our second. We've seen a bit of the island and spent all the dollars that we had so we couldn't stay any longer even if we wanted to. Besides which, $10 a day seems too much, although it was worth it to have come here.'

`Oh, you don't need to worry about that,' said Christian. `The Port Captain does not have a boat and as long as you keep out of his way during office hours, you won't need to pay. We're thinking of staying another couple of days. Someone said that the boat is due on Monday and we need to buy some fresh fruit and vegetables for Pablo. As soon as we have them, we're going to Salvador.'

`How often does the boat come?' Pete asked.

Maria replied that it came once a fortnight, from Recife. `We've been told that you have to be there when it arrives,' she added, `because the fresh food goes straight away. Like everything else here, it costs twice what it does on the mainland, but by European standards, it will still be cheap! If it doesn't come, we will head on down for Salvador anyway and manage with tins for a few more days.'

`Will you be there for Carnaval?' we asked.

`I hope so,' said Maria. `What about you?'

`We've not made up our minds, yet,' Pete said, `but we'll probably be there well before Carnaval, so we'll look out for you.'

`You may as well stay tomorrow, anyway,' said Maria, `because it's Sunday and there will be no one even to see that you are still here, let alone take any money from you.'

The Tempter whispered and we fell. The next morning saw us still at anchor and we went ashore once more, this time to look at the reef, which with the spring tides, was almost dry at low water. We saw people walking around on it and wondered if we could walk across to the island, but it was breached at one point and we decided against it, instead having an interesting time looking at some ruins and trying to determine what they had been and taking some good photographs of the boats at anchor, with the menacing finger of Morro do Pico in the background.

The next morning we prepared to leave for Jacaré. We would have liked to see more of the islands, but you need to obtain permission to anchor in other places and we were not sure as to whether we would also be charged. As we were getting ourselves ready, we saw a sail approaching the anchorage. Of course, we had to wait to see what boat it was and when we saw the handsome wooden cutter, obviously American, we felt that we had to go and meet its owners before we left.

The boat sailed smartly in and anchored some distance in front of us. When we were sure that they were settled, we rowed over and apologizing for not giving them a bit longer, explained that we intended to leave shortly, but had wanted to say hello and tell them what a lovely boat they had. We introduced ourselves and asked about their yacht. *La Fomalhaut* was a Sam Crocker design and Charles and Maggie seemed pleased that a couple of Limeys had heard of him. They invited us on board for a cup of coffee and, when we were sure that they would not have preferred us to leave them in peace, we accepted. We stayed for about half an hour and gave them some information on Fernando. They were tired after their Atlantic crossing and were a little upset to find the anchorage so rolly, but we reassured them. It was high water and the sea level would soon be below the reef again, we told them.

`Where are you heading?' we asked and discovered that they too, were bound for Jacaré.

`We'll probably see you there, then.'

`I expect so, we won't stay long here anyway,' said Charles, `especially at $10 a day. After all, it's only another island!'

Slightly nonplussed at this comment, we made our farewells and rowed back to *Badger*. We lifted *Skip* on board, raised our sails, got the anchor and were soon running out of the anchorage and along the island, admiring the beautiful beaches as we sipped our morning cup of coffee and discussed what to have for lunch. By the time we had eaten it, Fernando de Noronha was diminishing astern and *Badger* was sailing once more in the perfect south-east Trade wind.

Chapter Five

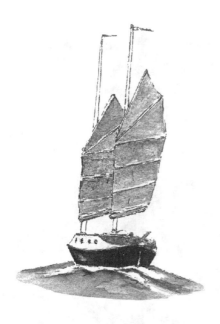

The first indication that we were approaching land was the gradually decreasing depths shown on the echo sounder. The coastline around Cabo Branco is so low that you are almost on top of it before you see it and at first I was unsure if the dim line in the distance was really land or merely some sort of optical illusion. We had slowed down overnight and now, sailing once again with full sail, on a sparkling, sunny morning, we could make out the buildings of João Pessoa in the distance and, in the foreground, what surely must be the port of Cabedelo. As we approached, we identified the first of the buoys marking the channel that wriggles in among the sand banks to connect with the Rio Paraíba. Following this we soon came to Cabedelo, where small ships lay alongside the wharves, but remembering what John had told us, we carried on, tacking up the river, using the echo sounder to warn us of shoals once we were past Cabedelo, where the buoys ceased.

The wind in this part of Brazil, rarely rises above Force 5 and generally blows less, so that our sail up the river was pleasant and relaxing and we had time to take in the scenery of this new land. After Cabedelo, the river was wide and wooded along both banks, not alas, with lush, tropical jungle, alive with the screams of monkeys and cries of parrots, but instead, with rather spindly broad-leaved trees, which were, nonetheless, attractive. The tide was ebbing quite strongly and so our progress was less than spectacular. Nevertheless, we were thoroughly enjoying ourselves and ate our lunch on deck, as we continued up the river. In due course we rounded a bend and ahead of us we could make out several yachts at anchor.

'That must be Jacaré,' I said 'and by the number of boats there, we're not the first people to have heard of it!' Ahead of us there was a large, hangar-type building, which we later realized was a storage facility for small boats belonging to the Yacht Club, which was adjacent to Brian Stevens' boatyard. Pete went up forward and pulled out several fathoms of chain from the locker, to ensure that it was ready to run. He walked back to the cockpit.

'Where are you thinking of anchoring?'

'Well, I suppose that there will be less stream by the bank and also less distance to row; on the other hand there'll probably be more mosquitoes. I think our best bet may be to go upstream of the ketch with the brown sail covers and outside that catamaran. He probably draws less than us and it might be shallow closer in.'

Pete was trying to concentrate on where we should go but, as ever, was distracted by the boats.

'I think it's one of those Philippe Jeantot designs, don't you?' I made some non-committal remark: generally speaking, large, fibreglass catamarans leave me cold, because I find them so unattractive to look at, and anyway I, too, was studying the area to see where we should anchor, concluding that Pete's suggestion seemed to be the best idea.

'The ketch is a Yankee,' I pointed out, 'so he's probably on rope. We ought to give him a good berth if we don't want him swinging on top of us when it starts to flood.'

'OK, then, we'd better go on a bit further.'

A few moments later, Pete went up forward again and I put the helm down a little and headed towards the beach.

Jacaré, on the Rio Paraíba.

`Here, do you think?'

`Looks fine to me.' A moment later, Pete nodded his head and I let the foresail drop, followed immediately by the mainsail. As *Badger* lost way and the tide started to make itself felt, we stopped and Pete lowered the anchor over the bow, paying it out as we moved backwards. He took a couple of turns round the bollard and we brought to with a satisfying snub.

`Feels like a good, mud bottom,' he remarked.

`It's what you'd expect, I suppose.' I was hauling in the sheets and tidying up the `snotter' and yard downhaul. Pete tied the fall of the halliards away from the mast and I hauled them taut on the winches. Once everything was more or less ship-shape, we went forward and put *Skip* over the side.

`I suppose that she'll be giving us problems when we get wind against tide', Pete remarked, cleating off the painter.

`Ah well, we can always haul her on board,' I responded, `but we won't want to put her on the foredeck; we'll need the hatch open.'

`We might as well go ashore and make our number with Brian,' Pete said and we went below to get our shoes.

While we had been sailing up, we had noticed a landing stage with several dinghies tied up and it was for this that we headed when we rowed ashore. As we scrambled out and made the dinghy fast I exclaimed: `Oh Pete, look! A dugout canoe!'

And so it was; the first that we had ever seen. We looked at it closely, intrigued by its shape and the graceful curve of the stern.

`It's absolutely identical with those shown in the engravings of that copy of Christopher Columbus' diary that we've got on board.' I commented. `How amazing!'

We climbed up the wooden stairway onto a bridge and stopped for a few moments to look once again at the canoe, before walking on to find Brian Stevens and his boatyard. Along the riverside were several bars with tables and chairs outside under thatched `umbrellas' or roofs and we felt that an ice-cold beer in the shade could prove to be quite a temptation in such heat. However, as we still had no local cash on us, it was a temptation quite easily resisted and we continued on our way. There were several children running about, with coffee-coloured skins and the sort of eyes that you see in those rather tasteless paintings sold in Woolworth's and knick-knack shops. They smiled shyly at us as we walked past and then turned and grinned at each other, before scampering away. A few minutes along a dirt track, with the dust lying ankle deep, we saw the boatyard, with a surprising number of boats lying around in various states of decrepitude and some obviously brand-new projects underway. We walked in through the gateway and, peering into a shed, were instantly overwhelmed by the stink of styrene and the rather startling vision of a large catamaran in the early stages of construction and a parrot on a perch.

Withdrawing, Pete said, `It looks like a Derek Kelsall to me. Didn't John say something about Brian being interested in multihulls?'

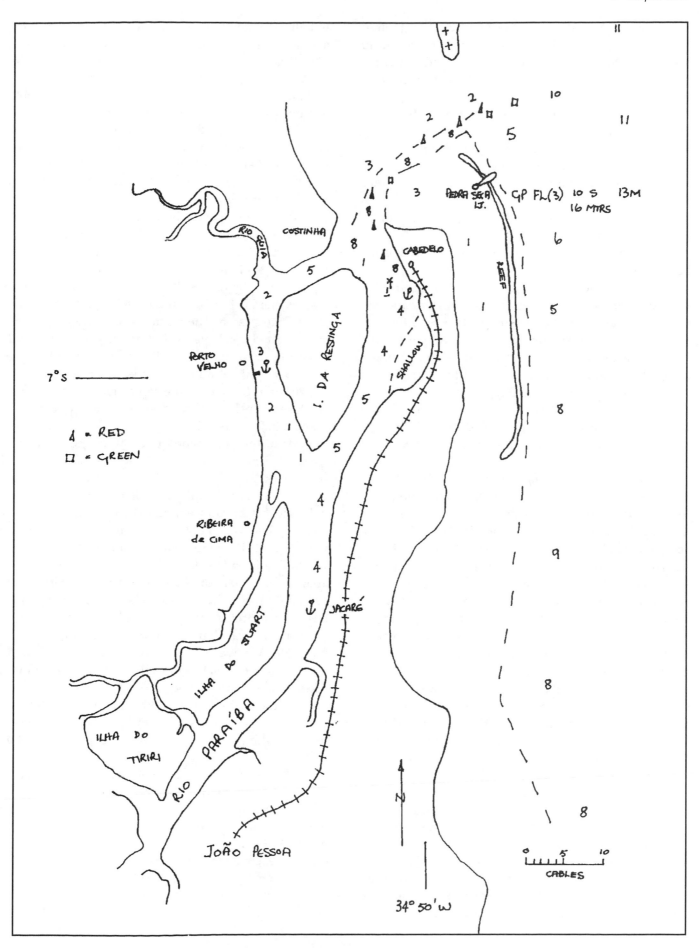

7°S

△ = RED
□ = GREEN

RIO SEIA
COSTINHA
PORTO VELHO
I. DA RESTINGA
CABEDELO
PEDRA SECA LT.
GP FL (3) 10 S 13M 16 MTRS
REEF
SHALLOW
RIBEIRA de CIMA
ILHA DO STUART
RIO PARAÍBA
ILHA DO TIRIRI
RIO
JACARÉ
JOÃO PESSOA

N

34° 50' W

0   5   10
CABLES

`Mmm, yes, I think so,' I responded, absent mind-edly, as I stared around me. We heard the sound of voices and following it, eventually tracked down the man we had been looking for. Tall, blonde and bearded, this had to be Brian Stevens.

`Excuse me,' Pete said, `are you Brian Stevens?' He turned round.

`Aha! You must be the people from the new yacht!' he said. `I watched you come in — she looked lovely.' From that moment on, we liked Brian very much.

`Come on', he said. `We'll go to the office and I'll tell you what you need to know.'

`Oh, but you're busy!' we protested. `We'll come back later on.'

`No, no. Not at all. They can manage perfectly well without me,' he said and without further ado, led us back towards the shed where we had seen the par-tially completed catamaran. By the time we were in the office, Pete and Brian were already deep in discussion about the building of multihulls and the comparative advantages of plywood and fibreglass.

`So tell me about yourselves,' Brian said, as we found seats. `Where have you come from? When did you leave England?' and so we all settled down for a good yarn.

Brian is still a cruising man at heart. He sailed his own yacht, a West Country Trading Ketch, into Jacaré in 1975. At the time, it was just going to be a stop on the way, but the boat needed work, it was an attractive spot and it did not take Brian too long to realize that he had found a place that he had no desire to leave. Although he had little money behind him, Brian had the vision and the capacity for enjoying hard work, which are two of the ingredients for making a success of life. The north of Brazil is not a wealthy area, by any stretch of the imagination, and unemployment is a way of life. In spite of this, there are affluent people about and Cabo Branco, on the coast, close to Jacaré, is a holi-day resort. To cut a long story short, Brian used his knowledge of boats and boatbuilding, combined with local labour, to set up a small yard, not only to repair the yachts of the well-to-do, but also to build new boats in a country that has a very limited boatbuilding indus-try. Brian is particularly interested in multihulls, an ideal craft for an area such as the Brazilian coast, strewn with reefs and shoals, and manages to find enough customers with the individuality and courage to go for a `one-off' boat. We were impressed at the extent of his achievement and could only guess at the determination that had been needed to overcome the problems of setting up a new life in a country that had

initially accepted him only as a visitor and whose ways and language were a completely unknown quantity.

Brian now had a Brazilian wife and daughter and spoke the language, at least to our ears, like a native. Although he was enjoying his new life, he still took a genuine pleasure in meeting cruising people and help-ing them in any way that he could. The yachts that stop at Jacaré all appreciated this and, by telling other people of their experience, made this a popular stop along the way, with the result that Brian came to meet and enjoy more voyagers.

After we had been there for twenty minutes or so, he stood up and went over to a filing cabinet.

`I've got a map of João Pessoa here, that might be useful,' he said, `and I'll write down for you the open-ing hours of the offices. It's a bit of a bind clearing in, because the Customs are in Cabedelo and the other two are in João Pessoa. The Customs are only open in the morning and you have to go there first, so you can't do anything until tomorrow. There is a train that goes from just up the road to both places, or you can catch the bus, which is a bit more comfortable, but further to walk from here. It's handier for the supermarkets though, in João Pessoa.'

Brian then proceeded to show us the places that we needed to go and then pointed out the market and supermarkets.

`We've heard all these terrible stories about crime in Brazil', I said. `Do we need to be very careful?'

`Well if you go to Rio or Recife, you need to be on your guard,' Brian replied, `but in all the years that we've lived here, we've never had anything stolen, apart from a pair of shoes that a visitor left on the verandah overnight. Cabedelo is very small and João Pessoa is a pretty safe place. Just use your common sense. By the way, have you got any money on you?'

`No. We were hoping that you might change some dollars for us, but the only cash that we had was taken by the authorities on Fernando.'

`Oh well, don't worry. I'll lend you enough to get into town so that you can go to the bank,' and so say-ing he pulled out some money and pressed 30,000 cruzeiros into Pete's hand.

`That's extremely kind of you!', we said. `We'll pay you back as soon as we can.'

Brian laughed. `I know it looks a lot, but it's only worth about three dollars,' he said, `so there's no hurry.' We thanked him again and then took ourselves off. As we left, he called after us.

`There's just one thing I'd like you to do!'

`Of course,' we said, `what is it?'

`I'd like you to fill in the visitors' book with a few details of your voyage and, if you have one, a photograph of *Badger*.'

`We'll be more than happy to do that,' we said, `and we'd love to have a look through the book, anyway.' With that, Brian went back to his work and we started walking back to *Badger*.

As we went out of the gateway, we could see a mast; the rest of the boat was hidden by the river bank. Because the mast was wooden, we were more than usually interested in what lay below it and went to investigate. A young man, up to his ankles in thick, black mud, scantily clad in a pair of sawn-off jeans and a torn shirt, was scraping assiduously at the hull. The boat was quite beautiful, a sleek, white hull with varnished cabin. As we looked at it, a young woman, wearing the most abbreviated denim shorts that I have ever seen, her mouth outlined in startling, scarlet lipstick, came out of the cabin and, seeing us, gave a bright smile.

`Hello!'

`Hello!' we replied. The young man looked up.

`Are you from the boat that arrived this afternoon?' We replied that we were and he straightened up and walked towards us.

`Where have you come from?'

`Fernando. What about you?'

`Oh, I've been in Brazil a while. I've been working on the charter boats around Ilha Grande and then I decided to buy a boat of my own. I got her for a good price, but she needs a bit of work doing on her and I'm trying to get her sorted out so that we can go up to the Caribbean.'

`She's a lovely boat. We were just admiring her. Is she an American design?' I asked.

`Well, yes she is, as a matter of fact. How did you know?'

`I thought that she looked very much like a Finisterre Yawl,' I answered.

He then told us a little about the yacht. *Majoy* was built in 1949, at a time when the Brazilians were taking up yacht racing with enthusiasm. They would go to an American designer, but the boat would be built in Brazil, where they had first-class woods and skilled craftsmen to use them. *Majoy* was one of about forty boats built to the same class and had, in fact, been designed by Sparkman and Stephens, which perhaps explained her resemblance to Finisterre.

`It's not a good climate for wooden yachts,' he concluded, `but fortunately, she seems to have been well looked after and there's not a lot wrong with her,' but as the days passed, Chris discovered that he had

perhaps been over-optimistic in his assessment of the boat, and she stayed on the drying-out frame for much longer than he had originally intended.

We noticed that the sun was approaching the horizon.

`We'd better shove off,' I said, `the mosquitoes will be out soon and I'd rather avoid them!'

`Oh yes. They can be pretty bad here, but where you're anchored, you shouldn't find them too much of a nuisance,' Chris commented.

`I daresay we'll see you around.'

`Sure, see you!'

We climbed back up the bank and walked along the track. The sun was already behind the trees on the far bank and looking at my watch I said to Pete,

`What time do you think it is?'

`I don't know', he replied, `six o'clock or so.'

`Half past five.' I announced, `and just about midsummer.'

This was one of Jacaré's few drawbacks. The shortness of the hours of daylight in the Tropics is one of the things I like least about them, and the fact that it was pitch dark by six o'clock on this part of the coast was a real nuisance. It curtailed our time in town, as we felt that we might be pushing our luck to walk around João Pessoa's dimly lit streets after dark, and anyway, there was no lighting at all on the track back between the railway station and the anchorage. It also meant that one had to do a fair amount of thinking ahead, because if I got caught ashore after sunset, I paid for it with mosquito bites, unless I remembered to take insect repellent with me.

There were several people in one of the bars, who called out greetings in English as we walked past. We exchanged a few pleasantries, but did not stop and were back aboard as the last rays of the sun left the sky. We shipped our mosquito screens, switched on the lights and sat down to talk over what we had seen and to enjoy a glass of rum.

`Here's to Brazil!'

The next morning we were up in good time to go and catch the train; Brian had thoughtfully pinned up the timetable on the wall of his office. We walked along the dusty tracks and climbed the dozen or so steps up to the ticket office and platform. A turnstile prevented access until a ticket had been purchased.

`Dos por Cabedelo,' I said in my best Portuguese, pushing across a 10,000 cruzeiro bill. The lady took it from me and frowned slightly as she went to the drawer for change.

`I hope I've given her enough!' I whispered to Pete. A whole wad of bills was pushed back to me, under the grille, and I took them from her, with no idea as to what they represented. We clattered through the turnstile and walked along the platform a little way.

`I'd better sort out this money,' I said to Pete, `will you see how much there is while I get my purse out, please?'

`There's 8,300 cruzeiros left!' Pete exclaimed in tones of disbelief.

`But I thought that Brian said that he only gave us three dollars.' I replied. `The fare must be more than seventeen hundred for both of us. What does it work out at?'

Pete thought for a moment.

`It's less than ten cents each,' he said, laughing. `I thought it would be a lot more. After all it's five miles or so and I hate to think what that would cost in England.'

`Well, it used to work out at tenpence a mile years ago,' I said, `so even at that rate we'd have paid seventy-five cents. Still, it makes a pleasant change to feel that we can just pop on the train whenever we want to, without having to count the cost. I wish all public transport were so sensibly priced.'

I stuffed the sheaf of notes back into my purse and we looked around us at the people on the platform. Several of them had huge bowls full of some sort of fruit, that they were obviously taking into town to sell and there were a few young people who appeared to be students. While most of the men were wearing long trousers, what surprised me was that nearly all the girls and women, with the exception of the elderly, were wearing shorts. In my skirt, I felt that I stood out like a sore thumb.

`I thought the books all said that a "certain decency" of dress was the order of the day,' I said to Pete, `but look at all the women! There's hardly a skirt or dress to be seen, and everyone has bare arms.'

`Not only bare arms, either,' said Pete looking along the platform to where a young woman stood in her shorts and a top that just came down to her waist.

`Well, that's a relief.' I said, `I was bothered that I might need to wear long sleeves. I wouldn't have dreamed of wearing shorts ashore, but in fact I'd be less obvious in them than in this skirt. A pity really — a skirt's cooler.'

`On the other hand,' said Pete, `I'd better stick with the long trousers. There don't seem to be many blokes in shorts, do there?'

`No, but it may be different in town. Sometimes people in the countryside are more conservative. For that matter, maybe it's the other way round and all the ladies in town will be wearing skirts.'

There was suddenly a mass movement and looking along the rail, we saw the train approaching. We waited for it to come in, rattling and clanging, and then climbed aboard with everyone else. It was pretty scruffy. Most of the glass windows had been replaced with a presumably cheaper plastic which was so badly scuffed that they were impossible to see through. The seats were of moulded, hard plastic and so designed that one slid off them, so that people tended to sit with one foot pushed forward, wedging them into place, but as the old saying goes, `third class riding is better than first class walking' and we were not complaining.

The train was fairly busy, but we could find a seat without too much difficulty and amused ourselves by alternately craning our necks to see through an open window or by observing our fellow passengers. After about a quarter of an hour, we arrived at Cabedelo and climbed down.

This was our first Brazilian town and we looked about us with interest. Our first impression was of incredibly shabby buildings, unpaved streets and children everywhere. The place seemed full of life and people were smiling, laughing and talking to each other as though they did not have a care in the world. Following the directions that Brian had given us, we walked through the busy streets until we found the Customs office. Here we were greeted by an immaculately dressed gentleman who spoke a little English, but was obviously more than pleased that my Portuguese was up to the formalities of entering. There did not seem to be a lot to it and we left after about ten minutes or so. It was rarely going to be so brief again.

Walking back through the streets, we looked into the doorways and open windows. Although this was no *favela* area, there was little sign of prosperity; children tried to sell us bags of limes, and in the end I succumbed, discovering later that I had been thoroughly ripped off. It was the only time that this happened to us, during the six months that we spent in the country. The experience did little to raise my already low opinion of children.

Back at the ticket office, we handed over a 5,000 cruzeiro note and asked for tickets for João Pessoa. To our astonishment, the charge was once again 1,700 for the two of us, this time for ten miles.

`Obviously, it's a fixed price,' said Pete. `That's a bit of information worth remembering. It's probably the same all over the country. With any luck, we'll be able to take a few train rides.'

En route to João Pessoa, we passed a huge rubbish tip and, through the scratched windows could dimly make out a number of people, gleaning the items that they could make use of. Poverty is the ultimate incentive to recycle. Nearby were shanty-type houses and we noticed more of these as we lurched along the track. Approaching the town, the houses became more frequent and a greater number were built of concrete blocks and even finished with plaster. We were obviously in a less poor area. In due course, we came to realize that the average Brazilian house would probably be considered a slum in the UK. They are invariably small, often have packed earth floors and are inhabited by a large number of people. I doubt that many of them have hot water and suspect that more than a few have no running water at all, although we heard that the Government has been trying quite hard to improve standards and now lays on water and electricity to any recognized housing area, including the infamous *favelas*. In spite of the obvious disadvantages in living in such cramped and over-crowded conditions, it never ceased to amaze me how incredibly clean and tidy the average Brazilian managed to be. Time and again I saw a woman in a pristine white blouse, or a man in smartly pressed slacks emerging from a tiny dwelling.

The train drew up at the station and we all got out. Following the crowd, we left the station and started walking up towards the town. The railway follows the river, but the town is built higher up the hill and its centre is quite some distance from the station. Once again, with Brian's map in hand, we could set off confidently in the right direction. It soon became apparent that Brazil still had the Latin tradition of having shops of the same type in the same area. The street that we were walking up sold spares for motor cars and, further up, became the area for furniture shops. We passed stalls selling green `drinking' coconuts with holes bored for a straw and, along the street, were dozens of hawkers selling flip-flops, earrings and all sorts of other items. Further on, we came to a square where several men were standing around with old plate cameras. Identity photographs are, of course, one of life's necessities in any South American country and this is where you could come to have them taken. We were amazed that such equipment was still being used, but in due course realized that the cameras were, in fact, simply the equivalent of a shop sign. On a later occasion, we watched someone having their photograph taken. He approached the photographer of his choice and apparently enquired as to what it would cost and then asked for the photograph to be taken. He was seated and the photographer produced a mirror and a comb and then walked over to one of the other photographers. This man then handed the first one an

SLR camera, which he then took back to his customer. He took the photograph, the customer left and the photographer returned to the man from whom he had borrowed the camera and handed it back. We concluded that either the camera was held in common, or hired out by the fortunate owner to those who did not have one of their own. No doubt the film was taken along every evening to a developer and the cost of processing and printing was shared out fairly. In a place where there is, to all intents and purposes, no social security, it made us wonder how anyone could earn enough money to live. This was a question that we were frequently to ask ourselves during the time we spent in Brazil.

Eventually we came to the Capitania, not as one might expect, down by the river, but right in the centre of town. Needless to say, it was an imposing building and there was a young matelot, armed, standing at the doorway. He asked what we wanted and either understood, or assumed that as foreigners we must be yachtsmen, and waved us in to a doorway. Another rating came to the counter and with much frowning and hard wielding of ballpoint pen, we managed to fill in his form to his satisfaction. We were given several copies (usually, as we were later to discover, the wrong ones) and then carried on to find the Polícia Federal.

On arriving at this establishment, we were shown into a large office, with a couple of hard benches. After a little while, a large man with a surprising red beard came to deal with us. Everything went smoothly and he obviously knew what he was doing. He spoke English, too, and so could explain to us what was required and the terms of the ninety-day visa. He emphasized that there would probably be no problem in renewing our visas, even a couple of weeks in advance, but that if we were in the country after it had expired, we could be fined or even imprisoned. With that warning, he stamped our passports and dated the visa. `Remember,' he said, `that this is for ninety days and not for three calendar months.'

Our next task was to go to a bank for money, but we discovered that the only bank that would take a VISA card, the Banco do Brasil, was shut for lunch. Having only spent just over 3,000 of the 30,000 cruzeiros that Brian had given us, we reckoned that we should see if we could get ourselves some lunch. Beers were out of the question, at 10,000 (a dollar) a bottle, but we went to a *lanchonette* and had ourselves a *hambúrguer* each and a *suco*. Nearly all Brazilian hamburgers are sold with cheese on them and are marked up on the menus as `X-burgers'. For some reason, this is pronounced `Shees-burger' and at first, we would get into endless difficulties trying to buy a `shees-burger' without cheese for Pete, who is not fond of cheese. *Sucos*, on the other hand, never gave us any problem, apart, that is, from selecting which of the many tempting varieties to buy. The *suco* is one of Brazil's better inventions: a beverage made from liquidized fresh fruit, water and ice. Offered ice-cold and with or without added sugar, they are sublime. Those concerned about the purity of the water often drink them made from milk (but is the milk always pasteurized and never diluted, I wonder, and what about the ice?), but we always drank the straight sucos, without sugar, and never had any problems. On this occasion, our money being in short supply, we ordered the cheapest on the menu, lime ones, incredibly refreshing on a hot day.

The rest did me good and I felt a little more human as we sallied forth again to the bank. It was astonishingly busy and we concluded that this probably had more than a little to do with the fact that inflation at the time, was running at one per cent per day. They did not deal with VISA transactions at the cashiers' positions, but instead at a desk, one of several scattered about. An extremely pleasant and obliging little man came forth to assist us and asked us how much we wanted. With inflation being so high, we didn't want to get too much out at once and had settled on US $20 worth of money, which would be the equivalent of 200,000 cruzeiros, which is what I wrote on the paper. He looked a bit puzzled and asked me if I was sure. I looked again in the phrase book and said it in Portuguese, but he then wrote down: 2.000.000,00. The full stops and commas seemed most confusing, but we reckoned that he probably thought that we were more likely to want $200 than twenty. For the avoidance of doubt, I told him that we wanted the equivalent of twenty dollars and that we would get more out when we needed it. He looked a bit puzzled, but then started telephoning. He seemed to have great problems getting through, then he started talking to someone else and eventually, he got up and walked away with this other man.

We waited with what patience we could muster, watching our friend as he appeared and disappeared amongst the crowds. He came back again, smiled at us, picked up the telephone and talked rapidly into the receiver. He put it down and smiled at us.

`O momento.' Then: `Americano? Allemanio?' I shook my head.

`Não, ingleses.'

`Ah! ingleses. Carlos e Diana, eh? No es bene?'

At the time, the Prince and Princess of Wales had just announced the break-up of their marriage and this little man obviously knew considerably more about it than we did. We made the appropriate tut-tutting noises and a rapport was by then thoroughly established. His telephone rang. More rapid conversation and then he leapt up and disappeared again. A short while later he came back with a sheaf of notes in his hand, which he handed to us after Pete had signed the appropriate forms. We shook hands.

`Ciao', he said, which we soon came to realize was the invariable South American word for `good-bye'.

`Boa tarde', we replied, more formally, `e obrigada', I added. The whole transaction had taken three-quarters of an hour. It was not surprising that he had suggested we should have more money. We were soon to realize that getting out our money on a VISA card could take anything between twenty minutes and an hour.

`Did you notice,' I said as we left the chilly, air-conditioned building and walked into the almost solid heat on the street, `that nearly all the ladies in the bank were wearing shorts and that a lot of the men wore jeans?'

`Yes, you're right,' responded Pete. `I suppose that jeans are the height of fashion here. I can't imagine that you could get away with wearing them in a British bank. Mind you, you are probably vetted to see if you are wearing the correct label.'

`The ladies' shorts were very smart,' I continued, `a lot of them had turn-ups on and I saw several ladies wearing a matching jacket. They must also be very fashionable here, but I saw some wearing jeans, too.'

Being somewhat out of touch with the rest of the world, I often speculate on local fashions, wondering if they are a world-wide fad or simply popular in the country that we are visiting. It seems that `city shorts' had caught on in other countries at this time and we were later to realize that many other obviously fashionable clothes were in vogue all over the western world. People are becoming depressingly homogeneous.

`I've put Brian's 30,000 to one side,' Pete announced, `so I suppose that now that we have some money, we can go and see about the mail and then we ought to go and find the market.'

`Do you think that we should buy our fruit and veg in the supermarkets?', I asked. `If you remember, that couple we met in Horta said that it was better shopping in the supermarket, because everything has its price marked and that, anyway, they seemed cheaper.'

`Yes, I remember,' replied Pete, `but I thought you might like to see the market anyway. You could write down some prices and if it is cheaper, we can always go back again after going to the supermarket. We've got to go there anyway, for rum. And we must try a bottle of *cachaça*, too.'

Once again, Brian's map was consulted and we found our way to the post office. It was an impressive building up a flight of steps, on and around which were hordes of people all trying to sell something. A popular item was packs of airmail envelopes. I wondered how many packs a day a man would have to sell in order to feed his family; a lot of them were trying to sell and there were not many people buying.

The post office had a massive queue, although it was well organized by posts and ropes and the empty windows were indicated by an illuminated sign, showing which number was vacant. Unfortunately, this had broken down, but a couple of young men were waving customers to the waiting clerks. It is a matter of constant amazement to me that in every country I have ever visited, there always seem to be too many customers and too few clerks in post offices. One always seems to end up waiting for ages to post letters and, as in the supermarket queue, the one I end up in always has a customer who takes forever to carry out his business. At least with the post office in João Pessoa, there was no risk of that happening, but the wait was long.

Eventually I was waved to an empty window. Phrase book to hand I asked in my best Portuguese for my mail, handing across a slip of paper on which my address was written, for the avoidance of doubt. The clerk smiled at me in kindly manner and then told me that I had come to the wrong place — the counter that I needed was elsewhere, out through the main doors, down the steps, turn left and left again and then in through the doorway there. I summoned up the manners to thank him courteously and then, exasperated at the thought of another long wait, fought my way back to where Pete was standing. He took the news stoically and we sought out the appropriate office.

The counter to which I had been directed, was tucked away among the post-office boxes and, of course, there were several people before me. Although I had not been in contact with my mother, who forwards all our mail to us, I was sure that she would have sent the package on the date that we had asked her to and, from what Brian had told us, we had high hopes of its having arrived by now. On the other hand, we had been filled full of tales of South American post, its unreliability, the chances of pilfering and its general inefficiency. When my turn came, I asked the lady behind the counter if she would please check to see if there was any mail. She disappeared for a few minutes, then returned, shaking her head, 'Nao.' Disappointed,

we were not entirely surprised and thanking her, we went out of the building.

'Never mind,' said Pete, 'we'll come back in a few days and ask again. It's probably delayed with the Christmas rush.'

The bright light was almost painful after the dimness of the cool building and we found that we had to push through considerable crowds on our way to the market, where the stalls were laid out with a mouth-watering variety of fresh produce to tempt us. But as we had been warned, prices were few and far between. We would like to have explored the large market area more thoroughly, but the afternoon was waning and we did not want to be travelling back in the dark, so we carried on down to the supermarket.

There were a couple to choose from, but the first one that we entered seemed to sell more clothes than food and so we went to the second on our list, which was more what we were looking for.

Due to the expense of having had to buy a new Seagull outboard motor before we left the UK, we had concluded that we needed to go on a bit of an economy drive, once we arrived in Brazil. This was based on the information that food prices were very low. Instead of our usual £25 per week, we were living on about £16, which, for the sake of convenience we translated to US$25 per week. With the present rate of 10,000 cruzeiros to the dollar, it was easy to do the sums and find out what everything cost. We heaved a sigh of relief. We could live comfortably on the money available.

The problem, in fact, was not what to buy, but what not to buy. There were so many things available: tomatoes, cucumbers and green peppers for salads, papayas, pineapple, oranges, limes, passion fruit and completely unrecognisable items for our breakfast or to be squeezed into rum for a sundowner. Beer was 75c a bottle, which contained 660 ml, rum was about $3, but for a dollar, we could buy a litre of *cachaça*. *The Lonely Planet* guide had told us all about this native firewater. The locals either drink it neat, or, if they are more civilized, they mix it with lime and sugar to make the typical Brazilian *caipirinha*. Limes, in particular, were especially cheap and, being very fond of our 'Limey,' we reckoned that *cachaça* and lime, without sugar, would probably be a very acceptable beverage. We tried to remember the long trek back to the railway station, that it was very hot and that there was another long walk at the other end. We know from harsh experience that plastic carrier bags cut into your hands and that they collapse when overloaded. We would only buy sufficient to fill our two rucksacks and our two shopping bags, we agreed.

At the checkout, Pete filled our bags, while I emptied the trolley. The bill, over 100,000 cruzeiros, was to me an incomprehensible number of zeroes. I examined the notes in my hand and tried to match them with what I could see on the till. In the end, I shoved a handful at the assistant, who smiled and counted out what she wanted before handing me back the change, which, to my astonishment included coins.

Aware that I might have been swindled, I kept the receipt and put it in my purse, thinking, `We started off with 200,000, Pete has taken out Brian's 30,000 and I still seem to have loads left. I don't think she took too much.'

Pete stood by the end of the counter, loaded up like a sherpa with a disconcerting number of bags around his feet.

`Oh God!' I said, `look how much we've bought!'

`What did it all come to?' he asked me.

`I'm not sure exactly,' I replied. `A hundred an odd something. I suppose that's somewhere over ten dollars. That seems a lot — half a week's money.'

`Yes, but on the other hand, look what we've bought. The *cachaça* alone cost a dollar!'

`Yes,' I groaned, `look at it!'

`I'll carry this rucksack and these two bags,' said Pete. `Can you manage the other rucksack? Those two bags aren't very heavy, really.'

As usual, Pete had taken the bulk of the burden, but it was a miserable walk back to the station, sweating freely, footsore and weary. I buoyed up my spirits with the thought of all the lovely food that we were carrying. A train rolled up a few moments after we arrived and we sat down on the hard, uncomfortable seats, with as much pleasure as if they had been stuffed with finest horsehair and covered in satin.

The twenty minute train ride was perhaps insufficient to make a new man of me, but it did have a reviving effect and our burdens seemed less heavy when we got off the train at Jacaré. We walked back to the riverside through the deep dust of the tracks and, by the time we were passing the entrance to Brian's yard, our loads seemed to weigh several tons. At the last bar before the Yacht Club's dinghy dock, where we had left *Skip*, there was a group of several people, obviously our fellow yachtsmen.

`You must be from *Badger*,' a large woman hailed us as we trudged by.

`That's right.'

`Well, there's only one rule round here, and it says that everyone has to meet here each evening for a sundowner!' she announced.

We smiled uncertainly and exchanged glances. Even at a dollar a bottle, our budget did not run to daily beers. Then Pete said to me,

`Well, I think we probably deserve a beer after today's marathon and we ought to appear sociable, I suppose.'

We entered the covered area where everyone sat and put down our loads.

`You go over there, to order a beer,' someone told us, so Pete went to a little hut and came back shortly with two bottles of ice-cold beer and chilled glasses. With the bottles were polystyrene covers, to keep them cold. We each poured some into a glass, took a swig and sighed gratefully. They were so good! Feeling slightly more human, we introduced ourselves and then met our companions.

The silver-haired man on the next table, turned out to be from the American ketch, next to which we were anchored. The lady who had hailed us was from the Danish catamaran and the well-built man next to her was her husband. Nearby sat a small, dark, rather stout man who turned out to be Spanish, from a little boat that we had noticed that morning, and which Pete swore had been in Palma de Mallorca at the same time as ourselves. As we were talking to them, Chris came in with his girlfriend, whose name we discovered was Vera. From Switzerland, she completed our League of Nations. As usual, the common language was English. This reflects not on the fact that the Empire still has its sway, but that the mighty USA is the strongest influence in the world and that its films, music and technology are doing away with any need for Esperanto, as people scramble to learn English in order to get on. Even in the UK, this is true, as more and more Yankee words and spellings are slipping into our programmes and publications.

By this time, half past five, the sun was sinking behind the trees on the opposite side of the river and a blessed coolness was descending. Too tired really to develop any opinions about our new acquaintance, we finished our beers, picked up our shopping and went back to *Skip*. Back on board, we brought everything below and then sat down for five minutes before starting the mammoth task of emptying out our bags. Needless to say, we sampled the bottle of *cachaça*, with a lime or two, just to check that it was potable.

Chapter Six

We stayed for three weeks in Jacaré, largely because we were waiting for our mail, but it was a congenial place, we enjoyed the company of the other yachts and we felt that it was a good place to get used to Brazil.

Most days found us busy: we made several shopping trips into João Pessoa, which always meant most of the day, because the town was spread out and a lot of walking about was involved. On the days that we had to change money, it all took even longer. Charles and Maggie had come in a day or two after us and they told us that we should cash dollars at one of the Câmbio houses. However, we had brought no cash with us, not wishing to have money on board when it could be earning interest in the bank. We also discovered that we could have changed it at one of the local bars, Gringo's. We had heard terrible stories of being ripped off in Brazil, but as time went by we realized that the danger lay in changing money on the street. If you went to a shop or a bar they invariably gave the correct exchange rate, often telephoning a bank to check first. Businesses were usually happy to change money: dollars kept their value until the end of the week when they could be banked, local currency did not.

We soon came to know our fellow sailors, a mixed bag, as is usual in any group of yachts. The big catamaran that we had noticed was owned by a couple of Danes who chartered it out. Jan said that he preferred a catamaran to a monohull since having had one break up under him near the Cape of Good Hope. He and Kristina had lived in Greenland and, having been there ourselves, we enjoyed talking about it with them.

'I would never take a yacht there,' Jan said, 'I have seen how bad it can be,' implying that we were more than a little mad to have sailed there ourselves. Kristina and I had quite a discussion about how the Greenlanders hunt. I can sympathize with their desire to maintain a traditional lifestyle, but shooting seals with rifles from motor boats is not what most of us think of as native hunting and such methods make it too likely that the rarer animals such as walrus will be hunted to extinction. It also seems wrong to hunt endangered species such as narwhal and then sell the meat in shops, but Kristina countered by saying that the KEP had a monopoly on selling, which was why we had seen narwhal meat in the supermarkets. I wondered how, if this were so, that we had seen people selling reindeer meat outside the stores.

'Would you have them starve?' Kristina asked, 'or rely totally on Denmark for everything?' It was not an argument that could be won by either of us. Kristina is of the opinion that the world is provided for human beings to use as they wish, preferably with sense, but invariably to their own ends. I, on the other hand, have the feeling that we have a duty to care for our planet and the fact that we are the most powerful creature does not make us any more important nor give us any greater right to be here than any other being. As far as Greenland is concerned, the real problem is that the country barely had the resources to support the native people when they lived off the land; it certainly does not have the resources to support a twentieth-century, western way of life.

Pete and Jan, who could appreciate both types of boat, enjoyed discussing the pros and cons of multihulls; it was a pleasant change to hear the various points talked over in a non-partisan manner. Jan and Kristina were often in the bar when we came by, their paying guests taking full advantage of the cold beers and local colour. The children adored Kristina, who spoilt them, completely beguiled by their winning and affectionate ways, for they were easily pleased and enjoyed the novelty of the visitors. It was a great delight to the children to be able to use the pool table in the bar, but they needed money because it was a coin-in-the-slot operation. Jan used to get a little annoyed with Kristina.

`You shouldn't give them so much money!', he would say.

`Why not? It's only a few cents.'

`Yes, but the money that you have given to these children over the past week or so, is as much as their fathers earn. You're spoiling them and they will get greedy.'

`But they enjoy it so much and they never complain if I don't give them anything. Besides, we'll soon be gone and they will have to find their own games to play.'

Kristina invited some of them onto their boat for a party. They were all delighted over it, but I wondered with Jan, if too many treats from the foreign visitors could spoil them. It had not happened yet. When Jan and Kristina sailed off they did not come begging from the other yachtsmen and still would run and fetch fallen mangoes for us when we walked past, simply to please us. It is difficult to know how to act in these situations. Their poverty is great, but they can so easily become dependent on visitors and vulnerable to the accidents that dictate which place is popular from one year to the next.

There were two singlehanders at Jacaré, Miguel and Bob, who in many ways were complete opposites. Miguel was Spanish and, as Pete had thought, had been in Mallorca at the same time as ourselves. His boat was about thirty feet long and he had fitted her out himself from a bare hull. Miguel was pleased to see us and remembered *Badger*, too, although we had never met. He was a convivial soul, but as poor as a church mouse and eked out his meagre income by selling earrings, pendants and so forth that he made from shells that he trawled up. Miguel got along well with the locals, of course. Portuguese and Spanish are by no means the same language, but Brazilians are always keen to communicate and Miguel could get by very adequately. He had been there some time, when we arrived, and had apparently had quite a lot of hospitality from the other yachts. He was about to leave and so arranged for a party at the bar that the yachtsmen frequented. He asked some of his local friends to catch a load of crabs and cooked them at the bar. Everyone

was invited to partake and Miguel was plied with beers. He got quite elevated and was prevailed upon to tell his best joke: one about a crocodile. I do not think that anybody managed to understand what it was about, but he had us all in hysterics with his imitations of the `cocodril' with its huge jaws. Not long after he subsided in a corner, worn out by his act.

Bob, on the other hand, was fairly affluent and would often offer to buy us a beer if we came past towards sundown. From the United States, he was both a loner and convivial. Although he apparently went ashore for company, if anyone visited his boat, he never offered hospitality, something that is almost unheard of among cruising boats. He had lived for some time in the Azores, where he had worked as a sail maker and was the owner of the large ketch near which we lay. As we had suspected, she was anchored on rope and wandered around all over the place at the change of tide. As we were on chain and there was so little wind, we barely moved and in the end we re-anchored to keep away from his yacht's advances. Bob had left the Azores a few years previously, largely at his wife's behest, but had not been happy in the USA and so had bought this boat to go off cruising. His wife, apparently, was not fond of sailing, so for most of the time he lived a bachelor existence, flying home occasionally to see her. He was not averse to the company of the local ladies and his command of their language, combined with an ample supply of dollars, obviously made him a more attractive proposition than poor Miguel. He still had his sewing machine aboard and would undoubtedly have been able to have made a comfortable living in a more popular cruising ground.

In the evenings, they would gather with some of the other cruising people to watch the sun go down, even though Miguel could not afford to buy a beer. I am afraid that we were less sociable and usually enjoyed our sundowners aboard, as we too were unable to afford a cold beer every night, but enjoyed watching the sun set with a glass in our hands. A quarter of a mile or so up the river was a bar that always opened in the evening and invariably played Ravel's *Bolero* at this time of night, so that the piece is now inextricably linked in my mind with Jacaré. It was the only piece of classical music that I ever recall hearing in Brazil.

We all had different ideas of what to do for Christmas. Bob had been invited out, Jan and Kristina had their charter party on board, and Charles and Maggie told us that they would go to Cabo Branco, the nearby holiday resort, and tour the bars for a while before finding a restaurant for the evening. It was not our idea of Christmas and, instead, we went the whole hog, except that we substituted a chicken for the traditional turkey. This meant a trip into João Pessoa on Christmas Eve, to give the chicken time to thaw out, without going off. We also hoped to pick up our mail, in which hope we were once more doomed to disappointment.

By this time we had sampled both the buses and the trains. General opinion was in favour of the buses, which cost twenty cents as opposed to ten cents on the train, but left from closer to the supermarket. Raúl, the Argentine, would not go on the trains.

'They are disgusting and dirty', he told us, so after that we did not really like to tell him that we preferred them. Disgusting and dirty though they may have been, at least we could usually get a seat, which was often an impossibility on the buses and, although the railway station was a long way from the supermarket, the station at Jacaré was a lot closer to the river than the bus stop and, to us, it was that final walk that was the killer. On Christmas Eve, everything had taken even longer than usual and it was nearly dark by the time we walked through the dimly lit streets to the station. We were a little concerned, but consoled ourselves with Brian's comments on João Pessoa's relative safety. Even so, I have to confess to being relieved when we finally arrived at the station. A train was soon to leave and we staggered aboard and sat down with a sigh of relief. Not long after we pulled out of the station, out of the corner of my eye I noticed a movement on the floor. Looking down I beheld an enormous cockroach scuttering along by the seats. If there is one thing that I loathe it is a cockroach, and the thought of this monster running over my bare feet was not one that I found pleasant. A moment or two later I saw another and lifted my bags off the floor onto the empty seat by my side.

'My God! Look at those things!' I said to Pete. 'You'd better lift your bags up, too, we don't want to take one of them home.'

'Not very nice, are they?' he commented, pushing his feet further away from the seats. A young lady sitting opposite, following the direction of my gaze, also saw the creatures and, giving me an embarrassed smile at her weakness, lifted her feet up and tucked them under her. I smiled back, glad to see that it was not only the gringo visitors who disliked cockies so much.

When we arrived back at Jacaré's station, it was dark, very dark, and it was with some difficulty that we found our way along the dirt tracks back to the river. We made a vow that we would not repeat the experiment; it was bad enough carrying half a ton of provisions without having to grope our way home.

Back on board, we had a cup of tea to restore our energies a little and then I started washing the fruit and vegetables before stowing them away. As I was doing this, there came a knock on the hull and Pete went out to see who it was. I heard voices and then the visitor left.

'Who was that?' I asked.

'It was the lady from *La Louisette*,' Pete replied. 'She rowed over to invite us round for dinner tonight.'

'Oh, hell!' I said, 'I feel absolutely knackered. The last thing I want to do is go out to dinner. What did you say to her?'

'Well, I said that we would. I couldn't really refuse.'

'No, no, of course not. Especially at Christmas and when they've only just got here, too. But when I talked to her yesterday, I thought that she really didn't speak English.'

'No, not really, but enough for me to be able to understand her.'

I had spoken to the lady the previous day, when she had come over to ask if it was all right to use the Yacht Club's dinghy dock. She had not heard about Brian, and I had suggested that she go over to talk to him. We had been speaking in French and she had asked me if Brian spoke her language and was delighted to hear that he did.

'My English is very bad,' she had explained, 'and my captain doesn't speak a word!'

I anticipated that the evening ahead would be quite hard work because my French is not so good that I really enjoy having to converse in it for any length of time.

'So what time are we meant to be there?' I asked Pete.

'Oh, about half past seven. We should have time to put most of the stuff away first.'

'Well, one thing,' I said, 'it'll be worth going over just to look at the boat.'

Pete agreed with that comment. We had been fascinated by the yacht since she had come in to anchor the previous day. *La Louisette* was a gaff schooner designed by a Frenchman called Daniel Bombigher and she appeared to have sailed straight out of a South Sea Island fantasy. We had seen some of Bombigher's designs in magazines and were aware of the extreme romanticism of his work, but it was quite an eye-opener to see it translated into three dimensions. From the exaggeratedly raked masts, to the wood-stocked anchor catted on the bulwark, the schooner represented the total antithesis of the stark, practical lines we generally associate with French yachts.

At half past seven, we rowed over to a very warm welcome. As we went below, we were struck with the amount of work that had gone into the boat and looked around us with great interest.

We sat down and introductions were made. *La Louisette*'s owner was called Daniel Mantovani and his mate was Susanne Louis. The third member of the crew was Daniel's eleven-year-old daughter, Céline. While Susanne was mixing *caipirinhas* for us, we asked about the boat.

Daniel had spent eight years of his life on the Ivory Coast, building the fifteen-metre, Shpountz design, cold-moulded of local woods. He had been helped by two or three African craftsmen, one of whom had carved her magnificent figurehead of a mermaid. Unusually for a cold-moulded vessel, at twenty-five tons displacement, *La Louisette* was a real ship and no light-weight. She had a beam of no less than five metres and a draught of two metres, with the centre-board raised.

`I believe that Daniel Bombigher insists that you don't make any changes to his plans,' I translated for Pete.

`Yes, that's right,' responded Daniel. `When you buy the plans, he gives you a choice of interiors and a choice of styles; for example, Louis Quinze or Colonial. We chose the "La Famille" interior in a Colonial style.'

I looked around. `Some family!' I commented. `How many berths are there?'

`Yes, he must expect you to have a lot of children,' Daniel laughed. `There are nine berths altogether. I think that he regards it as a family design because it is very open inside and there is only one private cabin. Perhaps that is intended for the parents.'

We asked about their voyage to date.

`We left the Ivory Coast not long after we launched *La Louisette* in late 1991.' Daniel told us. `We sailed directly to Rio and then up to Vittoria. We had to beat all the way. It was very rough and when we arrived at Vittoria, there were many repairs to make.'

`How many sails do you normally set?'

`Six.'

`She's a big boat. Don't you find that the work is very heavy.'

`Oh yes, she is really too much for us. But you see, before we left the Ivory Coast none of us had had much sailing experience. We did not realize what *La Louisette* would be like and I learnt to sail very quickly, I can tell you. *C'etait un apprentissage dure*,' he added, with a wry smile.

By now we were ready to eat and Céline came out of the galley, where she had been helping Susanne, and proudly passed us a menu that she had made. She had worked hard on it and I felt so glad that we had not turned down their invitation and even more so when Daniel explained that in their part of France, Christmas Eve is generally celebrated by the family getting together for a special meal. With just the three of them, the atmosphere would not be the same and, as they had no family in Brazil, they had decided to invite us instead, knowing that I, anyway, spoke some French. They had taken a lot of trouble and it would have been a big disappointment for them, and especially for Céline, had we turned them down.

The menu commenced with *kibe*, a local dish that we ate quite frequently during the following months. It is a cross between a faggot and a skinless sausage and quite delicious. This was followed with an African stew that Susanne had learnt to cook on the Ivory Coast. To conclude, we had a delicious cake that Céline had baked.

As the evening progressed, Susanne and Pete managed to converse very effectively with a few common words and gestures. Pete always makes me laugh when we are with people who barely speak English, because his method of assisting them is to speak in a similar manner, using a sort of pidgin and talking with the appropriate accent. On this occasion he sounded a little like Peter Sellers in the role of Inspector Clouseau.

Daniel went out into the galley and came back proudly bearing a bottle of champagne. Céline gave a squeal of excitement.

`Is it time then?' she asked.

`Very nearly,' replied Daniel. Pete and I looked at each other, puzzled. Admittedly it was quite late and we were tired, but try as we might, we could attach no significance to eleven o'clock. Still, Daniel had told us about the small village that he had come from and where he had celebrated so many Christmas Eves and we thought that perhaps this was a local tradition. With great showmanship, Daniel uncorked the bottle and filled the champagne glasses. There was one for everyone and Céline's eyes were sparkling at this special treat. The electric lights were switched off and in the warm glow of the oil lamp, we wished each other a Merry Christmas and a *Bon Noel*. Glasses were clinked together and the wine sampled and pronounced very acceptable.

After we had each had another glass, Daniel asked, `Do you like Martinique rum?'

This was a facer. The only Martinique rum we had ever drunk had been absolutely foul.

`Well,' I said, `to be honest, we've only ever had Martinique rum once. It was a white one and we didn't really enjoy it on that occasion.'

`Ha!' exclaimed Daniel. `That was not rum. What you had was the raw spirit, a little like *cachaça*. *This* is Martinique rum,' and with a flourish he produced a bottle of golden liquid.

`But it's called *St James*!' I protested.

`Well, perhaps St Jacques would be more appropriate,' Daniel admitted, `but it is from Martinique and it is very good. A little like one of your special whiskies. Would you like to try some?'

`Oh, please,' we replied.

`We must have clean glasses for this,' Susanne said and found some while Daniel poured the last of the champagne into Céline's glass. He had not exaggerated. The rum was excellent: smooth and mellow, to be sipped with appreciation rather than drowned in Coca-Cola.

When we had finished our glasses, Daniel offered more, but we refused. The rum was obviously a special treat for them and would be difficult to replace. Besides, we could hardly keep our eyes open and it was nearly midnight. Susanne and Daniel did not protest too forcibly and we guessed that they, too, were feeling that they had had a long day and, indeed, had probably not yet recovered from their last passage.

`Come and see us tomorrow afternoon,' we said, `and have tea with us.'

`Real English tea?' asked Susanne.

`But of course.'

Laughing, we climbed into *Skip* and rowed back to *Badger*, tumbling into our bunk to sleep like logs.

When Daniel, Susanne and Céline came over the following day, Daniel said:

`You must have thought we were crazy last night!'

`What do you mean?' we asked.

`Why, opening the champagne at eleven o'clock!' he exclaimed.

`Well, we did wonder,' we admitted, `but felt it was some special tradition.'

`Non, no. I thought it was midnight! We are still on Vittoria time and it is an hour different from here. We did not know there was any difference until today, when Brian mentioned it!'

One of the pleasures of this anchorage at Jacaré, was watching the local *canoas*, which we had noticed on our arrival, sailing back and forth about their daily business. About half of these were dugouts and the other half had been built out of planks, due to the unavailability of large trees. The dugouts were the more refined of the two, boats of beauty and grace, with a most elegant, swept-up stern on which the paddler sat. They were rigged with sprit sails and also had leeboards, which intrigued us. As leeboards are rarely found on native boats, we wondered if these had been introduced by the Dutch, who were in this part of Brazil in some force in the past, hoping to get some of the wealth of the New World themselves. On Sundays, the *canoa* owners took the day off and often ran races with one another, several of the crew well out to windward, hiked out on long boards, with a rope to the mast. We were never quite sure if the rope was to support the crew or the unstayed mast. Painted in gay colours, and tearing through the water, they made a joyous sight.

Watching these *canoas* sailing back and forth up the river made us wish to do a little exploration ourselves. Pete had recently made a little green lugsail for *Skip* and here was a chance to try it out. The sail was rigged to one side of the boat and we had a leeboard that was fixed onto the same side. *Skip* is a very small boat, only two metres long, and her sailing characteristics proved to be unusual to say the least. Easing the sheet seemed to make her head up and hardening it in caused her to bear away; or at least on some points of sailing. The steering oar was sometimes effective and sometimes useless, but we progressed through the water in a satisfactory if, initially, a somewhat erratic manner. As we got to understand her, the sailing became more pleasurable although at best, we were `killing time, rather than distance', as *Skip*'s designer, Phil Bolger, would put it. She has a central seat running fore and aft. Reclining on cushions on either side of this, we were very comfortable and had a good view of our surroundings.

We rushed up the river with a fair tide and then sailed around the top of Ilha do Stuart, into the network of creeks on its far side. Fortunately, it was easy to make out the main part of the river along the shore of the island, so there was no risk of getting lost. At one point we saw a *canoa* hauled up on the beach. Men dressed in mosquito veils and clothed from head to foot were ashore in the mud, catching the little crabs to sell to the locals. These were the same crabs that Miguel had given to us at his party; small and muddy, they were hardly a gourmet delight, but were undoubtedly cheap. The mosquitoes we knew about, but we were unlikely to experience them if we got back before dusk. What we had not come across before were the *pium* flies, vicious insects, not unlike horseflies, but more tenacious. It was not sufficient to wave a hand at them, you actually needed physically to brush them off, as I soon discovered to my cost. The bite that they left not only hurt at the time, but bled copiously and itched unpleasantly afterwards. We had applied insect repellent, but not in sufficient quantities, it appeared. We had a tin with us and a second, more generous application did the trick, although we found that they were very clever at discovering any area not completely covered.

As we sailed along, we ate our picnic and drank our beers watching the interesting scenery and from the sketch chart, with which Brian provides all visiting yachtsmen, trying to work out how far we had come. There were one or two villages on the mainland side, less than desirable sites, muddy and infested by the pium flies and mosquitoes. The children who ran down to the riverside to watch us sail by were covered with bites.

About half way round the island, the tide turned against us and we had to start working for our progress.

'Never mind,' we consoled ourselves, 'we had the last of the tide going up from the anchorage and should have the first when we go up again, or at least be there at slack water.' Unfortunately, as we came around the bottom of Ilha do Stuart, the wind freshened up, straight from the anchorage, and we also discovered that there was a tidal eddy against us, down the island. We either had to cross this, which meant going out into the comparatively rough and open water on the river, or creep up against the eddy in calmer water, but against a foul wind and tide. As I have already mentioned, *Skip* is not really designed for beating to windward effectively.

We beat about for what seemed hours, making pathetically little headway and in the end, we abandoned sailing and Pete rowed us manfully back to *Badger*. The wind was really quite fresh and the chop raised by wind against tide enough to soak us from head to foot. As the afternoon advanced, we became thoroughly chilled, but the tide strengthened, making for faster, if wetter progress. It was almost dark by the time we got back aboard, but we stayed only to collect towels, before going back ashore to use the hot showers, generously provided by the hospitable Yacht Club. Thawed out and refreshed, we concluded that the 'voyage' had probably been worthwhile after all.

A few days later we went over to have supper with Charles and Maggie on *La Fomalhaut*, a fine example of one of Sam Crocker's designs. Thirty-five feet long, with ten feet of beam and a five-foot-four draught, she was built by the very well-known Bud McIntosh, in 1939 at Dover Point, New Hampshire.

After a varied career, she had spent the last seven years as a cruising home, exploring the Caribbean and Central America. Charles and Maggie found her in St Thomas in 1985 where she had just completed a substantial refit, including new planking and decks. She was built of mahogany on oak and rigged as a bermudian cutter.

Charles and Maggie seemed to be an odd couple to own such a classic, wooden boat. They were both New Yorkers, city people through and through, and we could never reconcile their worldliness and sophistication with owning and living aboard this comparatively simple, wooden boat. Although she had an engine, they were some of the rare people who prefer to handle a boat as though the motor is not there and they did not even have an echo sounder. That they had very little money behind them, might have explained their choice of material: wooden boats in the Caribbean sell for a lot less than glass fibre, but in no way would it explain their contentment with their lot.

It was a pleasure to sit in the roomy, American-style cockpit, watching the sun go down. Charles and Maggie were excellent hosts and good company and took great pleasure in our obvious delight of their special cocktails. One of their luxuries was a twelve-volt blender. Charles went into some detail as to the choosing of one.

'A lot of them are just jokes,' he explained, 'and although they are sold for making drinks aboard, they are useless. But this one is the goods. It's solid and powerful and will crush ice and that's what you need.' This he proceeded to demonstrate and with the addition of pieces of several different fruits and, of course, *cachaça*, the most marvellous cocktails were soon whizzed up and being sampled.

'Wonderful!' we exclaimed.

'I think that one of the best things about Brazil is the fruit here,' said Maggie. 'We usually have *sucos* when we are ashore, don't you?'

'Well, when we are in town and have to buy lunch, we normally buy a lime *suco*. But I have to confess that we still regard an ice cold 'Antarctica' as more of a treat and we can't bring ourselves to pay more for a more exotic *suco* than we would for a beer,' I said.

Charles laughed at that. 'Well there's no doubt about it. Brazilian beer really takes a lot of beating and at a dollar a pint, you can't say it's expensive either!'

Charles and Maggie were also a fairly low budget outfit. Maggie had been a nurse in New York and Charles had met her there not long after leaving university. He was obviously a very clever man because he had studied mathematics at Cambridge, UK, but he had not really been able to cope with the combination of a different society, the pressure of studying and his comparative youth, and had packed it in. Maggie was several years older then he and had her feet planted firmly on the ground. They seemed to complement one another very well.

`You must find cruising a lot different from New York,' we commented.

`It certainly is!' They went on to tell us some stories about New York and particularly its night life until we felt like a couple of country bumpkins:

`You must be joking! I can't believe that! Really! You're not pulling my leg, are you?' Charles and Maggie had been ready for most things and had experimented with drugs and visited some of the sex clubs in the sleazier parts of New York. Some of the stories that they told us had our hair standing on end, but are not the sort of thing that could be published for a family audience. Sufficient to say that in one of the clubs that they went to, they saw a young woman hanging, naked, in chains, while a man nonchalantly flogged her with a whip. Another feature of the club were the `Glory Holes,' but good taste forbids me to enlarge on these.

Maggie and Charles were undoubtedly amused at our innocence and, perhaps feeling that they had shocked us, assured us that they no longer used drugs, although `we smoke a little pot from time to time.' As with all other pot smokers that we have met, they also seemed to enjoy alcohol, which always amuses me, having heard so many apologists for pot saying that is only really the same as `the businessman's martinis.' Apparently pot was of good quality and readily available in Brazil; the drawback was fairly severe punishment for those found possessing it. We voted to stick to *cachaça*; I have quite enough vices.

We had a very pleasant evening and a good meal. When we had eaten, Maggie said,

`Raúl and Nidia are having a party tonight and invited us along. We told them that you were coming round, but they said to come later if we wanted to. Do you fancy it?'

Raúl was an Argentine whom we had met the first day we arrived in Jacaré. He and his wife had `dropped out' of the mainstream, middle-class, Buenos Aires lifestyle, no longer enjoying the Argentine way of life. Raúl had been the owner of a company that built yachts and before he gave up his former lifestyle, had them build him a hull and decks that looked suspiciously like a Freedom 40. They had had a couple of children, and had added to the family regularly since they left, so that by now, there were four or five little ones running around. This made life slightly more

complicated, particularly as Raúl was still fitting out *Samadhi*, in spite of the fact that they had been living on her for four years. He was fascinated by junk rig, and was very interested in *Badger*.

As Raúl had already asked us to call round sometime, we agreed that this evening would be a good opportunity and so we all rowed ashore and walked round to the small house which they rented in the village, while Raúl continued to work on the boat.

When we arrived we were greeted with obvious pleasure and led round the back of the house to a barbecue area. To our consternation, there was food waiting to be cooked and it became apparent that Charles and Maggie had got hold of the wrong end of the stick — we had been invited round to eat. In spite having already dined, by the time the chicken was cooked, the tempting smell had been sufficient to enable us to eat some more. Pete, as ever, had no problem at all in making a second meal and we sat down, eating, drinking and talking.

As the evening progressed, the other guests left so that only Charles, Maggie and ourselves remained, talking about boats. The night was dark and warm, lit only by the glow from the dying fire and I was in a state of mellow relaxation so that I did not really question the odd gesture of Raúl, passing his cigarette around. I took a whiff,

`It's like Portuguese tobacco,' I said and passed it on. After a while, Charles started to get very giggly and rather silly and as it was now very late, Pete and I thanked our kind hosts and pushed off back to the boat. Picking my way along the dark road, I was thinking of the evening.

`I didn't think that Raúl smoked,' I said.

`That was pot.'

`You're joking! After all these years! I've always wanted to try it and when I got the chance I never even realized what it was. I could have at least tried to inhale!'

`Never mind, Annie, you might have ended up like Charles. It made him very silly.'

`Yes, that's true. Still, I wish I'd known. I'll probably never have another chance. It seemed to work very quickly on Charles.'

`Didn't you notice? They were both smoking when we went over this evening.'

`I don't think I'd want to risk it. Imagine if you got caught. I know that it's unlikely, but I'd rather not take the chance.'

`I suppose that you don't think about it after a while,' Pete concluded. `Still, we'll stick to *cachaça*. I expect it's cheaper, anyway.'

Another occasion that Charles had us amused was on New Year's Eve. Gringo had invited everyone round for a party and we all took food along to share. Around midnight, a car pulled up and half a dozen people got out and came over to us all to wish us a `Happy New Year.' With typical Brazilian warmth, they hugged everybody and then jumped back into their car and drove off. The next day Charles discovered that he had lost his wallet.

`It must have been those guys in the car,' he said. `One of them was a pickpocket and the other distracted our attention. It's just the sort of thing that would happen in New York.'

`Oh no!' I said, `I'm sure you're wrong Charles. They were just happy and being friendly. I can't believe that they would have done that.'

`Well I'd like to know where my wallet is, in that case!'

After he'd left I said to Pete, `What I can't understand is that Charles is meant to be so street-wise. What on earth was he doing carrying his wallet in the back pocket of his shorts. He was advertizing it — asking for it to be stolen.'

We saw them again a little later, when we were rowing ashore.

`Hey! Charles found his wallet,' called Maggie, with a malicious glint in her eye.

`Oh good! Where was it?'

`It fell out of his pocket when he used the head at Gringo's. Someone handed it in, but Gringo forgot about it until he opened up at lunch.'

We laughed. `I'm really glad it wasn't those people in the car.'

`Yeah, well. It's the sort of thing that would happen in New York,' said Charles, smiling a little shamefacedly.

A couple of days later, we had our chance to repay the hospitality of the others and also to thank Brian. We offered everyone a day out on *Badger*, which they seemed delighted to accept. It was, of course, a lovely day with a pleasant breeze. There were seven guests aboard, but by towing the dinghy we had lots of deck space for everyone to spread themselves around. We had a delightful sail down the river and anchored for lunch, a cold collation that I had spent most of the previous day preparing. Everyone made the right noises and the food was obviously enjoyed. Raúl had endless questions to ask about the rig, which he was thinking of putting on his boat and Brian was equally interested in *Badger* herself, so that we enjoyed talking about matters close to our heart.

Brian thoroughly enjoyed his day out. He has a small, Jim Brown-designed trimaran which he often sails, but said that he rarely got the opportunity to sail in other boats.

`It's something that I've often noticed,' said Pete. `The average cruising person does not seem that interested in sailing. Most people seem to go and anchor somewhere and then stay put until they move on to a new place. They never go out for a day's sail.'

`I think that a lot of boats are just too much work,' Brian said. `You've got the right idea keeping things simple. It's much easier for you just to pull up the sails and go, then it is for a lot of the boats that I see here.'

Suiting the action to the word, we cleared the debris away and sailed back up the river again, bringing up to anchor in our old spot.

One of the things that we had been discussing in the afternoon, was the threatened advent of *Trios Elétricos* at the weekends.

`Whatever is one of those?' we asked.

`They are very popular at holiday places here,' said Brian. `You've no doubt noticed that Brazilians love music and dancing. Well, the *Trio Elétrico* is a way of bringing music to the people. What they do is to get a large van, the size of a furniture removal lorry, and then they cover it with speakers and drive it to a popular spot, where they park it. They then plug into the mains — hence the

Daysail from Jacaré.

name: three pin plug — and there you are, an instant outdoor disco.'

'It sounds horrendous,' I said, at the same time as Charles said, 'That sounds kinda neat.'

Brian laughed. 'Well, I must say that I agree with Annie. We've complained to the local council and say we don't want it, but I'm afraid that we'll be outvoted. It'll bring a lot of trade to the riverfront bars. The thing will be parked right next to our house and will be unbearable.'

The next weekend, Brian sculled out to *Badger*. 'Would you like to come for a sail with us, tomorrow?' he asked. 'It's about time I took *Jelinha* out and we've heard that there is definitely a *Trio Elétrico* coming tomorrow, so I want to be away.'

'Great! That would be wonderful!'

'OK, we'll give you a call when we're ready to go.'

The following morning saw a great bustle in the village and a huge van drove down to park just outside Brian's yard. Before long they were plugged in and the technicians were blowing down the microphones saying *um, dois* over and over until the sound quality was to their satisfaction. When we heard the volume at which the music was played, we wondered why on earth they bothered about its quality. You did not hear it: you felt it. Céline was jumping up and down with excitement.

'She loves music,' Susanne explained, 'and knows all the latest hits. She can sing them, too, even though she doesn't understand all the words. It helps her Portuguese, but I don't think it's good for her ears when they play it so loudly.'

Even on *Badger*, the noise was excessive, and it was with relief that we saw Brian getting his boat ready. With his wife and daughter aboard, he was soon alongside and we stepped over. Pete was delighted at the thought of sailing on a Jim Brown design and he and Brian were in their element as we sped down the river on the light breeze.

Silvia spoke very little English and my Portuguese is virtually non-existent, but we somehow managed. She and Patricia were content to stretch out in the sunshine so that soon, I was happily ensconced at the helm while Pete and Brian looked at the little boat's construction details and discussed building methods.

'I love plywood,' Brain said, 'but it's almost impossible to get decent stuff in Brazil. It all seems to be infected with some sort of rot. When you buy it, it looks perfect, but a couple of years later it starts to crumble away. I don't know what causes it and, of course, I can't treat it because it's impossible to get

preservative into the inner cores. It makes building a real problem.'

'That's interesting', Pete remarked. 'I was wondering whether to get a couple of sheets so as to have a kit of parts in case anything happens to *Skip*, because the wood seems pretty reasonably priced. But from what you say, I don't think it would be worth while.'

'It wouldn't — for the quality, the wood's far too expensive. I'm hoping that someone will start manufacturing or importing decent stuff. It would certainly make my job easier.'

With her shallow draught, *Jetinha* could explore places that were impossible to get to in *Badger* and we sailed up the river, off which we had anchored the previous week. As it got narrower, we beat up in shorter and shorter tacks until we could really get no further. Here Brian dropped anchor and we had something to eat. Every now and then a vagrant shift in the breeze would bring the sound of the *Trio Elétrico* to us, despite our now being several miles from Jacaré and surrounded by trees.

'Are you going to have to suffer that every weekend?' we asked.

'I'm afraid so. I don't want to make too much fuss about it at present, because the fact that so many people will be coming to Jacaré gives us much more leverage to have drinking water piped to the village. They are now promising it for next year.'

'What do people do now?' I asked, 'They surely can't afford to buy bottled water.'

'Well, they are told to boil it, but I suspect that they just get strong stomachs or ill,' Brain replied. 'Which reminds me, I have a car going for spring water for us in a few days. Bring some jerricans along if you want some.'

By now it was time to turn back and we retraced our steps with some difficulty, running aground once or twice, the tide having fallen. The wind went light and it was growing dark by the time we got back. Silvia and Patricia were feeling cold and being bitten by mosquitoes and left in short order when we picked up the mooring. Pete and I helped Brian to tidy up *Jetinha* and then went ashore to see what was happening around the *Trio Elétrico*. We met Charles.

' Man, these Brazilians are really wild!' he exclaimed. 'You should have been here while they were dancing. My God, they dance so hard that the sweat is just flying off them! You really missed out.'

'Too much noise, I'm afraid, Charles,' I said, 'and I don't really like the music, anyway. I thought that Brazilian music was meant to be a little special, but it just sounds like any other pop music to me.'

`Oh no! the rhythm is quite different. In fact they have several. It's really unique.'

`You're obviously a connoisseur,' I said, `but I'd much prefer peace and quiet to amplified music. We're ready to leave anyway, but we'll certainly be off before next weekend. I could put up with the power boats, but I draw the line at *Trios Elétricos*.'

With Jacaré being such a popular centre, our anchorage was invaded by motor boats every week-end. A lot of them were dry-stored at the Yacht Club and on Friday evening and Saturday morning there were scenes of frantic activity as those that were required were launched and anchored off. Where we were, well out in the river, they were no problem, but some of the yachts closer in had to fend them off as the tide turned and the light power boats swung on their rope cables. Later in the day they could be a nuisance, as the macho owners, well loaded with *caipirinhas*, showed off to their wives and girlfriends and postured in front of the other men. At night they were a real menace, tearing along with no lights, but by Sunday evening they had disappeared, leaving the river to the yachts and *canoas* for the rest of the week.

Before we left, Pete went and talked with Raúl and with Chris, from *Majoy*, whom we had met on our first day. As they had both sailed further south in Brazil, they had information about anchorages and harbours that we would be visiting. They were happy to pass on their knowledge and it proved very useful in time to come. Poor Chris was having a hard time. The `bit of work' that he had had to do on his boat daily increasing as he started looking closely and discovered pockets of rot; his engine did not work — he had known this, of course, but had not realized the extent of its problems until he came to fix it; his leg had been badly nipped by a crab and had started to fester; Vera's sister was staying with them and had her purse taken out of her handbag — with a thousand dollars in it, a fortune to the locals and sitting in full view, the temptation had proved too much. As if all this were not enough, the house in the village that they had rented, because they were feeling overcrowded on the boat and having difficulties getting on with their work, was broken into and some things were stolen. Chris complained to the police, but he was angry at the treatment that they had given him.

`It's his own fault,' Bob said. `He went straight up to the police from working on the boat. Dirty and wearing sawn-off jeans, bare feet and no shirt. They refused to talk to him until he'd put a shirt on and then of course, he was in a bad temper and nobody was trying to help anyone at that stage.'

We felt sorry for Chris and it was an incident that upset everyone, particularly Brian, who felt that it reflected on the village, towards which he had protective feelings.

`That's the trouble with the bars and more tourists,' he said. `They are attracting people from outside Jacaré. But she shouldn't have left a wallet with that sort of money on the table, and Chris has lived here long enough to know he should look after valuables more carefully — and that the police expect to be treated with respect.' Vera's sister left shortly after.

By now we felt that it was more than time for us to move on and see what the rest of Brazil had to offer, even though our mail had still not arrived. Brian had been surprised that it was lost.

`I bet they've put it in the wrong place,' he had said and so I was determined to get them to look properly. We went into João Pessoa to clear out and I left Pete to it while I went to the post-office. I entered the huge building and walked into the cool room where the post-office boxes were situated and along to the Poste Restante desk. Once again I asked for my mail and handed over a slip of paper showing exactly what would be written on the package.

`Não, nada. Desculpe.'

I had practised several responses and now, in Brazilian Portuguese I said,

`I am sure that it is here. I know that it was posted over a month ago. Please look again. It is very important to me.'

They looked again. Nada. I felt so disappointed and was almost in tears. Then another lady walked in. She saw me and obviously realized that there was a problem.

`What is it?' she asked

`Mail was sent from England to me over a month ago,' I explained. `I am sure it must be here, but they say it is not.'

She took the slip of paper with my name and address on it and went and looked behind the stack of post-office boxes that hid all the parcels and packages from view. In a couple of minutes she returned, triumphant.

`Aqui!'

`Oh, obrigada! Obrigada!' I cried, delighted.

`De seu esposo?

`Não, minha mamãe!' They beamed at that. How touching that the *inglesa* lady should be so pleased to hear from her mother! Of course I was, but the package also contained all our mail from our friends, too, which we would have hated to lose.

Smiling from ear to ear, I left the post office and walked gaily along to the Capitania, where I expected Pete to be waiting for me. Instead, I found that he was still inside and one look at his face told me that my feeble Portuguese was going to be tested again.

'What's the matter?'

'The Port Captain won't clear us. I think it's something to do with our clearance from the Canaries.'

'But they didn't give us any clearance.'

'That's the problem.'

I put on my best smile and asked the uniformed officer behind the desk if there was a problem. Pete was correct. It turned out that the young man who entered us should not have done so until he had seen our clearance papers. I explained that we were not given any papers. Nonsense, all ships received clearance papers. Well, yes, of course that was true, but in the EC they often did not bother with yachts from member states. 'But the Canaries aren't actually in the EC,' Pete said, when I told him what I'd said.

'Oh for God's sake! He won't know that. Don't make life more complicated.' I hissed back. The Port Captain was not convinced. Rummaging back through his documents, he produced a paper of a ship that had cleared from Greece.

'Greece is in the EC, is it not?' he challenged me.

'Yes, but that is a ship. We are a yacht and yachts are treated differently.'

'That cannot be so.'

'But it is. That is why we have no clearance papers, apart from one from the UK. See! This is it.'

He looked at it. 'But that is September. It is now January.'

'Well, it's the last document we were given and we have to keep it for when we go back. It is for the Customs.'

He looked at it again and then checked the details on it against those in his book and on his sheaf of papers.

'Well,' reluctantly, 'if you have nothing more, then this will have to be sufficient.' And with bad grace, he filled in a form that cleared us out from João Pessoa to the next port on the way.

'Whew! What a performance! I thought he'd never let us go!' Pete exclaimed.

'Ah well, I suppose that's part of the experience of being off the beaten track,' I said. 'As well, most of the other yachts come in from the Cape Verde Islands and I'll bet that they give clearance papers — and in Portuguese, too!'

We lugged our loads of shopping back to the railway station, hurrying to make sure that we caught the last train of the morning.

'I'm never quite sure if the advantages of lots of cheap food are not outweighed by the disadvantages of having to carry it back,' I said.

'Never mind, it will be a while until we are able to go shopping in supermarkets again,' Pete told me. 'Maceió, probably.'

After lunch, we went ashore to say our good-byes to Brian. I handed him a letter that I had written to the Commodore of the Yacht Club.

'I don't know if he calls himself that,' I said, 'or whether he can read English, but I thought it would be a nice gesture to thank the Club for letting us use their showers, dinghy dock and other facilities.'

We had taken Brian up on his offer to get drinking water for us at ten cents a gallon. When we tried to settle up he waved our money away.

'It's not worth it,' he said. 'You only wanted a few gallons and Franco was going anyway.' We thanked him again for his kindness and walked for the last time along the dusty road to the dinghy dock.

'It's time we were moving on,' I said, 'but I don't think that we could have chosen a better place to start our stay in Brazil, do you?'

'No, we did well coming here. I think it would have been more difficult going straight to somewhere like Recife. Brian makes it a lot easier and I feel that we know something about Brazil now and will find it much more fun to cruise than we would otherwise have done.'

Back on the boat, we hauled *Skip* aboard and shortened in the cable. Then the sails were hoisted, *Badger* pointed her bows downstream and, with the sun descending once more towards the treetops, we set off to see some more of Brazil. I could just hear the sounds of *Bolero*.

Chapter Seven

It was a good feeling to be underway once more and the thought of sailing along this unfamiliar coast and exploring new anchorages was exciting. The tide and fair breeze soon brought us to Cabedelo and before long we had negotiated its slightly tricky entrance channel and were out once more into the open, if shallow sea: although we gave Cabo Branco, the most easterly point of South America, a good berth, the depths were still around thirty feet. If leaving Jacaré seemed to be an important step, rounding the Cape felt like a deliberate plunge into the unknown. In spite of our agreeable introduction to Brazil, we still felt a little bit nervous, a little haunted by the horror stories we had heard.

We were heading for Forte de Orange, sixty miles down the coast from Jacaré and a little way north of Recife. It appeared to be about low water when we arrived and although Brian had given us instructions on crossing the bar, we still managed to touch bottom a few times. The less-than-clear water looked deeper towards the reef, so we apprehensively edged over, to find ourselves back in the comparatively narrow channel. Once over the bar, we were in plenty of water and we continued up the river, sailing past the impressive fort and around a beautiful bluff, on which sat a handsome church. Further on, the river became shallower and the channel narrower so that we blessed our digital echo sounder, which is so easy and unambiguous to read. A bridge across the river effectively prevented us from going further, so we brought up off the small town of Itapissuma. It was well past eleven and we went ashore forthwith in case everything shut down at midday.

There was a road alongside the river with occasional steps coming down to the water and we rowed across to a flight of these. Itapissuma was a very small town; with a few shops and a market that was closing down as we got there. As in João Pessoa, there were no prices displayed on the stalls, but we enjoyed wandering round and looking at it all and in the small supermarket, I saw a bottle of green chili peppers in brine, which were so cheap and looked so appealing that I could not resist buying them. A large tree stood in the main street and this was obviously the gathering place for

Forte de Orange, its beach lined with jangadas for the tourists.

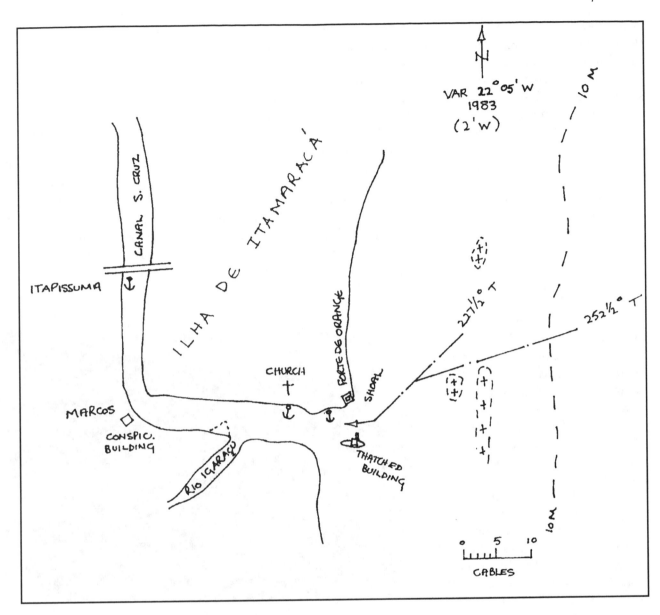

the locals, who lounged in its shade exchanging news and gossiping. This just about exhausted the attractions of the town and so we went back to *Skip* and rowed back aboard.

The tide was still flooding and the light head-wind made for a slow, but pleasant beat back down the river. Eating lunch underway, we had ample time to admire the scenery before bringing up under the old fort near the entrance. All around us were scenes of immense activity. On the opposite side of the river to the fort was a smaller island with a bar built on it, which seemed to be a tremendously popular place and there was a constant to-ing and fro-ing of *jangadas* fer-rying people about. They all had brightly coloured sails, many of which had the names of companies writ-ten on them and as a form of advertizing, I have seen a lot worse. Buzzing around overhead were two or three microlight aircraft, fitted with floats, taking tourists for

a spin, using the river as a runway. Amplified music was coming from a variety of sources, including a large number of thatch-roofed bars along the beach on the fort side. The scene was anything but peaceful and I began to wish that we had anchored further upstream. Hoever, as the day drew to its close, the lit-tle planes landed for the final time and were hauled up on the beach with the *jangadas*, most of the bars closed down for the night, and the noise gradually died away. In the quiet twilight, we sipped our sundown-ers, able at last properly to admire the huge fort that dominated the scene.

Constructed by the Portuguese in 1654, it was on the site of an earlier one built of wood and mud by the Dutch in 1631, hence the name. In those times, the Dutch were trying to get a foothold in Brazil and after they were driven out, a number of their own forts were taken over and fortified by the Portuguese in order to ensure that they did not come back. In most countries, the building would have been regarded as a national monument, but Forte de Orange had been allowed to go to rack and ruin, had become partly buried under sand drifts and used as a home by vagrants and animals. It had been restored to its present impressive status due solely to the work of one man, José Amaro.

Although it is not immediately apparent, Forte de Orange is in fact built on an island, which still has a prison on it. José Amaro was incarcerated on Ilha de Itamaracá for a number of years, convicted of murder. During his time there, he became fascinated with the fort and upon his release, set to work to restore it. This was an immense undertaking and there must have been times when he was close to despair, but now his achievement has been fully appreciated and many tourists come to walk round the ramparts and examine the old building. The work is by no means finished and once restoration is complete, or as complete as it can be, the running of the fort will still be a heavy burden.

When we went ashore the next morning to have a look round, we discovered that visitors are charged a nominal fee to enter, but that sales from a small craft shop provide most of the wherewithal to keep the fort going. We were impressed at the quality of the work, especially when we realized that most of it is made by the local prisoners. There is also some of José's own work — he appears to be a talented artist. We bought ourselves one or two things: a straw hat for Pete, decorated with a string of painted shells and a *carranca* for *Badger*. *Carranca* means `frown' or `scowl' in Portuguese and the carving that we bought had a most ferocious expression. They were originally made to be put on the stem of a fishing boat, where their fierce expressions would scare away any evil spirits. Our *carranca* was attached to the windvane, in the hope of frightening any ill wind that was thinking of coming our way. By and large, it seems to have done a pretty good job. After walking round the fort and again noticing that the cannons had the British broad arrow cast into them, we strolled among the *barracas* selling food and drinks, all seeming to be well patronized.

To ensure arriving at our next stop some fifty miles away, in daylight, we were to make a night

passage of it and just after four o'clock we got our anchor and sailed out, not entirely unhappy to leave all the bustle behind us. Our departure was easier, for the tide was higher and we had a better idea of where the channel ran, but Pete took careful bearings, which he noted down. Our passage was made by the light of the full moon and I watched with interest and some regret as we sailed by the town of Olinda. This has the reputation of being an extremely attractive place, filled with beautiful buildings, but there was no anchorage off the town itself and to visit it, we would have to go first to Recife. We thought it best to try to avoid large cities, wherever possible, and so Olinda would have to wait for another time. I felt no qualm at all at watching the lights of Recife slip past.

The ruins of Forte de Orange.

At about half past five we were approaching the River Suape and Pete got me up. As we approached, we could see another fine fort, considerably smaller then Forte de Orange, on the starboard side. Our chart was inadequate, but a mile of so further on, were several fishing boats on moorings and, although they were all fairly small, we hoped that there would be sufficient depth for us to anchor near by. Sailing under Forte de Nazaré, we had eighteen feet of water, but this suddenly shoaled to under a fathom and we were in imminent danger of running aground. We could see no obvious channel and discretion seemed the better part of valour, so we turned tail, but with the breeze blowing directly into the harbour, there was little room to spare. The ebb created a few heavy overfalls and one of these caught *Badger* fair and square when I tried to tack.

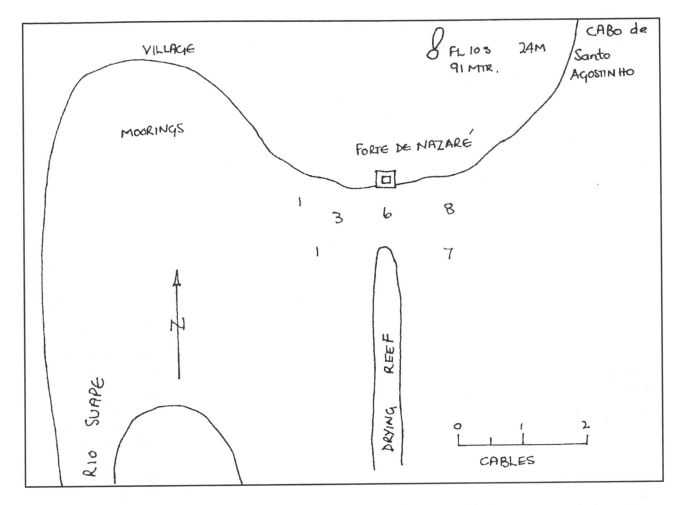

'Wear round!' shouted Pete and with my heart in my mouth, I put the helm up. Our bow seemed to hang suspended over the coral and then the ebb took her clear as she paid off on the other gybe. Moments later, we were beyond the narrows with all the room in the world, but it took a little longer for my heart to stop its pounding.

Pete and I looked at each other.

'Phew!' I said. 'Isn't it a bit early in the day for this sort of thing?'

'It was a little tight back there,' Pete admitted. 'I suppose we'll have to give River Suape a miss. We'll go on to Ilha Santo Aleixo, shall we, and see what that's like? Just steer about 210°, along the coast, and I'll go and start breakfast. According to the *Pilot*, there's a large artificial harbour near here. That looks like the breakwater over there. Give me a shout when we're a bit closer and I'll have a look at it through the bottles. I can't imagine that it will be available for yachts, though. Or suitable. I think it's some sort of oil terminal.'

'OK', I said. 'And seeing as how it's only half past six, I might have two eggs for breakfast this morning. I feel like I deserve it after all that excitement!'

For the next four hours or so we sailed merrily on our way. The artificial harbour was as unpromising as we had suspected and we were not sorry to pass it by. As we were about to have our morning coffee, a rain squall descended on us, sending us scrambling for oilskins. When it left, it took the wind with it and we drifted the last few miles.

Ilha Santo Aleixo was mentioned in the *Pilot* and sounded as though it would give good shelter from the prevailing south-easterly winds. We studied the directions, but when we came to sail in, found them rather misleading. A reef stuck out from the south side of the island and while we were negotiating this, we noticed a large catamaran anchored in the lee. As we tacked up to anchor nearby, an orange inflatable appeared and came bounding over the waves towards us. It was manned by a Frenchman who warned us that there were several coral heads about. They showed up relatively clearly, in fact, but we appreciated the kindness of his gesture. Waiting until we were in the anchorage itself, he showed us where he thought the best spot was and then returned to the catamaran.

When we had completed tidying up, we had leisure to look about us. The small and attractive island looked as though it had been spirited from the Caribbean: sandy beaches, palm trees and blue skies made for an idyllic picture and the owner of the little holiday home situated there must be an object of envy to his friends and acquaintances. Turning our attention to the catamaran, we saw that it was not quite what we would have expected to find cruising in Brazil. It was about sixty feet long and looked like a high-tech racing machine. Wishing to thank our `pilot' for his assistance, we had the perfect excuse to row over and find out more about it.

We were welcomed aboard by a young Englishman, who explained that he was a friend of the owners, also cruising on his own yacht.

`You can just see her,' he said pointing to where a boat was anchored, a short way back up the coast.

`I met Jacques and Clothilde when we were in the Canaries together and we've sort of teamed up since then. They're running beach charters here, and I help them a bit and get a few bob as well. They'll be back in a couple of minutes — they've just gone to pick up the charter party who are diving off the reef.'

As he spoke, we heard the sound of an outboard motor and saw the Zodiac returning, laden down with people. Philip went to take the painter and everyone climbed aboard, heavily encumbered with snorkels and flippers and the occasional underwater camera. The cat's two owners spent a few minutes sorting out their guests and distributing beers and then came and sat beside us.

`'Ave a beer,' they suggested, passing us a couple of dewy bottles. We accepted gratefully and then asked them about their boat.

`She's not the sort of boat the you'd expect to find cruising,' Pete commented, `where did you get her from?'

`We build 'er ourselves,' Jacques replied, `at a place in Brittany, called La Trinité. Perhaps you know it?'

`Isn't that where all the racing multihulls are built?'

`Yes, that is right and that is one of the reasons that we build there. It is a good place to fit out a catamaran. As you know, Grand Prix racing boats throw away their sails and ropes long before they are finish and also such things as winches. When we are building this boat, we make friends with a lot of the skippers and they offer us their old equip-

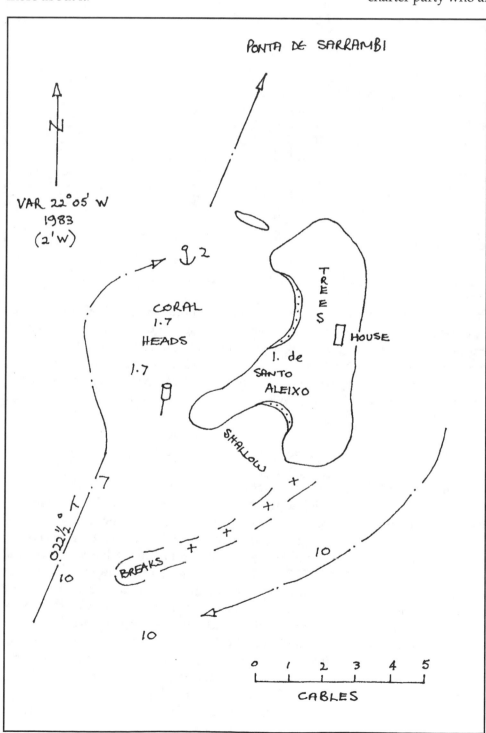

ment so we build the boat very cheap. Just 'ave a look at our mainsail, when we sail out — it is all Kevlar.'

`But isn't the boat very hard work to handle?' I asked, `How many crew do you sail with?'

`Normalement there is just Clothilde, myself and our son, Marc-Louis, and it can be difficult, but we do not drive the boat and only use a little bit of sail, but now I am chartering and,' leaning forwards and lowering his voice, `all these good people who pay to come sailing; I ask them to raise the sail. We tell them it is part of the day out, the *experience*, and so I get a good and fresh crew every morning. They enjoy it, too.'

`How did you find this place? Did you know somebody here?' we asked.

`Non,' replied Jacques, `but we build this boat to charter you know. So when we get to Brazil we look for a good place, a beach where we can anchor safely, with a big hotel that has many people. Then we go to the manager and offer to take out some of his guests. "What a wonderful idea!" 'e says, because, you know, the people on 'oliday, they soon get bored. Of course, it is not legal, what we do, but we will carry on and when we 'ave to leave, we will go to another beach, with an hotel and try again. We make enough money and we 'ave fun.'

By this time, Clothilde had disappeared into one of the hulls and we noticed their little boy coming out with dishes and plates of food and arranging it for the charter party.

`Please,' said Jacques, `'ave some food with us. There is plenty and maybe some things that you do not get too often!'

`Is it not a tremendous amount of work for you, making all this food every day?' I asked Clothilde.

She laughed, `Ah no, not at all. The hotel, they provide all the food, and the beer too. All I do is put it together and serve it. We eat well every day we 'ave a charter! But I make some extra things, too, so that it is different from what they eat in the hotel every day.

As we ate, we asked Philip about his plans.

`Well I think that I'll stick around these good people for a while', he said, `It's still fun, I'm getting some money and I found out when I crossed the Atlantic that I don't really enjoy single-handed sailing, but eventually I want to go into the Pacific.'

The meal over, it was time for the party to go back to the hotel. Our offer to help clear up was smilingly refused.

`No, no. It is not a trouble to us and we enjoy meeting you. We miss being with cruising boats.'

Thanking them for their hospitality and their help when we sailed in, we jumped into the dinghy. We rowed across to have a look round the island and, pulling the dinghy up the white, sand beach, we heard the sound of the sail being raised. The charter guests were hauling lustily at the halliard, while the huge and heavy mainsail made its slow way up the mast. When it was set, Jacques ran forward and got the anchor, the sheets were hardened in and seconds later, the big catamaran was racing across the sparkling sea, towards the distant hotel. The holidaymakers were having an unforgettable day out.

Ilha Santo Aleixo was as attractive as it had appeared from the anchorage. According to Jacques it was privately owned, but it was permissible to walk around it and boats would come over at the weekend to hold barbecue parties on the beach. It was partly wooded and, as we wandered about, we discovered two pretty beaches: one facing into the cool Trade wind and the other in the lee, quite protected. A truly perfect little island.

Thirteen miles down the coast, lay Tamandaré our next port of call, so for once we could have a night in bed and get underway after breakfast. It was easily identified by its lighthouse, but we were disconcerted to find that the bearings to enter, shown in the *Pilot*, were incorrect. Despite this, we managed to find our own way in and just before midday brought up in twenty feet, in a palm-fringed bay. The anchorage was protected by reefs and the golden beach on which we landed the dinghy, appeared to stretch for miles in both directions. The strip by the village was crowded with people on this sunny Sunday afternoon, but

Tamandaré

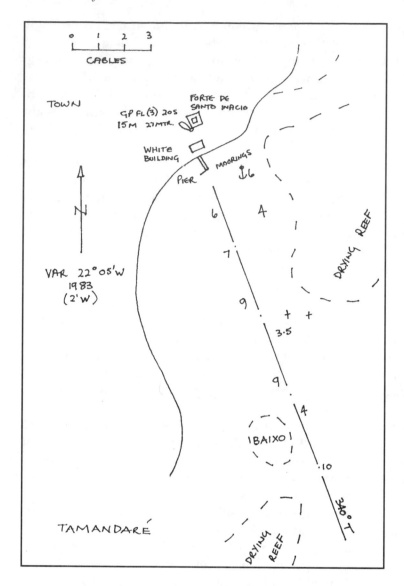

sails coming towards us — Maceió's *jangadas*, off for the day's fishing, and they were quite a sight, as they came out of the lee of the bay and gathered speed. Maceió was a centre for them and we had seen one or two the previous day, well offshore and out of sight of land. Simply a raft, with two or three benches across, providing support for the mast and steering oar, they appeared to be too flimsy and insubstantial a craft to sail such distances. We appreciated seeing them being used for their original purpose, as distinct from the tourist boats at Fort Orange, and every morning and evening, during our stay in Maceió, we had the pleasure of watching these strange craft going out at sunrise and returning at dusk.

The line of *jangadas* indicated where we should go and we sailed into the harbour, trying to judge the best place to anchor. Noticing some small boat masts behind a fence ashore, we guessed that this was the Yacht Club and headed in that direction. We dropped the hook in eight feet of water, not far from another foreign yacht, among the fishing boats, a little concerned as to the proximity of a sizeable *favela* nearby. `Never anchor near *favela* districts!' had been one of the dire warnings that we had heard before coming to Brazil. On the other hand, there was that other yacht and Raúl had spent time in Maceió and spoke well of it. Anyway, there was nowhere that looked any better.

As it was still only about six o'clock, our immediate priority was to have breakfast and, while Pete went below to light the cooker, I looked around us. Our anchorage, to be honest, was less than prepossessing. We were some distance from a rather grubby-looking beach; there were a number of scruffy workboats on moorings, but as I looked more carefully, I also noticed one or two small yachts, a reassuring sight. Ahead and to starboard as we lay, was the *favela* already mentioned, while around on the starboard quarter was a large building, that reminded me of the Tate and Lyle sugar warehouses in Liverpool. Away off the port bow the beach ran along in front of the town itself, which was not easy to see from the anchorage. The contrast with the beautiful surroundings in which we had spent the last few nights, coupled with the fact that in this town, there would be no friendly Brian to tell us where to find everything, made me feel rather dispirited. It was the sort of feeling that comes upon most sailors from time to time: `what on earth am I doing here, when I could be safe ashore back "Home"?' The glass of freshly-squeezed orange juice

twenty minutes walk either way would bring you to an entirely empty beach, to lie under the palm trees and imagine that you were on a desert island.

Going ashore the next morning, we discovered that the town itself was really just a few buildings on either side of a road, with bars and the odd *pousada* and in the centre, several tiny stalls selling vegetables. We visited a shop and bought a piece of unidentified frozen fish, sawn up on a bandsaw, for our supper and then had a look around the little fort by the lighthouse that guarded the entrance. Again we noticed British cannons — we were beginning to wonder just how many must have been sold to the Portuguese all those years ago.

It was to be another overnight passage to Maceió, nearly eighty miles away, so having eaten a substantial lunch first, we got our anchor not long after three o'clock and then tacked out through the reef. The gentle and reliable Force 3 Trade wind eased us on our way and by dawn, the city was in sight, with a fleet of

that Pete handed up to me was an effective restorative.

Undoubtedly one of the worst aspects of cruising in Brazil is the bureaucracy. As soon as you arrive in a harbour of any size, you have to go and fill in sheaves of forms. Admittedly other countries are just as bad, but what makes it such an ordeal in Brazil is that the offices tend of be vast distances away from one another and they have to be visited in the correct order. As we did not have a clue where to start in Maceió, the obvious thing to do was to go ashore by way of the other yacht, who would surely know where everything was. Accordingly, we put on our tidier clothes and rowed over. Their ensign had been fouled, but we could now see that she was French and as we came alongside, a man appeared from down below, followed by a woman and a little girl.

Maceió

`Bonjour.'

`Bonjour.'

They invited us on board and we talked for a little while. They were just about to head on north, having spent a week or so in Maceió and gave us directions as to how to find the Customs and the Port Captain's office.

`The Polícia Federal is a long way out of town and you have to catch a bus. They run from the Rua Comercio and if you ask there, someone will tell you which one to catch. I forget the number.'

`We should be back fairly soon. Will you come over and have some coffee with us later on?'

They laughed. `We cleared out yesterday and the Port Captain can probably see us here. If we don't leave this morning, they might ask us to do it again! But anyway, we want to go as soon as possible, now that we are ready.'

And so, with expressions of mutual goodwill, we went our separate ways. A brief meeting with people we would have liked to know better, not untypical in our way of life.

As we rowed ashore, a crowd of children gathered to watch, but when we climbed out of the dinghy, they all scampered away, laughing. A young man came over and helped us to carry *Skip* up the long beach. The Yacht Club was fenced around, but someone came and opened a gate for us, indicating that we should bring the dinghy inside for its security. We asked if it was all right to leave it there while we went to clear in. Of course, *não problema*, and we were invited to fill in a book at the bar, which we gathered made us temporary members; but my Portuguese was not really up to the details.

Going out of the Yacht Club gates, we crossed the road and turned left. Following the directions that we had been given, we soon made out the Customs office, and after a wait of some time, managed to complete the formalities. From there it was only a short walk to the Port Captain's building. The official at the desk was very helpful and also told us that the Polícia Federal was outside town, but that if we asked for the `Forene' bus, the conductor would tell us where to get off. He made the suggestion that we clear in and out at the same time to save ourselves the problem of having to catch the bus again in a couple of days, advice that we appreciated.

We had acquired a rather inadequate map, which did not show the names of many streets, but indicated where we would find the centre of the town and towards this we turned our steps. In a short while, we found ourselves in a traffic-free area, lined with shops and packed with people. The `modern but relaxed' feeling, cited in the *Lonely Planet Guide*, was not readily apparent. While the buildings were certainly modern, I doubt that even someone from the heart of Manhattan would describe Maceió or any other sizeable Brazilian town, as `relaxed.' Nevertheless, we rather enjoyed working our way through the crowds and discovering where such things as the Banco do Brasil were situated. In due course, we found the bus that we wanted and climbing on board, paid our fare, asking the conductor to tell us when we arrived at the Polícia Federal.

Several other passengers took an interest in us so we felt assured of success. The bus was crowded, but we managed to find a seat and looked through the windows at the passing scene. After a while, we seemed to be getting well out of the town and at every stop, we looked questioningly at the conductor, but she invariably shook her head. Eventually, after a journey of about half an hour, the person behind us tapped Pete on the shoulder and said that we should get off at the next stop. By now, we were on the extreme edge of the town, on a main road, and after the bus had left, we could see no sign of any building that remotely resembled what we were looking for. I asked a passerby if he knew where the Polícia Federal was situated and he pointed to a small brick and glass building in the centre of a large roundabout.

`Oh dear, that doesn't look very promising, does it? I think that we've come to the wrong place.' I said.

`Well, everyone seems to think that this is the Polícia Federal, so we'd better give it a try,' responded Pete.

We crossed the road and went into the building where we were greeted by a stout policeman.

`Good morning.'

`Good morning'

`We are on a foreign yacht, in the harbour,' I explained in hesitating and ungrammatical Portuguese. `We have cleared with the Port Captain, but ...' I stopped as I saw an expression of complete incomprehension on his face.

I tried another tack.

`Somos estrangeiros e está necessário por nossos passaportes ...' I stopped, absolutely clueless as to what the Portuguese for `to be checked' was. This was not the time to get out the dictionary.

At last he spoke: `I do not deal with passports. I am here for the traffic. You need to go to another place.'

I translated this for Pete.

`Ask him where it is, then,' he said. Understanding directions is always difficult and by this time, my mind had seized up and I could only comprehend about one word in ten.

`Obrigada,' I said when he had finished, `és muito gentil.'

`So, where do we go?' asked Pete.

`I've no idea, I'm afraid. I couldn't understand what he said, but I think he was saying that we should go back towards town.'

`Well, we're fairly sure that we were on the right bus, so we'll go back to the bus stop and ask someone there.'

`There's no point — I can't speak Portuguese. I don't understand what they're saying. It's no good. I don't want to ask.'

`Come on, Annie, you've done fine up to now,' Pete encouraged me.

We walked back to the bus stop, where several people were gathered.

`Ask one of these people,' suggested Pete.

I approached a lady and, with a sense of desperation, put my question to her. Unusually for a Brazilian, she did not want to help.

`Oh God, it's useless. Anyway, even if they know, unless it's really straightforward I won't be able to make out what they are saying! I think that the best thing, really, is to catch the bus back into town, throw a six and start again.'

`Well, I suppose that you're right. If all else fails, we can go back to the Port Captain and ask for fuller instructions, but just ask the conductor when we get on the bus will you? He might know — after all, we're pretty sure we are on the right bus and the police surely won't be any further out of town.'

`All right, I'll do that.'

We stood with the other people by the bus stop and about ten minutes later, the right bus pulled up. We climbed on and as we passed through the turnstile, I asked the conductor if she knew where we could find the Polícia Federal, `for our passports'.

But certainly! We were on the right bus and would go to their bureau. I did not catch everything that she said, but we both understood her crystal-clear gestures that told us she would let us know when we were to get off the bus.

`Maybe we'll have better luck this time,' I said, as we took our seats.

`I'm sure that there can't be three different sets of Federal Police along this road, anyway,' said Pete, `so if the last one was wrong, it *must* be the next one.'

`I hope she doesn't forget.'

But about ten minutes later, the conductor asked someone to tell us we were nearly there. When the bus stopped, several different people made sure that we knew that we were to get off and that we should find the Polícia Federal over *there*. As the bus pulled away, they were still waving their hands, and pointing at the building and this time we knew that we had found the correct place because we could see the crest on the wall. The actual paperwork seemed a piece of cake after what had passed.

`They don't make it easy for you, do they?' I said as we left the building and crossed the road back to the bus stop. `It's almost enough to make me wish we were back in the Caribbean, surrounded by other yachts and with officials who are used to yachts and where everyone knows what to expect.'

By the time we were back in town, Pete had bounced back, while I still felt as though I had been through a mangle. I tried to sound enthusiastic as we wandered around and actually felt almost human after we had stopped at a *lanche* and each had a *suco*. Walking past the railway station, Pete suggested that we go in and find out what time and to where the trains ran. We discovered a timetable and wrote down the names and times on a piece of paper. Leaving the station, we followed the railway lines as they ran down the centre of the main street, Avenida Maceió, and back in the direction of the Yacht Club. Still somewhat jaded from our morning's adventures, we called it a day and went back to *Badger*, where we spent a lazy afternoon.

After a good night's sleep, we felt ready to face the new day and this time, we turned to the right outside the Yacht Club and in due course, came to one of the main holiday beaches. It was a lively spot. There was a large market selling clothes, curios and `ethnotat' to the mainly Argentine tourists and we spent a pleasant hour sauntering around and seeing what was on offer. Further down the beach, several *jangadas* were drawn up. They were for hire and I dare say that the owners made more money from tourists than they ever had from fishing. These days, many of the boats are built of plywood boxes or even from large blocks of polystyrene foam, roughly held together in a framework of wood. However, there was an example of a genuine balsa *jangada* lying on the beach, its sail set. A glance was sufficient to tell us that this craft was no longer seaworthy and when we saw the dimensions of the logs from which it was built, we were not surprised that such timber is no longer available. Someone had obviously taken a certain amount of effort to see that it did not deteriorate any further, and we guessed that it had been salvaged when already condemned and tidied up to show the visitor what a *jangada* really should be. Although it was sad to realize that such craftsmanship as had been put into this balsa example was no longer required, we could only admire the resourcefulness of fishermen who made use of such scrap materials as they found around them to make themselves a working vessel that could earn its keep and provide them with a livelihood.

Leaving the market, we crossed over the road and went a further block away from the beach, before turning back towards the Yacht Club. In due course we found the *Bom Precio* supermarket that the French yacht had told us about, and it seemed both cleaner

and more sophisticated that the one that we had frequented in João Pessoa. Before long, we had our basket filled with fruit and vegetables and ingredients for lunch.

Back aboard, I washed the fresh stuff, while Pete leant against the chart table examining our little map of Maceió.

`You know, if we make proper notes about the places we go to, there'll be enough for a new folio for the FPI. For example, if we hadn't met *Idée Fixe* yesterday, I don't think that we would have found the supermarket. And I've been thinking about the *Pilot* — we've already discovered several errors and there might well be more. I suspect that it's a direct translation of the Brazilian one, because it's unusual to find mistakes in any Admiralty publication. I'm sure that other members will be coming to Brazil in the future and would make use of it, and be able to add to it, too.'

The FPI, to which Pete was referring, is a service that the Royal Cruising Club provides for its members. It consists of a number of `folios' of information, gathered by various people over the years and compiled by an editor. We had made use of one when we were in Greenland and had enjoyed adding some items of our own. On arriving in Brazil, we continued to make notes, because although there was no FPI for this area, one of the rules of the Club is that you collect and disseminate pilotage information among the members. It added extra interest and it encouraged us to visit places that we might otherwise simply have passed by.

`What do you have in mind? We already do notes about the anchorages and a sketch chart if the real one isn't good enough.'

`Yes, that's true, but I was wondering whether we shouldn't do more. Describe how to get to the various officials, for example. I mean, it would have made a real difference yesterday, if we'd known exactly where to get off the bus, wouldn't it?'

`You're telling me!'

` What I'm thinking of is something more than just a few notes, in fact more like a cruising guide. I think that people would like general information too, more about Brazil, for example. Wouldn't it be nice to have a few facts — rather than rumours?'

`Yes, you're right there. I mean, we were really worried about coming here and even now, we're not exactly confident about it all.'

`That's more or less what I'm saying. We're still affected by all the rumours and I think that even the *Lonely Planet Guide* is a bit hysterical, really, although I suppose that it's aimed towards people who will be spending a lot of time in cities and so on. But we have a much more positive outlook towards Brazil than we did when we first came here. Admittedly, we've only been to one or two places, but even so . . .'

`There's still time for us to be mugged,' I teased, `but if you wrote down what you wanted to say, I could type it all up and then we'd have something decent to send to Sandy.'

`I'll have to give it some more thought, but it would be nice to do a proper job, something more complete than just notes.'

The next morning we investigated another supermarket that we had been told about. This one had the advantage of being nearer other shops that you might want, but either way, it was a long walk. We returned to the Yacht Club by a different route and walking along a side street, we came upon a little market selling fruit and vegetables. We went over to look at it and discovered that, for once, everything was priced.

`These prices don't seem that high. Hang on a minute while I get out my notebook and check them,' I said to Pete. I had taken the precaution of noting down what we had been paying so that I could make comparisons. It is never easy to remember what we have paid for all the different things that we buy and in Brazil, with prices increasing almost daily, it was even worse. On this occasion, a glance along the stalls told me that we were on to a winner. The market was obviously designed for the local people whose houses were far from grand, and the prices were very reasonable, as was the quality. We shopped to our hearts' content, in the blessed knowledge that we were only a short distance from the Yacht Club.

`This market is really worth knowing about,' commented Pete. `It's ages since we bought any papayas because they're too big and heavy to carry, but with this place virtually just around the corner, we can

buy what we want. It's just the sort of information you'd want in a cruising guide.'

`Yes, you're right, it'd be really useful. Not only would you know where things were when you arrive, but you could also plan around it. We ought to work on one. Anyway,' I added facetiously, `it will stop us from getting bored!'

Back aboard, I put away what we had bought while Pete started writing up some notes about Maceió.

A little before half past nine, on Friday morning, we arrived at the railway station, picnic in hand and boarded the train for Albuquerque, the end of the line. The carriages were pretty much kicked about and again, many of the windows had been reglazed with plastic, but we found a seat next to a glass window from where we could watch the passing scenery. We wanted to be on the left hand side of the train, going up, because the map indicated a lagoon on that side, which we thought would be interesting. The seats were wooden and not upholstered, but they were reasonably comfortable and had the advantage that they would not be hot as the day progressed. We settled ourselves in and a few minutes later, the train jerked into life.

It was not the sort of railway journey that would have been recommended to tourists but, although there was neither picturesque nor beautiful scenery on the way, it was full of interest. The first stage was across the centre of Maceió and the line went through the heart of the municipal market. There was barely room for the train to squeeze through and it was fascinating to move by and be able to see everything from a slight elevation. Normally, in a crowded market, all I can see is other people's backs, with the occasional glimpse of a nearby stall, but here I could watch the buyers and sellers, examine the goods for sale and look into the distance at the other stalls. It was an enormous market place and it took quite a while to pass through. The train moved at a slow walking pace, but the area was so crowded, that to have gone any faster would have resulted in injury. Some of the stalls were in such proximity to the line that people were pressed against them as we passed, the steps of the carriages missing them by inches. It was all very different from Europe or the USA with their stringent safety rules and regulations.

In due course, we left the town behind and passed through the suburbs. The scenery became more rural and soon we caught sight of the lagoon, olive green around the edges, deep blue in the middle. *Canoas* were drawn up on the muddy beaches and now and then we could see fishermen working their nets, which appeared to

The train we took.

be stretched along stakes. Thin woodland covered the area between the lagoon and the railway line and people had made their homes in clearings — shanty houses of scrap materials, with the inevitable washing hanging out. The kitchen was outside, with a lean-to roof overhead and, occasionally, a second wall on which a few poor bits of kitchen equipment were hung. Oil drums substituted for sinks and food was cooked over a wood or charcoal fire; not a barbecue of chops or steaks, but a long, slow

Rio Largo, a railway ride from Maceió.
Above: the old cotton mill.
Left: the vultures hop about the river rocks.
Below: a memorable picnic.

process of cooking black beans and vegetables with, rarely, a piece of meat. Scrawny hens scratched round and any that ended up in the pot would probably need longer cooking than the beans. There was an abundance of half-clothed children who halted in their play as the train went by, to wave and to laugh in delight

when someone waved back at them. The women at their washing would also straighten their tired backs for a moment to watch us pass. I wondered how many of them ever went more than a mile or two away from their homes. In spite of all the obvious poverty, there were few signs of misery and throughout our time in Brazil, this early impression of a generally happy and carefree people prevailed. Perhaps it is true that blue skies and sunshine compensate for many things.

As the line started to swing away from the lagoon, the woodland gave way to more open countryside where some farming was carried out. There were small herds of cattle, not the infamous beef cattle for MacDonald's, who are grazing the ground once covered by ancient rain forest, but the beautiful and placid animals of India, with their long dewlaps and large, brown, wise and gentle eyes. Beyond these, small hills stretched into the vast distances that are the interior of Brazil. Climbing gently but steadily all the time, we came to great fields of sugar cane, interspersed with tracks leading to the occasional building. The villages went by: Bebed, F. Velho, Satuba, Utinga and then we came to the penultimate stop, Rio Largo. There was a river running here and we had just passed some intriguing-looking ruins. In an instant, we decided to go no further, but to explore this little town and to wander along the river until we found somewhere to picnic.

There was no real platform and it was quite a jump down from the train. As it pulled away, we headed towards the centre of the town to have a look round. Rio Largo was only small; there was nothing at all special about it and therein lay its interest, because it was simply a place where ordinary Brazilian people lived and worked and no tourist would choose to go there. We pottered around its streets and ended up in a small square where we bought a doughnut each, and had it with the coffee we had brought. Back near the railway, we crossed over towards the river and came to a small street market which, as well as the usual fruits, vegetables and eggs, sold everything from woven baskets to live hens, from garden seeds to pots and pans. At the end of the street was a bridge and leaning on the low parapet, we looked at the wide, shallow river, strewn with rocks and boulders, where great, black vultures, hopped from one rock to another in the slightly sinister fashion of these birds, picking through the rubbish and squabbling over the choicer morsels. Houses, whose balconies hung out over the water lined both sides of the river, mostly in a sorry state of repair with here and there, unfinished projects of breeze block, perhaps awaiting the time when the builder got some more cash, perhaps totally abandoned. In truth, it was hardly a scene in which 'Every prospect pleases,' but the traveller differs from the tourist in being interested in all aspects of an area, while the latter is wishing only to view the beauty spots and quaint scenes.

Retracing our steps back through the market, we walked towards the ruins that we had noticed from the train. According to some faded lettering, it was an old cotton mill and we spent some time examining the buildings before continuing on a little further down the road, admiring some of the few, grander houses that had been built in Rio Largo's prime and then crossing over the river to investigate a complicated system of sluices. Speculating on how they had worked, we guessed that the water had needed to be diverted as required, for processing the cotton. The factory was long-closed and its demise apparently brought an end to Rio Largo's days of prosperity. Perhaps the river level fell as a result of destruction of forest land further upstream, or maybe some other industry, sugar for example, proved more profitable. It might have been a depressing scene, but under a bright blue sky, dotted with fluffy, white clouds, greenery all around, butterflies and birds and the sound of the rapids swirling and gurgling around the rocks and sluices, it was very attractive. Finding a comfortable spot from where we could watch the water, we sat down to eat our picnic in the warm sunshine.

The road followed the railway and away from the heat of the coast, walking was pleasant, so we continued on down to the next station. There was no hurry and we strolled along, stopping as our fancy took us to look at things. There was a wait of about half an hour at Utinga, then the train grumbled and clanked its way in, we climbed into the high carriages and slowly returned to Maceió. The tenpenny train fare had been money well spent.

It was time to move on. After an early breakfast, Pete rowed ashore with all our empty jerricans for filling with the clean, sweet water from the Yacht Club tap. Having cleared in and out at the same time at the Polícia Federal, we had only Customs and the Port Captain to visit. On the way back from the Customs, we passed a shop selling superior white rum at a mere three dollars a bottle and then bought a few more bits and pieces at the little market that we had discovered. After we had shopped at the market, Pete said,

'I think we ought to buy a case of that rum, you know. It's a very good price, because it was more like four dollars in João Pessoa and we don't often see it.'

'Yes, but it's white rum and I really prefer golden.'

'Well, we could still buy the odd bottle to drink just with water, but the white we could have with lime or orange juice. It's not that much more than *cachaça* and it tastes a lot better.'

'Have we got enough money? We don't want to have to change more.'

'No, we're OK at the moment. We got out enough to see us to Salvador.'

`Well, then, let's do it. But how can we carry it back?'

`I could fit quite a few bottles in the rucksack and he'd probably give me some other bags. Could you carry the stuff that we've just bought?'

`It's not that far — I could probably just about manage. We'll have to see if everything in the rucksack will fit in these other bags. I'll wait here for you — it's not worth walking all that way and back.'

`OK, I shouldn't be too long.'

I felt a bit conspicuous, standing on the corner waiting for Pete to come back, sure that I must look like a tourist, and remembering the stories of robbery and theft. Pete, with his brown hair and eyes and dark tan could easily pass for a local, but my reddish hair and fair skin make me stand out like a sore thumb in most countries; yet this time I obviously looked the part, because a middle-aged lady stopped and asked me for directions. Unfortunately, I could not help her, but enjoyed passing for a native. I told Pete about it when he came back, staggering under his burden.

`It's probably because of all the shopping,' he said. `Most tourists don't buy in loads of fruit and veg.'

`You bought the rum, then,' I said, picking up my bags.

`Yes, though it turned out that he only had eleven bottles left. But I even got a ten per cent discount for quantity!'

`How did you manage that?'

`I just said, "es descuento por mucho" and he said "Sim" and something else, which I suppose was "ten per cent",' replied Pete.

`The language of business,' I laughed. `The Portuguese is desconto and muito!'

`Well, he understood what I meant, anyway. And I even managed to imply that I was disappointed that he only had eleven bottles. Actually, it was just as well, because I don't think that I could have managed another one!'

We really felt rather embarrassed as we went back to the Yacht Club with all the rum. We piled up our bags and carried *Skip* down the beach, where Pete loaded all the bags and bottles, while I held the dinghy in the shallow water. Most of the fishermen had never even tasted good rum, let alone seen so many bottles at one time and we felt ostentatiously wealthy and hoped that no one had noticed.

Stowing things away, we heard the sound of an anchor chain and I looked out:

`Good heavens! It's Raúl,' I exclaimed.

`He finally got away then,' said Pete.

All the time that we had been in Jacaré, Raúl had been intending to fetch the wood for his masts, a couple of trees that a friend of his had cut down for him, so we were quite surprised that he had actually done so.

`We'd have missed him if he'd been an hour later,' Pete said. `As soon as you're ready, we'll go over and have a few words with him, shall we?'

When we rowed over, Raúl greeted us. `I'm so glad that you are still here. My friends who came down with me from Jacaré are wanting to meet you. They are interested in building a plywood boat and going cruising, too.'

He introduced us to his friends, also from Argentina and speaking excellent English. They were pleased to be able to talk to someone with first-hand knowledge of building and sailing a plywood boat and

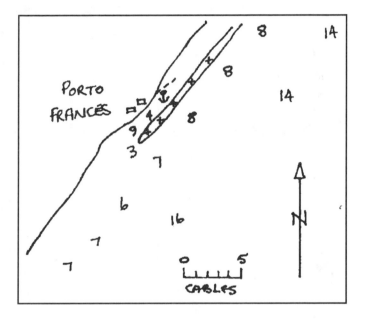

as they were also considering a Wharram catamaran, they were delighted to hear that we used to have one. We could all happily have spent the rest of the day talking boats, but they had to get ashore in a hurry, to fit in with a lift that they had arranged and we wanted to get underway, so we took our leave and a few minutes later, *Badger*'s anchor was at the bow and we were heading out of the harbour.

It was a lovely sail and with a Force 3 breeze, steady on the quarter from east northeast, it took only an hour and three quarters to cover the ten miles to Porto Francés. There was a beach here, protected by a narrow strip of reef, reasonable depths and room to anchor several yachts. The beach was full, this Saturday afternoon, with one or two speed boats and pedalos moving up and down the anchorage. Later in the afternoon, our peace was shattered by a wet bike,

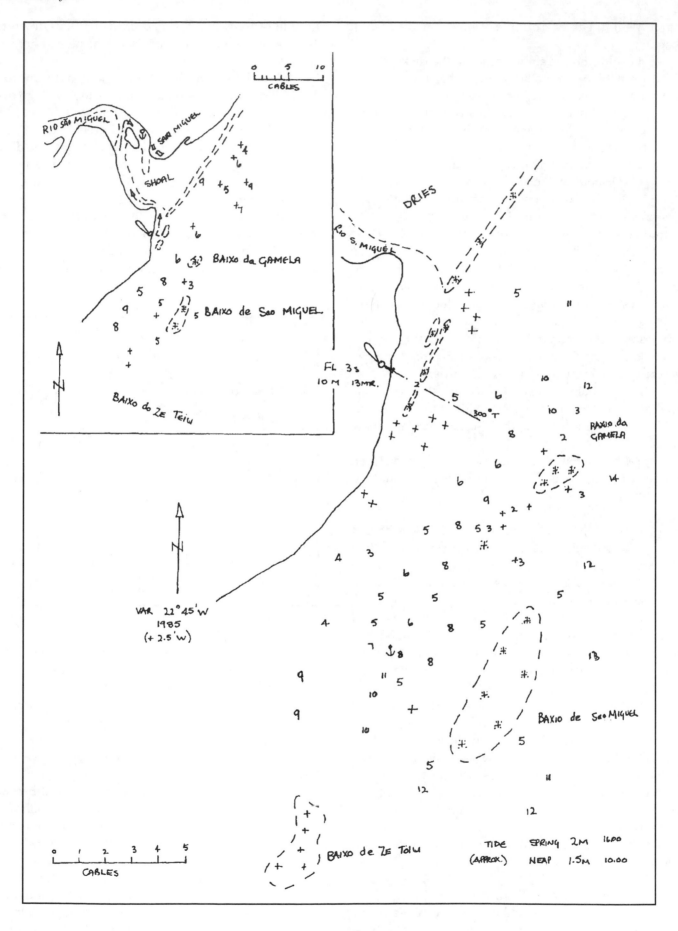

those vile machines that turn the most gentle of people into potential homicides. Fortunately, the rider quickly got bored and we were left with the comparative silence of radios, shouting people and engines. Brazilian beaches are generally crowded and the people full of verve and energy, which makes them anything but restful, but as soon as the sun nears the horizon, the bags are packed, towels rolled up and the beach empties, as once more the open skies and distant horizon are exchanged for a small, crowded house, overlooking countless others just the same. Most Brazilians live along the coastal strip, which is generously provided with glorious beaches where they can enjoy a bit of fresh air and elbow room, at least at the weekends. We have the great good fortune to spend most of our life surrounded by the beauties of the world and yet we never tire of watching the sun set and delighting in the changing colours of the sky. By the time the last of the afterglow had disappeared, the beach was entirely deserted and only a few sounds from a nearby *pousada* came across the water to remind us of our proximity to other people.

Seven miles further down the coast, Barra de São Miguel, another beach protected by a reef, and something of an up-and-coming tourist resort for the wealthier citizens of Maceió, sounded interesting. Raúl had warned us that it was a tricky entrance and that although there was a gap in the reef, this was not shown even on the most recent chart. He had indicated its approximate position and we had marked it on our chart. The *Pilot* mentioned three breaks in the barrier reef, opposite the entrance to the Rio, but no further details were given.

Having found out about the local tides in Maceió, we knew that in order to arrive at Barra de São Miguel with the flood, we had to leave Porto Francés at dawn. An hour and a half's sail brought us near to the mouth of the river and Pete climbed up the battens on the foresail to try and identify the entrance. It was going to be a dead run in, and *Badger* would be going too quickly, even well-reefed, so we dropped the sails and started the engine to approach as slowly as possible. Watching the echo sounder I noticed the depth suddenly decreasing, so shouted a warning to Pete, who told me to turn round and head out again. As we turned, he jumped from the sail bundle and came aft, saying that he could see that it was a dead end ahead. The motor was cavitating in the swell and then a bigger wave came and swamped it completely. The sails were up in a matter of seconds and we beat offshore for a quarter of a mile or so, while Pete read the book of words and got the engine running again.

About half a mile further along the coast, we identified the correct entrance. Judging it prudent to investigate from the dinghy, this time, not wanting the poor Seagull to suffer from another ducking, we anchored while Pete rowed off with the leadline, checking the depths, finding ten feet in the break in the reef. The channel was narrow, but there was sufficient room to sail *in* — the difficulty would be leaving again. The prevailing wind was onshore and if the present swell was anything to go by, there was no way that we would be able to motor against it and the channel was too restricted for tacking. Once we were in Barra São Miguel, there was every chance that we would be there for the foreseeable future! Admittedly, we could probably have arranged a tow out, but we did not like the idea of relying on that, nor of putting *Badger*'s safety in the hands of total strangers. After a few minutes discussion, while we pitched in the swell, we concluded that the only sensible thing to do was to carry on for Salvador, two hundred and fifty miles further south. We brought *Skip* aboard, sailed out our anchor and by coffee-time, were under self-steering gear with the lighthouse at the river entrance disappearing astern.

Chapter Eight

Having been contemplating a quiet night at anchor, mentally running through menus and wondering if I would finish my book, it was rather a shock to the system suddenly to realize that, on the contrary, I was about to make a passage, even if only of two hundred and fifty miles. I had to switch into sea-going mode and think about life at sea, instead, but with a boat like *Badger*, where the only real difference between harbour life and sailing life is keeping watch, the change is easy to make and one's body is soon attuned to the swing and lift of her deepwater motion.

For two days we ran before the Force 3 breezes, hot by day and warm at night. During the hours of darkness we picked up the loom of the occasional town or a rare navigational aid and all through the small hours of Tuesday, we could see the glow of Salvador ahead. Peter Pye's account of the entrance, in *Backdoor to Brazil*, filled out the *Pilot*'s terse description and we identified landmarks as we sailed along the coast.

With a population of some 2,000,000 people, Salvador was definitely in the category of being potentially dangerous and we had no intention of staying long there, but as we dearly wanted to explore the Baía de Todos os Santos, it was necessary to clear in. Moreover, the city has a reputation for being totally different from anywhere else in the world and we believed that to miss it would be a mistake. Not fond of cities and indifferent tourists, we nevertheless intended to to walk around the historic part and view the churches and houses built during the seventeenth and eighteenth centuries, when Salvador was the splendid and wealthy capital of Brazil.

There was a small boat harbour in the city, reputed to be unsafe for dinghies and even for unattended yachts, so we anchored outside the moored boats off the Yacht Club, the best anchorage being filled with moorings, in twenty-seven feet with a fairly strong tidal stream.

Rowing ashore, we found nowhere obvious to leave the dinghy so pulled her out of the water. The Yacht Club was obviously a very superior establishment, with a beautiful swimming pool and a large shower block, immaculately kept. Near to the pool, under cover, was a bar that also sold snack meals. The roofed area extended over part of the terrace and there were also tables and chairs out in the sunshine, thus catering for both sun worshippers working on their tans and smartly-dressed business men, taking a lunch break from the office. There was also a more formal restaurant, which apparently provided first-class cuisine. Wandering round, we came to a guarded gate leading to the upper part of the Club, where, the gateman indicated, we would find the Secretary, so up we went. When we explained our situation, we were made very welcome by the Secretary of the Club and given full membership for ten days, for which no charge was made, after which it would cost us ten dollars per day per person. He also told us where to find buses into the city or down to Barra, a half mile or so in the other direction, where we would find shops, bars, restaurants and so forth. Cards were made for us there and then, with the explanation that we needed them not only to enter the Club premises, but also to get from the main building to the pool area. We did not understand why there were two security checks, but it would have been very embarrassing if we had gone up after office hours, as without cards, we would have not been allowed back through the gate and would have been cut off from *Badger*.

Somewhat overwhelmed by all the luxury and distinctly gratified by the hospitable attitude of the Club, we deemed a cold beer appropriate while we relaxed on the terrace and enjoyed the sensation of belonging to an expensive and exclusive Yacht Club. I sat down and Pete went to the bar where a slightly shocked barman took his order: in this place, the staff came to the customer, not the other way round. The beer was cold, delicious and reasonably priced and we savoured every drop of it as we contemplated the fact that we were now in Salvador.

Bahia, as it is also known, is in many ways the soul of Brazil. The official capital is now Brasília, the industrial capital, São Paulo, and the place `where it all happens,' Rio, but Salvador, the original capital, is older by far than these upstart cities and it is here that Brazil has its roots. Failing to keep up with a changing world, for many years Salvador stagnated and decayed, living on memories of past glories while the new wealth went elsewhere. Because of this, the old traditions not only survived, but flourished. Bahia was the centre of the sugar and tobacco plantations, the great slave area of Brazil. Its ambience is African. Here is the greatest concentration of black people; their music; their food and their arts and crafts. The economic backwater, virtually ignored for a century, is now once more asserting its importance as a centre of culture, unique and vibrant. Now officially 'discovered', its tropical climate, its beaches and its history are proving extremely appealing. We anticipated that whatever else, Salvador would not be dull.

The thought of going into the city and doing the rounds of the offices in the heat of the afternoon was less than appealing, so deciding that the officials would have to wait we walked into Barra to see what it had to offer. Leaving the Club, we kept to the shady side of the street, protected by a high wall. Before long we found ourselves on a wide pavement between the road and the beach and noticed, with some surprise, the plethora of uniformed police walking in pairs, patrolling the area. Apparently, Bahia's bad reputation for street crime was affecting its burgeoning holiday industry and, in the tourist areas at least, some effort was being made to reduce the threat.

Barra was not for us: it was a place for foreigners to spend money, crowded with places to eat, expensive shops and even a mall, where the visitor could be tempted to part with his

cash. A little off the main thoroughfare, we found a supermarket, which did not appear to be particularly expensive and was not too far from the Yacht Club. They had cream crackers *em oferta* and we immediately bought several packs, knowing that if you see a bargain in Brazil, you do not put off buying it until later because by then it will be gone. By now dusk was falling with its usual rapidity and we returned to the Club; it was dark by the time we were back on *Badger*.

Although protected from the Trade wind, the anchorage is wide open to a cold front. We were unlikely to encounter one of these at the end of January, but preferring somewhere more sheltered we did not plan to linger. The following morning, we made use of the Club launch to get ashore, to clear in and explore the city.

The previous day, we had noticed that the buses displayed the cost of the fare as well as the destination, but that some were cheaper than others, the prices apparently varying in relation to the comfort and speed of the vehicle. Needless to say, we selected the cheapest one; it halted at every stop and we were not quite sure just where we would end up, but Pete thought that the bus should take us to the lower city, near to the Port Captain. Salvador is built on two levels, the one dramatically higher than the other, so that many years ago a huge lift was built to carry people between the two. There are also flights of stairs, but rumour had it that they were unsafe, even in broad daylight. Pete was right — the bus stopped right in front of the Port Captain's building, an imposing white, stucco edifice on the edge of the small boat harbour. The forms were soon filled in because this Port Captain was used to dealing with foreign yachts and he gave us directions to the Polícia Federal and

The Yacht Club at Salvador.

Customs House, both in the same building. We could see no sign of them and we trudged the whole length of the dock area and back before we finally located the offices, inconspicuously marked and up a flight of dingy stairs. With the ship's business finally concluded, we could now explore the city.

The *Cidade Buixa*, the lower city with the commercial area and the port, is busy during the day, the streets filled with business men in their suits, with sailors, dock workers and ships' agents and with tourists who visit the large craft market not far from the Port Captain's building. At night, things are very different and it is a foolhardy yachtsmen who rows ashore intending to have a night on the town.

Although the craft market is considered a highlight, we discovered little of appeal, finding the dark wood carvings at best ugly and often downright sinister and only rarely was anything for sale out of the ordinary. On the other hand, there were some beautiful laces, such as is traditionally worn by the ladies of

Salvador, whose dresses include or are even entirely composed of superbly made white lace. I wondered how on earth they managed to keep them so immaculate, especially as they often sit by the side of the road, cooking *Acarajé* or some other dish to sell to the passer-by. There is no need to find a restaurant in Salvador, the streets are plentifully provided with vendors of freshly cooked food.

We made our way to the historic area in the *Cidade Alta*, the upper city, where the priests built their churches and the wealthy their houses. Although defaced by the odd tower block, Bahia's skyline is still dominated by twin towers typical of Portuguese churches. While the good citizens might well differ from me, I can only rejoice that for so many years there was no interest in the city. Because of this, the beautiful buildings remain standing: whole streets of them facing onto cobbled roads and unchanged in two hundred years. While it would have been no bad thing for these houses to have had a bit more maintenance during this

time, the colonial past is now being appreciated. People have realized wherein lies the true wealth of Salvador and the marvellous, baroque buildings are being renovated. Many of the churches have never been neglected and these are a truly astonishing sight, with their gilded altars and silver chandeliers. Often built by slave labour, no expense was spared in their construction and ornamentation, and the ostentation and vulgarity of their interiors has to be seen to be believed.

There was a tremendous amount of restoration work being carried out, often upon both sides of an entire street. The fine, old buildings were recovering their former glory with the

The churches of the Cidade Alta in Salvador.

stucco painted in a variety of glowing colours and the wrought iron picked out in contrast. While the ground floors were being converted into bars, restaurants and shops, obviously tourist orientated, it appeared that the upper floors would be used as dwellings. Going up a couple of side streets, we would soon find ourselves in the untouched parts of the city, where the buildings were dilapidated and crumbling, with grass growing in the gutters, where gutters remained, and the balconies were in imminent peril of losing their hold altogether. Here we could begin to appreciate the sheer enormity of the task that faced the restorers and wondered how the decisions are made, which building to save and which to let go.

An afternoon sufficed for us and I realized once again that the natural world holds far more fascination for me than do the works of men. On our way towards the bus station, we crossed a square where we stopped to look at

Views of the older sections of Salvador.

some drawings for sale. The artist, a young black man, approached and greeted us.

`Hello. These are yours?' we asked. `They're very good.' As indeed they were; studies of the city, not only the tourist scenes, but the old and decaying areas through which we had just walked.

`Would you like to buy one? Name your own price. Just pay me what you think is fair,' he said, displaying several of his pictures to better advantage.

`No, thank you,' I said. `We only stopped to admire them.'

`Where do you come from?'

`England.'

`Oh, England. How wonderful! Perhaps you would like to take one home as a souvenir?'

`We don't have room for anything like this,' I smiled at him. `We live on a boat.'

`I have some smaller ones here,' he responded. `Look — here, just tell me what you think they are worth. You fix the price.' We were somewhat embarrassed. His importuning ways did not fit in with his

truly charming personality and smile. We wondered what he would say if we offered him a dollar. Or a hundred. We had no idea what he should be paid for his work; we only knew that we admired it, but had no real desire to own any. With some difficulty, we extricated ourselves, feeling vaguely guilty that we had bought nothing from him.

A couple of days later, we went and filled up our water containers, and discovered that the taps were high up on the end of the Club building. Most of the members had power boats, and the taps were perfect for filling their tanks but not so easy for us to use without a hose. That afternoon returning from shopping, we saw that another yacht had anchored, which we recognized as *Steradenn*. Christian, Maria, Pablo, Anne and another lady, all dressed in bathing suits, had already settled down on the terrace, sitting in the sunshine. We went over to greet them and were introduced to Christians's mother.

`Ah good,' said Christian, when we had caught up with each other's news, `now you can tell me what 'appens 'ere. 'Ow long can we stay before we must pay?'

We told him about the arrangements and then I had a sudden thought. `You'd better go and sort out your passes,' I suggested. `It's Saturday tomorrow, and there may be no-one here to give you one.'

`Yes, you are right. I will go up now,' said Christian, rising and picking up his bag.

`Don't you think it might be an idea to put a shirt on?' I asked him. `They may object if you go to the offices just in shorts.'

`I suppose so,' sighed Christian reluctantly, `it is very bourgeois, this Club.' He rummaged in his bag, drew out a crumpled T-shirt and pulled it over his head. We all laughed: the front was full of holes.

`Ah yes, I 'ad forgotten. I spill some battery acid down it. Never mind. It is still a shirt,' and he went off to see the Secretary. When he returned, he commented, `I thought you said they give you ten days for free?'

`That's right.'

`Well, they only gave us five. It is very strange, is it not.'

Maybe Christian would have been made more welcome without the holes.

Sunshine and a light breeze made for a pleasant, if slow, sail the following day. Approaching the anchorage off the small town of Itaparica, we were confused by a complicated series of yellow buoys, which apparently marked a degaussing range. Among the local yachts at anchor, we were surprised to see about half a dozen boats wearing foreign ensigns. It explained why we had not seen any in Salvador: this was obviously the favoured alternative. Originally people came to Itaparica for their health, as there is a spring in the town that is supposed to have medicinal properties, but now it is frequented by trippers who want to escape from Salvador for the day and the whole island is a popular holiday resort. The water is now bottled and sold in the town.

Selecting a place to drop the hook was slightly difficult, because of a few odd and intrusive concrete structures, possibly concerned with the oil industry, and the local boats, obviously here just for the weekend. A further obstacle was that the shoal water was

more extensive than we had thought. The bleeping echo sounder warned us, we executed an unplanned tack which took us into the thick of the fleet and there were a few tense moments as we wriggled our way to a likely looking spot and dropped the hook in sixteen feet. With no room to sheer about, I lowered the sails as soon as Pete snubbed up and then called the depth, so that he could let out the correct scope. We tidied the boat up, trying to look as though we normally entered an anchorage with such panache.

A voice hailed us from the water. `Nice to see another red ensign! Why don't you come over and have a drink? We're on that yacht,' he continued, indicating the immaculate Nicholson 35, *Encounter*, anchored next to us.

`Thanks very much, we'll be over as soon as we're sorted out,' we replied. It was the start of a most sociable month. Several yachts based themselves here at Itaparica, and we enjoyed being able to spend time with the people on them. As well as a couple of French boats, Bob and Miguel, the single-handers from Jacaré, were both here and then *Steradenn* turned up a few days later.

From that first afternoon on *Encounter*, we spent quite a lot of time with Mike and Christine. She was German but spoke perfect English, and we all enjoyed being in the company of people with whom we could converse so easily and who shared a similar sense of humour. We ate with one another, often had our sundowners together and always found plenty talk about. One evening we ate some tuna chunks on toothpicks, which were delicious. Christine had pickled it herself and taught me how to do it. It sounded too good to be true when she first explained it.

`You cut up the fish into one inch cubes, fry it in oil and then put it into a jar. In another pan you have a mixture of fifty-fifty vinegar and water, which you boil for five minutes with whatever spices you like. If you want, you can add some onion to the jars and then you pour the hot vinegar over the fish until the jars are full and then put the top on.'

`Do you need proper preserving jars?'

`Oh no, any type will do.'

`Really? And how long does the fish keep?'

`For ages. It's like tinned food — it only goes off once the jar is opened. It's a wonderful way of keeping fish if you catch too much.'

Christine and Mike kept their boat in beautiful condition and one afternoon, I admired the leather on the rim of the stainless steel wheel.

`There's quite a story to that,' said Mike. `We found it in the Bahamas.'

`Found it?'

`Yes. We were anchored off a small island with an abandoned house on it and went to have a look around. We couldn't believe it, because it was a really expensive looking place and when we went inside, all the furniture was still there, in good condition and obviously fairly new. We couldn't understand how anyone could just go off and leave it. Some of the windows were broken and the weather was getting in. In the living room we saw a settee covered in this leather, all going to waste. When we went back on board, I said to Christine, "I'm going to cut that leather off the settee. It'll get ruined anyway and we might as well make use of it." She didn't think I should, but in the end you agreed, didn't you? It broke my heart to do it, really, but it seemed worse to leave it. There was quite a lot. I'll show you.'

He went below and came back shortly with several large pieces of leather.

`Look! Feel it — it's lovely stuff.' It was, too, soft and supple, obviously of high quality, an attractive shade of fawn. `Originally,' Mike continued, `we were going to use it for chafing gear and so on, but it's too good for that.'

`Oh no, you couldn't!' I exclaimed, `it's probably too soft, anyway, even if you could bring yourself to cut it up like that. You could use it on sails, perhaps but you ought to make a skirt or something. It's beautiful.'

`Why was the house abandoned?' asked Pete.

`Apparently it belonged to a drug dealer who was arrested. When that happens they confiscate everything. I suppose that it really belonged to the Bahamian Government, but they weren't doing anything with it.'

A few days later I was talking to Christine who had been visiting a nearby Swiss ketch. `They speak German and it's rather fun to be able to use it again,' she told me.

`You must miss that,' I said.

`No, not really because Mike and I speak English all the time and I think in it now. It's just a pleasant change. I like languages and the next one I want to learn is French. We meet so many French people, I'd be able to use it quite a bit.'

`Would you like to have a French language course?' I asked her. `We bought one ages ago, for Pete, but it's just taking up space. You can have it if you want.'

`I'd love it. What are you asking for it?'

`Oh, nothing, I'll be glad to get rid of it. The only reason we've hung on to it for so long was because we wanted to give it to someone who was certain to make use of it.'

Christine obviously felt that she should pay for it, because the next day she rowed over with a bag. `Here, take this,' she said, `I think it's a fair swop.' Inside was a large piece of the leather that we had been admiring. It was more than a fair swop.

Itaparica city had a fruit and vegetable market. Prices varied and some stall keepers were more friendly than others, but it was convenient. The little supermarket in the town was very expensive, so if we needed to buy anything else, we would catch a bus for twenty cents to the town of Bom Despacho, where the Salvador ferry docks, and which had two large supermarkets. The bus ran from just outside the gates of the Yacht Club, where we could leave our dinghies; it was all very convenient and perhaps explained why some yachts spent so long anchored at Itaparica.

We wanted to dry *Badger* out for antifouling and Mike and Christine suggested that we use the wall next to the bottling plant, where they had seen other boats dry out. On inspection, it looked a bit dubious and we preferred to use a nearby sand spit and dry *Badger* out on her legs, waiting until just after high water and then running her gently aground, an operation which caused a certain amount of interest in the anchorage. The legs are purpose-made of marine grade aluminium, and Mike and Christian both had a good look at them. They were particularly impressed by the way that the legs telescope up and Mike was, I think, quite tempted, although Christian reckoned that they were too expensive.

Christian, who used his ensign to tie up his cockpit awning, considered us terribly proper, because we wear a burgee, take in the ensign at sunset and display an anchor ball. He was unconvinced by our explanation that that the former is a good wind indicator, the

Badger *beached for antifouling at Itaparica.*

ensign lasts a lot longer if it only flies half the time, and that without an anchor ball, we might be blamed if someone collided with us. So when we put *Badger* onto the sand spit, I immediately hoisted the signal flags J and H, which means `I am aground. I am not in danger.'

`There,' I said, `now Christian will *really* believe that we are proper yachties!'

The sand spit proved to be ideal, with enough rise and fall that the paint had a chance to dry before the tide came back in and as the bottom was still fairly clean, the job was done quickly.

Most of the other yachts were quite content to stay at anchor in one place, but having been in Itaparica for nearly a week, we were ready for a change. It was noisy during the day: the nearby jetty either being used by tourist schooners or by children diving off it with the usual screams and shouts, which also made it fairly perilous to approach in the dinghy. The other drawback of Itaparica was an inexplicable plague of flies, which I spent half the day swatting. After Pete had studied the chart of Baía de Todos os Santos and talked to the other yachts that had been anywhere else, we had settled on the River Paraguaçu for our first cruise.

`See you in about a week,' we called as we sailed out past *Encounter* on Friday morning.

`You're doing the right thing — we'll be colliding with the locals all night!'

We suspected that they could well be right. Itaparica was best avoided at the weekend.

That first day, the afternoon breeze that usually sprang up in this area gave us a splendid run so that it took just over two hours to cover the eleven miles, anchor to anchor. We dropped the hook into a mere fathom of water in a little bay, the complete evocation of The Perfect Anchorage. The golden beach, palm-fringed, curved in a flawless crescent, broken in places by artfully situated boulders. Behind it rose a steep hill, clothed in lush, tropical growth and above that was the blue sky, dotted here and there with white clouds. Here, at the bend of the river, was total protection, although such safety would not be required, for the climate is generally too benign for the mariner to have to worry about lee shores or dragging anchors. After the noise and bustle of Itaparica it was sublime.

A further advantage of river sailing was brought home to me the next day. When we are exploring, Pete enjoys sailing from dawn until sunset, which gives me

no time for many of the chores that have to be done on a regular basis, but here we could not consider going further until the tide was in our favour, because the morning breeze was too light and variable for us to fight a foul tide and many places were really too deep to anchor. Thus it was that we only got underway after half past three, when we sailed in leisurely fashion up the beautiful river, admiring the scenery and looking with interest at the occasional house that we passed. After about seven miles, we sailed out into an area of shallows, where two tributaries joined the Paraguaçu. Over to starboard, we could see an old church and headed towards it.

Dedicated to São Francisco, the building was handsome but decaying and looked anything but prosperous. Around the back we could just make out the priest's house with a pig and several hens rooting and scratching in the yard. A few poor shacks stood nearby, fishermen's homes, apparently, and brown children were running around and playing in the shallows. Several dugouts were pulled up the beach. It was a lovely spot. We sailed a few cables further, entering the mouth of one of the tributaries and dropped the hook.

São Francisco, on the Rio Paraguaçu.

We had a really special meal, this evening, to celebrate *Badger*'s tenth birthday. Contemplating our wonderful little ship, we agreed that she did not look her age and indeed, still felt relatively new. Although we chose the design with care and built her to the best of our abilities, she is by no means a conventional yacht and there were many who criticized our ideas when she was in build, so that we sometimes wondered if we really *did* know what we were doing. Now, we feel extraordinarily fortunate to have such a boat.

We woke with a start the next morning, hearing, through the hull, the sound of cracking ice! That was

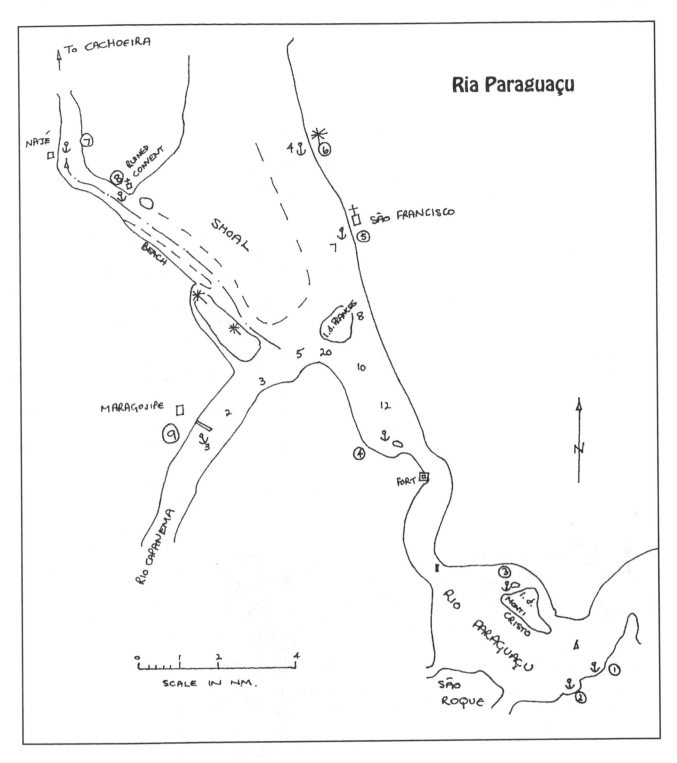

Ria Paraguaçu

obviously impossible and we lay there wondering what on earth it could be. It came again and a third time, but this time there was also a muffled explosion and we realized that the fishermen were dynamiting fish. With declining fish stocks, this is strictly illegal, with large penalties for anyone convicted, but its extreme efficiency makes it too tempting a proposition. It is also quite a dangerous practice and several people have been badly injured, but with fish hard to come by and a large family of hungry children, the risk does not seem that much and there are more important worries than the state of the world in years to come. Later, as we ate our breakfast in the cockpit, to the accompaniment of the cracked bell in the church, some *canoas* came back with their fish. They did not have many.

The wind seemed unlikely to come and so at half past ten, we started the Seagull. Sitting under the awning it was very pleasant and we picked our way carefully through the shoal water, relying on our echo sounder because we were now off the chart. At times we only had an inch or two under the keel but managed to avoid actually touching. Just before noon, a light breeze filled in, but the sun was so fierce that we left the awning up and proceeded under foresail only, happy to proceed slowly in these shallow waters. We knew that it was possible, but difficult, to get up the river as far as the town of Cachoeira and intended to give it a try. Having safely negotiated the large area of shallows, probably from the silt that the rivers carry, we found a channel and headed towards the upper Paraguaçu.

The channel was taking us closer and closer to a beach, full of people. Several of them were standing up to their necks in the water, so assuming that it should be just deep enough, we crept forward through the turbid water, gazing intently at the echo sounder, with only a couple of inches under the keel. Then we touched. Immediately dropping the sail, we started the motor, putting it hard astern, but nothing happened. The young men that we had been using as a tide mark, stood up, revealing water only waist deep and the horrible realisation that we had run aground hard by a popular beach, at Sunday lunch-time, sunk in. The younger male element now noticed that free entertainment had been laid on. Laughing and shouting, the men came to try to `help' us while the boys did their best to capsize the dinghy. Pete was worrying about all his soft antifouling coming off, I was worried about losing our oars, and around us was mayhem. I dealt with the boys by hauling *Skip* aboard and with the men by thanking them, but pointing out that the paint that was covering them contained poisons, which discouraged them from renewing their several efforts to move *Badger* left, right or sideways, while Pete scrabbled in the lazarette, extracting the legs.

Somewhat distracted by youngsters swinging on the outboard, we fitted the legs and then *Badger* was safe, so long as we kept a lookout to swat away any children who reckoned that the legs made good climbing frames. Having pulled the motor out of reach, we settled down, with what shreds of dignity we could muster, to await the flood that would release us from this ridiculous predicament. The sun seemed stationary in the sky and it was an eternity before the beach started to empty. At low water, we realized that our 'channel' was a dead end, but laid out the anchor upstream, believing there would be enough rise of tide to allow us to pass over the slight elevation ahead.

By half past ten, there was sufficient water to float us and we pulled *Badger* back into the main channel. At first, there was just enough breeze to sail, but we had to motor for the last couple of miles. To port was a small village from which some extremely loud music was issuing, but when we tried to go further, the depths fell off and in the dark, we were not really sure of

Najé, on the Rio Paraguaçu.

what we were doing. It was nearly midnight, we had had enough, so we dropped the hook off the village, hoping that the music would stop.

Up early, we cleaned and put away the legs ready to continue our attempt to sail up the river. After ten minutes underway, we ran out of water and could discern no obvious channel, so re-anchored to consider our next move. A fisherman sculling by in his dugout canoe, saw us in the cockpit and came alongside. His eyes wandered over *Badger*'s brightwork with delight: `muito lindo, muito lindo.' He picked up a bight of our artificial hemp sheet and felt its soft texture with appreciation. `Está bom, não, este cabo?' but it was said simply with admiration, without envy. We talked with him for a while. Yes, it was possible to get up to Cachoeira, he would even pilot us if we wanted, but it was not easy, there were many rocks and it would take a long time. Perhaps, too, our beautiful boat might receive hurt, he did not know the channel so well. We thanked him and said that we would not try; it was not so important. As he sculled away, I turned to Pete,

`Well, at least we tried, but it's not worth risking the boat, is it?'

`No. Obviously the river is badly silted up compared with the old days. If we only drew two or three feet like the local boats, I'd give it a go, but even if we didn't damage *Badger*, it would take forever. Let's go and have a look at Maragojipe and on the way we can stop off at that convent down near the mouth of the river that we saw yesterday.'

With barely a breath of wind we resorted to the Seagull for twenty minutes or so, then anchored in the shallows off the ruined convent of Santo Antonio do Paraguaçu, where we would have been aground at low water. The nuns had selected a choice site for their convent, bordered by water on three sides, with open views over rural scenery and hills in the distance. Most of the buildings had crumbled into complete ruins, but the chapel, with some exquisite mosaic work on the gable end over the main doorway, still stood; perhaps it was used as a place of worship even after the convent fell into disuse. We looked inside, but a huge sow challenged our right of entry, snorting with irritation and glaring at us belligerently out of her hard, tiny eyes. Her entrancing, diminutive piglets snuffled around her, but not wishing her to mistake our intentions, we confined ourselves to the entrance. The walls were washed with pastel colours and the altar, now totally unadorned, still stood. There were niches where effigies of the saints and the

Virgin had no doubt stood and overhead was an elaborate candelabrum. Although I am not, by the wildest stretch of imagination, a religious person, it seemed a shame that this pretty little chapel should have sunk so low as to become the home of pigs.

More pigs grunted and huffed in the shade outside and, as we rambled about examining what was left of the convent, we heard a thump. This was immediately followed by a squealing from the pigs who scrabbled to their feet and all charged off in one direction. Watching them with great curiosity, we saw the one in the lead pick up something from the ground and start to munch it with evident enjoyment. Walking over, we realized that it was eating a mango and then noticed several more trees, scattered about in a small grove.

`Mangoes!' I exclaimed. `Let's find a stick and knock some down, shall we?'

We soon had two or three heavy pieces of wood and started throwing them at the ripe fruit. Thump, thump, thump. They hit the ground and rolled away in several directions. The pigs once more leapt into life, and, laughing, we raced them for the fallen fruit. For such cumbersome creatures, they had quite a turn of speed and some of them managed to get to a mango before we did. With soft grunts of pleasure, their eyes glassy in ecstasy, they chewed the ripe mango, juice dribbling from their mouths. We could hardly begrudge them their delight; besides, the trees were laden and we soon had more than we could carry. In the end, Pete took off his T-shirt and used that for a bag, to its eternal detriment. With twenty mangoes, we returned to *Badger*, well-pleased with our morning's exploration.

Our passage to Maragojipe was not without its trials. Again we were faced with extremely shoal water

The ruined convent of Santo Antonio.

and no chart and, knowing that it was around high water, we erred on the side of caution when we started to run out of water, anchoring and launching the dinghy, so that Pete could row away with the leadline. After about twenty minutes, and at a considerable distance, I saw him gesticulating. Having no idea what he meant, but even from afar, inferring impatience, I at last divined that he wished me to get underway. What! All by myself? I spoke kindly to the Seagull, which obligingly started at first pull, and then fisted in the anchor. With an undeniable feeling of `Master under God,' but a sharp eye on the echo sounder, I steamed down to where Pete sat in *Skip*.

`You took your time!'

`Well!' I said indignantly, `it took me ages to work out what you wanted. You never said I was to come after you when you left.'

`Yes, but I didn't realize that I'd go so far. Anyway, as you discovered, there was sufficient water and it's been getting deeper for some time, so I think that we're over the watershed.'

With the afternoon breeze filling in, we had a slashing sail to Maragojipe, anchoring off the pier in time for a late lunch. The anchorage was crowded: Miguel, Mike and Christine and *Steradenn* were all

A saveiro overtook us as we sailed up the river. With their gaff rig and baggy sails, they look unmipressive but many a yachtsman has been surprised at their turn of speed off the wind.

there. We rowed over to *Encounter*, who said that they had come in a couple of days ago and were about to go ashore. We all went across to *Steradenn*, who were also getting into their dinghy, while Miguel's tender was already tied to the dock. There was a causeway built over the mudflats from the town to the jetty, where there was deep water for the ferry. The others told us

that they were trying to find out the where and the when of the local market, but had all been given different information.

We enjoyed the rather down-at-heel town, so typical of Brazil, with a character all of its own, much enhanced by the local habit of riding in on horse or donkey or, better still, an ox. Iron rings were attached to the kerbside, where the animals were tied up while their booted owners sold their produce or bought a drink at a bar. There was a minuscule street market of about a dozen stalls, by the river, a few shops and a town square, where we had hoped to find the main market. Not much perhaps, but the winding streets and the *saveiros* along the causeway, all added to its charm. We spent some time gazing at one *saveiro* that had just been unloaded. It was as clean as a whistle inside, the owner having swept out every trace of his last cargo. A small caged bird sat singing on the foredeck and the two crew were nearby relaxing in the sun until such time as the water returned and floated them once more.

While the word *saveiro* is used to describe any working boat in Brazil, including the many tourist schooners, we were looking at one of the last real, sailing workboats, now found only round Bahia, whose good breezes still allow a sailing boat to be an economic proposition. The sight of a *saveiro* underway in a brisk breeze is enough to stir the heart of any sailorman. For windward work, *saveiros* set a tiny jib, which seems more as a gesture than in any real hope of improvement, but in spite of their great beam, shallow draught and primitive rig, these boats manage to get where they are going and may even beat a pleasure yacht, due to their ability to take short cuts. With a fair wind they show an impressive turn of speed and Mike, for one, had reconsidered his first impressions of them, when he had sailed against one in *Encounter*.

Generally around forty feet long, drawing about three feet and invariably sloop-rigged, *saveiros* have a sharply raked transom, with a large rudder, are decked to the mast, with a one plank's-width side-deck and a coaming around the well. They used to carry all the cargo around Bahia, but now roads are making fewer cargoes available and we saw them carrying building materials, particularly sand or fresh produce.

Like most Brazilian boats, they are gaily painted and beautifully kept by the crew whose home they are. They live under a cuddy, forward and the rest of the boat is empty — we could clearly see the massive structure of the hull whose workmanship was, of necessity, simple. The frames more accurately described as `hewn' rather than `sawn'; but where a ceiling was fitted in the cargo area, the planks were smooth and true. The stem post and the first two frames were made with extra length to provide mooring bitts and her stern lines were taken to the mainsheet horse.

Examining the rig, we noticed a relatively short gaff and a loose-footed sail, laced to the mast with a single line. The mast was tall, longer than the boat, unstayed and very spindly, appearing precarious and not too permanent, an obvious illusion, because the large mainsail cannot be reefed and the beamy *saveiros* are very stiff. We had noticed how their skippers enjoy driving them when the wind gets up, and the masts seem unperturbed by the loads on them. Also brightly painted, it had a kink a few feet from the masthead and having noticed this on other *saveiros* we wondered at its purpose. Pete pondered for a while.

`I'm not sure, but I suspect that by placing the blocks slightly abaft the mast, it may make it easier to raise the sail. The mast's pretty rough and maybe it stops the halliard binding.'

Later, the *saveiro* glided past us. Innocent of an engine, the skipper was poling it along in the evening calm, using a length of bamboo as a quant.

We saw Miguel coming along the causeway. His Spanish being more readily understood than our various efforts, Maria excepted of course, we asked him about the market. `Tuesdays, they tell me, definitely Tuesdays.'

`Tomorrow? Oh, that's a nuisance — we were going for a day out.' Our attempts to get to Cachoeira by water having failed, we had planned instead to go by bus the next day.

`Don't worry about it,' said Christine, `I'll buy you anything that you need while you go and see what Cachoeira's like. If it's any good, we'll go.'

Our *Lonely Planet* guide fairly raved about this old town and a visit might be a good dose of culture in our benighted lives. In fact, the bus ride was the best bit of the day, apart that is, from seeing a couple more *saveiros* alongside the quay at Cachoeira, where we also noted plenty of depth of water; it was a shame that we had not found the channel. The town itself, while certainly old, did not seem to justify its description as a `jewel,' and `a living museum.' Concluding that we are undoubtedly Philistines, our regret was that a hydroelectric dam had ruined the

rapids after which the city had been named. But we had had a grand day out and salved our consciences by having attempted some serious sightseeing.

We made our report to Chris and Mike, who decided to save their energies for some other place. Apparently the market had failed to materialize. `Maybe tomorrow.'

There was no market on Wednesday, either. When we met up in town in the morning, we elected to move on. Mike and Christine were undecided and the others were staying a few more days, with Miguel determined to find out when the market was held. He invited us all back to his boat for a drink, in the company of a gorgeous young local girl. She seemed disappointed when she saw his yacht: it was perhaps not exactly what she had had in mind. Miguel generously invited everyone to lunch, but, wanting to make use of the ebb, we declined and I was rather relieved when I saw what was being cooked: tiny fish, like whitebait. I am foolishly squeamish about such things and Mike looked less than enthusiastic, but Miguel's hospitality was so genuine that I almost wished we were staying.

We had a wonderful sail that afternoon. At a narrows in the river was a ruined fort facing a small island to one side of the main channel. We went and anchored upstream of this, had our lunch and then beat through the channel behind the island, with barely enough room to tack. Later, we followed an ox-bow in the river, which brought us to two more islands and an anchorage between them, that was secluded and sheltered from the fresh afternoon trade wind. The smaller island had a perfect palm tree and there was another next to a shack on the larger island of Monte Cristo, but this was the only sign of humanity. Reluctantly, we tore ourselves away and at tea time dropped the hook

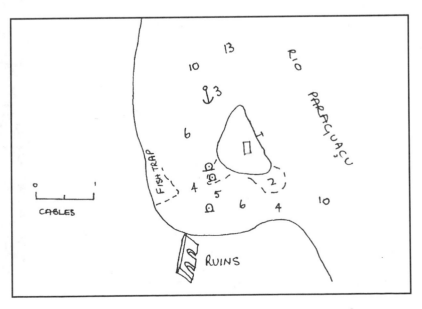

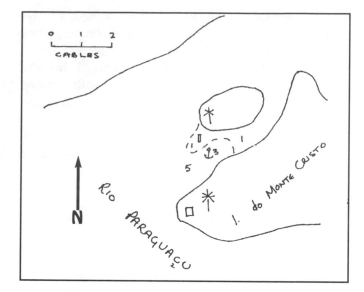

in a bay adjacent to the one where we had first anchored. It was an indifferent anchorage, with the middle obstructed by an area of rock, but Mike had told us that we could find some large bamboos ashore here, which we wanted to improve our awning.

Once again we were woken by an explosion: this time the fishermen were dynamiting our anchorage. While we ate our breakfast, we watched them diving time and again after the stunned and dead fish, with neither flippers, masks nor snorkels, and wondered how they could find their victims in the silt-laden water. After they had left with about twenty fish, as we needed to rinse off all the mango juice from breakfast anyway, we put on our snorkelling gear to see what we could find. We swam for quite some time but neither of us saw anything other than one little fish, about four inches long, twitching on the bottom. Unsporting and damaging to fish stocks it may have been, but these fishermen could not have been accused of being wasteful.

We dried off and went ashore and after a hot and sweaty climb up a steep hill, found our stand of bamboos. The three that we selected took a bit of sawing down and we were constantly brushing off flies, so it was with a pleasant sense of achievement that we dragged them back to the beach. Three six-foot lengths would do for the awning, and we kept the thin ends to one side for such things as a spare burgee stick.

Back at anchor off Itaparica city, we held a party to celebrate *Badger*'s birthday. We went into Bom Despacho and bought some *kibe* and other things for snacks. In the afternoon, Pete scoured out our deck bucket and made a wonderful *cachaça* punch, squeezing fruit, mixing and tasting, until he was sure that it was perfect. Christine and Mike had made *Badger* a card, which we cherished for a long time, and Christian

and Maria brought *Badger* one of the wood carvings that were sold in Salvador, to mount on the bulkhead. It was a rather malignant-looking woman's head whose presence did not add to *Badger*'s ambience as she leered at us in the saloon. A good time was had by all and Pete had to mix up another bucket before the evening was out. Astonishingly, no one had a headache the next day.

In Itaparica, it was possible to get water, which tasted of chlorine, from the marina or take your containers to the bottling plant and get them filled there. More interestingly, Mike and Christine had told us of a waterfall where you could take your jerricans and get pure spring water, so Saturday saw us escaping the weekend crowds and heading off again. We discovered that "waterfall" was something of an exaggeration for the small spring that dribbled over a low cliff into a shallow pool. From the amount of carved graffiti, we gather that we were not the first to visit, nor to feel that it would have been less tedious had the stream flowed with more generosity, but as we had brought our lunch ashore and it was a pretty spot, it was no real hardship. We collected nineteen gallons of water, had a cooling splash in the pool and then went back aboard.

The waterfall at Itaparica.

Our chart showed another river, the Jaguaripe, with a small town of the same name. With no more information available, we had to go and see for ourselves. The chart was unclear, but we managed to wriggle through the shallows and find a channel, which we then followed as far as the town, arriving at dusk. It was one of our better anchorages: Jaguaripe was little more than a village and during the night there was barely a sound. Ashore in the morning, we found a delightful, totally unspoilt place, with handsome, old buildings. Women were cooking breakfast behind the shacks, almost hidden from us by banana trees, which provided both shade and sustenance. People smiled and greeted us as we passed, probably wondering where we had sprung from, as, so far off the beaten track a stranger must have been something of a novelty.

Above, a house in Jaguaripe.
Below, a view of the village from the river.

The spring ebb was running strongly as we beat back down the river and we reached the entrance earlier then we had anticipated. Anchoring until the flood commenced, we then sounded our way across the shallows, establishing the path of a channel, which Pete noted down. At the back of Ilha de Itaparica, we joined the main river, noticing a flotilla of boats heading in the same direction. As they drew near, they proved to be brightly decorated with streamers, flowers — natural and artificial — flags and greenery. We sailed with them, calling and waving back and forth, but after a couple of miles, they all brought up to anchor off a small, white church where a crowd had gathered. No doubt it was some festival of blessing for the boats and we had been lucky to be involved, however briefly.

We had to pass under a major road bridge and some power lines, but between the two, we dropped the hook

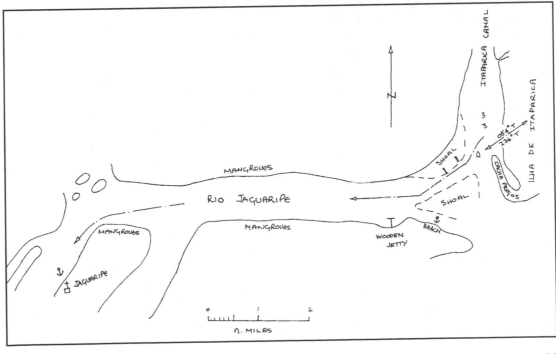

Festival day parade of sails at Ilha de Itaparica.

off a tiny, sand beach, by a magnificent mango tree, which was fairly groaning under the weight of this delectable fruit and which we had noticed the previous day. We collected no fewer than twenty-eight mangoes, but with some for chutney and some for our friends in Itaparica; there was no risk of any being wasted. We lingered over lunch, sitting in the cockpit under the awning, the road bridge so high up that we could barely hear the traffic, but eventually we dragged ourselves away to sail back to the waterfall anchorage for the night.

Just after dawn, we topped up our water, enjoyed a refreshing shower in the little grotto, with a fine, open view up and down the river and were underway by ten to eight. With days so short and so hot, we used to get up as soon as it was light enough to see, but as soon as the sun peeped over the horizon, its strength could be felt. Once it was fully risen it was literally scorching and, although over the past twenty years I have spent a lot of time in the Tropics and believed that my skin had become acclimatized, Bahia apprised me of my mistake. I could not come to terms with the fierceness of the mid-summer sun so close to the Equator. Its rays burnt me, totally disregarding sun blocks and barriers. In desperation, I resorted to wearing my Chinese `happy suit' to sail in, which with long sleeves and loose fit was the equivalent of wearing pyjamas. I also wore a large straw hat that we had found floating in the sea one day and, while this outfit was somewhat lacking in style, it did prevent me from getting burnt, so long as I kept my feet in the shade.

The windless mornings were the worst and this day was no exception. We could not work out how to fit a bimini top to *Badger* to shade us from the sun and when there was no wind the heat was intense, the temperature *under the awning* reaching 40° C and far higher in the sun. We drifted along for a couple of hours or so and as we passed a sand spit, Pete suggested that we

stop to see what sort of anchorage it provided. Carefully sounding our way, we found a bight just big enough for a yacht, with ten feet of water. It was rather pleasant, out in the middle of nowhere with distant vistas, and we drank our home-made lime *suco* with appreciation.

After a further two hours we drifted the six miles remaining to Itaparica and were anchored in our old spot by lunch-time. A breeze was just beginning to fill in as Pete put up the awning and with the scuttles and hatches open it was almost cool below. Christine rowed by later.

`Is the sun bothering you?' she asked, `I noticed that you were all covered up when you sailed in.'

`I'm afraid so,' I replied. `It's really too much. And the heat's even worse.'

`Yes, I know! It's almost unbearable, isn't it? We leave the forehatch open, when we go ashore now, otherwise the boat's like an oven when we come back. I'd rather be robbed than have that! Will you come and have a beer with us this afternoon?'

`I'm sorry, but the Yacht Club's too expensive.'

`Oh, I quite agree — I didn't mean there. Mike and I have found a bar in town that has Antarctica *em oferta* at the moment — under a dollar a bottle.'

`Of course, I'd forgotten that you have an instinct for cheap beers! We were going ashore anyway, so that sounds like a good excuse to try your find!'

On our way into town we saw the *Steradenn*s sitting having a late lunch at the Yacht Club.

`It's just as well that someone does more than just leave their dinghy here!'

`You should come 'ere sometime. It's very good.'

`Yes,' said Maria, `but the best thing is that it is so close! You know, it takes all four of us to carry Pablo's gear. I don't know how we'll manage when we lose Marguerite.'

`Ah yes, I 'ave to go back to France next week,' Christian's mother sighed, `and it will be so cold there.'

Mike, Christine, Pete and I went to the bar that they had found, a tiny place with two, small steel tables and four metal chairs along one wall. As all the other customers were standing up, we commandeered these and drank our icy beer Brazilian style, sharing a bottle between the four of us, so that it didn't have time to get warm.

Mike and Pete had been talking about *Badger*'s rig: `The easiest way to show you how it works is to take you for a sail,' said Pete. `We were planning to go shopping tomorrow. How about Wednesday late morning, when there's a bit of breeze blowing? We'll go somewhere, anchor for lunch and then sail back.'

This we duly did and all enjoyed our day. Christine was convinced by the rig, instantly appreciating its ease and simplicity, but Mike was more ambivalent.

`I must say, though, that you do a lot more day sailing than we do, and I think that's partly because it's so much hassle to get the sails ready, but round here, the problem is also our draught. As you know, we have an encapsulated keel — it's easy to maintain, but I'm always rather worried that I might knock off a lump of gelcoat and then the water will get in. We're only in six feet, aren't we? I couldn't anchor here.'

`Yes, we've only got four foot six draught, but I'd love to have even less,' Pete responded. `Unfortunately, the only way to make a real difference would be with a centre-board, and I don't want one of those.'

We cleared away the remains of lunch, got our anchor and sailed back. We were leaving Itaparica for the last time in the morning, so we went over to *Encounter* for sundowners. Christine produced a few nibbles and then we agreed that having had a substantial lunch it was hardly necessary to cook dinner, so we had some more nibbles and yarned the evening away.

`Maybe we'll see you down in the Falklands, then,' joked as we rowed off: Mike had briefly been tempted by the thought of the Southern Ocean.

`I think I like wearing shorts too much!'

`Ah well, we'll see you along the way. Take care.'

They were such *simpatico* people; there was a lump in my throat at the thought of parting. I hope that we cross tacks again some day.

The advent of the breeze late the following morning saw *Badger*'s sails being raised and we romped off towards Ilha do Frade, the island that we had visited the previous day. This time we wanted to have a look at another anchorage. We had lunch underway and up at the north-west end of Ilha do Frade, dropped our anchor in eleven feet of water with a good mud bottom. It was a pretty spot, tempting us to spend the night, but the afternoon was still young, we should soon be heading south and there was still a lot to see, so we got our anchor and sailed over towards the island of Bom Jesus. There was an obvious anchorage between it and the next island but the chart was a bit vague about details, contenting itself with showing that the depths were generally under a fathom. By looking at the areas of deeper water,

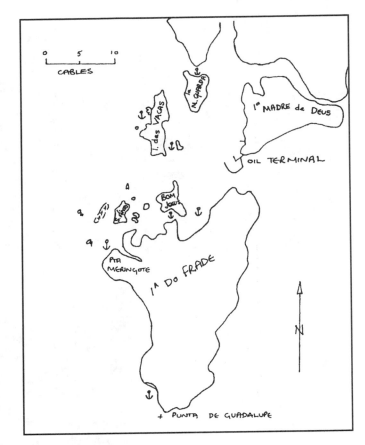

we inferred the presence of a tidal channel and at slow speed, sounding all the way, we determined its course, working our way in with some difficulty as the channel was only just wide enough to tack through. In the narrows where we anchored were nine feet of water, several moorings and a hard at which we could land. As the day drew to its close, small *canoas* were pulled up there, but the larger, heavier ones had to be moored, while the owners either hitched a lift or swam ashore.

We went to look at the island before it went dark, finding that it was essentially one, densely populated village. There were no cars, which made it a pleasure to

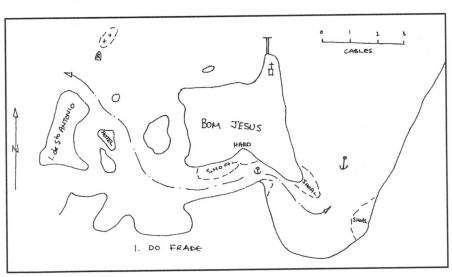

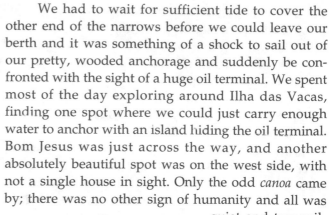

We had to wait for sufficient tide to cover the other end of the narrows before we could leave our berth and it was something of a shock to sail out of our pretty, wooded anchorage and suddenly be confronted with the sight of a huge oil terminal. We spent most of the day exploring around Ilha das Vacas, finding one spot where we could just carry enough water to anchor with an island hiding the oil terminal. Bom Jesus was just across the way, and another absolutely beautiful spot was on the west side, with not a single house in sight. Only the odd *canoa* came by; there was no other sign of humanity and all was quiet and tranquillity. A third place, Ilha das Fontes, was quite choppy in the afternoon breeze, so we went back to the west side of Ilha das Vacas and enjoyed a night of perfect peace.

Bom de Jesus, above, its pier, centre, and the lovely anchorage, below.

Saturday found us looking at a further three potential anchorages. At Santana, Ilha da Maré, a little village at the southwest corner of the island, where we stopped for lunch, we only found five and a half feet even well offshore, and concluded that it was not a place to spend the night. We could see a path going to a tower and onto a beach on the island. We were quite tempted to take a walk, but the heat was too much for me and after due consideration, Pete opted to go sailing instead.

We had read that Baía de Aratu was a highly industrialized area and not really worth visiting, but reckoned that we ought to go and see for ourselves. We approached the entrance with several other yachts whose crew stared in amazement at this bizarre black-hulled apparition, with green, strangely-shaped sails. It was not easy to concentrate on the long, poorly-marked entrance channel because we were busy looking at the Navy ships in the dockyard on either side and waving back at the other yachts. Then the bay opened out, lined with mangroves, with only one factory in sight and a large marina at the end. Sailing down towards it, we could make out a couple of foreign yachts, but preferring to anchor, we turned back. A railway ran along the bay on one side, but we did not see many trains. Near the entrance, on the far side, we found a quiet

walk around, and the accepted way of transporting goods was obviously by wheelbarrow, on which theme there seemed to be endless variations. Although there were several bars and restaurants, there were few shops, with only very basic food supplies. Judging from a ferry that we saw returning from the mainland, the islanders went there to do their shopping. Along the sandy beaches were many signs of fishing: nets being mended and the boats being worked on. There was a surprising amount to see and the sun had set before we started to wend our way back to the dinghy, almost getting lost in the maze of unplanned roadways.

bight in the mangroves where we dropped the hook and spent a peaceful night. Far from being ruined by industry, we found this, our final stop in Baía de Todos os Santos before going back to Salvador and on south, was one of our quieter anchorages and if not the most beautiful, nor was it ugly.

Armed with more information from the other yachts, we considered that the advantages of going to anchor off Salvador in order to clear out and stock up outweighed the disadvantages. The small boat harbour was very crowded with tourist schooners and their moorings, making it difficult to find anywhere to anchor. Our berth gave us a good view of the city and Pete noticed the

View of Salvador from the anchorage.

bright colours of some houses in the lower city and the quaintness of the older buildings, while I found the obvious squalor of the modern blocks of flats depressing and that Salvador had a threatening aura that I had not experienced on our previous visit. As the sun went down, the tourist schooners returned to their moorings, some coming perilously close, but handled with such skill that we soon relaxed and watched with admiration as the long-keeled craft were manoeuvred into a space that seemed to be little more than their own length.

The next morning, we discussed our plan of campaign. We had to clear for our next port and wanted to shop at the supermarket, about half a mile away. With no safe place to leave the dinghy, we felt that even our little plywood pram might prove too much of a temptation to one of Salvador's notoriously light-fingered, dockside loafers. There was a convenient flight of steps leading down to the water from grounds of the Capitania, but yachtsmen were not permitted to land there. This seemed unreasonable: the Port Captain was responsible for the well-being of the craft under his jurisdiction and no one would have been inconvenienced had we been able to tie up there, to keep our dinghies safe from the thieves in his harbour. Alternatively, we could use the the pontoon near where the ferry tied up and which was relatively safe because you needed a thirty cent ticket to get to it. Cheap insurance perhaps, but one or two dinghies had even disappeared from there and besides, we could buy pineapples or avocadoes with that money. The paperwork was dealt with by my rowing Pete ashore to do the

rounds of the offices, keeping an eye out for his return, but it needed both of us to do the shopping, as there would be too much for one person to carry. We also needed to discuss whether to take advantage of any offers available and to make decisions about fresh food depending on what was available.

In the end, we went and anchored in a tiny cove right next to the supermarket. There were several power boats on moorings and we found a good spot just outside these, in ten feet of water and well out of the fairway. Pete rowed me ashore and collected me after I had had a look round. We then drew up a shopping list and Pete was detailed off to shop, being the superior pack horse, and we rowed back, well laden, just before sundown. The anchorage was quiet, but with one or two people on the motor yachts, the dinghy would probably have been quite safe, left on the beach unattended. Remembering the noise and bustle of the small craft harbour and with an early start planned for the morning, our present anchorage, opening onto the bay, seemed much more attractive. Thus it was that our last evening in Bahia found us sipping our drinks watching the ships passing by, silhouetted against the afterglow and gradually becoming transformed into a dark and mysterious mass, with red, green and white lights.

Chapter Nine

Our intention to leave at first light was frustrated by a total absence of wind. We ate breakfast. Still not a breath. At eight o'clock came the lightest of zephyrs and an optimistic eye could perceive catspaws on the smooth, blue water. Without further ado, we raised sail, got our anchor and, turning our backs on Salvador, set course for Morro de São Paulo, thirty-four miles away. After several weeks of daysailing, this short passage felt almost like a voyage; clearing the bay our eyes rejoiced to rest once more on an horizon, uninterrupted and infinite.

With such gentle conditions I could make mango chutney and, although a lot of mangoes produced a rather disappointing number of jars, I was well-pleased

The anchorage at Morro de São Paulo.

with their appearance and it certainly tasted as good as I had hoped. After lunch, the breeze picked up to such good effect that our day's average was over four knots; we dropped the hook not long after four o' clock.

Our anchorage at Morro de São Paulo, one of the prettiest that we have ever visited, was tucked into the side of an island and protected on three sides. Facing us was a coral reef, partly awash; to starboard a golden beach and astern rose a high hill, covered in thick scrub and surmounted by a handsome lighthouse.

We were frankly disappointed to find another yacht anchored there, but perhaps they felt the same, because unlike most Brazilian sailors they evinced not the slightest interest in us; we were selfishly pleased when they got their anchor towards sundown and powered away. There was an exquisite sunset and the steady, reliable flash of the lighthouse created a great sense of reassurance and contentment. The glow of Salvador illuminated the sky to the north-east enhancing our pleasurable remoteness.

`Come on, wake up! You haven't drunk your orange juice yet!' Pete's accusing voice sounded in my ear and I realized that I had gone back to sleep. `I thought you wanted to walk up to the lighthouse early, before it's too hot.'

The sun had barely risen, but when I went on deck I almost winced. `It doesn't make any difference what time you get up,' I grumbled to Pete, `if you can see the sun it's too hot! I hope the trees and shrubs will provide some shade when we climb up.'

We rowed ashore and pulled the dinghy up the beach. A clear trail led towards the hill on which the light stood. Although the track was relatively shady, the dense vegetation killed any vagrant air that might have refreshed us and I was relieved when we arrived at the top of the Morro. It was well worth the effort. Pete took a stunning, calendar-type photograph of *Badger* sitting amongst the various colours of deep water and shoal, sand and coral, all enhanced by the early, but intense sunlight. From this height we could clearly identify the coral patches in our anchorage, which Pete memorized for a sketch chart and there appeared to be another place for a yacht to lie if the usual, rather restricted one were crowded. We walked right round the lighthouse, where we could make out the channel in the river.

`I must try and remember its route,' said Pete, `and then we'll know roughly where to go when we get underway.'

We went down to the village. Although now almost entirely made over to tourism, having become popular with wealthy jet-setters in recent years, it was tranquil at this early hour. No cars pollute the island and the less-used, unpaved side streets were grassy. Almost every building was a bar, *pousada*, restaurant or shop, but they were generally attractive and simple and the village was surprisingly unspoilt. Across the island from the anchorage was a ferry landing, with a shop nearby, selling odds and ends, suitable for campers or people in self-catering places — so long as they generally ate out!

As we got back to the beach, the heavens opened and from having been far too hot we were suddenly covered in goose pimples and shivering with cold. By the time we had rowed back, we were soaked to the skin and dashed below to towel off, but the sun was drying the decks before we had changed.

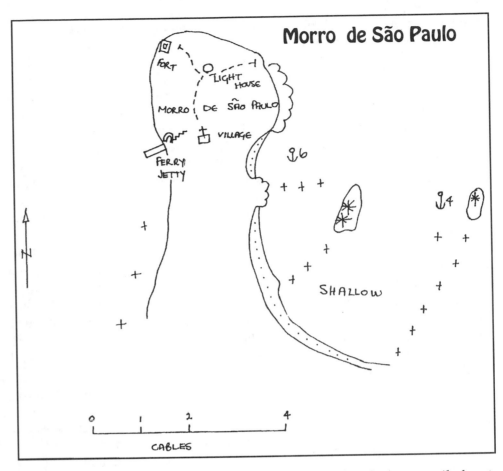

The anchor came up cleanly as we sailed out. Morro de São Paulo marks the wide and rather pretty entrance to the River Una. Sailing up, we noticed several yachts, including one or two foreign ones, at anchor near the village of Gamboa, a rather out-of-the-way spot to spend any length of time, but without the appeal of true remoteness. The river divided in two around a couple of islands and caused us some head scratching over which channel to take.

About twelve miles from the entrance was the island of Cairu and here we anchored off the town of the same name and went ashore. It was rather an interesting and appealing little place, with a factory where people were busily engaged in making brooms, the raw materials for which were being brought in by donkey, and a hill with a church on top, from where we had a clear view up and down the river. Returning by a different route, we sauntered along the bank in hot sunshine past a bar, shaded by an awning and overlooking the water. It was irresistible. The young couple who ran it were delighted and fascinated by our custom — foreign yachtsmen were not their normal clientèle and, as we managed a fairly intelligible conversation, I felt that my knowledge of Portuguese must be improving. With a struggle, we resisted the temptation to buy a second cold beer, and rowed out to *Badger* to head back down river.

On the north shore is a small town called Valença, connected to the main stream by a creek. Seeing several motor boats entering, we believed that there would be sufficient water for us, but soon discovered our mistake. We sounded around for a while, but in the end had to accept that, at this state of the tide, *Badger* drew too much. It was disappointing when we could actually see the place, but it was too late in the day to leave the boat at anchor and row in. Indeed, it was a race against nightfall getting back the couple of miles to Gamboa, with wind and tide against us and it was quite dark when we finally dropped the hook, having had a fine day and enjoyed the novelty of sailing so far up a river.

Up at first light to sail to Porto de Camamu, Pete shortened in the cable and we hauled the sails up. As I bore off to sail out the anchor, *Badger* snatched round on the end of her chain before I could put the helm down. I was astounded: we should still have about thirteen fathoms out and had only anchored in fifteen feet.

`What's wrong?'

`The chain's fouled. Let go the sheets and I'll try and see where it's lying.'

As we lay quietly to wind and tide, Pete peered over the bow.

`Oh hell! It's caught round a coral head. I'll have to dive on it.' He came back aft. `You'd better drop the sails, Annie, we may need to use the helm to help. There seem to be a few coral heads; it probably explains why no-one else is moored here. That'll teach us to anchor in the dark when there's coral about!'

Pete found his mask, snorkel and flippers and lowered himself over the side, diving and surfacing several times, kicking, splashing and puffing like a seal and then swimming towards the bow, where I was perched on a bollard.

He took out his snorkel. `It must have got wrapped round with the tide,' he said, `but I've managed to get it loose now. Can you just crank in a little — we're almost over the coral head and if we get in front of it we won't need to worry about snagging it when we get underway.'

I wound away at the windlass handle until Pete signalled for me to stop. A couple of minutes later, we had the sails up and were away.

`It makes you glad that we anchor on chain, that sort of thing,' Pete commented. `The coral head was about forty feet from the anchor; if we'd only had three fathoms of chain, it could have cut through. We could have done without it though — I wanted to get underway early. We've got quite a long way to go, today.'

We made a slight detour to investigate the alternative anchorage by Morro de São Paulo — fine in settled weather, with unusually clear water, and continued on our way in the lightest of breezes.

`Do you think we'll get there before dark?'

Pete considered the matter. `The *Pilot* mentions a couple of lights and the channel is buoyed. They'll be lit, or at least some of them will. Let's press on — if we can't identify the lights, we can always carry on to Itacaré.'

The wind picked up later, but the sun was nearing the horizon before we could make out the entrance to the river. There was an improperly surveyed reef across the direct route and as we thought that we had given it a wide berth, it was something of a shock when I noticed breakers some distance off, but right ahead. My cry brought Pete on deck.

`Head off shore of them. I'll take a fix.' A moment later he was standing in the hatch with the hand-bearing compass, then disappeared back below.

`According to that fix,' he said, sticking his head out again, `we should be at least half a mile clear of the reef.'

It was now almost six o' clock and the sun was too low to read the water, but looking at the echo sounder, I saw the figures suddenly decrease, dropping from fifty feet to fifteen feet in seconds. The water around us was darkening as the coral came up to meet us.

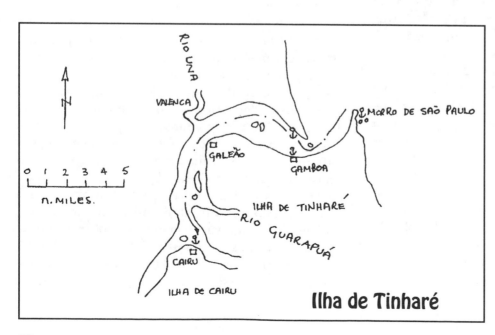

Ilha de Tinharé

`Fifteen feet — less! What shall I do? Which way shall I head?' I shouted.

`Just head right off shore. The reef obviously comes out a bit further than on the chart.'

I swung *Badger* further to port and the depths increased again. I was starting to relax when I noticed that once more it was shoaling rapidly.

`Oh God, Pete,' I wailed, now thoroughly frightened, `we're right in the middle of it.'

Pete jumped to the sail and climbed up a couple of battens.

`Starboard a little! It's all right, I can make out enough to see where to go. OK, back offshore again. Port now — no, a bit more. That's fine, keep her like that for the moment.' A wave broke nearby and I imagined I could see coral showing in its trough. Tears were streaming down my face. *I don't want to lose* Badger *on this cruel reef*, I thought.

`Offshore again, now. How are the depths, now?'

`They went under twelve feet but we're in twenty feet now, no twenty-five,' I hardly dared hope. Pete stayed aloft for another few minutes while the water got deeper. There were no breakers now when I looked to one side or the other.

`All right, Annie, we should be clear now. Head up again for the river, will you?'

`We're not still going there?'

`Why yes! We're clear of the Sorocuçu reef now and the lights will be on soon.'

`But the chart's wrong. There may be more reefs about. I don't want to risk it again. I hate coral when I can't see it.'

`Don't be silly, Annie. The chart's not *that* wrong and anyway, the echo sounder will tell us if it's getting shallow again.'

`Just before we hit — it rose out of nowhere last time! There wasn't any warning apart from seeing those breakers and now it's going dark.'

`Yes, but we're past it anyway. My last fix showed that.'

My nerves in shreds, I steered on, casting anxious glances at the echo sounder.

`Do you want me to steer?'

`No, it gives me something to do.' Perhaps too, as I was expecting a breaker ahead any minute, I would react that much faster.

`Aha! there we go — Quiépe Light. Good, I'll take another fix.'

`You can relax now,' Pete announced, `we really are well away. Have you seen any sign of the channel buoys?'

`No, not a blink, but they may not be very bright.'

Pete reached for the binoculars. `We can sail quite safely until Quiépé Light is bearing 250°, but if we can't make out the buoys by then, we'll have to give it a miss.'

By half past seven, the light was bearing 250°, but there was no sign of any buoys.

`I'm sure of our position,' Pete said, `and if we carry on, we'll probably be able to make out the buoys, don't you think?'

`No,' I declared, with determination.

`Don't you want to try?' asked Pete, sounding surprised.

`No,' I repeated, even more firmly.

`Oh. Well, I suppose it is getting a bit late and we might not be able to pick up the buoys, but it seems a pity to miss it.'

`I'm not fooling round with unlit buoys. My nerves aren't up to it — they're as bad as bloody coral. Come on, give it a miss. Let's head on for Itacaré and I can get us some supper.'

`All right then. I suppose it might be a bit difficult to find the channel in the dark. We'll carry on if you like. I'll go and work out the course.'

I turned *Badger's* head offshore with a deep feeling of relief. Far, far better a night at sea than groping up a channel, strewn with unlit and undoubtedly large and solid buoys. My idea of sailing is bimbling along, quiet and tranquil, without too many surprises or adventures.

I was cooking the chickpea curry for supper, when Pete called down: `At this rate, we're going to get there well before daylight. I'm going to pop a few reefs in.'

With Force 4 on the quarter, it needed three reefs in each sail to make an appreciable difference to our speed, and a further reef to bring our speed down to two and a half knots. For the rest of the night, we continued sailing between two to three knots, gradually shaking out the reefs as the wind died away. We picked up Itacaré light just before five o'clock and were off the entrance at six.

Jim Gattward, a friend of Brian's whom we had met at Jacaré, lives at Itacaré and had given us a rough sketch of the tricky entrance channel. We approached very cautiously; the tide was ebbing and as we wanted to enter on the last of the flood, we were obviously in for a long wait. We anchored off a rocky spit surmounted by a lighthouse on the south shore, to await the tide and have breakfast.

About half an hour later, a fishing boat motored out of the river and towards us.

`Bom dia! Tudo bem?

`Sim, obrigada.'

`Por que razão estão aqui?'

We explained that we were waiting for enough water to enter.

`But you can enter now!'

`We draw one metre and a half.'

`Yes, yes. There is enough water.'

`And the current? Our engine is very small, it is not strong.'

`No, you will manage. Follow us. We will show you the way.'

It seemed worth the chance. If there was not enough water, the ebb would flush us back out, there was no wind to speak of and we could always retreat.

`OK, thank you. We will follow you in.'

They waited while we got the anchor and under the Seagull we made good progress until we started to round Ilha de Contas. Here the ebb flowed rapidly and I revved up the engine to its maximum. Pete was watching the echo sounder, our pilot and the channel. There were overfalls and I was worried about swamp-ing the engine, but we were directed around the worst of them.

`It's bloody shallow here,' Pete said, `we've got less than six inches under us.'

In the troughs we must almost have touched: swirls of sand could be seen in the water astern. The Seagull struggled manfully but we were almost station-ary, the fishermen were obviously wondering if we needed a tow and, as that was the last thing we wanted, we prayed that the engine would cope. Then we were moving once more.

`Six and a half feet now,' Pete announced with relief. There were smiles and waves from the boat ahead. Avoiding a shallow spit, we came to a pool of water off a small beach and although the fishermen continued to wave us on, after another quarter of a mile the water started shoaling again.

`It's down to five feet and getting shallower — we'll go and anchor back there,' Pete declared. `Turn round towards the beach, I think it's probably deeper that side.'

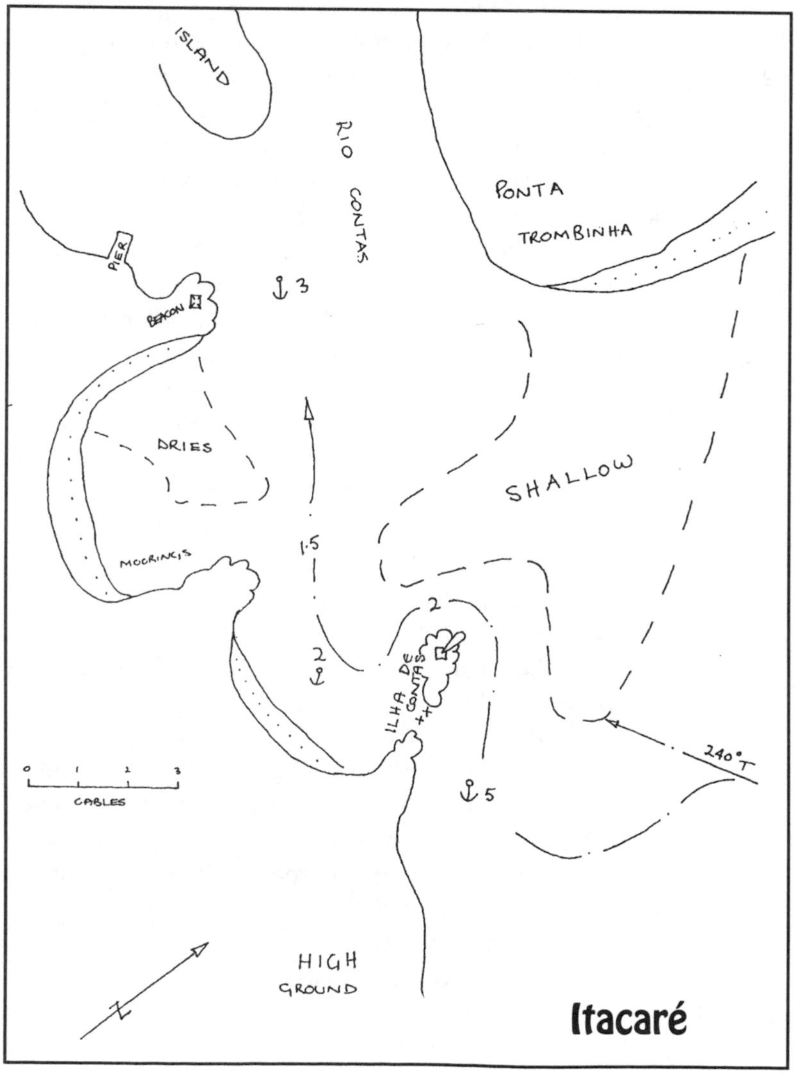

We back-tracked a short way and Pete lowered the anchor. Our pilots returned.

`It is better to anchor further up, past the town. You will not be comfortable here.' With graphic gestures, he depicted how we would roll at high water.

`Thank you, we will do that, but now it is too shallow.'

`No! There is enough. See, we went there.'

`We will wait until later anyway. It will be more easy then. Thank you for your help. Would you like this?' I passed them a coil of new rope, which I hoped they could use and they roared away back to their mooring.

`Well,' I said, `I'm glad it wasn't any shal-lower.'

`I don't think that they believed how much we drew,' Pete commented. `Just as well we don't have six foot draught — I'm sure they'd still have said we'd be all right. Any-way, we're here now. The tide's still ebbing and I don't suppose that we will be able to move on till eleven at the earliest. I think I might turn in and catch up on my sleep.'

That sounded like a good idea, so I did the same. By midday there was enough water to go further up the river, where we managed to find anchorage in four feet six inches, just touching at low water.

We found Jim's butcher shop, but were disappointed to discover that he had gone to

Itacaré

Rio for Carnival. Itacaré was another town untouched by tourism and we enjoyed our couple of days at anchor in the attractive and interesting river with its wooded shores. It was divided in two by an island, with several villages upstream and we watched with interest the *canoas* that came by at frequent intervals, often with whole families aboard, to pull up on the nearby beach. In fact, the only drawback of this spot was the excessive number of flies. It was a puzzle because, if anything, Itacaré was cleaner than other places we had visited, but each evening we slaughtered about twenty flies after shipping the mosquito screens for the night.

The town was preparing for Carnival. A huge *trio elétrico* had parked by the cobbled square, a myriad of wires leading away. There was a feeling of excitement with stalls being set up and people running around in masks and clown-style suits. Perhaps we should have stayed there for Carnival, but in the end we went to Ilhéus, thirty-odd miles away.

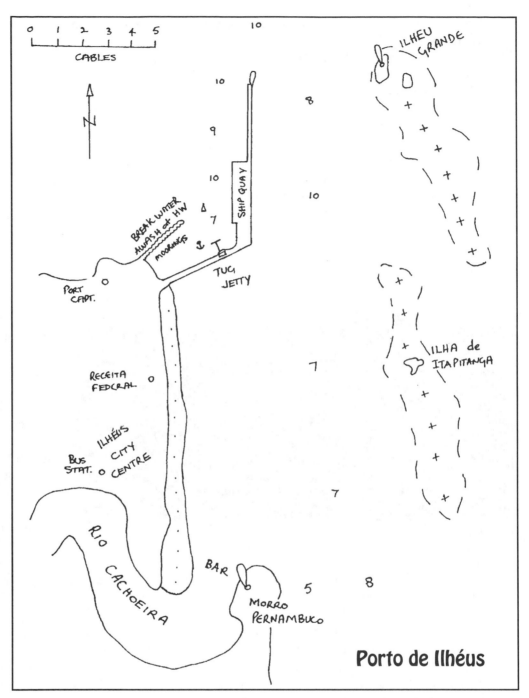

Porto de Ilhéus

We slipped away at first light on Sunday morning with an ebb tide and going over the bar, the fickle breeze deserted us altogether, so that we had to start the engine. Offshore it regained its enthusiasm and we were soon out in sixty feet of water, admiring the scenery as we sailed along jungle-clad coast, with rolling hills rising behind.

The *Pilot's* warning of a bar at the entrance to the Rio Cachoeira persuaded us to anchor in the commercial harbour, to the north of the town at Ilhéus. Protected by a half-mile long breakwater, it is just over a mile out of town and surprisingly attractive, with views over hillsides only partially built up. A jetty at the south end looked like a promising place to land, with a tug alongside and people coming and going. If nothing else, they could probably suggest where we should leave the dinghy.

In the morning, we made fast at the foot of a rickety ladder and climbed up. The tug crew were very friendly and assuring us that *Skip* would be in nobody's way, showed us where we could get water, described how to find the Port Captain and warned us to make our number with the guard in the gatehouse so that he would let us back in. We thanked them and headed for the Capitania.

Finding the office with only one false start, we were disconcerted by a sign informing us that it was only open in the afternoon. With Carnival starting the following day, if we did not clear in today there could be problems, so we opened the door and entered, prepared to claim that we could not read Portuguese. It soon became clear that the notice only applied to the general public and not to Ships' Masters or other grand personages, such as ourselves. The Port Captain was friendly and accommodating and when we had done our paperwork, we asked him how to get to the Polícia

Ilhéus, where we spent Carnival.

Federal. As usual, it was a long way out of town and when the Port Captain realized that we were going to take a *bus*, he was so appalled at such unbefitting behaviour that he summoned one of his minions to drive us there. Thanking him kindly, we were soon bouncing along the road in a Jeep. The young *marinheiro* pointed out the bus station for our return journey and a few moments later, pulled into the parking area in front of the Polícia Federal. Kindly explaining the reason for our presence to the appropriate people, he gave us a grin and a wave and disappeared in a cloud of dust.

After kicking our heels for a long time, our papers were duly stamped and we walked back to the bus station. Although it was the long-distance terminal, there was a connection back to Ilhéus town centre, making it very convenient for visiting the Polícia Federal.

`It'll be a lot easier to describe this one than the bus to the Maceió Polícia Federal,' Pete commented as we entered the building. Everything was clearly

marked and in a matter of moments we found the right bus. In Ilhéus, the bus station was near the river and we walked down to look at the bar.

`I suppose that it might be possible to cross it', said Pete, `but it looks pretty shallow.'

`And there's a safe place to leave the dinghy in the harbour,' I said. `If you *could* get up the river, you'd have to worry about finding somewhere to land. You'd be tide rode, too.'

`I don't think we'll recommend trying it, or even bother ourselves.'

I laughed, `You're really getting quite keen, aren't you?'

`Well, I've always fancied the idea of doing a cruising guide — do you remember we thought of doing one for Iceland, at one time? The FPI is the best of both worlds, because you don't have to bother about covering everything, like where to find cooking gas. And you're aiming it at real cruising people, with the Club, so you don't need to spell everything in words of one syllable.'

Finding some supermarkets, we did some shopping and continued towards the harbour. Booths were being erected left, right and centre, selling beer or food — there was going to be some serious eating and drinking going on.

It was well over a mile back to the tug jetty and there was not a vestige of shade along the way.

`I'm really finding the heat difficult, Pete. I can't really cope with it and I'm getting some sort of a rash on my arm.'

I showed him my left arm; it had a red, tender area that was starting to itch.

`That's not so good. Do we have anything that you can put on it?'

`I'm hoping an antihistamine cream might work.'

`Instead of renewing our visas at Rio, should we go down to Uruguay instead, for a couple of months? It would be cooler and perhaps we'd appreciate Brazil more too, when we came back. After three months, we're probably taking things for granted.'

`Mmm, that sounds tempting. In fact the only drawback that I can see is that I'll have to get back into Spanish again!'

The next day was Mardi Gras and we went to see what it was about, but it was a disappointment.

Supposedly Ilhéus had a good Carnival; it was certainly a lively affair, but we felt that the replacement of the traditional Carnival bands with *trio elétricos* was a retrograde step. There were two or three of the old-style groups, who had gone to a tremendous amount of trouble with their costumes, their dance and their music, but *trio elétricos* were led by a crowd bounded by a thick rope held at waist height by the outer members, who wore one or two items in common and just shuffled along to the rhythm of the pop music as their fancy dictated. Compared with the other bands, they were merely a noisy and motley mob and the *trio elétricos* themselves were a nightmare. As they passed, you could *feel* the bass notes and, even with my fingers stuffed in my ears, I found the noise almost unbearable. To add insult to injury, the groups atop the vans were all playing one of about six tunes that we were already fed-up of hearing in every building that we entered.

The atmosphere was good and we did enjoy what might be termed the fringe events and we were fascinated by the transvestites; they are anyway completely tolerated in Brazil, but at Carnival they come into their own. They varied from tattooed, mustachioed, hairy-legged specimens, to tall, glamorous and beautiful beings who came under suspicion largely because they were so overdressed and, at times, perhaps rather self-conscious. Carnival, we concluded, is basically just a gigantic street party and we thought it overrated, although maybe we simply do not have the right mentality to appreciate it.

Back aboard, we could still hear the *thump, thump, thump* from the *trio elétricos*.

Leaving with a very light breeze on Thursday morning, it took so long to beat down the harbour that I lost interest and went below to polish brass. Suddenly I heard Pete call:

`Quick, Annie, come on deck!'

I rushed out to find that we were practically on the breakwater.

`We've lost way. Grab the boathook and see if you can fend us off while I start the Seagull!'

Even with the twelve-foot boathook, I despaired of keeping us off the huge stones at the base of the breakwater, especially with the surge caused by the backwash, so I tried to tack again — impossible with so little way on. Two fishermen were staring at us, mouths open in astonishment. As Pete lowered the Seagull, one of the men dropped his rod, apparently intending to try to help us. Abandoning the tiller, I untied the boathook and, as we crept along on port tack, I willed the wind to give us a little lift. The motor roared into life and Pete put it into full ahead, but a

moment later the propeller screamed as the surge cavitated it out of the water. As it went back in, the terrific shock load broke off the support for the bracket and the whole thing fell in the water. The fishermen looked even more shocked than we were, while Pete hung over the side hauling up the motor by its safety line and I helplessly held the boathook against our imminent impact.

At this stage, *Badger* lost patience with her incompetent crew and, finding a breath of wind, luffed herself into it and sailed past the breakwater. The man who had come to assist us grinned hugely, the colour coming back into his face, which had gone grey with concern. I put back the boathook, shouted, `Obrigada' and went to help Pete while *Badger* sailed away from the breakwater.

`Here, hang onto this while I anchor and we sort out this mess.'

He ran forward and dropped the hook and after the engine was back on board I asked Pete: `Whatever happened? One minute we were sailing along and the next we were on the breakwater.'

`It was my fault — I can't imagine how I let it happen. I knew the wind was fluky and that we might miss stays, especially in the backwash, but I just went too close and didn't leave enough room to wear round. And then, instead of dropping the anchor, I started the bloody engine instead!'

`Oh.' I said. `Anyway, we're clear now. Let's get the engine cleaned up. Is the bracket support broken?'

`Yes, it's a real mess and we've lost one of the bronze strips, too. I don't suppose that'll be easy to replace — we had to order it in England.'

`We'll worry about that later. The important thing now is the Seagull. Poor thing — it's having a bit of a hard life. I bet it wishes it had never left Cornwall.'

`I can't run it, but I'll do everything else and then just pull the cord a few times. It should be all right.'

Having sorted ourselves out, we got underway and when I went below to make coffee I noticed that the carving on the bulkhead looked even more malicious than usual.

Baía Cabrália, just over a hundred miles from Ilhéus, sounded an attractive anchorage from the *Pilot*, but with winds getting lighter and lighter, the further along the coast we progressed, we only averaged two and a half knots, taking a day and a half to get there. Just as it was going dark, another unpleasantly close encounter with coral found us caught in a bight of Recifes Arajipe, which again seemed more extensive than indicated on the chart. We tacked out on the echo sounder, my nerves once more jangling, but soon iden-

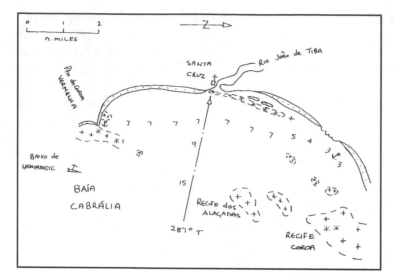

the coral heads stood out clearly and we piloted *Badger* through as easily as if the passage had been buoyed.

Porto Seguro is the site of the first landing by Europeans in Brazil, when, on 22nd April 1500, Pedro Alvares de Cabral, generally regarded as the man who 'discovered' Brazil, anchored here on passage to the Indies. Until recently, it was a quiet fishing village, but is now totally overrun by tourists. The passage to the inner anchorage behind the reef was only passable at high water and very tortuous, the alternative anchorage was rolly and uncomfortable and there was a great deal of noise from motor boats and music. All in all, the only thing in favour of our visiting Porto Seguro was that we could write it up and warn other sailors to keep clear. Unless, of course, they happened to like rowdy holiday resorts!

The first of March is officially the first day of Autumn, but it seemed hotter than ever as we hauled up the sails and thankfully left Porto Seguro astern, and although the breeze was somewhat steadier today, it did little to cool us. The rash on my arm had flared up and was itching appallingly, so to soothe it, I plugged the cockpit drains, filling it with seawater and taking a tepid bath, with my arm underwater. It felt wonderful.

Piloting our way through the coral, we found a delightful, isolated anchorage in a bight of Recifes de Pitiaçú, sheltered by the reef from both waves and swell. A more pleasing contrast with our previous night's berth would be difficult to find. So far offshore, there were no mosquitoes and we sat on deck after sunset, anchored in a mysterious and romantic setting, seemingly in the middle of nowhere.

Inside another reef, we followed the Canal dos Itacolomis, the broiling day persuading us to stop and bathe in the cool sea for a while, before sailing on to anchor for lunch at a village called Cumuruxatiba, where there was an abandoned wooden jetty:

A long, straight pier that widens to a wharf,
. . . At the pier-base, a beach and tiny town:

It seemed deserted: a few fishing boats swinging to their moorings under a blazing sun, dazzling water and no relief ashore where the beach glared with reflected light, the very air shimmering with the fierce heat. We cowered under the awning until late afternoon when, raising our anchor from its bed of golden sand, we lethargically beat out through the gap in the reef.

Our bows were turned towards the Arquipélago dos Abrolhos, the Isles of Thorns, or Troubles, depending on the translation. Either would apply to these five

tified the lights of the small town of Santa Cruz Cabrália. Pete, looking through the binoculars, recognized the Igreja Imaculada Conceição.

'Oh good,' quoth he, 'the *Pilot* gives a bearing on the church, clearing the reefs on either side of the bay. We continue until it bears 293° and then steer that.'

'But it's pitch black!' I objected, 'What if this bearing's wrong, like some of the others? We won't see any coral until it's too late!'

'No, no, we'll be fine. The reefs are over three miles apart and the bearing ties in with the chart.'

I sighed, 'Oh, all right then. But I wish you wouldn't keep doing this to me.'

'What are you worried about? It's perfectly safe.'

'Well that's as maybe, but I feel that I've had more than enough of coral dodging recently. It really frightens me, the way that there's no warning.'

'But we *won't* be dodging any coral! We have a bearing to steer on.'

A jittery mass of nerves, I had lost faith in bearings and *Pilots* and sailed on in fear and trepidation, expecting at any minute to be entangled with an unmarked reef. In point of fact, the entrance is perfectly straightforward and when, about three hours later, we brought to in nine feet, our greatest difficulty had been steering an accurate compass course.

Saturday was a lazy day. Getting up much later than usual, we lingered over coffee after our boiled eggs. Around eleven o'clock we sailed to a more comfortable anchorage a couple of miles away, where we spent the rest of the day, lounging under the awning, reading or just looking about us. The following morning, we headed for Porto Seguro, looking at one or two possible anchorages on the way and passing inside Recife de Fara, close to a wrecked ship: a stark reminder of the dangers lurking along this coast in wait for unwary mariners. Under a blazing, high sun,

islands surrounded by a huge area of coral, thirty miles off the coast. We wanted to arrive in daylight, but the wind, light for so many days, filled in and sent us on our way at five knots. We raised Abrolhos Light around midnight and Pete reckoned that the bearings of this, used in conjunction with our log, echo sounder and a careful compass course, would guide us up the Canal dos Abrolhos and explained it all to me, when I came on watch at 0100.

Arquipélago do Abrolhos

`You ought to raise the loom of the light on Ponta da Baleia before too long,' he concluded, `and that will give you a good cross bearing.'

My ludicrously active imagination was not calmed by having to study the chart each time I fixed our position, but I managed fairly well until I realized that we were getting set by a current and I still had only the Abrolhos Light to guide me. At each fix, the water was shallower and sixty feet felt like six whenever I visualized what was around us. The *Pilot* did not help me:

> *Arquipélago dos Abrolhos is surrounded by dangers, and it is probable that many uncharted shoals exist in its vicinity, in addition to the very large number already charted. . . . The only approach to the islands which is comparatively clear of danger is from SW.*

We were entering from the north. Of the Canal dos Abrolhos, it remarked optimistically that:

> *. . . there are numerous dangers in it ... The dangers in the channel are steep-to, and little or no reliance can be placed on the soundings as a guide.*

It was no good. All of a dither, my brain refused to function reasonably and in the end I woke Pete.

`I'm sorry, but I just can't cope with this.'

`Why? What's wrong?'

`Well we seem to be getting set sideways, it's going shallower and I'm not really sure what I'm doing. I've seen no sign of the other light and I'm terrified that we're going to hit a coral head.'

`But Annie, the channel is ten miles wide.'

`I know that, but it doesn't seem like it on the chart and all I can think about are "the numerous dangers in it." I'm sorry, love, but I'm hopeless at this.'

Pete sighed, `OK then, I'll take over.'

Looking back and re-reading the *Pilot*, I wonder why I was so worried. Certainly I should have been concerned because the pilotage required was fairly tricky, but after all, the channel *is* ten miles wide and we were only making a couple of knots or so. I know that our recent brushes with coral had upset me, but there was no need to get things *quite* so much out of proportion. I despair! Pete woke me just before seven to help him anchor off the lighthouse on Ilha de Santa Barbara, the passage perilous safely won. After breakfast, Pete turned in for some well-earned sleep.

Arquipélago dos Abrolhos is a marine national park and, being one of the few places in Brazil where the water is clear, is very popular with divers. From the anchorage, the island of Santa Barbara looks higher than its actual 121 feet and the black-and-white striped lighthouse on its highest point adds to this effect. Some schooners steamed over from the mainland, there were a solitary palm tree, several red-roofed buildings and a couple of boats, one of whom called by, in

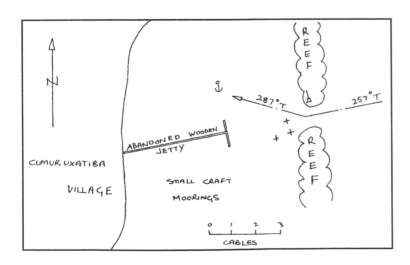

order to record our visit. The air was filled with birds and I realized anew how few seabirds we had seen along the Brazilian coast. Here were boobies, frigate-birds and terns and I sat under the awning for a couple of hours, entranced by their glorious beauty, freedom and diversity.

It was a place to linger, but with our visas due to expire, we ought to be on our way to Cabo Frio, where we could clear for Uruguay and escape the heat for a while. So, later that afternoon, we got our anchor, heading south-west towards Búzios, three hundred and fifty miles away. With the breeze stronger than usual, we were soon reeling off the miles, averaging over five knots for the first time in what seemed like months. The sun set just before six o'clock, rewarding us with a spectacular and lengthy green flash.

In the small hours of the morning, the towing generator fouled something and when I stopped to investigate, I discovered a fishing net. It needed both of us to get free and eventually we had to drop the sails and stop completely, to cut it away. Realizing that we were still only in twenty-five fathoms. we left the rotator on deck, in case there were any other nets in our path. By morning, the wind had dropped right away and it was uncomfortably hot again. I had another couple of cool, cockpit baths to soothe my arm and after dusting the rash with talcum powder, it was quite comfortable for an hour or so.

The passage was one of showers, ships and oil-rig flares, light winds and oppressive heat, but on Saturday, we caught our first ever dorado, about three feet long and as delicious as we had heard. Nine o'clock on the 7th March saw us dropping anchor off the little resort of Búzios.

Another quiet fishing village that one day woke up to realize that it had been `discovered' — by Brigitte Bardot — and could never be the same again, Búzios is crowded in the season with self-proclaimed "beautiful people." It was our good fortune to arrive after the season had ended, but before all the shops, boutiques, *pousadas*, bars and restaurants had finally put up their shutters for the winter, and we found it an attractive little place, with many pretty buildings. B.B.'s taste cannot be faulted: the whole of the Cabo Búzios peninsula is quite delightful, with a rocky and indented coastline, miniature coves and low, craggy cliffs providing quite a contrast to the long, sandy beaches and coral reefs of recent weeks. The coves were sheltered on the north side and had quite impressive surf on the south side, each having its own golden beach, some of which were little gems that would tempt anyone to find a large towel and lie down in the sun. A very enjoyable afternoon was spent wandering around the northern end of the peninsula and Búzios was colourful with flowers in gardens, baskets and window boxes.

The anchorage being a relatively sheltered spot, Pete suggested we repair the broken outboard bracket.

`We may need the engine when we get to Uruguay and we don't know when we'll be in another safe anchorage,' he explained.

`But you won't be able to buy another piece of bronze here. What'll you use instead?'

`I'm thinking that I could try laying up a strip of glass and epoxy.'

`Will that be strong enough — and stiff enough?'

`Well, it's the forward piece that takes all the load, so if I move the strip of bronze there and put my fibre-glass one aft, it should be all right. Anyway, it's worth a try and we've got enough wood for the rest of the repair.'

These little jobs always take longer than anticipated and we were held up by rain on one day, so were four days in Búzios. I was pleased to be able to get on with the washing and letter writing, but Pete had a frustrating time, working from the dinghy, bouncing about in the little waves in the anchorage and the washes from the many fishing and tripper boats. At last the job was done and we could press on towards Cabo Frio.

One afternoon, there was a great bustle on the nearby Yacht Club terrace, which kept us looking across, curious as to what was happening.

`It's a hot-air balloon!' Pete exclaimed.

`So it is. Whatever are they doing with it?'

It was a few hours before we found out. There was a wedding reception and the balloon had been hired for the occasion. Having absolutely no shame, we took it in turns to look through the binoculars. The bride, in all her finery, climbed into the gondola where she posed with the groom for photographs. Anticipating that this was the dénouement, I was impressed at their style — a hot-air balloon is definitely one up on a white Rolls-Royce or an open carriage pulled by matching cream ponies. The photographs taken, more gas was fed to the burner and the balloon slowly started to rise, but as it was still tethered, it could go no higher than to about fifty feet. We waited for the ropes to be cast off, but alas, instead the balloon descended, the bride and groom climbed out and a number of guests made equally decorous ascents. The bride and groom probably went away in a white Rolls-Royce.

The day we left was overcast, unusually, without a breath of wind. After waiting until ten o'clock for a breeze that never came, Pete suggested that we use the Seagull. `We could do to try out the new bracket, anyway.'

With perfect motoring conditions, we chugged along over a smooth sea, while Pete scrutinized the bracket.

`What d'you think,' I asked. `Does the glass strip seem strong enough?'

`I don't know really. It *looks* all right, but I think we'll need to use it more before we can be sure.'

Passing between Ilha Branca and Cabo Búzios, we found a faint breeze that let us stop the engine. The breeze seemed untrustworthy and we were occasionally on tenterhooks, sailing between a group of islands and the mainland, where the currents ran quite strongly across our course. Would our little wind abandon us and leave us at their mercy? But it was not until well after eight that it finally died and by then we were almost at the anchorage off Arraial do Cabo, where the land would have cut off the breeze anyway. We motored the last half mile or so and anchored just outside the boat moorings.

We had come here rather than to the town of Cabo Frio, because of a bar across the river there and the possibility of nowhere to anchor. The next day was a busy one. We rowed ashore and walked through the small town, a long, thin place, straggling along the road. We wanted to do a bit of reprovisioning, to take

us down to Uruguay and, not relishing the thought of bringing mountains of food back from Cabo Frio, we had a good look in Arraial's few shops. Vegetables were reasonably priced, *cachaça* was at the going rate; we would manage quite well here.

We found the bus stop for Cabo Frio and in a few minutes one came along, but on discovering the cost of the fares, we were outraged — fifty cents each way!

`Good heavens!' I exclaimed, `They weren't joking when they reckoned that you have to be wealthy to live here!' I was half serious: when the minimum wage is fifty dollars a month, fifty cents for the bus is quite a lot of money.

It was six miles to Cabo Frio, across arid countryside looking like drained salt marshes, an impression reinforced by the great heaps of salt scattered around. It was one of the least attractive areas that we had visited, which was surprising because it is also one of *the* places to live, but the town was pleasant enough, with a river running through it. This made for an agreeable walk, which was just as well considering the distance from the bus station to the *Capitania*.

The Port Captain was frankly surprised to see us and completely uninterested in our papers. We explained that we needed clearance from him to take to the Customs and Federal Police.

`But in Cabo Frio there are neither *Polícia Federal* nor *Receita Federal*. They are in Niterói.'

`Niterói? But that is the same as going to Rio. We did not want to sail there because it is dangerous.'

`I understand, but you could go by bus from here.'

`We will have to think about it, but thank you for your help.'

`*De nada.*'

`Well,' I said to Pete as we came out onto the street, `that's tricky one — what do you want to do? If we catch the bus, we'll both have to go because the captain has to sign everything and we may need my Portuguese and long-distance buses aren't that cheap. On the other hand, if we go there ourselves, we'll have to get a wiggle on, because it's already the 12th and our visas run out on the 16th.'

Pete thought for a while. `I don't think the bus is really on: it's expensive and if we get held up, we'll end up wandering round in the dark. I think our best bet is to go in *Badger* to Rio, where we know there's a marina we can use, which is supposed to be safer than it was. We shouldn't have any problems, if we're careful.'

`Yes, you're right, but if we're going to Rio, we ought to leave tomorrow and I must get some stores before we go down to Uruguay.'

`I want to look at the anchorage off Cabo Frio Island for the FPI, so we'll have to go there today. What do you say to having a look at that place near the bus station where they were selling fruit and veg?'

`We can see what they have, but I really don't want to get too much here — it's quite a hike from the bus stop back to the dinghy.'

`I can carry most of it.'

Anchorage at lha do Cabo Frio.

`Well, let's see what they have, then.'

Back at the stalls, the prices were not only marked, but reasonable, the stallholders probably hoping for out-of-town customers to buy there, rather than lug bags all the way back from the supermarkets. We bought things that in Arraial had been unavailable or more expensive and then caught the bus back.

After a hasty lunch aboard, we sallied forth once more to buy a variety of stores in various shops, which were then piled into *Skip*, to be dragged down the long, soft sand beach and rowed back to the boat. We picked over everything to check for cockroaches, but even so we managed to get underway just after five o'clock.

The breeze was extremely light and I put things away and washed the fruit and vegetables while Pete steered the two miles to Ilha do Cabo Frio, a beautiful anchorage off a pretty, sandy beach, dropping the hook in twenty feet. This would be our last real anchorage in Brazil and we felt that we could hardly have done better. After our somewhat strenuous day, we reckoned we owed ourselves a stiff sundowner and savoured it,

contemplating the narrow, white beach, with the sand stretching further inland, covering the undulating ground and drifting round the trunks of the trees that grew in that sheltered spot. Not unlike casuarinas, their presence here, instead of the usual palm trees, might be due to the current, which gives Cabo Frio its name. This current brings frigid water up the coast of South America, from the Falklands to this point, where it heads east into the Atlantic.

In the morning, local fishermen came into the bay and two *canoas* each took one end of a net setting it in a slight curve. They then rowed in towards the beach and the men who had been landed there waded out to take the ends of the net, hauling it further into the shallows. Even from *Badger*, we could see the turmoil of the frantic fish, trying desperately to escape, but they were dragged ashore and the catch divided. Either the fishermen totally disregarded the ban on going ashore or they had the neces-

sary signed permit from the Port Captain in Cabo Frio. It was with reluctance that we left this unspoilt anchorage for the problems and noise of Rio.

There was just enough wind to sail through the narrow gap between the island and the mainland. Little, castellated clouds out at sea bespoke the Trade Wind, but in spite of pushing us along at a couple of knots, it was too light to be cooling. With dark came the loom of Rio's lights and by nine that evening, the statue of Christ on Corcovado was easily discernible twenty-five miles away. An unforgettable dawn slowly revealed a truly breathtaking scene as the mountains of Rio were defined against the lightening sky, the amazing shapes of the peaks and Sugar Loaf, dominated by spectacular Corcovado; the colossal statue of Christ surmounting all, arms upraised in blessing — or despair? — over the city. In an almost non-existent breeze, the silence disturbed only by the low rumble from the teeming life ashore, we ghosted in, sad that such a beautiful setting should be marred by the ugliness of the masses of concrete.

The traffic on the water slowly increased and we resorted to engine for three-quarters of an hour to keep out of the way. It being a Sunday, we could do no paperwork until the following day and fearing that the marina might be expensive, we anchored off the Rio Yacht Club until tea-time, so that we could limit our stay in the marina to twenty-four hours. We sailed the couple of miles to Marina de Glória and had just started the motor to enter when a local boat came speeding across the bay towards us with someone on deck frantically waving and calling. Over the sound of the Seagull, it was hard either to understand or even to hear him, but suddenly Pete cried:

`Peter Pan! He just said "Peter Pan"! It's Nils, Annie!'

As recognition dawned, we waved vigorously back at the fast departing figure, now heading off in the direction of Niterói and had barely realized what had happened before we were at the entrance, wondering where to go. A number of yachts were alongside the walls and there were several finger docks, but what caught and held our attention were two large mooring buoys, each with a `sunflower' of yachts, bows to. *Peter Pan*'s spindly masts were immediately recognizable near the red stern of an unmistakable cruising yacht.

`I'll bet those buoys are cheaper than a pontoon berth,' said Pete, `and easier, too. Let's go to the far one, with *Peter Pan* on it. We'll go alongside the outermost boat and hold on, while we take a line to the buoy.'

The outer boat proved to be *Peter Pan*, which has alarmingly low freeboard, but it was calm in the Marina and we have good, fat fenders, so the little boat should take no harm.

`We can help Nils move to the other side of us, if he wants to,' said Pete, after securing us to the buoy.

Not long after, Nils turned up:

`I couldn't understand why you didn't recognize me!' he exclaimed as he scrambled onto his boat, `because I knew you right away. But then I realized that you would not expect to see me on this Brazilian

Rio de Janeiro's Sugar Loaf.

boat and it was then that I shouted "Peter Pan" and you knew who I was!'

He beamed at us from behind his glasses and then we were all talking at once. He and his tiny boat, a twenty-foot canoe yawl, had shared many adventures since we had met in Madeira in 1991. Perhaps *Peter Pan* was too delicate and too complex for ocean crossings because she had been dismasted and many of her electronics had failed, but Nils, with the rose-tinted spectacles that most boat-owners wear, was still convinced that she was the Perfect Yacht. We had nearly missed him because, with nowhere suitable in Rio to carry out the considerable amount of work that needed doing, he was moving over to Niterói the next day. We asked him to dinner, but he had promised to spend the evening with the owners of the boat he had been sailing earlier.

`You should come with me to Niterói,' he suggested. `Rio is a terrible place. It took me eight days to enter and it is full of thieves. I have had my credit card stolen and twice someone has tried to pick my pocket on the bus.'

`We don't want to stay more than a couple of days,' we replied, `and then plan to go on to Uruguay. How long have you been here?'

`Oh, I don't know — several months. And now they want me to leave Brazil because I have been here more than six months, but my boat is not ready to go. They will have to let me stay. I may need to contact the Swedish Embassy, but I think I have found someone who can help me.'

We never heard the full story, but poor little *Peter Pan* certainly did not look seaworthy. Nils, large and well-built, moved clumsily, like someone unused to small craft and seemed quite unsuited to such a dainty yacht. Accident prone, in Madeira he had dropped his wallet containing money and his ill-starred credit card overboard when he came back from the bank. Fortunately, another yachtsman was a keen diver and, generously donning his scuba gear, went into the dirty water to look for it and now Nils had overstayed his visa. We were a little worried about him, but Brazilians are kind people and Nils was no doubt given the time to make his little boat seaworthy again. I hope that at our next meeting, we will spend longer together.

After we helped him leave, we met the couple from the red cruising boat. Peter and Anna Liese were an interesting and pleasant couple. Although both were German, they had lived for many years in South Africa, where they built *Nori*. Having spent quite some time in Brazil, they were now planning to go down to Patagonia.

`It sounds rather frightening to me,' I told Anna Liese, `especially all the wind.'

`Oh we are used to wind, from sailing in South Africa. It doesn't worry me at all.'

We mentioned that we were about to clear in and they gave us directions to the offices, warning us that it was not straightforward. There followed dire stories of robbery and muggings, `although the park is much safer than it used to be. Now there are always policemen, but I still would be careful at night.' The park was notorious but was the only route from the Marina to the footbridge that crossed the main road. Apparently one yachtsman who arrived in Rio from the Canaries, having secured his boat, went ashore to see the sights and was set upon at the bridge, robbed of everything and left stark naked in the park. He returned to his boat, dressed in fresh clothes and got out a few more dollars. Going ashore, he started to cross the bridge when the same thing happened. The third time he saw another gang waiting, so he turned round, went back aboard, cast off and sailed straight to the Caribbean, or so the tale goes.

Relieved to hear that we at least had a sporting chance of reaching the city before we were robbed, even if we did not have much chance of returning in one piece, we assembled our papers putting the passports and credit card in a pocket that I had sewn inside the waistband of my shorts.

March 15th is Pete's birthday and it was a shame to spend a large part of it embroiled with officials. In the marina office, a man speaking perfect English informed us that the price of our berth was a mere two dollars a night and told us where to find the other officials. The rest of the morning was spent clearing in and out and not made any easier by the fact that everyone gave us conflicting advice and information.

`I'm going to make a careful note of all this procedure,' Pete declared as we dragged ourselves wearily from the last office back into the torrid streets. `We've done really well — we've seen everyone and it's only just lunch-time, not like poor old Nils' eight days. I think it helped that you can speak Portuguese, too.'

`Get by, you mean! Anyway, that's all done now. It's your birthday and I think that we should have lunch out, don't you?'

`You wouldn't prefer to go straight back?'

`Not really. We're very careful and quite honestly, it doesn't feel any worse than Salvador to me. What about you?'

`I agree — if it weren't for the fact that we'd have to renew our visas, I'd be tempted to stay a few more days. We could take a train ride this afternoon, if you want.'

`I'd like to get rid of the passports first — they're hot and uncomfortable in this pocket and show when I'm sitting down. Have we time to go back to the Marina first?'

Pete looked at the map. `Only if we give lunch a miss.'

`What would you rather do?'

`Well, we can come back to Rio when we revisit Brazil and it's quite a walk to the Marina and then to the station. I don't think you'd enjoy it. Let's find a *lanche*.'

In the business area, we soon saw a *lanche* that we liked the look of. We sat down at a table and looked at the menu.

`I think I'll have *frango* and chips,' Pete decided.

`Chicken sounds good, but I'd like to try something different. I think I'll have a *milanesa* — I've been wondering what they are — with potato salad.'

`Shall we have a beer?'

I laughed. `I don't think that needs an answer!'

We ordered and the food soon came, the plates piled high with rice and black beans, as well as what we had ordered. My *filé à milanesa* was a thin piece of meat, covered in batter and fried. Herbs and spices had been added and it was surprisingly moist. Pete's quarter chicken looked very good and the more-than-welcome beer was tooth-achingly cold. Pete managed to eat everything, but although I made a determined effort, I was defeated.

'If I'd known about the rice and beans, I wouldn't have had the potato salad,' I said, 'but it was a good one, so I'm glad that I did. Can you manage any of this?'

Pete looked doubtfully at my plate. 'I'll see what I can do,' but even he was defeated.

The bill came to 101,000 cruzeiros, four dollars fifty: a bargain.

On our way back I said, 'We've enough money left for another night in the Marina, but it's probably quieter out at anchor. If we spent the night off the Yacht Club again, we could have a cold beer in the bar, before we leave.'

'It's tempting. And after all, it is my birthday. Let's do that.' There is nothing like walking round a hot and noisy city to make you appreciate cold beer.

Late in the afternoon, we moved out to anchor and celebrated Pete's birthday with an avocado followed by spaghetti with tuna and mushroom sauce washed down with one of our Spanish briks of wine, saved for such an occasion. We also drank to the next passage and sat up late talking.

With a nine-hundred-mile passage ahead of us, we brought the engine below, so inevitably, by the time we came to leave, the wind had almost gone. In fact we re-anchored for about an hour before it returned to let us sail out of the bay, under a scorching sun, surrounded by a thick haze.

As I cooked our lunch of black bean chili, I said to Pete, 'I'm sorry to be leaving Brazil, but I'll be so glad to leave the Tropics. I bet this rash of mine will disappear as soon as it starts getting cooler.'

Progress was less than spectacular until the small hours of the morning when a tremendous thunderstorm was accompanied by squalls of F5 winds, which felt alarming after months of light airs, and as I seemed to have lost faith in our lightning conductors, the night was anything but tranquil. Although we left the Tropics, next day, it seemed hotter than ever and we sweltered and drifted until about six o'clock on Thursday, when a F3 breeze filled in, by which time we had collected a small shoal of fish under us, apparently sheltering from the sun in the shade of the boat. A whale spouted in the distance; we saw a shark, a rare and exciting event; in places the water was covered with great rafts of yellow-brown flotsam and another terrific thunderstorm brought wind and rain, upsetting

our breeze and sending it round to the north-west, in direct contradiction of the Routeing chart, and then sou'west. Now we were close-hauled and had to shut the scuttles and forward hatches, so that it was almost unbearable below, even hotter than Rio, and I fretted that my vegetables would get spoilt.

I started the Uruguayan flag, not the easiest, consisting of blue and white stripes with a multi-rayed sun in the upper hoist, but I enjoyed making it and was pleased with the finished result.

The wind became a fresh southerly but it was not unpleasant to have such boisterous sailing again and at 80°F/27°C, it seemed almost cool. We had forgotten to put the caps on the forward cowl ventilators (which, since we discovered that water-trap ventilators are just that, are no longer Dorade types and can let water down) with the inevitable result that we ended up with a wet bunk for the second time in four months, something that had never, ever happened until this voyage. Although it was Saturday, it was really too rough to enjoy our usual glass of wine.

Sunday brought a free wind and, as we settled down to enjoy a pre-prandial snorter and popcorn, I noticed that we had caught a fish. The drinks and popcorn went below and in came a fine, two-foot dorado and then, streaming the line to untangle it, we caught another one of about eighteen inches. This rather put the kibosh on the spaghetti bolognese, so I put it aside for the morrow and tried out Christine's soused fish recipe on the small fish. The large one was cut into chunks, fried in batter, and made excellent eating with 'sea-going chips.' With wine to wash it down, it was quite a feast.

The wonderful sailing continued, more birds about and I saw my first small albatross, or 'mollyhawk' as the old sailors called them — only the great Royal and Wanderer were known as 'albatross.' While we were having lunch, we saw a sail on the horizon, which altered course to close with us. In all our years of sailing, this had never happened, so we were thrilled when they dropped their jib so that we could talk. The yacht, *Nora* of Buenos Aires, had two men and a woman aboard who told us that they were going to La Paloma, Uruguay and then on to Buenos Aires. Unfortunately, it was too rough to talk properly, so we went our separate ways, but we were delighted at the meeting — it was truly heart-warming.

'Did you notice they had a Brazilian courtesy flag?', I asked Pete.

'It's obviously where they've come from.'

'Yes, but it implies that you can clear in at La Paloma. It might be fun to go there, too.'

Our one-eyed visitor, a white-chinned petrel.

Pete went below and looked at our charts.

`We've got one for La Paloma. OK, Annie, let's go there. I'll work out our course. Two-three-five,' he announced, coming back on deck.

The following morning saw my first yellow-nosed mollyhawk and also several white-chinned petrels and I felt that we were definitely getting south. The light wind encouraged me to bake a ginger cake and I was just making chapattis when Pete called that we had caught another dorado. We had fishcakes for lunch and with about a pound and a half of fish to three medium-sized potatoes, they were absolutely delicious. In the early part of my first night watch, I stood for a long time in the hatchway admiring a glorious sunset, but before it was quite dark, I had to tack to avoid a ship who did not seem to have noticed us. His radar was going, but maybe there was no-one on the bridge.

When Pete woke me up the next morning he said: `I've got some bad news. I found a large cockie in the galley, while I was getting the coffee out.'

`Oh no! What happened to it?'

`I gave it a zap with Combat and that seemed to do the job. I didn't see any others — it probably came aboard in Rio.'

`That means that it's been on board a week and had time to lay its eggs. I hope it hasn't — I really don't want bloody cockies on board. Oh, Hell. Damn the Tropics.'

I cleaned out the galley lockers under the sink, looking for signs of more cockroaches but saw none. We never had another, I'm glad to say.

One afternoon we heard a thump on deck and discovered a white-chinned petrel aboard, blind in its right eye. After taking a photograph and giving it time to recover, we gently persuaded it back overboard, where it landed in a fluster of feathers, righting itself a couple of moments later and apparently none the worse for its experience. It must have approached on its starboard side and hit the sail.

The evening was perfect for a green flash, but just as the sun was about to disappear, an ugly ship steamed in front of it. The night was beautiful and tranquil and it was definitely becoming cooler — we slept under a blanket for the first time in months. We were surrounded by dozens of white-chinned petrels and the occasional sea lion, and Pete caught another fish.

We sighted land around tea-time, the quiet day mellowing into a gentle evening. After dark, a land breeze filled in enabling us to reach La Paloma by midnight. It was a rather small and crowded harbour, but eventually we found somewhere to drop the hook, out of everybody's way, but ten minutes later, we heard someone shouting. Reluctantly, we put the dinghy over and went to see what they wanted. The details were unclear, but the gist was plain: we had to move onto the wall with the other yachts.

`But we are not in anybody's way.'

`No anchoring in the harbour.'

`Is it necessary to pay on the wall?'

`No, no. It is not necessary.'

`We only have an outboard engine. Can we stay where we are for the night and move in the morning, when it is light?'

`OK. You stay on your anchor for the night. And sleep well.'

We went back to *Badger*, had a cup of coffee and a glass of rum and gratefully turned in.

Chapter Ten

The sun shining from a bright blue sky woke us and we commenced moving forthwith: it was calm now but might be breezier later. Starting the motor, we raised anchor and moved over towards several mooring buoys, by the wall. Pete caught one with the boathook and attached a long warp. Taking another line from the stern, he rowed to the wall and cleated it off and we then adjusted the lines until we were far enough back, secured and shipshape alongside the ketch, *Nora*, that had spoken us at sea.

We had breakfast and walked to the town, wondering if there were an open bank, where we could change money. The wide road was almost empty and everywhere was very quiet and clean, especially when compared to Brazil. The banks were shut and did not take VISA, but we saw a board showing exchange rates. With this information, we could get an idea of prices in the shops.

`Things don't seem quite as cheap here as Brazil,' remarked Pete.

`Quite the opposite — it's positively expensive!' but after thinking about it, I added:

`In fact it's not so much that it's expensive - prices are about the same as Europe — it's that in Brazil, things were generally so cheap.'

Although most of the holiday places had shut up shop until next year, it was still hot enough to feel like summer to us. Walking back along the mole, a young man, standing on the bow of a blue, Uruguayan yacht hailed us.

`Are you the people on the English boat?'

`Yes, that's right.'

`Where you have come from?'

`Brazil — Rio. We got in last night.'

He asked us on board and made us coffee.

`My name is Leo and I am at University. Now I study to be doctor, but it is good for me to speak English with you.'

`Is this your boat?'

`No, it belongs to a friend of mine who builds it. Perhaps when he comes back, we both come and see your boat?'

`Of course.'

As we climbed back onto Badger, we noticed people around on *Nora* and spoke to them. To our surprise, the young woman, Sarah, was English.

`I met Guido in Brazil and mentioned that I wanted to get to Argentina. There's a chance of a job for me in Buenos Aires. He was looking for a third person, so I more or less hitched a ride.'

`Had you done any sailing before?' I asked her.

`No never, I didn't know anything at all about boats or sailing, but I really enjoyed it. The boys told me that we had perfect conditions and I can believe it. I was really sorry when the trip ended and they say it won't be as nice sailing to Buenos Aires.'

`We were thrilled when you came and spoke to us.'

`So was I. As soon as I saw your boat I said to Guido: "That boat's got to be British!" and I was really excited to see you.'

`Why on earth did you think that?'

`I just knew. Only a Brit would have a boat like yours. You looked so *different* from all the other boats I'd seen.'

Leo duly brought his skipper round and we gave them tea. Jorge was taking his boat up to Brazil soon and thought we were crazy to come down to Uruguay in the autumn.

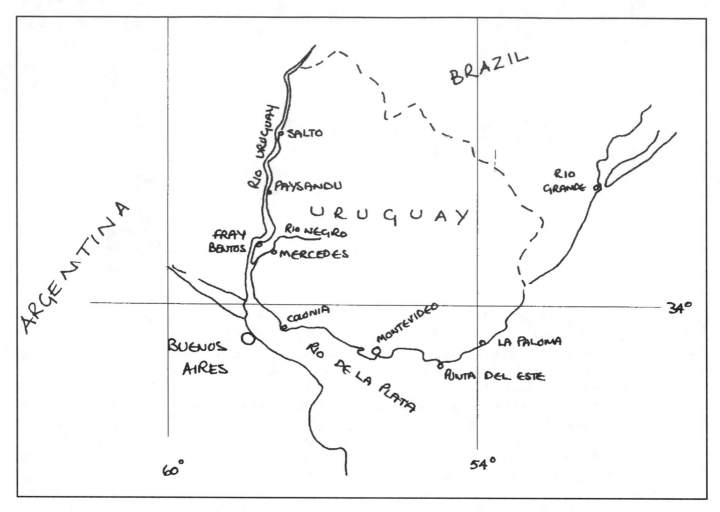

'It will soon get cold,' he said, 'maybe only twenty degrees and less at night.'

We laughed. 'That's just what we're hoping. It was too hot in Brazil for us and we're looking forward to some cooler weather.' Jorge shook his head, but Leo looked delighted to find that the English really are eccentric. It seemed more than usually difficult to understand them when they spoke Spanish and then Leo used a word that I should have known from the context, but did not recognize. We resorted to the dictionary.

'There,' he said in triumph, *Moo-ejay*!'

'Oh!' I exclaimed, 'but I learnt to say *moo-elyay*, that's why I didn't understand you. Are all words with double L in them pronounced *juh*?'

Leo looked puzzled, so I asked him to say some more words: *allí, parillada, bello, llamar*. They all had a J sound for the double-L, which reflected Brazil, where I had noticed that often, by substituting a J sound for the double-L in the Spanish word that I knew, I could make myself understood; but it took a while to learn to speak South American Spanish.

Sunday dawned fine and sunny, a good day for a walk and picnic. While I was making samosas to take with us, I heard Pete talking to Sarah and a few minutes later he came below.

'*Nora's* leaving shortly. They've run out of gas and can't replace their cylinders here so are going on to Punta del Este.'

'Oh, that's a shame. I was hoping that they'd come round for a drink. I promised Sarah some of those *Wildlife* magazines — would you mind popping them over? I can't leave these.'

After about half an hour, Pete came back.

'Guido has been giving me some information about the Plate. He also reckons we'll have to pay here — about a fiver a night!'

'Five quid! But it can't be. The blokes in the Prefectura's told us we didn't need to pay.'

'Yes, but Guido said that you have to pay everywhere in Uruguay. He's just settled up here. Apparently only a few Uruguayans have yachts and they're generally wealthy. Sailing is much more popular in Argentina and he reckons that the Uruguayans simply get as much as they can out of the Argentines, who're often rich, anyway.'

'But we've been here two nights already — that's ten pounds! Half a week's money! They might let us off the first night, when we were at anchor, but a fiver's bad enough.'

'Worse still, we've no local money and the banks here don't take VISA. Even if they did, we couldn't afford to stay until tomorrow.

'We must go and find out what it's all about. Perhaps we should ask Leo to come along — to translate for us and avoid misunderstandings.'

'OK, Annie. But do you think that we should involve Leo?'

'I'd rather not, but my Spanish probably isn't up to explanations about VISA cards and I'm hopeless out of the present tense.'

After seeing Leo and explaining the situation to him, we all went to the office of the *Hidrografia*, where we spent a most embarrassing ten minutes. It was soon apparent that Leo understood less English then we had thought and his attempts made matters worse, because having taken on the rôle of translator, he would not let me speak at all. I understood what he was saying, which was not what we wanted and, coming from a fairly well-to-do background, he simply could not believe that we only had an income of thirty dollars a week and translated this as our only having thirty dollars on us. In the end I intervened and tried to explain how we could not get money out on our VISA card in La Paloma, that we had just come from Brazil and that we had been led to believe that no charge would be made to tie up. We would leave immediately, I told the officials, because we could not afford an extra night and if they would give us a bill for what we owed, we would post the money from Punta del Este.

'But you cannot leave without paying. The Prefectura will not allow it.'

Dear God, I thought, why will they not try to understand?

'We have no money. We cannot get money here. No bank takes VISA in La Paloma. It is very expensive here. If at the hour we arrive, the Prefectura says, "you must pay eight dollars a night", we say, "It is too dear, we go to sea again." But the sailor we speak to says there is no charge and we stay until now when we speak to *Nora* who tells us we must pay.'

Maybe my words about going back to sea rang true. Or perhaps they were weary of the whole thing; certainly they did not believe that we would send them the money, which was rather insulting. Whatever the reason, they let us off and gave us a note for the Prefectura saying that we owed no money. We must have caused them a real headache, because the bill already had been prepared on a numbered form. We were mortified. We would not have dreamt of putting in to the harbour had we realized that we had to pay and because we were not *permitted* to anchor, it seemed plausible that it would be free to tie up.

Thanking them and Leo we got underway, heading for the small anchorage of José Ignacio, twenty-seven miles away. Our handsome Force 4 breeze fell light so that we did not arrive until midnight. Although it was not easy to make out the details in the dark, there seemed to be rocks further offshore than the chart indicated. We managed to find a reasonable spot in which to anchor, only to be rudely awoken by the

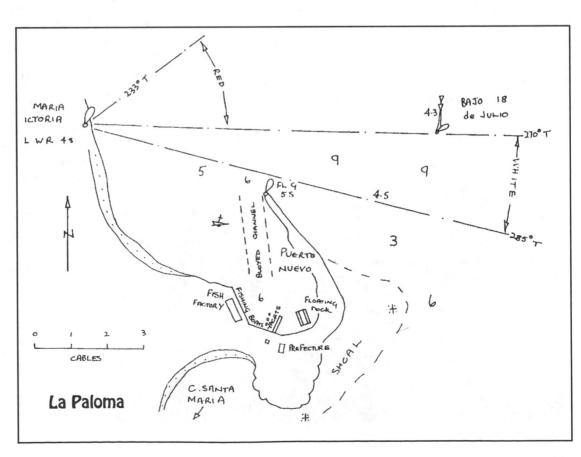

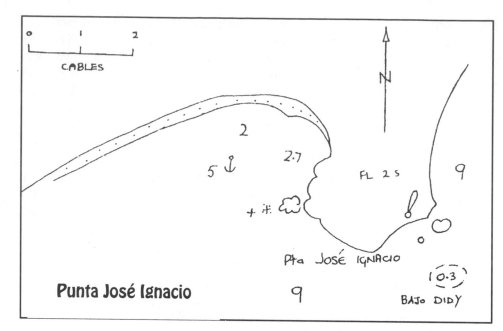

Punta José Ignacio

CABLES

N

2

2.7

5 ⚓

+ ⚓

FL 2 S

Pta JOSÉ IGNACIO

9

9

9

BAJO DIDY

(0.3)

twenty-one miles in six hours. Sailing into the lee of the point, we noticed that in the area protected by the wall were scores of moorings and a fair-sized marina. We had to anchor in a more exposed position, wide open to the south-west, but *Nora* had picked up a mooring.

The large bay, fringed by a dazzlingly white beach is now largely given over to pleasure craft, but was the anchorage for Maldonado in the days of the Conquistadors and looking across towards Isla Gorriti it was not difficult to visualize the bay filled with caravels at anchor.

The caravels had a distinct advantage over us: they did not have to deal with endless paperwork each time they arrived in a harbour. We rowed ashore after lunch tying up near the *Prefectura Naval* building, as imposing as any *Capitania* in Brazil, which stood at the head of the harbour, the town stretching away to the north. For once, it was a relatively painless procedure with only the one stop. Perhaps the necessity to clear in and out of every harbour might be less onerous than in Brazil. Our paperwork completed, we were told that we must also clear out at the *Hidrografia*.

`Why is that?'

`We cannot give you clearance until you have paid for your mooring.'

wind, which had shifted round to the south and was blowing into the anchorage. After a quarter of an hour or so, we came to the reluctant conclusion that the breeze was staying and we had better leave. We put a reef in each sail and the short, steep waves, kicked up by the new wind, stopped us going about while we were trying to sail the anchor out. Pete had quite a struggle to bring it aboard, but without its drag, *Badger* beat out without difficulty. As we left the bay, we noticed a lot more rocks off the point, where the chart showed none at all.

Close-hauled to a good Force 5 we thrashed along to Punta del Este and we enjoyed the contrast with the easy sailing in Brazil. No doubt the novelty would have worn off had we taken longer, but we covered the

`But we are at anchor. Surely we do not need to pay for that.'

`At anchor? Where? Show me your boat,' the port captain responded incredulously. We pointed *Badger* out to him.

`OK then. You do not need to pay anything, but if you move into the marina, you will need a paper from the *Hidrografia.'*

We turned our steps towards the town.

`You realize that no-one's stamped our passports, yet?' Pete commented as we walked away.

`I know. It really seems to be rather civilized doesn't it? Apart from their desire to charge yachts, that is!'

Punta del Este from Isla Gorriti, Uruguay.

Noticing several inflatable dinghies tied up a few minutes later, we were even more impressed by their civilization.

`Good heavens, Pete, look at that! The dinghies aren't padlocked up and nor are the outboard motors!'

`They've either got incredibly good security or the locals are very honest,' Pete commented, `and I can't see any armed guards.'

Inflatable dinghies, with outboard motors are horribly vulnerable to theft. The demand for such craft being limited, the inevitable conclusion is that they go to unscrupulous yachtsmen who do not inquire too closely as to their antecedents.

As well as being an important yachting centre, Punta del Este is a large holiday resort and we soon found a bank where we changed a hundred pounds, relieved to be in a country where inflation was at a more normal rate. We did some shopping and met Guido and Sarah while walking back.

`You had a bit of wind when you came in this morning,' Guido greeted us.

`Yes, we spent the night at José Ignacio but we had to leave when the wind came in.'

`The Prefectura asked us where you were, when we cleared in this morning. We said we had no idea. Why should we? They said that you were reported as overdue.'

`Overdue? but we never gave an ETA — they didn't ask us for one.'

`No, but you had cleared for Punta del Este, so they were expecting you. How long are you staying?'

`We're not sure. What about you?'

`I must get back soon. We will go as soon as the weather improves.' We walked on until they left to find a restaurant for a late lunch.

`My god, Pete! Talk about Big Brother!'

`No doubt they'd say that it's for our safety. Imagine if the weather had continued fine and we'd stayed put — they'd probably have instituted an air-sea rescue. It doesn't bear thinking about.'

We slept like logs that night, in spite of *Badger* rolling from time to time. Next morning, having found only a couple of small supermarkets in Punta del Este, we set off to walk up to Maldonado, some five or six miles away. I had reservations about this idea — it would be a long way to carry shopping, but the walk

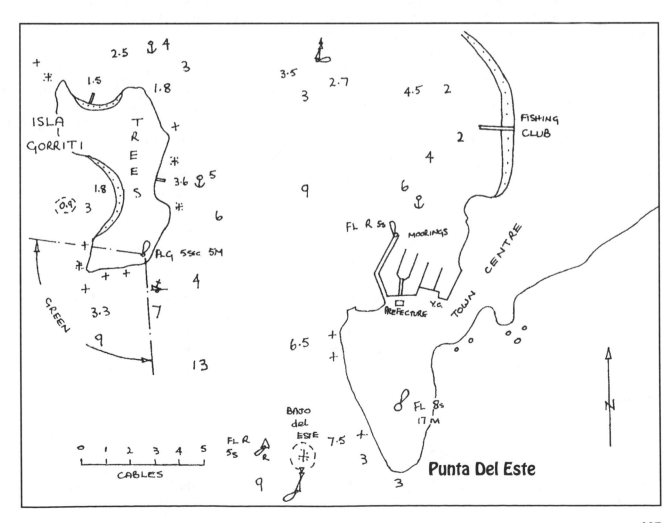

Punta Del Este

should be interesting and we took the makings of a picnic with us.

It was another hot day and I was frankly relieved when we found a large supermarket a mile or so out of town. They sold wine at just over a dollar a litre, half the price of any that we had seen. There was plenty to choose from, but fresh food was no more expensive in the supermarkets near the harbour, where we later bought lovely oranges for seven cents each. We had our picnic on the beach and a sea-lion followed the dinghy back to *Badger* as we rowed, rather splashily, in the fresh breeze.

Another sunny day followed a calm, cool night. While I was doing a pile of washing, Pete fitted a new burner in the cooker, which reminded him to buy paraffin. He went to a nearby petrol station that sold it from a pump and coming back aboard, said:

`The bloke who sold me the paraffin tried to cheat me!'

`You're joking!'

`No, I'm sure he did. I'd worked out how much it would cost, but you know what it's like with new money: I was concentrating on counting it out and it was only when I had handed it over that I realized it was too much. Anyway, I told him and he obviously caught my drift, because he eventually worked it out correctly. But I'm sure that he was trying it on.'

Well, you may be right, but perhaps he just can't add up — even with a calculator.'

After Pete had put the paraffin away, he went back for more.

`You won't believe this!' he exclaimed as he passed the containers up to me, `that bloke tried to cheat me again. He must be stupid as well as dishonest. Surely he must have recognized me — there can't be that many foreigners buying paraffin from him.'

It seemed strange that we had never been cheated in Brazil, so notorious for its crime, whereas here in Uruguay, where they do not even lock up their outboard motors, someone had tried to swindle Pete twice.

We had some pleasant walks ashore and, much more importantly, discovered that we could buy wine at the two bakers' shops, sold *suelte*, translating as `loose'. We took our own container, which meant that there was neither rubbish to dispose of nor a deposit on the bottle. We bought a litre to sample, but the shop assistant was somewhat taken aback when we returned with a five-litre jerrican.

One afternoon, a young man came by, trying to sell us charts, but we promptly lost interest when we heard the price: twenty-one dollars each, the same as for an Admiralty chart, but with inferior paper. Nor

were they particularly accurate, because the chart of José Ignacio failed to show the rocks that we had observed. The young man blotted his copy book when he told us that it was he who had reported us `overdue' and left, mentioning a gale warning, but not saying from which direction. Had we been wealthy and extravagant, we might have picked up a buoy at eleven dollars a night, or we could have spent twenty-eight dollars for a berth in the marina. In the Summer, the charges would have been twenty-eight dollars and an incredible fifty-six for the marina. We stayed at anchor.

Our supper of omelette and chips was all cleared away when the wind came, fortunately out of the east. During the windy and rainy day that followed, a number of Argentine fishing boats came in to shelter. Sunday was another wet and windy day spent aboard, but it seemed a little better the next morning and we were ready to move on. Going ashore to clear, we were told that we must stay put, as the harbour was closed. The wind having moderated to Force 6, this seemed excessively prudent on the part of the Authorities, but possibly they knew something that we did not and as it was no use arguing, we went back to Badger.

`I don't think I'd like to sail in a country where the harbourmaster makes the decisions for you,' said Pete.

`They've probably heard a gale warning or the sea's still rough, but I'd rather make up my own mind — though it's not easy until you know the weather and the River Plate has a nasty reputation.'

`But we're not really in the Plate yet and could still get out to sea if we met a gale. Let's hope we can go tomorrow.'

I strongly suspect that the harbour was closed on Tuesday, too, because at five in the morning, the change in motion woke us when the wind started to blow out of the west. With no protection from this quarter we shifted berth straight away. The wind never blew much above Force 5, but our anchorage off the north-eastern end of Isla Gorriti was more comfortable than the old one. When the wind went further north, we moved again.

`Do you think that was a *Pampero*?' I asked Pete.

`I don't know — I was wondering that, but it was too dark to see what the cloud looked like.'

`Whatever it was, it's certainly brought the rain with it! It's coming down like stair rods.'

`You've got your break from the scorching sun, anyway,' said Pete with a laugh.

We took the precaution of sleeping in the saloon, but it went calm and the next day dawned fresh and sunny, although the harbour still looked rough. In the afternoon we went for a walk on the island, which is quite beautiful and well-wooded, with several paths winding around, leading to old batteries on each corner of the island. On the west side was a sandy beach and a summer-only bar and restaurant stood nearby. We saw quite a few birds, including parrots and a great grebe. Several little brick *parilladas* had been built for the Uruguayans to indulge in their national pastime. The *parillada* looks like a barbecue, but instead of the food being cooked quickly over hot coals, the fire is to the side of the grill and the glowing embers are raked under the meat, which cooks very slowly. Rather more relaxed than a barbecue, it is still very much a masculine province and the sight of all these fireplaces was too much for Pete.

`Shall we have a barbecue, tomorrow? If we got up early, we could buy the meat and sail back here for lunch. Then go on to Puerto Buceo in the afternoon.'

`OK then. Let's do that, but it might be an idea to sail over to the harbour this evening. I suspect that it's going to be calm again, in which case we might spend half the morning getting there.'

We did as I suggested, but my weather forecast proved incorrect; this time it was three in the morning, when the nor'westerly wind woke us up. Pete considered the matter for a while.

`It mightn't blow up until daylight, but I suppose we'd better be safe than sorry.'

`When in doubt, get on out!' I quoted.

We beat back to our old spot off the pier on Isla Gorriti, but in the dark, we did not get so far in. By half past eight, it was blowing great guns, but the island gave us adequate shelter. The wind continued to increase and in the middle of the morning, we started to drag. When Pete paid out more cable, he observed that the water level had noticeably risen, thus reducing our scope.

`Shall we put out a second anchor?'

The time to put one out is the moment that you think about it, but on this occasion we were worried that it would hinder us if we had to move. The wind was blowing from well south of west and would make our situation very uncomfortable, if it went further south. As it was, the motion was enough to make me seasick. Or maybe I was just worried sick?

We were soon joined by four fishing boats, who anchored further out and we relieved the monotony by watching them slowly dragging out into the main part of the bay until they were no longer sheltered, when they got their anchor, steamed back to the anchorage and started again. Some of the gusts were quite fierce and it was distressing to watch three small boats, near to where we had lain in the harbour, all drag their moorings and end up on the beach. We wondered why no-one from the Prefectura sent a boat to assist. I could not eat any of the curry I made for supper, and as it was still rough, we settled down to anchor watches for the night. Pete took the first watch and the wind had abated when he woke me; by the end of my watch there was no longer any reason for anyone to stay awake.

The following morning was sunny and breezy, with a big sea still running, so we stayed where we were until Saturday, when it had moderated sufficiently for us to return to our usual spot and get ashore

'Parillada' on Isla Gorriti

for some shopping. Pete was still keen on a barbecue, so we went to the hypermarket whose meat had seemed inexpensive. This was a lucky choice, because we passed a wonderful market selling fresh produce, all of beautiful quality. We bought plenty, as it might be a while before we found anywhere else as good.

In the *Prefectura* they looked surprised at our loads, probably wondering how we would eat so much between Punta del Este and Montevideo, but at least they let us leave. I asked if the previous day's gale was unusual, after all, three boats had ended up on the beach, but apparently such winds were not infrequent. The Plate estuary obviously needed to be treated with a great deal of respect.

I wondered if our lovely island would be overrun with trippers on a sunny, Saturday afternoon and the multitude of boats anchored off confirmed my fears, but we sailed over, anyway, while I collected the wherewithal for the barbecue. When we rowed ashore, the island was almost deserted; everyone had gone to the beach on the other side. Finding a suitable site in the sun, we collected firewood, lit a fire and had an excellent barbecue. The big pile of meat (which had cost under two dollars) with a loaf of bread, made an adequate repast; there was a litre of wine and time to enjoy it in the warm sunshine. It was hard to believe that, a couple of days ago, I had been frightened that we would lose our boat.

We planned to sail the sixty miles to Puerto del Buceo overnight, so food eaten and wine drunk, we tidied up and rowed back. There was just enough wind to give us steerage way, but when even this light zephyr failed us, we dropped the hook off the north end of the island. It was then that we realized that we had left the grill at the barbecue site.

`I'll row back for it,' said Pete.

`Row back? But it's over a mile. Why don't we motor over in *Badger*?'

`I don't want to use the engine. Come on, we'll put the dinghy over. It won't take long.'

`Oh honestly, Pete, you do like to do things the hard way. I hope the wind doesn't pick up while you're gone.'

We put *Skip* back over the side and Pete rowed off. He got smaller and smaller and I worried about him rowing back, especially when a breeze filled in, but all went well, the grill was put back in the oven, the dinghy on deck and we got underway, gently reaching along at a couple of knots in the light norther.

Although we were sailing at three knots, our fixes showed a fairly strong current against us and progress was pitiful, but it was delightful yachting with hazy sunshine, a balmy breeze and several yachts, to add interest. It happened to be Easter Sunday and we celebrated with the following slap-up menu:

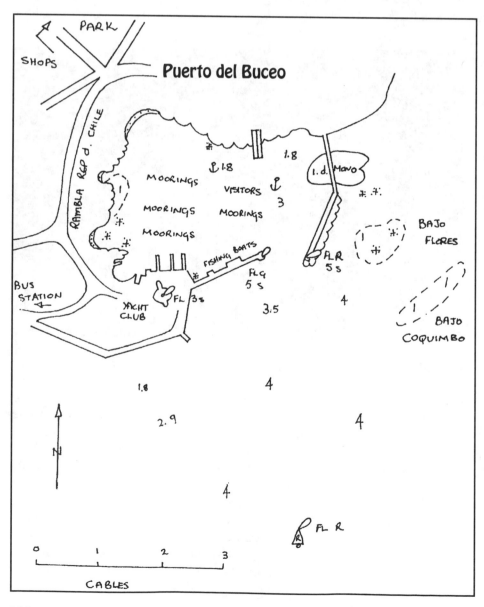

rum and lime (2), popcorn
sardine paté, crackers
stuffed peppers, brown rice
Christmas pudding
rum sauce
lots of wine

With that under our belts and the relief of finally escaping from Punta, we were unconcerned about our slow passage.

Taking calms philosophically sometimes brings its rewards, and this was such an occasion, with the breeze picking up during the evening. Knowing that the breakwaters at Puerto del Buceo had lights, we carried on. The *Pilot* stated that there was also a light on the roof the Yacht Club del

Uruguay's clubhouse, but even with the binoculars we could not pick it up against the confusing plethora of city lights. Eventually we identified the lights on the breakwaters, but they were so dim that by then we were almost on top of them; there was no sign of the light on the Club. We sailed in and anchored in the rather restricted space outside the moorings.

Not having received any mail since Ilhéus, we were keen to get into Montevideo, but had first to clear in. A mooring was offered, but no difficulties were made about our staying at anchor. Formalities completed, we set off on the four mile hike from the port to the city centre, but collecting our mail was compensation enough. We sat in a park to read it and eat lunch, by which time we had the energy to walk back.

We liked Montevideo, a small and accessible city, with the unmistakable air of having seen better days. Uruguay used to be a wealthy little country, making large sums of money from the sales of corned beef during and after the Second World War, but with increased competition and changing eating habits, demand has fallen, so that Uruguayan towns now tend to be rather seedy and down-at-heel. Time seems to have stopped half a century ago; we found it appealing to be transported to another age. Many gracious old buildings were still standing, even in town centres; butter and cheese were sold from the slab, in minute quantities, if required; horses and carts were commonplace but the most remarkable phenomenon was the cars. The streets, especially away from Montevideo, were like a museum, full of cars with running boards and headlights perched on the front wings and so many Model T Fords that we stopped commenting on them. The Uruguayans must be marvellous mechanics. Although these ancient motor cars are generally valued as a cheap means of transport, a few, still in everyday use, had been completely restored to their former glory.

At forty cents a pound, Pete had meat for dinner, stir-fried with some of the lovely vegetables we had bought at the market. After he had washed up, we recharged our glasses and discussed our plans.

As usual, there was no shortage of ideas and things that we wanted to do, and as usual, we had to find the time to do them and it was one of those situations where you have to think a long way ahead and then work back.

`Right, Annie, to be able to spend as much of the summer as possible in the Falklands, we want to be there by mid November and I like the idea of leaving from Puerto Madryn, where we may be able to see some whales, so we want to be there by the end of October. Now I'd like to spend another three months in Brazil and fill in as many gaps as possible in the guide, but to give ourselves a bit of time, we want to be leaving Brazil about mid September. That gives us from now until about the beginning of June to see something of Uruguay and Argentina, which is nearly two months. We also need to repaint the topsides and you want to do the varnish, either here or somewhere quieter. Guido recommended a river Rosario, further up the Plate, as being a good anchorage and I wondered if you'd fancy going there.'

`So your idea is to get the work done and then go further up the Plate and then on to Buenos Aires?'

`Yes, it would be nice if we could make it as far as Fray Bentos don't you think?'

`Oh definitely! I can't resist the idea of going to the home of corned beef. It would be lovely to be able to start a letter, "Aboard *Badger*, At Fray Bentos", wouldn't it? I'm all for moving on to your river, too. Buceo is too much the city for me and after Punta, I fancy escaping from "the madding crowd" for a while.'

The plan was made, but as so often happens, proved easier to envisage than to enact. We ended up staying eleven days in Puerto del Buceo, instead of the intended four or five, due to a combination of factors, all to do with the weather. Initially we were held up by a really unpleasant gale, but after that, either a bad forecast would deter us, or the Prefectura had closed the port, occasionally for no obvious reason. By the time we left Uruguay, we had come to the conclusion that the forecasters were rarely caught out by bad weather, possibly because they expected the worst from every ripple in the isobars. Not infrequently we were forced to remain in harbour, even with blue sky, a rising glass and the south-west wind dying away — the gale warning had not been cancelled and the fact that it had already passed was irrelevant. At this stage, too, the weather patterns were still so new to us that we had no confidence in our own forecasts.

We met two foreign yachts here, one Swiss, with a couple on board to whom we chatted briefly and one under the Red Ensign, but manned by a Kenyan and a German. Jan had gone away for a while, to sort out his affairs, but we spent some time with Britta, who was troubled with engine problems and other jobs that needed doing. I think that she quite appreciated our moral support because she had a lot of decisions to make and discussing problems helped clarify her ideas so that she knew what to do. It was not easy, dealing with engineers, sailmakers and so on, in Spanish, but she said that her fluency had improved tremendously since Jan, a good linguist, had left.

Sunny days with warm sunshine were sandwiched between days of strong wind and rain. Before the first blow came, the Club boatman suggested that we would be more comfortable, tied bows to the harbour wall, alongside the fishing boats. Dragging our CQR in a moderate squall had given us severe reservations about the holding, so we were not reluctant to do this. He assured us of `mal tiempo' and, his local knowledge mirroring our own suspicions, we took

ity to cope, stood by until we were actually alongside one of the fishing boats, a courtesy we much appreciated. We came also to appreciate his advice because the swell, which soon entered the harbour, would have made our previous berth excessively uncomfortable, if not dangerous. Instead, we lay snug and secure while the tops from waves crashing against the wall, landed cold and heavy on our decks.

Tired of waiting, I started work on the foredeck brightwork and Pete sanded down the hull and when the weather was unsuitable, we would wander up to town and find out where things were, passing a large and expensive mall, with a North American style supermarket. We preferred the local shops.

Above, the Yacht CLub at Puerto del Buceo. Below, workmen's lunch being cooked.

One day, when we were working on *Badger*, a couple of men on a small motor-bike came along the mole.

`Have you seen a boat called *Zarifa*?' one of them called. Pete was in the dinghy, so rowed over to the steps to converse more easily. A few minutes later, he was rowing them aboard. Although they were big men, *Skip* still had quite a lot of freeboard — not many dinghies of six foot six inches would happily carry such a load.

Our visitors introduced themselves as Rudi and Manuel. Rudi was from Czechoslovakia, `at least that was its name when I left. Now I am from the Czech Republic,' whose boat was moored in Montevideo. Manuel, his Uruguayan friend, was greatly interested in boats and dreaming of going cruising one day. Pete would have asked them aboard anyway, but hearing that Rudi had sailed in the Falklands, I guessed that there was a reason beyond mere hospitality for the invitation.

heed of what he said. Having laid out the sixty-five pound Luke anchor, as well as the Bruce and CQR, it was quite a palaver getting everything in. It was blowing pretty freshly and the boatman, who obviously shared our (unspoken) doubts about the Seagull's abil-

Rudi could fairly be described as a `character' and had built his own boat, which, we gathered was far from being a yacht. He had made a splendid circumnavigation in the Southern Ocean visiting many islands, including Heard Island and the South Shetlands in the Antarctic. His crew consisted of a couple of friends, neither of whom was a sailor and there did not seem much money to spare. They sounded a hardy outfit for whom comfort meant little. Rudi thought *Skip* was a bit of a joke and would be useless in the Falkland Islands, where light winds are the exception rather than the rule, but Pete had confidence in her. They stayed for about an hour and we saw Rudi once more, when he revisited Buceo to see if his friends had turned up. They had parted in the Falklands arranging to meet in Montevideo and he was a little worried about their safety, but as is so often the case, they had simply been delayed. On this second occasion, Rudi turned up with his own transport: a child's push scooter. `It is much smaller than a bicycle and a lot faster than walking,' he explained. Rudi was not much bothered about other people's opinions.

We came to know Manuel rather better. He and his mate, Irena, had a very small boat, but wanted something larger. For hours we would discuss ideas with them, but Manuel's problem was that he wanted a yacht. He laughed at Rudi's galley: `It's hard to believe it, but he has no proper cooker, only a couple of Primus burners!' and his rigging `it is held together with bull-dog grips!' not appreciating that Rudi was making exceptional voyages, while Manuel was dreaming. He wanted to build a wood and epoxy boat, `but epoxy is so expensive in Uruguay and we import all our hard-wood.'

`But Manuel, why don't you build a boat like Buehler designs? They're very simple, you can use soft-wood and iron fastenings — they're intended for people on a low budget. He tells you how to make your own galvanized hardware. If you went for gaff rig, your rigging could be low-tech and simple. I'm sure that you could get almost everything you need locally.' Pete's practical suggestions fell on deaf ears.

`Yes, but it is not so easy. A softwood boat will not last so long, you can't buy equipment like your nice lamps here — you have to import them and an aluminium mast is so expensive and the rigging must come from overseas.'

`But the boat will last for twenty or thirty years! You could use hurricane lamps, build your own mast, use galvanized rigging — if you look after it, it will last as long anyway.'

Manuel was not to be persuaded. He looked at yachts and wanted one. A strong, simple boat that would take him anywhere was within his grasp, but an elegant, cold-moulded yacht was way beyond his means and he set too much store by appearances. Our first boat had a single burner Primus stove, our second had galvanized rigging and it is infinitely preferable to

build something simple but adequate and go sailing than to stay put, wishing for The Perfect Boat. Think of the many happy years the Pyes spent with *Moonraker*, of Rudi's circumnavigation of the Antarctic. Those who want to do it enough, can and will. Manuel was not obsessed and unless one is wealthy, it is only by being obsessed that the necessary sacrifices and compromises can be made, to acquire a boat and go sailing.

At last the weather and the Authorities cooperated to let us leave. I had pulled my back a few days previously and was more or less hors de combat, but Pete cheerfully volunteered to go shopping. When he returned he was so burdened with bags that I wondered how he had carried it. Loading it all in the dinghy he pulled out to *Badger*.

`I found a street market!' he told me triumphantly. `It was very cheap and I bought lots of good things for you.' His eyes were sparkling as he showed me his purchases: tomatoes, peppers, aubergine and squash for my favourite ratatouille; hard onions, garlic and a lovely, leafy cabbage; salad greens and fruit. He piled it all on deck and, with a final flourish said:

`And *asado* for a barbecue at the river Rosario, tomorrow!'

I laughed. `We'd better get going, in that case. I'll wash all this as we sail and just have a quick check for cockies first.'

`Where are the oranges?' Pete asked.

`Oranges? I didn't see any.'

`But I bought three kilos. Hell! I must have left them at the supermarket. They were in a separate bag and I put them down at the check-out. I'd bought you a *chorizo*, too. I'll have to go back and look for them.'

`Oh, Pete! What a shame! But it's no good going back, darling. Someone will have taken them, thinking the bag was theirs.'

`No, I'll go back. It might have been handed in and there was the *chorizo*.'

He went back ashore. I felt so upset for him — he had already done so much — but there was no sign of the bag.

We eventually got away around half-past three and Pete settled down to steer while I washed all the fresh food and prepared an early supper, or a late lunch, depending how you looked at it. It was delightful sailing, with the sun pouring into the galley, *Badger* gliding gently along and the gorgeous smell of the bubbling ratatouille, which we ate with pasta, while sitting on deck.

The breeze never failed us and Pete using the excuse of pilotage, took more than his fair share of watchkeeping, so that I could rest. Not long after eight o'clock, he identified the entrance to the river and woke me up. We approached a buoy and searched unavailingly for the leading beacons described in the *Pilot*. Tacking, we discovered that the channel was very narrow, so we started the Seagull, dropping the sails. With both breeze and current against us, progress was slow, but at least this made it easier for us to stay in the channel. To starboard were what looked like the remains of two ship's boilers and as we brought them abeam, Pete, looking through the binoculars, suddenly said: `Those two buoys ahead each have a triangular topmark. I think that you're meant to keep them in line. Can you do that and we'll see?'

`OK.'

The buoys proved to be leading marks and we found the deepest water close to them, then followed a right-angle bend into the mouth of the river and another one into the river itself. The setting was quite lovely, with tree-lined banks, almost hiding an abandoned factory to starboard, where a handsome iron, steam-tug was moored to a decaying dock, appearing at first glance, ready to get underway at a moment's

notice. Closer examination revealed the red paint to be rust and there were weeds growing on deck between the planks, but the old, abandoned ship added to the feeling of tranquillity and peace that was the great attraction of this river. Passing a creek, we brought to at another bend in a very pretty spot.

After Pete had had an afternoon nap, we prepared for a barbecue, taking a bag of popcorn, garlic bread, the *asado*, a litre of wine to wash it down, and *cachaça* and orange juice, which Pete mixed up to have with the popcorn. We rowed downstream and found a delightful little beach not far from the tug, where we landed, only to be set upon by a cloud of huge and voracious mosquitoes.

`I think we'd better find another site!'

`Too right! Come on — get back in the dinghy.'

Back upstream, was a less attractive spot that we had earlier dismissed, but apart from a large number of cow pats, it seemed quite suitable, until we looked for dry wood. In the end we made do with damp wood, so that the meat took a long time to cook, not that we minded: perfectly happy to sip drinks, nibble popcorn

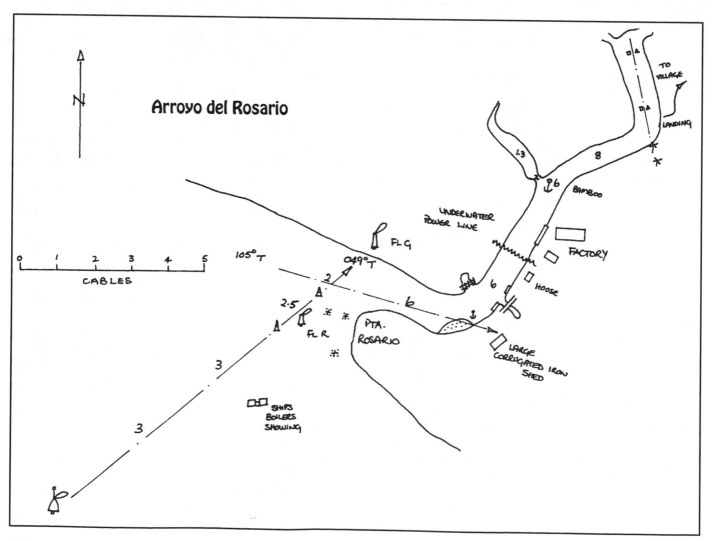

and enjoy the peace and quiet of the country. It was dark by the time we got back aboard.

Nearly three weeks were spent in this beautiful river and apart from the occasional weekend yacht and sometimes a barge, that took on sand at the mouth of the river, we remained in splendid isolation.

We had perfect weather for the first week, with warm, sunny days and light breezes, so that I could varnish while Pete pottered around crossing jobs off the list, fitting the big locker in the heads with dividers and, after much

Above: Another 'asado' at Rio del Rosario.

Left: Abandoned tug at Rio del Rosario.

cogitation, devising a method of putting bars across the openings to the lockers behind the backrests, so that their contents would stay put in a knockdown. With my back slowly mending, our evenings were made even more pleasant when we discovered a radio station that played only classical music.

The mornings were glorious, clear and crisp and the wild, shrill cries of a flock of plovers would waken us not long after sunrise, as they flew downstream to their feeding grounds. One day a calf fell in the water when the bank collapsed under it. The foolish animal kept trying to climb up where it was impossibly steep until I got into the dinghy and bullied it into swimming to an easier spot.

One Saturday, a yacht dried out on the sand spit near the entrance. The owner, speaking excellent

English, came to ask us to pull him off, but we explained that our six horsepower outboard motor was not up to it. He seemed unconvinced, so Pete suggested that he try kedging off, but he had lost his only anchor and anyway was hard aground. We then suggested that he borrow our CQR and attach it to the masthead, in order to heel the boat over. As he obviously did not have a clue what we meant, Pete got out the anchor and went to assist while I carried on sanding.

He came back unsuccessful, but buoyed up by Campari, gin and soda and a glass of wine to tell me all about it. Apparently Alberto, missing the channel in the dark, had anchored and in the morning, finding his anchor fouled, had cut his cable, motored into the river and run onto the sand spit so that he could take a rope to a stake ashore. The wind had been blowing him off, but after turning in to recover from the stresses of the previous night, he had awoken to find they were aground. He was a surgeon and had to be back for an important operation and was desperate to get off, so Pete had promised to go back and help near high water. In the meantime they had laid out our CQR.

I went with Pete, in case I could help and we were greeted with delight by Alberto's wife, Marta, who shook our horny paws with incredibly soft, pink little hands. Because she did not understand what was going on, she was very worried and I think her faith in her skipper had been a little shaken. In truth, I suspect that Alberto only grasped what we were attempting when we had finished, so I did my best to explain everything to Marta in my inadequate Spanish. Not really listening, she showed me photos of her house and children, gossiping happily away in rapid and incomprehensible Spanish, while I smiled and nodded. When Pete had organized everything so that we could start, Marta and I went out into the cockpit to 'help,' but she had badly hurt her foot in February and I had my back, so we were a rum bunch. Pete and I ended up doing most of the work as they were both so unfit and bewildered and after enormous amounts of effort and long after Marta and Alberto would have given up, we got off. There were cheers all round and Alberto opened a bottle of champagne. They were a lovely couple, more than appreciative of our assistance and Marta started bustling round digging out bottles and nibbles. Pete needed to speak quite firmly to Alberto to check that his boat was securely anchored before we sat down to crackers, *chorizo*, ham, smoked cheese and more wine. It was quite late when we rowed home.

'Alberto has asked me to pilot them out,' Pete said when we were back on board.

'But I thought he'd been here before.'

'So he has, several times, but apparently he didn't realize that there was a tricky channel. It must have been sheer good luck that he never ran aground before.'

'Fancy a foreign yacht acting as pilot to a local!'

Badger with new paint and varnish, Rio Riachuelo.

'It's as well I took careful bearings for ourselves. His boat draws a full six feet and he hasn't as much room to play with as we have.'

The next morning Marta and Alberto came alongside to hand over our anchor and Pete went onto their boat. When he returned, he said that he was not surprised that they had run aground coming in.

'I suggested they keep their speed down, but they steamed out at six knots,' he recounted. 'Alberto told Marta to mix Camparis all round when I'd asked her to watch the echo sounder, which is down below and he couldn't steer the compass course that I gave him! I was really worried that we'd run aground again and it was more by good luck than good management that we got out.'

Later, Pete went to see if he could find their anchor, but had no success.

After this, the weather became more unsettled, but when we could not work outside, we could do our notes for the FPI and one day went to the nearby village to see what it had to offer. Apart from mosquitoes and empty houses there was little more than a tiny shop that probably sold basic provisions. The mosquitoes were the only drawback of our anchorage; they were a nuisance ashore and forced us to stop work and ship the screens as soon as the sun went down.

There was a tremendous thunderstorm one night and the next day, the river rose after all the rain that had fallen, causing a fierce current, which ran against the wind. At times it was quite alarming and that night we slept in the saloon because the boat was moving so much.

The current still ran strongly the following day, measuring one and a half knots on the log, but the next day it was back to normal and we were once again swinging to the tides. As we were getting low on vegetables and had run out of wine, Pete decided to row to Juan Lacaze, a town four miles west of the river entrance and also take the opportunity to have a look at the harbour. He had a full and tiring day and by the time he was home, was more than ready to sample some of the jerrican of wine he had bought.

At last our jobs were finished and my back was about better. I did a month's washing, we put away our tools, brushes and tins of paint and varnish and on a morning of hazy sunshine, motored down the river and away from the delightful anchorage that had given us so much pleasure.

Out of the entrance there was too much chop for the Seagull so we hoisted the sails, finding that we could just make headway against the light wind. It was a long and tedious beat to Arroyo Riachuelo, our next destination, and dark when we arrived, but the entrance was clearly lit, so in we went. Rushing along the dimly-perceived and disconcertingly narrow channel in the pitch dark, with a following breeze, was quite unnerving, but our powerful searchlight helped immensely, even if it did hammer the battery. Sailing up as far as the yacht basin, we found no room to anchor, so turned round and went half way back to the entrance, where the river widened out a little. Dropping the hook, we took a line to a tree, pulling *Badger* out of the fairway.

We had hoped to sail on to Colonia the next day, but Pete reckoned that the fresh breeze would be blowing into the anchorage there and make it rather uncomfortable, so we stayed put. The previous day's washing was hung up to dry and after lunch, we rowed up to the moored yachts. There was yet another office of the *Hidrografia* and if we had found room among the other yachts, we would have had to pay. Incredible though it sounded, we were apparently supposed to pay to anchor half way down the river, but now it was the middle of May, the office was shut up and we could walk past with a clear conscience. The road took us to the `village,' consisting of a general store, a butcher and a baker straggling along the main road to Colonia, an attractive, palm-lined avenue which led through pleasant countryside. It was good to be able to stretch our legs again.

The next morning, Pete dragged me out of bed at some dreadful hour, to set off for Colonia, my only consolation being that he at least put the kettle on. With barely any wind, we motored down the river until near the entrance, where there was enough to give us steerage way and sail out. We could lay Colonia and had a lovely, if rather cold sail

in the bright sunshine. Anchoring in a rather uncomfortable spot off the old harbour, we went ashore to change money, post letters and do some shopping. A charming, old-fashioned shop sold us eggs and some local cheese and the elderly man who served us said that his grandfather was an Englishman, by the name of Walter Scott. The old part of the town was really beautiful and we explored its cobbled lanes for some time, before returning to *Badger*.

The following morning we continued up the river and after a day of light headwinds, we headed for Rio San Juan for the night. It was after dark by the time we arrived and as entering looked rather dicey, we had popcorn and a drink while considering what to do. Being only in sixteen feet, we finally dropped anchor where we were, I could cook the spaghetti to go with the lentil sauce, already prepared and we had a surprisingly comfortable night.

Monday was another sunny day of light winds. Pete got up at dawn, saying that there was a northeast wind.

`It'll go nor'west after the sun's properly up,' I commented, but he wanted to press on for Carmelo and suggested that he get underway on his own. I believe that he rather enjoyed it. By the time I emerged,

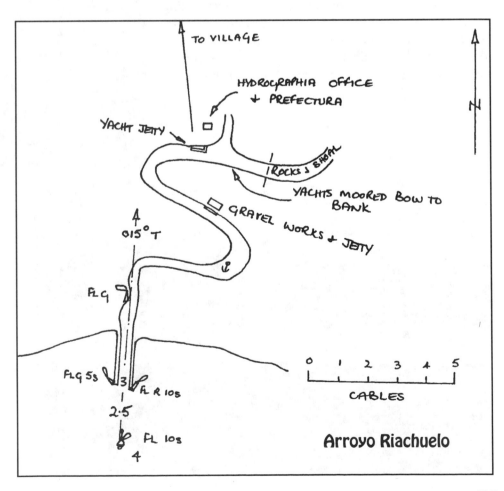

Arroyo Riachuelo

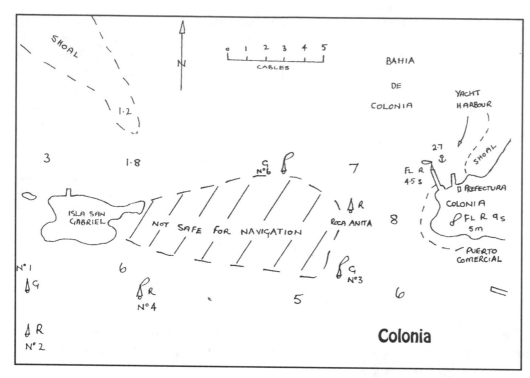

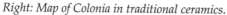

Colonia

pile of fishcakes and (tell it not in Gath) mushy peas, Pete screwed it all down with ginger pudding and custard, while I enjoyed a piece of the excellent cheese from Colonia. The cool weather was reviving our appetites.

Pete again got underway on his own, before seven o'clock while I slumbered on. He lit the heater so that I could get up to a warm cabin, but the valve in the heater's carburettor stuck and I got up to a fire! *Badger* was only heeling slightly, but burning oil was trickling out from

the wind was north-west, and unfortunately there was quite a current, which delayed our progress by about a knot. As we were either just able to lay the course, or having to beat, we did not get very far and when around tea-time, we were sailing slowly and standing still, out came the Seagull to get us to Punta Dorado, where we hoped to be out of the worst of the current. We anchored in a glassy calm and for once I could cook dinner in a leisurely fashion. After polishing off a

Right: Map of Colonia in traditional ceramics.

Below: Square in old part of Colonia.

underneath and when, even after shutting off the fuel, the fire showed no signs of burning itself out, we took the galley fire extinguisher from the bulkhead and, following the instructions printed on its case, turned it on the fire. Nothing happened. We tried the second one from the lazarette and again nothing happened. Wrapping the fire blanket round the heater, to smother the flames which were beginning to leap out of the top, I suggested somewhat belatedly that Pete put the bi-carbonate of soda from an extinguisher down the chimney.

Making a hole in the top of one of them, he ran on deck, removed the stack and poured some of the powder down. It was an instant success. We were left with a filthy boat, some scorched varnish, but no serious damage and I spent the rest of the morning washing down, alternately cursing the manufacturers of the fire extinguishers (which looked like new and had no `best before' date) and thanking our lucky stars that we had barely been heeling. The carving on the bulkhead looked as though it was mocking me.

`I don't like that carving, Pete. I think it's bad joss on *Badger*.'

Above: Carmelo street scene and riverside park.

`Anyone would think you were superstitious!' Pete responded, with a laugh.

Light headwinds being the order of the day, we trickled along and in the afternoon, Pete worked on the stove, managing to salvage the carburettor. Eventually, again in the dark, we made it to Carmelo after a certain amount of guesswork, anchoring miles off the beach. We were more than ready for a good supper and a night's sleep.

Another sunny day convinced us that the weather improved as one left the Plate estuary behind and going ashore to see Carmelo, our first stop was necessarily the *Prefectura*, who not having noticed *Badger*, were surprised to see us and when they were told where we were lying, informed us that we could not anchor there. I translated this and Pete's reply, fortunately in English, was that we already were. On being instructed to come into the river and pick up one of their moorings, for a fee of twelve dollars, Pete refused, so after arguing back and forth for a while, they reluctantly allowed us to stay for a couple of hours, which was all we wanted anyway. We had an agreeable stroll into the town accompanied by a very friendly dog. Carmelo was a nice place, with lots of old cars and pleasant, old-fashioned shops. Going into one of these in search of eggs, I asked for *huevos* and the girl behind the counter offered us a little, rectangular newspaper package. I tried again — and again — the girl pointing to most things in the shop and me shaking my head at them. Coming back to the newspaper parcels, I asked her if she would mind opening one. Not at all. It was unwrapped to reveal six eggs, neatly packaged, and occasioned much hilarity. They were only about a dollar a dozen, so we bought four packages and paid for some milk and delicious cheese while we were at it. Further on, a baker's tempted us to buy an appetizing-looking loaf, but at another's, the bread looked even better, so we bought some there, too: lovely french sticks for only thirty cents each. Our allotted time being up, we returned, cleared out and had a luxurious lunch of bread, *chorizo* and wine, before leaving our *prohibido* anchorage and continuing up the river.

Still the light headwinds and a noticeable current against us, but there was sunshine and pleasing scenery in consolation. At Nueva Palmira, where the rivers Uruguay and Paraná-Bravo meet, becoming the River Plate, the breeze started to fill in.

`Let's carry on, now that we have a breeze,' suggested Pete.

`Do you think so? In the dark? I'm a bit worried that the buoys won't be lit or will be different from the chart.' The British Admiralty chart for the river Uruguay is only a guide, because pilotage is compulsory for `all sea-going vessels'; for some reason, this did not apply to *Badger*.

There was no need to make a hasty decision, for although `the shades of night were falling fast,' the wind was still barely sufficient for us to stem the current, but when it got dark the next buoy proved to be lit, so we carried on to check that the one after was visible. Pete has better sight than I, especially at night and soon picked it up, but we were some way past the first one before I could make it out. This convinced Pete to continue, not wishing to waste the first decent breeze

for days, but he kept watch until four o'clock, when the buoys became rather more frequent.

It was distinctly chilly when I came on deck and I was more than grateful to feel the first rays of the sun, but as it grew warmer, the breeze faltered and died. By lunch-time, we had to resort to motor and were none too sure of our position, the buoys, supposedly showing the number of kilometres from the Paraná-Bravo, being all too often blank. Trying to tempt the breeze, we dropped the hook for lunch, but there was still insufficient wind to make against the current, so once again we resorted to the Seagull, with whose assistance we reached the Rio Negro by half-past five and anchored for the night just inside its entrance.

It was a beautiful spot, completely tranquil, with only natural sounds to be heard and a little way up the river, a *hacienda*, surrounded by lovely shade trees. As the sun set, huge mosquitoes emerged and forced me below behind screens, where Pete was sound asleep, making up for the previous night. I had time to make something a bit special for supper and as I pottered in the galley, I heard a low rumbling sound and looking out, saw several scores of Hereford cattle trotting by on the opposite bank. They were followed by a couple of gauchos, who shortly returned and in the silence, I could hear them talking quietly to each other and the jingle of harness as they unsaddled their horses, who stamped their hooves and swished away the mosquitoes with their long tails. Soon smoke was rising from the men's fire and I turned

Above: Soriano street scene complete with gauchos.

Right: the long pier at Soriano on the Rio Negro.

back to my galley to stone the avocado and stuff the cabbage leaves.

Underway before eight o'clock, we had a further day of beating against wind and current, though there must be a better word than 'beating,' when the wind is only Force 2. The chart showed a small town by the name of Soriano, where we stopped to have a look round, arriving mid-morning and dropping anchor in about twenty feet, off a long jetty. We went ashore to a real one-horse town, the most impressive building of which was the *Prefectura Naval*, whose charming representative suggested that we go and see the town while he did the paperwork.

Soriano was interesting and although founded by the Portuguese and the oldest town in the area, giving its name to the province, it is now obviously past its prime. The main street was paved; all the rest, whether at right angles or parallel, were simply dirt, with cows grazing at the ends, but they were lined with bitter orange trees and I gathered some fallen fruit to make marmalade. A gaucho rode by and turning into a side street, stopped outside a house, tethered his horse and went in.

Pete had been hoping to buy *asado* for a Saturday night barbecue, but the butcher was shut. In compensation, we bought two inexpensive and large *chorizos* in another shop and could buy fresh milk. Normally fresh milk is sold in plastic bags, *bolsitas*, but here beyond the reach of civilization, we were expected to supply our own bottle, to be filled from a large basin of 'genuine cow's milk.' Of course we had no bottle and when I explained this, the gentleman serving us, realizing that we were going to be disappointed, called to his wife, asking her if she could find an empty bottle. From noises offstage, it seemed that the contents of the only bottle to hand were being transferred to another container, but a few minutes later, a beaming lady handed us a full litre bottle of fresh milk. The twenty-seven cents and our fervent thanks seemed scant reward for all their trouble. Did they sell bread? No, but a shop back towards the river had some.

No baker being immediately apparent, we asked at a pharmacy, about the only shop not yet visited, for a *panaderia* and to our surprise, were told that there was no such thing. Thinking back to what the lady had said, I tried again. Was there a *casa* that sold bread? The helpful young man came to the door and gestured: 'There! the house with the red shutters.' Instead of the usual french sticks, we were offered loaves made of little rolls, all stuck together and bought a kilo before returning to the *Prefectura*, where our friendly official had completed his forms. Talking with him, we were taken outside to see the various levels to which the river had occasionally flooded, the record being five metres above low river level. It must have caused tremendous damage, with the land on either side of the river stretching flat and level for miles. On the office wall was a framed chart of the Rio Negro.

'Do you sell these charts?' I asked

'Excuse me, but no.'

'We would like to have one because we have no chart of the river.'

Immediately getting to his feet, he took the chart off the wall and opening a filing cabinet, extracted several sheets of thin paper, produced a pencil and invited Pete to make a copy. We were delighted at his thoughtfulness and, the copy completed, we shook hands all round. Rowing back to *Badger*, I saw him settle down in the sun and wondered how long it would be before another foreign yacht came to disturb his peace.

The light breeze of the morning had all but vanished, so the Seagull was once more pressed into service. I made marmalade, we managed to run aground — it felt like a sunken log — but got off without difficulty, we had scones for tea. Five hours of motoring and eight miles further on, we found somewhere to anchor for the night.

The following morning I utilized the boundless, if rather brown fresh water, to wash the settee covers, filthy from the fire, while Pete painted *Skip* and repaired the fendering. Because we had chosen to stay at anchor, it was a breezy day, so after lunch, with the washing almost dry, I suggested that we carry on, but after sailing for a couple of hours, it went calm and we anchored. We sat in the cockpit, enjoying the last of the sunshine and the abundant bird life, which made this stretch of river particularly interesting.

We were underway by nine on Sunday and a good breeze gave us one of the best sailing days that we had enjoyed for some time, which was just as well, the current being pretty strong in places. Either the river was low or some of the buoys misplaced, because one or two places were unpleasantly narrow and, needless to say, we were beating. The town of Mercedes finally gained, we found a delightful anchorage between an island and the town shore. Ponies were grazing, pre-1950 cars driving past and it was like being in a 'time warp,' so astonishingly tranquil that it was hard to believe that we had brought up at the edge of a fair-sized town.

Although rain fell overnight, we thought the worst had passed when we went ashore. We were wrong. The rain came down like stair rods and, the streets having no proper drains, turned into little torrents, shallower in the middle where the road was cambered, deep and fast-flowing by the kerb. Getting thoroughly soaked, we found the shops we needed, treating ourselves to cakes to have with coffee and after some difficulty, we also managed to find the *Prefectura*. Back aboard, cold and damp, we were ready for some hot coffee and Pete got the heater working again. Its heat was welcome, but we looked at it with jaundiced eyes and no longer quite trusted it. The rest of the day brought little improvement and for supper we had huge, steaming bowls of thick, home-made soup.

The returning sun brought washday. Having noticed a picnic area on the island, Pete rowed over to see if there were any *parilladas* and locating a pleasant, if rather damp spot, he came back asking if I wanted to have a barbecue.

'I must finish the washing, first.'

'But you won't be much longer, will you? I can go and buy the meat and get everything together.'

'All right then. I should be about done by the time you're ready.'

Pete was quicker than I, but at about two o'clock we went ashore and had a great time, in spite of the cool weather and needing to wear wellies. Pete was master of ceremonies and we dined sumptuously, not to say greedily, so that by the time supper time came around, we were still full.

That evening we discussed our next move. Progress had been slower than we hoped, we certainly no longer had time to go to Buenos Aires and it was still quite a way to Fray Bentos. Reluctantly, we concluded that we should really start back downstream on the morrow.

'It's a shame,' I said, 'I don't suppose there is much worth seeing at Fray Bentos, but I'd have liked to go there, just for the sake of it.'

Another 'asado' at Mercedes.

Above: Fray Bentos, spiritual home of corned beef.

Below: a riverside picnic at Fray Bentos.

'I'll tell you what, Annie, why not take a bus? I had a look when I was ashore yesterday, and they go there regularly. We ought to take a bus ride anyway, while we're in Uruguay and could take a picnic lunch with us. If we went early, we could be back in time to clear out and get a few miles down river.'

This seemed like a good compromise and the morning saw me packing *chorizo*, coffee, wine and bananas into our rucksack. Ashore, we bought a couple of cakes for coffee and bread for lunch. The bus ride was interesting and my day was made when we stopped for two gauchos in traditional dress, to climb on board. Arriving at Fray Bentos, we found quite a pleasant town, certainly nicer than I had anticipated and strolled around, had a picnic down by the river and caught the bus back. We passed a gaucho and his dog, herding cattle along the road and felt that we had seen something of the real Uruguay.

Leaving by half past four, we sailed for about an hour, but covered six miles: it was a lot easier than sailing upstream. Although our anchorage was pretty, we had no time to enjoy it being under-way before sunup, with, to our chagrin, light headwinds all day. Even with a fair current we only averaged about three knots, but it was a lovely, sunny day, if very cold. Pete was all for sailing overnight, but I was not sorry when the wind died after sundown and as there was no point in motoring, we brought up, again near the mouth of the river. We saw the gauchos, but it was too cold for the mosquitoes.

Estancia near the mouth of the Rio Negro.

As we were trying to get back to the river Plate by Friday evening, I felt guilty for preferring to spend the night at anchor with a long way yet to go, but my conscience was some-what salved with a seven thirty start. The early morning mist thickened and losing the chan-nel, we had no option but to anchor, so took the oppor-tunity to eat a substantial breakfast of fried egg sand-wiches. Soon, the fog had cleared and the light north-east breeze picked up to about Force 4, speeding us down river, at times doing six and a half knots with the current and covering in ten hours what had taken over two days, sailing upstream. It was a glorious, sunny day and although quite cold after sundown we kept on, past the place we had intended to spend the night and approaching our second choice, feeling it a pity to waste the splendid breeze, Pete went below and did a few sums.

`We should be able to make Rio San Juan by about half past seven, and there are enough lit buoys to try the last bit in the dark. What do you think?'

`Let's go for it! From what we saw last time, it looked a lovely place, and as we are a day ahead of schedule, we could spend the day there if it's nice.'

`Right, we'll press on then.'

The breeze faltered, but held and we arrived at the entrance to the river at eight o'clock, too late to try to negotiate the unlit buoys in the channel. We anchored for the night, about a mile offshore relieved that the echo sounder, which had been reading erratically, behaved when we needed it.

When we got the anchor, the light breeze was dead on the nose for sailing into the river, so it was under Seagull that we worked our way up the tricky channel. As some of the buoys were only small plastic bottles and the echo sounder on the blink, it was as well we had not attempted it at night. Once inside, we found a beautiful river with a lovely calm anchorage.

Before going ashore, we checked all the connec-tions in the echo sounder yet again and it seemed to work perfectly. On the left bank of the river are the grounds of the Presidential Palace, which is situated at the junction of the Rio San Juan and the Rio Plata. This beautiful spot is also of historic importance, being the site of the first settlement by Europeans on the River Plate. Sebastian Cabot, son of John Cabot, built a fort here in 1527, the site being marked by a stone tower resembling a light house and incidentally making a magnificent navigational aid, usually showing a fixed white light at night. An amiable cat accompanied us around the delightful and deserted grounds for half a mile or so and down by the river bank, we found a per-fect barbecue spot, which caused Pete to change his mind about sailing in the afternoon. We rowed back to *Badger*, assembled vege-burgers bread and wine and, returning ashore found ample good, dry wood for a super fire. The burgers were at their best, cooked that way and it was a truly memorable afternoon, sitting under the trees admiring *Badger*, serenely at anchor in the lovely river. It had fallen absolutely flat calm, so we felt no qualm of guilt at `wasting' the afternoon in this exceptional anchorage.

Sunday also dawned windless, but we found light headwinds outside the river and progress was so slow that it was seven in the evening, by the time we dropped the hook in the rather open anchorage in Colonia. When a breeze started to fill in about ten o'clock, it seemed prudent to leave, and although I sug-gested saying that we had sailed right past, Pete felt that we should clear in and out first, having told the people at Mercedes that we were going to Colonia. He

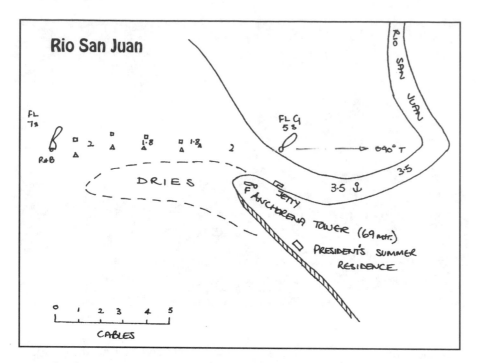

Rio San Juan

day and with eighty-eight miles to go, settled into our sea-going routine.

Montevideo's main harbour had a bad reputation, but wanting to see for ourselves and knowing that yachts had anchored off the rowing Club, we sailed into it. Threading our way through hundreds of laid-up fishing boats, we recognized the Club from Manuel's description. With no room to anchor, when a man suggested that we pick up his mooring, we somewhat reluctantly accepted, although normally, we never pick up a strange, private mooring. Going ashore, we discovered that the stories of Montevideo were not exaggerated. The harbour was filthy, with everything covered in thick, black oil, its stench hanging in the air and, landing at the Club's wooden float, it was difficult to put a hand down without getting oil on it. We hauled the dinghy out, viewing with disgust the black shiny covering on every surface. Although we needed to provision and Puerto del Buceo was a long way from Montevideo, it was a bad decision to come here.

Certainly all types of shops were close by and we noted the ones that we needed. Passing a metal stockist, we enquired about a bronze strip for the outboard bracket, the fibreglass one proving inadequate, and were able to buy it off the shelf for twenty-one dollars, at which Pete nearly fainted, whether from the shock of its availability or the price, I was not sure. We also

came back saying that we would have to stay because not only was the *Prefectura* refusing to let us leave without a receipt from the *Hidrografia*, (even though we were anchored!) but that there was a forecast of west-southwest Force 7-8.

To the impecunious — or even thrifty — yachtsman, the harbours in Uruguay are a real problem, rarely providing anywhere to anchor, sheltered from *Pamperos*, vigorous south-west winds that come through with monotonous regularity. Although we tried to find better shelter, there was nowhere satisfactory and finally, we resigned ourselves to picking up a buoy, selecting one away from other boats and sheltered by the wall. It seemed close to the next one and concerned that it had been laid for a smaller boat, we also put out an anchor, then, satisfied that we were now secure, turned in.

The gale duly arrived and our decision was vindicated. All day it blew and as it was still breezy at sundown, we decided to bite the bullet and stay another night. We could leave by Tuesday morning, but first went ashore to buy bread and milk and have a final look around the beautiful, colonial town. There were no problems with the *Prefectura*, the *Hidrografia* only charged us for the one night and we felt very pleased with life, as we got underway on a lovely, sunny

Badger at Rio San Juan.

passed several butchers and felt that at a dollar fifty a pound, we ought to splash out on some fillet steak and on the assumption that a successful cruise up and down the River Uruguay was cause for celebration, ensured that we had all the ingredients for dinner, *viz*: *chorizo* slices in batter; steak au poivre, baked potatoes and Brussels sprouts; bananas au cognac with cream; a litre of Argentine wine; coffee with cream; brandy. Even we occasionally live the high-life.

Needing to replenish our wine, as that which we could afford in Brazil was quite undrinkable, I washed out and sterilized several jerricans. We shopped for paraffin, potatoes (a sack), seven dozen eggs (reasonably priced), some bacon (to put by in salt) and, of course, wine — fifty-five litres of it. It was rather embarrassing, trundling it through the streets of Montevideo, in our cart.

Noticing a bag of leather offcuts in the street, put out as rubbish, Pete brought it back, to take out any that might of use. Manuel and Irena came by on the way to their boat and when we invited them aboard, Manuel was rather shocked at our explanation of the leather: it was not very `yachtie.' I suggested using some of the leather to make me a patchwork rucksack, coveting the ones sold in Montevideo, but Pete had the much better idea of using the leather that Mike and Christine had given us and in a saddler's, we found some seamanlike brass buckles for it.

The shops being shut on Sunday, Pete fitted the bronze strip for the outboard bracket; it was a relief to have it trustworthy again. Manuel and Irena came round for dinner, bringing some *alfajores*, a Uruguayan specialty, Irena had made, a biscuit similar to shortbread, but with *dulce de leche*, a fudge-like spread, between them and very good. We enjoyed our evening, learning about Uruguay and discussing boats.

By Tuesday, we were ready to go, but the glass was falling and there was a gale warning, so we had another look at our mooring, reassured by its stout chain and the fact that it was designed for a heavy, steel, thirty-foot motor launch. The wind got up and it became so uncomfortable, that we turned in on the saloon settees, only to be awoken around midnight by the noise of a boat alongside. Going on deck, we could not understand what had happened, but then came the dreadful realisation that we had dragged the mooring, ending up against the bows of a workboat and less than a hundred feet from a ruined, concrete jetty, with lengths of rusty, steel reinforcing sticking out. In the howling wind, we managed to haul *Badger* alongside

*Right: Monument tower at Rio San Juan, visible in background of the photo of **Badger** on the opposite page.*

Below: Another happy barbecue.

the workboat and make fast, forcing our fenders between the gaps in the tyres around our neighbour, to protect the starboard rail which had already taken a beating. After taking two lines to a fishing boat ahead, there was nothing else to do but to wait for daylight and listen to the horrible noise of squealing tyres.

At first light, the wind having somewhat diminished, we prepared to row out an anchor, but this was easier said than done, because our anchor chain was shackled onto the mooring buoy, which was submerged because we were now in deeper water. In fact, the mooring chain was very short and when the storm caused the water level to rise six feet, we simply lifted the mooring and floated it away. While we were struggling to get the buoy to the surface, Pete saw the mooring's owner and rowed over to ask him how we should get it moved back. Apart from being surprised that we had shifted it, he did not seem too concerned and said that he would deal with it.

Unable to raise the buoy, we had to saw through the anchor chain and while Pete was doing this, the boat to which we were tied started to get underway. Explaining what had happened and that Pete would row out an anchor so that we could move, our engine being too small to use in such a strong wind, I asked him to wait until we were safe before moving. Pete buoyed and cast off our chain to the mooring, lowering another anchor and chain into the dinghy, but the boatman insisted on leaving and despite my pleas, undid all our lines, while Pete was actually rowing out the anchor. Seeing what was happening, he dumped it where he was to come back and help me. The work boat forced her way out, doing more damage and as he went clear, *Badger*, still held by the ropes to the fishing boat ahead, swung round through 180°, her bow heading towards another workboat's stern. We frantically shifted fenders, but were now stern to the anchorage and it was killing work to get out without the stern swinging onto the ruined pier. Taking a bow line to a moored boat, Pete rowed the anchor further out and then brought the cable to a deck winch, where I ground away with all my strength, repeating the operation as necessary. By midday, we were anchored away from all the boats and Pete went back to release our other cable from the mooring.

Not being ideally situated, we put on the Seagull, thankful that Pete had been fitting the new bronze strip without which it would have taken the full impact of the collision and moved outside the yachts. When we dropped the Bruce anchor, it promptly dragged, so with infinite care, we laid it out again and it seemed to hold. Secure at last, we had the leisure to examine the damage: two bent stanchions, the rubbing strake badly chewed up, the cream paint covered in tar and oil from the workboat's tyres and requiring repainting, a crack in the bulwark, by the front of the cabin. After all our recent work painting and varnishing, it was heart-breaking, but at least it was largely superficial and a harsh reminder that we had broken our own rule of never trusting a strange mooring.

In need of cheering up, we had thought to try a *parillada* in the meat market, but did not like to leave the boat, being dubious about the holding, so I helped Pete lay out the CQR and went ashore to collect the mail, and also bought bread and freshly a roasted chicken, a favourite of Pete's, because we had not yet eaten. Back on board, Pete told me that we had been slowly dragging again, and although the thought of

more anchor work was intolerable, by the time most of the chicken was eaten, washed down by a glass or two of wine, we were sufficiently restored to relay the anchors. About three o'clock, a boatman came past and told us that they were forecasting another gale and although the barometer was high and only climbing slowly, not daring to take the risk, we laid out the Luke. Physically and mentally exhausted, we made an early night of it.

Fully revitalized, we woke to a calm, sunny morning and after getting in the Luke, went ashore to buy me some warm boots for sailing down south and to clear out. I soon found just what I needed, felt-lined and only eighteen dollars, but the only ones in stock were all left feet! Eventually, we had to squander forty-eight dollars — more than we could really afford — to find any suitable, but they were a beautiful pair of soft sheepskin boots and wonderfully comfortable.

`You can have them for your birthday and even if they don't keep your feet warm, at least you'll enjoy wearing them,' Pete commented.

`Well all I can say is that if I get cold feet now, I'll never cure them,' I replied.

Buying the boots had taken ages and we still had to see the *Prefectura*, and do some last minute shopping so, ravenously hungry, we bought sausage and bread in the market. The *Prefectura* had a forecast of south-south west Force 6-8, becoming south 6-8, but as this was obviously yesterday's weather we cleared out, which also took ages. Astonishingly, the port was not closed.

Manuel was waiting to say good-bye and after Pete had been up the mast to fit the windsock and we had hauled a disgustingly filthy *Skip* onto deck, at last we got underway while Manuel took photographs of us sailing out. Six o'clock saw us waving him a final farewell and working our way out through the moored fishing boats. Montevideo was a fine town, but we were glad to leave such a foul, dirty harbour. A tug called to us, wanting to know our name, destination, etc. and outside the walls, a *Prefectura* inflatable warned us that we were sailing towards the rocks, which we knew, staying with us until bored with our slow progress, they roared off to leave us finally in peace. It was good to be at sea again.

Chapter Eleven

I lay in my bunk listening to the quiet sounds that accompany a gentle night's sail, rejoicing to be once more sailing the ocean, away from the noise, dirt and problems of land. These passages become addictive and even three or four days at sea cleanse the system, allowing the brain to absorb and process the impressions it has received.

A clear, sunny day and light northeasterly winds, quite the opposite of the forecast, allowed me to wash the decks, cabin sides and after bulwarks, swilling down with buckets of clean seawater. A couple of hours and a bottle of detergent, saw *Skip*, who had oil *all over her*, as good as new.

The wind increased and headed us the following day, but the delightful weather held and we were both overjoyed to be at sea once more. For much of my watch, I gazed entranced at the birds surrounding us: yellow-nosed and black-browed mollyhawks, white-chinned petrels, Cape pigeons and great rafts of Magellanic penguins. A large frond of kelp would wave and transform itself into a fur seal, lying on its back like a sea otter and although by midnight it was blowing Force 6, cold and rough, we had still not got over our euphoria. All day Sunday we beat and on Monday the main tore, so Pete tied three battens together. On Tuesday we caught a fish, ate some and pickled the rest and a squally night with thunder and lightning was probably what caused the bottom batten on the main to break. It was no real problem to fit the spare and the broken one could be mended at anchor.

On Wednesday, we saw the lights not only of Rio Grande, but of dozens of ships at anchor, but it was new moon and near the solstice, and not liking to enter in the dark with the probability of a strong current, we anchored. Totally open to the south, it was not a reassuring spot, even though the onshore breeze was no more than Force 3, but we hoped that in daylight we could work out when the tide started making.

The wind increased and at about half past two, Pete woke up and decided that it was getting rather rough.

`I don't like this Annie,' he said, `I think we'd better get underway.'

Having not slept a wink, I was more than happy to leave and we soon had a few panels of each sail up. It was the devil's own job getting the anchor which was as well set as if someone had poured quick-setting concrete round it! After a fierce tussle, Pete eventually secured it at the stemhead and we beat out.

Back in the cockpit, the skipper said: `I don't fancy trying to enter Rio Grande with such rotten weather, especially as we've no idea what time the tides are. Should we go on to Florianópolis?'

`Good idea!' said I. `I'm getting a little weary of cold fronts and Florian-op is four and a half degrees further north', so off we went, bowling along merrily all day with the wind staying at Force 5-6. On my first watch, I picked up the occulting light at Mostardos, which gave us a good fix, showing that we had a knot of current *with* us: a pleasant change.

By morning, we were under fairly easy canvas, with only the top of the foresail drawing and a well-reefed main, the wind logged at Force 7. Polishing a lamp, I caught sight of the Salvador carving, its expression as malignant as ever. I looked at it. It leered at me. Thinking of the misfortunes in the past few months: breaking the outboard bracket, the fire, dragging the mooring, even the unrealized visit to Rio Grande, I became convinced that they were connected with the carving and that it was an unlucky thing to have on board. It was valuable as a gift from Christian and Maria, but if I explained it to them, they would understand and I told Pete how I felt.

`The horrible thing is malevolent! I think we should get rid of it or give it to somebody else.'

`No, we can't give it away, Annie, because if you're right, we would be passing on bad luck. We ought to throw it out.'

Although it was only attached to the bulkhead with *Blu-tack*, it seemed reluctant to come away and as I carried it to the hatch, its expression was as wicked as ever. Looking at it one last time, I said:

Above: a fine example of a dugout canoe. Left: more canoas and nets hung out to dry on the beach at Pinheira.

`I think you were carved by some horrible person who had a grudge against tourists and made you to harm people, so you'll have to go. Don't worry, though, you'll float, but I hope you end up somewhere well away from other people. Perhaps after weeks in the pure ocean, the evil will be cleaned from you and if someone takes you home, you won't bring them bad luck.' With a feeling of relief, I threw the carving overboard watching it float off in our wake. The saloon looked better without it.

`I think you're superstitious, Annie,' Pete joked when I came back.

`Not at all. It's just that some things are unlucky!' But I don't think Pete ever regretted its departure.

The wind eased with the dawn and the day revealed land in sight: a scene of splendid mountains. We kept Badger sailing at full speed and eventually came to anchor at Pinheira, south of Santa Catarina Island, a very pretty spot, tempting us ashore. We found an attractive fishing village, with a few rather better houses around it and a most delightful beach where several, beautifully maintained *canoas* looked very picturesque among the fishing nets hung out to dry. In a small supermarket we were gratified to see that everything was as cheap as we remembered. We appreciated Brazil anew after a couple of months absence.

After a good Sunday breakfast, we sailed up the sound between Santa Catarina and the mainland, in light headwinds, but with a fair tide through the narrows and anchored off the Yacht Club just after sunset.

Next morning we went and made our number, but unlike most clubs in Brazil, the one at Florianópolis proved to be less than welcoming. When we asked if we could leave our dinghy in the safety of the Club precincts, we were informed that we could, but it would cost five dollars a day for the first two days and eight dollars after that, but we could also use

Enseada da Pinheira, Brazil.

the WCs, showers, *lanchonete*, and restaurant (at lunchtime, not in the evening). The Secretary then told us to go back to *Badger* and await the doctor who had to give to give us a clean bill of health before we went ashore.

In due course, the doctor came and solemnly inspected our drinking water (a five-gallon polythene container), washing water (a one-gallon jerrican) and rubbish disposal (a plastic carrier bag hung behind the companionway ladder), then drove us off to the other side of town, to fill in forms. A very pleasant man, he explained that his visit was due to the recent outbreaks of cholera in Brazil. It seemed a little topsy-turvey to examine a boat coming from a country that had no cholera, to one that had, but the ways of bureaucracy are strange indeed, and not to be questioned too closely.

The form filling was no bad thing, because the office of the *Polícia Federal* was situated not far from the medical centre and the doctor gave us directions. As they were shut for lunch, we changed money, bought ourselves hamburgers and a beer for a mere two dollars, but then in the elation of being back among Brazilian prices, bought too much in a supermarket that we found. The *Polícia Federal* satisfied, we then had a great hike back to the Island, passing a shop selling fire extinguishers. We bought just what we wanted for thirteen dollars, whereas in Uruguay they had been both very expensive and far too big.

We arrived at Customs in the late afternoon and although very pleasant, they were slow, so that the Port Captain had shut up shop by the time we got there. Back at the Yacht Club, we went to the Secretary to say that we would pay for our day, but could not afford any more. A member kindly translated for us, persuaded the Secretary to let us off any payment and apologized for the apparent inhospitality of the Club, explaining that a recent visitor had `paid with the main sheet'. This is an all too common phenomenon and I wonder how many of these selfish and dishonest people realize what problems they leave for those in their wake.

It had been a long day and cooking had little appeal, but after a couple of cachaça punches and the obligatory bowl of popcorn, I stuffed a huge avocado with tuna, green pepper, onion and lime juice, which we ate with bread and butter. Replete and contented, we crawled to bed.

The following day we left *Skip* near some fishing shacks on the beach while we went to clear in and do some more shopping. We picked up some bargains in Florianópolis: as well as vegetables, we bought several bottles of rum and ten kilos of dirt cheap popcorn.

We had been planning to do some sail repairs in Brazil — after the last passage, they were needed — and a place called Enseada de Brito, looked suitable on the chart. After a fine sail, we arrived in the bay, to find that the soundings did not match the chart, so anchored and had a look at things. As there was no obvious alternative, Pete rowed off to sound around and found a route with enough depth. It was around low water and with the new moon and the solstice, the tides must have been about the biggest of the year, so even with only inches under us, we felt fairly safe.

Unfortunately, we were still in range of the cold fronts and next morning, a south-westerly breeze forced us to move to the south side of the bay. A few days later, a fresh north wind caused us to shift berth just as we were about to have dinner and, overnight some gusts reached gale force, with a repeat performance next night and strong gusts all through the later part of the afternoon, dying away again at sundown. By this time we were really getting fed up for although our anchorage was very pretty, it was by no means

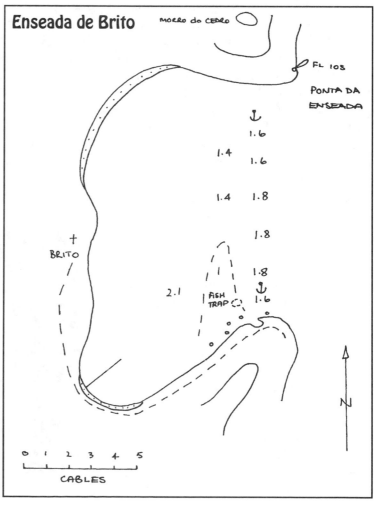

Enseada de Brito.

ing three avocadoes and a small pineapple, and only the fact that we were spent up prevented us from buying more. Because we had started from a different point, it was with some difficulty that we found the *Polícia Federal*, but at last we got there. It was a long, weary walk back and nearly dark when we went aboard *Badger*, but a good dinner of cabbage leaves stuffed with *kibe* and washed down with Uruguayan wine did a lot to alleviate our tiredness.

The following day, with the breeze blowing right up the sound, we left north about, the wind occasionally reaching Force 6, but outside there was not a breath and a vile sea for hours. Eventually, a fresh breeze filled in from the south-west, with rain, making for a rough night and when I got up, it was overcast, raining and blowing.

`Why does the weather never read the *Pilot*?' I complained to Pete and then grumbled again when he told me that we had finished the *dulce de leche* and could have no more on our porridge until the weather turned cool again.

`I wouldn't call it exactly tropical now,' I commented.

`No, I know it isn't, but it will be when we get to Ilha Grande and then the *dulce* will go mouldy and you'll be annoyed,' Pete replied.

`Well, I think it's a rotten swizz!'

`Cheer up, Annie. Wait until you look out of the hatch: there are lots of birds around again!' and after breakfast I stood watching mollyhawks, white-chinned petrels, Cape pigeons and storm petrels, soaring around the boat. Then the wind eased down, the last of the reefs were shaken out that night and Saturday

tranquil and we felt vulnerable with the sails off. However, Pete had now mended them and the batten and I had done a month's washing plus our sailing clothes, still filthy from fending off in Montevideo.

With the mainsail back on and having shifted berth again, we allowed ourselves a holiday, taking a pleasant stroll ashore. A track, shady with trees, led into a village, clean, pretty and obviously prosperous, with much new building underway, after which we found a view point, where we could enjoy our tea and scones. On our way back, we had to fend off two or three noisy and unfriendly dogs and Pete, who is not fond of dogs at the best of times, unceremoniously pushed me in front of them. `You like dogs,' was the explanation for his pusillanimity. The attack was as surprising as it was unprovoked, most Brazilian dogs being as amiable as the human population.

The following morning, our intention to explore a little was thwarted by a fresh south-west wind, which made many of the potential anchorages untenable, but a spot called Ponta Caicanguçu was both better and deeper than it looked on the chart and well protected with winds in the south, so there we anchored. After lunch, an interesting walk took us up quite high, to reveal some good views.

Concluding that we were still too far south for good weather, we sailed back to Florianópolis to clear out, finding a pleasant anchorage on the *Continente* side, off a beach, surrounded by houses. Ashore, we found a *Cesto de Povo*, where everything was priced at 13,000 *cruzeiros*, the equivalent of twenty-two cents a kilo and for two dollars, we filled two carrier bags with fruit and vegetables, includ-

Sailing under the bridge at Florianópolis.

dawned almost calm, although a large swell was still running. It gradually became warmer, the sea became bluer and the birds left us. We were out of the Falklands Current.

The passage ended with a brief southerly blow from a clear sky and we raced into Baía de Ilha Grande, to bring up in a pretty anchorage off Ilha Gipoia, sheltered from the south and out of sight of the bureaucrats. We sailed to Angra dos Reis the next day.

Angra, a pleasant and well-provided little town, has all the necessary shops and services. Although not particularly pretty, it is small enough to make everything accessible and in spite of being only fifty miles from Rio, it feels perfectly safe.

We had some fun and games when we came to clear in at the Capitania. Several officials stood behind a long counter dealing with people and after a short wait, one turned his attention to us. After we had shown him the appropriate papers, he asked:

`Where is the captain's certificate of competence?'

I translated this for Pete and told the official that we did not have one.

`But the captain must be qualified!'

`In your country, yes, but not in England.'

`That is impossible! Show me the certificate.'

`We do not have one. It is not necessary to have a certificate to sail an English yacht.'

`All captains must be qualified. For any boat. It is the law!'

`Not in England,' I repeated, by now considerably nettled at the official's hectoring manner. `England,' I added, perhaps unwisely, `is a free country.'

He was thoroughly irate by now and turned to one of his colleagues for support. I could not understand the whole conversation, but I gathered that the other man believed my statement to be true. Our official, a small and plump man, by now somewhat red in the face, glowered at me and reached for a telephone.

`I am calling Rio,' he told me. `Then you must produce your certificate.'

By now the whole office was interested in this confrontation. Pete and I, while certain of our ground, were becoming seriously concerned that we might be refused entry. We made an active decision to sail without qualifications because we feel very strongly that individuals have a perfect right to do whatever they wish with their lives, so long as they do not harm others. If we want to sail off in the wide blue yonder and

drown through our own folly, that is our problem and not any one else's. Besides, there is no proof that mandatory qualifications make for better amateur sailors — they merely serve to satisfy the bureaucrats' thirst to control our every move.

Contact was made and the official put his question. `From England', I heard him say. Then, `Are you certain?'

Ilha Gipoia.

He slammed the phone down and seized our papers with one hand and a rubber stamp with the other. Wordlessly, he banged down the stamp and scrawled his signature over it and then thrust the papers back at us. One of the other officials asked `Do they not need the certificate, then?' and received a curt reply. Behind him, two or three people were sniggering, but we remained wooden faced, thanked him and left as he flounced away from the counter in a towering rage. It had not been a pleasant experience.

At least now, we were free to walk round the town and in one of the supermarkets we found *Melita* coffee at a silly price, sixty cents for two hundred and fifty grams. Remembering bargains in Brazil have to be snapped up, we bought twenty-five vacuum wrapped packages, regretting later that we did not buy more. We suspected that some of these bargains were the result of high inflation, because if for some reason an item had not been repriced, a couple of weeks later it would be really cheap. It seemed a bit unsporting to take advantage of these mistakes, if such they were, but I am afraid that we never pointed them out. On this occasion my conscience was somewhat salved: looking at the bill, with its bewildering row of figures (and I defy anyone to multiply 68,380 x 25 in a crowded and noisy supermarket) I felt that it was not enough and

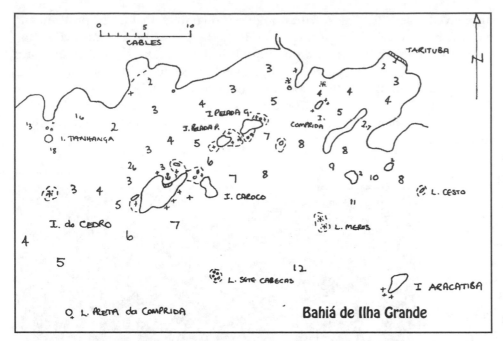

Bahiá de Ilha Grande

realized that the young lady at the till had undercharged us. A short tussle with cupidity and my conscience won — she might have had to make up the difference — so I pointed out her mistake. She looked both incredulous and relieved when I had paid over the outstanding notes.

Having noticed a German yacht at anchor, we were eager to see them, fellow sailors having been few and far between since Salvador. We met them while we were buying the coffee and later that day rowed over to *Tiama*. Helmut spoke perfect English and his mate, Pauline, came from the UK. They too, were pleased to meet fellow yachtsmen and we stayed, drinking tea and wine, until about nine o'clock, enjoying their tales of cruising South America and fascinated by their account of sailing up the Paraná, almost to Bolivia. We swopped books and invited them to dinner the following day. Pauline, came over in the morning: a good and interesting talker, she also came from Lancashire and we had a lot in common. She was a teacher and had always wanted to travel, but at first, even going to the other end of the country seemed rather daring. Then she spread her wings and went to Germany and, emboldened by this success, she eventually went further and further afield and had travelled around China on her own, thoroughly relishing the experience. A `mutual friend' introduced her to Helmut, several years previously and he invited her to join him for a few weeks. Despite suffering very badly from seasickness, which made offshore passages nothing less than Purgatory, she loved the life and never left. They seemed to make a good team and we thoroughly enjoyed their

company. Unlike us, they travelled inland and indeed, Helmut was quite shocked at our narrow attitude.

`But we travel in order to sail,' Pete explained, his tongue only slightly in his cheek.

`No, no, that is the wrong attitude. You must see more of a country when you visit it!' Helmut protested.

`We're all different, Helmut,' Pauline reminded him. `We like to travel inland, but not everyone does and even here, you need spare money to do so.'

In truth, Pete and I are not great travellers and the additional expense is enough generally to deter us, but their tales of the Falls at Iguaçu made them sound very tempting.

`It would only cost you a hundred American dollars,' Helmut told us, `and they are the sight of a lifetime.'

We even discussed it, but we were still recouping the cost of the Seagull and would have had to sacrifice too many other things to afford the journey. Our loss, no doubt, but what the eye doesn't see, the heart doesn't grieve over. I sometimes have the somewhat depressing conviction that Pete and I are really rather Philistine.

We left in the hot sunshine that had been our lot for the past week or so; perhaps we had finally found the good weather. We ghosted to a deserted little anchorage on Ilha Grande, but had to clear out early in the morning when the breeze started blowing in, uncertain of the local weather and worried that it might be a cold front. But it was just a vagrant breeze which deserted us a little later so that was not until eleven o'clock that we dropped anchor off Abraão, Pete's refusal to use the Seagull being more than a little irritating. My temper was not improved when I discovered that all our muesli had gone bad and as Pete is in charge of breakfast, this was his responsibility, so he was really in the doghouse. But in the warm sunshine, such aggravations are soon forgotten and we spent a pleasant afternoon loafing about, doing very little.

Another German yacht came in and we went over to speak to them. Welcoming us aboard, they introduced themselves as Heinz, on the last leg of a circumnavigation, and Katia from Rio, who had joined Heinz for a holiday. Heinz had a wonderful sense of humour, they were good company and spoke excellent English. They had been at Saco de Ceu, which sounded a delightful place and we wondered why they had moved over to the less pretty Abraão.

'We were lying in bed last night and I heard someone moving about in a small boat,' Katia explained. 'I woke up Heinz and told him, but he said not to worry, it would be the fishermen going out. I tried not to worry, but in the end I said that we must move.'

'But why were you worried?' we asked, 'it seems to be safe here and we haven't heard of anyone having problems.'

'It is because I come from Rio,' she replied. 'To live there and survive you have to suspect everyone. It is terrible — even the children are murderers.'

'Children! Murderers! Surely not!'

'Yes, in fact the bad people deliberately use children to rob and to kill because the law cannot touch them. You have heard about the many children who live on the streets and have no homes. They live in gangs and have their own area, each one. Even small children carry guns. I have heard of nine year old children boasting that they have killed someone.'

'But stories get exaggerated,' I protested. 'A nine-year old child in the tale that you hear was probably fourteen or even older, in truth.'

'I know it is difficult to believe, but it is true. Listen, I will tell you a story that happened to a friend of mine, a man I have known for many years. It shows you why when you live in Rio you are always frightened. This man, my friend, is a teacher and he has a nice house out in the suburbs. He came home one day with his family and another friend. Carlos and his family walk into the living room and there are three or four boys, children, with a gun. They are robbing the house and they point the gun at Carlos. "Go and lock up the others," they said "and then show us where all your valuable things are kept." Carlos' friend was delayed for some reason and as he is going to enter the living room he hears these voices, so he stops. He sees Carlos taking his family into another room and the boy with the gun. He goes back to the car in the garage and takes the gun out of it and goes into the house again. Then he enters the living room with his gun and tells the children to hand over their gun to Carlos.

'"OK", says the oldest boy, still only about ten or so, you know, "so you have stopped us, but you will not take us to the police because we know who you are and if anything happens to us, the other boys in the gang will make you pay. They will rape your wife and

hurt your children. You must let us go, but, of course, give us the money first."

'The friend says to Carlos, "Tie these kids up while we think what to do." After this is done they talk about it. What these children have said is true. They will hurt Carlos and his family if he takes them to the police, because even if these children are locked up for a while, others will have revenge. The children are bad boys. They will never be better. They have shot people before. So my friend, Carlos, the teacher, and his friend settle that there is only one thing that they can do. They must take the law into their own hands and execute these boys so that they will not do any more harm. So they put them in the car and drive out into the country and they kill the boys.'

'That can't be true!' We were horrified.

'Yes, but it is! And Carlos was right. These children had already killed, I told you, and would do it again. His family would get hurt and the police could not protect them. Even if they locked up these boys, it would be for only a year or so and then they are out again and full of the bad things that they learn. It was the only answer.'

We had heard of the vigilante groups that roam around Rio shooting the street children like so many rats, but had never dreamt of anything like Katia's story. She told us other tales of the dreadful lawlessness of the city and of how its citizens live barricaded in their own homes, in fear of the gangs that come down from the *favela*, commit their crimes and vanish back among the slums before anyone can catch them; of the children of wealthy parents that have always to be guarded against kidnap; of the impossibility of protecting vast wealth from people who have literally nothing to lose by trying to take some of it for themselves. Placing no value on their own lives, why should they value any one else's?

'So you see,' Katia concluded, 'even here, on Heinz's boat where I know it is safe, I am frightened of any strange sound and only feel safe among other people.' And yet, it is in the cities, among so many people, that the danger lurks, while rural Brazil is as safe as anywhere and the small towns rarely harbour anything worse than a bag snatcher. Stories like Katia's explain why so few yachts visit Brazil, but although we did not doubt their truth, in the six months that we spent there, we only felt uncomfortable in Salvador and Rio and in the latter it was due to its reputation, rather than to any feeling that we had. For all that, Katia's tales made us glad that we had decided not to return there.

We wanted to visit Ilha Jaguanum, where Peter and Anne Pye had spent some time in *Moonraker*, many

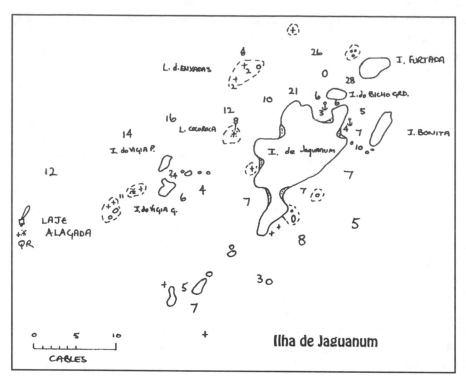

Ilha de Jaguanum

0   5   10
CABLES

anchorage and drank a cup of coffee and, having exhausted the possibilities of Jaguanum got underway for Saco de Ceu, another anchorage of the Pye's, where Heinz and Katia had been anchored. It sounded pretty and secluded and worth investigating. It was pouring with rain, but the pleasant breeze was still blowing and we had a good sail, close-hauled with occasional tacks. By tea time, both rain and more regrettably, wind died away so that progress became slow and painful and, having abandoned Saco de Ceu in favour of Abraão once more, to my astonishment, Pete used the engine for ten minutes so that we got in not long after the sun had set.

There is a path from Abraão across to a bay on the other side of the point and although it was cloudy and damp and did not look too promising, it was not actually raining, so I suggested that we go for a walk. Pete reckoned that the paths would be muddy, which was probably correct, but I was getting fed-up with dull weather and dull sailing. There was no breeze and when it started drizzling again, there was no point in sailing, either, so having cheered myself up by writing letters, we both settled down to a good book for the rest of the day.

But winter in Brazil is not a serious affair and despite it being cloudy, next morning it seemed to be brightening up, so we sailed to Saco de Ceu, which lived up to expectations. The bay was small and enclosed with steeply wooded sides and at one end, a beautiful house almost hidden among the trees. The

years ago. The morning was miserable, grey and drizzling, but with a good fresh breeze from south-west, a rare commodity around Ilha Grande, so we got underway and had a fine sail even if the rain meant that we could hardly see anything. By the end of our stay in this area, we had realized that it was a case of a good sail or admiring the scenery; the chances of enjoying both a decent breeze *and* sunshine seemed virtually nil.

Anchoring in the afternoon, we sat for a little while, comparing Jaguanum, with the Pye's description in *Backdoor to Brazil*. It had not changed dramatically although there were, of course, more houses than thirty years previously. Although there were still showers about, we went ashore anyway, having noticed an inviting-looking track leading into some thick woodland. The trail petered out at some houses, but one to the east went further and was a pleasant walk, possibly continuing right round the island, but the day was getting on and around dusk, we went back aboard to a supper of warming chili.

At the end of the beach was a spring flowing out of a pipe, where people could fill up water containers, have a shower or wash their clothes and before leaving, we filled our water containers from it. Motoring through a gap round the corner between Jaguanum and Ilha Bonita to give the engine a run, we had a look at the

Saco de Ceu, Ilha Grande.

place has a bad reputation for *borra-chudas* and Katia said that she had been bitten, so rather than stay the night, after lunch we sailed for another anchorage. It took ages to beat out of Enseada de Estrela, as there was a lumpy little swell, but then a nice breeze took us round Ilha de Macacos, before dying away so that we had to resort to the Seagull for the last few minutes, to get in before dark.

With fresh food starting to run short, it was time to go back to Angra dos Reis for some shopping and noticing that *Tiama* was at the other side of the harbour, we went and anchored nearby, spending a pleasant evening with them.

Private island near Angra dos Reis.

Talking about the necessity for speaking at least some Portuguese in Brazil, Pete said:

`Annie does all the work as translator. I can't speak a word of Portuguese — or any other language for that matter.'

Helmut was shocked: `You mean you only speak English?'

`Yes,' Pete replied, `and I don't speak that very well.' Pauline laughed, but Helmut was not mollified.

`It is very bad to speak only one language,' he declared, `uncivilized. It makes you very narrow, because when you learn to speak another language, you learn to think in a different way.'

`I'm sure you're right, but I just don't seem to be able to learn. I spent a couple of years in a French-speaking school when I was a little boy, in Montréal. All my classmates learnt English, but I never learnt a word of French and when I was in secondary school in England, I once got a school report where the French teacher wrote: "Peter has been fighting a losing battle and lost"! I'm afraid that I'll have to put up with speaking just English.'

`But you must try. If you try, you will learn.'

I kept quiet. I can stagger along in French and Spanish, but no-one would call me a polyglot and Pete's earlier comment having given me a spurious claim to being civilized, I was not going to jeopardize it. Of course, Helmut was correct and it is our misfortune that English, or maybe American, has become the *lingua franca*, especially of the sailing world. There is no longer any need for Esperanto.

Enjoying the *Tiama's* company, after crossing over to Angra for shopping, we returned to stay and do some work. Pete started repairing the rail that had been damaged in Montevideo and I did the usual washing, typed up notes for the FPI and spent some time with Pauline, discovering a common interest in birds. The weather was fine again, but was very warm and humid and when on Saturday, Pete was ready to glue on the rail, it was really too hot, with the cabin at 84°F and the glue probably the same. That evening, we went over to Helmut and Pauline, where we ate a delicious curry and she showed me the new pressure cooker that she had bought in town. It was well made and of a good size, but I was even more impressed when she told me the price: ten dollars! I needed some spare parts for mine, which had to come from England, and suggested to Pete that we buy one.

`Surely you don't want two pressure cookers!'

`Well, actually, I've sometimes thought that it might be useful because I often use mine two or three times for one meal and the record is five times. I'm sure that I'd make use of two, and even if I don't, my other one isn't working properly at the moment and Mum may not be able to get the spares out to me. I can't live without one and at ten dollars, you can't really go wrong, can you?'

`Well, if you can find somewhere to keep it, it may be worth thinking about. But let's wait until we get the mail.'

`You ought to consider it, Annie,' Pauline said. `Helmut had a huge one on board, which he was always nagging me to use, but it took so long and used so much fuel to heat up that it was hardly worth it. This little one is quite thin and heats up really quickly, which is worth a lot, I think, even if it means it mightn't last so long.'

'My God!' said Helmut, 'Listen to these two! They'll be talking about washing detergents next. And people think that we sailors must be such interesting people!'

After dark we noticed a fire on the hillside, obviously out of control and we worried that it would threaten the houses. It came very close and we could see men silhouetted against the flames, frantically beating at them, trying to establish a firebreak. They seemed to be losing ground, but fortunately it died down of its own accord. Helmut and Pauline told us that such fires are common and usually started deliberately, in the belief that burning off the grass encourages new growth. Apparently they often get out of control and do a vast amount of damage and worse still, the theory is quite wrong as burning the old growth does not help at all.

It turned drizzly again and as we could not work and had been a long time at Angra, we decided to go sailing. Helmut and Pauline were also supposed to be leaving, but there were no signs of life and we suspected that after looking out of the hatch, they had turned over again! In light winds, we had a pleasant enough sail and were anchored at Ilha Comprida by

tea-time, staying there the following day, while rain fell steadily from a grey sky. Pete started making the rucksack for my birthday and I spent the day typing up more notes on anchorages. Next morning, it was still raining and flat calm, to boot.

'Honestly!' I exclaimed, having had a look round, 'it's as bad as England, here!'

'Well, it is mid-winter, you know, and I don't think you'd be wearing shorts in January,' Pete responded.

'True, but the rain's as bad as July in England.' I said, laughing, 'Well, Scotland, anyway.'

'It'll probably clear up tomorrow — it only seems to rain for about three days at a time,' was Pete's prophesy.

A light wind came later, encouraging us to make sail and we anchored off a pretty spot at Ilha Itanhanga, where some lucky people had a beautiful house, but, judging by the number of signs saying 'private,' they did not wish to share their place. It had actually stopped raining by sundown.

As Pete had forecast, Wednesday morning was fine and we took advantage of the relatively cool temperatures to glue on the new length of rubbing strake. A little breeze sprang up and, as there was no risk of putting the rail under, we set off for a new anchorage, but sadly, the breeze soon died away and the rest of the day was nearly calm, any wind we had coming from ahead. It looked a little murky to the north-west, so we sought an anchorage sheltered from that direction and at last a nice breeze allowed us to get to the island of Gipoia once more and we were anchored in a new bay before dark.

Baía de Ilha Grande is a marvellous, sheltered cruising ground, protected by the mainland on one side and Ilha Grande on the other, strewn with numerous islands and indented with many small coves. Less than a hundred miles from Rio and a popular holiday area, it is still largely unspoilt, although reading Peter Pye's book made us wish that we could have been there thirty years earlier. It was a wonderful place to spend several weeks, or even months, with full-blown gales being extremely rare and the only drawback from a sailing point of view was the almost complete lack of wind. In winter, the breezes were supposedly at their best, but unless there was a depression about, the average wind was Force 2 or less. We usually got up with the sun, to make the best of the short winter days, but rarely had enough breeze to get underway before mid morning, so that a run of ten miles was considered a good day. Pete had agonized about using the engine more, hating to motor at the best of times and loth to

Baía de Ilha Grande

spend much on petrol, but in order to explore the area thoroughly, the Seagull was brought into use more often than was desirable.

We set off in a flat calm, with the intention of investigating anchorages on the south side of Ilha Grande, occasionally turning off the Seagull and sailing. An hour or so after lunch, a breeze filled in from the south-east, picking up to about a Force 4 and rounding the western end of the island, it was very choppy with two opposing swells. There was an anchorage that we dearly wished to visit, but if our wind died, we would be unable to motor in the sea that was running. After some discussion, we were forced to conclude that we might be trapped in the anchorage, unable to leave due to calms and the swell, but also exposed to a front. The other anchorages were similarly situated; we would have to leave the south coast for another time and another season. I suggested going back, but Pete thought that the breeze should take us down to the east end of Ilha Grande, which we had not yet seen. The wind backed from south to west and not only continued to blow, but increased so that our original destination may well have been uncomfortable, anyway. Eating supper in the cockpit, we charged along in comparatively rough and windy conditions, but the breeze eased off as we came into the lee of the island. This area being fairly well trafficked, there were navigational lights and also aided by those ashore, we headed for Enseada das Palmas, getting in about half past ten. After anchoring and tidying up, we felt that we deserved a warming cup of coffee and a tot of rum.

We woke to a fresh, sunny day, ideal for walking to the beach on the south coast and we followed a lovely path to a long white beach where we had a picnic. Poor Pete had a rotten cold, which he had probably picked up in Angra, but was still glad to have come ashore. Returning by a different and even more attractive route, with delightful views through the trees, we passed some wild bananas and Pete picked a bunch, while I got bitten by horseflies, wondering if it was an excessive price to pay.

Back at Enseada das Palmas, an Australian boat had just come in to anchor, so we went over to meet them.

`G'day mates, have a beer!' was the greeting. Few things could have been more acceptable on that hot afternoon, so we climbed aboard and introduced ourselves.

Canoe at Enseada das Palmas.

`So you're from the Pommy boat — well, you had to be really. I'm Graeme and this is Erika who is also a Pom. Good to meet you — we haven't seen many other cruisers for a while now.'

This was the Australian boat, *Zarifa*, for which Rudi had been looking in Puerto del Buceo and we told them that we had met.

`I believe that you came round Cape Horn,' I said, `What was it like?'

`Well, I was glad when it was over, I can tell you. We were OK but then we hit a really big storm. The seas were enormous — about fifty feet high. I'm not exaggerating either, we met guys from the *Endurance* who were in the area at the same time and they confirmed it. We spent some time in the Falklands, because we needed to repair the Aries, but we were just so glad when we turned our bows north.'

Graeme was still high on the voyage and we were happy to listen to anything he had to say about an area we were planning to visit.

`My god! What do you want to go to the Falklands for? There's nothing there, it's freezing cold and it blows a gale all the time, mate.'

`Well, I'm looking forward to seeing the wildlife — penguins and so on.'

`Yes, we went to see a penguin colony, but you know once you've seen one, that's it!'

As the afternoon became evening and beers kept coming, Graeme mellowed and showed a different side. I had been fascinated as to why he had attracted Erika, a ravishingly beautiful woman in her early twenties: tall, with black hair almost to her waist. She had had an excellent job in London but, meeting Graeme while on holiday in Costa Rica, had thrown it all up to go sailing with him. She was educated and sophisticated and they seemed like chalk and cheese, but when Graeme started to relax with us, I began to understand it. Like many Australians, he apparently had to present himself as super-masculine, but he was actually an extremely generous and affectionate man, with a good sense of humour. His genuine wish to enjoy our company and his obvious attachment (which he tried to hide) for Erika, more than compensated for his wanting to impress us. Anyway, I reckon that anyone who has sailed a small boat around Cape Horn has something to boast about!

We might have survived the afternoon with dignity intact, if Graeme had not mentioned his rum locker.

`I always have a glass of rum first thing in the morning and last thing at night,' he declared, `and often during the day, too, if I feel like it!'

`That's all right here,' we said, `but how on earth do you manage in places with strict Customs allowances.'

`Oh that's not a problem. I thought about that. In the heads I have a tank and I tell the Customs that it contains oil for my refrigeration system. It holds a couple of gallons and no one ever checks.' His eyes twinkled. `But come and look — it's actually my rum store.'

We went down and examined the innocent-looking stainless steel tank.

`Pass me the bottle, will you, Erika?' She passed over a half-full rum bottle and Graeme turned the tap.

`There you are, see. Good, golden rum. I can even get it in bulk with a discount!'

`Here, Pete, try some and see what you think.'

Pete took a sip, `Very nice. See what you think, Annie.'

`Hey, come on! Sheilas don't drink rum!'

`This one does!' I announced, sampling Pete's and pronouncing it satisfactory.

`I don't believe it! Well, I guess you'd better have your own glass.'

Pete was right, it was excellent rum. But we should not have had it after all that beer and certainly, we should have not had a second glass.

`I'm sure it's doing my cold good,' I recall Pete saying.

We woke up feeling somewhat jaded and with little appetite for breakfast. Late in the morning, Erika and Graeme came over to swop books.

`Here you are — take these!' said Graeme as he came below and passed over a couple of packets. `One of them gets rid of the headache and the other settles

the stomach,' he explained. His kindness was appreciated. It was a rotten day, blowing and raining, and we spent it aboard, yarning, eating lunch and then playing *Trivial Pursuits*.

`Hey now look, you've got a Pom version, so I'm not going to answer any questions on your sports and entertainment.' Graeme declared, as we opened the box.

`Yes, but I may be able to answer them,' protested Erika.

`Play as a team, you mean? No way! that's still two Poms to one. It'd be better to play individually. And I'm not answering any Pommy history questions, either.'

Pete and I were in stitches.

`What's up with you two, then?'

`For heaven's sake Graeme, does it matter who wins?'

`Oh Graeme hates to lose,' Erika said laughing. `He's so macho he can't bear it.'

`Now come on — I only want to have a fair chance.' He seemed quite hurt at the suggestion.

`Play it your way,' I said, `I'm sure you'll enjoy it more, but you've actually got an advantage because I know nothing about sports and haven't watched television for twenty years, so I'm a dead loss on either the "pink" or the "orange" questions.'

The play was dilatory, to say the least, because the questions kept leading us on to topics of conversation until one or other of us remembered what we were doing.

`OK, Graeme,' I said, `your question: "Which island did the Dodo become extinct on?" My God! their grammar is always so appalling!' I didn't even bother to look at the answer.

`Madagascar!' he answered immediately.

`Wrong!' I said, laughing, `it was Mauritius.'

`No it wasn't!'

`It was! Look, it's here, written on the card.'

`Well, I don't believe it. They've got it wrong.'

`Come on Graeme,' Pete expostulated, `everyone knows it was Mauritius.'

`It was Madagascar!'

`Look, I'll tell you what, we'll check in the dictionary,' I said and getting it from the shelf, passed it over to Erika.

`What do you bet?' I challenged Graeme.

`Well, I don't know. Ten thous ...'

`Sweetie!' Erika looked up from the dictionary, her voice was gentle, but her eyes were sparkling. Graeme glared at her. `Don't bet too much!' She showed him the book.

`Well they were in Madagascar, too. They probably flew from one to the other.' This caused a howl of laughter and Graeme was both nonplussed and irritated.

`Come on! What's the joke?' he demanded.

Erika wiped the tears from her eyes. `Oh, Graeme, you're wonderful. *Dodos couldn't fly!*' and we all started off again. We had to smooth his ruffled feathers down again before we could carry on. Pete won the game.

Going into the galley, I happened to look out of the scuttle, only to see that *Zarifa* was slowly dragging. Graeme managed to express total disbelief and shoot out of the hatch at the same time. Leaping into his dinghy, he started vigorously rowing towards his boat, but a moment later, an oar broke.

`Grab one of ours from the dinghy!' Pete shouted. Fortunately they were of a similar length and he got to *Zarifa* without further mishap and was soon re-anchored.

`I can't believe it.' Erika said as we stood and watched him. `We stayed anchored all night and this morning when it was blowing quite hard, but now the wind has dropped and she suddenly starts off. What on earth can have caused it?'

When Graeme returned, he was wondering the same thing. `The only thing I can think of is that the anchor's bent. Maybe that's something to do with it.'

`What type is it?'

`A CQR — but a real one.'

`I remember reading, or hearing, that the angles on CQRs are critical,' Pete commented, `so maybe you're right. It's a bit of a worry, though, when you don't know. You won't really be able to trust it now.'

`We've got another one though, haven't we?' asked Erika.

`Yes we have. And I'll put that out later and change it over to the main chain, when I have the chance.' Graeme said. `Anyway, one good thing — I got the bottle of rum while I was back on board!' The rest of us groaned, but Graeme was made of sterner stuff. They stayed for the rest of the evening and a bite to eat.

The first of August came in overcast, but with a light south-westerly breeze and we got underway mid-morning, sailing past *Zarifa* to say goodbye. Noticing an object on her stern, Pete called, `What's that?'

Graeme replied, `It's a "Sea Squid" — a sort of sea anchor — do you want it? My boat's too heavy for it.'

So we sailed back again and he chucked it to us, while Erika appeared like Venus de Milo, standing in the forehatch, her long hair covering her naked body and causing a passing fisherman to have acute difficul-

ties with his steering. We waved goodbye to each other, thanking them for the *Sea Squid*.

`See you along the way!' we called, wondering if we ever would. We had so much enjoyed them, but a sailor's life is full of such brief encounters. We were touched by Graeme's gift, that knowing where we were bound he had generously thought to pass it on to us.

`It'll be interesting to see how it works,' said Pete.

`I hope we never have to,' I replied.

For an hour or so we romped along, but then the wind died, so that we drifted all day, anchoring about six o'clock in pretty Santana Bay. After supper, we each started a new, big paperback, courtesy of *Zarifa*.

Ashore, the following morning, we discovered a few houses, some shy people and a delightful little church: it was a charming spot, but as there was a decent breeze for once, we continued on to Angra, for shopping. I had caught Pete's cold and was feeling less than energetic, which may explain why we did not do all that we wanted in town, but Pete selflessly suggested buying some of the special sausage for *churrascuro*, easy for me to cook for dinner. When I reminded him that we had no barbecue, he replied that it would probably fry quite adequately!

Tuesday, bright and sunny, saw us finishing the shopping. We inquired about mail and, hoping for some birthday cards, I was particularly disappointed that there was nothing for us. On the way back to *Badger*, we stopped by a Dutch yacht, *Do-Do*, that had anchored the previous night. Busy working in the cockpit, Bettina paused to chat and discuss plans, her skipper, Hank, being ashore. They were hoping to go through the Beagle Channel, but might well visit the Falklands first. She seemed full of enthusiasm for the idea and as I was still more than a little frightened at the thought of going south, I wondered anew at these bold and dauntless spirits. *Do-Do* was a classic steel yawl and very beautiful, but the doghouse had large windows, which looked rather vulnerable to our eyes. Bettina seemed a lovely person: it was a shame that we never crossed tacks again, although we passed them a few days later, both going in opposite directions.

Having thoroughly explored the area around Angra, we cleared for the other end of the bay and Paratí, leaving in very light winds, but lovely sunshine. We had guacamole for lunch, one of five large avocadoes that we had bought for sixty cents. The breeze was fickle and finally failed us before our anchorage at Punta Grossa and we had to motor in, yet again. To our surprise, there were quite a few yachts, but they were all local and none of them seemed occupied.

Even Brazil suffers from winter and Wednesday was the fourth miserable, dull day in a row and as it was flat calm, Pete suggested staying to sew my rucksack, but later, a breeze filled in and we sailed, stopping at an island called Ilha Sandri for lunch. Despite the breeze continuing, the skipper wanted to carry on sewing, so we stayed put. We had a grand view of the nuclear power station, but apart from that, it was a pleasant, if not quite birthday-class anchorage.

As well as being my birthday, the next day was also our wedding anniversary and I had a day off, loafing and reading, which felt like a holiday, while Pete put the finishing touches on the bag. The sun came out occasionally and we had lunch in the cockpit, treating ourselves to a bottle of beer each. Our celebratory dinner, preceded by rum punch, was avocado stuffed with egg mayonnaise, chick pea and aubergine stew and, a real treat this, *strawberries* and coconut cream. We did not stint on the alcohol either, with `champagne' and Uruguayan red wine. It was a veritable feast.

This seemed to mark the end of the poor weather and the next day saw us sailing with a gentle, breeze in warm sunshine to a place by the name of Ilha Cedra, recommended by Helmut and Pauline. We arrived mid afternoon at what proved to be my favourite anchorage in the Ilha Grande area. The atmosphere was Bahamian as we sailed into a sheltered bight, behind a low island edged by pure, golden beaches and in the shallow water, the colours were exquisite. A house stood on the island, its walls washed in faded pink and apparently unused. Two or three fishermen in small boats, were tending their nets but towards evening they pulled away leaving us alone. At sundown, the haze cleared, giving a view of distant mountains while beyond the beach, the dense woodland provided roosts for a host

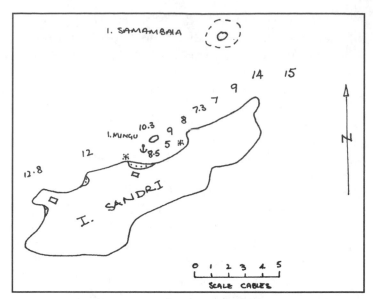

of birds: royal and Cayenne terns, frigate birds, snowy and great egrets and night herons. It was a lovely spot.

Having found such an attractive harbour, we spent another day there to do the washing and the only unpleasant event was being bitten by borrachudas, nasty little insects, similar to sandflies, but with an even more vicious bite. Such a beautiful day demanded beer with our lunch and later, a yacht sailed in, thoughtfully anchoring some distance away. We drank a sundowner in the cockpit, admiring our lovely setting.

When a light breeze came in after breakfast on Sunday, we got underway. As we were sailing slowly out, the skipper of *Biba*, our neighbour, called to us recommending one or two places to go. We tacked over to hear him more clearly and misunderstanding our intentions, he put out fenders so we sailed alongside. William, from the United States, and Ana introduced themselves and invited us aboard, proving very hospitable and friendly. Offering us a beer, they asked us where we had been and all about our way of life;

Ilha Cedra proved to be a favourite anchorage.

towards lunchtime, Ana made *kibe*, hummus and pita bread for us all. We talked of boats and anchorages and William gave us a chart, so that we could explore the eastern end of the bay more thoroughly.

`We must pay you for it,' protested Pete.

`No, no. I don't need it. I always buy a new one every year, so I've got several spare. I'd be pleased to think that you managed to see more of the area because of it.'

They pressingly invited us to stay with them at their home, but sadly, the problems of finding somewhere secure and affordable to leave *Badger*, combined with the fact that we needed to start working south fairly soon, prevented us from accepting their offer. William was shortly to retire and they were thinking of running their boat on charter, combining a cruise aboard with some time spent at their house, which was in a beautiful area within reach of Rio.

`I feel,' said William, `that a lot of people from the States would like to be shown round Rio by someone who knows the city, could guarantee their safety and speak their language. We know the good restaurants and the places to go and when they're tired of Rio, we can come here and sail for a while.'

`It sounds wonderful,' we agreed. `There must be lots of people interested in such a holiday.'

`Well, I thought so, too, but my ads in *Cruising World* don't seem to have met with much response.'

`That's interesting' Pete said, `because we have friends in the UK, who run a charter boat, and they discovered that they get a much better response from advertizing in newspapers than the yachting magazines. In fact one of the Sunday papers did an article about them, and afterwards, they were flooded with enquiries. Maybe that might be worth a try?'

`I hadn't thought about that, but it sounds like a good idea. Maybe I could have the same sort of feature as your friends did — one of my classmates at Yale writes for the *New York Times* — we'll offer him a sample holiday, should we, Ana, and see what he can come up with?'

The breeze was calling, the sun high overhead and we had to go our separate ways, but as we cast off our lines, they passed across four chilled beers.

`You said that you had no ice. Enjoy these!'

Already full of beer, we managed another one each as we sailed along; ice cold beers are a rare treat.

`We must save the other two,' said Pete. `We'll drink them when we get to the Antarctic.'

`What? Oh yes, "Antarctica" beer! But the Falklands are hardly the Antarctic, Pete.'

`Oh, well,' he said, suspiciously vague, `but we should save them for a special occasion, I think.'

`OK, I'll put them away.'

And we did drink them on a special occasion, much as Pete had hinted, but that is another story.

A steady breeze gave us a delightful sail to the pretty island of Ilha do Pico, and we congratulated ourselves on leaving the best part of the Bay until last, for in this area we were in sight of the distant mountains, there were picturesque islands everywhere and fewer houses. A perfect morning of light easterly breezes had us underway just after sunrise to visit an island called Araujo, which we walked round. I christened my new bag, putting in my purse (you never know), camera, spare film, sun screen and insect repellant. Once ashore, we also put the rowlocks and keys in it, as always in Brazil, locking up *Badger* and securing the oars in the dinghy with a padlock and chain when we went ashore. I am sure that this was rarely necessary, but on the other hand, it seemed unfair to put temptation in people's way.

The island was unusually high and with a clear path to follow, it was an excellent walk with good views. After rowing back, we set off for Paratí enjoying the interesting pilotage round the numerous shoals and islands in this part of the Bay. An astonishing house of yellow domes and turrets and flying buttresses, stood on one island, looking like something out of a fantasy. At anchor off Paratí in time for tea, we noticed a yacht flying the Brazilian flag coming towards us and watched while they picked up a nearby mooring.

`Her name's *Hummel*,' I commented. `Must be a German.'

A little while later, we were invited over for a drink. Jorgen and his son, Claus, were Germans and with them was Nelson, their Brazilian paid hand. Jorgen had come to Brazil thirty-seven years previously, after serving in submarines during the Second World War and added the interesting comment that most submariners had disagreed with the extremes of the Third Reich, `but we were sailors in the German Navy and it was our duty to obey orders and to defend our country. It was not a good time.' It reminded me again of the appalling waste of such wars where good and decent men on both sides end up killing each other.

Claus was fascinated by *Badger*, wanting to build his own boat and go cruising and asked us all about her. They were very friendly and hospitable, Jorgen even inviting us to his *fazenda*. We should dearly have loved to have accepted, but were almost relieved that we could not, because it was impossible to repay such hospitality. Disappointed in our refusal, they insisted

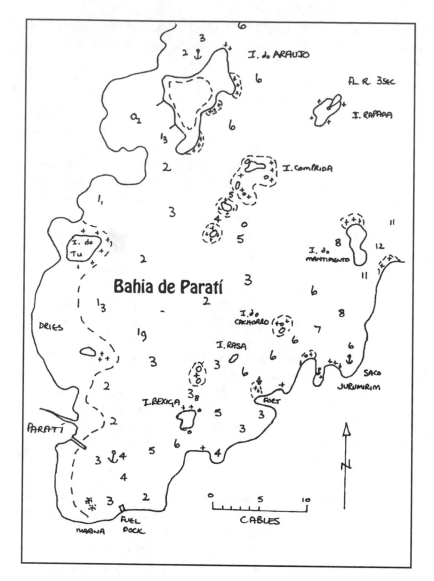

Bahia de Paratí

are tourist shops, *pousadas* and restaurants, too, it feels like a real town. A strange little church stands near the beach. At least, the church is quite normal, but what is peculiar is that instead of the usual flight of steps up to the door, there is a steep slope down, which is the more extraordinary because Paratí's streets flood at spring tides. We had our doubts about the theory that this was a primitive sanitary system, because the tidal stream in the streets is insufficient even to take back the sand that the flood brings in, let alone to carry away other débris.

The streets were fascinating and admiring the splendid, old architecture, I felt that while Salvador may have many more buildings of the Colonial period, Paratí's were much more pleasant to wander round, not in the least because the town was so small and so safe. Only twenty years ago all trading goods were carried by water or on pack animals, but the new road has changed everything, bringing holidaymakers from São Paulo and Rio. However, the City fathers ban motor traffic from the historic area and tourism, while obviously important to the town's economy, had not yet spoilt its atmosphere.

Being tired of waiting for VISA transactions in Brazil, we had bought dollars in Uruguay and went to the bank, to change some. They would only handle sums over fifty dollars, so against all advice and common sense, we changed it on the street. As the young man offered us a fair price, did not haggle, was on the main road in broad daylight, and did not try to entice us down a back alley, it did not seem unduly risky. Although he obviously had no intention of cheating us, we felt rather pleased with our daring: we are not generally such intrepid travellers.

Assuming that our mail was waiting in Angra and, with the prevailing light winds, judging that it would take quite some time to get back there, we investigated taking a bus. Unfortunately, the cost was twelve dollars and as we were still having to watch our money, we unwillingly accepted that we would have to sail back, having first seen as much as we could of this end of the Bay.

Back on board, with indications that a cold front might be on its way to make our anchorage uncomfortable, we left for Saco Jurumirim, which on the chart, looked very sheltered. It started to rain and although

instead, that we share their dinner with them, even though I suspect they went on short rations to do so. It was cooked by Nelson and we ate in the cockpit, while he dined below. He had been with *Hummel* since they first owned her and spent more time on the boat than in his own home. Apparently happy with his lot, a few days later, we saw him washing her down, whistling away to himself, seemingly delighted to be left alone with `his' boat once more.

Claus and Jorgen came over next morning, to have coffee and look at *Badger*. Claus was very impressed, especially with the amount of room below and took a note of the designer's name and address. They were due to drive back to São Paulo and before they left, we were once more invited to go with them.

Paratí was supposed to be something special and, going ashore, we found it a lovely, unspoilt town. UNESCO money has helped restore it, but because most of the buildings are simply homes, although there

the wind only increased to about Force 5, we were pleased that we had left Paratí. The rain soon turned to showers and the most recent of these had just died away to be replaced by bright sunshine, when we sailed around the rocky headland into the anchorage, to be met by a picture-postcard scene. High hills covered in lush and dripping vegetation lined two sides of the almost rectangular cove and at the end was a pristine little beach, overhung by shaggy palm trees, with a barely perceivable house beyond this. We anchored near two yachts already in the bay and Pete looked through the binoculars at them:

'I thought so,' he observed. 'They're *Paratí* and *Rapa Nui*. We've seen the names — they've both been to the Antarctic, sailed by a Brazilian — he overwintered in one of them. I think his name's Amyr Klink.'

I gazed at the two boats in silent wonder. At present they rested quietly in the tranquil, tropical harbour, with the wind from the cold front blustering overhead, but they had seen very different harbours, very different winds. What tales they could tell! In imagination I saw one frozen in, surrounded by snow-covered, hummocky pack-ice, a screaming blizzard turning the air white and, below, the solitary man listening, feeling the shudder of the boat assaulted by the furious wind, aware of every flex of its thin, steel plating, with only his own ardent spirit to encourage and reassure him.

Above and left: peaceful street scenes in Paratí.

Below, Paratí's pretty little church.

Seeing these boats was a reminder that it was almost mid-August and time for us to go south, but firstly there were jobs to do on *Badger*, the most important being to scrub the bottom. After consulting the calendar for the state of the moon and the charts for a suitably sheltered beach where we could dry out, Pete suggested that Ilha de Cotia looked like a good bet, being well-sheltered and fairly steep to.

It was with regret that we left the perfect harbour of Saco Jurumirim, to sail round, but with a light wind and no hint of swell, it was easy beaching the boat, and we could fit her legs, calmly and without hurry. Several days were spent here, scrubbing off, antifouling and at last finishing the repair on the rubbing

strake. At low water, we were completely dried out and excavated under the wing of the keel to paint the bottom. Safe as houses, we could take off the sails, check them over and make good any chafe. Because Pete had been unable to do all that he wanted in our anchorage near Florianópolis, he was pleased to be able to work on them at leisure. But a serpent lurked in our Eden in the form of *borrachudas*, whose bites drew blood even from Pete's leathered hide. One mosquito bite can keep me awake half the night, so those from the *borrachudas* almost drove

Ilha de Cotia

me demented and Pete nobly did the bulk of the work on the beach, but his legs were a dreadful sight by the time he had finished.

We were lucky with the weather. One day looked like rain, but I `took a chance' and varnished, which usually guarantees a downpour and to my amazement, it even brightened up later.

A Brazilian yacht sailed in during our stay, whose skipper, Mark, had been at school in the United States and spoke perfect American-English. He invited us over for beers on his boat one night and ate curry with us the next. Mark intrigued us. He had long wanted to go cruising and was obviously a clever business man, because at the age of forty, he had just sold a restaurant, which had realized enough for him to retire in some style.

`When are you setting off, then?' we asked, `and where are you heading?'

`Well, I dunno. That's the problem. Now that I *can* go, I'm not sure if I want to. Not on my own, anyway, and I don't know anyone I want to go with. I may use the money and open another restaurant. I'm not sure if I'm really ready to go cruising, yet.'

Although to us, who strove and struggled for years to get away on a minuscule amount of money, this seems an almost incredible attitude, at the same time, perhaps we do understand. The power and excitement that come from setting up and running a successful business, must make cruising in a small boat seem rather small beer and then there is the temptation for those with money to spare, to spend it on making the whole thing easier. But if you make it too easy, you take away the challenge: outboard motors, electric windlasses and marinas reduce the physical labour;

Barbecue at Ilha de Cotia.

144

a powerful engine can often compensate for poor judgement; radar and GPS take the strain from thick visibility; HF radio and a dedicated emergency transmitter ensure that someone will bail you out if everything else goes wrong. None of this encourages self-reliance and therein lies the greatest satisfaction of cruising. In the old days, it was `a truth, universally acknowledged' that the object of the exercise was to go out, to stand on your own two feet and do everything yourself, but old-style voyaging is a totally different ideal from the retirement home afloat.

On Wednesday we floated off again, hastening away from the *borrachudas* to Parat-Mirim, where we would stay and go for a good walk, but a breeze springing up during the night persuaded us to try sailing to Angra. Needless to say, the breeze died, but fortunately, we had the sense to sail back to Parat, although Pete was disappointed about missing his walk.

Again, we discussed getting the bus to Angra, doing what we needed and then continuing on south and eventually, on the dubious grounds that we had promised ourselves a bus ride in Brazil and the one from Parat to Angra was said to be very scenic, we managed to justify the expense.

Although it was a dull day, we enjoyed the ride, a run of an hour and a half with some quite spectacular views of the bay, from an elevation that showed it laid out below like some beautiful mosaic in shades of blue, scattered with green and golden islands. To our delight, the mail had arrived. I had asked my mother to send me a new valve for the pressure cooker, but `the man in the shop' had told her that I could not possibly need one and persuaded her to buy the wrong part, which meant that my pressure cooker was still useless. As I was cursing the shopkeeper for an interfering busybody, I remembered seeing a Brazilian pressure cooker like Pauline had bought, in a shop that we had passed. We went back, had a look at one and confirming the price of ten dollars, bought it. I was delighted, because with a diet based on dried beans and brown rice, the lack of a pressure cooker means much longer cooking times, thus using considerably more paraffin.

We took full advantage of Angra and staggered back to the bus station, well laden down, arriving at Parat to find that the tide had flooded the streets, so

that we had to do some paddling, not to say wading, while trying to keep all our shopping dry. Back on the beach, we discovered that some kind soul had moved *Skip*, who had obviously been trying to commit suicide, to a safer spot. We had sausage, cauliflower and new potatoes for supper, the vegetables being cooked in the new pressure cooker, which was voted a complete success.

As Saturday was gloriously sunny, we took advantage of it to record some of Parat's more outstanding buildings on film and discovered that the town was dressing itself *en fête* for a *pinga* festival (*pinga* being the polite term for *cachaça*). Although

Setting up stalls for the pinga festival.

tempted to stay and enjoy it, we would have lost another couple of days and it was time to move on. Pete bought petrol and topped up the water, I washed the fruit and vegetables and put them away and then we had a pleasant, gentle beat to Parat Mirim.

The following morning, while I was doing the washing, a man paddled by in his *canoa*. We greeted one another, commenting on the cold weather and about an hour later, I saw him again, this time coming over to *Badger*. Stopping alongside, he passed me a lovely, yellow flower that he had picked and with a shy smile at my startled thanks, he sat down and paddled off again. I was very touched by this gesture — the only face of Brazil that we ever saw. Crime and violence were so many stories, the kindness and friendliness were our reality.

With the washing pegged out to dry, we could at last go for Pete's walk along the river. We talked about the mail that we had received and an idea in the Junk Rig Association newsletter, for a side-by-side, junk-rigged, Wharram-designed catamaran. The concept was tempting, not that we have any complaints about *Badger*, but we like to discuss schemes for Another Boat. Who knows? One day we may want to spend a year or so in the shallow Bahamas or circumnavigate in the Trade Winds. Or, perish the thought, we may lose *Badger*; but these discussions always make us end up appreciating her anew and unable to visualize a boat that would suit us better, all round.

The following morning in rain and cloud, we sailed to Praia Grande, an anchorage that Chris, at Jacaré, had recommended to Pete and the last one we intended to visit in Baía de Ilha Grande. We rowed ashore to find the waterfall that Chris had mentioned and had to wade across a quite deep and fast-running river. We felt like explorers. The waterfall was lovely with rapids that reminded me of the Duddon Valley, in Cumberland, a favoured picnicking spot for my family when I was a child. Somehow the atmosphere was very English in spite of the palm trees and the `beastly *borrachudas*.' It made me feel quite homesick; I wondered why I was in such an alien place as Brazil, dreaming about the fresh greenness that is England and forgetting, for a

while, the noise and overcrowding that eventually overwhelm me whenever I go `home.'

Back on board with the sun brushing the horizon, melancholy thoughts were banished by the simple pleasure of an avocado at supper and a glass of wine or two, because it was Sunday.

At half past ten, I was sitting, relaxed, replete, reading and vaguely contemplating going to bed when Pete said:

`There's a bit of a breeze sprung up. Do you think that we should get underway for Ubatuba?'

Knowing that this was a strictly rhetorical question, I sighed and put my bookmark into place. Before I had even found a sweater against the cool of the evening, Pete was on deck and shortening in. I hung up the wine glasses in their rack, climbed out on deck and prepared to get underway. My own doubts as to the breeze were realized when we came to a halt half-way down the bay, where, with not the faintest indication that the breeze would return, we dropped anchor, but the greater swell had us sleeping in the saloon until dawn, when a light wind returned. I offered to make breakfast and treated us, or at least myself, to poached eggs on toast, Pete believing that the subtleties of poaching eggs require the skills of a *real* cook. The breeze was fickle and we got nowhere fast for hours and hours with a vile swell that nearly

Waterfall near Praia Grande.

drove me mad, but a miserable breeze filled in later, from ahead, of course, bringing Scotch mist towards midnight. As ever there was some compensation: we were visited by dolphins and although we could not see them, we heard them talking back and forth. They must have been different from previous visitors, because instead of squeaking, they buzzed. I wished they would return in daylight so that we could make their acquaintance. In the small hours of the morning, the Scotch mist turned to real rain and continued for most of the day, but it cleared at sunset, revealing the land and we eventually anchored about two in the morning.

The sun had returned when we got up, to find ourselves in an attractive anchorage, with very different scenery from around Ilha Grande. We walked into Ubatuba, a nice little town, but rather pricey, but whether this was because it was a holiday resort or because we were now officially in Southern Brazil, we were not certain. Not a few of its inhabitants regard Brazil as two separate countries: indeed there is a movement for the South to secede. We gathered that, historically, the wealthy lived in the South and made their fortunes in the North, but nowadays, the North does not have so much to offer. Coffee and sugar are all very well, but more money can be made from manufacturing, and the people of the South are of European descent and more amenable to working in factories than are the Indians and Africans of the North. Now, the North is seen as a drain on the wealth of the South and many Southerners would like to be rid of it.

We left later on, with a fair breeze, which true to form, went and headed us, but it was pleasant sailing for all that. We had coffee; we ate lunch; I put out the fishing line and Something took our penultimate spinner; we put the last one out on a wire trace, but caught nothing and at five o'clock, we brought to, off Ilha dos Porcos.

This was a delightful spot in spite of there being a prison ashore and we could not help feeling that many of the prisoners were probably better off 'inside' than they were in their *favela*. At any rate, to be incarcerated in such beautiful surroundings must make it more bearable. Sitting in the cockpit, admiring the scenery and eating pre-prandial popcorn, Pete bit down on an unpopped kernel and cracked his tooth. Having been granted very good teeth by a benign Providence, I thought that he was exaggerating, but when Pete showed me the lump that had come off, I was quite concerned.

'Leave it for tonight,' I said. 'We've got Peter's dental repair kit on board, but I think that we should wait for daylight. I'll get it out tomorrow and glue the broken bit back on. It isn't hurting is it?'

'No, it just feels a bit strange and sharp, but I don't want it to get infected or anything.'

The following morning, I read the instructions in the Dentanurse kit. It all seemed fairly straightforward so, following them to the letter, I stuck the piece of tooth back on and it promptly came away. I tried again and it stuck a moment longer before coming off. Disregarding finesse, I mixed a larger amount of the glue, which squodged up nicely when I pushed the broken bit on top, and stuck a little longer. Unfortunately, when it came off this time, Pete swallowed it!

'Oh honestly, Pete, you don't make things any easier, do you?'

'I couldn't help it,' he protested, 'I didn't even realize that it had come off until I swallowed it.'

'Anyway, this dental kit's useless!' I exclaimed in disgust. 'Next time I write to Peter, I'll tell him about it — he could probably make up something better himself.'

I had another look at his mouth. 'The glue's still there — it's a bit like a crown. Let's keep that on to protect the tooth until we can get to a dentist. It should be all right — if it's not painful, it can't be down to the dentine or anything.'

Later, this piece came off and Pete tried underwater epoxy, which stuck for several weeks.

Next day, we set off for an anchorage on the island of São Sebastião, but when our jolly little breeze died away, we carried on. The highlight of the day was catching two or three glimpses of a La Plata River Dolphin, which looked like a delightful little animal; they are not common, so I was thrilled to see one. Our decision to continue paid off, with a breeze that returned, faltered, but never quite died. With our curry at supper, we had sliced banana — one of those that we had picked at Ilha Grande a month ago, and at last ripe. After a sunny morning, we ran into fog in the afternoon, the first that we had seen for ages, but certain of our position and with no shipping around, it caused us no real concern. It rose later, leaving quiet, cloudy conditions. The sun broke through about noon, bringing a fair wind and the birds with it: yellow-nosed mollyhawks, brown boobies, white-chinned petrels, occasional black-browed mollyhawks; a strange combination of tropical and temperate. On Sunday we crossed the bar and sailed up to Ilha do Mel, a National Park in the Baía de Paranaguá, about an hour after sunset. Not much of an anchorage, shelving from forty feet to four feet in no time at all and pretty open, too, but in such light conditions, we could always clear out if necessary and were glad to get the hook down.

We had read that Ilha do Mel was a place that should not be missed because there were some good walks and `excellent beaches.' Not being a beach person, I felt that I could do without them, but the idea of a good walk was appealing and we planned one for the morrow. The morning broke bright and sunny, but a decent breeze persuaded us to go on up to Paranaguá — we could always visit Ilha do Mel on the way back. It was perfect, beating up the river, with the spring flood under us, but just off the docks, a blast of wind hit us and we tore on, frantically dropping reefs while trying to locate a way into the town itself. The only option seemed to be to back track and go in behind the docks and we tacked up some narrow creeks, at every bend expecting a cul-de-sac, suddenly to find ourselves heading towards an anchorage off the town, where we smartly dropped the hook.

Cup of tea in hand, we gazed around our anchorage, one of the most interesting that we have visited. On one side, and hidden behind tall reeds, was a large and apparently populous island; upstream was the entrance to another creek and *canoas*, some paddle and others motor, were constantly entering and leaving. Their cargoes were many and varied: gas bottles, bricks, fruit, potatoes, passengers and fish. On the other side lay the town, its low quayside, with steps at intervals, lining the river and a road along it, with all sorts of vehicles: ancient jalopies, donkey carts, wagons and wheelbarrows, passing to and fro or stopping to transfer their loads. Facing onto the quay were bars and shops, where the proprietor stood, whiling away the time between customers by watching the activities on quay and river and hailing his acquaintance. It was a wonderful spot.

Rowing ashore, we pulled the dinghy up a flight of steps and went to look round and clear in. The Port Captain was conveniently situated on the waterfront, the *Polícia Federal* in town not far off, but the *Receita Federal* was miles away, by the docks. Time was getting on, it would probably be shut, so we dismissed it and wandered round, finding a supermarket with some good buys and many interesting shops along the waterfront.

We had thought to stay at anchor and do some jobs, but the next day was overcast and miserable. Talking over our plans for the next few days, it occurred to us that with shops being so close, we could stock up here with milk, flour, oil, and so on, especially as the *Real* supermarket had some good offers and sold brown flour and distances were shorter than at Florianópolis, the obvious alternative.

First we had to see the *Receita Federal*, but they were shut, so we went shopping and did very well, finding cheap butter and two-kilo cabbages at twenty-eight cents each in one shop, a sack of potatoes at thirty cents a kilo and onions for the same price in another. After bringing it aboard, we had lunch and Pete went back to the Customs and although there had been some showers, did not take a jacket and returned looking like a drowned rat. That night there was a terrific thunderstorm, whose initial gust had us anxiously checking our bearings: the weather was `unsettled', as the forecasters say.

One of my jobs was to salt the butter we had bought, which came in plastic containers. I scraped it all into one bowl, added ten grams of salt to every two hundred of butter and put it

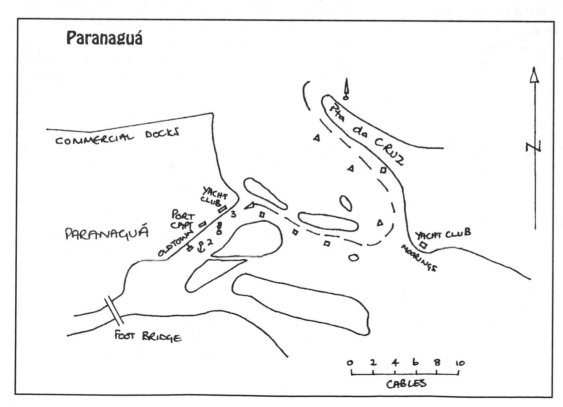

back in the containers with a layer of salt on top; it kept for many weeks.

The next day, discovering a shop selling spares for my new pressure cooker, we bought some gaskets and a couple of new safety valves. The shopkeeper looked a bit surprised at the latter asking if I had problems with them and when I replied that I wanted them `in case' obviously thought that I was prudent to a fault.

It took us until tea-time, to stow everything the following day and the lazarette was bursting with food, a sack of onions and one of potatoes on either side of the companionway ladder, the rest of the potatoes in a locker and the onions in baskets in the lazarette.

I would have liked to spend a day sitting on deck watching the world go by at Paranaguá, but there were still places to visit before our visas expired and late afternoon saw us underway for Antonina. With a fair breeze, we carried on after dark, anchoring off an island in a strong tidal stream, just in time for another thunderstorm.

Having lost his barque, *Aquidneck*, on the bar at Paranaguá, Joshua Slocum had taken his shipwrecked family to Antonina and built the *Liberdade* to take them back to the United States. Joshua Slocum, the first man to sail around the world on his own, is of interest to all sailors. We have a particular interest in the *Liberdade*, however, because Slocum chose to take his family home in a junk-rigged dory, essentially the same as *Badger* and so we wanted to visit Antonina. One of the ferry boats at Paranaguá was called *Aquidneck* and we wondered if her skipper knew the story behind the name.

Our chart was totally inadequate, this far up the river, and Pete did not want to go close to the town.

`I'm sure it'll be all right,' I said. I am always optimistic about such things when I sense that the alternative is going to be a long, hot walk.

`I don't want to go much further, Annie. There doesn't look anywhere to land and it shows a rock and shallow water on the chart.' The skipper can be irritating. At times he scares me to death with his lack of caution, but then suddenly chooses to act with an almost excessive prudence, but I could not really argue, because if we had difficulties, we could not back-track against the powerful flood tide. We ended

up anchoring off a small village some two or three miles from Antonina.

We waited on board until after lunch, hoping the rain would stop, but when the weather showed no signs of improving, we donned our oilskins and went ashore, walking along a cobbled road along which very little traffic passed. The buildings were largely turn-of-the-century, with little done to them since and it

Main road, Antonina.

seemed quite natural to be overtaken by a horse and cart, but there were some motor cars about, one of which stopped to give us a lift. Antonina was an interesting town: beautifully restored in some parts, totally decrepit in others and Slocum would still have been able to find his way around it. Although on a nice day, it would have been attractive and photogenic, it was rather depressing in the prevailing cold and damp, but we were pleased to have been there.

Saturday was another cloudy, cool day and we headed back downstream, much cheered by seeing some of the tiny little dolphins known as Tucuxi. We also enjoyed looking at all the ships alongside the docks, or anchored and awaiting their turn, and trying to identify the new flags of the old USSR. Needing to get on with our jobs, we had to forgo Ilha do Mel, intending to press on to São Francisco. I was looking forward to this, because Pauline had described the area as full of marshes and mangroves, with exceptional bird life; it sounded a pleasant place to stop while we prepared *Badger* for the Southern Ocean. The breeze picked up about tea-time and as the anchorage at Ilha do Mel looked uncomfortable, we felt quite happy to pass by.

`We'll stop there next time we come to Brazil,' Pete promised, with a laugh.

With an onshore breeze and the ebb tide, the bar was quite rough and although it is now buoyed and dredged, it could still be very unpleasant and it is not difficult to understand how Slocum's barque was overwhelmed here. Once out of the channel, we had dinner and I turned in. When Pete woke me, he said:

`I've re-read the *Pilot* and I reckon the current in the channel out of São Francisco will too much for us to make up against. It's narrow and even on neaps, it runs at three or four knots and there's no slack water, except at high water springs. And it says the entrance isn't passable with fresh north-east winds and it's blowing about a 4 from north-east, now.'

I was so disappointed, but without a powerful auxiliary, I realized that it was not even worth trying.

`Porto Belo looks like a possibility, but if that's no good, I'm sure we'll find somewhere else,' Pete told me.

Picnic lunch near Porto Belo — rather cool!

`I hope so — surely there must be somewhere to stay safely for a few days. I feel like the Wandering Jew!'

The day broke overcast, but soon brightened up and we caught a fish, but it was too small to eat, so wetting my hands, I took it off the hook, placing it in a bucket of water to recover. When it started swimming about, I held the bucket at an angle until it jumped back into the sea and swam off none the worse for its adventure. A brave wind wafted us on our way, `wing and wing'. For once we risked waiting until we were anchored to have dinner and got away with it, drop-

ping the hook just in time for a sundowner. Porto Belo seemed to be well-sheltered, with a narrow entrance between quite high cliffs, partly blocked by an island. We anchored at the north-east end, near a small yacht club marina, protected from any cold fronts that might come through.

Waking to a bonny day, we set to on our jobs: washing; unbending the mainsail; checking over and varnishing the battens; repairing the saloon post at the deckhead where the glue joint had cracked with the pressure on the topsides as we bashed our neighbour in Montevideo; filling and painting the damaged cabin sides; painting the outboard bracket; making waterproof shut-offs for the ventilators in the galley and heads in anticipation of the Roaring Forties, etc. We also discovered the drawback of Porto Belo, for next door to the yacht club was a fish plant whose ice machine made the most appalling racket all day, but otherwise, we had no complaints, working until seven in the evening, to take full advantage of the fine weather.

Tuesday was a holiday, with quite a few boats coming and going to the Yacht Club, but the fish plant was shut and mercifully quiet. A couple of days later, a cold front came through, proving the anchorage to be good, with a moderate amount of rain but not so much wind as usual. Being well into September, the sting was going out of them.

Porto Belo was about half an hour's walk away, a nice, clean little place, with a varied selection of bars and restaurants attesting to its popularity as a holiday resort.

We took Saturday off, sailing *Skip* across the bay to have a barbecue on the beach. A motor boat named *Maiorca* steamed by and the man on board complimented us on the dinghy's pretty rig. `Here you are,' he said, leaning over the rail and giving us each a cold beer.

We enjoyed our picnic, but got chilled when the cold breeze picked up, finding us in T-shirts and shorts. We had just got back aboard, when we were called ashore.

`Where you come from?'

`England.'

`All the way in *that*?' The comment is well meant, but always makes our hackles rise.

`Why yes. She's a fine boat.'

`Yes, but so small.'

`Not when you have to work on her!'

`I believe you! We do not see many visitors, but we want you to know that you may use our jetty. We will give you four days here, if you want. There is two and one half metres along the dock here. Please feel free to use our club, the showers, fill with water. Whatever you want.'

`Thank you. That is most kind of you. We appreciate it, but we were hoping to leave tomorrow.'

`That is a pity. But if you decide to stay longer, please come alongside.'

Going back to *Badger*, I commented, `It's a bit different from Florianópolis, but then I suppose that no-one's cut and run yet.'

Later on, we had a chat to the people on *Maiorca*, Claus and Tania, interesting people, Claus having a prosperous business nearby.

`I do quite well,' he told us, `but we have so many problems with taxes, with the government and their rules and regulations. Our politicians are all corrupt, as I'm sure you know.'

`It seems to be the same the world over,' I said. `Whenever you speak to anyone, from whatever country, they all complain about their politicians. I suppose that anyone who *wants* to be in power is almost by definition, unsuitable.'

`Yes, you are right. There should be some way of training them. A qualification, if you like. They could be tested, pass or fail. In the south, you know, we pay all the taxes and it is spent up north where people don't work.'

`But we heard that there are no jobs.'

`Oh there are jobs all right. But people want too much money, they don't want to work anyway, most of them. And the government does not care about us, the people who make the wealth. I keep out of politics, but a lot of people in business think that we should have the military back in power. I agree.'

`The military? You mean a dictatorship?'

`If you like, maybe it is. But at least when the military run a country you know where you stand. There is order and the rulers are not corrupt and getting rich as quickly as they can. Our army is disciplined, you know. It's not like some of those Third World ones you hear about.'

Claus, and no doubt many of his friends, genuinely felt that the military would do a better job of running his country than the democratic government did and other people told us that the Brazilian army was well-run. If they took over, maybe they would have the country's best interests at heart. The British, with their well-developed sense of fair play, feel that everyone should have a democracy, but if the citizens do not also have a sense of fair play, democracy may degenerate into mob rule. It is rather arrogant to impose our way of government on another country because we feel it is best. Who knows? Maybe the military in Brazil would be a benign dictatorship: the ideal form of government. Or maybe not.

Tania was interested in our way of life.

`When did you leave England?'

`Well, on this voyage, just over a year ago.'

`*This* voyage? You have made others? How long have you been sailing?'

`Since we got married, more or less.'

`And when was that?'

`1975.'

`1975! But that is nearly twenty years! You mean that you have been married for twenty years? That is incredible.'

`But a lot of people stay married even longer.'

`Not in Brazil,' Tania stated with assurance. `No-one stays married for twenty years in Brazil. Look at me. I have been married three times already and Claus twice!'

`Three times! But you don't look old enough.'

`Ha! You can make a mistake very easily when you are young you know. But how can you stay married for so long? *I* never could. I would get bored with someone after all that time!'

I stole a look at Claus, but he seemed quite unperturbed by this announcement. Tania was gazing at us both, shaking her head in astonishment.

`Twenty years. That is truly incredible.'

While we were on board, another man, Vitellus, came by and asked us to visit him on his yacht and we went along and talked about cruising. He was interested to hear about our long passages because, like many yachtsmen, he dreamed of taking off into the blue one day and, as a surgeon, had hopes of being given a sabbatical year. He invited us to join him and his three-year-old son, Lucas, for a *churrascaria* at eight o'clock and we accepted with delight, agreeing to meet him at his boat. Excited at the prospect, we had glorious, really hot showers at the club, before treating ourselves to a drink in the cockpit in the quiet warmth of the evening. Just before eight, we duly went ashore, but there was no sign of Vitellus and after waiting half an hour or so, we gave up. Perhaps he had been called to the hospital for an emergency and had tried to call us on VHF, but his dinghy was inflated; he could have come out or sent a message to us. We were disappointed, for each other as much as ourselves and going home, we changed back into our usual clothes and I cooked supper.

We set off for Florianópolis the next day. I was worried about staying there because the anchorages were exposed in a cold front, but at least for our first night, we found somewhere sheltered in the northern bay. The following morning we ran down the sound, hoping to anchor in a bay north of the huge suspension bridge, connecting the *Continente* with the island, but it had a nasty tide rip and no protection, so we went and anchored off the Yacht Club, protected from the northwest wind. Having cleared out at the *Polícia Federal*, we did some more shopping and, even more heavily laden than usual, caught a bus and were back about sundown. A fisherman came down and chatted to us as we were loading up the dinghy, a pleasant man, and we asked him if the beach was a safe place to leave the dinghy. `Não problema,' he assured us, there were usually fishermen around, who would keep an eye on it and no-one looking to steal anything would come to this beach — there were too many people about.

My lists of provisions to get us to South Africa, were fully drawn up in the knowledge that buying groceries in the Falklands would be an expensive business and fresh food difficult to obtain. We could top up in Uruguay and Argentina, but Brazil was cheaper and it was better to rely on getting things here than in Uruguay. Several trips were needed to carry the seventeen kilos of oranges, three and a half kilos of carrots, four kilos of green peppers and ten dozen eggs, which at sixty-five cents per dozen and huge, too, were a good buy and unlikely to go off in the cold waters we would soon be entering.

There were a score or so of wooden sheds on the beach, where fishermen kept their gear and nets and a vast number of cats that presumably lived off fish waste. One drizzly afternoon we were pulling the dinghy up the beach and heard a kitten mewing. The poor thing was wet and bedraggled having obviously wandered and got lost, but was very friendly and tame and all for following us, when I put it down near the other cats. I was concerned that it would wander off again; Pete was more concerned that I might take it back to *Badger*, but in the end, common-sense (that most boring of virtues) prevailed and I was relieved when later on we saw it playing with some other kittens.

With most of the food bought, we now purchased fleece material to make me some trousers, a T-shirt, paint, paintbrushes and petrol; alcohol for pre-heating the cooker and *cachaça* for warming ourselves and twenty-five metres (and one for luck) of twenty-five

millimetre polypropylene rope, in case we needed strong docklines in Stanley.

By Thursday morning, we were about stocked up and spent up and went ashore with our last few hundred thousand *cruzeiros*. Crossing towards the town centre, we saw a *Cesto de Povo* and went to investigate. Everything was priced at twenty-two cents a kilo, which was incredible value and, as we still had almost four dollars in hand, we bought a total of seventeen kilos of fruit and vegetables including tangerines, aubergines, courgettes, tomatoes, green peppers, pineapples, avocadoes, spinach and bananas. Fortunately, we had taken all our bags ashore and could just about carry it, spending our last pennies on two more oranges.

As we put everything back into the dinghy, our friend on the beach warned us that it was going to blow hard from the south. Having a touching and totally unjustified faith in the locals' ability to forecast the weather, we were a little shaken at this, but as the anchorage was exposed to the south, we had to leave, anyway.

The skipper wanted to leave at once, to clear the Island by dark, so I persuaded him to go north about, which would make it easier for me to put everything away than if we were beating, and avoid the risk of having to negotiate both strong wind and tide through the narrows, maybe in the dark. In the end, far from howling from the south, the breeze disappeared and we anchored for three hours to eat dinner, salt down some peppers, and put the rest of the grub away.

The cloud clearing and a south-west breeze setting in, we set off for Uruguay, a pleasant gentle start. Standing under the pram hood watching the sea enfold us once more, I reflected that yet again I had wasted an appalling amount of nervous energy worrying about chimerae: there had been no wind while we were in Florianópolis.

Chapter Twelve

With light headwinds and sunshine, we relaxed, recovering from the busy times in Porto Belo and Florianópolis and dining on salad, chicken and cauliflower soup, and bananas, revelling in the abundance of fresh food on board. Overnight, drizzle set in, but the wind freed, at last letting us lay our course. I re-read Weston Martyr's *The £200 Millionaire* and we discussed how closely the philosophy of the character in the story coincides with ours. We first read it in 1982, and wonder if we would have done things differently had we come across it sooner. An inspiring little tale, it gives me fresh enthusiasm whenever I read it.

The wind picked up to Force 6, it clouded over and turned into a rough and very black night, a great contrast to the last couple of months' weather, but by dawn, the wind had eased off again and *Badger* was under full sail in bright sunshine, when Pete woke me.

In spite of seeing two big flying fish, the birds were indicating the presence of cold water, for instead of boobies, we saw storm petrels, white-chinned petrels, Cape pigeons, great shearwaters and yellow-nosed mollyhawks. I became very fond of the attractive little Cape pigeons (a type of petrel).

It being a Sunday, we had rum punch before lunch and two each, to use up the oranges, which were of disappointing quality. As some of the other fruit was likely to get overripe quite quickly, we were having delicious fruit salads of banana, pineapple and orange for breakfast. Out at sea, radio reception often seems better, and I could enjoy the *Short Story* and *Letter from America* on the BBC. Although I long ago rated our cheap, digital watch as gaining three-quarters of a second a day, I pick up a time signal most nights, generally listening to the news bulletin that follows and recounting the headlines to Pete so that we stay abreast of current affairs. With a quarter-hour of news being sufficiently depressing I try to find a time signal that precedes one of these programmes. Sometimes I wonder why we bother, being unconvinced that the world is a better and happier place because we know the details of man's inhumanity to man and of his cynical disregard of other living things. `Where Ignorance is Bliss 'tis Folly to be Wise.' We hardly ever listen to the radio in harbour, disliking the mindless adverts and `music' that punctuate most radio stations and, apart from feeling vaguely guilty, never miss being out of touch.

Lightning and a falling barometer had me worrying, but the wind was from astern and only touched Force 5; the cloudy day was vastly improved by seeing my first wandering albatross, with its impressive wingspan. A kittiwake is a small bird, compared to a great black-backed gull; a mollyhawk dwarfs the gull in the same way and the wandering albatross makes the stately mollyhawk look insignificant. Close-hauled in a rough sea, we had to eat our lunch from bowls and it was difficult sleeping with the noise and motion. It was becoming distinctly chilly and we needed more bedclothes; we had entered the Falklands Current. I watched for Wanderers, sitting on the board under the pram hood, but although none appeared, there was generous compensation in the other birds, soaring and swooping, wings held stiffly to harness the blustering wind and use it to glide effortlessly over countless miles of ocean. I sighted an Antarctic fulmar, the silver-feathered sister of our cherished companions of the North Atlantic: graceful and exquisite. There were so few birds in Brazil that I could not get over this feast.

But it was cold. I changed the menu from salad to chili and broke out warmer clothes for us. Pete filled up the porridge container. We were used to the warmth and although the thermometer was reading 55°F and we were sleeping under the duvet, I was still too cold to sleep and asked Pete for a hot water bottle. In the morning, despite the sunshine, we dressed in sweaters, trousers and *socks*. To need so many clothes at such a low latitude was quite a shock and must have been due to the very cold water. I was beginning to wonder how we would cope in the Falklands.

We had seen a corvette and several fishing boats; at the change of watch during the night, Pete had pointed out two warships nearby, one of which he suspected was an aircraft carrier and this morning, a frigate, *F 42*, 'pinged' past us. We heard them again several times, but soon the navy disappeared, leaving the merchant ships and ourselves in peace.

On Wednesday afternoon we were back in soundings and the seabirds deserted us; the wind and sea had died down, we were again under full sail and even laying the course. I was busy making the Argentine flag, because once we were in harbour, I probably would not have time and we finished the last of our Uruguayan wine, which had been a good investment, hoping that we could replace it in a couple of days. We continued to bound along with a fine breeze and at breakfast, dared to suggest that we would get in; by tea time, it was clear that we would and at nine o'clock we were dropping the hook in our old spot off Punta del Este, sea lions cavorting around as we tidied ship. After eating a bowl of soup, we both read for a while, savouring the quiet and lack of motion.

When we went to clear in on Friday morning, the two pretty girls at the desk seemed to be quite shocked at the idea of us sailing so early in the year. After strolling around window shopping, we posted our letters, changed money and bought fresh milk and five litres of wine — *suelte*, of course. While Pete went for paraffin, I put away shorts and T-shirts and pulled out our woollies.

Now that we were back in Uruguay, Pete put in for a barbecue, so we went and bought the best part of a kilo of meat for just under two dollars. Being English may have something to do with it because in England, it is usually a disaster to plan a barbecue in advance, as doing so just about guarantees rain. The same still holds true for us, even in countries with much better climates and this occasion was no exception, with Sunday coming in grey and breezy, later turning to rain. Although the glass was high, we went to check for a forecast because we had developed a great deal of respect for the weather in the Plate estuary. There did not appear to be anything nasty about, so we cleared out intending to leave after lunch. It was still raining when we went back to *Badger*, so we fried the meat and had our 'barbecue' anyway. With popcorn and rum to start, tons of meat, bread, coleslaw and wine, it was a real blow-out. For dessert we each had a banana and rounded it all off with a tot of brandy. It was a celebration after all: exactly one year since leaving Falmouth.

After Pete had washed up, we left for Puerto del Buceo with the forecast north-easterly wind. It soon headed us, bringing fog later and although at first we had the current with us, even that turned against us so that we did not arrive until mid afternoon. A man in a dinghy was photographing us as we entered and after clearing in, we went over to visit a Nicholson 38, wearing the Red Ensign because we saw the dinghy astern of it. The photographer was on board with the owner, who was from the States, with an Argentine wife and baby. We never discovered why he was British registered; it seems to be something of a flag of convenience these days. The owner chatted to us, but did not invite us aboard. He had spent a lot of time in the Southern Ocean, on bigger boats, but sadly was not as forthcoming as most cruising people; we would have been interested to talk about the places he had been. After we went

Puerto del Buceo, Uruguay.

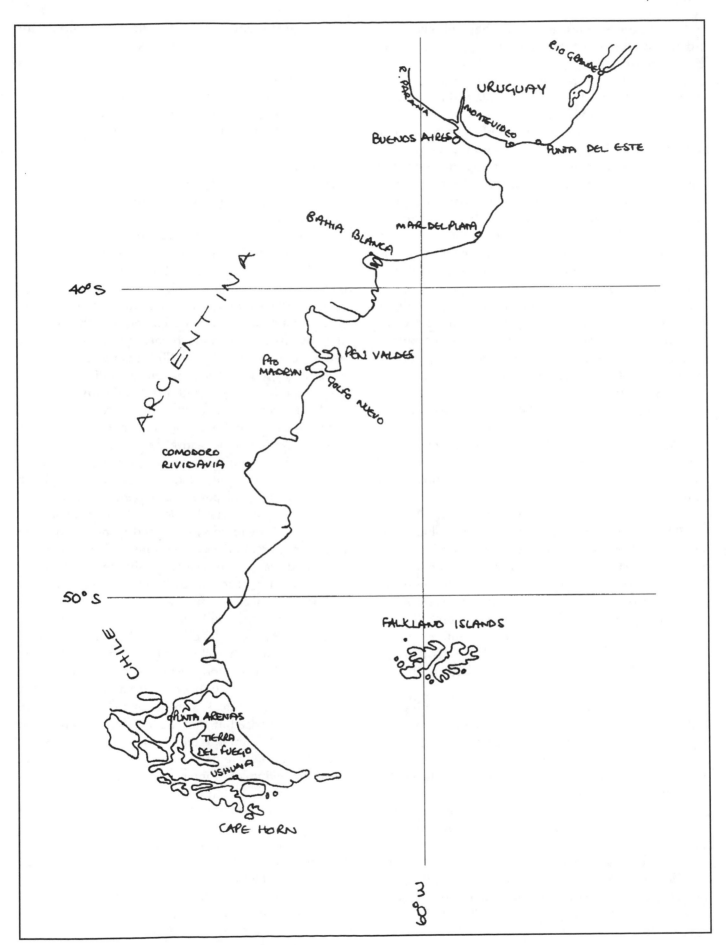

back to *Badger* we moved over to the wall where we had stayed on our last visit, which was just as well, as it blew up later.

One of the well-known French charter boats, *Kotick*, who plies his trade in Patagonia and the Antarctic, came in while we were at Puerto del Buceo and we spoke to them briefly. They were re-rigging the boat and a couple of days later she sailed for the south.

With the normal jobs and shopping to do, we stayed about a week, enjoying the usual mixed bag of weather. One of our projects was to finish up the pilotage notes that we had been doing on South America, to photocopy what we had done and send them to the Club, keeping my much-corrected originals. We found our notes on Buceo useful, with the days of the market up in town, where we could top up our egg supply, buy some cheese for me and replace the oranges that had gone bad. We sterilized several five litre jerricans again and Pete went into Montevideo to fill them with wine. While there, he could not resist the incredibly cheap fillet steak, so that night we had another feast: popcorn, of course; garlic bread; fillet steak à poivre vert; strawberries and cream; coffee and brandy.

Monday was the first sunny day for ages, so we went into Montevideo to do the photocopying. As we were walking, Pete suggested giving Buenos Aires a miss.

`It sounds like a really big city, not like Monte, and if that's the case, we probably won't be able to see much of it. For a start, the Yacht Club is a long way from the centre, which seems to be well spread out. Argentina doesn't have a reputation for being cheap, so we'll end up spending a fortune on buses if we want to see anything of the place. Besides, you don't like big cities. The other drawback, is that it's a hundred miles up the Plate and back again, which means that we won't be able to see much of anywhere else in Argentina.

`Hmm, I wondered when you'd be coming up with some good line to put me off. I knew that *Kotick's* departure would set your feet itching — it's not so much that you don't want to see Buenos Aires, you want to set off south. I must say that I don't fancy the idea of the trip up and down the Plate, but I was quite looking forward to going to B.A. because of the people that we would know there, like the chap from *Nora* and Marta and Alberto.'

`Yes, but the trouble is that unless we actually see them at the Yacht Club, we'd have to 'phone them up and then they'd probably end up having to fetch and carry us. The other thing is, if we don't go to B.A., we can spend longer in Mar del Plata, which is a lot smaller and probably more interesting. They don't get so many foreign yachts there, either, so we'll probably meet more of the locals.'

`Yes, that's true. And you're right about the difficulty of seeing anything of the city anyway — if we wanted to. In truth, I'm not sure that I'm interested in doing the tourist bit. It's funny though. We didn't have time to go to Buenos Aires last time we were in the Plate and now you'd rather press on. It looks like we're doomed not to go there. OK. We'll give it a miss, then and carry on south.'

We enjoyed our walk into Montevideo and found a photocopying place for the FPI notes. Having had dismal results at similar establishments in Brazil, we first checked the quality and, finding that it was first class, had the job done. The price was very reasonable, at six dollars for over a hundred and fifty sheets. In an attractive park, we had lunch, then did some shopping, had a film developed by the Chinaman in Calle Andes, who did a good job last time and who did an equally good job this time and, with great difficulty, we managed to get some flints for the galley lighter. My dictionary had the word, but no-one understood what I was after, until a lady overhead me at a tobacco kiosk and directed us to an old-fashioned, proper tobacconists, who sold us what we needed. Then we changed our money for Argentine pesos and, having six Uruguayan pesos left and knowing that Pete had been enjoying the odd piece of dead cow, I decided to buy him some more. Finding a butcher, I told him we had exactly six pesos and wanted entrecote. He sharpened his knife, selected a piece of meat, cut a slice off and it came to 5.84 pesos. I was impressed.

It had been a busy day and about a mile from Puerto del Buceo, it clouded over, the wind picked up and it became rather chilly. Having detoured to the Club to look at the non-existent forecast, I was really cold by the time we got back aboard and glad to warm up by cooking the steak with egg and chips for dinner. We were surprised at the quality of the meat, which was not much inferior to the fillet and half the price.

`It's as well we don't live in Uruguay,' Pete said, `you'd get fed up of eating meat.'

I laughed. `I don't think so. It's still expensive compared with beans and we couldn't afford to eat it anywhere near as often as we have been lately. But I dare say that we'd manage it once a week. We don't live too badly, really, do we?' I added as Pete topped up my glass of wine.

`It makes you wonder why people bother working,' was his response.

In the morning, I made bread and marmalade and filled up the ready-use pots in the galley, while Pete sorted out charts. He was standing at the chart table and noticed that the solar panel was not charging and checking everything through, he eventually discovered some corrosion. As a last resort, he covered it with plastic contact film saying: `This will never work.'

Impatient to be off, we went to see the forecast, but there was none up and the port was closed.

`Come back later,' suggested the *marinero* at the desk. We had lunch and then returned and found a good forecast pinned up, but the port was still closed.

`Por que no es possible para sortir?' I asked.

`No se.'

I explained that we were keen to leave and that the forecast gave no reason why we should not. He called up his bosses, who gave us permission to go, so he filled and stamped the appropriate documents and we went on our way, rejoicing. We had a mass of ropes to sort out and then Pete could not break out the CQR from the dinghy so we had to take *Badger* to the anchor and winch it up. It was in an area that occasionally almost dried out, but fortunately the water level was high. A man on the quay was obviously hoping that we would require his help, so we started the Seagull and I asked him to let off the line. He did so, I pulled it in and the engine stopped. We swung to the main anchor, luckily hitting nothing and got the engine going again after a few minutes of fruitless swearing. We motor-sailed out of the harbour just before seven on a lovely evening with a gentle breeze and, putting *Badger* on course, we ate a late supper and settled into our sea-going routine.

We pottered along all night and the following day was hot and sunny, with the same light, variable breezes. I did some bosun's jobs and although Pete's repair to the solar panel was a success, we decided to use the Walker log until the battery was topped up. I checked it, moving the weight where it had chafed the line and then put it over, losing the whole lot because the hook to the log had come loose. The skipper was not pleased.

After dark, the breeze picked up a little and steadied down. Some seals followed us for a long time, racketing about, chuffing and splashing and the next day I was delighted to see penguins around again. In the

hope of arriving at Mar del Plata in daylight, we used the Seagull for a while when the wind headed us and died away, but our progress was so slow, that guessing at a foul tide, we gave up, somewhat consoled by catching our first fish in months. Coming into the harbour, we were surprised to see *Kotick* tied up, just outside the yacht basin. Not quite sure where to go, we motored slowly along and when a swing bridge opened at our approach, went through and were signalled to a berth in the Yacht Club Argentino. By the time we had tied up, the Club employees had gone home, so we went and asked Alain on *Karadec* where we could find the *Prefectura*, discovering that he had

Yacht club at Mar del Plata.

been forced to stop in Mar del Plata due to engine problems and was worried that the delay would make him late for his charter. We did not envy him.

We had no joy at the *Prefectura* and, although we would have to return during normal hours, were relieved to have avoided a mass of paperwork. Back on *Badger*, I cooked our fish and a great pile of chips for supper and feeling tired, we turned in early.

The following morning, as we were walking out of the Club, one of the members stopped and asked if we were from the visiting yacht and could he help us at all. When we mentioned that we were on our way to the *Prefectura*, he offered to give us a lift, but unfortunately, his car ran out of petrol before we left the Club, the petrol gauge being out of order. Apologizing profusely, he gave us explicit directions and told us that the Health and Immigration offices were on the way.

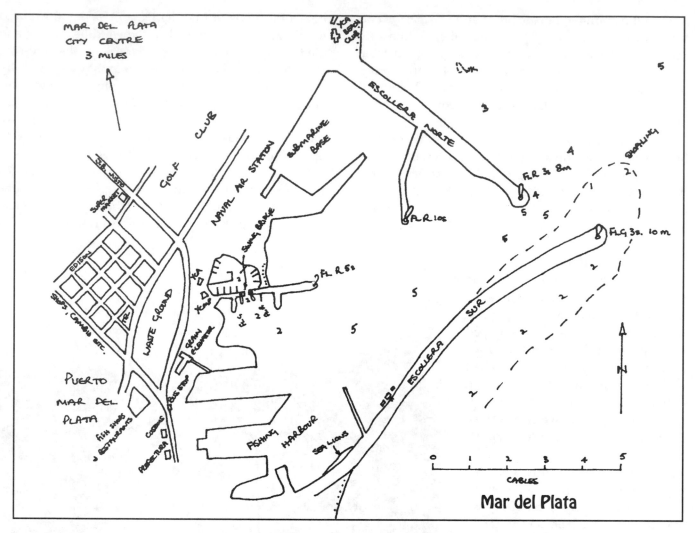

Mar del Plata

They were shut, so we went on to the *Prefectura* and after about an hour, were sent back aboard to await the doctor. Not having too much faith in his imminent arrival, we got on with some jobs.

In the afternoon, the Club Nautico boatman came by to chat with us. He had been a merchant sailor for many years and spent time in both England and the USA and spoke very passable English. Atilio was quite a character and claimed that he was the man who brought the boogie-woogie to Argentina.

'See! I can still dance it now,' he said, giving us a spirited rendition in his dinghy, which was mercifully stable. 'It was during the Second World War and we take many cargoes to the States in those days. I go to the clubs and learn how to dance and when I come back to Argentina, I show them all how to dance to the music that the bands are playing. You should see me dance in those days! Hey! You heard of Vito Dumas, hey?'

'Why yes! He was a marvellous sailor. We have his book on board.'

'You do, hey? Well, me I know Vito Dumas, we are friends, him and me. When he comes down here I drink with him and, I tell you, he enjoy a drink. Like you say, a good sailor! Ha ha! Once, after one or two, he set off out to sea in his boat, but you know what it is like, a few drinks and the hot sun and Dumas he goes asleep. Yes! he does! Just up the coast he end up on the beach. He has to get some fishermen to pull him off. But he is a good man Vito and yes, a good sailor, too. You ever see his boat? *Dios mio*, I would not sail round the world in that. I like your boat though, lady. You must come and see mine. She is just like yours. Not so big, no, but like yours. I give you a photograph. You must come up and have *asado* with me some time hey? Now I better go, I don' belong yacht Club Argentino, I work for Club Nautico. *Hasta luego*.' He rowed off, calling: 'Don' forget — I'm the man who bring the boogie-woogie to Argentina!'

The doctor never arrived, of course.

The following day, unable to go anywhere until the doctor had cleared us, we carried on with our jobs. We had lunch and still there was no sign of the doctor.

Later in the afternoon, Alain came round saying that the *Prefectura* had called him on the VHF, unable to get through to us and wondering why we had not completed clearing in. We told Alain that the doctor had not arrived and he offered the use of his VHF so that we could explain the situation. We all went round to *Kotick*, Alain called the *Prefectura* and they promised to call back. About twenty minutes later they did so, informing us that the doctor would be coming at seven o'clock and while we were waiting, Alain gave us a beer and we talked about his engine and chartering around Patagonia. He and his mate, both Bretons were very likable men. After the *Prefectura* had called back, we thanked Alain and returned to *Badger*.

We had just got back on board when two people from the Club office came to tell us that the doctor was coming and would we please fill in five forms ready for our departure. At half past seven, fed up of waiting, I started cooking dinner and the doctor arrived about half an hour later, stayed five minutes while he filled in the forms and without looking at anything, ourselves included, he left, telling us to go to Immigration, who would have someone in the office until nine o'clock. I turned off the cooker, we got our papers together and found that the Immigration office was shut. We traipsed along to the *Prefectura* and after some telephone calls, they told us that the Immigration officer would be there at nine o'clock. To our amazement, he actually arrived and after half an hour's form filling, asked for thirty-two pesos and twenty cents, to be paid either to the bank or to him. The fee should have been sixteen pesos, but our query was met with the bland explanation of `overtime.' With us, we had a twenty, a ten, a five and a single one peso note and when Pete offered him these, he took thirty-one pesos, put them in his pocket and without giving us a receipt, shook our hands and ushered us out of the office. Thirty-one dollars worse off, and we still had to complete clearing in; the Customs were next. I finished cooking supper and we turned in.

One of the few advantages of being alongside is that hoses and fresh water are generally available, and on Monday morning I took advantage of these to wash down the boat, after which we warped her right round, to make it easier when we came to leave. The Customs were closed — it was a Public Holiday.

Concerned as to the stresses on the running rigging in the Southern Ocean, we checked it over and although most of it was in good order, we thought it prudent to change the halliards, which are spliced to a fitting at the top of the masts; it can be embarrassing if they come adrift in the middle of the ocean. Several people came by to chat and come aboard and one of them, Rolo, was very keen to see below, but on his way to another boat for lunch, so we suggested that he return later. He arrived with José, who had offered us the lift to the *Prefectura*, and we asked them aboard for afternoon tea. Rolo owned *Malon*, a handsome forty-six foot, wooden ketch that we had been admiring at the end of our jetty and turned out to be a real anglophile. He had been educated at Cambridge (it was a little while before we realized that it was a school that he had attended and not the University) and had been bowled over by all that he saw. He owned a Triumph TR7 motor car for general use and also had an estate car for carrying around his lovely golden labrador. Dressed in a fine, wool sweater and corduroy slacks, sandy-haired with a neat moustache, he looked the complete Englishman and was obviously flattered when, referring to his fair colouring, I asked him if he was of British ancestry. By no stretch of the imagination could I be described as a fervent patriot, but I felt absurdly pleased to find someone with such a high opinion of my country. Our offer of afternoon tea could not have been better directed and it was satisfying to be able to do it properly with crockery cups, saucers and sideplates, teaspoons, sugar bowl and spoon, milk jug, tea pot and cosy, warm scones, butter (in a dish) and home-made jam. Rolo obviously thoroughly enjoyed the whole ceremony as did José. The Club had made us so welcome, that it was a pleasure to return some hospitality.

We talked about famous sailors that had been to Argentina, of which there were surprisingly few until the recent media-inspired races, and mentioned that we knew of and greatly admired Vito Dumas.

`It's unlucky to say that name!' said Rolo and, twisting sideways, put his hand in his pocket.'

`What do you mean? What are you doing?' asked José.

`I am turning over my keys, to undo the bad luck!' Rolo replied.

`What nonsense is this?'

`Oh José! Surely you know that to say that name is bad luck?'

`I have never heard this! Vito Dumas was a great man — the best sailor that this country has ever known. What is this about bad luck?'

Rolo explained that, when he learnt to sail in Buenos Aires, it was a generally held superstition that it was unlucky to pronounce the name of Vito Dumas and that if someone did so, you had to turn over the keys in your pocket. José, quite a lot older than Rolo, seemed offended that such a notion should be held about this Argentine hero. It was an interesting side-light and later on, Pete and I conjectured whether the superstition had been deliberately planted in order to stop people discussing this highly individual person and perhaps getting the idea that there was something to be said for jumping into a yacht and sailing around the world. Such concepts would not have suited the old regime and even now, yachtsmen are kept on a very tight rein and hedged about with restrictions before they can go sailing. Not only do they have to have qualifications, but they cannot even leave the harbour unless the boat is inspected, has a functioning VHF that is always switched on and informs the *Prefectura* of its movements. Our friends explained that this was for security: `If a ship is in trouble, then the *Prefectura* knows that you are nearby and can ask you to give assistance.'

`Yes, but in the UK, they put out an "All Ships" call on the radio, which has the same effect.'

`But you need a license before you can drive a car.'

`But a car is a lethal instrument — you can kill someone driving carelessly. It is difficult to do a lot of harm at five knots.'

`The *Prefectura* keeps an eye on us.'

`We would rather be independent.' And therein lies the difference, not only between the Latin and the Anglo-Saxon, but also in the way that we want our country to be run. Although we spent only a short time in Argentina, it appeared that the majority of people had no understanding of democracy, as we see it, and no desire for the liberties that we take for granted. South Americans, at least to our eyes, prefer a strong government. At that time, there was a lot of discussion as to whether President Menem should be allowed a second term of office. The Constitution, drawn up perhaps, with the thought of dictators in mind, wisely prevented a President from putting in for more than one term, but it was being argued that Menem was the only man who could do the job, although it seemed unlikely that no other fit person could be found, from a population of some 33,000,000. José, a true democrat who took his right to vote seriously, certainly was not too happy about this and other ideas that were being debated and would soon be put to referendum. Rolo and José were cultured and articulate men; it was a delight to exchange ideas with them and learn about their country and we felt distinctly gratified when José, as they left, promised to ask his wife to arrange an *asado* for us.

It had been misty and cool all day and in the evening we lit the heater and hot pot was very welcome for supper, but the next day came in with hazy sunshine. At last we saw the Customs, who gave us a form to be filled in by the YCA. When we showed it to Toni, the marina manager, he explained that the form ordered the YCA to take responsibility for our yacht for the duration of our stay and that they would refuse to sign it. That was understandable: why should they? But it did not help us complete the entry procedures. The morning was now well advanced and having been invited on to *Malon* for coffee, we shelved the problem while we paid our visit. As we went on board, Rolo, explaining that he runs a nursery, gave me three pots of herbs: tarragon, chives and marjoram. They were lovely, but I could not imagine what I was going to do with them down in the Falkland Islands. Over coffee and croissants, we mentioned our problem with the Customs and to our embarrassment, Rolo promptly gave José a call on the VHF, who soon arrived, breathing fire and brimstone. He explained that the Customs were convinced that every foreign yacht came to Argentina with the sole intent of offloading all their gear to Argentine yachtsmen and had insisted that any foreign yacht visiting the YCA should put down a bond to the amount of its value. The YCA had protested that this was completely unacceptable and the Customs has responded by saying that the YCA was responsible for ensuring that no visiting yacht sold any of its gear while on Club premises. This, of course, was also totally unacceptable, and they were now at stalemate. The Swiss couple that we had met in Puerto del Buceo had mentioned this, saying that they would not visit Argentina because of the cost of the bond to Customs. We were in something of a quandary and when José offered to come round to the Customs with us and sort out the problem, we accepted gratefully, although we felt very embarrassed about the inconvenience that we were causing.

`No, no, you must not think about it. We are delighted to have you here. We have so few foreign visitors. But that is why the Customs do not know what to do. They are not used to yachts entering here. Rolo! I will see you later about when we go sailing, eh? Now come, let us go to these stupid people and tell them to fill in their pieces of paper.'

José was a man in late middle age, patrician and with great dignity; we had the impression that he had come down in the world. He talked of all the places he had visited, of holidays in London and Paris and of the estancia that his family had owned when he was young, of the racing yacht he was given for his twenty-first birthday. Now he no longer owned a boat and the car he drove was the most disreputable wreck of an Argentine-built Fiat. We climbed into this and, after some hesitation, it deigned to start and we rattled round to the Customs. Most of us tend to be over-awed by Government officials, but José was a true hidalgo and told them that the YCA would *not* be responsible for us, emphasizing his point with a clenched fist pounded on the counter. The cowed official was not inclined to argue and this seemed to be an end to it.

José turned round and with gracious courtesy, ushered us out of the office.

`These people do not really understand,' he explained. `The Yacht Club Argentino is going to welcome visitors and that is all there is to be said. I am going to collect my wife from where she teaches. Will you come with me? I do not think that you will have been able to see anything of Mar del Plata yet.'

`Why, thank you, that's very kind. We'd enjoy that.'

We drove along and José pointed out places of interest to us.

`My wife is an artist and she teaches, in the mornings, at her studio,' he explained, stopping the car. `Come and see, I think you will like the building, it is very old.'

He showed us round the outside of a handsome, sprawling, single-storey building, slightly shabby, but the more charming because of it. His wife seemed shy and said little to us. The car was ailing, so José gave it a rest at his house and asked us to come in and have a glass of wine, but we accepted somewhat diffidently, as Alicia was obviously not prepared for guests and probably had plenty to do. The house was small, but beautifully furnished and with what even I could see was some fine art: paintings, collage and sculpture were all represented. I asked Alicia if they were her work. She seemed pleased at my attempts at Spanish.

`Uno o dos,' she replied.

When we came to drive back, the car's problems seemed terminal and we offered to make our own way. José seemed quite upset, but we explained that we enjoyed the exercise and had been unable to leave the Club precincts since we arrived, so a walk would give us chance to see a little more of the town. Still looking doubtful, José accompanied us to the end of the road and gave us directions. `We'll see you tomorrow, will we?'

`I think so. We are sailing on *Malon* if the weather is fine.'

We strolled the couple of miles back to the Yacht Club, looking around and getting our bearings. After a bite of lunch, we went to see if we could find a lady to whom we had been given an introduction by a shared friend and walking through town, we came to the con-

clusion that Argentine women must have a passion for sweaters, because we passed countless shops selling them in all colours, styles and varieties of wool. A pretty, rose pink, angora turtle-neck caught my eye, but Pete continued remorselessly on his way. José had told us that the road we wanted was near Alicia's studio and after finding that fairly easily, we lost the trail, so asked at an estate agent who directed us to Rioja. Lorna lived in an apartment, apparently a quarter of an old house, where we had another problem because the entrance was equipped with an intercom, which we did not know how to use. Moreover, there were no names, only apartment numbers and we only had the address of the house. In desperation, we pressed buttons at random until we got a reply, which fortunately turned out to be Lorna. At first she was very surprised, not having heard from our joint acquaintance for a long time, but she invited us in, gave us tea and was very cordial; she perhaps enjoyed speaking English for a change. Having given her the news of our friend and drunk our tea, we made a move to leave and were pleasantly surprised when she invited us to dinner in a few days' time. English she may have been, but Lorna had all the warm hospitality that seems to be characteristic of South Americans.

We returned through the centre of Mar del Plata to the Yacht Club, a matter of some two or three miles, which distance is undoubtedly the greatest drawback when visiting this city. On the other hand, the genuine warmth with which we were received more than compensated for any inconvenience, for we had been invited to stay, free, gratis and for nothing for a month. After that, the Club would have to make a charge of five dollars a day, which seemed reasonable for a clean and secure mooring, with an attractive Club House and good showers. Going back on board, we noticed a big bunch of rhubarb had been put through the scuttle onto the shelf in the heads and correctly guessed at Rolo's kindness.

As ever, there was washing to do and I also took the opportunity to make the Christmas cake, which seemed to take the best part of a day. Friday brought our engagement with Lorna and we decided to have a proper look round the town, see a couple of museums and then round the day off with our visit. I made sausage rolls for a picnic lunch and we left about mid morning, but as we went through the Club gates, a young man stopped us.

`Are you going into town?' he asked and noticing our puzzled expressions, explained: `My father has a yacht at the Club and I saw you the other day so recognized you. I thought perhaps you could use this.'

He passed us a map, ideal for our purposes and we thanked him gratefully for his consideration. Smiling away our thanks, he walked on, leaving us to study the street plan. The road we chose, gave us an attractive view and led us past the Golf Club, a grand Tudorbethan place of astonishingly English pretensions, and on past the large Public Gardens, where people lounged in the sunshine gazing across the boundless blue ocean, towards Africa. We had our lunch in a park and after consulting the map, set off for a couple of museums, at which point, our luck ran out: one of the museums had been pulled down and the other was being rebuilt. So much for my efforts at culture, but we bought six kilos of grapefruit for three dollars and some asparagus at two dollars per kilo, which bargains gave Pete more pleasure than would an afternoon amongst artifacts. We arrived at Lorna's on time and had a very pleasant evening. She had gone to a lot of trouble with dinner: melon and *jamón crudo*, *sorrientos* (pasta stuffed with ricotta cheese), and fresh fruit salad and with our usual hearty appetites, we polished off everything, so that I think that Lorna wondered if she should have done more because she mentioned that she was used to catering for her friends who were all quite elderly. Mercifully, I had seen an expression of doubt cross her face and turned down a second helping of fruit salad, claiming that I had eaten more than enough so that, like Mrs Cratchit, Lorna could console herself that 'they hadn't ate it all at last!'

Our conversation was interesting. Now widowed, Lorna had been married to a fairly high-up army officer in the days before the Falklands Conflict, who must have been involved in the so-called 'Dirty War.' Needless to say, we felt that this was a sensitive subject, but were a little taken aback at Lorna's bland assertion that 'no-one was arrested or imprisoned who did not deserve to be. There were a lot of terrorists and violent criminals around then.' That her son had moved to England during the late seventies and refused to come back to Argentina, even now, seemed to contradict this, but we all tend to believe what our rulers wish us to. The talk moved on to less controversial topics and it was half past twelve before we left to walk home. Lorna was a bit shocked at the idea and wanted us to take a taxi or the bus, but our route was through prosperous suburbs and well-lit streets and we made it home without being assaulted.

Saturday was blowy and rainy and Pete got out the sewing machine to do a few jobs while I bottled asparagus and made bread and asparagus soup for lunch, but the following day, a lot of people came down to the Club, many of whom had a look over *Bad-ger*. While I was busy, painting the inside of the dinghy, Rolo came along and said, quite casually: 'I've bought the meat for the *parillada* tonight.'

I had almost forgotten about José's offer to have us round for dinner and when I finished painting, I told Pete who was delighted, as he loves barbecues.

That afternoon we replaced the top line of the guard rails, which are of polyester rope, cheaper and more comfortable to lean against than the usual stainless steel. They looked a lot better.

After a hot shower and changing into our best clothes, we were collected by Rolo at the typical Argentine hour of half past eight and drove to José's house. Alicia, expecting us this time, was much more relaxed than at our first visit and we met another lady, Marta, an old family friend. Everyone could speak some English, so Pete was not left out of the conversation, but I practised my Spanish with Alicia and Marta who preferred to speak their own tongue, and were probably amused at my efforts. We were offered a glass of Argentine whisky and although José apologized for not having Scotch, we found it very good and indistinguishable from the real thing.

It seemed that Rolo had done a deal: he provided the meat and the others did the cooking, but José was in the doghouse because although Alicia had done *her* share, he was late returning from the Club and had not lit the *parillada* in time. This problem was circumvented by the simple expedient of lighting a fire in the living room fireplace and cooking the *asado* over that and we learnt that this apparently eccentric procedure was not uncommon in Argentina, especially in the winter when no-one fancies going outside. As well as the meat, we also had cooked *chorizo*, which was delicious, and there was salad and an apple pudding to follow. The food was accompanied by some Argentine wine, with the Lopez label, which was regarded as a very reasonable bottle. The Argentines are not heavy drinkers and I suspect that eyebrows were raised when we also accepted a brandy with our coffee, but not having tasted Argentine brandy before we were interested to see what it was like. Delicious. All in all, we had a delightful and memorable evening.

The following day we started replacing the lazy-jacks and mast lifts, which are spliced to eyes at the top of the mast. Although I am *Badger's* bosun, I have a poor head for heights and spend so much time simply clinging on, that it is a lot faster if the skipper works up the masts. The wind picked up, it became decidedly chilly and Pete was glad to get back down and thaw out with a lunch of buttered baby new potatoes and a glass of wine. In the cockpit, out of the wind, it was so pleasant that we were not keen to carry on, but our consciences prevailed, and we were quite pleased when, a little later, Rolo asked if he and Hector, his paid hand, could come and look at *Badger*. While they were on board, Rolo asked me to show him how to make custard. I usually use custard powder and it was a long time since I had made it with eggs and with my reputation as cook at stake, I was concerned that I would make a hash of it, but it turned out well. In the meantime, Hector and Pete had been getting on very well, in spite of having few words in common and when I called them back below, we all had a cup of tea and sampled the custard with some date and walnut loaf. An odd, but not unpleasant combination.

By Tuesday, we had been at Mar del Plata for ten days and were nearly ready to leave, but first, we had to finish clearing *in* because the Customs had recently sprung back into life and now wanted to see us on board so that they could complete their paperwork. They made an appointment to come and see us, but needless to say, did not turn up, so we went for a walk along the outer breakwater. In one corner of the none-too-clean harbour, a group of sea lions was hauled out. They were mainly males, obviously the younger, older or generally unsuccessful ones and it has to be said that they had looked much more glamorous swimming than they did ashore in somewhat squalid surroundings. It was still a thrill to see them and also to observe some sheathbills, the first that I had seen.

Although damp and grey, it was not an unpleasant afternoon and at the end of the breakwater, we had our tea and cake. The breakwater was in pretty poor shape, with the light tower at its tip quite rusty and rotten; we had a good view of the bar, which looked anything but inviting in the strong north-easterly wind. Quite a few hulks lay along the wall and we pottered back looking at these and watching the sea lions, who had now abandoned the shore for the water once more. In an empty and deserted watchman's hut, a local chart was pinned up, by the broken window, a corner flapping in the breeze. It could not survive much longer, and was newer and of a larger scale than ours, so we liberated it. It was a shame for it to go to waste.

The wind had moderated sufficiently by morning for us to change the topping lifts on the foremast and while Pete was aloft, tucking in splices, a Customs officer came along with his form to be completed in triplicate, so I filled it in and he went away happy, leaving us bewildered as to why it had had to be done on the boat.

The jobs were almost completed and Pete put the fendering back on *Skip*, topped up the water and changed the paraffin container for a full one. Later on, we went to *Malon* for tea and Hector toasted lots of bread, which we had with Rolo's home-made jam. There was an elegant silver service and Rolo was pleased to show that it was not only on *Badger* that a proper afternoon tea was served. He and Hector had a pleasant relationship, managing to be both master and servant as well as friends. After preparing tea, Hector sat down with us and Rolo carefully translated anything in the conversation that would interest him.

That evening, we were in a supermarket about half a mile away, when we met Roberto, who had been on *Badger* once or twice. He invited us back for a drink and we drove round to a very modern and elegant house in one of the better suburbs, where we were introduced to Marian, his wife, while Roberto poured glasses of ten year old whisky. They were both in their early forties and during the next half hour or so, we met the rest of his family, one girl and five boys, courteous and pleasant young people and in spite of our protests, we were invited to stay for dinner. After we had dined on soup followed by steaks, cold potato croquettes and pumpkin, Roberto, Marian and ourselves went back into the living room where one of the children brought us coffee. Apart from the youngest children, everyone could speak some English and the older ones enjoyed practising it. They were all very friendly, but we were amused when Roberto tried to convince us of Argentina's perfection: a country with no race problems, and no real poverty. And yet only a few blocks away was a family living in a cardboard hut on a vacant piece of land, worse than anything we had seen in Brazil. Roberto also explained that the 'Dirty War' was nothing but a myth put about by left-wing extremists.

'I lived in Buenos Aires throughout those years,' he told us, 'and not once was I stopped by the Guardia nor did anyone ever want to examine my papers or ask me where I was going.'

But then, an obviously prosperous young man, driving a motor car such as a Mercédès would rarely be regarded with suspicion by a Government that had done its best to keep the wealthy happy. He went on to tell us why the Falkland Islands ought to belong to Argentina, but as we were his guests we did not argue, contenting ourselves with saying that we thought that it was a matter to be decided by the inhabitants of the Falklands.

'Exactly so, and when you get there you will find that they really want to be part of Argentina. I know.' We had our doubts. For all that we disagreed on one or two matters, we were very interested to hear about

Grand houses at Mar del Plata.

The Club to which he referred was the YCA's main clubhouse, where the major functions were held. Apparently, `in the old days' whole families used to stay there in the summer, when they came down to Mar del Plata for their holidays and Papa went sailing. It was on the main beach, a very splendid building and the side facing the sea was entirely French windows. José excused himself and we gazed out at the excellent if uninviting view of the sea. When we wandered round, looking at the pictures on the wall, I noticed that the room was lined with radiators, all of which were on and that the windows were not double glazed. There was only one person in the huge, terrazzo-tiled room, it was far from warm outside and we were not surprised when José told us that the Club loses a lot of money with this building; the heating costs alone must have been tremendous. Many of the members in Buenos Aires want to sell it, but people like José, who remember a more gracious era, would not like to see it go. I suspect that José was hoping that some day people would once more come to appreciate the virtues of Mar del Plata and that wealthy people would again have their summer homes there.

José drove us up some of the roads where the entire block (the town is largely laid out in a grid system) had only one house on it. Many of these houses were of Bavarian style and most of them had heavy and ornate stonework.

`These houses were built in the days when the Club was always full.' he told us. `In those times whole families shut up their home in Buenos Aires and came down here for the summer. They sent their servants in advance so that everything was prepared for their arrival. Then they would stay for three months and the house would be shut up again. Buenos Aires is impossible in the summer — it is so hot and humid, but here, with the cold current, it is never too hot.'

We gazed at the enormous houses. `You mean that these were only holiday homes?' I asked.

`Yes. My family used to have one — not as big as these — just for the summer, but now things are different. People have air-conditioning, they go for a holiday in Brazil, the women work. No-one can afford a house like this any more. In fact they are too big even for people who retire down here. They are not easy to sell.'

their country and their opinion of the new government. We got the idea that Roberto thought it an improvement on the previous (socialist) one, but was still not impressed with the way things were going; but then, how many people are satisfied with their government?

After a late night, we were almost relieved when we woke up to a strong breeze from the south, which persuaded us to wait another day. José, Rolo, Hector and Roberto all came to see if we were leaving, but were not surprised that we had postponed our departure. Rolo gave us a jar of raspberry jam and Hector a miniature life ring that he had made, very neatly, with tiny stitches seizing the rope onto it and *Malon*, her registered number, YCA and Mar del Plata painted in tiny letters, a thoughtful and delightful souvenir, which I stuck onto the beam shelf in the saloon, where it has stayed to this day. This giving of miniature life rings may be a South American tradition, because in one of his books, Miles Smeeton mentions that they were given three by some friends in Chile.

After they had left, we walked round to a tower on the other side of the basin, used for working on yachts' masts, in the hope that we could see what it looked like `outside', from the top. In my pocket, I had an RCC burgee for José to pass on to the YCA and seeing him, we took the opportunity of giving him the flag. He seemed to be delighted with it and insisted on giving us one from the YCA in exchange.

`You are probably a bit fed-up with waiting to leave,' he said. `Why do you not come for a drive up to town with me. I have to go into the main Clubhouse to see someone and I do not think that you have seen it yet. You will get a much better view of the bar and the sea from there than you will from that tower.'

We collected Alicia and stopped outside a bakers while José went in. In front of the car, a young man was pushing a broom about in a desultory fashion. Alicia turned round to me.

`Es Malvineiro,' she explained. I said that I had not heard of this word.

`He is a young man who went to the Malvinas,' she said. `You know that a lot of the men who went there were not trained soldiers, they were boys from the country. One day they had never seen a gun or a uniform and the next day they were on their way to the Malvinas. I think it is very cold there, the war was hard. Many of the young men ended up like that one. No-one knows where he came from. He lost his mind in the Malvinas. They are given work sweeping the streets.'

We looked again at the tragic figure: a good-looking young man, but with a blankness about his face that confirmed Alicia's story.

José bustled back to the car, his arms full of packages. `Here, try these,' he offered, passing a bag containing little hard pastry biscuits. `Have some, they are good.'

He started the car and drove us back to their house. The next thing that we knew, we were invited for lunch.

`No, no,' we objected, `we can't eat with you again!'

`Oh but you must, we have just bought the pizza, it is in the oven now. Come, it is only a snack.' We were embarrassed at their kindness. Of course, it was out of the question that we help wash up, but at least we managed to persuade José to let us walk home instead of him driving us back as he wanted to.

Back on board, I wrote a letter of thanks to the Club, for we had really appreciated their welcome and the use of the marina. Settling down for the evening, we noticed that the wind seemed to be shifting to south-east.

`It's not ideal,' said Pete, `but we'll leave tomorrow if it continues to ease off, even if it's still south-east.'

But when we woke up the wind was back in the south.

`It looks like we're going to be stuck here for another day,' Pete sighed. I cannot say that I was enthusiastic at the idea of going out into a fresh headwind, but on the other hand, you feel rather a fraud when you have announced a departure date and then keep postponing it. Rather than be cooped up on the boat all day, we went for a walk, heading south, as we had not been that way.

Past the the docks was a beach, with sand so soft that our feet sank in at each step; huge drifts impeded our progress and the wind blew the fine sand into our eyes and mouth. It was not ideal walking. The edge of the beach was lined with beach clubs, interspersed with shops and cafés, but all the cafés were shut and the interconnecting walkways were closed off so that we were forced back to the road. We gave up the idea of a beach walk and instead wandered back through the suburbs and edge of town. We had a good stroll and did not get back until about lunch-time. The wind had moderated and convincing ourselves that it really was backing south-east, we decided to leave. I suggested that Pete go to the *Prefectura* while I started making lunch and although he was rather dubious, because no-one there spoke any English, he had no problems.

After lunch, we prepared to get underway. I gave Atilio a picture of *Badger* to remind him of his boat's big sister and he then insisted on taking me to the Naval Club to see a photograph of his boat under sail. As we were walking back, he told me that he had believed that we were staying longer and was disappointed because he had been going to invite us to his house for an *asado*.

`Next time, hey?'

`Yes, next time, Atilio.'

We took our last hot shower and then went to see Toni, to give him his copy of our clearance papers and the letter for José to give to the Club committee. The envelope also contained some recipes for Alicia, who had been asking me how to make ginger snaps.

Back on *Badger*, we cast off and with the help of a little plump man who always seemed to be about, warped to the end of the dock and Seagulled out of the basin when the bridge opened. We made sail, adjusting the new lazyjacks, and put a reef in each. The bar looked much less daunting today and we were soon safely past and heading out to sea. The wind had shifted back to the south, but once we had made a bit of an offing, we tried tacking and found that we could lay the course of 220° and occasionally even higher. When we had settled down, Pete turned in and I was left on my own to take in the fact that we were now heading down towards the Roaring Forties.

Our destination was Puerto Madryn, situated in northern Patagonia, about 43°S. I was quite apprehensive and did not take a lot of comfort from the knowledge that South America was a weather shore. I felt that while the lee that it gave might stop the huge swells of the Southern Ocean, it would have no appreciable affect on storm force winds. Whatever lay in store, at least we had a gentle start with the wind falling away during the night and the following day one of light winds and near calm. It was warm in the sunshine, but whenever a breeze sprang up, it was icy and the temperature fell quickly after dark. There were several ships about. In the small hours of the morning, a large school of dolphins came to keep us company and there was so much phosphorescence that I could clearly make out their shapes.

Sunday was another gentle, sunny day. Alicia had given us an avocado, which I intended to have at lunch, with a bottle of wine to accompany the meal. Such plans are usually a recipe for disaster, but to our astonishment, it stayed calm and we could eat the avocado and the spaghetti bolognese that followed it, at the table, without having to hold on to our glasses. Pete was rejoicing in the cooler weather, because it meant that he could have steamed puddings again. Later on, the wind picked up and filled in from the north-east, noticeably warmer, and we started to make progress.

The next day was a red letter day, for bowling along in the sunshine, with a fair breeze, we entered the Roaring Forties, which we celebrated with an extra tot of rum.

`If the Roaring Forties were always like this,' I commented to Pete, `it would be no problem.'

`If it was always like this, it would be full of yachts,' was his reply. We really enjoy cruising in places where there are few other yachts, but have to pay the price and generally, what keeps people away is the weather. No-one really enjoys being cold or sailing in gale force winds, but in such places, Nature is often at her most splendid, to compensate for the discomforts and occasional frights. The cold water that had us reaching for our warm clothes provided food for the wonderful birds that surrounded us. The night was beautiful, tranquil and moonlit.

The following day also brought sunny and gentle weather, although the wind shifted to south-south-east and while I was cooking dinner, I noticed hazy sky away to south-west.

`Oh-oh,' I said, `it looks like our good weather might be coming to an end.'

I was right. The wind backed round and by tea time we were starting to reef. It was a good Force 5 when I went off watch and increased slowly but steadily through the night, backing northerly, the barometer falling steadily and the day came in with pouring rain and the wind at Force 7 — we were in the Roaring Forties. We were rapidly approaching Golfo Nuevo, in which Puerto Madryn lies, and sighted land just after we finished our morning coffee, making our

way towards it while Pete identified the headlands. It was quite rough, with the gusts occasionally touching gale force, but by mid afternoon the wind had started to ease off and by tea time, all the reefs were out. Perhaps due to the proximity of land, the breeze died away completely, apart from the occasional squall to keep us on our toes and we debated going to Puerta Piramides in order to get in before dark. Progress became so slow that it seemed unlikely that we would save our daylight to any anchorage, so we carried on for Puerto Madryn.

It was a fortunate choice, because the night that followed was literally marvellous, with a nearly full moon, which turned the barely undulating sea to black. Silver dolphins and sea lions surrounded us, splashing and chuffing, and invisible whales surfaced, the sound of their immense exhalations travelling from afar over the still water. All around us, terns were chattering and penguins mooing.

We approached the harbour as day broke and there were southern right whales in the bay, lazing on the surface and occasionally sounding, their tails coming right out of the water as they dived. They seemed unconcerned at the proximity of boats, some of which approached quite closely, their fascinated passengers almost forgetting to take photographs in their excitement. It was the knowledge that these huge, slow-moving and gentle beasts were often to be seen here that had decided us to call at Puerto Madryn and we were delighted that they had obliged.

We dropped the hook at half past eight under the intense scrutiny of a large sea lion and while Pete went below to make breakfast, I took stock of our surroundings. We were in a large bay with dun-coloured hills stretching away in all directions and little else to see but Puerto Madryn, which did not look like much of a place.

`From what we can see, Rolo may have been right,' I commented.

`What do you mean?'

`Well, if you remember, he said that most people believed that beyond Mar del Plata, "all is desert" and that you had to be a mad man or wanted by the police to live further south. Certainly, the houses here are not quite in the same class as those that José showed us in Mar del Plata.'

Pete popped his head up. `No, it does look a bit like a frontier town, doesn't it? It is literally desert too, from the look of things.'

It was with simple pleasure that I noticed that at either end of the town, the road was no longer asphalted, because coming from super-civilized England where an `unmade road' is a rare sight, I find something romantic about dirt roads, a feeling of being at the edge of civilization and amongst pioneers. Of course, the real explanation is a prosaic one, involving costs, weather and distances, but for me, the aura remains.

Breakfast over, we rowed to the beach. It was quite warm in the sun and we sauntered along to the conveniently situated *Prefectura,* made our number there and then looked round the town, which was more attractive than we had anticipated. It was small, with the centre only a couple of blocks wide and about five blocks long, but there were two or three supermarkets, one of which was very stylish and, of all things, a first-class health-food shop. The area around Puerto Madryn and the town itself were originally settled by Welsh people and, until fairly recently, a number of people still spoke Welsh as their first language. This dry, sparsely vegetated region is about as different from Wales as it is possible to be and we speculated as to why the settlers should have chosen such a place for their sheep farms, rather than further south where they would have felt more at home. Perhaps, by the time they got to Patagonia, this was the only land unclaimed. There was not much to indicate their presence now, apart from one or two gift shops exploiting the Welsh theme. I wondered what the Argentines made of the foot-long witches on broomsticks.

I spent most of the afternoon cooking, baking a cake for the passage, scones for tea and sausage rolls for a picnic we planned for the next day and found dead maggots in the brown flour that we had bought in Brazil. The cold had killed them off and they were easy to sift out, but Pete suggested that I was being over-fastidious — the extra protein might be good for us.

About sundown, a boat from the *Prefectura* called on us, but I told them that we had cleared in and waved our piece of paper at them. They seemed satisfied and went away, but next morning, the noise of a boat very close to *Badger* woke us up and we looked out to see that they were back again. They wanted us to go ashore, so, without stopping for breakfast, off we went. We had decided to change another twenty dollars and buy some supplies, because it was unlikely to be cheaper in Stanley and we did not expect that there would be too many temptations to part with our money once we were cruising round the Falkland Islands and Pete suggested that we shop while we were ashore. We spent ages in the *Prefectura,* having to do everything again because they had not done the job properly the previous day, so we cleared out at the same time.

When we told the *marinero* where we were bound, he made his right hand into a gun: `They will shoot you, if you tell them you come from Argentina!' he said, grinning.

Pete had done right to bring the shopping list and money. We went to the health-food store for popcorn, because although it was the same price in the supermarkets, I preferred to buy it loose and not have plastic bags to throw out. I discovered that principles sometimes pay, because when I asked the lady if she would give me a discount for buying six kilos, she reduced the price from a peso fifty a kilo to a peso twenty. We spent the rest of our money on four dozen eggs, fifty oranges, four kilos of carrots, a brik of wine and some *jamón crudo.* Laden down, we staggered back to the boat for our belated breakfast.

It was too late in the day to go for a walk and a picnic, so instead, we sailed up towards Puerta Loma where, according to a poster that we had looked at in town, we had a good chance of seeing sea elephants. It was a truly glorious day with a gentle breeze, making a sail far more appealing than walking in the hot sun, with dust blowing in our eyes and not much idea of where to go. With everything put away, we raised sail and set off across the bay. Although the wind headed us, it was a lovely sail and we drank our tea and ate our scones enjoying the afternoon and taking in the scenery, so different from our environment of the past year.

The hilly land was parched, desiccated by the pitiless sun, with no greenery or shade, just rock, dust and scrub and never a sign of the sheep that presumably lived there, although we wondered how. In the distance, the odd house occasionally had a hint of verdure, suggesting a constant struggle to create a reminder of another, fresher world, where mosses and ferns burst forth amidst a superabundance of moisture. This land was sere and barren, with a beauty of its own, but a beauty that must be difficult to appreciate by those trying to wrest a living from it. It was a true desert landscape.

Approaching the far side of the bay, we stood close inshore and worked our way up in short tacks, to see the coast more clearly. In a cove, under the cliffs an unidentifiable something was moving and, as we sailed closer, it took on a pinkish hue. I went for the binoculars and stood in the hatchway, focusing them.

`They look like flamingoes, Pete, but I can't believe it! In a desert, for heaven's sake.'

`I'm sure that's what they are, a whole mass of them,' agreed Pete, who has superb eyesight.

Flamingoes fly above while sea lions bask on the beach at Golfo Nuevo.

close to us, snorting and puffing, curious and ebullient. Those that remained on the beach watched warily, relapsing into somnolence once we had gone about and moved away. It was all very wonderful and although there was no sign of the sea elephants — it was probably the wrong time of the year — the other wildlife more than compensated for their absence. It had been an unforgettable afternoon.

We came to anchor in Ensenada Avanzado, a mile to the south-

There were about fifty birds and as we approached, they began moving in an agitated fashion.

`We're upsetting them, Pete — we'd better tack,' but even as he put the helm down, they all took flight. It was an astounding sight: a flurry of rose, coral and black, long legs dangling and slender necks stretched out, seemingly too delicate to support their bizarre beaks as they circled overhead, glaring down on the strange craft that had trespassed on their solitude. We felt guilty at disturbing them, especially when instead of settling back in the cove, they flew off in another direction.

`I didn't realise that there were flamingoes here, did you?'

`No. Gerry Clark saw them in the Magellan Straits, though.'

`Yes, I remember the photograph in his book, but I'd have thought that it was too dry for them here. What an unforgettable sight! I wish they'd circled again — by the time I got the camera they were too far away.'

We had to make another couple of tacks inshore, before we got to Pta Loma and at each one, there was something to see. Rock shags were nesting on the cliffs and craned their snake-like necks, looking at us first with one eye and then the other, while those flying past the boat would stare over their shoulders at us until their curiosity became too much and they came round to examine us again. On the beaches below the cliffs, groups of sea lions heaped together and some of them, possibly the younger ones, excited at seeing us and with a fine disregard for their companions in the way, made a bee-line for the water, leaping in to emerge

west of Pta Loma, rather gingerly because the north-easterly wind was blowing into the anchorage. The glass was still rising and we would expect bad weather to come from a westerly quarter, from which the bay was sheltered, but it was nevertheless a relief when the wind died down. We had a rather curious dinner of the *jamón crudo* and grapefruit, followed by the sausage rolls that had been intended for our picnic, with carrots and chips, washed down with a glass or two of wine.

Saturday was cloudy, but we went ashore in the faint hope of finding some sea elephants, but to gain access to the beach where they gathered, we had to enter a wildlife reserve which had a charge of three dollars each. This was a bit of a facer, because we had no money on us. I explained to the young man who had come out of his house to stop us, that we were on a boat at anchor and had not realized that we would be charged to look round. He was a friendly person and, perhaps because I had been playing with his two lovely dogs, waived the fee. A short way past the gate was an `Interpretation Centre,' but it was closed down, so we followed the track and came to a beach, covered with sea lions. A wooden rail ran along the edge of the cliff and we leant on it, with a good view, fascinated with the way they went back and forth, climbing over one another, dozing and yawning, bickering and squabbling; they certainly seemed healthier and better looking then the ones at Mar del Plata. The path looped back, but there was nothing else of much interest and although it did not seem much value for three dollars, I suppose that such parks are very expensive to set up and maintain. We enjoyed coffee and scones, in a sheltered spot overlooking the bay and then strolled back to the boat.

As we were rowing out, the breeze picked up quite freshly from the west, a fair wind, so we hastily sorted ourselves out and got underway with such despatch that we were out into the Gulf before I had time to realize that at last, the log entry read *Towards Stanley.* As it turned out, we might as well have left at leisure, because twenty minutes later, the wind dropped away and remained messy and of variable strength for the rest of the day and all night, but the cloud cleared away after dark and there was a beautiful full moon. Pete woke me to see a small school of killer whales, which were leaping in the distance and we wondered if they were the ones that are known to live in Golfo Nuevo. There was a male in the pod whose enormous fin stuck straight up out of the water like an attenuated, submarine's conning tower, but as ever with killer whales, the pleasure of seeing them was tinged with apprehension, due to the stories of their attacks on yachts. Soon we were surrounded by scores of black-browed mollyhawks, resting on the

Lonely Patagonian anchorage at Golfo Nuevo. **Badger** *is visible at left.*

water and, like ourselves, awaiting a better breeze. The wind increased in the afternoon, but the sea stayed smooth for the rest of the day.

Overnight the breeze headed us, then backed right round so that from being close-hauled, we were on a dead run at tea-time. The wind was not only uncertain in direction, but variable in strength, too. By Tuesday morning, we were bouncing along in Force 5-6, with a lot more birds about. After debating having our morning coffee on deck as usual, we drank it below, neither wanting to be splashed nor to bother with oilskins, and for the first time spent the entire day below; it was getting noticeably colder again. We were getting south and indeed, that afternoon we picked up *Calling the Falklands* on the BBC and afterwards, discussed how we would spend the six weeks that we would be there.

I woke up to a Force 6 wind, from south-west, which Pete said had come suddenly with the sun, so that one moment it had been calm and the next he was dropping two reefs in each sail. I could no longer ignore that I was feeling cold and broke out my thermal underwear.

`I didn't want to start wearing it yet,' I told Pete.

`Why not, if you're feeling cold?'

`Well, I'm worried about what might happen if it gets any colder. I wanted

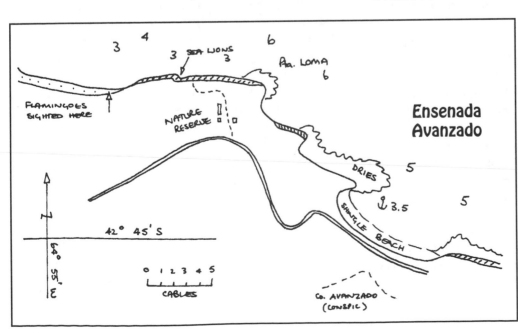

to wait as long as possible before putting them on and try and get acclimatized.'

'I shouldn't worry too much, Annie. I doubt that we'll find it much colder than Scotland and we didn't even *have* thermals the first time we cruised there.'

It blew a steady Force 6 for most of the day and although it was Half-Way Day, it was too rough for celebrating, so I made a one-pot meal for lunch. I spent a lot of time under the pram hood looking at all the birds. There were masses of Cape pigeons about and, to my delight, I also saw a wandering albatross and although we came to see many of these sublime birds, I never took them for granted.

Pete woke me up: 'Not much of a night, Annie, but the wind's eased off. We're back under full sail again, so unless it picks up there shouldn't be too much for you to do.'

We slopped along, the breeze boxing the compass again, but even I could not describe adjusting the wind vane as arduous work.

We were approaching the islands and, the previous day's sights having been taken in rough conditions, Pete was keen to confirm our position. A morning sight was taken in the drizzle, but when it cleared up after noon he was able to get a good fix, which showed us to be more or less where he reckoned and that the morning sight had been reasonably accurate.

'More by good luck than good management, I suspect,' was his comment, but I think that he was secretly pleased with himself.

We were quite excited when in the afternoon, a Fishery Patrol vessel came to pay us a visit.

'We must be getting close, now, ' I said.

'Well, you know that from the sights.'

'Yes, but actually having some sort of contact is different.'

It was a lovely, sunny evening, with clear sky and did not really get dark until ten o'clock and I mentioned it to Pete when I got him up.

'That's one of the best things about high latitudes,' he commented. 'It's really good to be away from long nights.'

Friday brought very light headwinds and in the morning we were buzzed by a large, four-engine, prop plane, with blue and red roundels, which Pete guessed was probably a Hercules, patrolling from the Falklands. The wind started to fill in and after Pete had taken the meridian passage he announced:

'We are now in the Fifties and I think that we should get in tomorrow. It's not been a bad passage, has it?'

'So far!' I replied, not intending to push our luck. The glass was high and steady and there was a hazy sun, not at all like the Furious Fifties of legend, but although we had managed the Forties without a gale, I did not believe that we would make it to Stanley unscathed.

The night was cloudy and rather boisterous and early in the morning, Pete sighted land. As always happens when land is in sight, *Badger* seemed to yaw about too much with the self-steering gear, so after breakfast, we togged up and went on deck. We had been travelling all night at six knots and carried on at the same rate, but as we approached, the wind got up to Force 7, touching Force 8 in the gusts. Through the scud and low cloud I could make out the land, low, grey and windswept, devoid of trees or any sign of life.

'Hmm,' I commented to Pete, 'the islands don't seem too inviting, do they.'

'Well, we couldn't really hope for light winds all the way. I don't suppose that it's always like this.' I hoped Pete's confidence would not prove misplaced.

The wind was from the north and was reputed to double in velocity through the narrows into Stanley Harbour. We were not quite sure what twice Force 7 was, but it sounded too much to handle, so after looking at the chart, we sailed instead to an anchorage in the lee of some higher ground, in Port William, the bay off which Stanley Harbour is situated, dropping the hook at half past eleven, in an anchorage that was anything but tranquil. *Badger* yawed about, heeling right over and although I eventually became convinced that the anchor would hold, I found it very unpleasant. It did not worry Pete. Once he was sure that the anchor was well dug in he was quite contented.

We had been seen: a harbour launch came by to check that we were OK and later on returned with a Customs officer, who came on board with another man. They were both very friendly and it was a delight to be able to speak freely in our own language again. We celebrated our arrival with a Christmas pudding and I started to relax when the wind eased off at night. We would move first thing in the morning before the wind got up, and as I turned in, it was with the comforting thought that tomorrow would find us in Stanley and in a snug berth. It was as well that I could not see into the future.

Chapter Thirteen

t went almost calm overnight and we woke to very light winds and sunshine. After breakfast, we had a shower and by the time we were ready to get underway, it was blowing a full Force 6. We had learnt our first lesson about the Falklands' climate: it may go calm overnight, but it rarely stays that way.

We had asked the man who came on board with the Customs officer about the wind increasing as it funnelled through the Narrows.

`They're really too short to affect the wind much,' he had told us, `but as you go through, you might find bad gusts whipping round the end.' I had also asked about predicting gales. `The weather systems are fairly straightforward: keep an eye on the barometer and you should be all right,' but as the barometer was fairly steady, I reluctantly concluded that the Falklands deserved their reputation as a windy place. After all, Force 6 is a `yachtsman's gale.' We ran down Port William towards the Narrows and passed through without difficulty into Stanley Harbour.

The harbour is a stretch of water, about three miles in length, running east-west, and very reminiscent of a Scottish loch with the town built on sloping ground along the middle of the south shore, where it gets the full benefit of the sun. Many of the houses have corrugated metal roofs, brightly painted and the effect is colourful and attractive. We were amused to see a roof with a huge Union Flag painted on it: at least one of the citizens preferred to be under British rule. The spire of a good-sized church, Stanley Cathedral, is by far and away the tallest and most conspicuous structure, but a sailor will instantly notice the number of hulks spread around the harbour. At the eastern end lay an iron ship, with masts still standing and looking, at that distance, almost seaworthy, while several other old ships formed the basis of wharves and jetties. Stanley is well known for its collection of wrecks: ships that put into the Falklands to recuperate after dreadful struggles to round the Horn, only to be condemned as being too expensive to repair. They are an astonishing sight.

Stanley was not established with yachts in mind and while the harbour is one of the best in the Islands for sizeable vessels, it is far too large and open for small craft. At the east end is a floating dock where we could find a berth, but we were chary of manoeuvring under power in strong winds, would have to pay to stay there and had a walk of over a mile into town. Off the town itself there were four large mooring buoys and a local yacht was lying to one of these on a long scope of chain. There was a fetch of over a mile from both west and east and although the town provided a bit of a lee so long as there was no north in the wind, and a gale from the east was not to be expected during the summer months, they looked very exposed in the strong northerly breeze sweeping right across the harbour. The west end looked like the best bet, and despite there being a walk of over a mile to the town, *Curlew* had spent a lot of time at anchor there, so that we were sure this was the best spot.

We had on board Ewen Southby-Tailyour's excellent book, *Falkland Islands Shores*, which, incredible though this may sound, is a cruising guide to the islands, but his sketch chart of Stanley Harbour showed no soundings at the western end and we were not quite sure where to go. With the wind in the north, we brought up on that side of the loch, with the thought that we could always shift berth if needs be and anchored in about ten feet. Although well-reefed, it had actually been rather a fine sail and much less

Badger, anchored at Port Stanley for the first time.

ated from what we had read, of an area with a very long and indented coastline, numerous islands, an abundance of wildlife, a small population and only one town, all in a latitude that ensures long hours of daylight during the summer months. The climate is a lot drier than the UK and, not being tropic birds, the fact that we would have to wear more than shorts and a T-shirt was no real deterrent. Indeed, the only drawback seemed to be the frequency and duration of strong winds.

cold than I had feared. People tend to make a big issue of the proximity of the Falkland Islands to the Antarctic, but the climate is moderated by the sea and we found that the temperatures compared with those in the west of Scotland.

A majority of people never even heard of the Falklands before the Conflict and their image is that of the television screens, of men fighting in the mud and misery of winter, circumstances that would make even Eden look appalling. Nearly everyone found it incomprehensible that we wanted to cruise there, but never having seen these programmes, our images were cre-

Safely at anchor, the scene was much more attractive than it had appeared the previous day. The land was washed in bright sunshine and overhead, white clouds scudded across a pale, blue sky, their shadows making patterns on the hills, covered in golden-coloured `white grass.' In the distance were the handsome, twinned peaks of the `Two Sisters' and the land rose gradually on both sides of the harbour. On the north side, white-painted stones recorded the names of the survey ships that had guarded the Islands over the

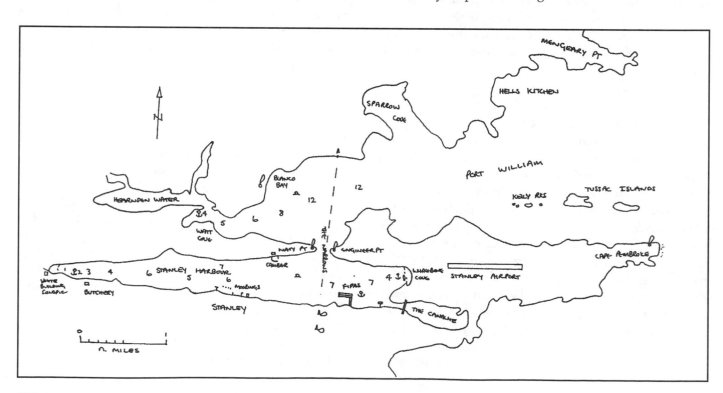

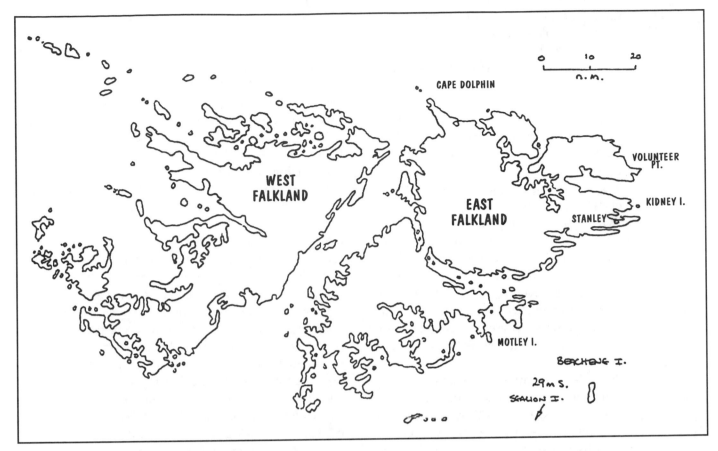

years, *Protector*, *Beagle*, *Endurance* and *Barracouta*. The blue water had little white horses running over it and the bracing wind was fresh and clean. A snow-white kelp goose was browsing along the shore with his brown mate, whose handsome plumage was barred with white, which transformed into large white wing patches when she flew. Steamer ducks abounded and had rushed noisily away from us when we sailed down, stirring up great gouts of water with their wings and reminding us of Bill Tilman's incomparable description of them, in *MISCHIEF in Patagonia*. The collective noun must surely be a `rout' of steamer ducks.

A friend of ours had cruised the islands and before he left, we had written to ask if we could borrow his charts. A couple that he knew in Stanley had kindly offered to take care of them until such time as we should turn up. After lunch, we found their address and had a stiff row ashore. Carrying the dinghy up the rocky beach, I commented:

`Well one thing, Pete. At least it looks as though Rudi was wrong about the dinghy.'

`I thought that he would be. I don't think that we could row in a gale, but then I'd be surprised if he could have. I wouldn't like to have to pull too far, though,' he added, feelingly.

We had landed on the north shore, about half a mile down to the bottom of the loch and a further couple of miles into town.

`I can't believe that Tim and Pauline did this all the time,' I said, `Do you think they found somewhere on the south shore to anchor?'

`Maybe. When we get Willy's charts, we'll have a good look and see if we can make out where they would have gone.'

The track soon joined a made-up road and went past some new houses towards the town, taking us right along the side of the harbour where we could admire the scenery and watch the steamer ducks and kelp gulls in the water. The Post Office and Town Hall marked the start of the town proper and a little further on we saw a bank.

`Let's find out how to get our money, here,' Pete suggested.

Although it was a Standard Chartered bank, they would have no truck with our Visa cards. We had been warned about this, but were not too concerned, having taken the precaution of bringing a certain amount of Sterling with us. The young lady behind the counter was very helpful.

`We can cash an English cheque,' she informed us, `so long as you have a cheque guarantee card.'

`That's fine,' said Pete, `next time we come in, we'll bring the cheque book with us.'

Continuing our walk, we passed the famous Upland Goose Hotel, and savouring the beautiful colour of the grass on the green, we walked over the road to look at a huge mast displayed there. It was from the *Great Eastern* that had been in Stanley Harbour for many years before being towed back to Bristol for restoration, but in interest it could not compare with the soft, green grass.

`Look, Pete! It's real grass, not raffia grass, like we've seen everywhere else. A real lawn at last!'

With its white-painted flagpole, neatly trimmed grass and bollard-and-chain fence, the green looked as though it had been transplanted from the heart of England and Stanley itself, had a truly British country-town feel about it, emphasized by the overwhelming majority of cars being Land-Rovers, and the neat gardens in front of the houses, where flowers, carefully sheltered from the wind, made splashes of bright colour.

With all the streets identified by signs, we soon found the road for which we were looking, but only a few houses had numbers. By counting from one of these, we worked out where to go. A long garden led up to a cottage and we passed through a wooden gate and up a rather overgrown path to where a lady was bending over some plants. She stood up at our approach.

`We're Pete and Annie Hill,' Pete explained, `and we've at last come to take Willy's charts from you. I'm sorry that you've had to look after them for so long.'

Dianne smiled at us. `It's as well you sent that postcard — we were beginning to wonder if we'd end up keeping them for ourselves! Would you like a cup of tea? I could do with one.'

She led the way round the back door that opened to a tiny yard next to the peat shed and into the house. A road ran close to the back and this was obviously the usual access. We followed Dianne through the living room into a large kitchen, dominated by a peat range. Moving the kettle over to a hotplate, Dianne riddled the fire and opened a damper.

`Where have you come from, then?'

We were all halfway through a second cup of tea when Carl came home.

G'day,' he greeted us.

`This is the couple that Willy left his charts for,' Dianne explained.

`Oh, you're friends of Willy's, are you?' Carl spoke slowly, seeming always to be considering his words; Dianne was brisk, almost abrupt. They both seemed rather reserved, but in time we realized that they were actually a little shy. Kind and generous people, who never hesitated to put themselves out for others, it was our good fortune that Willy had left his charts with them.

Carl and Dianne had sailed to the Falklands in 1980, from Australia, by way of Cape Horn. Their boat had started out twenty-three feet long, but Carl, a skilled boilermaker and a magician with steel, had lengthened the boat to thirty feet, after which they set off cruising. Finally, they sailed from North Island, New Zealand, non-stop to Stanley, but never made much of this epic passage and appeared to think it a perfectly normal thing to do. When a baby girl was born, they sailed with her to South Georgia, but here they came unstuck because their little baby was so appallingly seasick that they were seriously worried for her health. For the time being, they swallowed the anchor and, returning to the Falklands, worked out in *camp*, the name given to anywhere outside Stanley, soon having another baby. When Tracey needed to go to secondary school, they settled in Stanley to avoid the family being split up during term time. *Qakstar* had been long sold, but they had soon bought a fifty-foot ketch similar to the Hiscock's *Wanderer IV*, which they had sailed to Uruguay for several months. *Compass Rose* had also been sold and when we met them, Carl was busy plating up a steel hull. They were both very enthusiastic and Dianne had already planned her first cruise.

We soon met Tracey and Rachael, whose initial shyness wore off after a few visits. Tracey, the elder was slim and blonde and much quieter than Rachael, who was also blonde, plump and at times boisterous. To Dianne's irritation, they bickered endlessly, trying to score points as sisters will, but we liked them both and the squabbling disguised their affection for each other. It was a happy family and we were enjoying it all, but with dinner time fast approaching, it was time we were off.

`We'll run you down in the Rover,' offered Carl.

`No, don't worry. It does us good to get some fresh air and exercise.'

`No probs. You've got all those charts and besides, we missed you sailing in and would like to see your boat.' So we all climbed into the Land Rover and drove back.

`I see that you're right over the other side, then,' Carl commented, `I think that you could come nearer this shore.'

`We needed Willy's chart to work out the best spot,' Pete replied, `but I think we'll probably move. Is there anywhere you'd recommend?'

`Well, we used to lie alongside the Government jetty, but it was pretty shallow and anyway, it's falling down now. There's always FIPAS of course,' he added doubtfully, `but that's not a good place to stay because it's so dark there — always in the shade. Stanley's not much of a place for a boat.'

At the bottom end of the loch, a gate barred the way, but Dianne hopped out and opened it before the car had really stopped and we bounced along the side of the harbour until we were next to the dinghy.

`An interesting boat, you've got there. Look forward to seeing her sailing, sometime.'

We thanked them for the lift. `No probs. Glad to see you.'

`And don't forget to bring up your washing sometime,' Dianne called as we said good-bye.

Back on board, Pete pored over the charts, while I cooked supper.

`There's just about a full set here: obviously Willy bought whatever Warren didn't have.' Willy had also borrowed some charts and his friend has been happy for us to use them. `We'll be able to go anywhere we want with these, but I don't know how we're going to fit everything in,' Pete concluded, happy to be planning.

It was a breezy night, but I turned in contented. `It's nice to meet some real cruising people again,' I commented. `I think I'm going to enjoy Stanley.'

We had to finish preparing our notes on South America and send them off, but soon completed this chore, as the next couple of days were very windy. Our anchorage was too exposed for comfort and as soon as it was calm enough we went to try anchoring off the town, hoping for more comfort and to save the lengthy hikes to and fro. We dropped the hook in the place recommended in *Falkland Islands Shores*, but we still had the Bruce bent on, and despite the breeze being only Force 3, it dragged, fouled by kelp. Recovering it, we picked up a mooring, which would allow us to change the Bruce for our sixty-five pound Luke, (a Herreshoff-designed, improved fisherman anchor) which would be infinitely better in kelp. The mooring buoy was a huge, steel one, but it was unlikely to go so calm that we would be bumping into it.

We went ashore to do some photocopying, having seen a place advertized on the door of the bank. It was shut however, so we asked advice of the ladies at the Post Office, who suggested the library at the school. They wanted twenty pence a copy, which was incredibly expensive to minds used to South American prices, but at least we could do it ourselves and make sure that it was just what we wanted. Back at the Post Office, wanting it to arrive within a month, we put the package on the scales and asked the price.

`You want it to go airmail, do you?'

`Yes please.'

`Well that will cost you £21-79.' We went white.

`How much?!!'

`It's an awful lot of money,' said the lady, `it would cost much less sending it surface.'

`Yes, but it just *has* to get there by the end of the month. We don't really have any choice.' I opened my purse.

The ladies looked at one another and one of them glanced through the door into the back room and nodded to the lady attending to us. In a low voice she said: `We'll charge you surface, but put it in the airmail bag.' She and the other two all blushed bright red at their plot.

She quickly stamped, cancelled and dropped the parcel in the bag. `Back in England, the Air Force throw out the ones that weigh over a kilo, you know,' she said, `even when people have paid the full rate. At least we're getting a bit of our own back. Don't worry, it'll go all right. No-one will check it.'

We did not argue, but thanked them with true gratitude. We hoped that they would get away with it and no-one would find out, but they did, because our package arrived a week later. It was a gesture that was typical of people in the Falklands and in every shop and business that we dealt with, we found that people always tried to help us, far beyond what one would normally expect.

Carl and Dianne had reiterated their offer for us to use their washing machine, so we went up when we knew that Dianne would have finished work.

`Oh good! I'm glad you've come. It's just sitting there most of the time — you might as well make use of it.'

I loaded up the machine and we all had a cup of tea.

`Carl should be home soon. Would you like to go and see the boat?'

`We'd love to, but it means him going back. Should we not just go down some time when he's there?'

`He'll be happy to run us down and I haven't been to see it for a while anyway.' So after Carl had come home and had a cup of Ovaltine, we all drove back to the boat.

`You're working full-time on her?'

`Yeah, but I'm not sure for how much longer. The guy who owns the place wants me to work for him. I'll still have a lot of free time and he says so long as I do my job, any spare time is my own. I'd rather not, but I don't see how I can refuse, really.'

`I suppose the extra money will be useful, anyway.'

`I guess so, but I don't want to be tied down.'

The boat was very impressive and even at this early stage of the plating, the hull looked very fair. She was round bilge and until Carl had been given a machine designed for the job, he had hammered the shape into the sheets of steel, but they were all so well formed that it was impossible to tell which plates had been curved in what manner. We stayed for quite some time looking at the boat and discussing its accommodation and it was about nine o'clock when we left.

Picking up the washing from their house, I said:

`We're planning to go off for a bit of a cruise, tomorrow, but I hope you'll all come over for supper when we get back.'

`We'll look forward to that. Sure you don't want a lift.'

`No, we'll walk, thanks all the same. It's not far.'

After a dull start, the morning faired up and we got underway, intending to sail east for the next big indentation in the coast, Berkeley Sound. We stopped on the way at Kidney Cove, a small anchorage off the wildlife reserve at Kidney Island. The mainland beach was dotted with gentoo penguins, but we could not land because it is one of the areas that is still mined.

During the Conflict, the Argentines laid several minefields in the Falkland Islands, especially around Stanley, but although the fields were recorded on maps, no account was kept of the number of mines laid. Afterwards, British bomb disposal experts tried to clear the fields, but the Islanders called an end to it after the second soldier had had his leg blown off, the plastic mines being extremely difficult to detect. The minefields are all fenced off and no-one can use them, which is particularly sad around Stanley, where many of the areas and beaches that used to be favoured places for picnics, walking or sunbathing are no longer accessible. Its effect is as though a small nuclear device had been exploded.

The Argentines had recently made some half-hearted offers to have them cleared, but the Islanders want the results guaranteed. As one of them put it: `If President Menem will bring his granddaughter to play on the cleared fields, then I'll believe that the job has been done properly.' *That* offer has not yet been made.

As we had sailed out of the Narrows, several Commerson's dolphins, locally known as `Puffing Pigs', had joined us. Their name is entirely appropriate, because they are small and chubby, have white saddles across their backs and spend a lot of time on the surface, breathing noisily between dives. About the size of the common porpoise, they frequently escorted us and on this occasion, stayed patiently waiting while we were at anchor before accompanying us to our first anchorage in Berkeley Sound, Johnson's Harbour. We gave them a good run for their money as we romped up the Sound in a full Force 6, but they left when we started to tack into the Harbour, bored with our slow and erratic progress.

A large stretch of water, Berkeley Sound has been a secure harbour for sizeable vessels for many years and during the squid season, is full of fishing boats. We had it to ourselves and after so many months of sailing in South America, the contrast was startling, with distant horizons, low, rolling hills, trees few and far between and hardly a sign of humanity. Of course, the landscapes would be different without sheep and the white shapes of buildings were dotted about at two or three places along the shore, but man had not shaped the scenery: the hills were not criss-crossed by roads, there were no bridges, no electricity pylons, no walls nor fields of grain and had the wind not been buffeting us about, we would undoubtedly have remarked on the silence. Outside Stanley, it is rare to hear an internal combustion engine, a sound that is ubiquitous in most places, except at sea, and for all the turbulent weather, my first and remaining impression of the Falklands is that of peace, a place not yet overwhelmed by man.

Dropping the hook in good time for tea, the harbour, although recommended in *Falkland Islands Shores*, did not seem particularly snug because we could not get close inshore and there was really too much fetch for comfort in a small boat. Overnight the wind increased and was a steady Force 7 by mid morning, although the day was sunny and bright. I do not like wind. In fact I would go so far as to say that I detest strong wind, which makes me tense, irritable and generally out of sorts and I am always anxious about an anchorage until it has been well tested. The day seemed to go on forever. As there was not much kelp about, we had anchored on the CQR and although we did not move and the Luke was ready to go, still I worried. But it was a mercifully brief blow, easing in the afternoon and dying away to a light breeze after sunset.

In the morning, we went ashore to the farm, to ask if it would be all right for us to wander round. A tall, long-haired lady answered the door.

`So you've managed to get ashore, at last. You didn't look too comfortable out there yesterday. Come in — you'll have a cup of coffee, won't you.' We followed her into the kitchen. `George! It's the people on the boat.'

Farmers in the Falklands have more jobs than they can ever hope to deal with throughout the summer, but Jenny and George gave us the impression that they had nothing better to do than to spend the morning yarning with a couple of strangers, which speaks wonders for their hospitality.

`We were off moving some ewes to another camp, yesterday,' Jenny told us, `and we saw you out there bouncing about.'

`Is it always as windy?' I asked.

`Oh the wind!' exclaimed George. `Do you know, I've lived all my life in these parts, but I've never got used to the wind. Sometimes it feels like you've spent the whole day just fighting against it.'

`Yes, it can be a nuisance,' Jenny added, `like yesterday with the sheep — they won't move if the wind's in the wrong direction, you know, and you almost have to force them to the camp you want.'

`The horses don't always like it either,' added George.

`Horses! George still sticks to rounding up on horse-back,' explained Jenny. `I don't like them myself, I'm not a good rider — and they're so much work.'

`Not really, Jenny. I don't think they are and at least you don't need to watch where you're going all the time, like you do on a bike.'

`Do people use motor-bikes, then?'

`Oh yes, there's only a few of us left who still use horses. It's true the bikes are faster and you can maybe get by with less people, but they're always breaking down, they cost a lot and they're dangerous. Jenny had a bad accident last year on hers.'

`Oh, that was just bad luck! But it has really slowed me down,' she continued. `I was on my trike and going quite fast over rough ground. I was watching what I was doing, but suddenly I was in the air and the thing fell on top of me.'

`What happened?'

`The wheels had got tangled in some wire — one of those weather balloon things they send up. I wasn't looking out for that sort of stuff. The worst thing was that the others were miles away and it was ages before they found me. I couldn't do anything, because the trike was on top of me and had broken my ankle.'

`It's taking a long time to get better, too,' said George. `She doesn't rest it enough.'

`I haven't got time to rest it,' Jenny said with a laugh. `But it's getting there.'

`I suppose one of the problems with the small farms is that you can't really afford for one of you to be unfit.'

`No, you're right. We've got Mike to help us, but quite a few settlements only have the husband and wife and if anything happens they have real problems.'

We went on to other things and soon, the subject of the Conflict came up. We had wondered if people would want to talk about it, but George and Jenny were typical in having their stories to recount and enjoying telling us all about it. Indeed, for many of the Islanders, it was the most exciting thing that had ever happened. George told us that after the initial contact, they had not been too much bothered by the Argentines, although now and then they would visit to check up or search for radios and they had set up an observation post on their land.

`Mind you, the SAS boys soon put the wind up them.'

`They were here, were they?'

`You wouldn't believe it. The Argies had hardly settled in before the SAS arrived and there was at least one of them here. I've lived here all my life, know the place like the back of my hand and I never saw a sign of him, but he was here all right. He got one of the Argies one night, and when the others realized, well, they were as jumpy as cats after that, wondering if it was their turn next. I don't blame them. This SAS bloke crept into their post and killed one of them without any of the others even waking up, or the sentries suspecting a thing. They were scared to death.'

`And you never saw a sign of him?'

`No, nothing and I wouldn't mind betting there was more than one of them.'

`I suppose that the war changed a lot of things around the Islands.'

`Oh yes, now we have all sorts of people coming in and telling us how to do things. Take tourism now. We have a track across our land to Volunteers, where they have the King penguin colony.'

`Oh yes, we've read about that. I'd like to see it.'

`You're not the only one — I think everyone who visits Stanley goes out there! Well, as I said, they come across our land in the Rovers, and sometimes we have to go with them, so they don't get bogged down, or tow them out when they do. Well, because they can be a bother and mess up the camp, the tourist board suggested that we charge them five pounds a head to come across our land. That's fine. They could come for free, as far as I'm concerned, but because we get that money, we don't mind if we need to look after them. The same thing happens at other settlements — cars come across to see some sight or other, and we all get paid five pounds. Well, now the Tourist Board wants us to start charging fifteen pounds. But what for? Five pounds is more than enough. I don't want to rob the visitors and anyway, if we charge that much, maybe a lot of them won't bother and then we all end up losing. But the Tourist Board blokes keep getting all these ideas from England and don't listen to us. Money,' he added in a tone of contempt, 'that's all they think about. Money! Not the people's holidays.'

Jenny looked at the clock and started bustling about.

'You'll stay and have dinner, won't you. It's just leftovers from yesterday and what we don't eat I'll throw out. It won't keep.'

'Are you sure? We seem to have spent half the day here already.'

'It makes a change to see a new face — we get fed-up of looking at each other, don't we George? Anyway, it's Sunday. Do you like fish? George has got a heart problem so has to cut down on the meat. Lucky we've got plenty of mullet round here.'

'I was wondering if it would be possible to do a bit of fishing,' said Pete.

'Of course you can. The best place is along up the creek away. You normally catch something up there.'

Falkland Islands houses were not ergonomically designed and in this, our first farm, we noticed the way that the domestic arrangements made a lot of work for the woman of the house, who already has more than enough to do. The peat range is in the living-kitchen, where we were sitting, but the food is prepared in a scullery, which is usually by the main entry into the house, the front door rarely being used. Here are the sink, a table for rolling out pastry or chopping meat and vegetables and all the pots and pans, but the food is cooked on the range and every time she wants to add salt, or check that the pan is not boiling over, the cook has to walk from the scullery and back. Dianne had mentioned this to me: in her house, the range formed part of a normal-style kitchen, but most houses were like George and Jenny's, due to the fact that the range is the main source of heat, as well as the cooker. We felt bad, seeing Jenny limping back and forth for plates and cutlery but our offers of help were smilingly waved away. 'It saves my leg from getting stiff.'

When everything was ready, another man came in: Mike who helped them run the farm. We sat down to fish and sausages, potatoes and savoury pastries that Jenny had baked for the previous day, with large mugs of tea or coffee to wash it all down. Helping to clear up, my frugal mind was a little shocked when the leftovers were scraped into a bucket to be thrown away and perhaps Jenny saw my face. 'I always make too much,' she explained, 'but it doesn't get wasted: we give it to the hens or the dogs.' The scullery was full of pies and pastries ready to go into the oven and I was greatly impressed by Jenny's energy and the amount of work that she got through, without complaint, as though it were the most normal thing in the world.

After we left, it was too late to go for a long walk, so we went to the creek for some fishing, soon catching a couple of mullet. We drank the tea that we had brought ashore and it was pleasant to sit on the rocks, out of the wind, watching the birds. After picking a load of mussels for Pete we rowed back to *Badger*, where we ate the fish cooked in a green peppercorn and tarragon sauce. We had seen Falkland mullet compared to the finest turbot, but this seemed to be hyperbole, for it is rather a coarse fish and benefits from a well-flavoured sauce.

There was still plenty of wind the next morning, but having despaired of ever seeing a nice Force 3 again, we headed further up Berkeley Sound, well-reefed. The wind eased off, we shook out most of the reefs and had a lovely sail up Stag Road, past Long Island in sunshine, with the rolling countryside and blue Sound making an attractive scene. Dogs and people on horseback were gathering sheep on Long Island: a picturesque touch. With Force 7 winds forecast, we anchored right at the head of the harbour, hoping to be sheltered from north-west to south-west. It was a rather drab and unattractive anchorage, with land sloping down gradually to the water's edge and a long, muddy foreshore, created by a little creek at the head of the bay. A bridge had been built over this, carrying one of the major roads on the islands and we saw *two* cars pass along it, both Land-Rovers of course.

It had clouded over and was quite cool, but Pete, fired with enthusiasm after yesterday's success, went to see if he could catch any fish, while I stayed on board, hoping for the usual sunshine tomorrow.

The Falklands' winds were knocking seven bells out of the burgee and in the hope of coming up with something bulletproof, I experimented with making a wind sock, with the appropriate design thereon. We have a small one on the foremast, as a wind indicator, which only ever needs replacing because the sun attacks the nylon; it is the flapping that destroys burgees.

Pete returned, empty-handed, the wind calmed down after sunset and we enjoyed a lovely, peaceful night.

The disc-jockeys on the early morning radio were very cavalier about the time that they read the scheduled forecasts, but they were so appalling that we could not bear to listen to them and so we managed to miss both the early morning forecasts. By seven o'clock, it was blowing freshly and we recalled Carl telling us that the wind does not normally pick up before eight o'clock, but that if it does so, strong winds are probably on the way. His theory was confirmed: it was a full Force 6 by nine o'clock — `when the wind fills in 'fore eight, you know 'twill be a day you'll hate.'

Our planned walk down to Long Island House was abandoned, as we were chary of leaving *Badger* in such conditions.

`Well that's another lesson learnt!' I commented to Pete. `There was nothing wrong with yesterday afternoon, apart from it being dull and cold and we should have gone for our walk then. In the future, if it's not blowing hard, I'll take the opportunity to get off the boat, regardless.'

`Yes, and it wasn't bad, once I'd got ashore, but I don't think we'll be going anywhere today.'

`You know, Pete, if we're going to be getting winds like this every other day, we're not going to be able to see as much of the islands as we were hoping to. It's just as well that Steve's coming, we couldn't possibly have seen anything in the six weeks that we'd originally intended.'

Steve is an old friend of ours and had mentioned that he was envious of our visiting the Falklands. Having people stay on the boat with us is not usually much fun: *Badger* is too small and we are used to our own routine and ways of doing things, which another person upsets. All too often, if we take another man sailing, he instantly promotes himself to Mate and demotes me to A.B., but Steve is different. He is quiet, tolerant, easy-going, with a good sense of humour and no ego and having spent several years living on a boat, knows what it is all about. Indeed, it would probably be harder for him than for us! We met him before we were married and after seeing his slides and talking to him, we realized that we not only could, but should go off for a voyage in the boat that we had then, rather than waiting until we had the `right one.' He sailed out again at the same time, was our mentor and always there when he was needed. We had no hesitation at all in asking him to join us in the Falklands and he had no hesitation in accepting, suggesting that he came over Christmas, avoiding all the family get-togethers! This had meant prolonging our original six weeks to more like three months, but having studied the Routeing charts we concluded that we could leave later than we had first thought, without risking worse weather.

`I hate to say it, Annie, but I think that we're going to have to get used to sailing in a lot of wind or, as you say, we won't get to see anything.'

`Well, yes, but not today, I hope.'

`No, we'll stay here today — I'd like to get on with that half model that I'm making Steve.'

It blew hard all day, with bright sunshine and scudding clouds. We listened to the news: half a dozen maniacs had raped, tortured and set fire to a sixteen-year old girl, who died in hospital after having been found wandering naked in the streets. Children in the United States were now carrying guns to school. Two boys were on trial in the UK for the murder of a two-year old.

`I don't care if I am an escapist — who wants to live in that sort of madness? God, it's bad enough *hearing* about it, I'm glad that we don't see the papers and TV. I'm not surprised that Carl and Dianne would rather bring up their girls in the Falklands than anywhere else.'

The wind died away and was down to a Force 3, which felt like a calm, by the time we turned in. It was a beautiful night, with a bright, new moon and although the forecast was for gales overnight and tomorrow, we hoped that they had gone through.

Wednesday also started off breezy, but with the forecast amended to Force 6, we got underway for Port Louis. Pete had problems getting the Luke anchor, whose shackle is too big to come over the stemhead roller, so later, we put some plastic over the capping rail so that he could be a bit more cavalier. The `Careenage', seemed rather exposed, so instead we headed for the anchorage off `Loggerhead Pond'. We had problems getting *Badger* to tack up to the pond and had to shake a couple of reefs out of the foresail, that had been reefed right down for running and we had made a big mistake towing the dinghy, because once we had to beat, she was swamped in the rough seas. After twenty years of sailing together and over seventy thousand miles in *Badger*, we now found ourselves in completely unfamiliar conditions, having to learn a whole new set of skills.

When we rowed ashore, there were a couple of gentoo penguins on the beach, and although they backed off at our approach I was delighted to see them at close quarters — this was what I came for. As we arrived at the settlement, we met the manager, Mike Morrison, with his wife, Sue. We introduced ourselves and asked if we could have a look round and maybe do a spot of fishing.

`Of course. If you follow the track round the bay there and across, you'll get to Fish Creek. I'm sorry we can't stop, we're tied up this morning. Is there anything you need?'

`No, thanks. Oh! You wouldn't have any milk that we could buy, would you?'

`No, I haven't picked it up yet,' Sue replied, `but if you go over to that house, Isabella will have done the milking and should be able to give you some.'

Thanking them, we set off along the track.

Port Louis is the site of the original capital of the Falklands. As the name implies, it was built by the French who are also responsible for the Argentine name for the islands. French sealers from St. Malo hunted around the Falklands, hence Malouines, Malvinas. The Manager's house, a handsome, whitewashed stone building, its gable wall covered with a luxuriant growth of ivy, dates from these early days. There was a sturdy tree growing next to it, a rare and welcome sight outside Stanley and, unlike most of the trees that have been planted around settlements, was not leaning sideways.

We tramped over to Fish Creek in the hazy sunshine and stood for a while, looking back over the settlement, snug and tidy, with its neatly-kept whitewashed buildings, red-painted roofs and the odd tree huddled in the lee of a house. At this time of year, the islands are at their most attractive, with splashes of vivid yellow around most of the settlements, where the gorse is in bloom. Usually, these large areas are a sombre green, but in early summer the bushes are startlingly bright and intensely eye-catching against the generally subdued hues of the landscape. On the rare, calm days, the scent is almost overwhelming and, trying to identify it, there is a shock of recognition: coconut at 52°S!

It was good to be able to stretch our legs and although we discovered that Fish Creek was a misnomer, we enjoyed our walk. Back at the Settlement, we knocked at the door of the cottage that had been pointed out to us.

`Come in, come in!' Isabella greeted us enthusiastically. Taking off our boots, we followed her in to a sparklingly clean kitchen, the walls covered with pictures and posters of exotic wild animals, the range gleaming with loving care. On a folding table stood a tray with mugs, a couple of canisters, sugar and milk. Isabella moved the kettle onto the hot plate.

`You'll have a cup of coffee?'

`Thank you very much.'

When the kettle had boiled, she indicated the table. `Coffee? Tea?'

`Coffee please,' we both replied. She looked at us. We looked at her.

`Well, help yourself.'

This was our introduction to an invariable camp custom: you make your own tea and coffee. Perhaps this stems from when the place is filled with the shearing gang and the confusion of catering for several strangers: `no milk and two sugars, please; one sugar and milk; I'll have tea, two sugars and milk; straight black, please.' How much more sensible to ask people to help themselves, but being used to not taking anything until specifically invited, it was hard to acclimatize.

Isabella had a straightforward openness about her, which made conversation very easy, even with very little in common and there was no need of small talk. After half an hour or so, Denzel, Isabella's mate, a pleasant and congenial soul, came in and settled down for a chat.

As we were leaving, I asked Isabella if there was any chance of buying some milk.

`No, no you can't *buy* any, but I'll give you some and happily. We have more than we know what to do with, but that's the trouble with a cow. It's all or nothing. Have you got a container on you?'

I had a litre bottle with water in it, so she emptied it out and filled it to the brim with milk. `It's this morning's, so should keep all right,' Isabella assured me.

The settlement at Port Louis.

`Are you sure you can spare all this?'

`Look how much we have!' It was a huge bowl, filled almost to the brim.

`That's wonderful, thank you so much. It's a real treat to have fresh milk — we usually have dried and couldn't even buy fresh in Stanley.'

`I've heard so. I don't know why people live in town.'

We walked back to the beach, which was covered with steamer ducks, loggerheads, as they are known locally, which explained the name of the pond. The gentoos were still there and watched suspiciously as we carried *Skip* to the water. Isabella had been surprised to hear about them, apparently they rarely came so far up the Sound. Mussels abounded.

`Why don't you get some, Pete? Here, put them in the bailer. You can have them for a starter tonight.'

Pete soon filled the container and we rowed back to *Badger*.

We sailed down Berkeley Sound, with puffing pigs joining us by Kidney Island, perhaps our friends of a few days ago and swept round Mengeary Point in fine style, with a fresh Force 5, only to find the wind screaming down Port William, blowing a full gale which was not pleasant, close-hauled. We made it to the Narrows, had a few moments with freed sheets and then girded our loins for a thrash up the harbour, dropping anchor on the south shore, just west of the butchery, having averaged five knots. We must really have been travelling down Berkeley Sound. The wind was still gusty when we turned in and I was ready for a calmer spell.

Thursday, however, was very windy all day and I felt very depressed and, unusually, wanted to get off the boat. There were reported to be a lot of penguins at Gypsy Cove, so we collected a picnic and rowed ashore to walk there. We landed on a suitable-looking beach below the Butchery, only to discover that it was covered in a disgusting mess of bones, skin, intestines and offal. Squelching through it, gorge rising, we were thankful to be wearing wellingtons and moved the dinghy down to the next beach. We had not gone far up the road when a tractor and trailer stopped.

`Hello! I'm Sam Miller. I saw you out there the other day when I was doing Fisheries Patrol. Hop in the back and I'll give you a lift.'

We did not hesitate to accept his offer and were soon trundling along. A Rover was overtaking us and Sam suddenly swerved out in front and back again. The car pulled over and I expected the driver to leap out full of abuse, but instead a pretty, dark-haired girl climbed out, laughing.

`You trying to kill me, Dad?'

Sam leant out of the cab. Give these two a lift, will you Julia? They'll be more comfortable than in the trailer here. They're off the boat.'

`Of course.' She smiled at us. `Shall I drop you down by the West Store?'

`We're going to the bank, actually.'

`OK, I'll put you down there.'

The bank had told us that our Building Society cheque, although backed by a guarantee card, was not acceptable.

`But the cheque goes through the identical clearing system,' we had protested.

`I'm sorry, but we only accept cheques from the major banks. I didn't even know that there was such a thing as a building society cheque account,' was the response.

We could hardly blame her for that. The majority of visitors probably bring cash or travellers' cheques, but it had not been much consolation to us with a bank draft being time-consuming and expensive to arrange and our need of money being fairly urgent.

`Perhaps we can arrange something,' the clerk had told us. `I'll just go and see the manager.'

She had returned smiling. `It's not perfect, but if you write out a cheque, we'll credit you with the money as soon as it's cleared, although you'll have to open an account with us so that we can put the money in. But that won't cost you anything.'

This had seemed a reasonable compromise, although we were amused at the idea of having a bank account there, when we were only staying a couple of months. Now, hoping our money was in, we went in to find out.

`Yes, it's come through.' Just write out a cheque for "cash", will you?'

`I was thinking,' Pete said. `We may as well use these cheques in town rather than carrying round cash. Could you give us a guarantee card?'

`We don't do them.'

`Do people just accept a cheque then?'

The girl looked at us with amusement. `This is *Stanley*,' she explained. `The Manager knows who's not to be trusted and won't let them open a cheque book account.'

`Of course,' Pete said sheepishly. `It never occurred to me. What a shame that everywhere doesn't work the same way.'

In the Post Office, we were delighted to find several Christmas parcels that my mother had sent on.

Following the main road, we walked on to the head of the harbour and stopped at the wreck of the

Lady Elizabeth, regretting the fact that the tide was too high to walk out to her. The very strong wind made walking something of an ordeal and although Pete was happy to continue, I had had enough, so we found a sheltered spot where we could have our lunch. Returning along the airport road was a real struggle, dead into the wind and we were more than grateful to be offered a lift half way. We trekked back through the town and glumly realizing that it was blowing far too strongly to row back aboard, sat on a bench near the Cable and Wireless station, in the lee of some gorse bushes. It was pleasant there, but we knew that it would get cold when the sun had moved round. A car stopped. `Do you want a lift back to your boat?'

We walked over. `Thanks so much, but it's too windy for us to row back aboard at the moment and at least we can sit down out of the wind, here.'

`Well get in anyway, and come and have a cup of tea with us. You can go down when the wind eases off and it won't be so far to walk.'

I could have hugged them.

`I'm Maud and this is Charlie,' the lady introduced them. `We live right along by Moody Brook.'

As we drove along the harbour we could see *Badger* sheering about at anchor.

`When Tim and Pauline stayed here, they were a lot closer to the shore and further up,' said Charlie. `They had cleared a slipway and anchored right next to that.'

`Ah yes, we've seen that, but couldn't row so far upwind this morning. I wondered how they used it. You know them then? You reckon that they were quite close to the slipway do you? Our chart shows it as being pretty shallow there, which is why we didn't come any closer.'

`They'd come and see us from time to time. When we get home, we can show you where they were. Standing up, we could just see their mast, but we couldn't when we sat down. Tim said that the landfill had made a bit of a bay that gave them some shelter.'

`I think I know where you mean,' Pete commented. `Certainly where we are is too exposed.'

At the end of the loch we turned up a driveway to a smallholding with a few sheds and a mobile home. Two or three sheep were ambling about and there was a splendid hen-run, with wire netting to keep out the gulls and giant petrels and one or two fine clumps of tussac grass to shelter the birds and give them something to scratch around.

`Do you fatten the sheep up?' I asked Maud.

`No, I'm too soft-hearted to do that,' she replied. `They're really pets. I was born and brought up in camp and we only moved to town when the children were growing up. The animals make it feel more like home.'

We went inside and Maud put the kettle on. The caravan had a couple of bedrooms, a living room and a dinette in the kitchen. It was in the latter that we sat.

`Look,' said Charlie to Pete, `you can easily see your boat from here. Now, see the aerial there? Well, if you take a line from there over the dump, that's where *Curlew* used to lie. When you're tucked in there, we shouldn't be able to see your masts without standing up. I suppose that you can use our place as a bit of a guide. If you can see us from on deck, you'd be too far out, wouldn't you?'

`Yes, that's right. Thanks a lot. We'll definitely try to get in *Curlew's* spot next time we anchor.'

Maud gave us tea and biscuits and we chatted back and forth, finding that Charlie had been keeper of the light on Cape Pembroke. `It had an unusual mechanism and all but one of the others built like that have been replaced, but it got smashed up during the war,' he told us.

`Did the Argentines destroy it so that it couldn't be used to help guide in British ships?'

`No, no. The Argies didn't touch it. In fact they really did very little damage to anything. It was the Paras that smashed it up. That and a lot of other things, too. They ran riot after the war and of course, no-one complained because after all, we'd just been liberated. But they went into the lighthouse, broke all the glass and the lenses of the lantern and wrecked the mechanism. I suppose they were having fun,' he added bitterly. `I spent years looking after that light, it was a beautiful thing.'

`Those Paras were meant to be crack troops,' Maud added, `but they were horrible. And the others were almost as bad. The reason that they moved the garrison out to Mount Pleasant was because of the way the soldiers behaved. No female between nine and ninety could walk along Ross Road without soldiers making nasty remarks. Even little girls! At first we were so pleased when they came here, but we were glad to see them go.'

`And the place was such a mess,' Charlie continued. `Of course they had to put up temporary barracks for them, but there seemed to be mud everywhere. It was like living in a dump. The war was bad enough, but it seems like the peace is no better. Everything's changed now. Stanley isn't the place it used to be at all.'

`That's what the Argies don't understand,' said Maud, `all that we ever wanted was to be left in peace. We don't want them interfering and we don't want the British interfering, either, like they're doing now. All these people coming in, all the new rules! We managed fine on our own before the war and we don't need them to tell us how to run the place now. But we have to have the garrison and because we can't pay for it, we don't really have a say any more.'

`You think you still need the garrison then? The Argentines have said they will only try to get the Falklands by diplomatic means.'

`Huh! If you believe that, you'll believe anything. You can't trust that lot. The trouble is, I don't trust Britain, either. They want to be rid of us.'

`I suspect you might be right there, but the Conflict is still fresh in people's minds in England. Too many were killed for the Government just to hand it over to the Argentines, without everyone getting upset about it.'

`I don't know why the Argies want the Islands anyway. None of them ever came to live here even when they could. And the soldiers who were here in the war — they couldn't wait to get back home. All they ever did was moan about the weather.'

`Talking of which,' I said, `we can't get over how windy it is here. We'd heard that it was, but I didn't really believe it.'

`Oh, it's a particularly bad year,' said Charlie. `It isn't usually like this. Your boat is still having a rough time of it out there, but normally the wind would have eased off by now.'

We had noticed a couple of tall aerials and asked about them. `I'm a Ham,' Charlie told us, `would you like to see my rig? It's in the shed out there.'

`In fact, that's where we spend most of our time.' Maud told me. `It's a sort of workshop. I used to do a lot of knitting and Charlie has his radio and all sorts of bits and pieces. Come and have a look.'

The shed was fitted out quite comfortably, with chairs, a TV, carpets and several workbenches. There were hanks and skeins of wool about.

`You said you used to do a lot of knitting. Do you make sweaters for the Home Industries?'

`No I don't like their designs. I make them for other people, but not as much as I used to. It hardly pays, really. People won't pay for much more than the cost of the wool. Maybe I'll do more when I retire. What I like doing is getting the wool, spinning it, dying it and then making something.'

`Do you use a spinning wheel?'

`Yes, it's over there.' Maud went over to a workbench and pulled the cover off, then she sat down and showed me how it worked. She was very skilled because she made it look so easy.

`The Government tried to set up a woollen industry,' she explained, `and a lot of women started spin-

ning and then knitting up the wool. You can charge a lot more for clothes made of home-spun wool than with the usual stuff, but most of the women got bored with it after a while and the scheme fell through. One of the problems, I think, is that people wanted to spin the wool so that it was as even as machine-spun, but the trouble is that if it *looks* machine spun, you've lost the nice appearance. I can spin it much smoother than I do, but I want it to look like it's done by hand.'

`You said that you dye it, too. What do you use?'

`Lichen mainly.' Maud got out a bag: it looked like dried branches from a bush. Some was sage green, some grey.

`And what colour does it turn out,' I asked.

`Oh it's much nicer than you'd think,' she assured me and then pulled out a couple of hanks. They were in two different, soft shades of yellow and she put them against the lichens. `The light one comes from this greeny one and the darker shade comes from the grey.'

`But how did you know about it?' I asked. `It's not an obvious thing to use for a dye.'

`I read about it somewhere. I read a lot, especially about wildlife. I love it. That's what we have the TV for — the wildlife programmes. They're all I ever watch.'

Pete and Charlie came out from the radio shack and we stayed for about another half hour, by which time the wind seemed to have abated.

`We should be able to get back aboard now, I think,' Pete said. Going outside we could see that the white horses were smaller and Badger was not sheering about as she had been. It was with real gratitude that we made our farewells and set off back to the boat.

`Call by any time,' they told us.

It was eight o'clock when we climbed back on board and after I had knocked up a curry for supper, we opened our mail. My mother had sent a box of gift-wrapped presents for Christmas, knowing that I absolutely adore opening presents. I put them away carefully, to be opened one by one, with due ceremony, on Christmas day. We had a pile of other mail too, and the rest of the evening was spent enjoying this and by the time we had turned in, the wind had died away, but its effect was still with me and I felt very tensed up.

We woke up to a fine, sunny morning and a forecast of northwesterly Force 4-6 and as we needed to shift berth anyway, we went back to the moorings, hoping that the wind would be far enough west for us to be sheltered. Carl, Dianne and the girls were due to visit the following day and it would be easier to ferry them from the Government Dock rather than the beach. By the time we got there, it was quite fresh, so we decided to pick up the buoy under sail, as *Badger* was completely unmanoeuvrable under Seagull in anything of a wind. The heavy metal buoy would damage us if we hit it and there was no pick-up buoy, so Pete was told off for foredeck work, being both stronger and with a longer reach than I. My first approach was too fast and the second time I missed by several feet, but by the third time I had the hang of it and stopped *Badger* as close to the buoy as I dared, but Pete tried to grab it with his hand and as the buoy was about four feet in diameter, we needed to be right on top of it for him to do so.

`Try the boathook!' I suggested and we went round for another try. This time Pete picked it up without difficulty, quickly attaching a line, while I dropped the sails. When that was made fast, we secured properly, at leisure, but it was still a struggle, with the eye too high to reach from the dinghy. Reluctantly, we hauled *Badger* right up to the heavy, rusty monster, so that we could bend on the mooring lines.

There is an entry fee of forty pounds for yachts, to be paid on arrival in Stanley, which we felt was pretty outrageous as, traditionally, charges are waived for yachts and it is wrong for governments to require payment for completing their bureaucrats' forms. When we protested, we were told that it was for Harbour Dues, but they still had to be paid even if you never came into Stanley. We said we would anchor, but were informed that it made no difference: the buoys were provided, it was our choice whether we used them; but they were particularly unsuitable for yachts, and our forty quid should have got us something a bit better. It is a great shame that the hospitable and friendly Falkland Islands should greet their infrequent visitors so discourteously. Sailing to the Islands is an arduous and uncomfortable process and while we do not expect any reward, neither do we expect to be welcomed with what is effectively a fine. For those who have just battled around the Horn and come into Stanley for a few days rest, the charge is really outrageous and as only about a dozen yachts a year visit the Falklands, it seems very petty-minded that the Powers That Be should create so much bad feeling and a reputation of being unwelcoming, for the sake of less than five hundred pounds per annum. Most yachts never visit anywhere other than Stanley and their impression from the charge for entering and the high prices in the shops, is that the Islanders are out for every penny they can get. We had already discovered that the Falklands is one of the friendliest of places, but sadly, those yachts that stay only a few days think quite the opposite.

It was time to be thinking about Christmas and so we went ashore to buy Christmas cards and several excellent postcards. Pete's epoxy crown had recently come off again, a timely reminder to do something about it. In Brazil, the cheap dentists are an AIDS risk and the expensive ones are United States prices, so Pete had waited until we got to Stanley, where the cost should be reasonable and he and the dentist would speak the same language. Having made an appointment we went round to the hospital, where the dentist had looked at it, complimented Pete on the epoxy job and tidied it up. Then he said to make another appointment as he would need a longer session to discuss what was to be done.

A Canadian cutter had come in, so we called by to see them on the way back. The big yacht was sailed only by a father and his daughter, who introduced themselves as Frank and Julie and over a cup of tea, Frank told us that he was slowly sailing round the world. Originally, he had set off with his wife, son and daughter, but after a few years, they all wanted to do different things and now he spent most of his time on the boat, with his family flying out to join him, from time to time and with regular visits back to Canada. He and Julie were heading off for Tierra del Fuego, very shortly, intending either to go round the Horn or through the Magellan Straits and back to Canada via the Pacific. *Niatross* was a powerful yacht with a wheelhouse, but a big boat and I did not envy them sailing her in heavy conditions. Although most people seem to think the bigger the better, we find *Badger* quite enough to handle in narrow waters and plenty of wind and certainly would not relish the thought of fighting large sails in heavy weather. Even if the large yacht were fitted with junk rig, the thought of the work and cost of maintaining it would put us off. Small is beautiful. As we left, Frank and Julie promised to call by for a cup of tea and to swop some books.

`But not in this wind!' Frank said laughing. It was a stiff row back and although he had an inflatable with an outboard, we understood his reluctance to motor up and see us. In a fresh wind, Stanley Harbour picks up a nasty chop and whatever type of tender you have, it is a full oilskin job to go anywhere.

Saturday was cloudy, with rain showers and a very fresh breeze. It was too windy to take Carl, Dianne and their family for a sail, as we had arranged, and we now realized that days suitable for a pleasant afternoon's sailing party were so rare, that they could only be planned a few hours in advance. We went to see them in case they thought that we might still be planning to go and I took the herbs that Rolo had given me for Dianne, who had a conservatory, thinking that she might be able to look after them there; they certainly were not thriving on *Badger*. No-one was around when we arrived, but Carl walked into the yard after ten minutes or so.

`Why are you sitting out here?' he asked, opening the door.

`Everyone's out — no-one answered when we knocked.'

Carl laughed. `The girls are still in bed! Did you bring your washing with you? Just shove it in the machine.'

A few minutes later Dianne came back from shopping.

`Are those two still not up?' she asked `I don't suppose that you're still thinking of going for a sail today, are you?'

`No, we're rapidly coming to the conclusion that it's no use even planning. However, maybe you'd all like to come round to dinner tomorrow?'

`Sure. We'll do that.'

A squall of rain hit the window and, sitting next to it, I could see *Badger* worrying at her mooring lines. It was not a consoling sight. We ended up staying half the day and got them to talk about their voyage from Australia and show us their photographs. Carl had taken one of Dianne sitting at the helm, Cape Horn in the background; she looked as though she were enjoying herself. The washing was pegged out, only to be brought back in about an hour later when the rain seemed to be settling in, but Dianne had one of those wonderful drying racks that work on a couple of pulleys on the ceiling, and we put the clothes on that to dry.

`That's a nice piece of Marlow rope you've got for it,' I commented.

`Oh that. It came off the dump.'

`I might have guessed.'

The Islanders tend to be a thrifty race and after the Conflict, virtually every house ended up with several ammunition boxes, well made out of fairly thick steel, with strong hinges and over-centre catches, that they use for all sorts of bits and pieces. Apparently the quality of storage paid off because nearly all the shells that the British fired did their unpleasant job without problem, whereas the Argentines had a very high failure rate, largely due to the way in which they had been stored. But it was when the Garrison came to be built at Mount Pleasant, that the Islanders really started to win, because there is the most incredible amount of wastage. It may be a rumour, but several people told us that *everything* used by the Forces has a shelf life, after which it is dumped. Moreover, the regiments at the garrison change every three months and when a new

one comes in, it brings all that it needs, which includes everything from shoes to shelving and as it is not economical to transport the old equipment back to the UK, that all gets dumped, too. If a soldier tears his jacket or his loose change chafes a hole in his pocket, the clothes are not repaired, but thrown out, even his work clothes. The Islanders made full use of this largesse until *They* put an end to it. The story goes that the local shops, which means the unpopular Falkland Islands Company, complained that people were taking things from the dump rather than buying them at inflated prices in the store, so now, when anything is dumped, it is first rendered useless by, for example, cutting right up the back of a jacket. The apparent waste makes for efficiency: everything works when it is urgently required, but it still seems like wanton extravagance to most people.

We left later in the afternoon, the rain having ceased for the moment, as had the wind; there was only a light breeze when we went back aboard.

But the wind filled in before eight o'clock the next morning and although we were half expecting Julie and Frank to come by, it must have put them off. The breeze often dies down in the evening, but if anything, conditions were worse when Dianne and the family arrived. Pete managed to fetch them, after a very wet row, but as soon as they got on board, the girls felt sick.

When he came below, Carl looked at them and said, `I told you that it would be too rough for you.'

Tracey managed a weak smile. `No, it's fine Dad, just a bit bouncy,' but a few minutes later she dashed into the cockpit and leaned over the rail. Rachael seemed less affected, but was not her usual boisterous self and even Dianne looked a bit green round the gills.

`It saves us a lot of walking, being on the moorings,' I said, `but I'm not sure if the discomfort is worth it. I wish we were down at anchor, it would be a lot better for you.'

Dianne smiled, `yes, but Pete would never have got us aboard — it was bad enough just to the jetty and back.'

Uncertain as to whether they would come to dinner, I had kept it simple and made spaghetti bolognese with a chocolate pudding to follow. Tracey quailed at the sight of food, in between her trips to the cockpit and we could not put the boards up so that she could stand in the pram hood for fresh air, because the diesel heater was lit and was too sensitive to draughts even to consider it; each time the poor girl went out, the fire threatened to follow suit.

Despite Rachael feeling queasy, she polished off a plate of spaghetti, but a few minutes later, she too dashed to the cockpit and fed the fishes. She bounced back below, smiling cheerfully.

`Well, I've got some room for pudding, now,' she announced and, perhaps because it was a little calmer by then, managed to keep it down. Dianne had recovered sufficiently to eat, but I was getting quite worried about Tracey, who was as white as a sheet and must have been getting cold.

`It's a lot calmer now,' I told her, `try coming below and lying down. You're going to get frozen there.' She cautiously came into the saloon and lay down with her head in Dianne's lap. She looked forward and started to go green again.

`Would you mind, very much, taking the globe down?' she whispered. The wild movement of the big, inflatable globe hanging in our cabin was impossible to ignore and obviously unsettling.

`Don't look at it,' Dianne suggested, but I took it down. We were both very impressed with the girls' gallantry; they must have felt extremely miserable, but made not a word of complaint and even did their best to join in the conversation.

`Tracey gets much worse than any of us,' Carl said, `don't you love? When we went up to Uruguay, she was sick nearly all the way there and then coming back was the same. I usually feel a bit off on the first day or so and Di and Rachael are both really ill for a couple of days, but we all recover. Poor old Tracey has a hard time.' She gave him a wan smile.

`And you're looking forward to when *Pale Maiden*'s finished?' I asked her.

She nodded her head. `I like being on a boat,' was her incredible comment.

`She's a great little sailor,' Dianne said. `I remember one night when everything was going wrong — we had to shift anchor, it was blowing a gale and raining and Carl and I were just about bushed when we'd finished. When we got below, Tracey had made a pile of sandwiches and flasks of coffee. She was only nine at the time. She's really sensible — when she wants to be,' she added, with the true mother's touch.

They stayed a while longer and Tracey was just about able to sit up by the time they left. Pete took them off rather more easily than he had got them aboard. `Thanks for letting us come,' the girls both said. `It was great.'

`I'm sorry that you had such a rotten time, Tracey.'

`No, it was fine, really,' she smiled.

Hope triumphing over experience, Pete left the washing up for the morning, but the wind picking up again about five o'clock, forced us to move into the saloon and fearing breakages, Pete did the dishes before turning in again.

It was with considerable reluctance that we climbed out of our bunks to a truly horrid day. It blew and blew and although the wind was from south-west, the waves seemed to be coming right up the harbour. It was really uncomfortable, with the boat pitching and heaving and we struggled ashore to post mail and to buy me some cord trousers for a Christmas present. Annie at the Pink Shop had a sale on, but I could find none that I liked and would fit. In the end she went round to her store room and brought out a pair in a lovely shade of raspberry, which fitted perfectly. They were size nine, and I teased Pete that the nervous strain of being in the Falklands had made me lose weight.

Later in the afternoon, we heard a boat's engine close by and looked out to see the harbour launch, *Speedwell*, with *Skip* on board. She had pulled out her stem fitting and started drifting down the harbour, where she had been seen by the launch's crew who picked her up and brought her back. They passed her across and we put her on the foredeck, where she could get into no more trouble. Our thanks were heartfelt and we gave them a bottle of good, Brazilian rum, in appreciation, for it would have been a disaster to have lost her. Looking at the fitting, we found that it had broken off and must have fatigued; I dislike and distrust stainless steel for just this reason.

Normally, we shackle on our anchor chain to a mooring, but with these being open to the north and east, we might have had to leave in a hurry, with the risk of damaging *Badger* on the mooring when we unshackled the chain, and so we had used rope lines, one of which had already chafed. When the time came to turn in, the wind had picked up to near gale force and it seemed sensible to keep `anchor' watch, but Pete never woke me because it had calmed down by one o'clock.

I woke up, still tired from so many broken nights.

`We might as well go sailing,' Pete said. `Obviously we're just going to have to get used to strong winds and we're unlikely to be more uncomfortable at anchor then we are here.'

I felt less than enthusiastic about the sailing bit, but was quite happy to get off that dreadful mooring. Nine o'clock saw us underway and heading for Port Harriet in a sou'westerly Force 5, aiming to get as far west as possible, before returning to Stanley in the middle of December to meet Steve. Although the wind eased once we were out of Port William, before long we had to reef again. It was a hard windward thrash but the skipper was sure that we could make Bluff

Cove, and, with the thought that it might be blowing even harder the next day, we carried on. The day seemed endless and I had lost interest by the time we eventually anchored at a quarter to midnight of a clear, moonlit night, foolishly having postponed dinner until we got in. Having hoped for a nice quiet evening and an early night, I was beginning to wonder if I would ever catch up on my sleep.

One of the consolations of the Falklands was the number of sunny, not to say sparkling days and despite our late night, we were up by nine o'clock, the fine morning tempting us out of our bed. We were anchored off a small bay, protected by a narrow entrance bordered with rocky cliffs, which would have made a perfect harbour, had it not been too shallow. Rowing ashore, we saw that the cliffs were lined with rock shags and at this state of the tide, hundreds of mussels were clinging to the rocks above the water. A fine walk brought us to the settlement, where a nearly-completed house sat on the sloping ground, overlooking a grand view. As we approached the house, a young lady came out to meet us.

`Hello! Where've you sprung from?'

`We're on a boat, anchored down off Bluff Cove.'

She invited us in, apologizing for the state of the house.

`We got fed-up of waiting for it to be finished and I wanted to be in for Christmas,' she explained. `We still need the doors on and a few other jobs, but at least we're in.'

Dianne was also English, an ex-nurse; her husband was a solicitor in Stanley. They had hoped to run the farm commercially, but the fall in wool prices had made it impossible and Kevin had gone back to his profession.

`The trouble is we can't live here as cheaply as we'd like to. We miss some of the things that we were used to in England.' She picked up some leaflets.

`We're members of several book clubs and can't resist buying them — we both love books. Poor Kevin hates working as a solicitor, but when we've finished the house and paid off the farm, he should be able to stop working. I hope so.'

We were delighted when Dianne offered to show us round. A large sheep bounded up to her when we went out of the back door.

`Go away! I've nothing for you.' It butted her in obvious

disbelief and she pushed it away as we dodged through a gate, leaving it on the other side.

`It was a pet lamb,' she told us, `but it's really getting to be quite a bully. I don't know what to do with it. I can't bear to kill it, but it won't have anything to do with the other sheep. We'll just have to take it to a far camp and leave it there, I think. *These* are my real interest.'

`What lovely ducks! Do you breed them?'

`Not yet, but I'm hoping too. I had a lot of problems earlier, because they kept losing condition. I'd hoped they would go down to the creek below the house, but they don't seem interested. Maybe it's too far from their food. Anyway, they were eating well, and seemed quite happy, but they looked so scruffy. In the end I asked the vet round and he said they needed water. "But they always have plenty!" I told him, but what he meant was that they actually need to be able to get into the water to wash themselves properly. We made a small pond for them and they've come on wonderfully since then. They're laying now. We have hens, too, for eggs, but ducks are more interesting.'

We went back to the house and had a very pleasant morning. Dianne was an intelligent and cultured person; we would like to have known her better. Hearing that we were heading out west, she asked if we knew the Poncets.

`No,' Pete replied, `but we're hoping to go and see them. I'd love to meet them. They've done some really remarkable voyages.'

`We used to see quite a lot of them,' Dianne told us. `They're really incredible. Sally is very good-looking — she could have been a film star. They must

Beaching **Skip** *at Bluff Cove.*

be very busy though, because they never come and see us nowadays.'

We were invited to stay for lunch of coffee and sandwiches and the afternoon was well advanced by the time we came to go. As we were putting on our jackets, Dianne asked, `Could you buy any eggs in Stanley?'

`No,' I replied. `I couldn't believe it! I don't think we've ever been anywhere where we couldn't buy eggs. Fortunately, we still have some left.'

`Well have some of ours,' Dianne responded, taking me back into the kitchen. `We've got far more than we need.' There was a stack of egg trays, well-filled. `Would you like some?'

`Well, ...'

`Go on. I've got some boxes here. I'll put in some duck eggs, too, they taste nicer.' Once more embarrassed by the Islanders' hospitality, we were very grateful to be given one of the things that was impossible to buy. As we walked away, Dianne came running after us. `Here,' she said, `take these. You probably don't have any on board.' It was a bag of tomatoes, a real treat, but when we got back to the boat we were mortified to realize that they were not home-grown, as we had supposed: they had been bought in Stanley. Dianne had guessed right that we had none aboard: at one pound fifty a pound, the were far too expensive and we were sure that Dianne and Kevin could ill afford such extravagance. Her thought had been more than generous.

With a couple of reefs in each sail, we set off towards East Road, a short cut that sounded quite complicated, but turned out to be a piece of cake, interesting and satisfying pilotage that made for a most enjoy-able sail. With only nine miles to go, the anchor was down in Fitzroy Creek at the more sensible time of a quarter to seven.

A breeze filled in after sundown, turning into a hard wind that had us crawling out of the bunk to the quieter saloon. The day came in extremely windy, with the boat heeling and yawing, the gale funnelling down the gap in which we were anchored and I was tense and worried, unhappy where we were. By mid-morning, there seemed to be a lull and, hoping to find better shelter, we started the Seagull and at full revs just managed to give ourselves enough power to assist Pete, struggling to get the anchor. Under bare poles, we tore down Pleasant Sound, a misnomer that day, finding no suitable anchorage and once outside, the wind increased even more to a steady Force 8-9. Wondering if we were going to have to put to sea for a day or so, if I had been unhappy at anchor, I was far from cheerful now. More in hope than expectation, we shaped a course towards Choiseul Sound and with just the fore-sail bundle squared off, we were doing four and a half knots. To our profound relief, the wind started to take off, we raised the top of the main, logging seven knots and by four o'clock, had a further two panels up, but perhaps we overdid it, because one of the battens broke. After a tremendously hard sail, culminating in a long beat, we dropped the hook in Pyramid Cove, to find ourselves in a marvellously secure harbour, surrounded by small islands and banks of kelp, which blocked the waves from just about every direction. To me, it had been an absolutely vile day, matching my worst visions of the Falklands and as I turned in, yet again in the saloon, my one consolation was that we would be leaving at the end of January.

Successful fishing at Pyramid Creek.

Having pushed me to the brink, the gods relented, the wind fell away overnight and we woke fully refreshed, to a sunny day. While Pete was making breakfast, I commented, `Do you realize, that before we came to the Falklands, in the ten years we've been sailing *Badger*, we'd only ever been forced to sleep in the saloon about half a dozen times? Since we've got here, it seems to have been about every other night!'

Ignoring this observation, Pete asked, `How about going ashore and seeing if we can catch some mullet here?'

This seemed an excellent idea. I made some Cornish pasties, by which time the wind had picked up again, and it was a stiff row ashore, but we had a fine walk to Pyramid Creek, finding a delightful spot, made perfect by the fact that it was *out of the wind*. The pretty creek had high banks on either side and a rocky foreshore and the fish were biting. Despite putting the small ones back, we ended up with eight mullet, but not having anticipated such good luck, had only brought plastic bags to carry them, whose handles cut into our hands. I had a length of string, which we passed through the gills, enabling us to pull the fish unceremoniously, over the diddle-dee.

`Next time we go fishing, I'll take a knife and clean them on the spot,' Pete declared. Even after a dinner of chinese-style fish and pickling six jars full, there was still some left for fishcakes for the next day's dinner. It had been a very good day and as we climbed into our own bunk I told Pete that I might stay after all.

It went flat calm and the sound of rain woke me in the small hours. I know of no feeling cosier than that of listening to the patter of raindrops on deck and I lay there, feeling snug and secure, revelling in the tranquillity.

In the morning, the wind was very light, which seemed quite incredible. By ten o'clock the sun had come out and with a Force 3 breeze, for once we had perfect sailing conditions, but it showed signs of faltering, so we set our sights on nearby Shallow Harbour on Lively Island. It was interesting to sail in, wriggling around a few shoals and tacking up a narrow channel; Ewen Southby Tailyour's sketch chart seemed more accurate than the new Admiralty chart.

Passing an island, covered with Magellanic penguins, we were inundated with little brown birds, which hopped about on deck, friendly and confiding, peering down the hatch and perching on the backrest, only a foot from where we sat. One landed briefly on my head. They were so charming that it was difficult to concentrate on steering for the anchorage off the settlement. I had completed my `bulletproof burgee' on the way, and we hoisted it after we had anchored. Rowing ashore, we reckoned that it looked very acceptable and it proved to be almost indestructible.

We pulled the dinghy up the beach and walked towards two people, busy painting, who greeted us kindly and introduced themselves as Alec and Elliott.

`Don't you have an engine, then?' Alec asked.

`Yes, we do,' Pete replied, `why do you ask?'

`Well, I've only ever seen one other boat actually *sail* in through that gap and I assumed his engine must be bust. When I asked him what was wrong with it, he nearly brained me! He didn't have one at all and I think I insulted him.' There was a twinkle in his eye, `so I didn't want to make the same mistake again.'

`I'll bet you're talking about Tim and Pauline.'

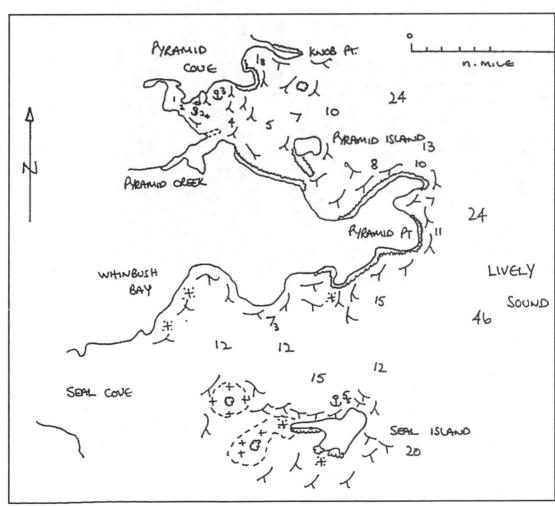

'That's right. You know them, then?'

'We've met them once or twice. They seem a great couple.'

'Yes, we liked them, too. In fact, you're the first boat to visit since they were here.'

Our first impression of good, kind and friendly people was reinforced after visiting Alec and Elly on several other occasions, and we became very fond of them. This morning, they both put down their paint-brushes and Alec lounged on the grass to talk to us, while we all enjoyed the unwonted light winds and sunshine.

'It's not often we get the chance to paint — usually, the wind just blows the paint straight off the brush,' said Alec. 'I often get up at dawn to work before the wind gets up, but then everything is covered in dew.'

'There's only the two of us,' Elly told us, 'and when we bought the place, everything needed painting. It's taking us a long time.'

'Would you like us to give you a hand?' Pete offered. 'We're both used to painting.'

Imperial shags on the headland at Lively Island.

'No, that's very kind of you, but you're here to enjoy yourselves.'

'We enjoy painting,' I said.

'No, you go and have your walk. But come and have a cup of tea with us when you come back, won't you?'

'We will. Thank you,' and we took ourselves off so that they could carry on painting. Lively is quite a large island, but although much indented with coves, they are usually too exposed or too shallow to be used

as harbours. The little brown birds were everywhere and, on a headland, we came upon a huge flock of imperial shags. They were difficult to photograph because being incredibly tame and intensely curious, they came right up to us, heads weaving up and down, back and forth on long, snake-like necks as they strove for the best view of us. Their black backs had a lustrous sheen and they had white breasts, gorgeous, bright blue eyes, startlingly orange knobs on their beaks and huge, pink feet, which constantly tripped them up.

It was late afternoon when we got back to the settlement and Alec and Elly seemed pleased to stop for tea. Their house was immaculately clean, like most of the houses in camp, but although the range was in the living kitchen, Elly had a huge scullery, which was more like a conventional kitchen, apart from the lack of a cooker. By the sink was a large jug of milk and I asked her if she made her own butter.

'I used to, but I broke my wrist last year and it's still giving me a lot of trouble.'

Alec overheard: 'Yes, the doctors don't seem to be able to do any more for it. Poor Elly gets a lot of pain from it and I don't think that it's going to get much better, now.'

'But you can buy an electric churner, can't you?'

'Yes, but if I do that, I'll feel like I've given in. I'm sure it'll get better eventually.'

We were told that the little brown birds we had seen were tussac birds, well-known for their fearlessness, which had been their undoing, as they were a prime target for rats who ate both birds and their eggs. To our surprise, Alec said that Lively Island was rat free.

'Yes, it's one of the best things about it,' Elly added. 'We both love the little birds — all the birds in fact. I have a couple of Upland Geese that nest every year just across the green here. In a lot of places the rats or cats would get them, but here they are quite safe.'

'We'd heard that farmers don't like Upland Geese.'

'Some of them don't. But if anyone asked to come and shoot *our* geese,' Elly added with feeling, 'I'd soon send them on their way.'

Alec and Elly were not what might be considered typical farmers.

'I hate killing the sheep,' Alec told us. 'When they are about seven years old, we have to get rid of them.

The young ones are growing up and the older ones don't give as much wool. We can't sell them — I tried to get them to buy our mutton for Mount Pleasant — Mare Harbour's only just across the way — but the soldiers can't eat *our* meat. It's not EEC approved. Us and the dogs can only eat so much, so the rest is wasted. When I take them off to kill them I think, "you poor beast — you've lived for me all these years, giving me your wool, having lambs and earning me a good living and now you're getting old, so I'm going to kill you." It doesn't seem right.' Then he laughed. `But as we have to do it, I hope you'll take some mutton back with you. It'll save it going to waste.'

And when we eventually said good-bye, we were laden down with a huge bag of mutton and a litre and a half of fresh milk.

`There's enough here for a week!'

`No, no — I'd eat that lot for breakfast, when we're shearing!'

`Come back and see us again, won't you?' called Elly.

`We will!'

It was calm when we turned in, and although the odd gust woke me and had me edgy, the morning broke with very light winds again, and we got underway with a nice Force 3 drifting in from southeast. As this was on the nose at the mouth of Lively Sound, we put into Motley Bay, where we rowed through the kelp to land on a white, sand beach. Motley Island was lovely, rising from the beach, with cliffs, topped by tussac grass down to the south. Tussac grass is found on

Motley Island birds: from top, Magellanic penguin, rock shags and a tussac bird.

most islands in the high southern latitudes, growing in large clumps, which can reach eight or nine feet in height. They can be of equal width and as the grass dies at the base it grows from the top, forming a pedestal. Both living grass and pedestals provide nests for dozens of different birds.

The beach was alive with Magellanic penguins, which were also braying in the tussac beyond the sand hills, where we found a big colony with lots of burrows.

There were birds everywhere, flying, feeding and looking after their nests: kelp and upland geese with their goslings, a hawk, skuas, rock shags, black and Magellanic oyster catchers, finches, thrushes, tussac birds, an owl and wrens. In the centre of the island was a pond, where ducks swam and on the far side, we startled a huge sea lion, who thundered off over the slab foreshore into the water. Further on four more sea lions, females this time, were sleeping peacefully in the sun, but took to the water when they heard us. It was

Sea lions sleeping peacefully in the sun on Motley Island.

absolutely marvellous and the sheer variety was almost unbelievable. Pete found a huge fender on the beach.

`We can use it if we go to FIPAS,' he said, `or give it to Carl — they'll need big fenders.'

The wind stayed light all day and although it was rather rolly at anchor, I had so enjoyed these last few days, the calm weather and the wildlife that I barely noticed it. Having dined well on mutton pilaff and figgy duff for Pete, we turned in to another calm, moonlit night.

A light breeze blowing straight into the anchorage had us away before breakfast. With only a fortnight to get back to Stanley, we debated whether to continue west or to content ourselves with circumnavigating East Falkland. Pete wanted to meet the Poncets, but I was uncertain, because they might either be fed-up of admiring yachties turning up, or feel themselves too good for mere mortals, but we could always leave if we were not welcome, so I agreed to give it a try. After all, it should be a fast passage back from west to east.

Rain set in and we lit the heater, which worked quite happily in these moderate winds, to keep the boat dry. With an early start and a rare, fair wind, we covered fifty-one miles to Halfway Cove on Speedwell Island by six o'clock that evening.

The rain having ceased, next morning we packed a picnic and set off to see the gentoo penguin colony that we had read about. There was no-one around at the settlement, so hoping that they had no objections, we headed towards the colony, passing a pair of Magellanic oyster catchers with two fuzzy little chicks who scurried around like clockwork toys. A kelp goose was nesting right next to the track and had been invisible until she moved. She flew away at the last minute and, feeling very bad at disturbing her, we watched from some distance to see that she returned. Disturbingly, a skua flew over, but the goose saw it and flew back to her nest.

The gentoos were on a level piece of ground well above the sea: scores of them nest-building, on eggs or with chicks. We were surprised to see a king penguin among them, looking lonely and misplaced, while handsome, dove grey dolphin gulls, their legs and beaks apparently dipped in carmine, loitered around, probably with no good intent.

Walking back, Pete nearly stepped on a steamer duck, who left her well-hidden nest of four eggs in the marram grass, returning as soon as we had passed. On a nearby beach, the penguins shot out of the water and ran up the sand before plodding the long trail up to the colony.

Back at the settlement, we met the owner and his wife, but unlike most of the Islanders, they were not at all interested in us and were contented to be by themselves. Having apologized for not asking their permission to walk around, and their having asked if we had managed to find the penguins and enjoyed our walk, the conversation languished, so we bid them good day and went back aboard.

The forecast was warning of northerly gales, to which Halfway Cove would be exposed, which caused us furiously to think. George Island looked possible, but not inviting and eventually we settled for an overnight sail for Albermarle Harbour, before the gale came. Pete carefully planned the courses and distances to run and we got underway. The moon was just past full, which not only made the passage easier, but much more pleasant.

Wanting to do the pilotage, Pete steered most of the night and the wind had increased from a comfort-

Speedwell settlement.

able Force 4 to a good Force 6 by the time we got to Albermarle, anchoring in a fine, sheltered spot, just after six o'clock. Although the wind picked up considerably, there was no fetch where we lay and we were hardly aware of it. By the time we had eaten dinner, the wind was easing off and with a reasonable forecast, we planned to get away first thing in the morning.

We were up at five-thirty to a lovely day and a light breeze, which never rose above a Force 3. Unfortunately, it was a headwind and with strong tides in the offing, we put into Port Stephens, as an acquaintance of ours who had once lived there had asked us to pass on her regards to the present occupants, Peter and Anne. It was a delightful sail up to Port Stephens, at the top

Gentoo penguins and a couple of dolphin gulls (left) on Speedwell Island.

end of a lovely bay and two people in an inflatable came by to talk to us: they were moving horses off one of the islands. After anchoring, we went to the big house to give Peter and Anne our message. They had all been neighbours, farming in Argentina, but not having seen An for donkey's years, they were more than a little surprised to hear from her.

`I didn't even realize that she was still alive,' Peter said. `She must be at least eighty now — it's forty years since we've seen her. Does she still drink her bottle of Scotch a day?!'

We laughed. `She sure does!'

Anne's mother still lived in Argentina and they had been unable to meet since the Conflict, but recently, the Falklands Government had given her permission to visit the Islands. Surprisingly few of the Islanders have any links with Argentina, but for those that do, it had not been easy over the previous ten years or so, but when I suggested that there might be a division of loyalties, Anne soon put me right.

`Certainly not! I have no wish at all to be Argentinian — I just wish that we could travel back and forth like we used to.'

A young man joined us for a cup of tea and as he was fascinated by our way of life, we offered to show him *Badger*.

`You must invite Mike, too,' said Mark. `He's mad about boats and I know he'd love to see yours,' so we went to find him, meeting Leon, who had been in the inflatable and who invited us round for a drink after supper.

Mike and Mark enjoyed their visit and Mark was full of questions, having just started to travel, the Falklands being his first stop. Anne was some sort of cousin, and he had many more scattered about the erstwhile Colonies so there was no shortage of places to go or opportunities for a bit of casual work, but when he realized how we took our home with us and had been sailing and travelling for years, he felt that we had the answer. By the time he left, he was planning to buy his own boat and go sailing. We wondered how long the idea would last.

After a hasty supper, we went ashore to visit Leon, his wife Pam and their two daughters. Their base was at Albermarle and they were disappointed to have missed us there, but, like Mike, were staying at Port Stephens for the shearing, bringing their sheep to the big shearing shed. Their farms had once been part of Port Stephens and they had been employed there before it was broken down into smaller units. It was poor camp, the sheep did not thrive and they had to work very hard, but felt that it was worth it to be inde-

pendent. Pam and Leon were nearly ready to move in to their `new' house at Albermarle, which had come from Hoste Inlet. When the Islanders talk about `moving house', they sometimes mean it quite literally for the prefabricated buildings are no great problem to dismantle and reassemble. Although we all had a long day ahead of us, Pam and Leon were still offering another round when we left, well past eleven; we had enjoyed the evening.

Up at half past five on Friday morning and underway before breakfast, we were chagrined that what wind there was came straight up the bay, but at least it would be fair when we turned west. It was not to be: by the time we worked our way out to sea again, the breeze had died away and when it eventually returned, it was back on the nose, but I was quite happy to enjoy such light winds and if we were not making much progress, at least it was peaceful. We headed for Rodney Cove, sailing the last hour or so with a cold fresh breeze and showers. It was a good harbour, with several spots to anchor: we dropped the hook near a Magellanic penguin colony.

Generally speaking, the tides are fairly weak around the Falklands, but they can run very strongly around Weddell Island and its environs and we had to get the tides just right to get to Beaver Island, where the Poncets lived. We had no tide tables, but *Falkland Islands Shores* gives the tides at full and new moon, enabling us to work them out with reasonable certainty. There was a time when Admiralty charts also contained this information, but the idea is now, unfortunately, considered obsolete, rendering tide tables a necessity, which is often easier said than done. They are, of course, much more accurate, but it is better to have a rough idea of high water than none at all.

Pete had worked everything out carefully, double checking it all, but we only just made it through Stick-in-the-Mud, a channel which was effectively the gateway through to Beaver Island. It is very narrow and the tide, which sluices through on springs, turned against us as we were beating up, so that we had to hug the shores and work the eddies to break out of it. It was quite exciting and very satisfying when at last we realized that we were going to make it and from there it was plain sailing to Beaver, where we anchored off the settlement. To Pete's delight, *Damien II* was there, which meant that probably both Poncets would be on the island.

Within a couple of minutes, a little boy rowed out and invited us ashore, introducing himself as Diti, Sally and Jérôme's youngest son. He took us to their yacht, where they were working and they suggested that we should look around and then join them for dinner, which we duly did. Diti acted as our guide, enjoying himself as he pointed out all the places of interest. As well as Sally, Jérôme and Diti, we met a young man called Frédéric; the other two sons were at school in Stanley. To my relief, Sally and Jérôme turned out to be very friendly and seemed unaffected by their fame. Jérôme could be very amusing, with an acid tongue, and in true French style ensured that his wife and

*Badger (in the background, left) anchored at Beaver Island with **Damien II** in foreground.*

family all spoke his language. Although he can read English as easily as French, his accent is still very strong and it is no exaggeration to say that he sounds exactly like Peter Sellers in the role of Inspector Clouseau, yet he would become quite irritated when people did not understand his occasionally incomprehensible speech.

Sally was particularly interested in our accounts of Motley Island, which was apparently for sale, as from what I told her, she thought it sounded like a natural wildlife reserve.

'We'd heard that it was eaten out and that all the islands to the east had rats on them,' she explained.

'Well, we certainly saw lots of tussac birds and, having seen them on Lively, I knew what I was looking at.'

'Did you see any wrens?'

'Yes — in fact I took a photograph of one,'

Sally went to her room and came out with a couple of bird books. 'Have a look in these and tell me what you saw.'

I pointed out the tussac birds, black-throated finches and a bird that was shown as a Cobb's wren.

'I'd really like Falklands Conservation to buy some land for a reserve, and these birds do seem to imply there are no rats.'

For dinner, we had Jérôme's *pièce de résistance*, tender mutton fillets, which I preferred to beef steaks.

Discovering that they were readying *Damien II* to go out on charter, we offered to help, which offer was accepted with alacrity.

I had a pile of washing to do, but Pete went ashore after breakfast and returned for lunch.

'What have you been doing?' I asked.

'Well, I seem to have ended up sailmaking. I get the idea that Jérôme is not too fond of the job, so he was more than pleased that I had some experience.'

'Has he got a good machine?'

'Not really. It's a big industrial one and powerful enough, but the handle isn't geared and there seems to be something wrong with the bottom tension. He must have had some bad weather on his last trip — the sails need a lot doing to them.'

In the afternoon, I made a huge, complicated curry and a ginger pudding for the evening, as we had invited everyone onto *Badger* for dinner. At least this time, our guests were not seasick. They brought a home-made loaf and a bottle of whisky with them, a very kind gesture. The food seemed to go down well and we had a wonderful evening, fascinated by their tales and stories of South Georgia and the Antarctic.

The next morning, Pete continued sailmaking while I did several outstanding jobs on board. Diti rowed over in the afternoon bringing us a cake. He had a sweet tooth and as Sally was not interested in cooking, had taught himself to bake, greatly encouraged by his mother, who also enjoyed sweet things. This was not one of Diti's better efforts, having a distinct taste of stale mutton fat and I rather suspected that the tin needed washing, but we each had a slice and I made the appropriate noises. He was rather a precocious little boy, clearly intelligent, but with a tendency to show off, perhaps because he was lonely. Although he squabbled with his brothers when they were home, he seemed to miss them when they were gone.

Invited up to dinner again, we spent quite a lot of time talking about South Georgia.

`We have *The TOTORORE Voyage* on board, and it makes South Georgia sound like a wonderful place,' Pete said.

`Ah yes eet is superb! But 'e is a madman! We 'ave been to all ze anchorages zat 'e 'as bin to and some of zem 'e should nevair 'ave stayed at when zair wair better ones near by.'

`Perhaps, but he was doing his bird counts.'

`Zen 'e should 'ave left as soon as it was done, or put 'is crew ashore and gone back for zem. 'e is a crazy sailor!'

`He certainly seems to have taken some risks and had his fair share of luck,' Pete commented, `but on the other hand, he spent three years in the Southern Ocean and brought his boat back, so he must be a fine sailor, too.'

The settlement on Beaver Island.

`'E did well, but 'e was vairy lucky, too'.

Sally wanted to know more about Motley Island. `Can you come ashore tomorrow and show me where the pond was? I'd be pleased, too, if you would check up on Imperial Shag rookeries while you're sailing round. I think I have them all marked, but I'd like to be sure.'

`Yes, of course. I'd be very interested in doing anything like that. I'll bring our small scale chart over tomorrow.'

Sally and I spent some time marking the chart and she asked me if we could go back to Lively Sound and have a good look at the islands there. To help me, she gave me a couple of wildlife identification books.

`But I was intending to buy some in Stanley, anyway,' I told her.

`You take them — I've one or two spare copies and you can regard it as payment for the sailmaking, if you want.'

`But you've fed us and offered us half a sheep already. Anyway, we're happy to help. We don't want paying.'

`Take them — you'll need them in Lively Sound.'

There were two houses in the settlement, the family's home and one for housing shearers and other visitors, generally referred to as The Other House. The long-term plan was to do it up for the family to move into, but although both houses were in a poor state and quite comfortless, Sally and Jérôme had so many different projects that a cosy home was well down on the list of priorities. On this afternoon, we were in The Other House, which had a glassed-in `conservatory' running its whole length: a lovely spot on a sunny day. Pete was still toiling away on the sails in the gloomy kitchen saying that if nothing else, it made him appreciate *Badger's* light and small sails, while Sally and I were in the conservatory, when a series of terrific squalls came through. Sally looked startled at their ferocity and Jérôme later estimated the worst at eighty knots. As we watched, williwaws tore off sheets of water, hurling them down the harbour and then *Badger* started to drag. Pete and I immediately started running down to the quay and met Jérôme, who had noticed what was happening.

`Get into ze Zodiac!' he shouted and we pulled it down the beach and leapt in. Jérôme's face was alight, Pete looked pale and I was frankly terrified. Racing out towards *Badger*, we leapt off a wave and I thought the RIB would flip, but Jérôme throttled back a bit. When we got to *Badger*, Pete and I scrambled on board and hastily put out the CQR, but as we still seemed to be dragging, we put down the Bruce as well, after which we stopped. The squalls had dropped to about Force 9 or 10, but with rocks astern, it was still very worrying and we sat in the cockpit checking that we were holding. In the meantime, Jérôme had been having troubles getting back and eventually had gone downwind to a beach, where he had ballasted the bow of the RIB with rocks, to prevent it from blowing up.

By about half past eight, the wind had eased sufficiently for us to Seagull back, inching our way in the squalls to pick up Jérôme's big mooring, as he had suggested. It had been a horrible and frightening experience.

`I remember why I didn't want to come here,' I told Pete. `If we are going to get winds like that again, what are we going to do? We were sure that the Luke would be man enough and we dragged. We can't stay if we can't trust the ground tackle and there was no warning at all of those squalls.'

`I was thinking about it, while we were sitting in the cockpit. Perhaps we should have had both anchors down, but I feel the real problem was that we didn't have enough scope. Five to one is OK for most places, particularly with the Luke, but maybe we should anchor on ten to one, here. It's not as though we're likely to hit a neighbouring yacht.'

I was still very shaken. *Badger* has many virtues, but it has to be said that the foresail creates a lot of windage on the bow, causing her to put heavy loads on her ground tackle, as she sheers about. The only real solution is lots of very heavy anchor gear, but we cannot afford to carry that sort of weight in the bow, where the anchor locker is situated. As they say, all boats are a compromise.

The following morning, we talked with Sally and Jérôme about what had happened and she very kindly tried to reassure me.

`But the South is really hard on boats and their gear,' she commented.

`We were worried about Jérôme getting back ashore.'

`So was I!' She laughed. `But it's just the sort of situation Jérôme lives for.'

Jérôme agreed with Pete that scope was the answer and told a story of when he and Gérard were on the first *Damien* and had come back on board after they had been stranded ashore by a gale. They had had a long line ashore to help pull themselves back and forth in the dinghy and when they came to leave, it was wrapped round the anchor cable. Untangling everything, they found the anchor totally fouled and that they had been moored solely by a vast length of light rope. Pete concluded that our tackle was up to standard, it was our technique that was at fault, but I had lost faith and if Steve had not been coming, I would have suggested leaving. Apparently Frank and Julie had dragged at Johnson's Harbour, but there was no more news and we hoped that they were not damaged. *Kotick* was apparently stuck at Saunders Island with damaged sails. It had been quite a blow.

`I've never seen woollies like that at Beaver before,' Sally said. `It was like the worst of our winter gales, yesterday.'

It had been suggested that we use Jérôme's workshop to repair the self steering gear, which had been damaged by the RIB when Jérôme put us aboard, and Pete mended the broken batten at the same time, before going back to finish off the sails. While I was cleaning up one of *Damien II's* galley doors for revarnishing, Jérôme came in.

`We are going to see ze fur seals. Do you want to come?'

`Oh yes, I'd love to. When are you going?'

`Now.'

`I'll just go and tell Pete.'

`Well I am going, so you 'ad better be quick.'

By the time I had seen Pete, Jérôme was already on his bike, so I climbed on behind him and, with Frédéric and Diti on another bike, we rode over the island. To get to the seals, we had to go down a gully and then climb down a cliff, which I found unnerving, but Jérôme somehow instilled confidence. Not daring to look up, which I find much worse than looking down, I eventually climbed down to where we could watch the seals. There were about ten pups, little black things, which I gazed at in wonder. The big bulls were a sort of olive green and the cows brown, with a light cinnamon belly. They are not easy to distinguish from sea lions, but have noticeably pointed noses, while sea lions have a square nose like their land counterparts. Climbing up again was even more alarming, but we had a wonderful ride back, with stunning views. Once again we were invited for supper and had *le ragout de la mère de Frédéric à la Falkland*, to which we contributed some Uruguayan wine, decanted into empty bottles. After dinner, Jérôme showed us some of the footage used in BBC's *Life in the Freezer*, with which they had been actively involved. There were unique recordings of fur seals eating krill and of a Wilson's storm petrel feeding her chicks.

It was time to get back to Stanley and Pete finished repairing *Damien II's* sails, giving them a final check over. Alain arrived on *Kotick* and Sally and Jérôme's natural pleasure in seeing their friend was enhanced by his cargo of Argentine wine. In celebration we were once more invited up to dinner, where we spent another pleasant evening.

On Saturday morning, as we went ashore to make our good-byes, Alain stopped Pete and asked him if he would do some sail repairs. It was the last thing that he wanted to do, as the sewing machine was still not working properly, but Alain was already behind schedule, so Pete felt that he could hardly refuse, especially as Alain had helped us out in Mar del Plata. I took the opportunity to put another coat of varnish on the batten and was in the workshop, when Jérôme came in to look for something.

`Ah hah!' he said, `I 'ave somezing 'ere zat might intairest you, Annie,' and pulled out a small bogey stove. We had been asking him how we could stop our diesel heater from down-draughting and he had told us that the only solution was to give it its own air intake, which was not practicable with our installation.

`That looks just the job,' I said laughing. `What do you use it for?'

`I 'ad forgotten zat eet was 'ere. It used to belong to *Baltazar* but zey dumped it 'ere. Do you want eet?'

`I'm certainly tempted. It's easy to find wood round here and I'm sure that it would work better than our other one. How much do you want for it?'

`Oh but you can 'ave eet, if you can use eet. I don't want eet — eet ees taking up space 'ere!'

The stove was obviously designed for charcoal, but looked promising and I showed it to Pete at lunchtime. `Well, it's not perfect, but I think it will be a lot better than the Reflex.'

`I don't suppose that it's worth it, for just a couple more months,' I commented.

`No, but when we go on to Tasmania we'll need a heater and I doubt that we can buy one in South Africa.'

I also painted Diti's *Optimist*, because although he was meant to be doing it, he found it hard work and wanted to be able to use the boat. Then I cleaned around *Damien II's* heater, a filthy job with the inevitable oil weeps invariably attracting a lot of dirt.

That evening we met another friend who had just flown in. Sandy was a fascinating person who had come to the Falklands with another girl by way of both Americas, cycling the whole length of the continent.

Pete finished Alain's sail the following morning and he gave us five *briks* of Argentine wine, which were very acceptable, after which we went to say our good-byes, Jérôme insisting that we take a whole mutton.

`Eet ees only a rabbit! You must not tell anyone eet came from Beaver. Eet is so small.'

Having thoroughly enjoyed our time there, we were sorry to leave, but promised to return to see Sally, if we managed to survey the islands in Lively Sound. With fair tides, it was straightforward sailing through Stick-in-the-Mud and Tea Island Pass and we made good time to Rodney Cove where we anchored for the night.

Incredibly, the next day brought light *easterly* winds: right on the nose for Stanley, but the wind came round to southwest after midnight and we then had a splendid sail, the wind never exceeding Force 4 and brought to off Pleasant Island the following evening.

We had a good romp back to Stanley, with the breeze increasing as usual as we turned up Port William, giving us a hard beat, the wind near gale force and right in our teeth. It was with a feeling of relief that we finally anchored in *Curlew's* spot at the top end of the loch, as well-sheltered as it was possible to be in that windy place. We had two days in hand before Steve arrived.

Chapter Fourteen

As well as meeting Steve, Pete also had a dental appointment, but when he went in the next day, it was to find it cancelled. Some poor soul out in camp had been flown in for emergency treatment.

I had to get *Badger* fit to welcome our visitor, cleaning up and polishing brass and with Steve coming for a month, I emptied a couple of lockers. This was easier said than done. Living on a boat, every space not only gets filled, but is usually overflowing and in one of his books, Eric Hiscock mentions that people continually put more things on to a boat, but very rarely take anything off. We are no exceptions to this rule, despite our best efforts and finding room for the tins and jars that I had taken out of the lockers involved a complete sorting out of half the others. Every time something like this occurs, I wonder what to jettison, generally finding nothing and, knowing that I could survive without most of the stuff we have on board, I realize how seriously I am possessed by my possessions. It is not an edifying thought.

Carl had kindly offered to ferry us to the airport, which we much appreciated, as it would save us the walk out to the airport, a distance of some five miles. Friday came in windy and showery.

`Not much of a welcome for Steve, is it?' I commented to Pete.

`Still, he won't be under any illusions about what he's letting himself in for,' Pete replied with a laugh.

We met Carl at his house, then drove up to the small airport, parking with all the other Rovers. After a short wait, the bright red Twin Otter came in over the airfield and touched down, looking very small; I rather envied Steve his flight from Chile. It was surprising how many people could be seated in such a tiny craft,

rather like one of those comedy films where fifteen people climb out of a Mini. Steve was instantly recognisable and looked unmistakably American, laden down with bags, binoculars and packages, with a pink jacket, over-size glasses and a hat. The usual formalities had to be completed and as he waited, there was a definite expression of relief on his face when he saw us on the other side of the barrier.

`You made it then. Great. Was the flight good?'

`Very interesting. Glad that *you're* here, too. I didn't really fancy spending a month in the Upland Goose.'

We went into the car park where Carl was waiting and made the introductions.

`Annie,' Steve said as we drove away, `I didn't bring any boots, they were too big to carry, so if I'm going to need them to get onto *Badger*, we'd better buy them on the way.'

`Is there any chance of stopping off at Falkland Farmers, Carl?'

`Sure, no probs. I'm not in any hurry.'

The shop is one of those that sells paint, ear tags, clothes, bloodless castrators, scrubbing brushes, saddle soap and anything else a farmer might require. It also sold wellingtons and Steve selected a pair of stout green ones, saying, `Pete should be able to use them when I leave. I seem to recall that we take the same size and I sure don't want to be taking them home with me.'

We climbed back in the Rover and drove along to *Badger*. Thanking Carl, we unloaded all Steve's kit.

`Don't worry, Annie,' he said, smiling, `It's not as bad as it looks.'

Pete took me back first with some bags, so that I could light the heater and then went back for Steve.

`Right,' he said, `let's do something about these bags. Now the binoculars, Annie, what did you do with them?' I passed them to him.

`OK, Pete, so long as I can use them to look at the birds here, these are for *Badger*.' Looking at him in astonishment, Pete took the glasses from Steve's outstretched hand.

`They've got a compass in them!'

`Yeah, and they're gas filled. *Supposed* to be waterproof, but I wouldn't want to take them swimming. I thought you might be able to use them.'

`But surely you need them on *Rosinante*.'

`Hell, Pete, it was enough trouble bringing them down here, without having to take them back again. If they turn out to be any good, I'll buy some for *Rosy* when I get back.' As Pete opened his mouth to protest, Steve added, `call it part of the charter fee.'

Pete grinned, `OK then, but thanks a lot, Steve, I've always wanted a pair with a compass in.' He went out on deck to try them.

`Fire!' I shouted, and he banged down the hatch. Steve looked startled.

`If we leave the after hatch open when it's windy,' I explained, `the fire downdraughts and it nearly gives me a heart attack when it relights. It stinks, too!'

`Hmm. Not a great success, huh?'

`It has its drawbacks.'

Pete came back down. `They're terrific, Steve. Thanks a lot.' I went and tried them out.

`They seem first-rate. How does this fixed focus work, do you know? It certainly makes it a lot easier when you're looking for something like a buoy.'

`Come on, Annie. I've got all this other stuff for you to sort out.' It was a bit like Christmas when he started unloading his bag. As well as several things that we had requested, such as a sou'wester and spare filters for our drinking water, Steve had brought film, thermal wear (`See what you think of it, Annie — if it's any good I'll order you some more') and lots of bits and pieces. I showed him the empty lockers and he unpacked his clothes. With travelling through the tropics, and intending to see a little of Chile before he went back to the USA, he had needed to bring more than he might have chosen and had also taken my warnings about the weather to heart, bringing plenty of good, cold weather gear. But it was going to be a squeeze.

`Don't worry Annie, I'll soon get back into living on a boat again.'

Somehow, everything was put away and Steve settled in. We spent the rest of the day on board, catching up on each other's news. Knowing our usual tastes, Steve had anticipated turning vegetarian for a month, so was quite stunned when I produced some of our Beaver mutton for dinner.

`There's plenty more left, too,' I told him.

`Really? Lamb's my favourite and I hardly ever get to eat it. Carol won't — she can't stand the idea of eating the sweet, little, woolly things.'

`Hell, Steve. When you eat a lamb in the States it's about a year old.'

`Yup. You tell her. She still thinks of the nice, little lambs and just can't face it.'

`Well, we can always buy some more, while we're here. You shouldn't go short!'

We made a leisurely start the following morning.

`Do you want hot water to shave, Steve, or do you use an electric razor?' asked Pete as he got breakfast underway.

`I think I'll just grow a beard again while I'm on board, Pete. It'll be easier and I'd quite like to see what one looks like after all this time.'

When we first knew Steve, he had a luxuriant black beard that grew high up his cheeks, but had shaved it off when he started working in the family business; men with beards are not really trusted in Ohio. We had never become accustomed to him clean-shaven.

`I hope you're feeling full of the joys of spring, now, because we have to go shopping today. We need to do some stocking up before going off sailing.'

`I'm looking forward to seeing the town,' Steve replied, so after breakfast, we rowed ashore. As we went along the harbour, we pointed out the wrecks to Steve, stopping to read the boards which the Museum has mounted in front of each one and which gives a brief description and history of the ship.

`You know, what amazes me is the size of these ships,' Steve commented. `When I think of "windjammers" I have a picture of massive vessels with great, tall masts, but looking at these wrecks, they're really pretty small, aren't they? And these are all Cape Horners.'

Pete agreed. `They couldn't have carried that much cargo, when you think about it. It's not surprising they were uneconomic as soon as the sailors were paid any sort of a living wage. The weight of the cargo must have made a hell of a difference in their sailing performance too. You read about them getting swept, but it's quite understandable when you see how little freeboard they had.'

`I reckon the super-yachts are much the same size as *Jhelum* there, Pete. How long is she, do you reckon?'

`I don't know. A hundred and twenty feet? Whenever you read any details, it's always tonnage and that doesn't mean much to me.'

`What fascinates me about the *Jhelum*,' I remarked, `is that she was an East Indiaman. I always envisage them as being huge ships and *Jhelum* just doesn't seem big enough. Can you see her battling round the Cape of Storms, laden down with spices, carpets and all the rest of it? And how on earth did they fit all the crew on, too? But the wrecks are a bit of a disappointment to me. We had a *Wooden Boat* magazine about ten years ago with an article about the Falkland's wrecks, but from what I remember from the photographs, they have deteriorated a lot since then.'

`I guess you're right. Still, I'm glad to have been able to see them before they disappear altogether.'

As we went into the West Store, Steve offered me the use of his wallet.

`Just buy what you need, Annie, and then add what you want,' but I found it a bit difficult to go on a spending spree, especially with prices being so high. All the same, we were well loaded down when we left. We went along to have a look at another yacht that had come in and was lying along the Public Jetty, discovering that it was *Dodo's Delight*, a fellow RCC member. `The Rev', as he is generally known, makes a practice of taking disadvantaged youths on adventurous sailing cruises and his latest venture was to circumnavigate by way of the Antarctic. His present crew seemed neither particularly young nor disadvantaged: one was on paid leave from the Army, one on unpaid leave from his job as a supermarket manager, one was permanent mate and although the fourth one *was* unemployed, he was in his early twenties. None of them could be described as small and it seemed an awful lot of people on a thirty-three footer. They had just got in from Rio and were sorting themselves out, so after a brief chat, we left them to it. and, picking up our bags, walked back to *Badger*.

Sandy, whom we had met on Beaver, was leaving the Falklands and had invited us to her going-away party. We broke the news to Steve, who is not a party man, but he actually seemed quite pleased to get the opportunity to meet some of the locals. We duly got ourselves ashore and walked into Stanley, soon finding the house, with the party already in full swing. We had a splendid time: there was a huge barbecue and the wine flowed like water. Steve soon got to know several people and as Sandy had come round on *Damien II*, we met up with Jérôme and Diti again. The latter had come in to town for a visit and told me that they had had a horrible ride through Tea Island Pass with wind against tide. With a powerful engine in his boat, Jérôme does not bother with tide tables, but perhaps Diti wished that he had.

`We went over a *huge* wave,' he told me, his eyes round as he remembered, `and then all this water came down a ventilator *right over my bunk*. I was mad at Jérôme!'

We found that the Rev was also at the party, along with his `lads.'

`It didn't take you long to find the right place to go!' I said to him. Poor Bob caused us some amusement when we realized that his initial awe-struck respect for us was because he thought that we were Tim and Pauline Carr, who had sailed their engineless gaff cutter, *Curlew*, from the Falklands down to the Antarctic the previous year. We were at cross purposes for some time:

`Have you got an engine in that boat of yours, yet?' he asked. At one time we sailed *Badger* without a motor, but I wondered how he knew.

`Why yes,' I replied, `we have a big Seagull.' Bob also commented about our odd rig, obviously thinking of *Curlew* and her enormous topsail, but as we have junk rig, his remarks did not seem too inappropriate. On introducing us to the `lads' he described us as `a couple who have been winning all sorts of awards and medals,' but even that comment was not incomprehensible, allowing for exaggeration, as we had won one or two Club prizes. In the end he discovered his mistake.

`As I mentioned, we're on our way to the Antarctic,' he said to Pete, `and I'd be interested in what you have to say about it — any advice that you could give us.'

`Well, I don't think I'm the person to ask,' replied Pete. `I've never been there.'

`But you got the Blue Water Medal! Last year! For going down there!'

The penny dropped; Pete realized Bob's mistake and disillusioned him. He hid his disappointment well.

In the meantime, I had met some interesting men from the British Antarctic Survey, who had been telling me all about the wildlife in South Georgia. It almost made it sound worth going there. They told me that they could arrange for us to see over the *Bransfield*, the BAS research ship that was presently berthed at FIPAS and I said that I would look forward to it.

Next day, Pete and I were both a bit hungover, but Steve, who hardly drinks, was only suffering from the effects of a late night. I had told them that about the invitation to look over the *Bransfield* and as she was due to leave the next day, we walked up to FIPAS. When we got there, it became apparent that I had got my wires crossed as the men that I had been talking to were not staying on the ship, but in digs in town. They had never mentioned that little detail, probably assuming that I realized it. The officer to whom we spoke was very apologetic: normally he would have tried to arrange something there and then, but with them being busy with preparations to sail, could not spare the time. It was a filthy day, blowing half a gale with heavy rain showers, but Pete and Steve did not make the comments that they must have been thinking. If nothing else, the walk did freshen us up a little and gave us an appetite for dinner.

We spent Monday morning doing our final shopping and on the way, we called on *Damien II*, wanting Steve to be able to meet Jérôme in a quieter atmosphere than the party. Steve was impressed both with

Anchorage at Pyramid Cove.

Jérôme and *Damien II*. Jérôme had been stocking up, too, and gave us a couple of mugs, with badgers on them, that he had seen in one of the shops. Coincidentally, they were identical to some that we had bought in England, but I was very happy to have a couple of spares and touched by the gift. Back on board, I stowed everything away, made some scones for tea, welcome on a cold, overcast afternoon and we discussed our plans.

`Treat me like a charterer,' Steve told Pete. `You arrange the itinerary and we'll go where you think is best.'

`We ought to get out west, the scenery is more impressive,' Pete suggested, `and it might be nice actually to go right round, don't you think?'

`Sounds good to me.'

The weather had been less than pleasant for Steve's visit, but Tuesday could not have been better, with hazy sunshine and a Force 3 breeze from the south. Steve was concerned about getting sunburnt and with a complete lack of self-consciousness, attired himself in a strange rig consisting of zinc oxide tape across the nose, several more strips across his face and a back-to-front sou'wester as sun hat. I had asked him to bring me a sou'wester, because I dislike using a hood and we were back in a climate where oilskins are the norm and he had brought two different designs. I had chosen the smaller of the two, but Steve's came with such a ludicrously long tail that it really needed a row of reef points. It looked even more ludicrous worn back to front, but Steve was impervious to our laughter and even put up with having his photograph taken. It was a lovely day's sail, with incredible weather and although progress was less than spectacular, we were at Bold Point, near Bluff Cove, in time for tea. Steve and I were going to row ashore to look at the Gentoo penguin colony, but the sight of the swell on the beach put us off and we contented ourselves with looking through binoculars. It was a rolly spot, so we upped anchor and took a passage through the kelp to anchor in East Road.

Not long after we dropped the hook, an orange inflatable whizzed out of Bluff Cove towards us, carrying Kevin Kilmartin and son, husband and offspring of Dianne. We asked them aboard, but he was worried about missing the tide; the dinghy and outboard were heavy to drag up the beach. We were sorry not to get to know him better: he was obviously a thoughtful person, because his main reason for coming out to speak to us was to warn us that people had reported poor holding where we were anchored. In such light conditions this did not concern us unduly, but we appreciated his concern.

We were away by half past six, next morning, on another lovely day with a light, north-easterly breeze, eating breakfast as we sailed, the idea being to go fishing and have a barbecue at Pyramid Creek. We anchored at midday and out came the rucksacks into which we stowed food, bottles of beer, a sharp knife, plates, cutlery, etc., and, complete with fishing rod, rowed ashore. We had collected some wood in advance and found that diddle-dee, a sort of heather that grows in most parts of the Falklands, made excellent fire lighting material. We enjoyed ourselves immensely: Steve and I built a fireplace from the conveniently flat stones lying about while Pete alternated between attending to the mutton and harassing the fish, catching several large mullet.

Steve was enthusiastic about checking on the wildlife at the islands in the sound for Sally, and he I went to Pyramid Island, later that afternoon. Steve offered to row, waving aside my offers of taking my turn, enjoying the exercise. He had taken the precaution of putting on some `sailing' gloves, but still had incipient blisters by the time we were back on *Badger*, for it was further than it looked. Pyramid was Steve's first tussac island and proved to be a fine example. He was delighted with it: tussac birds were all over the place, their complete fearlessness never ceasing to amaze us and a pair of crested caracaras, locally known as *caranchos*, were obviously nesting. They flew over us screaming abuse, trying to head us away from their nest, on a clump of tussac, with the young, almost-fledged bird standing on it. Steve had a powerful telephoto lens on his camera and took some photographs, but as we carefully moved away, it flew off. With the parent birds still swooping around, I lost track of it, but it landed in the kelp and it was a few minutes before Steve mentioned it. It was flapping its wings trying to take off and the parents were flying over calling frantically. I raced back to the dinghy, but with my non-existent sense of

Kelp geese at Pyramid Cove.

direction went the wrong way and had to go around two-thirds of the island. I rowed round to where I could see it tangled in the weed, but it was no longer moving and when I got there it had drowned. I felt terrible. The parents were flying and crying overhead and I carried the fledgling to the beach, unable to bear the sight of it in the water. They flew down to it after I rowed away, trying to get it to respond and move to a safer spot. It was heart-breaking. They generally only rear one chick, putting so much effort into it; this one was just about ready to start its own life and now it had all been in vain. After that it was difficult to remain enthusiastic about noting down the other wildlife, but I finished the job and we rowed back in the near calm. I could still hear the caranchos keening over the death of their young one.

The anchorage at Pyramid Island is beautiful in these gentle conditions, with low, golden islets and rafts of kelp, mysterious against the tranquil water. Steve sat in the cockpit watching the steamer ducks swimming around. Steamer ducklings tend to dive in moments of stress and cause great consternation to their parents when they come back up, as they tend to set off at a great rate in all directions until they are rounded up into a group once more, where, weighing hardly anything, they bob over the tiniest of wavelets as they paddle furiously to keep up

Steve and Pete tend the barbecue.

with the others. But I could not enjoy the evening, aware as I was of Pyramid Island, where the young carancho would still be alive had it not been for our well-meaning intrusion.

To our astonishment, Thursday also came in with light north-east winds and as the day progressed it became positively warm. We were quite incredulous as to how lucky Steve was with his weather.

`If this is the sort of luck you have, Steve, you'd better stay with us until we go,' we quipped.

Flourishing clumps of tussac grass grow to seven feet and provide hiding places for sea lions as well as birds.

`I'm not complaining. After what you've told me, and what I saw the first few days I was here, I don't mind if it stays like this. I'm interested to see how *Badger* behaves in heavy conditions — but not *that* interested.'

Because it was so calm, we took the chance of stopping to look at Seal Island, although it was so unprotected that Pete stayed on board, in case the wind picked up. It was very rewarding, alive with tussac birds, which fluttered around us constantly and we also saw several Cobb's wrens, that other clear indicator of no rats. One, nesting on the shingle beach, popped in and out quite unconcerned about the fact that I was only a yard or so away. Seven-foot plants of tussac grass flourished, sheltering quite a few sea lions, which we nearly fell over, to our mutual alarm. I noted down all that I saw, wondering if *that* bird was a snipe and trying to get a closer look at the beak of a little brown bird to establish if it were a pipit or a siskin. The

pictures in the books were not particularly accurate and as I was seeing some of these birds for only the second or third time, I was uncertain of some identities. I am not a trained naturalist, but I knew that I had to be positive before claiming to have seen any particular species. Steve was busy banging off film and we were having a wonderful time, so that it was nearly midday when we got back aboard.

By the time we were underway, the wind had increased to Force 4, which gave us a lovely sail down to Motley Island, where we anchored about lunchtime. Steve declined coming ashore with me, for in spite of playing a lot of tennis and golf, all the walking, rowing and sailing were starting to catch up. Pete rowed me ashore and left me to it, arranging to be back on the beach at six o'clock.

Motley is a fairly large island, about two and a half miles long and half a mile at its widest. The north end still bore signs of over-grazing, with very little tussac. The middle had the sandy beach rising to sand-hills on the east side and going west, there was a boggy plain, grassy on either side, with a pond; at the far side the beach was shingle. The southern end was totally covered with tussac, which followed the shore up to the middle both east and west. Sally was hoping that my survey would confirm that there were no rats on the island, in which case, she would try to persuade Falklands Conservation to buy it as a reserve. Because most of the larger islands have been used for cattle or sheep in the past, sooner or later rats have come in with the boats and very few are free of the pest.

Badger *at anchor off Motley Island, watched by sea lions.*

My afternoon was a success, insofar as at the end of it I was convinced that there were no rats about, but it was astonishingly hot work pushing through the tussac, which was so thick and high that it completely blocked out the wind, while its vertical growth allowed the sun to shine right down. It is not surprising that so many birds nest in it, for as well as providing nesting materials and food, the micro-climate that it creates is considerably warmer than the one outside, which must make the young birds much less vulnerable to exposure. With tussac as dense as I was finding, it was also very tiring, because I could not see beyond the next plant and was constantly coming to dead ends, where two plants grew so close together that I could not force a passage through.

I also had my fair share of adventure. Looking over a cliff, I found myself almost on top of a Casson's falcon's nest. Even as I noticed the chicks, who glared with fierce yellow eyes and hissed at me, the parents attacked with ear-piercing screams that scared me witless, until I discovered their source. It was still quite frightening as they swooped down at me, claws extended and aiming at my face, forcing me to grovel away through the tussac to escape them. I sat for a while waiting for my heart-rate to subside before carrying on. Further south, the tussac was almost impenetrable and I started to worry about falling over sea lions, which I could hear growling away and I was not a little concerned about falling over the cliffs because I could see nothing ahead and at times had difficulty locating the sun to help orientate myself. Sally had asked me to

sketch in the details of the island, cliffs, sandhills, etc., but it was getting extremely difficult to ascertain my whereabouts as I could see neither the anchorage nor The Mot, a small island to the south of Motley, that I had been using as a reference. Time was pressing, so abandoning the geography to concentrate on the wildlife, I took a short-cut across to a point opposite The Mot. I soon realized the error of my ways when I was dive-bombed by skuas. I know now that a stick held above head height will keep them at bay, but having no hat and feeling that they meant business, I had no choice but to stay on the edge of the tussac. Just before I got to the pond, there was another shriek from behind me: this time a brown owl reckoned that I was too close to *its* nest. My nerves jangling, I was happy to sit down for a few minutes, have a cup of tea, and watch the ducks and a Chiloe widgeon on the pond. It was a hell of a trek back, because having checked the shingle beach to confirm that there were Cobb's wren about, I then had to make a forced march across the bog to get back for six o'clock.

Steve had recovered sufficient energy to come ashore, Motley looking too appealing to miss, and had seen kelp goslings, sea lions and penguins galore and as we rowed back with Pete, we agreed that it had been a most satisfying day.

We slept like logs in the peaceful anchorage and made sail at about half past seven, hardly able to believe our luck: a fair light wind and sunshine, but by tea time it was blowing Force 5 with rain. In went the reefs and then the wind came round and headed us and it was with few regrets that I went below to commence cooking supper. Pete held on to a long tack and for once, the gods were with us because just as he went about, the wind shifted so that we could lay Fanny Cove Creek, our destination. Steve was most impressed with Pete's meteorological knowledge.

`I was expecting the wind to shift as the cold front came through,' he claimed. I was frankly stunned, because Pete generally takes the weather as it comes, not bothering too much about what may happen and to this day, I am not sure if it was good luck or good judgement.

The anchorage, recommended in *Falkland Islands Shores*, did not look exactly snug, but by the time we got the hook down, we were more than happy to get below into a warm, dry boat, away from a filthy evening, pleased to have made thirty-three miles to the west.

Christmas day came in wild and got worse, with the best part of a gale blowing for most of the day, bringing torrents of rain with it. Consoling ourselves with the thought that it was a suitable day to be harbour bound and that with better weather we might have felt guilty about not sailing, we settled down to enjoy Christmas. Pete cooked a splendid breakfast of grapefruit and orange cocktail; fried mutton, fried bread, eggs and tomatoes; bread and marmalade and a large pot of coffee for Pete and myself, (Steve has no truck with caffeine) and when this had been tidied away, we followed our tradition of pouring a sherry all round and opening our presents. Pete had made a half model of a double-ender, similar to *Rosinante* for Steve and he gave me the boots that we had bought in Uruguay and the trousers that we had got from the

Pink Shop. I gave him some fish hooks and a tape measure and we found that we had each made the other a Christmas card with a penguin on. My mother had sent us loads of goodies which took a deliciously long time to open and A Good Time Was Had By All.

The weather deteriorated and poor Steve was not happy. The dreaded seasickness had struck with yesterday's stronger winds, and the bouncy anchorage did not make him feel any better. For lunch I made *empanadas* filled with wild mushrooms and mutton, but Steve waved them feebly away. During the afternoon we sat reading and our oft-repeated comments of `I think it's moderating, now, don't you?' started to have a bit more conviction after tea time. By six o'clock, Steve was sitting up and taking notice again, so I pulled the stops out for dinner and we had a real feast:

popcorn and rum punch
curried mackerel fillet
roast leg of mutton, roast potatoes
asparagus (home-bottled)
Christmas pudding and rum sauce
Rioja.

I had decorated the boat the previous evening and we even had crackers to pull, so that we could take photographs of ourselves wearing silly hats. Christmas day had been a success; perhaps the weather even made it better, in the end.

Boxing Day came in `somewhat less revolting than yesterday', although it continued to rain. We togged up in oilskins and boots and went ashore to look for an enormous gentoo colony, that was reported to be quite close. After a lot of hard tramping over diddle-dee and having seen no sign of them, we concluded that either we had duff information or that the gentoos had vanished into the ether. However, the day had improved marginally and as the morning's forecast had been for fair winds and our anchorage was neither particularly comfortable nor scenic, after a quick cup of coffee, we got our anchor. Before long, the winds went light and variable and in the leftover slop, Steve succumbed once more to seasickness and turned in. When the wind went south, allowing us to steer our course, Pete and I discussed what to do with this unforeseen chance. On the one hand, Steve was not having much fun, but on the

The Christmas feast aboard **Badger***, complete with crackers and silly hats.*

other, if we took the opportunity now, we could get right out west and return at leisure, sailing more or less as it suited us. We asked Steve what he felt.

`Let the skipper do what he thinks best. I'm not going to die and we shouldn't waste a fair wind.'

We carried on and with a cold breeze, it seemed a good opportunity to try out my new boots. I sat in the cockpit.

`Hey, Pete, guess what?' I said after an hour or so.

`Go on.'

`I've got warm feet!'

`So they work, do they? Well, in that case we can go to South Georgia.'

Pete had been talking about going to South Georgia ever since we had been at Beaver. We would not have time to go this year as it was already mid-summer, but his idea was to over-winter in the Falklands and go the next season. Sally and Jérôme might possibly let us stay at Beaver: it was useful for them to have someone to look after the island when they left it, as they usually did for a month or so every winter and they appreciated that staying in Stanley would not be much fun for us. I, still wondering if I had bitten off more than I could chew with the Falklands, was not at all keen on the idea — South Georgia would be a lot harder.

`I think we should carry on with our original plan, Pete, or the whole voyage is going to take an extra year.'

`But this is the perfect opportunity; we may not get another like it.'

`South Georgia isn't going to go anywhere.'

`No, but it sounds as though there may be more rules and regulations in the offing and it may become more difficult in the future.'

We left it at that. Remembering the day we dragged at Beaver, I was sure that I did not want to go through that sort of thing again.

Steve opted out of dinner and Pete and I settled down to watches after we had eaten and cleared up. With a clear sky, an almost full moon and sure of our position, we had no fears of running into anything on this unlit coast. Besides, the nights were mercifully short at this time of the year, with only two or three hours of real darkness and for once, the forecast was right and the wind stayed fair.

Whilst on watch, I realized in what luxury we normally sail. The person off watch sleeps with the leecloth up on the windward side of the boat and the watchkeeper has the lee settee at his disposal. Even coastal sailing, much of the time it is perfectly safe to stay down below reading, getting up for a look round every few minutes. In fact it is arguably safer: sitting in the cockpit for three hours tends to be both cold and boring. There is a good risk of dozing off and, trying to keep out of the wind, you tend to huddle up in a corner — not the best position for keeping an all round look-out. Lethargy tends to prevent you from trimming the sails or even, if it is poorly situated, checking the compass course. Sitting below you are warm and rested; a book holds your attention and keeps you alert and the vague feeling of guilt that you are *not* keeping a constant lookout ensures that each time you get up to check things, you do a thorough job: course, speed, lights, sail trim, anything looming out of the dark ahead, all are monitored and appropriate adjustments made. Tonight, with both bunks occupied, it was not much fun keeping watch for although I sat under the pram hood, sheltered from the wind, there was no light to read by and the seat was not as comfortable as the settee. Once it was light, there was the land to look at and Cape pigeons, black-browed mollyhawks and sooty shearwaters flying around, but I was glad that we did not always keep watch like this. In the dark and unpopulated waters of the Tropics, passages would get monotonous: I am not the sort who can contemplate the infinite for hours on end.

Everything was in our favour on this passage: we saved our tide through Governor Channel, the alternative to Tea Island Passage and came to anchor off Staats Island just before ten o'clock. Steve had been up for some time and completely revived as soon as the hook was down, all the better for plenty of sleep. Staats Island is inhabited by guanaco, a type of llama, which were introduced in 1937, perhaps for `sport' or as an alternative to mutton. The island belongs to Beaver and the guanaco are something of a dilemma for Sally and Jérôme. Some people say they should be eradicated as alien species (should the sheep go, too?), some that they should be farmed, some that they need culling, some that no-one should interfere with them. Usually, they are left alone, but the odd one is shot occasionally to add variety to the Beaver larder. Another species that was misguidedly introduced to several of the islands, is the Patagonia Fox. The idea was that they could be trapped for their fur, but this did not prove economic and they are now simply a pest. On Beaver, they seem to find plenty to eat scavenging along the shoreline, but on the much larger Weddell Island, with its relatively shorter coast, they are a real problem, attacking the ewes when they are lambing and killing young lambs or weak sheep. It is impossible to eradicate the foxes, who can find endless cover amongst Weddell's `stone runs,' large tracts of loose boulders

A guanaco on Staats Island.

After lunch, the tide and wind being in our favour, we continued to Beaver Island, with no problems in Stick-in-the-Mud. Fish Creek is a deep anchorage, with a good fetch in sou-westerly winds and a lot of kelp about and as our last visit had taught us to be cautious, we picked up the empty mooring. Diti rowed out to greet us and we gave him some sweets and toys from our crackers: little plastic frogs, that jumped a surprising distance when you pressed down on their tails. After solemnly assuring me that he 'really wasn't all that fond of sweet things', he carefully

and rocks that feature largely on the Island's landscape. In desperation, a fox-proof fence has been erected, at great expense, enclosing a large area of land, in the hope of exterminating the foxes trapped within.

Several guanaco were in sight, so we launched the dinghy in the hope of being able to get a better look. Because the animals rarely see people except to be shot at, they are very shy and difficult to approach, but we were lucky enough to see them quite clearly. Climbing a hill to look at the view, we found ourselves just above a group of three guanaco, which we watched for some time before they noticed us and made off. It was a sunny day, with excellent visibility and magnificent vistas. In the foreground the small islands and passages between them were laid out like a chart and further east we could clearly see the strange stack of the Horse Block Rock, and past the Sea Dog Islands all the way to Cape Orford. To the west, beyond Governor and Beaver Islands, were the extraordinary and impressive cliffs on the west side of New Island, while below us in the horseshoe bay, with its dazzlingly white beach and its blue and turquoise waters, lay *Badger*, quietly swinging to her chain. Making our way back, Steve was delighted to encounter a jackass penguin at the mouth of its burrow, two chicks peeping out curiously from behind.

stowed them away from the sharp eyes of his brothers. We all had tea and went ashore, introducing Steve to Sally and meeting Leiv, the middle of the two sons, a quiet, friendly boy. Sally was very interested in the results of my survey of the islands in Lively Sound and I told her the story of the young carancho.

'Oh yes,' she said, 'that does sometimes happen — it's difficult not to disturb something now and then.'

Beaver has a sizeable colony of gentoo penguins and Sally showed us its location on the map.

'Is it OK if we go and look at them, tomorrow?'

'Of course. It's a nice walk, but quite a long way.'

*Below, **Badger** at Staats Island. Facing page: Hilltop view from Staats to Cape Orford.*

The next morning, I made a picnic and we had a lovely walk in the sunshine, Steve and myself assiduously picking mushrooms and gathering several pounds, including some puff balls.

`If I dry even half of these, I'll be able to use them whenever I want to. We can't get much in the way of fresh stuff,' I explained to Steve, `and something like dried mushrooms adds a bit of variety.'

The colony was in three separate groups and we settled down to watch. A steady stream of penguins trudged back and forth from the distant sea — quite a walk for human legs. Different penguins colonize distinct niches in the landscape: Magellanic penguins, or jackasses as they are called locally, choose peaty land where they can dig burrows, preferably among the tussac; rockhoppers, as their name implies, nest on cliffs; gentoos prefer higher ground, often some distance from the sea, which seems a strange choice, but perhaps they are latecomers on the scene. Their nests are hollowed-out mounds of mud, sometimes lined with pebbles and they spend much of their time guarding their own nests and filching pebbles from their neighbours, so that each nest tends to be just beyond pecking range of the next. After regarding us with suspicion when we arrived, most of them ignored us, but several were somewhat intrigued and

Gentoo penguins nesting and rearing young on Beaver Island.

waddled hesitantly up to have a better look, then curiosity satisfied, returned to their nests. They were at various stages of breeding, ranging from birds on eggs, through little grey chicks guarded carefully between the parent's feet, to well-grown young birds, marked with a washed-out replica of the adults' colouring. These were rather odd-shaped little birds, their fat seeming to flow down and gather over their feet so that they resembled those toys that can be knocked right over and still come back upright.

We sat for some time, eating our picnic and watching the penguins watching us. When we walked round, we were surprised to come across a couple of rockhoppers in among the rest, looking less than comfortable, but perhaps feeling the security in numbers.

Returning along a different route, we scrambled over very badly eroded ground. No-one is quite sure if the degree of erosion is natural or exacerbated by sheep and Sally had fenced it off and was watching to see how it progressed. As we walked

past the house, Sally sent Diti out to invite us to join them for supper.

`Do you think she would like some mushrooms?' I asked Diti.

`She might.' I offered Sally some of what we had collected and, to my chagrin, she took the lot. I always went over them carefully and cut off any that was a little suspect or maggoty, but Sally took the best and threw out the rest, there being plenty more where those came from. That was the case on Beaver, but I had already discovered that on most of the islands mushrooms did not flourish in the same way. Still, strictly speaking they were Sally's mushrooms and I could hardly complain.

There was yet another visitor, a friend from Stanley called Ian, an ex-BAS man, who often came out to Beaver. A skilled cook and engineer, he was even more welcome in Jérôme's absence, as Sally's talents lay elsewhere and she had little time spare from her many projects to tinker either with tractors or *haute cuisine*. We met Ian on several occasions and always enjoyed his company. A Derbyshire man, straightforward and outspoken, with a dry sense of humour, he had a good brain and was knowledgeable on many different subjects, all of which made him good company.

Wednesday was another sunny day, and as Pete had offered to repair the sail on the *Optimist* so that Leiv and Diti could use it, I took the opportunity to get on with some washing, while Steve took a picnic and went off for a walk. Pete came back for lunch and the wind was blowing so freshly by the time we had eaten, that he decided to stay on board to keep an eye on things. South Georgia was mentioned and although in such conditions, it was not an auspicious time to discuss the matter, Pete said:

`I really want to go there, Annie and I don't think that it would be as bad as you think. You managed in Greenland, after all.'

`I know that, but it sounds like the weather can be even worse in South Georgia and that gales come from any direction, which means that you end up on a lee shore. Besides, we had an inboard engine then. I keep thinking of the time we dragged in Godthaab and wonder if we'd have managed with only the Seagull.'

`Yes, but we have the Luke now, and anyway, we're unlikely to anchor anywhere that has rubbish all over the bottom, and that's what caused us to drag. Tim and Pauline have managed up to now without *any* engine.'

`That's true, but we're not Tim and Pauline. You're impatient and I'm easily frightened.'

`I don't underestimate South Georgia, Annie, I wouldn't take risks.'

`But I don't particularly *want* to go there. Why should I?'

`Well, there's the wildlife.'

`But the wildlife here is wonderful — there's more variety, too.'

`No wandering albatross.'

`I know. But I can hardly cope with what we're doing now. I'm a bag of nerves this afternoon ...'

`What for? It's a good mooring — it's not even blowing that strongly.'

`That's what I'm trying to tell you!' I almost shouted at Pete's obtuseness. `Can't you see? If I'm frightened here, in the Falklands, what's it going to be like in South Georgia. I don't want to spend a winter here, for that matter, with gales blowing sheets of wriggly tin round like leaves.'

`Oh Annie! that doesn't happen all the time.'

`Look Pete. The blow we had here was enough for me. I don't want to live through that sort of wind again. I've come down to the Falklands. We're staying longer than we planned. Isn't that enough? Why do we now have to consider South Georgia, for God's sake?'

`Because I want to go there. You'd enjoy it, Annie. Most of the time,' he added, trying to sound convincing.

`Steve doesn't reckon we should go, either. In a boat like *Damien II*, perhaps, but not in *Badger*.'

`Yes, well *I* think that we'd be OK in *Badger* — she's probably more suitable than other boats that have been there.'

`I don't want to go, Pete, and I don't think that I'm up to it.'

`Well, I think we should.'

By this time, it was far too windy to get back ashore for Steve and we hoped that Sally would not mind an extra mouth for dinner. Later on, the wind eased off a little and Pete rowed ashore to collect him, only to find that he had been offered a bed for the night and accepted, so he was left to enjoy his night's rest.

It was still blowing strongly the next morning and when it eased off in the afternoon Steve had disappeared, so we stayed ashore and I did a bit of weeding with Sally, until Steve returned, having had another good walk.

As I cooked dinner, Steve told us that he had talked for some time with Sally the previous evening, about Falklands Conservation and how they could obtain and manage their money more efficiently. He was in a good position to discuss these things, being a partner in a successful family business and Sally's comments had made Steve very interested in conservation in the Falklands.

'This place is really a bit special. If you do conservation work here, you can immediately see the results — buy an island and it's a nature reserve. The wildlife seems well able to look after itself just so long as no-one interferes. Like at Motley Island — we could see at one end how damaged it was and at the other, the tussac was really flourishing. If it's bought by a farmer, I suppose the tussac will go, but bought for conservation, there's a guarantee that no rats would ever get there, the tussac would grow and all the birds would thrive.'

'I know. It would be wonderful to be able to get hold of Motley.

Above: Wind kicks up the anchorage at Beaver Island.

Left: Beaver Island cliffs.

Maybe I'll write a bestseller and buy it one day, although as it's for sale now, I'd better not pin my hopes on it!'

'We'll find you another one, Annie. But I think islands are the way to go. You can't turn the whole of the Falklands into a nature reserve — people have to earn their livelihood, after all, but if the islands are uneconomic to farm, it seems like a good compromise.'

'Will Falklands Conservation put in a bid, do you think?'

'I don't think that they have enough in the coffers. I liked Motley though, it would be a shame to put sheep on it.'

On the subject of wildlife, I told Steve about Beaver's fur seal colony, and we planned to go there next morning, but by the time we had eaten breakfast and I had made some sausage rolls for a picnic, the wind had filled in again and Pete did not feel that he should leave the boat.

'We're probably all right here, but I'd prefer to stay on board, just in case. You two may as well go — I may get a chance some other time, but Steve should see as much as he can while he's here. You've not had too much walking, yet?'

'Well, put it this way, Pete. I'm fine now and I'd like to walk across the island, but I sure hope we go sailing tomorrow.'

With this settled, Pete rowed us ashore and we set off. It was a fine day, sunny and almost warm out of the wind and we enjoyed our walk, but as we got to the far side of the island, we realized just how strong the wind was.

'Did you say you have to climb down a cliff?' Steve asked, doubtfully.

'Yes, that's right. I can't say it's particularly easy, but I don't have much of a head for heights, which didn't really help.'

'I don't like heights either.' We looked at each other and laughed.

Above: Spilt Creek, Beaver Island.

Right: Annie surrounded by prickly gorse.
Photo by Steve Spring.

`They seem interested in him, too.'

Steve spent a happy half hour stalking and photographing the penguin while I lounged and enjoyed the show. After walking along the shore of the creek, we climbed up to discover a long strip of gorse right across our path and stretching a considerable distance in both directions. After casting about for a gap, we had to bite the bullet and force our way through. It was not the happiest moment of the day. The bushes were incredibly dense, so that we walked over the top of them, but every now

`Do you think it might be a bit foolhardy, Steve, I mean with this strong wind?'

`Yeah. A strong gust, just at the wrong time — well, you might get blown over.'

`Hmm. Perhaps we ought to err on the side of prudence. After all, we should be able to see fur seals at New Island.'

`Will we? D'you have to climb down any cliffs there?'

`I don't think so.'

`We ought to play safe, Annie. No sense in taking unnecessary risks.'

We both heaved a sigh of relief at not having to face the cliff. Because of the wind, of course. Instead, we shaped our course towards Split Creek, an inlet on the far side, that was popular with previous occupants for fishing expeditions. The completely sheltered creek was like a millpond and we found a comfortable spot in the sun to eat our lunch. A jackass penguin, uncommon on Beaver because their burrows, in which eggs and chicks are generally safe from predators, are easily entered by foxes, was wandering round, not sure which he fancied less: us or the two sea lions that were patrolling in the bay.

`I read in one of my books that sea lions occasionally take a penguin,' I told Steve, `and judging by this fellow, it looks as though they may. He certainly doesn't seem too keen on them, does he?'

and then a thinner patch could not take the weight and the sudden descent was an exceedingly uncomfortable experience. Steve managed to stop laughing long enough to photograph me, surrounded in all directions by prickly gorse; but Beaver has some pretty fine cliffs of its own, and the glorious views that we enjoyed were almost compensation for the gorse. Several foxes came near and I took a photograph of a cub that I noticed dart under some boulders, keeping well out of my way, but cautious rather than frightened. We gathered a few mushrooms and were back about tea-time, well-contented with the day's outing, if somewhat tired.

With it being New Year's Eve, the children wanted a party and Sally invited everyone to dinner, including George and Michelle, from another visiting yacht, *Metapassion*, who despite living in Tasmania, were very French. Neither Steve nor Pete wanted to go, but I like a New Year's Eve party and felt that it would be churlish to refuse, so we took some Uruguayan bubbly and I picked out the best of the mushrooms, for those who like them raw. Ian had left that day, but while he had been staying, they had gone over to Staats and shot a guanaco and an upland goose. He had made these into a `game' stew, which only needed cooking and had left Sally with strict instructions as to how this should be done, but she had merely left it to cook, without moving the meat around, so that what was on top was pretty tough, while those who went back for seconds had the most tender and toothsome pieces.

`Oh, is that why some of it was tough?' asked Sally, `Ian was saying something about making sure

having killed a few mutton before he left, Sally kindly gave us half a carcase asking us if we would mind taking the other half for Ian Strange, who owns New Island, South.

`Of course, we'd be delighted to. I should think he'll appreciate it, not running his own sheep anymore.'

`Oh! I've just remembered something. Don't go!' Sally ran back to the house and returned a few minutes later with two copies of a booklet that she had written, *Southern Ocean Cruising*. She handed one to Pete and one to Steve. `By the way, if you plan to go to South Georgia next summer, you'd be welcome to stay her for the winter.'

`That's really very kind of you,' Pete replied. `At the moment, we're still intending to go on to South Africa, in a few months, but we appreciate the offer.'

`Oh, well, anyway, I dare say that we'll see you again before you go.'

`I'll make a note of any shag rookeries, too. I'll get them to you eventually,' I promised.

Back on *Badger*, I quartered the large and rather fat mutton, in order to be able to get it out of the way. Steve was most amused at the sight of a vegetarian carving up a sheep and took a couple of photographs.

`They for blackmail purposes?' I asked. Neither Sally nor Jérôme could tolerate vegetarians, so I had not

Above: the cautious fox cub, Beaver Island.

Right: New Year's Eve party.

that everything was covered, but I didn't really listen properly.'

George and Michelle upstaged us by producing a bottle of *French* champagne, which was voted a great improvement on our bubbly. Leiv and Diti each had a small glass and ended up in giggles for the rest of the night. It was a good party and Steve and Pete were pleased to have gone.

We had accepted Jérôme's generous offer of the heater and, Ian

Annie tackles mutton in the cockpit. Photo by Steve Spring.

mentioned my preferences and as both Pete and Steve enjoyed the mutton, it was worth having for their sakes. In the early afternoon, we sailed off towards New Island, passing two oddly shaped stacks known as The Colliers and indeed, from a certain angle, they do look like a couple of clumsy sailing ships. Anchoring in the bay off the settlement, we tidied up and rowed ashore.

I was looking forward to meeting Ian Strange, a local naturalist who has done a lot to raise people's awareness of the importance of the Islands and the author of one of the wildlife guides that Sally had given me. We took his mutton in the dinghy and he came to meet us as we walked up the jetty.

`We've just come from Beaver and Sally sent you half a sheep.'

`That was kind of her, I could do with some fresh meat.'

`Well, they reckon that Beaver mutton is the best!'

Ian looked a little sheepish. `It's not actually for me. My neigh-

bour left me his dog to look after and she has just had puppies. He didn't realize and we hadn't got in anything extra for it.' He led us into an outbuilding, where a sheepdog lay suckling several puppies; she looked up at us warily when we went in.'

`Don't go too close. She's usually a gentle little bitch, but she's very protective.' He hung up the mutton.

`Now,' he said, `would you like to come and have a cup of tea?'

We went up to his house, where there were splendid views from the windows, down the harbour and over to the distant islands. Moving the kettle onto the hotplate, Ian introduced us to his wife, Maria, and his daughter who had a friend staying with her. To our astonishment, they were dressed in T-shirts and shorts, of which Ian did not really approve, feeling that they were courting skin cancer, with the hole in the ozone layer not far way and their skin unused to the sun. Ian and Maria had turned their half of New Island into a nature reserve and also had two small houses that they rented out, often to naturalists, a couple of young, American scientists studying penguins, being the present occupants. We found the Stranges very interesting and talked about wildlife for some time with them. New Island is one of the few places in the Falklands that has breeding fur seals and Ian told us that they could be observed very easily, their colony being on rocks, overlooked by low cliffs.

`You can sit up there very comfortably and watch without disturbing them,' he told us. `They are very shy, but don't really seem to notice people over their heads.'

Passing The Colliers.

Getting out a map, he showed us how to find them and where to see the penguins and black-browed mollyhawks nesting.

`You seem to know how to behave,' he told us, `so I don't mind you going anywhere you want and hope that you enjoy it all.'

After tea, Ian showed us round the settlement, taking us to see the fine, new house that he had built and on our way back, we met the young scientists. Introductions were made, but as they obviously had

Squabbling skuas mug for the camera.

matters to talk over, we thanked Ian for his hospitality and left them deep in discussion.

The morning came in nearly calm, with hazy sunshine and several skuas were hanging around the boat, looking hopeful. As not many yachts visit New Island, we wondered whether they remembered those that had, or simply associated humans with food and while I prepared a picnic, I gave Pete and Steve some bits of meat to tempt them to show off for Steve's camera, which they duly did, squabbling and screaming abuse at each other. Completely fearless, one even came aboard and swaggered about on deck in the hope of stealing a march on the others.

We had a glorious time ashore. Past the settlement was a hut that had been built many years previously by a marooned sailor and subsequently used by sealers. An old Canadian minesweeper, the *Protector*, brought out to the Falklands for sealing, lay grounded at the head of the bay, looking in re-

markably good order: an ideal `fixer-upper' as the Americans would put it. Climbing away from the settlement, pausing to admire the view, we were delighted when a `Johnny Rook', the local name for the striated caracara, landed on a fence post close by. These large raptors are extraordinarily tame and he allowed us to approach sufficiently closely to admire the orange skin round his beak and on his legs. New Island is plagued with cottontail rabbits, introduced no doubt, by American sealers, and we saw plenty of them as we tramped across in the direction of the fur seals. There were many prion burrows and all too often, the pathetic heaps of blue feathers where a sharp-eyed skua had spied one coming out. The petrels nest underground, entering and leaving only under cover of darkness, but in the short summer nights, the increasing demands for

*The **Protector** lies grounded at New Island.*

Fur seals on the rocks of New Island.

not instinctively to cower when a screaming dervish comes out of nowhere straight for your head. Steve and Pete had a little more sympathy for my stories of the skuas on Motley Island after this.

We found Ian's vantage point, close to where the fur seals were clustered together round some cliffs and sat for ages, looking for the little black pups and watching the adults. Many of them were in the water, disporting themselves with great verve, full of energy, swift and graceful, chasing one another and

food from their chicks sometimes cause them cut it too fine and the skuas are there, waiting. It is very hard to like skuas. They did nothing to add to their appeal that morning, because at all too frequent intervals, considering us too close to their nests, they would dive down to attack us. It is not easy to be indifferent when a large and aggressive bird comes screaming down at you, its sharp beak agape, and none of us had the sangfroid to stand up to them. Maria later explained that the worst thing to do is to duck, because they assess your height and come in lower next time, but I defy anyone walking peacefully along, minding their own business

playing in the kelp. The big males, masters of harems, spent most of their time dozing, but now and then a younger male would push his luck and approach, which resulted in the other getting quite worked up. At a certain stage, they started making *chuffing* noises, which seemed to indicate that they had had enough, because the challenger generally retreated at that moment. We could happily have stayed all day, but there were other things to see and Steve's time was limited.

Tearing ourselves away, we headed for the impressive cliffs, the highest in the Falklands, where the birds nested. Rising seven hundred feet sheer out of the sea, they stretch

The impressive cliffs of New Island.

away into the distance and are quite magnificent to behold. They were speckled in black and white, which resolved into thousands of birds, sitting on, walking and flying around their nests. Rockhopper penguins, black-browed mollyhawks and imperial shags all share the same ground, their nests indiscriminately mixed together: a quite astonishing scene. Mollyhawks sat with gentle dignity on their nests, constructed of dried mud, occasionally shifting their single egg or standing up and tending

Above: Mollyhawks tend their nests, surrounded by rockhoppers.

Left: A rockhopper penguin and chick in the tussac.

Below right: rockhoppers tolerate a visitor.

Below left: Imperial shags also tend their nests in the midst of rockhoppers.

the fluffy grey chick they protected, seeming too aristocratic to be forced to share their environment with the plebeian and quarrelling rockhoppers clustered about them. Some of the chicks were on their own, an odd sight, tall and thin, the gape of their

beak sharply defined in black, giving them a perpetually surprised expression. These chicks were now sufficiently well-grown to be safe from the skuas that patrolled the colony, alert for the momentarily unprotected egg or chick. We saw one swoop in on a penguin nest, causing the whole colony to stretch up threatening beaks and set up a clamour, but it was in and out before the unfortunate parent had realized its mistake.

The rockhopper nests were even more rudimentary than those of the gentoos, but

The settlement at South Harbour, New Island, with windswept tree.

peninsula in South Harbour, while watching the waders. Continuing our explorations, we passed countless cottontails on our way to the old whaling station, dismantled many years ago and moved down to South Georgia. An incredible amount of stuff had been left behind, including boilers, an anvil, anchors, a marine railway, lathes and metal working machinery; asbestos lagging stuck out of the grass and we found pieces of coal. New Island has no peat and for many years, the inhabitants cooked and heated with the coal abandoned at the old whaling station. Ian told us that the island was put up for sale when this started to run out: a marginal farm at the best of times, the extra cost of buying and transporting fuel swung the balance. Making our weary way back to the settlement, we saw Ian and Maria and thanked them for letting us look round. It was one of

most pairs seemed to have brought up a couple of chicks and were now wearing themselves out fetching food for the voracious youngsters. From under yellow, war paint-like eyebrows, their little red eyes glared belligerently at us, if we approached too closely, but they tolerated us sitting down four or five feet away.

On mud mounds, lined with dried tussac, imperial shags craned their necks, gazing at us from their exquisite blue eyes, with the gormless curiosity so characteristic of cormorants, before settling down once more to preen their feathers, their scrawny chicks keeping well down in the nest, under the parent bird.

New Island had yet more to offer, so we picked up our lunch from where we had left it in the dinghy and picnicked on the little

Remains of the whaling station.

the most interesting and rewarding days that we had ever had.

With so much to see, we needed to get on, so when Monday dawned sunny with light winds, we were up early and away just after six o'clock, and when the wind disappeared, the skipper broke our rule about doing everything under sail, motoring for five hours to save our tide through the Woolly Gut. Several Peale's dolphin joined us, entertaining us with acrobatics and very interested in the boat, contrary to what we had read. Whales and dolphins seem to be little understood and it is strange to realize how much scientists comprehend of the working of the Universe and how little of the inhabitants of our own oceans. Chugging on over a glassy calm, we enjoyed our visitors and admired the splendid scene of

Westpoint Island. Above: Long view of **Badger** *and settlement from the hillside. Top right:* **Badger** *anchored at the settlement.*

sea and islands, but the Seagull was able to take a well-deserved rest when a breeze came about tea time, allowing us to sail through Woolly Gut, having saved our tide. We brought to in a sheltered horseshoe bay, with a sandy beach and a pier, its shore lined with red buildings of 'wriggly tin' and at the far end, an old wooden ketch lay stranded on the beach. On the hillside, could be seen the houses of the settlement, the white walls and green roofs nestling among cypress trees. We were made very welcome by Roddy and Lily, who invited us in for a drink, and while we were there, several other people came in: Alan, Cora, Ruth and Caroline, who were renting a cottage from Roddy and Lily. Westpoint Island, like most out west, has spectacularly beautiful scenery and for those who live in Stanley, it is a real boon to be able to rent somewhere for a week or two. Westpoint has a large colony of black-browed mollyhawks and we asked Roddy if it would be possible to go and see them.

'Of course,' he answered, 'in fact you sailed past them — they are right at the end of the island.'

Roddy had a large piece of teak that he had given to Alan for carving and they had been discussing how to get it back to Stanley.

'If you don't mind waiting a couple of weeks, we can take it back for you,' offered Pete.

'That would suit me fine, but it's a long piece and I'm not sure that you would want it in your boat.'

'We can carry it on deck. It won't come to any harm.'

'But won't it get full of salt?'

Pete laughed. 'Not in a couple of weeks — especially teak. Under the surface it will still be full of oil. As it's an old piece anyway, you'll probably be planing off the surface and that will get rid of any salt.'

Alan considered the offer, but in the end, feeling that the wood might be damaged by the sea, had it sent back to Stanley by ship.

When we came to leave, Roddy sent us off with some milk and a big jar of cream, a marvellous treat. To make use of this largesse, the planned menu was altered to steak *au poivre vert*, and very good it was, too. The rest of the cream went on our breakfast porridge.

Steve's luck was still holding the next morning and in the calm, sunshine, he rowed round photographing steamer ducks, while I made sandwiches. To reach the dramatic cliffs at the west end of the island, we had to climb a fair way up Mount Misery and the views were nothing short of sensational, the land dropping away sheer to blue sea, where mist-

View from Mount Misery.

mate's return. Sitting on their nests, tranquil and gentle creatures, there was rarely any bickering between them, unlike other birds that nest in large colonies. Most seabirds have immaculate plumage, but the black-browed mollyhawk stands out even among these. The brow is caused partly by shadow, but close observation reveals dark feathers, which appear to have been tinted with eye-liner pencil.

We had to make our way back through thick fog, but a Rover trail helped us keep to our course and back at the settlement, we walked around the wonderful garden, of which Roddy and Lily are justifiably proud. Roddy invited us in for tea and cake and we enjoyed talking to him, for he had done a lot of cruising around the Falklands in his boat before it was wrecked and had useful information to impart. He was also very knowledgeable about the mollyhawks.

'We started ringing them twenty-six years ago,' he told us, 'and have found out some interesting things. They mate for life, as we'd suspected and always come back to the same nest site. The young ones lay their first eggs when they're about five years old, but often they lose this chick — it's a bit like a trial run. After that, they're generally quite successful at rearing them.'

covered islands stretched away into the distance. Then the fog drifted in, but we found the mollyhawks and spent a couple of hours watching them, sitting amongst hundreds of nests and so close that we could observe how they tended and fed their chicks, how they took off and landed. The colony was on steep, grass-covered cliffs and when the birds came in to land they simply stopped near their nest, stalled and landed, walking with clumsy, awkward gait, negotiating yellow, lichen-covered rocks and neighbours' nests. They greeted their mate with an elaborate display of bowing, out-stretched wings and calls and were answered in kind, before carefully changing places on the nest. The other bird manoeuvred until it had a clear path uphill and then, wings outspread, it bounded along inelegantly for several paces until airborne once more, it was trans-formed into a creature of grace, at home with the winds. Meanwhile, the chick in the nest had been peck-ing away at its parent's beak, which stimulated it to regurgitate the food it had caught. It looked a highly uncomfortable operation for the parent, which opened its beak to an astonishing extent in order for the chick to reach its crop. Feeding completed, the parent settled down over its offspring and sat patiently awaiting its

Mollyhawk nesting colony.

He had been interested to discover how long they lived and apparently a large number of the ones that they had originally ringed, were still returning to lay their eggs. `That's already twenty-six years and I wouldn't be surprised to find they live at least another ten.'

Back on *Badger* we had a relaxed evening and I gave Steve stir-fried mutton, to make up for the one that he had missed when we had been on passage.

The fog lingered overnight and when we woke up, we could barely see out of the bay. Wanting to carry on to Carcass Island, we made a careful study of the chart and what tidal information was available. At half

Carcass's anchorage.

past nine, needing to catch the tide, we could wait no longer, but there was little danger and indeed we enjoyed the challenge while Pete managed the intricate pilotage without any problems. We were almost disappointed when the fog lifted about half way there, to be replaced by a thunderstorm.

`I reckon that you've had just about everything in the way of weather now, Steve,' I said.

`Apart from snow, and I'm quite happy to give that a miss!'

Carcass's anchorage, although reasonably well protected, is open to the south-west, but Roddy had given us detailed directions and following these, we anchored with shelter almost to the south. Sailing in,

we had passed *Niatross*, the Canadian yacht that we had met in Stanley and just as we were about to get into the dinghy, Frank came out in an inflatable and, with a proprietorial air that I found very amusing, invited us ashore. Carcass is one of the most attractive settlements, with some large and well-established trees and bushes, turning the gardens into sun traps, alive with tussac birds that even come into the kitchen. We went to make our number and were warmly welcomed by Rob with tea and biscuits. A fair number of cruise ships call at this island and one could be forgiven for expecting Rob to be tired of visitors, but he was the personification of hospitality, making us comfortable and showing us a map of the island.

`I see there's a place here called "Elephant Flat",' I commented. `Are there sea elephants there?'

`Yes, we get quite a few on the island — I saw some a couple of days ago when I was over there. We've two pairs of giant petrels nesting right on the point there — the first we've had in years. I'm quite excited about it.'

`How wonderful! Is it far? It looks about three miles.'

`About that.'

Pete, Steve and I discussed whether we would have time to go,

Elephant seal female sunning herself at Elephant Flat.

as we had to push on the next day and it was now well into the afternoon.

'Would you like me to drive you over?' Rob offered, 'I can't take you all the way, but it's not a long walk from the airstrip and I was going there anyway.'

We accepted with unseemly alacrity and were soon bouncing along the track, where there were superb views of the Jason Islands, the westernmost outliers of the Falklands and the most romantic. Rob dropped us off, pointing us in the right direction and in due course we came upon the sea elephants. The first three were a young male, a female and a pup, not as one might think, a family group, but simply three companionable individuals. Elephant seal pups do not have much of a family life: they are weaned at less than a month old, after which the mother returns to sea to recover all the weight that she has lost feeding her insatiable baby, whose birth weight of a hundred pounds will have trebled or quadrupled in this time. Crossing the thin neck of land to the other side of the island, we found several others, extremely placid animals, who did little more than raise their heads as we walked by, although if we went too close, they started moving back towards the sea, humping themselves like huge caterpillars. I was surprised how small they were, but subsequently realized that the mature males were all at sea. Steve was cursing the fact that he had not brought his camera ashore; we had not expected to see anything so spectacular, but fortunately I had brought mine, so took photographs for both of us. There were dozens of birds about and we also caught a glimpse of the giant petrels.

We must have wandered near the nest of a couple of Johnny rooks, for they attacked us, but finding some sticks, we held them over our heads and the trick seemed to work. Evening was fast approaching and it was a long walk back, but it was with reluctance that we left the great seals to slumber in peace once more. As we stopped by to thank Rob, he invited us in for a drink and sitting in the cosy kitchen, sipping our beers and relaxing, we enjoyed the comfortable bustle around us. Frank and Julie seemed to be very much at home, and Rob's aunt and mother and his wife, Lorraine, were staying there. Lorraine spends the school terms in Stanley, running Stanley House, where the camp schoolchildren board. She was a warm, motherly lady: the children must be very fond of her and indeed, the whole family were very friendly, kind, people. The two older ladies helped out with the catering when the cruise ships come in and had such energy that it was hard to credit that they were both well over seventy. When we came to leave, we were invited to stay for dinner, our polite refusals met with: 'it's only a few bits and pieces; you'll help us get rid of the leftovers; there's plenty for all.' So we accepted gratefully and spent a very pleasant evening there.

Twelfth Night also started fine and gentle and we set off for Saunders Island, but what wind there was deserted us, forcing us to motor, once again. We soon agreed to abandon this unsatisfactory form of progress and go to Low Island instead, to have a lunchtime barbecue. Low Island is a nature reserve, belonging to Roddy and Lily at Westpoint and going ashore we could see why, with sea lions, Johnny rooks, tussac birds and Cobb's wrens all to be seen. There was plenty of driftwood for the fire and we also found some hardwood, which Pete sawed up in anticipation of our having a solid-fuel stove. As he knelt on the beach, a huge sea lion approached, coming very close before giving himself away with a big *chuff*. Pete got quite a shock when he turned to see what the noise was. A very cheeky Johnny rook reckoned that our leavings were just right for his chick back at the nest and did a good job of helping us tidy up.

Pete's work being overseen by a sea lion.

The wind filled in, blowing into the bay, so we went back aboard, got the anchor and set off, but the delightful, wholesail breeze eased off as the afternoon progressed. The obvious route left Calf Island to starboard, but with the fading wind, Pete felt that it was worth taking a short cut, leaving the island to port. The pilotage was tricky, but satisfying, with perfect conditions and a couple of puffing pigs joined us as we went through Reef Passage. We could clearly see them as they teased Steve, darting to the stern or under the

Magellenic penguin (jackass) and chick by their burrow. Photo by Steve Spring.

boat as soon as his camera was focused on them, but eventually they relented and allowed themselves to be photographed. Our progress became slower and slower, so I went below to cook dinner and with the galley scuttle wide open, I could look out at the passing view as I chopped mutton and fried it with onions, garlic and spices.

'Is that curry you're making?' came Steve's voice.

'It's Twelfth Night,' I replied, 'so we're having your favourite. Crème Caramel to follow.'

While the meal was cooking, I took down the Christmas decorations and put them away for another year. The cabin looked strangely bare without them. We anchored at nine o'clock off Saunders Island, with the very last of the breeze, well content with our day.

The next day could not have been more different, coming in breezy and staying blowy all day and as we could not get ashore, we had a relaxing day which, indeed, we rather needed. Every time we looked out we noticed that our puffing pigs were still swimming around us, no doubt discussing our sloth. But the blow was a short one and it had calmed down enough to cook chips for supper.

'I think we ought to make an early night of it,' Pete announced, clearing away the plates. 'I've been looking at Ewen's notes and reckon that we need to get underway at five o'clock tomorrow to take our tide through Rock Harbour and on to Pebble Island.'

Steve and I both groaned. 'Maybe it's just as well we had a lazy day,' Steve commented.

We were up as planned the following morning, but the skipper, in benign mood, let us have breakfast before we made sail. Possibly the fact that there was not a breath of wind had something to do with it, but even so, we were underway well before six. To our astonishment, the puffing pigs were still swimming around and formed into an escort as we sailed out of the anchorage.

Rock Harbour is an area abounding with rocks and shoals, reefs and kelp and Frank had hit a rock here, complaining indignantly that it was not where his GPS had shown that it should be. As the area had last been surveyed between 1843 and 1847, it is probable that the position of the various rocks and shoals were laid down with bearings to other points rather than from sun or star sights. It is easy to forget that GPS is an *aid* to navigation rather than the solution to all problems, the satellites fixing one's exact position on the planet without taking into account the accuracy or otherwise of the chart. We managed to find our way through the maze without too many problems, wishing we could stay longer and explore this wonderful cruising ground more thoroughly. Pete having worked out the tides correctly, we covered twenty-six miles in under four and a half hours. What a difference a fair tide and breeze can make!

There were hundreds of jackasses on Pebble Island and Steve got quite side-tracked with trying to tempt them out of their burrows for a photograph. It was hard walking in diddle-dee and white grass, but we enjoyed the exercise and drank our cup of tea, sitting by a lake, before girding our loins for the long tramp back to the boat.

The end of Steve's holiday was in sight and although the forecast was not brilliant, we felt that we had better press on. We needed a fair tide through the Tamar Pass and another early start was indicated. The day came in overcast, with a north-north west wind blowing at almost Force 5 and we headed out, some overfalls in the Tamar Pass making tacking a bit dodgy. Having no real choice, we tried to look relaxed, in the hope that Steve would not appreciate just how tight it was.

`It might we worth standing by the foresail,' I suggested casually.

`Hmm. Maybe,' Pete replied, walking with assumed nonchalance to the foredeck.

I watched the waves. Our information was not correct and instead of it being the last of the flood, the tide was already ebbing, creating nasty waves as the wind blew against the tide. I waited until there was a bit of a smooth:

`Ready about? Lee-oh!' I put the helm down, heart thumping. The bow went into the wind, hesitated for a heart-stopping moment and then the foresail came across even as Pete reached for the sheet. I swallowed, my mouth dry. *Badger* gathered way, but in a horribly brief space of time, we were approaching the other shore.

`Ready ...' my voice sounded shrill. I cleared my throat. `Ready about?' I caught Pete's eye. `Lee-oh.' This time she did not even falter and the tide was taking us through. One more tack would do it and with Pete just holding the foresail sheet for a moment as we went round, we were clear. The butterflies folded their wings and Pete walked back aft.

`She tacks well, doesn't she?' said Steve, but he had not been fooled by our assumed composure.

As we cleared the land, the wind increased to Force 6 and we dropped a couple of reefs in each sail. We could lay Cape Dolphin, but could not head up far enough to clear the Eddystone Rock and the race that runs between it and the Cape. According to *Falkland Islands Shores*, it was possible to go inshore of the race and we set the course accordingly. Pete had set up the self-steering gear before we left, but a strand of kelp had caught the servo rudder and broken the break-away coupling, an all too-frequent occurrence in this area. The coupling was only a length of line, but had to be replaced when the boat was stationary, so we had to steer by hand. *Badger*'s cockpit is too small for three people to sit on one side and it was far too cold to sit to leeward. As Steve had started feeling seasick again and

reckoned that he was better off outside, I went below, intending to read a book and enjoy the warmth of the heater. Sadly, conditions were too rough and it kept smoking and when I began feeling queasy, I turned it off and put up with being cold. It was quite a wild sail and as we approached Cape Dolphin, the race could clearly be seen, although there was no sign of the passage inshore, but it was too late to turn back, so we carried on. Enormous, toppling seas ran in every direction, heaped up by the strong wind and the sight, as I peered out through the bubble, was really quite alarming, so I sat down again. Entering the race, *Badger* plunged into these waves and although she was thrown around, battled on resolutely. We were completely swept by one wave, and Steve and Pete both looked quite rattled when I dashed to check that they were all right. Both they and the boat were streaming with water and Steve had wrapped the foresail sheet around his left hand while holding onto the tiller for dear life with the other. It occurred to me that they ought to be wearing safety harnesses, but it did not seem a suitable time to suggest it.

With the Cape abeam, we could bear away and *Badger* tore through the rough seas, leaping and crashing through the waves at top speed, so that we were soon out of the worst of it. Our intention had been to make for Big Shag Island at the entrance to Salvador Water, but in such boisterous conditions, it did not promise to be a comfortable berth. Other anchorages were considered and discarded until all that was left was Stanley. It was a long and wild sail, but we made it to Port William before dark where, contrary to its usual habit, the wind eased off. Rather then continue all the way to Stanley in a failing breeze, we drifted up to Watt Cove, at the top of Port William, although it was very nearly too dark to see what we were doing. It was twenty past ten before we dropped the hook, having covered eighty-nine miles since leaving Pebble Island at seven o'clock that morning: an average of nearly six knots.

Leaving Pete to tidy ship, I went below to light the fire and the cooker.

`I think we all deserve a stiff drink,' Pete announced as he came down the hatch and even Steve felt that a tot would not go amiss. It was so late that as we sat down with our glasses, we agreed simply to ignore the time, eat a leisurely meal and relax for a while before turning in.

`Well, Pete,' Steve commented, as we started to thaw out, `I wanted to see how *Badger* behaved in rough weather and I sure found out. You've got yourself a good boat here. I was surprised how well she did in light conditions and I was impressed with the way she went today. I don't think many boats would have been happy going through that tide race.'

`I don't think *I* was too happy, to tell the truth,' commented Pete, `and it will be a while before I trust any information about passages inside races again!'

But when Pete re-read the directions, he noticed that Ewen Southby-Tailyour had written that when sailing along the north coast, the `advice is to cover this distance as quickly as possible, but not at all if there is likely to be a strong onshore wind. . .' and that the track south of the race was to be attempted when `the winds are not blowing strongly onshore.' Pete's memory had played him false on this occasion.

After a long lie-in and a late breakfast, Steve and Pete went ashore to walk up to Sparrow Cove, hoping to find a colony of gentoo penguins that apparently nested there. It seemed a long way to go and as I had been doing more than enough walking in recent days, I stayed on board and had a pleasant time, baking bread, reading

Views of the **Lady Elizabeth**. *Photos by Steve Spring.*

Emma, mending the ensign, which had got somewhat frayed the previous day, writing a letter to my mother and boning a leg of mutton to pot roast. When Steve and Pete returned, it was to report a noticeable absence of penguins, so for once I had made the right decision.

On Tuesday morning, we got our anchor and sailed back to Stanley, actually able to lay down the harbour and with only two reefs in, having a fine morning's sail. In the afternoon, we then went ashore and noticing that *Dodo's Delight* had not yet left, invited the Rev round for supper the following day.

We woke up to a glorious, sunny day, which seemed ideal for our planned walk to see the wreck of the iron-built *Lady Elizabeth*, so we were disappointed to hear a forecast for strong southwesterly winds. Not fancying the idea of a five mile walk back to the anchorage, into the teeth of a gale, I stayed on board while Steve and Pete went, but the forecast had been wrong, the wind stayed light and I would have enjoyed the walk. When the other two came back, they told me that they had managed to get on board and climb all over the ship.

'It's in surprisingly good condition, Annie,' Steve told me. 'A lot of the deck's intact and the winches and fittings are still there. We went below, and saw the remains of the bunks in the forepeak. It was well worth the walk.'

'Don't rub it in. I've been kicking myself all day because I didn't go!'

The Rev turned up in due course and we had an enjoyable evening. A very interesting person and a good talker, he seemed to relish the curry I had made, although privately, I reckoned that the mutton was a bit gamy. *Dodo's Delight* would be setting off any day now and her crew were looking forward to their passage to the Antarctic; I think that we all rather envied Bob. When I saw Pete's face I realized that I had to reconsider my position about going to South Georgia: being frightened of an undertaking is a rotten reason for not doing it. We talked far into the night, but fortunately the Rev had been lent a Rover and did not have to face a long walk back to his boat

After a leisurely breakfast the next morning, we all went into town.

Pete had a dental appointment and Steve wanted to look for one or two things to take back to the States with him. The Rev had suggested that we pop round and see him, so we arranged to meet at *Dodo's Delight*. It was a lovely, warm day and Steve and I sat under the whalebone arch by the cathedral and had a bottle of beer in the sunshine. Having had a look round the church, we wandered down to where *Dodo's Delight* was tied to the Public Jetty.

'When d'you think you'll get away, Bob?'

'We're ready to go now, but someone's offered to get us stores from the NAAFI, though nothing seems to be happening. It'd probably have been easier to go to

the West Store, instead, as it turns out. Either way, we should be away in the next couple of days.'

When Pete came back he had bad news.

'Apparently the Government has just declared that with effect from the beginning of January, they'll only do emergency treatment to visitors' teeth.'

'Why's that?'

'It sounds like a lot of the contractors have been saving up their dental work until they come down here, because they don't have to pay anything, while to get it done on the NHS is expensive.'

'But I thought the dentist had said he was going to put a crown on.'

'That was before the New Year and the new decision.'

'What a nuisance. If you hadn't had the other appointment cancelled, you'd probably have had it done.'

The picturesque cathedral at Stanley. Left: Bottle of beer under the whalebone arch. Above: View from the harbour with the hulks in foreground.

`Well, I asked him if he could do it privately and he reckons that it might be possible, if we pay for the materials — after all his salary is paid anyway and he often has appointments free. I'm going back to see in a couple of days.' However, it proved to be impossible: there was no system to deal with private medicine, but as the `temporary' repair would last indefinitely, it was more of a nuisance than anything else.

We stayed a while longer and had a cup of tea and a yarn with `the lads' before getting a lift home in `their' Rover. Back on board I wondered aloud what to have for dinner, as it was Steve's last night.

`Don't worry, Annie, I'll take care of it,' Steve said. `I'm taking you both out to dinner tonight.'

`Really! What a lovely thought. I'm afraid I'm not going to refuse politely, in case you change your mind.'

`It's about time you had a night off. I won't change my mind. Don't worry'.

Having changed into more respectable clothes and rowed ashore, we walked to the *Upland Goose* and all ate smoked haddock, washed down with some very good Muscadet. After we had eaten, we adjourned to the lounge and had a couple of drinks while talking over all that we had seen and done while Steve had been with us. It was a lovely evening and even the discovery that it was drizzling, when we came to walk back, did nothing to spoil it.

The wind picked up overnight and by the time we had had breakfast it was blowing very freshly. Carl had offered to drive us all to the airport and both Pete and I were going to see Steve off and help him tote his bags to Carl and Dianne's house. As Pete rowed me ashore, I asked, `Are you quite happy about leaving *Badger*? It really seems to be blowing up.'

`I don't think that we should go off and leave her,' Pete replied, `but the trouble is that there's quite a load for just two people.'

`Well it's no use me staying behind. There's no way that I can handle the Luke on my own,' I pointed out, `so Steve and I will just have to manage the best we can.'

Poor Steve looked less than delighted at the prospect of carrying more than he had anticipated the two miles to Carl and Dianne's house, but understood Pete's decision.

`You're right to stay with the boat, Pete. I wouldn't leave her unattended in this.' They said their good-byes, Pete walked back to the dinghy and Steve and I set off under our burdens. Before very long it started to rain and it was not a pleasant walk. As we approached the town, an army Rover stopped and offered us a lift. The driver was a Major and introduced himself.

`Simon! Then your wife is Devina, Pauline's friend!' Incredibly, Pauline, on *Tiama* had a friend from her time in Germany, whose husband had just been posted down to the Falklands. Half jokingly, probably wondering if we had ever got there, she had written to Devina suggesting that she look out for us and she had come down to the loch a couple of days previously. Pete had rowed over and talked to her and we had promised to get in touch after Steve left. Now, by chance, we had met Simon. He drove us to the Falkland Island Company's office, so that Steve could find out about his flight, as we were rather concerned about the effect the weather might have. There was no news, so we took the luggage up to Carl and Dianne's. They were out and as it was still pouring with rain, we left the bags in the peat shed and went to the *Globe* so that we could sit down somewhere warm and dry. When Dianne's lunch hour came round, we went back to their house and rang the FIC, but there was still no news of Steve's flight.

`What do you think? Will they fly?'

`They don't usually cancel the DAP flight,' Carl said, `but it might be delayed for some reason. Look, I have to go back to work, but when you hear what time the flight's due in, call me and I'll come and get you.'

`No, you've done enough,' Steve told him. I'll call for a taxi when we find out what's happening.' Carl was reluctant to accept that, but in the end Steve persuaded him and we were left in the house while they went back to work. Steve and I sat on, browsing through magazines. At last the telephone rang and Steve answered it.

`They're going to fly from Mount Pleasant,' he told me `and are sending a car for all the passengers to drive them up there.'

`I wonder why that is. It must be too windy at Stanley, I suppose.'

Within a couple of minutes we heard a horn.

`Here,' said Steve, `I won't be paying a taxi now, so don't need any English money. You take it!' and he shoved a handful of bills at me. Before I could thank him, there was a knock at the door and we gathered up Steve's bags and coat and staggered out.

`Good-bye. Take care. It's been marvellous seeing you again.'

`Thanks for inviting me — it was even better than I'd hoped.'

The car door shut, the Rover accelerated away and I was left standing in the wind and rain, a little taken aback at the suddenness of Steve's departure. Going back in, I collected my waterproofs and bag and then left the house, checking that the door was locked. I started to walk back and as I came onto Ross Road, by the edge of the harbour, I realized that the wind was much stronger than it had been in the morning, but could not really assess the situation until I could see *Badger* properly. One look was enough to tell me that it was blowing too hard for Pete to get ashore. Until it eased off, and it showed no signs of doing so at the moment, I was stuck. I turned round to trudge the weary distance back into Stanley once again. We had already asked enough of Carl and Dianne, the pubs were all shut and I was not sure what to do. Then I remembered Devina and in the hope that she might invite me in for a warm and a cup of tea, I went to her house and knocked on the door. It was opened by a slender, fair-haired lady, who looked at my bedraggled appearance with a puzzled expression.

`Devina?'

Light dawned. `Are you Pauline's friend? Come in, you look soaked!'

`I'm sorry to call round like this and on such a day, but in fact I've just seen our friend off and I can't get back on board, so I thought that perhaps I might come and seek shelter with you for a while. I hope that you don't mind.'

`Not at all. What a dreadful day. Let me make you a cup of tea.'

I disrobed in the front porch and then went into the house, where I was introduced to Devina's three children, Michelle, four and a half, Peter who was three and eighteen-month old Adèle. Watching Devina trying to cope with the demands of these three on a wet afternoon made me feel that being marooned ashore was a pleasure by comparison. I was made very welcome and we found plenty to talk about, starting from Pauline and finding out a little more about each other. Devina was a quiet and gentle person and must have had a difficult time moving her family down to the Falklands and having to start a new home there.

`What do you think of the islands?' I asked her.

I'm really starting to enjoy them now, but it was hard at first, before I got to know anyone. Michelle will be starting school soon and that will be a relief. She's very good actually and helps me quite a lot, but Adèle still hasn't settled down and wakes up every night needing attention and Peter is very demanding. Trying to cope with all three is almost too much, at times. We've managed to get about a little bit, and are hoping to get out to West Falkland or some of the other islands. It must be wonderful to be able to see them like you've been doing.'

I am neither used to nor, to be honest, particularly fond of children, but my presence was an interest for them and Michelle was soon showing me her favourite book, while Peter wanted me to read to him, which gave Devina time to get on with one or two jobs.

I was still there when Simon came home and his face when he saw me, was a picture.

`Good heavens! I know we said we'd see each other again, but I didn't think it would be so soon!'

Simon was an extremely tall man, dark-complexioned, with a hearty voice and manner. He was good fun and enjoyed controversial topics of conversation, arguing cheerfully and without rancour. Devina, so quiet and gentle, seeming almost fragile, was his complete opposite. I explained my predicament.

`I don't think the wind has eased off much at all this afternoon,' Simon said and indeed from their window with a wonderful view of the harbour, it looked very wild. `I'll 'phone MPA and see what they have to say.'

After he put the telephone down, Simon commented: `I don't think you'll get back on your boat tonight. They reckon it's going to carry on until tomorrow and it's been blowing 72 knots up there.'

`Why don't you stay and have supper with us?' suggested Devina, `and stay here for the night, if you'd like to.'

`I can't do that — why you hardly know me! It's a terrible imposition.'

`Wouldn't throw a dog out on a night like this,' boomed Simon, `let alone an attractive young lady,' he added gallantly.

`It's no trouble, Annie, honestly,' Devina reassured me, `as long as you don't mind taking pot luck with us.'

`Well, if you're sure, I'd really appreciate it. In truth, I don't know where else I could go!'

`Good. That's settled, then,' Simon declared, `and now, can I get you ladies anything to drink?'

As I sat in their warm, comfortable living room, glass in hand, listening to the howling wind seeking out the house's weaknesses, I felt a deep gratitude to these two kind people, who cheerfully gave up one of their rare evenings alone to succour a poor sailor.

Chapter Fifteen

To my relief, the wind had moderated in the morning and Simon drove me back to the boat about half past eight.

`That doesn't count as a visit, you know,' Simon told me as I climbed down from the Rover. `Come and see us again, won't you?'

`We'll both come next time — I can't thank you enough for looking after me last night.'

`He laughed. `We enjoyed it.'

I managed to attract Pete's attention and he rowed out for me. After recounting my tale and having a bite to eat, we went back ashore with our new heater; Carl had offered to do some welding for its chimney. It was smaller than the one for the diesel heater and needed a flange to step it up. On the way, we stopped at *Dodo's Delight*, who had intended to leave the previous day; I had been unhappy about the thought of them setting off on a Friday.

`Your God obviously doesn't think you should leave on a Friday, either, Bob,' I teased him.

`Well, we're hoping to get away today, anyway. It'll probably be a bit uncomfortable for a while, but we ought to go while we can.'

`In that case, we'll wish you bon voyage and fair winds. Good luck! I dare say that we'll see you again along the way.'

Carl and Dianne were both in and after a cup of tea, Carl and Pete went off with the heater to Carl's workshop while Dianne and I had a pleasant, domestic afternoon, doing my washing, going shopping and discussing our plans and projects. Carl and Pete came back about mid-afternoon and we had tea together. As usual, Carl offered to run us back and with having the heater to carry, he was more than usually persuasive. In truth, I was not sorry to accept — I felt that I had

walked the length of Ross Road more than enough, just recently.

On Sunday morning, we went to look for some green hose that Pete had seen on the beach towards FIPAS, something that the military had used, a tough-looking combination of plastic and canvas. It would make good anti-chafe protection for the battens. As we walked along, we saw that *Dodo's Delight* had left.

`Well, at least Bob and "the lads" have had a good start,' I commented, `It will be quite something if they actually get to Faraday.'

`I don't find the idea of the Peninsula all that attractive, you know.'

`Don't you? I'd have thought it would have been even more appealing than South Georgia.'

`Some parts of the Antarctic, yes. But most of the Peninsula and the South Shetlands, too, for that matter, have too many bases, too many cruise ships and charter boats like *Damien II*, whizzing about. It's not my idea of a remote cruising ground. In fact, given the choice, I'd rather go to South Georgia than the Antarctic.'

`Well, according to Sally's book, South Georgia *is* the Antarctic — it's within the Antarctic Convergence.'

`I know, but I don't think I agree with that definition. South Georgia has tussac and grasses and seems too green to me, to be counted as Antarctic. Especially as it's so far north.'

`But Greenland was pretty green, too.'

Pete laughed. `Ask Erik the Red! But at least it's truly into Arctic latitudes. Remember those shots we saw from "Life in the Freezer" of South Georgia — it was positively lush and more so than Greenland. Anyway, it doesn't really matter. The main reason I'd rather go to South Georgia, is because it looks like a much better cruising ground. In the Antarctic there aren't that many anchorages and you can't get ashore at a lot of them, or you can only go a little way. But South Georgia has dozens of anchorages and you can actually get ashore and go walking. At the moment, anyway. But who knows? There are enough tourists going there, already. I bet before long several of the anchorages will be out of bounds.'

I sighed. `OK, OK, you win. I'm not going to spend the rest of my life feeling guilty because I deprived you of the great ambition of your life. We'll go to bloody South Georgia if you must, but I'm not going along the south coast. I'm not that brave.'

`There are some reasonable harbours along there, too.'

`Come on, Pete! Can't you compromise on *anything*?'

`All right. Just the north coast then. I'm glad you've changed your mind. I'm sure you'll enjoy it.'

`Hah! I'm only going because I can think of no good reason not to. Feel free to change your mind at any time — I won't be upset.'

`No chance of that! It sounds a marvellous place.'

I made some non-committal noise to that and we walked on, Pete's mind undoubtedly full of enthusiastic plans, mine full of forebodings, wondering what I had let myself in for. On the other hand, I felt sure that it was the right decision to have made: Pete must have ended up feeling bitter at my preventing him from doing something that was so important to him and that sort of resentment will eventually destroy a relationship.

We found the hose and picked up one or two long lengths. On the way back, we went as usual into the West Store, having discovered that they sometimes had offers or that fruit had arrived that we had not heard about and with prices being so high in Stanley, we did not want to miss any opportunity to snap up a bargain. Today we were in luck and found that they had wine on offer at one pound fifty a litre — a couple of dollars per box. We enjoy wine at the weekend and having our rucksacks with us for the hose, promptly bought twenty-two litres, all we could carry, and transferred the hose to carrier bags. We walked back to *Badger* feeling smug.

That afternoon, Pete took out the old heater and we offered up the new one in several ways until it seemed satisfactory. While Pete was fitting it, I emptied out the locker next to the starboard settee, so that we could put wood in it. This was originally built as a coal locker, back in the days when we had a *Tor-Gem* solid-fuel stove, but was now filled with paperback books for swopping. I put them on the shelf in the forward cabin and was surprised at how many there were.

`I don't know Pete. We always seem to end up putting too much weight up for'ard.'

`Ah well, we'll just have to keep the wood back aft, I suppose. OK, Annie. It's ready to light. Who's going to have the honour?'

`You've done all the work. You do it.'

Pete filled the firebox with small bits of wood and then poured paraffin onto the wick in the ash collector. He lit it and then went and looked out of the hatch.

`Plenty of smoke coming out. It seems to be drawing OK.'

`Gosh, Pete! There's heat coming from it already. It'll certainly warm the boat up a lot faster than the Reflex!'

`Hmm. It *seems* to be a success, but I suppose we can't really tell until we have a lot of wind, but so long as we can keep up a wood supply, we may be on to a winner.'

`Yes, that's the problem I foresee. If we go back to Iceland, we'll be in the same situation we were with the *Tor-Gem* — needing a fire but unable to buy wood or coal for it.'

`Yes, I'm not sure how to overcome that problem, but we'll cross that bridge when we come to it. Most of the time I'm sure we'll be able to get wood or coal and I don't suppose this little thing will use much.'

`As well, we can always keep a weather eye out for something better and until we find the perfect stove, we've got something very acceptable.'

We kept it going for the rest of the day, not because we really needed it, but because it was just so nice being truly snug, warm and dry for a change. I cooked dinner in my shirt sleeves.

The following day was sunny with light winds and by afternoon it was so warm and pleasant that we were tempted to go ashore. In the West Store, we noticed that all the cheap wine had gone, but today they had nectarines and plums from Chile, so we treated ourselves to some, unable to resist their heavenly scent as we walked past. It was our lucky day, because when we looked in at Leif's, we saw that she had some eggs and managed to buy a whole two dozen. Obtaining eggs was a perennial problem in the Falklands. Before the Conflict, the majority of people had their own hens and of those who did not, many had family in camp who made sure that they were never short. Since the Conflict, however, Stanley has become regrettably more bourgeois and some of the `New Islanders' as they are called, complain about the hens and regard them as a health hazard, so that they are no longer kept in the way that they were. In addition, the new housing plots are too small. Before there was any town planning, each plot was situated on the sloping land so that it looked over its neighbour at a view of the harbour and it was large enough to have room for a substantial peat shed, a hen run and a vegetable garden. Nowadays the houses face one another so that there is no privacy, on winding `Drives', `Ways' or `Avenues' laid out to English suburban standards on pokey plots. The net result is a perpetual shortage of eggs and of vegetables, for that matter. When the locals' hens are laying, it is usually possible to obtain eggs *somewhere*, but never in any quantity. Pete is extremely fond of eggs and we had got used to them being cheap and plentiful in South America. It hurt enough having to pay over twice as much for them, but it really seemed to add insult to injury when it was impossible to buy any.

Before Steve had come to visit us, I had gone into the *Upland Goose* to ask if it would be possible to buy a bath there, in case he might prefer a touch of comfort now and then. Renting out the bathroom to yachtsmen is common practice among the hotels on the West Coast of Scotland and I had not thought about the strangeness of my request, until I noticed the startled expression of the lady at the Reception desk. This had led to explanations and before long we discovered that Vera came from the same town as my mother and felt that we were almost related. She had asked us to call by some time, and as it was a pleasant day for a stroll, nothing was to be lost by looking her up. We found their house and knocked on the door.

`Hello? Oh, it's you — from the boat. Come in, come in! Frank's here — he'll want to meet you. I'm sorry about the state of the house — we're waiting for stuff from England and it's all a bit upside down at the moment.'

The house was a typical Stanley dwelling: a kitchen, living room and scullery below and two or three bedrooms above. The bathroom was on the ground floor and had been fitted at a later date. Most of the houses had steeply-pitched roofs and were clad in `wriggly tin', but the new bourgeois tastes inclined to plastic `wood' cladding, although to be fair, with most people it was probably that they fancied a change. Frank and Vera's house was much modernized and they were still doing a lot of work to improve it. They had chosen to have a peat range, but had done away with the scullery and had turned the old living-kitchen into a large, modern dining-kitchen. Such is the appeal of a range, however, that while they used the living room, particularly in the evenings, the kitchen was the heart of the house where everyone gathered.

`Do you like the peat range?'

`I really can't understand why people are changing over to oil,' Frank replied. `Even if you get some-

one to dig your peats, it's cheaper and, as you probably know, the Council allots diggings so if you do everything yourself, all it costs you is the petrol to get it home.'

`Isn't it a lot of work, though?'

`It's not that easy and I can understand old people not doing it. But I enjoy getting out and doing some manual labour. It keeps me fit. And as for bringing it in for the fire, all that needs is for you to be organized and make sure it's there for the morning and topped up during the day.'

`It does make a lot of dust, though,' said Vera, `and I like to keep everything nice, but as Frank says, we save a lot of money and it doesn't kill me to have to do a bit of extra cleaning.'

`To me the peat is part of living here,' Frank added. `This isn't England and that's why I wanted to come here. I wanted the different way of life because I think it's a lot better than the life we had at home. I love the garden and my hens and I like the peat, too.'

`What about you, Vera? How do you feel about the move?'

`Well, our children are here, too, which makes is a lot better. Without them, I don't know. I miss being able to go shopping, you know and there isn't so much to do here. But Frank's right. It *is* a better way of life. You know everyone, there's no drugs or crime or violence. I miss some things about England, but on the whole I'm happy here. At least I will be when we get the house sorted out.'

We seemed to find plenty to talk about: they were both energetic people and Frank had all sorts of plans for what he was going to do with their house when the kitchen was finished. He was obviously the sort of man who enjoyed projects, but I got the impression that Vera would be encouraging him to find another outlet for his energies: she did not want to spend the rest of her life in a home that was always being `improved.'

We had finished a second cup of tea when Vera said, `Look, it's a bit silly making a date for some other evening when you're here already. Why don't you eat with us tonight. Nothing special, but you're welcome to stay.'

We ended up having a very pleasant evening, once again realizing our good fortune in being able to spend time in such an hospitable and friendly community.

The following day was one of planning, for having made up our minds to stay over winter in the Falklands, we now had a lot more time at our disposal to explore them.

`We should really be able to use *Falkland Islands Shores* properly, now,' I mentioned to Pete as he stood poring over the small-scale chart of the archipelago.

'I've been thinking about that,' he responded. 'Ewen's book actually has quite a few gaps in it and some places are only treated superficially — obviously it was impossible for him to get everywhere or to spend much time when he did visit. We should try and fill in the gaps. I'm sure the Club would like to have the information for the FPI and it'd be really quite useful for any other members thinking of coming down here. Some of Ewen's book needs updating — things have changed so much since the War — and if someone was planning to stop at the islands just for a fortnight, say, on the way north, the more information they had, the more likely they would be to get out and see more.'

'I honestly believe, Pete, that you're the only person in the world who buys a cruising guide in order to go to places that aren't mentioned. But I don't think there'll be that much "exploring" to do. As far as I can see, there aren't that many places that aren't mentioned.'

'Well, I think that most of the more interesting places are covered, but on the other hand, there's hardly anything about Adventure Sound, nothing on Queen Charlotte Bay, and Port Philomel looks worth further investigation. The other thing is that Ewen did most of his work from the *Forrest* and she is a small ship, not a yacht. I'm sure the reason he recommended Fanny Cove was because it was comfortable in the *Forrest*, but it's not a small boat anchorage. We ought to investigate some more of these anchorages — those that don't look so good on the chart, for instance. The opposite is true as well — something too small and shallow for the *Forrest*, could be perfect for a yacht and Ewen might not have had a chance to investigate them, or been told they were no good. I'd like to check out some of these for myself.'

'We need to work out some sort of itinerary then. How long have we got before we need to lay up? I think we ought to be snugged down by early May — don't you? That's the equivalent of November in England and the days will be getting very short — we won't be able to do much sailing anyway.'

'Yes. With luck we'll be sailing again in September. I don't want to leave for South Georgia before December, so we'll have another three months in the spring. One place I think really needs looking at is Salvador Waters.'

'But there's a whole chapter on that — and really good sketch charts.'

'Yes, but the west end and south end are completely ignored and there are probably more anchorages to be found than are shown. Anyone coming to Stanley who is short of time, should be able to visit Salvador. It's not far away. There's a lot to do. I want a look round Bay of Harbours and Adventure Sound, too.'

'We'll need to come back to Stanley at regular intervals to re-provision. I mean we could stock up as though we're going on a long passage, but it does tend to make the lazarette over-crowded and it would be nice to be able to get some fruit and less robust vegetables occasionally. Besides, I'd like to see more of the people we know here.'

'I'm not sure how long it'll all take. We'll be stuck at anchor for bad weather, but if we sail on the good days, we should be able to cover quite a lot of ground. Probably the thing to do is to go out to Salvador and get some idea of what's involved. We can come back here and stock up and then go west and we should certainly have a look up Falkland Sound before coming back here. In fact, you know, there's a tremendous amount to do. We really ought to set off as soon as possible.'

'We must stock up first — I haven't bought any stores since Steve first came. We've still got plenty of spuds and cabbage, but the onions haven't kept that well, so I wouldn't mind having some more. With having soup for lunch so often, I get through them. We need more carrots, too. We're almost out of porridge oats and bread flour and I really need some new oilskin trousers. My waist-highs are leaking badly now and I can't put on chest-highs just to walk ashore. We're knocking seven bells out of our oilies, here — with wearing them nearly every time we go ashore, they're starting to get worn. My jacket isn't going to last much longer. We must keep any eye out for some cheap waterproofs, instead.'

'Anything else we need?'

'I ought to do a stock check — I haven't done one since we left Uruguay and it's ages since I've looked at the bean supplies because I wouldn't buy them where they were going to be full of wildlife. With staying on, it puts rather a different light on things. Leif has most of what we want, but not everything. I wonder if she could order stuff for me?'

'Why don't you do that today, as we're not going ashore. I'll go and saw up some wood.'

'The fire's burning well, isn't it? The wind doesn't seem to affect it.'

'Yes it does — it burns even hotter!'

Pete got into his oilskins, picked up his saw and rowed ashore to the beach where we had cached a pile of driftwood. I sorted out my lockers, checking on our supplies and refilling the ones I had emptied for Steve. After lunch I roughed out weekly menus and did sums.

We did not want to run short, but on the other hand, with food being so expensive in Stanley, I did not want to buy too much, either.

Pete had also been doing calculations and the next day, he put the little cart together and trudged to the other side of Stanley to buy petrol and paraffin. Knowing that he would have to make two trips, he took all the empty jerricans ashore. When he came back from his first haul, it was too windy to row back aboard, so he unloaded the full ones, put in the empty containers and went back again. By mid-afternoon, when the wind had eased off a little, he struggled back with his purchases.

`You poor thing,' I greeted him. `What a rotten time you must have had.'

`Well, it wasn't entirely wasted, Annie. I got all the fuel we wanted and coming back the second time, there was still room in the trolley, so I thought I'd have a look in the West Store and see if there were any bargains. They'd stocked up the shelves with boxes of the *Santiago* wine again, and I just about cleaned them out. I've got to go back for another load. I'll show you when I come back.'

I helped him offload the jerricans and he rowed back across the loch and filled up *Skip* up once more. Pulling mightily, he made it back to *Badger* and passed me up the trolley, a couple more jerricans and wine briks galore.

`Mostly red, but some white, too.'

`My god, Pete, how many boxes did you buy?'

`I'm not quite sure. All the red that they had. About forty, I think. With what we bought the other day, we should have about a year's supply, with a few extras for entertaining.'

`That's brilliant. Well done! You'll have saved a fortune — the other stuff is at least fifty pence more. They must have done some deal on this — I can't see why it's so much cheaper, otherwise.'

`Well the other thing I thought was a lot of other people seem to like it, too, and if we come back between ships, it'll all be sold out. By the way, I saw Dianne in town. We're invited round for tomorrow evening.'

`Oh, good!'

The rest of the day was spent packing wine away and shuffling round paraffin and petrol containers. Wednesday was another shopping day and this time Pete went for onions and carrots.

`Oh yes,' he said when he came back, `I picked up a letter at the post office. It's from the Club.' He opened it. `It's from the Pilotage Foundation. They want us to write up notes on the Southern Ocean and — you won't believe this Annie — they're offering to lend us a word processor!'

`Honestly? A word processor? That would be marvellous! What a difference it'd make. Imagine the job we could have done on Brazil if we'd had one.'

`I wonder if they'd be interested in updating *Falkland Islands Shores*? I'd do it anyway, but it would be great to be able to give them something useful right away. I'll write to them and see what they have to say.'

Pete was given the rest of the day off while I took the brown skins off the onions and put them away in baskets. He was poring over charts once more and making more plans of places that we `must' visit before we left.

`There's an incredible amount to see here. I reckon you could spend several years exploring the islands and not have to repeat yourself too often.'

When we walked up to Carl and Dianne's, we took our old heater with us.

`You may as well have it. We're hardly likely to be able to sell it here and don't want to carry it around and anyway, we were given the other one, so can't really sell this one,' I told them.

`It's a bit on the small side,' Pete explained, `but you might find it's OK for the after cabin. The heat from the saloon may not work its way back there. If you find you can't use it, I dare say some visiting yachtsman who didn't think ahead might take it from you!'

We spent most of the evening discussing their rig. Carl had not yet designed it, but had thought of doing something similar to the one on his last boat, but Pete felt that this was a bit hit and miss and offered to look through some of his books to see what he could come up with. I suspected that he would be quite involved in the design of this: it was just the type of problem to intrigue him. As ever, we had a good time: Carl and Dianne always made us feel welcome and we all enjoyed talking about boats.

The following morning came in with strong rain squalls, but they eased off after lunch and we went into town to buy oats and bread flour: the Co-op sold lovely stuff, full of malted grains that made delicious loaves. *Homecare* had some cheap waterproofs and I had a look to see if there were any trousers for me. They were all too big, but I noticed a sailing jacket.

`Here, Pete, try this — you need a new one.'

Pete took off his other one and tried on the bright red jacket.

`It's the same material as the last one you had,' he commented.

`Yes I know. It probably won't last *that* long, but it's in the sale bin and you should get a couple of years out of it.'

`It's certainly comfortable although I could probably do with the size up with a thicker sweater.'

`Beggars can't be choosers. Let's see what they want for it.'

While Pete was putting his jacket back on I walked over to the counter.

`We're interested in buying this jacket,' I told the lady, `but can't find a price for it.'

`It should be on the bag.'

`Yes, but it was loose and I don't know which bag it came from.'

`I'll come and have a look then.' She walked over to the shelf and rummaged about. `This'll be it. It's empty and the right size.' she looked at the price label. `Six pounds fifty.'

Pete and I gaped at each other. `Six pounds fifty?' I asked.

`That's what it says. Do you want it?'

`It's not too small, Pete?' I teased him.

`No, no. It'll be fine.'

I handed over the money before the shop assistant changed her mind, but she seemed quite satisfied. We took the jacket and left the shop.

`Well,' I said as we got outside, `that must be the bargain of the century. I reckon you'd pay sixty quid for that in England.'

`Surely not so much.'

`We paid thirty for my last jacket in 1987 and *that* was in a sale,' I reminded him. `This one is the same sort of quality.'

`I suppose you're right. Anyway, it felt very comfortable and at that price, it doesn't matter if it doesn't last as long as the PVC ones do.'

Pete had arranged to go up and talk rigs with Carl; having several jobs to get on with, I went back to *Badger*, and was lucky enough to get a lift half way. The novelty of the walk along Stanley Harbour had long since worn off and although we never thumbed a ride, we always appreciated it when someone stopped and offered us one.

The following morning I just about managed to squeeze in the oats and flour into our lockers. With all the wine that we had bought, there was not a lot of spare space and by the time I had juggled things about, most of the morning had gone. Pete wrote some letters and in the afternoon went to post them, while I spent some time in the galley preparing supper for Carl and Dianne. The wind had eased right down by the time we saw their Rover coming along the road and Pete had no problems bringing them ashore. Tracey was away with some friends for the weekend, but both Dianne and Rachael were completely unaffected by the boat's movements on this occasion. It was a real relief.

Although there is nothing that we can do about it, we still feel upset when our visitors are seasick. Stanley Harbour is not the ideal place for elegant entertaining aboard.

We had seen a stainless steel tank on a beach in Port William and had mentioned it to Carl. He thought he could probably use it and we had planned to sail over and pick it up the next day and also sound round `*Curlew's* anchorage' so that we could draw a sketch chart, but the breeze had filled in again from southwest. As we were invited round to Simon and Devina's that evening, we did not want to find ourselves in Port William with a hard beat back, so had to scrap the idea. One is always affected by the weather on a boat, but in the Falklands we found it almost impossible to make definite plans, so likely were they to be wrecked by the weather.

To our relief, the wind died down later in the afternoon and we managed to row ashore that evening without getting completely drenched. We walked to Simon and Devina's house, arriving rather late, not too concerned, as we thought that this would be correct, only to realize that we should really have been on time. We usually are prompt and hope that other people will be the same, but the etiquette varies not only from country to country, but from group to group and this time we had guessed wrongly. Simon and Devina had invited another couple, Bernadette and Barry, both doctors from the UK, who told us that they loved living in the Falklands and were hoping to get permanent jobs there. Devina's social talents were displayed, when we discovered that Barry and Bernadette had sailed a *Catalac* catamaran across the Atlantic in 1986; she had ensured that we had something in common to talk about. We had an interesting and pleasant evening, but it reminded us of how formal life ashore is, compared with the cruising world. Subsequently, we invited Barry and Bernadette round for dinner on two or three occasions, but they always put us off. We rather suspected that Bernadette did not want to rekindle Barry's enthusiasm to go off cruising once more, as whenever we saw him, he always seemed keen to `talk boats.'

We planned to leave on Tuesday morning, weather permitting and, expecting to be away for about a month wrote letters that needed had to be sent, including one to Sally, warning here that we were hoping to accept their offer of a winter berth. Pete sawed up a load of firewood and we had two sacks full on the foredeck, by the time we came to leave.

When we went for our final shopping on Monday, we noticed a Yankee yacht, *Shingebiss II* alongside the Public Jetty, so went to make our number. Larry,

Maxine and their crew, Gary, seemed pleased to see us and immediately invited us on board. Larry and Maxine were very good talkers and although Gary could barely get a word in edgeways, we soon found out all about their cruise. They had sailed down the west coast of America, through the Magellan Straits and across the Drake Passage to the Antarctic, where they had the misfortune to suffer an engine failure. Not wishing to carry on under sail alone, they turned back, within sight of the Peninsula. We felt very sorry for them, realizing anew how reliance on engines makes one very vulnerable. Not many of us would have either the courage nor the necessary skills to visit the Antarctic under sail alone, but at least then, you would not have to rely on gear that you could not repair yourself. In Larry and Maxine's case, the bolts on the coupling between gear box and prop shaft had sheared and there are very few boats that would have been able to repair that sort of damage. Now it was too late in the season for them to do the repair and return south and they were hoping to be able to leave their boat in the Falklands for the winter. Gary and Larry were both willing to give it another try next season, but Maxine felt that they had achieved their aim of getting to the Antarctic and did not want to face the Drake Passage again. The sudden changes in wind strength that they had encountered there, had made for a lot of strenuous sail handling. They, too, were planning to go to South Georgia the following summer.

We tend to a perhaps regrettable Luddism in our attitude to modern technology, besides preferring the sense of achievement gained from doing things `the hard way', whereas Larry, an ex-airline pilot was almost of necessity a great believer in such things. For all that, we completely had the wind taken out of our sails when Larry asserted that the Smeetons `were lucky to get away with it' when they cruised the Aleutians without radar or electronic aids to navigation, the fact that most of these things were unavailable at the time, notwithstanding. The Smeetons happen to be heroes of mine and whatever else Miles Smeeton relied on, he certainly did not push his luck. Larry and Maxine were from the Pacific Northwest and were rightly proud of a cruise that they had made in the Aleutians, but we remained unconvinced that it was foolhardy to the point of insanity, to navigate in that area using only traditional techniques. But Yankees tend to be dogmatic and we enjoyed meeting some new sailors and hearing their yarns. After we left them we went up to Carl and Dianne's to pick up our washing, Dianne having taken a load back with her when they had come for dinner the other night. I was embarrassed to find that she had washed one of my sweaters by hand.

`Oh, Dianne, I just shove it in the machine! I'd never have given it to you if I'd thought you'd have hand washed it.'

`Well, I wasn't sure. Don't worry, it only took a few minutes.'

`But I feel bad enough about you doing all our laundry anyway.'

`Why? The machine's here. It's not being used most of the time and the girls often help.'

Dianne really did not seem to mind doing our laundry, although I always felt rather ashamed of myself for letting her. I let my reluctance to do an unpleasant job overcome my scruples about taking advantage of her kindness and with so many heavy clothes to handle, I really appreciated the use of the machine. As if they had not done enough, Carl then ran us home: there was too much to carry with our shopping and laundry, he claimed. They were good friends.

We woke up to a flat calm and took advantage of it to survey the anchorage and confirm bearings by which another boat could be sure of anchoring in the best spot. The breeze filled in from the east at about Force 3 and we were delighted at the thought of a beam wind once clear of Port William. We tacked over to see *Shingebiss II*, Maxine took a photograph and we headed out of the narrows. A mother and baby Peale's dolphin played with us for quite some time and later two more adults joined in. It took a long time to reach Mengeary Point and by the time we could turn up the coast, the breeze had become light and variable and stayed that way for the rest of day.

`It doesn't look like we're going to get very far today,' I said to Pete.

`No. In fact I was wondering if we shouldn't take this opportunity to try Volunteer Beach. We should be able to find a clear patch to drop the hook in these conditions and we may even be able to get ashore.'

`That'd be marvellous. I'd really love to see the king penguins there.'

It was well after six o'clock by the time we entered the bay, where there was not as much kelp as we had anticipated and Pete easily found a spot for the anchor on the hard sand bottom. With it being so late, we went ashore straightaway and as we rowed to the beach, a fur seal took a look at us, an unusual event with these shy creatures. It was tricky getting ashore, but some handy white stones made a marker at the only possible spot. Passing through a large colony of Magellanic penguins, we went on to the perfect, white sand beach where we could see several king penguins, which let us approach very closely to admire and take photographs. Their colouring was so rich as to be breathtaking: the head was sooty black with a shocking

Badger anchored off Volunteer Beach.

appeared to be very delicate and helpless, their heads drooping on long, thin necks and their parents tended them gently. A number of chicks from the previous year could be seen, grotesque in appearance, covered in thick brown feathers, like teddy-bear plush, and with black, boot-button eyes and downward-curved, black beaks, which gave them a somewhat disconsolate expression. They looked so solid that their feeble cheeping seemed incongruous. Every now and then, one of the adults would throw back its head in ecstatic display and, beak pointing

pink or golden yellow stripe along the lower bill; behind the ears and under the chins was the same glowing yellow, shading through primrose to a snow-white breast and the back was a shimmering, silvery grey, separated from the other colours by a finely-drawn line of jet black. They were extraordinarily attractive, dignified birds and in spite of my best efforts to treat them objectively, it was impossible not to make the comparison with elderly gentlemen in morning suits.

Climbing from the beach, we passed groups of gentoos and eventually came to the kings' breeding colony. There were about sixty adult birds: a beautiful sight, the grey and white accented by bright yellow flashes. Many of them were nesting, with either an egg or a tiny chick on its feet. The chicks were slate grey, their down so smooth as to look like suede. They

King penguins' breeding colony.

skyward would emit the most glorious trumpeting call, a unique and thrilling sound.

Two American photographers were there, surrounded by large amounts of very expensive equipment, waiting for the right light and worrying that their time would run out before they got the perfect conditions. They told us that it was not unknown for photographers to use stuffed animals: most people never noticed and where time was money, not everyone had the patience to wait for the lighting to be just so and the mountain goat actually to appear where it was wanted in the composition. Sometimes, to ensure that all eventualities were covered, the stuffed goat would be replaced with a moose and then a wolf, or anything else that seemed appropriate. After the Falklands, they were going on to South Georgia and needed to book two cruises to do so: one ship to take them there, one ship to carry them out. As we walked back, Pete and I reflected that the magazines must pay very generously to compensate for that sort of investment and that perhaps it was not entirely surprising that some photographers were tempted to cheat.

Passing the gentoos once more, we noticed one had blood on it and wondered if it had had a close shave with a seal that was patrolling the beach. A man and a boy came out of the shanty on the beach. They had brought the photographers and were waiting to take them back to Stanley. Apparently it was he who had laid the white stones that had guided us to the landing place: occasionally he brought people round by boat and landed them on the beach by inflatable. The stones made it a lot easier to find the only safe place, as we had discovered. By now the evening was well advanced so we returned along the beach and rowed back to *Badger*, who looked as though she was rolling her sticks out, but it was not quite so bad on board, although we took the precaution of sleeping in the saloon.

We were up at six o'clock to an overcast day and a north-westerly wind. We started the long beat towards Port Salvador, investigating a bay near Dutchman's Island and finding quite a good anchorage, with shelter from north-east to south-west. It was a pretty spot and not too rolly; we were tempted to stay, but having named it 'Dutchman's Bay', carried on. To our dismay, the wind started backing so that after we had painfully rounded

M'Bride Head, we still had to beat. The cold front came through very quickly, reminding me of the passage of a Bahamian 'Norther' and it made me wonder what it must be like in the Southern Ocean when it has been blowing Force 9 for a day or so and then switches round to the south-west in a matter of minutes. We beat and we beat and I was beginning to get cold and tired, so instead of going on into Salvador, we tried the anchorage behind Big Shag Island. It was a very attractive spot, although as it was well after nine when we dropped hook, we did not really have the opportunity to admire the view. While I was cooking dinner, Pete dozed off.

'Not surprising that he always has energy,' I thought uncharitably as I chopped vegetables and pumped up the cooker, 'he keeps grabbing forty winks whenever he has the chance!' In spite of the

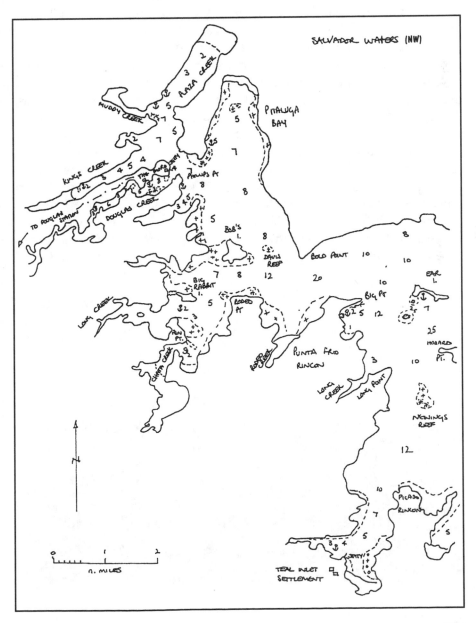

fire, we were both cold from long hours on deck and appreciated the inner warmth engendered by our supper of chili.

In the morning, the bad news was that I was not allowed eight hours sleep because we had to catch the tide, the good news was that it was sunny once more. Our progress was pleasing at first, but gradually it dawned on us that the tide was making against us, meaning that our information was incorrect. As there was no way we could fight the increasing tide, we anchored in the mouth of Sheila's Creek until it turned, Pete using the time to go wooding and make a survey of the creek. With the young flood, we set off to explore, going first to Ear Island, a delightful little tussac isle, with sea-lions, night herons, a pair of caranchos, tussac birds and a partly-fledged Cobb's wren, all of which I duly noted down, hoping one day to collect it all together and send the information to Falklands Conservation. The shores were covered with wood of which we gathered a goodly amount before rowing back to *Badger* and sailing around the east end to Salvador settlement. The wind was stronger than we had realized and we ended up anchoring with somewhat excessive panache, but fortunately without mishap. Once secure, we went ashore and up to the house, where we were welcomed by Jean Pita Luga who gave us tea and cakes. Originally from London, she must have found the Falklands a startling contrast and times have changed dramatically there, too. There was a time when her husband, Robin, ran the farm with more than thirty people, whereas now he has almost the same number of sheep, but is helped only by his son, Nicky, whose girlfriend, Antoinette, spends part of her time back in the UK helping *her* parents run *their* farm, and part of the time helping run Salvador. We found these three busy with sheep down by the shearing shed and talked for a little while, gathering the impression that Robin actually preferred the harder life of today to his previous work. Now he was actively involved with the sheep, while before he was dealing mainly with people, more manager than farmer. Antoinette had introduced several ideas from the UK.

`In the Falklands,' she explained, `people *ranch* sheep. We are trying to improve our standards, and farm them.'

`It seems to pay, too,' Robin confirmed. `It makes more work in some ways, but the sheep are a lot better for it.' We would have liked to stay and talk longer, but they were obviously busy, so we said that we would return at smoko the next day, when they could sit down for a few minutes.

`I'll get a mutton for you,' Robin promised as we left.

We had asked about fishing and been told where to look for mullet, so went down to the old fish trap and spent some time spinning, catching two fish. Nearby was a tangled, completely overgrown strawberry and raspberry garden and I scrumped the tiny, beautifully-flavoured fruit to take back for supper.

We woke to a howling, north-wester and although well-protected where we lay, the forecast warned of a cold front with westerly winds. We had our doubts, expecting that they would swing round to the south-west, in which case we would be completely exposed. We dressed and got underway immediately, Pete having a dreadful struggle with the anchor, which had fouled a large bunch of kelp. It was a very hairy sail in pouring rain, with the wind increasing to Force 8 and we were pooped twice in the race between Ear Island and Big Point, where the seas were steep and breaking. Punta Frio, about three miles away, looked promising and we found excellent shelter there, anchoring in a mere eight feet, with tons of scope out. We quickly tidied up and got below and out of our streaming oilskins. I lit the fire, Pete made breakfast and we settled down to make the best of the day. The wind shifted west, staying very strong; the forecasters were proved right, but we were still glad that we had shifted our berth because we would have been worried had we stayed.

Punto Frio.

Saturday dawned bright and sunny, but the wind came in before eight o'clock, warning of another very fresh day. After a lazy morning, we went to see if we could find any wood and although it did not look too hopeful from on board, we in fact found plenty. The shoreline, shown on the chart as mud, was actually rocky and we noticed an outcrop and a rock, neither of which were charted. In the afternoon, the wind eased off enough for us to go sailing again, the chain once more coming up covered with kelp.

Salvador Waters are a marvellous cruising ground, reaching right into the heart of east Falkland and entered through a narrow channel.

Plaza Creek.

This opens out into an extensive area of water with creeks and islands in every direction and while there is enough tidal stream at the north end to provide interest, in the farther reaches only the rise and fall affects navigation. The survey was old and patchy and we suspected that *Badger* was the first yacht ever to anchor in some of the places that we visited. Being landlocked, the wind raises very little sea, except where the tide runs strongly, and we appreciated this fact that afternoon, when the wind picked up again to about Force 7. An anchorage off Big Rabbit Island looked attractive, but turned out to be a bit exposed, so we went to an alternative at Chata Creek. We had only sailed for a couple of hours, but with such strong winds were as tired as though we had been out all day. Our anchorage seemed like a good spot, but just as we were about to turn in, it became a little popply, and we decided to sleep in the saloon. A little later the jobble disappeared as quickly as it had come: one of life's mysteries.

The next day, 30th January, was *Badger*'s eleventh birthday, which demanded a celebratory blow-out meal. The wind came in quickly and was soon at Force 6/7 and with more west in it, our berth proved to be less comfortable. We discussed looking at some more anchorages.

`What do you think, Annie?'

`You know my views on sailing in strong winds, but on the other hand, it's not that comfortable here and there's so much to see. We seem to be spending a lot of time at anchor — not that I'm complaining mind you — but if we're going to get anything done here, we're just going to have to make up our minds to go sailing in half a gale. We want a good anchorage to celebrate *Badger*'s birthday tonight and she should go sailing on her birthday.'

`You want to go sailing then.'

`Well, put it this way, I think we *should*.'

We togged up and went on deck. When Pete was hauling up the sails, I persuaded him to put one more reef in each than he really wanted to, but as we managed to tack without any problems, we kept them in and had a relatively pleasant sail to Plaza Creek, which provided an attractive and sheltered anchorage. Having looked at another possibility on the way, we felt that we had done a good morning's work and as our present spot was so comfortable, we stayed there for the rest of the day, spending the afternoon ashore. We walked to a house shown on the chart, but it was quite hard going. A common feature of Falkland's terrain is the cushion plant, an hemispherical mound which can grow to a couple of feet in height. They are very dense and unyielding and as they are all different heights and sizes, make the ground very uneven. Then there is the white grass, which grows in clumps of just the size to catch an unwary foot and in most areas there is diddle-dee, which like most heather, is dreadful stuff to walk over. We usually wore our wellingtons ashore, as we generally got our feet wet landing in the dinghy but they did not really make ideal footwear for walking in these conditions, although they were useful when we stumbled into a bog.

At last we sighted a peat stack and moments later the house itself, where to our surprise, smoke was coming from the chimney. As we approached, we could see a couple of men. The Pita Lugas had mentioned that some scientists were staying at one of their outside houses and obviously these were they. Dick and Peter, who were both geologists greeted us with surprise, but seemed pleased to see us and made us very welcome and we were joined a little later by Roy and Neil who were biologists. The house was not in particularly good order, although it was weatherproof, but they were obviously enjoying themselves, cooking on the open fire, provided with a rack and a piece of cast iron for supporting pans. There was plenty of well-dried peat to burn and they quickly stirred up the fire and moved the kettle over it. All of them, except for Peter were retired and two of them came from within a few miles of where we had built *Badger*. Roy actually thought that he could remember seeing us building the boat. He, Neil and Dick were paying for their trip out of their savings and although Peter was being paid his salary, he had no other financial assistance. They were really likeable men, Roy and Neil being retired teachers of the kind that were always respected and popular with their pupils.

Amongst other things, they were studying aquatic organisms, some of which they believed were unique to the Falklands. We were shocked to hear that there is no longer any system in the UK for ensuring that new species are identified and catalogued.

`We're really returning to the Victorian times, in many ways,' Neil explained. `Professional scientists are more and more being forced to work in applied science, their achievements measured solely in terms of financial return. Pure research, knowledge for its own sake, is increasingly carried out by amateurs — people like ourselves in fact.'

`Do you feel this is a bad thing?'

`Not entirely, no. The dedicated amateur can achieve a great deal, but the real problem is that he has limited resources. The equipment exists to help us analyse our findings, but most of us can't afford to buy it or get access to it, which means amateurs can only work effectively in certain fields. On the other hand, there's a great deal of satisfaction in setting up your own studies and carrying them out the way you want to, without being answerable to anyone else. There's still a tremendous amount of scope for the amateur in science.'

They pressed us to stay for dinner, and I was very tempted, but we had been looking forward to our celebration for several days and I thought that Pete might be disappointed if we stayed. It seemed churlish to refuse, but we could hardly discuss it, so we made our excuses, saying that we did not like to leave the boat unattended for too long. They were going to several other places in the Islands and I made a note of the dates, hoping that we would catch up with them again and perhaps I could go on a field trip with the biologists.

Walking back to *Badger*, we had wonderful views over Salvador Waters and beyond to the hills, radiant in the bright sunshine. The landscapes of the Falkland Islands are straightforward and uncomplicated, open and uncluttered: there is little

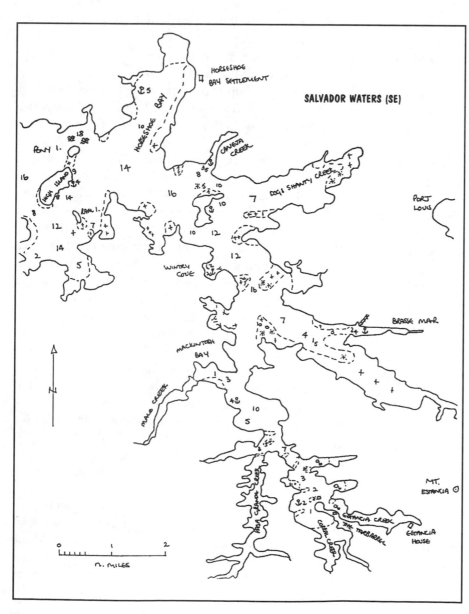

SALVADOR WATERS (SE)

of the picturesque or romantic and in their simplicity lies their appeal. They speak directly to the spirit, needing no aesthetic interpretation via a sophisticated intellect, and to stand as we were, with all this beauty spread before us gave an ineffable lift to our spirits and a feeling of spontaneous joy. I was being amply rewarded for my tribulations.

To celebrate *Badger*'s birthday, we had a splendid meal. Before dinner we had rum and orange, with home-made crisps, which was followed by mussels that we had picked off the beach for Pete, and olives and *chorizo* for me. For our main course, I `roasted' a couple of vacuum-packed chicken legs that my mother had sent us for Christmas and we ate them with home-bottled asparagus and `roast' (in fact, deep-fried) potatoes. Pete finished off with chocolate pudding and custard, while I had some cheese and the whole lot was washed down with a litre of Argentine wine. I hope that *Badger* enjoyed it as much as we did.

It was raining when we woke up, but by the time we had finished breakfast the sun had come out and the wind, which had blown all night, had dropped to about Force 4, which made it an ideal day to do some more exploring. We anchored four times and looked at one or two other places, including an uncharted inlet. If we dropped the hook rather than simply heaving-to at a place, we could ascertain the quality of the bottom and gain a better impression of the shelter obtainable. We also tried to take advantage of these stops for coffee, lunch or tea, more enjoyable consumed at anchor than when well heeled, or, worse still, actually having to tack. The wind had increased to what we were coming to regard as the `usual Force 6' by the time we came to our final anchorage in Douglas Creek. The chart was not very accurate and as we entered the creek, we discovered several shallow patches and that our chosen anchorage shoaled very rapidly. Taken by surprise we gybed round, a hairsbreadth from a Chinese one, which with junk rig has to be seen to be appreciated. As it was, the yard caught behind a topping lift and it took some sorting out before we could get the main down, grateful for the fact that at least it did not flog.

Postponing the four mile walk to the settlement until the morrow, we had time to sit down and read our books for a change, enjoying the good anchorage, which was made even better when the wind died away to a calm, after sunset.

Rising to a day of strong winds and squally showers, we put off our visit to the settlement for another

Douglas Creek.

day. We found plenty to occupy ourselves; I worked out what provisions we would need for the winter and kept the fire stoked up, while Pete started writing up his notes on the Islands and late in the afternoon, the wind died away, backing south-west and we even saw a little watery sunshine.

With a sunny if breezy morning, we at last managed to make our visit to Douglas Settlement, finding a few mushrooms on the way. Mike Clarke, an attractive-looking man, with black hair and intensely blue eyes, met us at the gate, accompanied by a small boy, Stephen, who turned out to be his grandson and not, as I had assumed, his son. It is possibly a sign of my own increasing years that I thought that he looked far too young to be a grandfather and that his daughter, Angeline, also looked too young to be a mother. We were invited in and introduced to his wife, Jeanette, their daughter and son, John. Mike was the owner of the handsome, fifty foot, oak-built MFV, *Penelope*, which came to the Falklands in 1930, two years after she was launched. He told us *Penelope*'s story and asked about our boat and when we told him that we were doing a bit of `exploring', confirmed that the anchorage was as good as we thought and also gave us some information about the Creek. Over a cup of coffee and some cake, we asked how the shearing was going and were surprised to hear that the Clarkes sheared all their seven thousand sheep without assistance. Apparently both Angeline and fifteen-year-old, John were near-champion shearers and Mike had carried off prizes in the past.

When we came to leave, Mike asked, `How are you off for meat?'

`Well, we don't have any at the moment,' I replied, `but we're used to being without.'

`Would you like some? We've got plenty.'

Mullet barbecue on Douglas Creek.

'That's very kind of you. A couple of chops would make a very pleasant change, if you're sure you can spare them.'

'I'll get some then.'

Saying good-bye to the others, we followed Mike out to where an almost full mutton, cut in half, was hanging up. Mike lifted off one of the pieces which lacked only the shoulder.

'Will this do you?' he asked.

'What? all that! We'll never eat it!'

He grinned, blue eyes looking at us with amusement. 'I know what it's like sailing. You're always hungry. You'll have finished this by the weekend.'

With a knife and a saw, he cut the piece in two, finding a couple of carrier bags to put it in. We thanked him sincerely and set off for the long walk back, the sheep seeming to have grown considerably by the time Pete put it down in the dinghy, with a grunt of relief. While he was getting his breath back, he noticed some mullet.

'Look at those. They're just asking to be caught!'

'I thought you wanted to carry on today,' I said mischievously.

'Well, yes, but it wouldn't take long to catch one or two.'

'What about all this mutton?' I teased him.

'But you could bottle what we caught. And we could have some for lunch. Barbecue it. I'll go and get the rod.'

At first the fish were not interested, but after the first one was caught, they came thick and fast until we had ten altogether, including an enormous one. When I was convinced that there would be something to cook, I rowed back for the barbecue equipment, having something of a struggle back to the beach, rowing against wind and tide. I built a fireplace and collected diddle-dee and Pete cleaned a couple of fish, which took a surprisingly long time to cook, but were very good, washed down with a can of beer. After we had eaten, I collected diddle-dee for kindling, while Pete finished filleting the rest of the fish.

'We really ought to get this fish bottled today,' I said as we rowed back to *Badger*, 'but if we go sailing now, I won't have time to do it and if we go sailing tomorrow, I won't be able to do it until the evening, by which time it won't be that fresh.'

'Time's getting on anyway,' replied Pete, 'and this is a good anchorage. You might as well do it now and we'll stay here the rest of the day.'

Pete had skinned the fillets, so all I had to do was cut them into dice and fry them. I filled a dozen jars and as we had become quite partial to our pickled fish, we were well pleased with our joint effort. By the time I had finished, the thought of cooking dinner was less than attractive and I blessed Mike's generosity, because it was a lot easier to fry steaks and make coleslaw than it would have been to cook one of our usual bean meals. We treated ourselves to some wine with it, as it seemed a shame to eat steak unaccompanied.

The wind was a light easterly when we got up and having done some sums about tides, Pete reckoned that it was not worth setting off until the afternoon. What wind there was shifted to the west, a fair one for us and it was a glorious day, positively hot at times as we sailed gently down towards the east end of Salvador Waters. A thunderstorm grumbled over the hills adding to the oppressive atmosphere, a state of affairs so rare in the Falklands as to be a reason for rejoicing: not my usual response to sultry weather. Our progress was less than spectacular, and eventually we brought to in a nameless cove, having enjoyed our rare day of warmth and calm, but in the small hours of the morning, things returned to normal: the wind came in at gale force, so that in order to get any more sleep we had to move into the saloon, where the motion was less noticeable. The day broke wild and wintry and the forecast promised more, so that once again a day by the fire was indicated. As usual, I found plenty to do, polishing brass, baking bread, writing a letter and putting wood on the fire. It was very cold with heavy showers of hail, but our anchorage was sheltered from the sea and we were quite comfortable and secure.

Pete, writing up some notes, commented: 'I've thought of a name for this bay.'

'What's that?'

'Wintry Cove.'

'Hmm, I think it'd be hard to come up with a more suitable one.'

Saturday broke cold, windy and showery, not encouraging us to get the anchor and we loafed around in the morning. By the time we had eaten lunch, we were feeling guilty and forced ourselves out for a sail and although it was cold, it was not as unpleasant as we had expected, as is so often the case. We explored a couple of anchorages and found that some of the information on the chart was totally out of date: the bay where we had planned to spend the night, was totally silted up. We tried the next bay, which was surrounded by low land, covered in dreary diddle-dee and neither pretty, nor particularly sheltered, but as the wind was easing, it was comfortable enough for the night.

The following day, hoping to reach Estancia, we ran aground on an unmarked spit, where we were forced to wait for two hours, which rather spoilt the schedule. We were using the leadline, a cold, wet job, instead of our now defunct echo-sounder, whose occasional lapses in the past had been a warning of total failure, but the lead was not a good indicator of rapidly shoaling water. At this end of Salvador Waters, the chart was nothing more than a rough guide, but even so we were somewhat taken aback when we found that we could anchor nowhere near the 'Tar Barrel', as we had planned, which meant that the walk to Estancia would be two miles longer. Reluctantly, we scrapped the idea and had lunch, after which we looked at some other anchorages, taking advantage of the rare moderate wind. About tea-time, we anchored off Green Island, where we went ashore to look for wood, having lately made some inroads into our supply, soon collecting enough to fill a sack. We walked around, but it was a sad little island. Having been badly over-grazed, it was almost entirely diddle-dee and appeared to be overrun with rats. The jackasses were standing about in disconsolate groups, there were no chicks and we suspected that the rats ate their eggs. A large flock of vultures, who perhaps made their home there, did little to improve the island's atmosphere.

After several cold and cloudy days, it was a delight to wake up to a fine day and light winds. So many people had told us that the Falklands were not usually so windy, that we wondered if the weather was at last on the mend. We had a delightful day, exploring anchorages and going ashore at High Island, which we found very interesting. Like Green Island, it had been over-grazed and become another diddle-dee desert, but here the tussac was making a comeback; unfortunately there were signs of rats and until they are eradicated, the island does not really have a chance. A shanty, in good condition and obviously used quite often, stood near the beach: a pleasant enough spot for a holiday. After anchoring once more, we had a pleasant sail to Teal Inlet, dropping the hook in what seemed like a good spot, to the west of the settlement.

The night was beautiful, clear, cold and quiet, but our hopes for another nice day dwindled when the wind filled in around half past six and we heard the forecast warning of a south-westerly gale. We stayed on board until mid-afternoon, but as the gale did not seem to be materialising, took a chance and went ashore, tramping along the pebble beach and up to the house. We were greeted by Gloria and Ben Thorsen, who invited us in and made us very welcome, surprisingly so, in fact, because Teal Inlet is one of the farms that is not cut off. The new road from Stanley passes the settlement and they probably get to see quite a few visitors; their hospitality confirmed our impression that the Islanders, are genuinely friendly people rather than welcoming us simply for the novelty of a new face. We stayed for a couple of hours, Gloria having some very interesting stories to tell about dogs' powers of extra-sensory perception.

Ben had a sheepdog that was devoted to him and although if he were away from the settlement, the dog would work for Gloria, if he were around it would have nothing to do with anyone but Ben. When he was in Stanley for the day, the dog would do as it was bid until he came home, when it would go straight back to the house. Considering the size of their camp and the fact that they could easily be well out of the range of even a dog's sense of hearing, it was a puzzling phenomenon.

High Island.

But Gloria had an even stranger story to tell. Ben had had a heart attack, which had required treatment in the UK and periodically he would call Gloria, but never at any particular time. When the telephone rang, she would know at once if it was Ben, because his dog went absolutely wild with excitement on the first ring. It never paid any attention to the telephone on any other occasion. It also knew the day that Ben was flying back from England and went to wait at the gate for him, but we agreed that it could well have picked up Gloria's feelings on this occasion. It was a fascinating conversation.

When we came to leave, Gloria loaded us with eggs, lettuce and spring cabbages, all of which were very much appreciated. The spring cabbage was particularly delicious and we had it that night with the last of the mutton from Douglas Creek.

We were hoping to pay another visit to Salvador settlement, but the following morning's forecast of south-westerly winds meant that the anchorage there would be untenable. It was a cold, squally day and after some discussion, Pete said that we ought to go back to Stanley, which is over fifty miles from Teal Inlet, stay there for a few days, get what fresh food was available and then go and see some of the other places that we wanted to visit. I was not enthusiastic about the idea and would have preferred to make the passage in less inclement weather.

It was eleven o'clock before we got underway and before long we were having problems with the fire. The chimney was really too narrow for burning wood and got easily blocked, but as charcoal was unobtainable, we had to make the best of it. I kept trying to get it going because it was so cold on deck that we would have appreciated some warmth below, but in the end, with a cabin full of smoke I abandoned my efforts. It was vile sailing, beating for several interminable hours against a Force 6 and a rough sea and I spent much of the day wishing myself *anywhere* but the Falkland Islands, fed-up of the wind and miserable because I was cold. So much for the improvement in the weather. To add insult to injury, we lost the 'bulletproof' burgee that I had spent so much time and trouble making: its ring had been insufficiently secured. We finally groped our way up Port William and anchored about two in the morning, almost too tired to eat supper before we fell into bed.

We had brought to off the beach where we had seen the stainless steel beer barrel and after breakfast, Pete went to pick it up for Carl, also finding a fifteen-foot length of douglas fir, which he brought back for ourselves, to make some new battens and replace some of those that had been repaired. Having anchored in kelp, we were not looking forward to getting our anchor, but amazingly it came up pretty clean and we had a pleasant sail to Stanley as it was only blowing about Force 5 and we could almost lay along the harbour.

We anchored in *Curlew*'s spot and after a quick lunch went ashore. At the post office, we picked up a load of mail and were delighted to find that it included an echo sounder, which Steve had sent us as 'part of the charter fee.' When we popped into the bank to speak to Dianne, she told us that *Dodo's Delight* had just come in, dismasted! Needless to say, we were itching to see them, but feeling that they would want to sort themselves out, withheld ourselves in patience and did our shopping first. There was a sale in the West Store, and I at last found my waterproof trousers. I had to buy a matching jacket, too, which I did not really need, but at two pounds fifty for the lot, could hardly complain.

The Rev had tied to the Public Jetty once more and we went along to hear the story. The yacht actually looked quite trim, with an effective jury rig and the burgee flying. The explanation was a simple one: stainless steel fatigue. Bob had noticed a shroud stranding and had backed it up with rope, well bowsed down, but a sudden lurch over a sloppy sea had caused the stainless to go and the mast had buckled before the rope had the chance to take up the strain. They had been near the Chilean base, but said with simple pride that the only help that they had required was a few pop rivets, although they had been happy to accept the offer of the odd meal. Neither Bob nor 'the lads' seemed daunted by their experience and were already wondering if the rig could be mended in time to have another try. They had plenty to do, so we left them to it and went home to read our mail.

That evening we spent at Carl and Dianne's and as she had invited all the *Dodos* around, too, it was quite a party. I had taken along my washing, but the machine was now being well utilized: Dianne had also told the distressed mariners to bring up their dirty laundry and from then until *Dodo's Delight* once more set sail, Dianne seemed to be inundated with clothes, but continued to insist that it was what the machine was intended for. There was nothing half-hearted about any offer that she made.

As ever, we ended up staying longer in Stanley than we had planned. Our first priority was to get the fire working and we soon realized that the chimney was blocked solid. In the end, Pete made a reamer from a piece of copper tubing, fastened to a bamboo with a jubilee clip. Used every day or so, this kept the chimney clean and the fire burning well, but if we forgot, we paid for it with a smoky cabin and a sulking fire. It was a lot better than the diesel heater, but not an unqualified success.

We did well out of the West Store's sale, finding Barbour proofed cotton clothes at a knockdown price. We each bought a jacket and overtrousers and came to wonder how we had lived without them. Not only did they save our oilskins for sailing, but they were much more comfortable for walking in and, as advertized, totally waterproof. The fact that the shoulder of my oilskin jacket came away a couple of days later made us realize how much wear they had endured since we arrived in the Falklands. Fortunately I had a spare.

The event of greatest moment came about, as such things do, almost by accident. I popped into the West Store one afternoon to buy something and while he was waiting for me, Pete, saw on the notice board an advertisement for an open boat with a twenty-two horse-power, Ducati, air-cooled engine.

`What of it?' I asked him when he told me, `we don't want a boat and surely you're not thinking of doing it up.'

`No, it's the engine I'm thinking about. The whole lot is only two hundred and fifty pounds.'

I stopped dead and goggled at him. `The *engine*! You mean you're thinking of putting a *diesel engine* in *Badger*? And twenty-two horsepower! I thought you liked having the Seagull.'

`I do, but this might be a good buy and it would make you feel happier about going to South Georgia if we had one.'

`Maybe. But wouldn't it be a hell of a job installing it?'

`Well, yes, but then we're having to lay up for the winter anyway, so we would have the time.'

I was so shocked at this idea that I was lost for words, so simply nodded when Pete suggested going to look at it. The man who owned the engine was out, but his wife let us see it and told us that it was in running order. It was an attractive proposition, but we wondered if we could actually fit it down the hatch. For the rest of the day, we talked of little else.

A couple of days later, *Damien II* came into the harbour and we went to see them, to hear about their plans and also to check that it was still possible to spend the winter at Beaver. Sally, Jérôme and Diti were on board, getting ready to go to South Georgia and we told Jérôme about the engine. He recommended that we buy it, believing that a good auxiliary makes the boat much

more useful and was full of ideas for helping us fit it, offering us the use of his workshop.

`I will put *Damien II* in my "marina" for ze wintair, so you could go alongside ze jetty and dry out. Maybe you can work between ze tides. I am sure zat we can do ze needed work zair wiz ze matérial zat I 'ave.'

With this thought, we felt even more inclined to pursue the matter. *Damien II* was leaving that day, so we took their letters to post and watched them sail out.

`Never mind, Pete. That will be us in ten month's time.'

Dodo's Delight.

That evening, we heard a car horn and looking out, saw Carl's Rover, so Pete rowed over to see what he wanted. He was soon back.

`Carl wants me to work tomorrow!'

`Doing what?'

`Unloading squid.'

`Oh god, Pete, you'll stink the boat out! Did you accept?'

`I did when he told me what I'd be earning — a chance of a bonus, too. If I get a few days, we'll certainly be able to afford this engine.'

`Don't you mind, though? We were hoping to be off again, soon.'

`It's worth it for a few days and besides, Carl can't find anyone else and is pretty desperate. I have to leave at six o'clock, though, so we'd better have an early night of it.'

Pete ended up employed for several days. Although he had expected to work in the hold, piling blocks of frozen squid into a sling, which was then craned out, he was asked to operate the crane. Somewhat taken aback, never having used one before, he was concerned that he might drop a fifty pound lump of frozen squid on one of his fellow workers, who were not provided with hard hats, but managed without doing any harm to either man or machinery. It also kept him at an acceptable distance from the squid. Dianne put Carl's overalls in the washer as soon as he came home, but they still reeked of fish when they came out. I would have been unable to wash Pete's, which would have had to stay below in case of rain, so I was relieved that he was on deck.

While he was working, I found plenty to do and just walking back and forth to Stanley on various chores, could take up half a day. One afternoon I was in the West Store and saw Andrèz, who now owned the boat that Carl and Dianne had sailed to the Falklands.

`Hi, how are you going?'

`Fine, and yourself?'

`I hear you're thinking of fitting Tony Jaffray's engine.'

I laughed. `Word soon gets round. Yes, we are. The trouble is it's on the large side, both physically and as far as horsepower goes. We're still trying to work out if it's possible.'

`Did you know I have a nine horsepower diesel for sale? It's also an air-cooled Ducati. It was in my boat when I bought her. It used to be in Zack's lifeboat, but he found it too noisy. It's too small for my boat, but it's in good order and has only done about a hundred hours.'

`That sounds very interesting. More the size we'd want. How much are you asking for it?'

`Oh,' replied Andrèz vaguely, `not a lot.'

I could hardly wait for Pete to come home to tell him about it.

`Well, that's a bit of a dilemma. I wonder what he wants for it.'

`It might be a better deal, because with Tony's engine we'd have to buy the boat too.'

`Yes, but we've told him we'll have it if we can fit it in. We must go and measure it as soon as I stop work.

Should we fit it to a `Sonic' saildrive do you think? That would be the ideal.'

We discussed this back and forth for several days, but in the end came down in favour of keeping the installation as cheap and simple as possible.

At last the weekend came and we could go and have a look at the engines. Tony was out when we went to his house, so we carried on to FIPAS to see Andrèz.

`Oh, hello there. You've come to see the engine. Did you know Tony has sold his?'

`You're joking!'

`No, he told me. In fact he wanted to know how to get hold of you because this bloke was offering cash. He couldn't believe it. He's been trying to get rid of it for ages and then suddenly two people were after it.'

`I don't blame him if he had a cash buyer,' Pete said. `Anyway, it saves us the problem of what to do with the boat. Is it possible to see yours, now?'

`Do you mind waiting a bit? There's this French film crew making a film here and for some reason they want shots of me and Ali working on the boat. The film's about island communities or something. I'm not really sure, to tell the truth.'

`We were thinking of going to see Larry and Maxine anyway, so we'll go along to *Shingebiss II* and see you in about an hour. Will that be OK?'

`We should be finished then.'

Larry and Maxine gave us a warm welcome. Gary had gone back to the States for the moment and they were also intending to pay an extended visit home, but in the meantime they had been enjoying Stanley and getting to know people, while sorting out their engine. They seemed to have met half of Stanley and knew far more people than we did, not in the least because they often had lunch in the *Upland Goose* when they were in town.

In due course, we got back to Andrèz and drove off to see the engine. Although it was only nine horsepower, it was not much smaller than the other one, but after taking some measurements, we reckoned that we could get it down the hatch, if we took off the gearbox and the rope starting mechanism. He still seemed unwilling to name a price, but Carl had told us that he probably wanted about two hundred pounds.

`But Andrèz is an Islander, he'd much rather trade than take cash,' Carl had told us. We did not really have much to trade and momentarily regretted not hanging on to the heater, as Andrèz would have been interested, involved as he was in a total refit of *Qakstar*. The only thing that we had was our fifteen kilo Bruce anchor, which we were going to replace with a twenty kilo one.

`Would you be interested in that?' we asked him.

`That seems like a fair trade.'

`Oh no! We'd give you money as well, but it's about all we have spare that might be of use to you.'

`No, it's fine, I don't want anything more.'

`Well, we can talk about that again, but we definitely want the engine,' Pete stated. Andrèz seemed pleased and I suspect that it hurt his engineer's heart to see a perfectly good engine sitting there doing nothing. He had started it up for us and had assured us that he had run it about every month or so. As it had leapt into life with alacrity, we had no reason to doubt him.

The following day was horrible, blowing a gale all day, but we were so absorbed in our new scheme that we hardly noticed. Having abandoned the notion of a saildrive, we had to work out how to install the engine so that we could still use the lazarette. It was not worth losing that enormous asset for something that would only be used for about thirty hours a year and after much calculation and measuring with a steel rule, we settled on mounting it with a conventional propshaft, but off centre. Obviously, this would mean that the boat would handle less well and, due to the asymmetry of the engine, we would have to mount it on the side which would exaggerate its tendency to turn us to starboard, but we felt that the compensation of a usable lazarette completely outweighed the other objections. We were also concerned about the fact that the engine's weight would be to port because the charts and pilot books under and above the chart table, already give *Badger* a tendency to list that way. For all that, we were happy with our compromise, although we regretted already the loss of our Seagull.

`I still can't get over you suggesting fitting an engine,' I said to Pete.

`Well, the Seagull is great for the purpose for which we got it, which is in a calm, but it's no use if there's any wind. The `Anchorman' is not man enough for getting in the anchor and chain when there's a lot of wind and everything is fouled with kelp. A decent engine might help there. If nothing else, it'll keep us head to wind and stop us going backwards. As well, Tony's seemed like a good bargain, even if it was rather on the big side, but this one of Andrèz's is even better and I doubt we'll ever get such a good offer again.'

One day we heard that Frank and Julie on *Niatross* had been knocked down on their way to the Straits of Magellan and had limped back to New Island. The Southern Ocean was treating them less than kindly; our own experiences had made us realize that there were a lot of new skills to be learned and *Shingebiss II, Dodo's Delight* and *Niatross* had all had their problems. Perhaps the most important lesson was that down here, it was not good enough to believe that everything was functioning as it ought, you had to be *certain* and not take anything for granted.

Pete had been asked to do some more work, so we stayed on in Stanley. It was often too windy for me to risk taking him ashore, in case I could not row back, so I was marooned on the boat. In the evenings, though, we had quite a social time visiting Carl and Dianne several times and invited round to Ian Bury's and we also took the Rev out for a sail and gave him dinner. He had somehow managed to persuade the RAF to fly down his mast and was planning another attempt at Faraday, but we were a little taken aback at his assumption that the days would still be longer down south than they were in the Falklands.

`But it will be after the equinox when you get there, Bob.'

He looked at us, puzzled. `The days were longer before. What difference does it make?'

`Ah well, Bob, never mind. At least you've got God on your side. He'll look after you.' And so he did. Bob and `the lads' succeeded in getting back to the Antarctic and visiting Faraday and completed the rest of a whistle-stop circumnavigation without accident.

Simon and Devina also came aboard one evening. It had been very windy earlier, but mercifully it eased off by the time their Rover pulled up on the road. Carl always put on the four-wheel drive and came as close to the edge of the loch as he dared, a rather alarming sight, but Simon and Devina were more cautious and I cannot say that I blamed them. Simon had knocked about in boats for a while before joining the Army, but Devina knew nothing about them and the evening aboard was a completely new experience for her. They both liked *Badger* and were intrigued at our floating home and our way of life and one way and another, there seemed to be plenty to talk about. Although they were different from us in many ways, we became very fond of them and always looked forward to seeing them again.

At last the squid were unloaded and we could leave, somewhat wealthier than before, in spite of having stocked up until the lockers were bursting and laid in a store of beer on offer at the West Store. We were more than happy to be off, for although we always enjoyed our social life in Stanley, the anchorage was far from perfect and a long walk from town.

Chapter Sixteen

Determined to get well on our way, we were off before six o'clock next morning, the day starting beautifully, with splendid sailing, but ending up with a very hard beat in a Force 6 breeze. We just managed to make it to Motley Island before sunset; the fifty miles made good had been worth the hard work.

The great event of the year out west is the West Games, celebrating the end of shearing and also, alas, the end of summer and we hoped to get there to watch the horse racing, sheepdog trials and sports, and enjoy the general conviviality. They were to be held at Hill Cove a few days hence, but when we woke to a day that was too windy for us to sail, we had to reassess our chances of arriving on time. Harsh reality forced us to concede that it was not possible: we had stayed too long in Stanley. It was a great disappointment, the West Games being a genuine Falklands event that few outsiders attend.

All in all, it was not our day. We had fitted Steve's echo-sounder in Stanley and now discovered that this one, an identical model to our old one, was not working properly either. Pete spent a large part of the morning testing the wiring, while I wondered if I should have moderated my language in the letter that I had sent off with our defunct unit.

`You know Annie,' Pete eventually opined, `there's nothing the matter with the wiring or the connections and the bloody machine's actually working at the moment. It's one of these intermittent faults.'

`It's funny that Steve had no problems and this one is playing up just like the other one, though.'

`Yes, that's why I thought the fault was at this end.'

`I know this sounds stupid, it's a bit like "Well the engine started fine last time we had the forehatch open — let's try that!", but do you think it might be the cold? It went on the blink when we were in Uruguay and then was fine all the time we were in Brazil. And now Steve's which has been working perfectly for him, ceases to function as soon as it gets here.'

`But surely it gets as cold as this in England — colder in fact.'

`True, but then not that many people sail in the winter, and of those who do, how many have a digital echo sounder mounted in the cockpit? I remember reading somewhere that digital watches can go on the blink if they get cold.'

`Hmmm. You may have a point, there, though it seems unlikely that anything designed for a boat would stop working because it got a bit chilly. The only thing certain is that this one is a load of rubbish. We should never have got rid of the whizzer.'

`Come on, Pete, that's not true. That was hopeless, too. OK, it worked, but it was hard to tell the difference between two metres and one, while we sailed with this one to the nearest couple of inches when we were in Brazil. I suspect this is one of the occasions when you get what you pay for.'

`Well it wasn't exactly cheap!'

`It was compared with the opposition. Anyway, either we buy a cheap whizzer and check all the depths with a leadline at anchor, or a better quality digital. We've got plenty of time to decide!'

Later in the afternoon, the wind died away, but it was by then too late to press on.

It was calm and drizzling when we woke up so we were delighted when a light breeze filled in around ten o'clock enabling us to get under way for Adventure Sound. While one might agree with Mrs. Elton that Birmingham `is not a place to promise much', only a bankrupt imagination could fail to be stimulated by the concept of Adventure Sound. The reality turned out to be less than inspiring scenically, situated in the 'plain' of Lafonia, whose name is the only romantic thing about it. Lafonia is an area of gently undulating rather than hilly ground, heavily populated with sheep which had eaten all but the diddle-dee, which made most things appear a drab grey-brown. In compensation for this lack of splendour, we had some very fine sailing and could 'explore' to our hearts' content among its myriad bays and backwaters.

By three o'clock, we were in Low Bay, after a sail that had been pleasant in spite of the rain, but I have to confess that the cold wind and drizzle put us off looking at any other anchorages. Pete, still trying with the echo sounder, had concluded that the co-axial cable to the echo sounder transducer was to blame, probably due to a faulty plug. He took this apart and rebuilt it, after which it appeared to be working, but I was becoming convinced that it just did not like being cold, especially as it seemed more reliable in the afternoons than the mornings. It was much harder to compile the quality of information at which we were aiming without it.

We went ashore next day, after the most tremendous hail shower, forcing our way through kelp which is vile to row through, to walk to Low House, only to find that it had been moved. The weather was so unpleasant that having abandoned our plans to get to the West Games, we had no hesitation in voting for a lay-day.

Over the next ten days, we investigated almost every possibility in the Sound, although we were sometimes much hindered by the conditions. The first of March, for example came in with every sign that Autumn was on its way and although I remembered to say 'White Rabbits' first thing in the morning, it did not seem to work, because the weather was appalling. I was horrified when, between squalls, Pete prepared to go sailing.

'You're joking! I expostulated.

'It should be all right, they're only forecasting Force 5 or 6.'

'And since when have we been able to rely on the forecasts? It was breezy well before eight o'clock!'

'Yes, but at this rate, we won't get anywhere. We can't spend every day at anchor. It won't be so bad once we get underway. It never is.'

But for once he was wrong: we had to wait for a lull between squalls even to get the anchor and when, about half an hour later, another fierce squall came

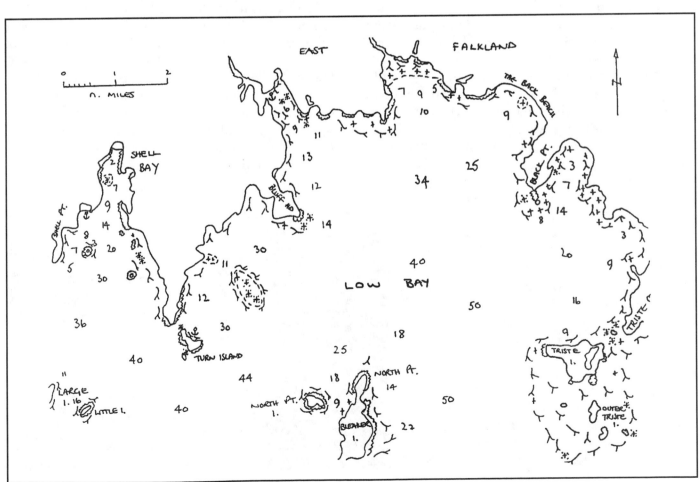

Sea lions frolicking on Turn Island.

so wild when we turned in that we had slept in the saloon.

Turn Island was as wonderful as it had looked. Sea lions were everywhere and about a dozen pups, who were absolutely charming, were playing in the shallows, mock wrestling with each other and chasing the steamer ducks, just like puppies. They were quite unafraid of us, but kept their distance, perhaps thinking that such big creatures might be as bad-tempered as the bull sea lions. The steamer ducks had a lot to put up with, the pups lolloping up to where they lay dozing in the sun and sending them waddling off indignantly in all directions. Walking through the flourishing tussac, we disturbed a huge, but very weary bull, who had probably fought his last fight. There were tussac birds, Cobb's wren and a carancho, but although we saw burrows, there were no jackasses, which were probably back at sea. It made us realize how the year was getting on.

Leaving with a very light wind, we thought that it would be fun to sail through Turn Island Pass, which was full of kelp. With a leading wind, there was no real problem, but it would have been impossible to tack through. To celebrate the good weather, I prepared a `barbecue' on board: well, vegeburgers and a tin of beer, all to be consumed in the cockpit, but as soon as the burgers were made, the sun went in. We anchored anyway and in the lee of the cabin, it was warm enough to enjoy a leisurely lunch. In the afternoon, the wind got up and it was distinctly chilly, with a fine, thin drizzle that made us glad to get the hook down and warm up below. It had got a lot colder during our

through we began to realize that it had come to stay. It was blowing a full Force 7, right on the nose for Bleaker Island settlement, which is where we were heading. The south-westerly wind was `like a whetted knife' as we plugged into it and when I went down to make some soup for lunch, I found that the fire had gone out. Pete yelled something down the hatch and I stuck my head out.

`Wait a bit, Annie, and we'll go in by Turn Island for lunch. It looks a likely spot and if the wind doesn't ease off, we can stay there.'

It was after two o'clock, when we eventually dropped the hook, having taken an incredible five hours to cover five and a half miles. The consolation was a lovely anchorage, well-sheltered by a delightful tussac island with lots of sea lions ashore, although at the time, I was far too cold to appreciate the view and wanted nothing more than to get the fire going and get thawed out. It had not been a pleasant sail and I mentioned this to Pete.

`I don't know why you get so fed-up,' he commented. `The sun will be out tomorrow and you'll be full of the joys. You know it doesn't last for ever and you wouldn't like it if it was always easy. You'd get bored.'

`Huh — just give me the chance.' But I knew that he was right. Unfortunately, I am anything but phlegmatic and while one part of me knows that without the bad times, I would not appreciate the good times so much, the other part of me refuses to listen and wants life always to be pleasant and comfortable.

And of course, the next day dawned sunny and flat calm, although it had still been

Sailing through the kelp of Turn Island Pass.

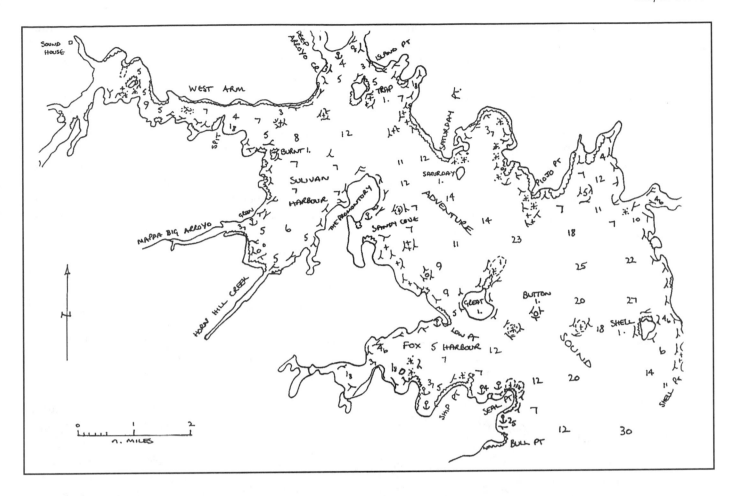

time in Stanley and that night I broke out the hot water bottle to take to bed.

On days of sunshine and light winds, we managed to cover a lot of ground and enjoyed all the new places with their odd names, such as Deep Arroyo Creek, a typical Falkland's tautology, *arroyo* meaning creek. In the western arm of the Sound, we discovered a lot of silting, but no decent anchorage, which I suppose was useful knowledge, even if in a negative way. At Sulivan Harbour there was a delightful green ashore and I picked over a pound of mushrooms, which were dried and put by. These greens are an interesting feature of the islands. In the settlements, they are created by the close grazing of sheep gathered for shearing, but out in camp, they just seem to occur. Bright in colour and covered in springy grass, they are just like a golf course, lovely places to sit in the sun and often a good source of mushrooms.

Sulivan Harbour itself, turned out to be a disappointment because after supper, the wind picked up and we found that the waves hooked round into the anchorage. After enduring a bouncy, windy night, our forebodings that the wind was to back south-west which would make the harbour even more uncomfortable, were confirmed by the forecast. With no obvious

alternative and the chart unreliable due to the area having silted up, we were forced to stay put, but although I worried that the wind would shift and increase, it dropped away little by little and went calm not long after sundown, which, we observed, was getting earlier and earlier at a dramatic rate. I tend to use up a lot of nervous energy anticipating evils which, thankfully, rarely occur.

The following day, Sunday, lived up to its name and with relatively light conditions, we did a lot of `exploring' accompanied for much of the time by up to twenty puffing pigs, which waited for us when we went in and out of the different bays and dropped the hook. It was almost warm and we even sailed without oilskins, something of a record. The highlight of the day was counting eleven giant petrel chicks at Mutiny Point.

Generally, it was rather different and on several days, we were forced to stay in harbour and often the wind blew all night. I was once awoken by a weird noise which I eventually identified as some kelp from the anchor warp flapping against the hull. At anchor, the sunshine would tempt us to further investigations and we would talk ourselves into believing that it was less windy than it appeared, but once under way, we were usually disillusioned and on such days our sailing could hardly have been described as fun. On the other hand, we really enjoyed anchoring off the little islands. Although several of them were diddle-dee deserts, with the demise of boats around the islands, we took a lot of pleasure in the fact that no-one visited them any more. With so many cruising grounds overcrowded, we could never get over our good fortune in having the Falkland Islands to ourselves.

One or two places in Adventure Sound had been surveyed in the seventies, but our faith in the modern Navy was somewhat shaken when we discovered that the gap between Adventure Island and the mainland was much deeper than the 1978 survey showed. This was the second important error that we had found on recent charts and we could not help comparing this with the older surveys, where inaccuracies were the result of time, rather than carelessness.

The shores of Adventure Sound often contained lagoons, most of which seemed to have at least one resident pair of black-necked swans, very elegant birds. Occasionally we saw them browsing among the kelp of which there were vast amounts in some of the bays. We became quite used to forcing our way through it, but nearly got stuck in one, where the weed seemed almost solid. It was good fun sailing through vast rafts of the stuff, so long as we were confident that there would not be any hidden rocks: it was tricky but not dangerous.

Our last anchorage was in Moffit Bay and when the wind picked up, we voted to stay put and have a barbecue ashore. Pete found plenty of wood, both for the fire and to take back, while I, though I says it myself as shouldn't, built a first-rate fireplace. We had a splendid time, but rowing back, a strong gust nearly blew us past *Badger* and we only just managed to grab her. It would have spoilt the day had we missed. After unloading the wood, we brought *Skip* aboard, to save worrying about her.

This was the first anchorage in several days to be open south of west and with the wind already due west, I started fretting. The pusser gave me an unscheduled tot of rum to calm my fears and had one himself to compensate for another night on the saloon settees. The next morning's forecast was quite dreadful, so we shifted further down the bay to get more protection from the south-west, but we ended up wasting the day. We were ready to move on to the Bay of Harbours and by the time the wind eased off, it was really too late to start what was going to be a long beat. Actually, the day was not a total write-off because I baked a sinfully rich fruit cake in preparation for Pete's birthday.

The next day also came in with warnings of gales, but as the wind seemed to be at an acceptable level and we had somewhat lost faith in the accuracy of the forecasts, we got underway, leaving through the 'not recommended' passage by Bleaker Island, known as Bleaker Jump. We did all right until after lunch when the wind picked up from Force 6 to more

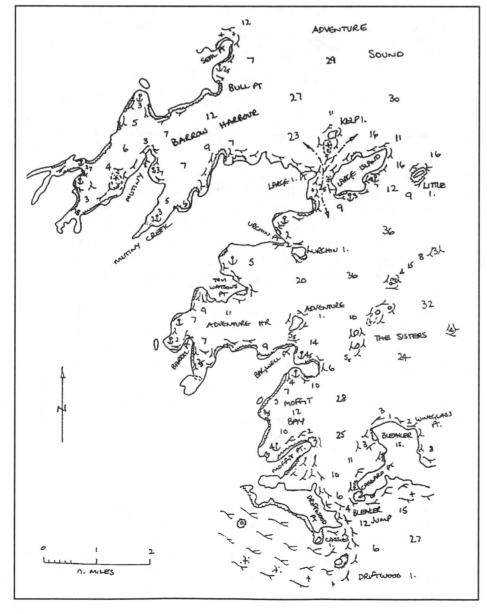

like Force 7. We were not making very good progress, the only possibilities shown on the chart were unsurveyed and there was no chance of getting to a guaranteed anchorage until after dark. The only alternative was to turn back to our previous anchorage and we had problems beating through the kelp in Bleaker Jump, finally resorting to simply barging through, sailing almost sideways. My afternoon was not at all improved when I realized that my behind was not only cold, it was soaking wet, too: my chest-high oilskin trousers had developed a leak at the crotch. I was not the only victim of the chilly conditions. As we beat into the anchorage, the echo sounder stopped working and we ran aground on a falling tide. In spite of our best efforts, we could not get off while the strong wind was pushing us further on. After my usual tantrum, I nobly made curry which we ate with the boat heeled at an angle of 50°. We turned in with a lee-cloth for the `uphill' bunk.

An obliging squall blew us off the mud in the small hours and Pete got up and sorted us out. Although we were by now heartily sick of Moffit Bay, whose only recommendation, admittedly not to be

sniffed at, was that it provided good shelter, we were forced to accept another lay day as it blew a gale for most of Friday. I started a new bullet-proof burgee for Pete's birthday, while he worked his way through an enormous stack of magazines that we had been given by Don Bonner in Stanley, and the only real compensation was that our sheltered harbour meant that I could make Pete toad-in-the-hole (in the frying pan) and chips for dinner.

The 12th March came in calm, cloudy and cold, but at the first breath of wind, we got underway to make another attempt at the Bay of Harbours. For the third time, we traversed Bleaker Jump and to our astonishment, the wind played fair and freed us when we tacked enabling us to reach the Fanny Islands about midday. On the way, we discovered that our stainless steel mainsheet horse had cracked, where a tang was welded on for the blocks, but it seemed to be strong enough for the moment, so we let it be. I do dislike stainless steel.

The Fanny Islands were a tempting place to anchor and explore. Shown on the chart as a single island, they were definitely two separate entities,

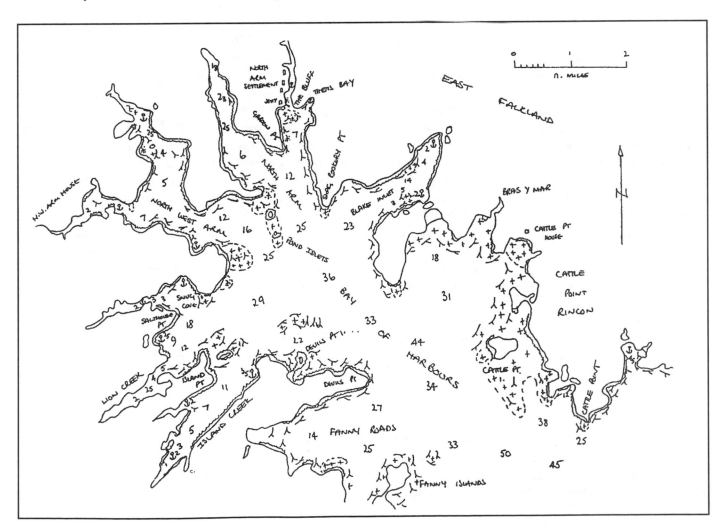

North Arm settlement.

side' house where farm workers stay when they are gathering sheep, was in good order and full of beds. The pantry contained such things as ketchup and Worcestershire sauce and the peat buckets were filled ready for lighting a fire. It was almost tempting.

The afternoon saw us underway for civilization in the form of North Arm settlement. One of the largest in the Falklands, we were particularly interested to see it, because it would give us an idea of what the Islands had been like before the Conflict and the breaking up of the big farms. It needed some interesting rock dodging to get in and the anchorage was long and narrow, so that to avoid swinging into the shallows, we had to moor on two anchors. It was strange to see lights again and we turned in to the sound of dogs barking.

The sun was shining when we rowed to the beach after breakfast. A young man passing on a motor bike stopped to greet us and told us that they were shearing. These were the stragglers, so that instead of professional shearers, it was the farm workers who were handling them. Many of the sheep objected strongly, and one or two of the men, obviously not enjoying the job, handled the animals roughly, so that they struggled even more and several of them had bad nicks. At the best of times, shearing is not for the squeamish as the electric clippers can do just as much damage as hand shears. Of course, a top-quality shearer takes a pride in his (or her) work and tries to shear quickly, cleanly and more or less in one piece, but watching less experienced hands is not a pretty sight. We soon wandered round to where they were sorting the fleeces, where Neil, the farm's mechanic, explained the importance of this job.

The fleeces are sorted initially by their texture: back, bellies and necks all being different. A good sorter can make a big difference to a farm because the bales are open at random when they get to the UK and the quality of all that grade judged on the one bale. If coarser wool is mixed with the fine stuff, the whole bale will be downgraded; conversely, if the sorter is too conservative the wool that should have been classed as top quality will be mixed with the next grade down and in that way be worth less. It is also important to have clean wool and any dung, skin or bloody wool must be separated or again, the wool will be devalued. Falklands' wool is valued for its whiteness and the

although there was possibly a spit between them that uncovered on big spring tides. Although we made three attempts to pass through the kelp between Fanny Island(s) and the adjacent Harbour Island, whose name made us wonder if the kelp was a recent phenomenon, we could find no anchorage. With a leading wind one could shove through the kelp, but then there would be no protection in the anchorage.

Disappointed, we went to investigate a particularly useful-looking cove to the north of Bull Island. There were no details on the chart, but it turned out to be a lovely spot, excellent and well-protected, open only from north-northwest through to east and backed by a lagoon on which we counted fourteen black-necked swans. It had no name, so we christened it Swan Cove. Pete had considered coming here for Christmas, but decided against it because it was too late in the day for exploring. It was a shame: Steve would have spent a much more pleasant Christmas day there. We only stayed to have our lunch before going on to Fanny Cove Creek, to see if we could find better shelter further up and although we found it to be very shallow at its head, there were one or two reasonable anchorages. We were extremely brassed-off when the echo-sounder started playing up again, the button to alter the depth alarm ceasing to function. The alarm is not a necessity, but a useful warning of unexpected shoals — a great asset in poorly charted areas with muddy water.

Carl and Dianne used to live at Fanny Cove House, so we went ashore to look at it the following morning and on the way there, I gathered nearly a pound and a half of mushrooms. The house, an `out-

least spot of colour is regarded with almost Biblical abhorrence. Mainland farmers who breed such exotic sheep as Jacobs are not popular, because should a ram escape and breed with another flock, that farmer's stock will be ruined.

Neil was ably assisted by a young woman called Sharon, from Gloucester, who was trying to immigrate to the Islands. She wanted a job at North Arm, that had been advertized twice with no takers, but the Government were still reluctant to allow her to have it. Originally from the English Cotswolds, she had become interested in farming through an uncle, had studied at Agricultural College and would undoubtedly have been a great asset to the settlement, but local politics were preventing it. Young people were becoming increasingly reluctant to work out in camp, a situation that was not helped by the inflated wages offered in Stanley, where completely unqualified school leavers were being offered salaries of £6,000; skilled men with an apprenticeship and twenty years' experience were not earning so much. Sharon wanted to live in the Falklands, because she was very fond of riding and there was plenty of spare land available so that she could keep her own horses. Living the rest of her life in the 'back of beyond' with neither the consolation of books, good conversation or even decent music, we thought a high price to pay and yet she appeared to regard us as a pair of ignorant yokels because we came from Lancashire!

When everyone stopped for 'smoko', Neil went and asked Mike, the under-manager if we could buy some meat, Pete having put in for a leg of mutton for his birthday. I had mentioned this to Neil and was embarrassed when Mike insisted on giving us the leg as a birthday present, saying that it was easier than working out what to charge us. Indeed, we came to discover that any request to buy milk, eggs, meat and so on, was likely to lead to embarrassment, as the food would be produced, but our offers to pay waved aside. In the end, we gave up asking but rather missed being able to have fresh milk.

We went and had a look at the pier before going back. The sides were lined in wire netting, to prevent oil drums blowing off, and a perfectly imbecile young rock shag was trying to get through it, not realizing that although his head and neck would fit through, the rest of his body would not. About ten feet away was a large gap, presumably where he had come up and in the end, I managed to steer him in the right direction. They really do seem to be 'birds of very little brain'.

North Arm is one of only two or three settlements to have a store and post office, so after lunch, we went to investigate. We were surprised to see that the prices were much the same as in Stanley so, pleased to be able

to make use of the facility, we bought some bits and pieces and also posted some letters.

'Can we buy some milk?' I asked.

'Buy it? Oh no, we don't sell milk. We each get an allowance from the farm.'

Other ladies overheard and a discussion ensued. A voice rang out:

'What? She needs milk? I've got lots to spare!' and a moment later I felt a hand on my arm. 'If you'd like to come with me, I can give you some milk.'

I accepted gratefully and Pete and I followed our new friend back to her house. She invited us in introduced herself and her children.

'These are Ivan and Eva.'

'Oh, so you're Ivan and Eva are you?' I asked, 'we know all about you!'

'What do you mean?' asked their mother, somewhat concerned.

I laughed. 'We're always hearing requests for them on *Children's Choice*. I wondered who they were.'

'Oh that's their Nan. They love hearing their names.' We then introduced ourselves. Arleen did not quite catch my name and by the time I realized, it was too late to tell her without causing embarrassment. I

Sheep shearing shed, North Arm.

left North Arm having been introduced all round as `Hannah' and although I would have liked to request a record for Ivan and Eva I never had the heart to let Arleen know her mistake or the courage to ask for it `under false colours'. We had a cup of coffee, Arleen asking us all about ourselves and as we left, she gave us the promised milk, suggesting that I come back the next day for some vegetables.

`I've got loads, truly. You know what it's like with vegetables. You get tons of the same thing and just can't get through them all. Let me drive you back and you can meet Oscar. He's down by the killing house.'

We recognized Oscar as the man we had considered the best of the shearers. A lovely man and, unlike the outgoing Arleen, quiet and reserved, he had come to the islands from Chile, reckoning that although their life was far from luxurious, he had a much better standard of living than he would otherwise have done. Oscar was obviously an intelligent man, apparently doing well at North Arm and highly thought of. Arleen told us proudly that he was the best horse handler on the settlement, which still used them extensively.

`Do you want some meat?' he asked us, gesturing towards the killing house. We thanked him and explained that we had already been given some.

`Are you staying long?'

`A couple of days,' Pete replied.

`Then we'll see you again.'

`Oh yes!' said Arleen, `Hannah's coming to get some vegetables tomorrow, aren't you?'

`That's good,' Oscar gravely commented. `We have more than we need. You're welcome to have what you want.' His comment reminded us of the one overwhelming similarity between the Falkland Islands and the rest of South America: the invariable hospitality that the inhabitants extend to strangers — *mi casa es su casa*.

We went our separate ways. The meat had almost thawed out and I was surprised at how much fat there was, but then remembered Dianne telling me about it.

`The islanders really love fatty meat. When they serve out the roast, they like to have plenty of "juice" with it, as they call it. That's the melted fat! When we were in camp, they reckoned that the stuff we ate was only fit for dog meat, because we got the pieces with the least fat on!'

North Arm sheep are enormous and the leg looked like it had come off a small cow, so I trimmed off a fair bit, leaving the rest to be boned and pot-roasted for the following day. With the anchorage being calm, we had a fondue on the heater. It made a bit of a mess, but was good fun and the meat went down well with bread, coleslaw and a glass of wine.

As it was Pete's birthday, I made breakfast the next morning: orange juice; bacon, eggs, mushrooms and fried bread; toast and marmalade all washed down with copious amounts of *café au lait*, using some of Arleen's bountiful gift of milk. One of the advantages of a limited budget is that this sort of breakfast, routine to most people, is a real treat to us and we appreciate it all the more for not having it too often. Indeed, if we could afford to eat according to our fancy, we would probably be as fat as pigs!

Pete spent the morning pottering round while I rowed ashore to see Arleen.

`Oh, hello, Hannah! Come and have some coffee.' I went out of the fresh air to roast slowly by the peat range, while we drank coffee and Arleen made ineffectual attempts to tidy up. Unlike most islanders, housework was not her forte and she appeared to be fighting a losing battle against the havoc wrought by two small children. She explained that they were hoping to get another house: there was some possibility of Oscar getting a better job, and I suspected that she was not fond of the one that they had. Her two children were exceptionally attractive, with their father's dark hair and eyes and Arleen's lovely skin and were as bright as buttons. Arleen told me that Ivan was doing very well at the settlement school and that Oscar was trying to ensure that they learnt Spanish from him, setting a great store by their education. The children in the islands have wonderful opportunities academically. In Stanley, the secondary school teaches a full curriculum up to GCSE level, after which the children can either leave school, or go to sixth form college in the UK for further education leading perhaps to University. In most secondary schools in England, class sizes are around thirty pupils; in Stanley, the year's *intake* was only thirty children, so that the teacher/pupil ratio was very small. In order to fit in with the British system, the children effectively took their exams six months early, at fifteen, but in spite of this handicap, achieved very high grades. The sixth form college was also excellent, offering a vast range of subjects and allowing the students to take the exams for which they were best qualified rather than forcing them to choose either `Arts' or `Sciences'. Arleen's children had the chance of a bright future, if they wanted to take it.

`I've got some milk for you,' she told me when we had drunk our coffee. `What vegetables do you want?'

`What do you have too much of?' I replied. `We can't buy much in Stanley, and most of that is old and poor quality, so we'd appreciate anything at all that's fresh.'

`Come on then.' Arleen grabbed several carrier bags and led me into their garden plot. It was a decent size and well laid out. I made admiring noises.

Yes, it's a good plot. We don't get much money out in camp and it's hard to save if you want to buy anything, but we have a good life. We're given mutton, some beef, milk and a garden plot. We can have hens, if we want or a pig. We had one last year for bacon, but Oscar killed it like they do in Chile, which he said you had to for bacon, but it was horrible and I wouldn't have another one. He digs over the garden for me and helps with the heavy work. Do you want some turnips? The golden ones are nice — and some of these, too? The white ones are just ready — have some of these. The potatoes are no good yet, though,' commented Arleen, as she grubbed some up.

`But they look lovely!'

`Oh, d'you like new ones? I know some people do. I don't really, though they're all right with Worcestershire sauce on them. I'm sorry I've no old ones for you ... Here, have some carrots — they're ready to eat now and some of these lettuce ought to be picked. They'll only bolt and I seem to have hundreds this year. Now, what else would you like?'

`You've already given me tons,' I protested, laughing at her determination to load me down. `You've got a family to feed!'

`You can see how much there is, Hannah, and we don't even have a pig to eat it now. Are you sure you won't have anything else?'

I managed to dissuade her from completely emptying the garden and after thanking her again, staggered back to *Badger*.

That afternoon, I finished Pete's burgee and then prepared his birthday feast. While we were each enjoying a bowl of popcorn and a pre-prandial drink, we heard the forecast. There were gale warnings.

`It looks like another day here,' Pete commented. `Let's bring the dinghy on board after we've had our drink, so we won't need to worry about it.' We had learned to think ahead on this matter, for during gales, the gusts were strong enough to lift the dinghy out of the water and capsize it as though it were an inflatable. It was then a real effort to get it on board, half full of water and with the wind trying to blow it away from us.

Back below, we took off our oilskins, Pete put some more wood on the fire and we sat down to enjoy dinner: stuffed eggs, followed by pot-roasted leg of mutton, with new potatoes and carrots. There was chocolate pudding for Pete and the whole lot was washed down with a litre of wine.

The forecast was correct and when we got up, finding that the fire was sulking, Pete took off the chimney and reamed it out ashore, while I went to see Arleen to pick up some eggs that she had found for us. She needed to go to the shop and I was pleased that I could look after Eva, while she was away as small recompense for her generosity. After she came back, I stayed for a while longer and when I went back aboard, it was to find a warm cosy boat, the chimney clean and the fire drawing well.

Going to see Oscar and Arleen before we left, we found that her mum, dad and Uncle Jimmy had all turned up, so introductions were made. We all had a cup of coffee together, Bert and Uncle Jimmy diluting theirs with rum and offering some to Pete. Ladies, of course, did not partake.

`You must have some more vegetables, Hannah,' Arleen announced, as we were leaving.

`No, really, Arleen, we've hardly started the others.'

However, both she and Oscar insisted and so we went out to the vegetable patch, where Arleen loaded me down again. I was glad that we had been able to bring something for her: it was only an old halliard for a washing line, but she had mentioned that hers kept breaking and seemed pleased with the new one. Her father looked at it.

`That's a nice piece of rope,' he said somewhat enviously.

`Well you can't have it, Dad. It's for my washing!'

After lunch, Pete went to get some water, which was in short supply and of dubious quality, due to lack of rain, so we sterilized it before stowing the containers.

Arleen's father wanted to photograph us sailing out and as we were getting ready to leave, I could see him standing on the pier. There was hardly any wind as we tacked across and I put *Badger* about, sure that she was turning and we had enough water. Pete thought otherwise and dropped the anchor, to prevent us going aground.

Coming back to the cockpit he said, `I don't think there's enough wind to beat out. We'll stay put for the moment.'

`But Bert's been standing on the pier for nearly an hour to take some photos of us, *for* us, Pete. We must carry on. He won't understand what's happening.'

`But there's no wind, Annie,'

`Then we'll just have to use the Seagull.'

`I don't want to motor out. There's no point if there's no wind outside, either.'

`I don't care. Bert's been standing there in the drizzle for ages and the least we can do is give him his photographs.'

Pete reluctantly agreed and we started the Seagull and motorsailed past Bert, who happily took his pictures and as there was no wind outside, we went into Thetis Bay, just around the corner from North Arm, which we wanted to look at anyway. Although it might seem to be of little interest, it was an anchorage worth knowing about if you had had enough of listening to the barking dogs!

When we switched on the radio to catch the evening forecast, we heard an announcement that there was mail for us at North Arm. We were quite excited to hear ourselves `on the radio' and much appreciated the thoughtfulness of the person who had collected our post for us and then gone to the trouble of trying to contact us when they found that we had left. The Falkland Islands Broadcasting Service is a truly local radio, with a great cross section of programmes ranging from `The Archers' to a most enjoyable programme of classical music every Sunday, which, along with a folk selection was our favourite. They broadcast late morning and in the evenings, the intervening time being filled with programmes from the military base at Mount Pleasant, which ranged from the merely bad to the quite appalling and were often quite unsuitable to be heard by children. The little television that we saw was of the same calibre. It never ceased to amaze me that, having a captive audience, the military did not try to introduce at least a little culture into the life of their people, whereas the entertainment provided was aimed at the lowest common denominator, than which there was little lower. Unfortunately, the morning shipping forecasts were broadcast during the programmes from Mount Pleasant and, the disc jockeys being of the intellect to suit, they were often given out several minutes late, or worse still, early, which meant that we had to tolerate what seemed like hours of witless and offensive drivel, interspersed with equally mindless disco music, while waiting. I found that it made for a poor start to the day.

The following morning it was still calm and drizzling, so we took our time over breakfast, hoping that the rain might stop before we returned to North Arm. We were just having our second cup of tea when we heard an engine and Pete put his head out to see a Rover driving along the track by the bay. We scrambled into our oilies, put *Skip* in and rowed ashore to greet North Arm's manager, Eric Goss, whom we had not previously met. He had brought our mail explaining that he had picked it up from Stanley the previous day, not expecting us to leave so soon. Wondering how to contact us, he had telephoned Carl and Dianne, who had once lived at North Arm, and they had suggested putting out a call for us before the shipping forecast.

`I guessed you knew them because you sailed into North Arm without difficulty, so they must have given you directions.'

`We do know them, of course, but we just used to chart to get into the harbour. The rocks and shoals are clearly shown.'

`Really! I always thought that it was a difficult place to enter. Every time a military boat comes calling, they always run onto the reef!'

`It was really very kind of you — not only to collect the mail but then to bring it out to us. We were just hoping that the rain would ease off before we came to pick it up. I'm sorry you've been to so much trouble.'

`I thought you might not have heard the announcement,' Eric explained, `and anyway, it's not much of a day. It was easier to come in the Rover.'

`Will you come back and have some coffee?'

`No, I won't, thanks. I'd better get on. Where are you off to next?'

We chatted for a while and then he drove off, while we rowed back to spend the rest of the morning reading all our letters, a wonderful way to spend a cold, damp day. Indeed, it cheered us up so much that after lunch, we went sailing despite the rain and mist, looking at one or two spots before anchoring in North West Arm.

The Bay of Harbours was also not particularly scenic, but was another interesting cruising ground, fully living up to its name, being a long, many fingered arm of water, with several islands. By now thoroughly besotted with the possibilities offered by the Falkland Islands, we were convinced that had it not been for the weather, they would have been infinitely more popular with yachtsmen, in spite of their isolation. As it is, they are only really of appeal to those who treat their sailing as a sport rather than a `leisure activity.'

For the first couple of days we had light winds, enabling us thoroughly to explore the western part of the bay, which has many lagoons just inshore of the beaches, again favoured by black-necked swans. We also found another breeding colony of giant petrels, not shown in the wildlife guide.

The calms, of course, soon gave way to more familiar weather and Monday saw us setting off with a nice breeze, which soon increased to more than the forecast Force 5/6. We went to a bay which appeared well sheltered from all directions except south, but had no soundings shown on the chart and it lived up to our expectations, and finding a moderate fifteen feet of water, rather than carrying on in the strong winds, we anchored and stayed put. Besides, having done some real exploration, we wanted to spend a little while gloating over it. Unfortunately, we could not survey our discovery as well as we would have wished, because Steve's echo sounder finally gave up the ghost as we sailed in and we could never induce it to work again.

We went ashore on a fishing/wooding expedition, having no luck with the former, for after our initial successes we had discovered that this fishing business was not as easy as we first thought. In compensation, we found the remains of a fairly large ship and a piece of its teak scrollwork, which was much more exciting than mullet. There was heaps of wood, so I gathered and Pete sawed, with some enthusiasm, as with the cool and drizzly weather we had the fire burning most of the time. At the head of the bay was a white, sandy beach, implying that a heavy swell could come in, where we picked up some aluminium tins of corned beef which seemed in perfect condition. There was another arm to the bay, extremely well protected, but very shallow: there is a lot to be said for shoal draught. Back on board, we stoked up the fire and spent a cosy afternoon enjoying our snug berth. I opened one of the tins and made a corned beef hot pot for dinner, it was of excellent quality: obviously military rations.

We left next morning in much better conditions heading for Blind Island. There are no details on the chart, which shows the surrounding area simply as blue wash, indicating depths of less than five metres and we felt that we were doing some real exploring again. There was a lot of kelp, which does not make using the lead any easier, but as the wind had eased right down, we were moving slowly, unlikely to come to any harm even if we hit anything. By the time we anchored it was too late to go ashore, but I was dying to see the island because we could hear and see a host of sea lions. The jackasses were still here and we turned in to the wonderfully evocative sound of their braying.

Blind Island proved to be an absolutely delightful, tussac-covered wildlife reserve. Although the jackasses were all moulting and a bit subdued, it was swarming with sea lions, including about twenty pups, with plentiful tussac birds and black-throated finches suggesting another rat-free island. I also saw two field mice, another introduced species, but quite benign and very sweet. On the point opposite the mainland, was an old corral, but because the tussac was in such good state and North Arm fully manned and able to make use of its islands, we concluded that only cattle had grazed here. Although cows do damage the tussac, they are not as bad as sheep, who nibble it right

down. On the south and west sides of the island were shingle beaches, covered in wood and other débris.

`You know, Annie,' Pete commented, `there's enough wood knocking about the islands to build a boat. There may not be many full sized-timbers, but you could certainly get enough for strip planking. It would be fun to do sometime.'

`Well, let's buy this island,' I suggested. `There's plenty here to make a start and the rest we can use for firewood. There's a good anchorage, no rats and we could use some of the wood to build a shanty. Then, of course we'd need a small vegetable patch... but's it's a long way to Stanley, for supplies.'

`We could get a motor bike and leave it by the old hut across the way, for using when we couldn't go round by boat. You'd soon be on the road from here. It's a beautiful spot — I could almost fancy settling here. You'd get good sunsets looking across Eagle Passage.'

Such is the stuff of fantasies, but I could never imagine us settling down anywhere, `like mud to the bottom of a pond,' as Tilman would put it. There are so many places yet to see and to see once more, that we would soon get itchy feet and after collecting some wood for the fire, we went back aboard. While Pete was looking at the charts, I made lentil soup and we discussed the afternoon's plans while we ate.

`I've done all I want in the Bay of Harbours, so I think we should have a look at East Falkland Sound. It's barely covered in the guide and there look to be several anchorages around Ruggles Bay and Great Island. There's a leading wind and not too much of it, so we could check to see if the passage between Blind

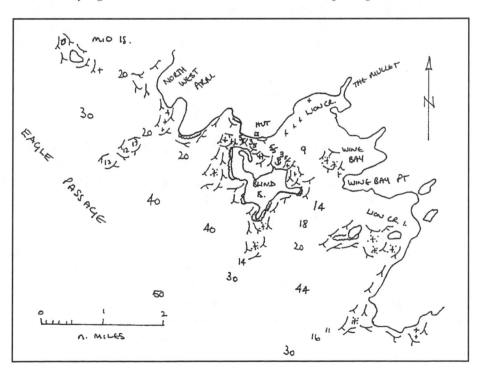

Sea lion bull and harem on Blind Island.

We felt that we were doing some useful work when an anchorage described in *Falkland Islands Shores* as `one of the finest in the Falkland Islands' looked anything but inviting in the fresh northwesterly breeze that was blowing. After investigating it more thoroughly, we concluded that it was another small ship anchorage, for although there is a reef that should stop the swell, there is nothing at all to stop the wind. It was a memorable place to visit because the area was teeming with tussac birds and we had a dozen at a time hopping over the boat. It would be a charming spot in settled weather.

Sunday saw us at anchor off Great Island in time for lunch. We went ashore to look around, seeing no sign of life, but on finding one of the sheds full of machinery, fuel, a Rover and so on, we assumed that the place must be occupied and walked quickly to the house to make our number. There was no answer to our knock and when we peeped in the window, it looked like someone had only just left, with bottles of ketchup and Worcestershire sauce on the table and fairly recent issues of the *Penguin News* on the windowsill. As we walked round the back of the house, a nice little pet lamb came up to us, baaing away and hoping to be fed. It appeared that the place was used as a holiday home and hobby farm, which we later found out to be the case.

On a beach on the west side of the island, were great heaps of wood, but apart from a couple of moribund and moulting jackasses and one lonely gentoo, it was deserted and with the island being all diddle-dee, the effect was rather depressing. On the strand lay the remains of a wrecked ship, which had obviously come ashore a long, long time ago and we picked up some large copper dumps from the timbers. While gathering some wood to take back with us, it started to rain. I was wearing my Barbour jacket and trousers, but Pete only had on his jacket, the excellent waterproofing of which made his trousers get twice as wet, the rain pouring out of the heavens and running in sheets off his jacket, but the trousers being woollen and still giving some warmth, he was quite prepared to saw up the wood before going back to the boat. We found a saw horse and hoping that the owners would not mind us using it for such a good cause, filled several bags, put them in the dinghy and rowed back aboard, where Pete dried and thawed out by the fire. It has to be said that Pete has the courage of his convictions: having always

Island and the mainland will "go", if you like. There may be some rocks in it, but the water's so clear that we should see any that could harm us, well before we hit them. What d'you think?'

`Oh yes, let's give it a try. It'll be a good short cut and give us more chance to get on.'

Accordingly, we raised sail and went out. It was great fun, in fact, sailing through the kelp, the only rocks that we saw were off the north end of the island and easily avoided and there was no shortage of water, the lead finding a minimum of about twelve feet. Despite the wind being so light, we were at anchor by six o'clock in an excellent spot: a bay called Jack's Well, across the passage from Speedwell Island, where we spent another quiet night.

We had a look at several anchorages during the next four days, with a mixed bag of weather and feeling the handicap of having to work by lead using such old surveys. We touched bottom on several occasions, where uncharted spits stuck out from the shore, but on one occasion it was really my fault. We were sailing into Findlay Harbour and Pete had just taken a cast of the lead which indicated that I could head up, but although I *saw* the spit I carried on, running us aground because I did not trust my own judgement. We were soon off and sat out a gale in this harbour, which provided such excellent shelter that it was only by looking at the scudding clouds that we could appreciate how much wind there was. Although the inlet is open to the west, there is an islet which together with large areas of kelp, completely blocks off any swell and seemed also to deflect the wind. We went ashore, but were disappointed to find that the romantically named Wreck House was empty.

claimed that he is perfectly happy to gather and saw firewood rather than buying diesel fuel, during our time in the Southern Ocean, he never failed to keep us well provided or complained about the work entailed. I asked him once if he was sure that he would not rather work a few days every year and keep that money for heating fuel.

`No I wouldn't,' he replied. `I don't mind sawing up wood and I don't like working for other people. Besides, there's a lot of satisfaction in heating for free, it gets me ashore and I get warm twice — once sawing it and the second time, burning it.'

If I had had to chop and saw up firewood, I would have chosen instead to do a few days' work and buy diesel, but Pete agreed to provide the fuel and has kept his bargain, so I have no complaints, especially as I prefer a solid fuel stove. For his part, he does not have to go somewhere and hang round until one or other of us has found work.

It blew a full gale all night, but the harbour proved well-sheltered and more protected than we had first expected. The wind had moderated when we got up, so after breakfast, we prepared to face the cold and made ready to go. As we were togging up, a strong squall came through, so we decided to wait until after coffee, but as we hung up our mugs, another squall hit the anchorage. Pete took out the *Ventimeter* and found it was blowing Force 7.

`If it's squally, now, it's probably dying down,' he declared as he came below, `but we might as well wait until after lunch now, and then we can eat in peace.'

`That's fine by me,' said I, trying not to sound too relieved.

Even after we had eaten, it was still breezy and, somewhat discouraged by a poor lunchtime forecast, we were trying to convince ourselves to leave when an earsplitting rattling on deck announced a violent hail shower. That finished us off. We stayed put and were sitting drinking tea and munching on parkin when the wind eased off and it seemed to get darker. I glanced out of the saloon hatch.

`Good Lord!' I exclaimed, `it's actually snowing, would you believe?'

We looked out at the flakes swirling round in quite a little blizzard.

`And it isn't even Easter yet,' I commented, as we sat down again and put more wood on the fire.

The wind picked up again as I was cooking up a big stew for dinner and for the sake of interest, I put the thermometer outside, bringing it in just before I dished up. The temperature was only a couple of degrees above freezing.

The next day being cold and windy, once more we stayed in harbour, consoling ourselves for our lack of progress at suppertime, with popcorn and a drink, despite the fact that it was only Tuesday. We were dismayed, therefore to wake to yet another rotten day and a poor forecast.

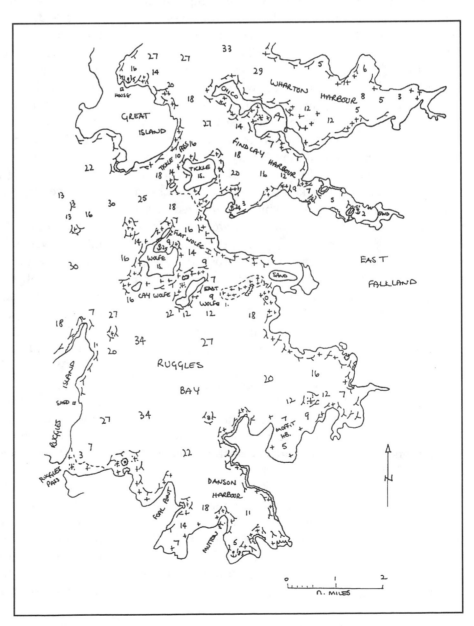

`We may as well turn over and go back to sleep,' Pete suggested.

`Good idea! It'll save wood.'

It seemed marginally better after breakfast and Pete talked about going ashore for more wood and then sailing after lunch, but there were still loads of Don's yachting magazines unread, so lunchtime had been and gone before he actually rowed off. I stayed behind cleaning up the cabin: the top-loading fire tended to make the boat very dirty and it seemed to be a real Forth Bridge job just keeping her looking half ways respectable. Pete came back about tea-time with loads of wood and a report of a gentoo colony on the island. I was disappointed because I would have gone to see them if I had known that they were there. We were both cheered up though, by a reasonable forecast, pizza for dinner and the `Messiah' on the radio.

We actually caught an occasional glimpse of the sun, the next day and when the wind moderated by mid-morning, lost no time in getting underway, racing across the sound under the mainsail only. We anchored off Port King, near a beach with a large gentoo colony and there were feathers everywhere, as they sat dejected and scruffy waiting for their new coats to come through. Many of them were preening, trying to remove the loose feathers and bits of white down were stuck to their beaks so that they seemed to be shedding, too. While we were watching them, we saw an animal in the distance, which looked like, but could not be, a large fox. After watching it a while, we realized that it was a ginger cat, obviously feral as we were miles from any settlement. It crept up on some unsuspecting upland geese and at the last moment, rushed in, leapt in the air as they started to rise and brought down a gander. The bird was quite dead and looked as though its neck was broken, but the rest of the flock soon settled down to graze again, quite unperturbed and as they have no indigenous land predators, they were possibly unsure of what had happened.

`Shall we take it home for supper?' I asked Pete.

`Can you pluck it and all that?'

`Well, I've probably got a book that might tell me how to. Dave and Candia used boiling water to loosen the feathers, when they did their Christmas geese. I'll tell you what, though. You pluck and draw it and I'll cook it. Can't say fairer than that.'

`Maybe we should leave it for the cat.'

`Perhaps you're right — we've got plenty of grub on board. I'll make you Mock Goose instead, if you like!'

Walking back, we saw a large number of oyster catchers.

`I think they're my favourites,' Pete commented `especially the black ones. I love their eyes and beaks.'

`Yes, and their call is so wonderful, too.'

We sailed round in decreasing winds to Cygnet Harbour, whose rather drab appearance was recompensed by its being a very sheltered cove. For the first time in several days we slept in our forecabin, with, if the forecast could be believed, the pleasant prospect of light winds on the morrow.

When Pete suggested that we get underway before eating breakfast, I hoped that it was an April Fool's joke, but, alas, he was quite serious. There was the merest zephyr from the southeast when I came on deck and it wobbled around, uncertain as to what to do before finally hardening from its original direction. Having read that Port Howard is subject to woollies in strong winds, we thought to visit there while the light conditions prevailed. This settlement belongs to Don Bonner's daughter Carol and her husband and having met Don in Stanley, we almost felt as though we had an introduction. Don is a well-known character: for years he worked as the Governor's chauffeur, a job in which he had taken great pride. He had an endless supply of interesting, amusing and, occasionally scurrilous tales about the previous incumbents and had been in Government House while it was besieged by the Argentines and defended by a handful of Marines in the opening hours of the Conflict. It was a real privilege to meet him.

It was a lovely sail and after the sun had burnt off the clouds, there was a stunning view of the mountains on West Falkland, covered in snow. We passed through the narrow entrance and sailed up the bay, anchoring off the settlement. It was about smoko time and, seeing what was apparently a welcoming committee of several young men on the jetty, we rowed over.

`Hello! Look, we can't stay — it's time we were back, but is there anything you need?'

`We could do with some water, if you could show us a tap,' Pete said, and secure in the knowledge that they were not in a position to *give* us anything, added, `and we'd like to buy a hindquarter of mutton, if that's possible, with Easter coming up.'

One of them said that they would be killing some mutton later and another showed us where to find a tap, then they looked at their watches and shoved off back to work. A young man called Bernie turned round and came back: did we want to use the bath and washing machine in the bunkhouse? Did we! Particularly with the weather being less than clement and our wanting to make use of light winds to see as much as possible, the laundry had been a real headache. I am sure that at most of the settlements a washing machine would have been gladly made available to us, but usually no-one thought to offer and as we would not ask to borrow a machine, I generally did it by hand. I came to loathe and detest Pete's favourite, heavy flannel shirt. A bath was also appreciated, but purely as a luxury, our shower arrangement on *Badger* being perfectly satisfactory.

Pete collected our empty water containers together and took them ashore while I started getting lunch. He returned, accompanied by half a sheep, saying that the lads had insisted he take it because it was so small and would only be given to the dogs, which probably explained why it was also mercifully lean. I cut it into two pieces and hung them in the lazarette.

Later we took towels and laundry and made our way up to the bunkhouse. Port Howard is one of the larger settlements, although nowhere near as big as it used to be and the single men all share a large bunkhouse, where they take their meals and have their own rooms. Bernie met us as we walked up the path.

`The generator won't come on for an hour, but I'll get a lead to heat the tank for a bath,' he said and was as good as his word. While the water heated, we had chance to talk to him. He asked us about our trip and was interested in our wanderings in South America.

`I got a place on "Operation Raleigh" a few years ago,' he told us, `and that got me interested in travelling. In fact one of my mates here, and me are hoping to go to Chile after the shearing is finished.'

`Sounds great. How long are you going for?'

`Oh, until the money runs out. It's cheap in Chile, so we should be able to stay for a few months. The boss says we can have our jobs back when we come home.'

`That's good news.'

`Yes, well it suits as both. He doesn't have to pay us for the slack season and we don't need to worry about another job. Jeff and me could both find work OK, but we like Port Howard, so it's good to know we can come back. I remember what it was like when we were on "Operation Raleigh", though and that's why I thought you might like to use the washer and have a hot bath.'

`It was a kind thought — and we do appreciate it.'

By now the heater had done its stuff, so after luxuriating in the hot water, we went for a walk round and to see what was on sale in the shop, Bernie having told us it would be open for a couple of hours. The settlement was built on moderately high ground and straddled both sides of a creek, which had cut its way through the soft earth, creating a fairly steep-sided valley. The buildings were well scattered and we

View of the mountains of West Falkland, covered in snow.

looked into the sheds that we passed. One, the size of a barn, had a full carpenter's workshop where just about anything in wood could be made and must have employed several men when the farm was at its height. The shop was situated across the stream and up the hill a little way and was surprisingly well stocked. I bought one or two things and we strolled back to the bunkhouse, in the hope that the generator would now be running. A young man, who introduced himself as Jamie, greeted us.

`Come up and have a beer,' he invited.

`Why, thank you. Is the generator running, do you know?'

`Yes it is.'

`Well Bernie suggested that we use the washers, so I ought to make a start.'

Jamie put down the case of beer that he was carrying. `Here, follow me and I'll show you how to use them. Then you can come and have a beer.'

I laughed. `OK, then. That sounds like a wonderful idea.'

Pete and I picked up the bags of washing and followed Jamie. One washer was running and the other full of clean clothes, which he unceremoniously turned out onto a table, before showing me how to use the machine.

`My room's upstairs second on the left,' he said as he left us to it, `see you in a few minutes.'

Assured by Bernie that we could use as much water and as many machines as we wished, I had brought several loads of washing. `You're not short of water?' I had asked him.

`Oh hell, don't worry about that. When the shearing gangs are here, they'll use a machine just to wash their tee-shirt and jeans for the next day. Help yourself.'

The machine loaded, we made our way, somewhat shyly, upstairs. A bottle of beer was pressed into our hands and we made ourselves comfortable in Jamie's living room, which he had decorated himself. He had done a good job of it and obviously took a pride in its appearance. He also had a separate bedroom; the bunkhouse had originally been designed for more people, but the present occupants had been told to make full use of it and so each had their own separate space. It was clear that Jamie appreciated having somewhere that he could call his own. As the evening progressed, we were joined by Bernie, Jeff, Roland and Ray. Later we were joined by Heather and Robin, known as Snoozer, who came from their own settlement some miles off. They always visited on a Friday night: party night at Port Howard, but we soon discovered how Robin had come to earn his nickname. Bernie, too was not called by his given name of Iain: his nickname came from his surname of Berntsen.

`We met a Leon Berntsen — he owns Albermarle — is he a relative?'

`Leon? Yes, he's my father's cousin's son. I don't know what relation that makes us.'

One of the others said, `His wife is my dad's first wife's sister's daughter from her second marriage, so I suppose that we're related, too.' Relationships in the islands are very complicated. The separation and divorce rate has always been high; unlike many island communities, the Falkland Islanders are not in the thrall of a fundamentalist religion. Indeed, we were told that if the Governor did not go to church on Sunday, thus providing an excuse for the more society-minded citizens to meet him, the Cathedral would only have about five members in its congregation.

Each time we finished a beer, another bottle was offered to us from one of the cases spread around the room: `Come on! It's Friday night!' Bernie and Jamie told us that they were pretty abstemious compared with people in their fathers' day. In times past, there was very little duty on alcohol, and the greater part of the price was due to transport costs. This meant that a

bottle of rum cost little more than a bottle of beer, with the obvious result that rum was the chosen tipple. An effort was made in most settlements to limit the number sold, but the boys told us tales of when they were little, seeing men when the rum was finished, drinking any sort of alcohol that they could lay their hands on and could remember seeing them sitting with the `horrors' on them, frightened to go downstairs because of what was awaiting them at the bottom. For a while there was a brewery in Stanley, which must have improved matters and now the government wisely put a reasonably high tax on spirits, with a much lower one on wine and beer. Together with cheap imports from Chile, this has altered the drinking habits of the younger people away from the much more damaging rum. We enjoyed talking to them all and finding out more about the settlement and their way of life and it was around midnight before we left.

The previous day, we had arranged to collect some milk, so went up to see Carol Lee, who was keeping it for us. When we arrived at her house, she invited us in for coffee.

`I believe you were up at the bunkhouse last night.'

`Yes, I'm afraid we drank them dry.'

`Oh, I shouldn't worry about it. There's not often any beer left for Saturday. They enjoyed seeing some new faces, I should think.'

A rather elegantly-clad lady walked in, an unusual sight out in camp.

`You know Don, don't you? Well this is my mother.'

We all sat down for coffee. `Have you seen our little War Museum, yet?' Carol asked us.

`No, we didn't know you had one.'

`It's just across the way,' she said, indicating with her hand. `Have a look in as you go past. It's not locked.'

`This is one of the places where the Argentines were stationed, isn't it?'

`Oh yes, they were all over the place here. You know, it was sad in many ways. The conscripts couldn't understand why we wouldn't speak to them. They had been told we were all pro-Argie and spoke Spanish, so they were upset when we didn't answer their questions. It was a while before they realized that we couldn't understand what they were saying.'

Carol settled herself more comfortably as she prepared to talk about those times and we were fascinated to hear what it had been like to be occupied. She told us that generally the soldiers had not interfered too much, but they had broken down fences and killed sheep for meat.

`That used to drive everyone mad. As you know, we usually have more mutton than we know what to do with, killing off the old sheep, but they just killed whatever was the nearest. Of course, they knew nothing about farming.'

`Did they not have plenty of food of their own? It seems bad PR to go around killing sheep!'

`They were terrible about food. The officers did all right, but they couldn't care less about the conscripts. They were starving — literally. They used to hang round the hen runs and dog pens to steal food. Then they discovered some of us had freezers and started stealing from them. It got to be too much, so we called the Commandant — we were really telling him that he ought to make sure they got enough food. They were only kids, you know. Anyway, he listened to what we said. "We will find out who these soldiers are," he told us, "and do something about it." A day or so later, he called us all together and led us out to the green. "We have found the culprits and they are to be disciplined," he said. We were a bit unhappy, because that isn't what we'd wanted, but when we saw how they were being punished, we couldn't believe it! There were two of them, only young boys, and they'd been buried in the ground with only their heads showing. This was in winter, you know. They were kept like that for twenty-four hours. It was absolutely horrible. The Commandant seemed quite pleased with himself, but all we could think was that if they treated their own people like that, how would they treat us? After that, we used to leave food out by the back door for the soldiers.'

`The worst part of it all,' Mrs. Bonner added, `was that there was plenty of food for them. It was all packed in containers in Stanley. After we were liberated, they found tons of food, but the officers couldn't be bothered to make sure that it got to the soldiers.'

`It wasn't just food, either,' recalled Carol, laughing. `Tell them about Dad and the televisions — you know, the ones he bought from the Argies.'

`Don bought things from the Argentines!' I exclaimed. `I can't believe he'd have had anything to do with them.'

`Ah well, this was a bit different.' Mrs. Bonner lit a cigarette before she continued. `You see I think the idea was that we'd all have a television and then they'd show programmes about how wonderful the Argies were so we'd want them to stay. Anyway, they were selling them, but to encourage people to buy, they offered them on hire purchase. You had them for a month before paying. Well, Don got three or four of them. I said, "What are you doing with all these? We can't afford them and anyway, I don't want to give money to the Argies!" "We won't," says Don, "by the time the first payment's due, the Argies'll be too busy fighting off the British soldiers to be bothered about their televisions. I thought we might as well get something out of them while they're here." And he was right, of course. So we ended up with four T.V.s as a gift from the Argies.'

`And Dad got a good price for them when things had settled down,' Carol concluded.

When we came to leave, Carol gave us two litres of milk and then handed us some of the ubiquitous West Store bags, known as `Stanley briefcases', in which were potatoes, carrots and cabbage. `I know what it's like getting vegetables in Stanley,' she said, waving away our thanks. We were very pleased to have them, having finished most of what Arleen had given us.

On our way back, we looked around the little War Museum, which was very well laid out. There is an exhibit on the Falklands Conflict in the main museum in Stanley, but somehow this one made it all seem more real, especially with Carol's stories fresh in our minds. We felt much sobered at the reflection of all the young men and boys who had died for the sake of their leaders' egos and remembering the youth in Mar del Plata, sweeping the street, recalled Carol's story that so many of the dead had no identification on them. They were simply pawns in a deadly game. If the Argentines had kept the islands, who would have gained? No Argentine people wanted to live there and with wool prices falling and all their extravagant promises to keep, the Falklands would simply have been a drain on the Argentine economy, inhabited by unhappy and probably uncooperative citizens. The Islanders could be very stubborn when they wished to be and in the early days of the Invasion, a directive was issued that all traffic must drive on the right side of the road. The reason behind this was to try to prevent accidents, because there were so many Argentine drivers who had never driven on the left. The Islanders thought differently, however, and insisted on sticking to their ways so that in the end, the Argentines gave up. Trying desperately to make themselves wanted, they could hardly imprison and fine every driver in Stanley!

After lunch, we went for a walk. Carol had told us about a small business in Port Howard, which made Falkland knitwear and we made a detour to visit Eddie and Anne, who also run the shop. They took us into their workshop where they made their sweaters, which were usually in a deceptively chunky-looking, fisherman style: deceptive because the Falkland Islands wool is remarkably fine. The bulky sweaters weighed only a few ounces and even holding one in my hands, I could feel how warm it would be. Like a good quilt, it was all air and the price being more than reasonable, I was very tempted to buy one, but the thought of my bursting lockers back on board dissuaded me.

The previous night, we had noticed an attractive tea-towel on Jamie's wall, which he had bought in the shop. Although collecting souvenirs is hardly feasible, living on a boat, I like to have plenty of tea-towels for long passages and often buy one when we visit a new country. I asked Eddie if he still had any, and finding that he did, arranged to come back after our walk.

The track led out into camp and while there was no real destination to head for, it was pleasant to stretch our legs and look around. We passed one of Port Howard's golf courses. The boys had told us that they were all quite keen golfers and assured us that Port Howard possessed no fewer then three golf courses! In due course, we stopped for a flask of tea, turned round and made our way back.

Eddie and Anne invited us in for a cuppa and we talked for a while about their life. Originally, Eddie had been a teacher in the settlement school and had obviously loved the work. He had no formal qualifications, which did not matter before the Conflict, but with the import of British ideas, it was decreed that all teachers had to be properly qualified. He seriously considered studying for his teacher's diploma, but would have had to go to the UK to do so, there was Anne to consider and the financial situation. Eventually and with considerable reluctance, he had to abandon his vocation and as he freely admitted to being no sort of a farmer

and wanted to stay in camp, they had to look round for something else to do. The shop and the knitwear business just about made ends meet, but the closing of the Lodge at Port Howard meant that he no longer had a captive market. Like so many Islanders, they hoped for more tourism, but the reluctance of the Military to allow civilian aircraft to use the airport makes it very difficult. The Tristar flight, run by the RAF is expensive, but perhaps more to the point for people coming on holiday, it is soon booked up and no attempt is made to ensure that the passengers have a comfortable journey. The cruise ships sell souvenirs on board so that the passengers have no need to shop ashore, but Anne and Eddie were getting a foothold at Mount Pleasant, selling to the military personnel.

It is very easy for people several thousands of miles away to tell the Islanders that they should diversify, but their efforts to do so seem to be thwarted at every turn. Even selling to the UK directly had its problems: because there is no VAT in the Falklands, it has to be paid on arrival in the UK and no-one is going to order something that is going to involve such complications. Eddie was also interested in boats, which gave us plenty more to talk about. We left with him, driving down to his shop, where I bought five tea towels, two for us and three as gifts.

Later that afternoon, I was getting in the washing, when I heard a call. Four figures ashore were trying to attract our attention, so Pete went to get them, while I frantically tidied the clothes away. After two trips, the saloon was filled with Bernie, Jamie and Jeff, together with the ubiquitous Julie from *Niatross*, for some inscrutable reason nicknamed `Fluff' for the duration.

They had brought with them an upland goose, cleaned and dressed, which offering I accepted somewhat dubiously, with an expression of forced delight. Apparently it would be ready to eat in a day or so. We were pleased to be able to return the previous night's hospitality and for once had plenty of beer on board. As no-one was showing much signs of moving, by seven o'clock, I invited them all for dinner and knocked up a large mutton curry. As I dished up, Bernie told me that he was not that hungry, but later came back for seconds. Afterwards, he told me that he generally hated curry and that mine was the first one he had ever enjoyed. I took it as a compliment. We had a very pleasant if late, evening, with them leaving at about three o'clock, having all signed our visitors' book. Our guests are usually requested to draw a picture of their boat. Julie obliged, but Jeff wrote: *I haven't got a boat so I will draw a picture of my Rover.* As Bernie had neither, he drew his sheep shearer.

In spite of our late night, we were up at a reasonable time and collecting together some of the magazines that Don had given us, took them ashore to leave at the shop for Eddie. From there we went to Carol's for more milk and then to bunkhouse to see if Bernie and Jamie were coming sailing with us. We planned to go round to Many Branch Harbour a little way north and the previous night they had seemed quite keen to come with us, but today they declined the offer because they could not get a lift back and like most Islanders, only walked under protest. It was also drizzling and rather cold, not what you might call inviting weather.

We just managed to lay up the coast to Many Branch Harbour, which was entered by way of a narrow cut. Our small-scale chart showed a rock in the middle, but seeing no sign of this, we concluded that its position was incorrectly marked simply because the scale of the chart made the rock appear to be a lot larger than it was. Through the narrows, the harbour opened out like fingers on a hand and we hesitated for a moment, wondering which way to go. With it being Easter Sunday, we wanted to be at anchor in good time, so selecting a site that looked to give the best protection, we headed for it and were settled down in time to have scones for tea.

We spent the rest of the following day exploring Many Branch Harbour, which had several good anchorages and was an interesting place to cruise. During the day, we were buzzed by a Hercules aeroplane, which flew so low as to seem below the level of the hills and following the steep-sided creeks themselves. With their four big propellers and the resonant throb of their engines, they always strike me as a real 'plane, while jet aircraft leave me cold.

If there had not been so much still to see and do in the Islands, we would have been tempted to spend longer in Many Branch Harbour, but with light winds forecast for the following day, we pushed on. We had to motor to get through the narrow entrance, but then had a splendid sail over to the San Carlos River. Eating lunch, we made our way up the beautiful river enjoying the intricate pilotage and after anchoring, we rowed upstream another couple of miles. About half way back, the tide and wind started making it hard work for Pete, so he put me ashore to walk along the bank until I was opposite where *Badger* lay, when he picked me up again. Pete went wooding although we had loads on board, because there was so much about that he could not resist it.

I had now to tackle the goose that we had been given. I was rather reluctant to bother, as with domestic goose there is an awful lot of bird for very little meat, but we could hardly waste it, so laying the carcass on the galley counter, I contemplated it. It was too large to fit in the pressure cooker entire, so I jointed it, pot-roasting the pieces and serving it with `roast' potatoes, carrots and cabbage. Unlike the domestic variety, there was a huge amount of meat on the breast and we found it to be delicious and much more tender than the one we had eaten at Sally's, but very rich and filling. We made a bit of an event of it with a pre-prandial snorter and a half litre of wine to wash it down and Pete had chocolate pudding to finish.

A calm sunny morning saw us motoring down the river, with the intention of visiting the settlement at Port San Carlos. The chart showed a depth of 4.9 metres, about sixteen feet or so, but we found it was more like 15 metres, even quite close in and wondered whether the 1 had been left off the correct depth of 14.9, when the chart was engraved. Whatever the reason, it was too deep for us to anchor and the jetty looked far from suitable. A little girl had run out of one of the

San Carlos River.

*At anchor once more in **Curlew**'s anchorage.*

houses and was waving to us from the shore, in obvious anticipation of our visit. I hate to think of her disappointment as we turned round and sailed out again and our own was probably not much less.

We now had to consider our next move. The forecast was for northerly gales for the next day: we had achieved most of our aims in East Falkland and although I wanted to visit Brenton Loch, largely because Conor O'Brien had been there in *Saoirse*, half a century ago, Pete reckoned that it did not look particularly interesting, so we decided to sail back to Stanley straight away. Finding a spot to drop the hook, we fitted the self-steering paddle and pulled *Skip* aboard. With the light breeze, we had a delightful little sail up the Sound, enjoying cold goose sandwiches for lunch. We found we could almost lay our course for Cape Dolphin, but despite the promise of a clear night, it clouded over later and the visibility closed down. Under self-steering, we could keep watch snug and warm below, more than pleased when the forecast gale failed to arrive, the wind staying light all night.

When Pete woke me for my morning watch, we were surrounded by thick fog and keeping lookout after breakfast, I was reminded of sailing in Greenland. Later on, the fog lifted when a light wind filled in from just east of north, soon hardening, so that from about nine o'clock, we averaged seven knots. The last of the goose went into a delicious (although I say it myself) game soup for lunch and for once, we had a glorious sail up Port William, the sun shining as we tore along. The hook was down in *Curlew*'s spot by three o'clock, in time for Pete to scurry ashore and collect our mail.

This was to be our last trip to Stanley for several months and our time there was fully occupied in stocking up for the winter and seeing our friends, but our major project was to arrange the deal with Andrèz for his engine.

We knew roughly where he and Ali lived, so went to see them. Still unable to come to what we considered a fair deal, we had another cup of tea and arranged to meet on Sunday. It was quite dark when we walked home, a reminder of just how advanced the year was.

We had been pleasantly surprised when we arrived in Stanley, to find a shop that sold what are commonly described as `health foods'; apparently our normal diet comes under this heading. Leif turned out to be a most helpful lady and when I gave her my large order, she offered to deliver the food to us and also gave us a discount. On the other hand, we were having terrible problems trying to get eggs and with the cold weather, a lot of hens had stopped laying and the dairy refused to sell them to anyone other than the few hotels, guest houses and restaurants.

The day that we went to collect the engine, we gave Andrèz our fifteen kilo Bruce anchor, having still a spare one on board. While we were dealing with the engine, I noticed a Taylor cooker in his container. A thought occurred to me.

`Do you have the hot plates for the top, Andrèz?'

`You mean those cast iron discs? No, we don't. The cooker's brand new, but I got it second-hand and they seem to have disappeared.'

`Well, mine are getting badly corroded. I was going to order some new ones. Why don't I order some for you, too, and we can count them as part payment?'

Andrèz was pleased at the suggestion and we were happy to be able to make the deal a little less one-sided. Loading the engine and its bits into his pickup, we went down to FIPAS, where we could go alongside in *Badger*. Andrèz drove us back to have coffee with him and Ali, continuing to insist that he was satisfied with the deal and did not want any more money, but in the end we persuaded him to accept another fifty pounds. They came round for dinner the following evening and not having seen the boat before, Ali was very impressed with the accommodation. We had a good evening, discussing their ideas for their boat and our various plans for the future. We mentioned the problems that we had been having with our echo sounder.

`Borrow mine,' suggested Andrèz. `It's brand new and came with the boat, but I'd like to be sure that it works properly before fitting it, after what you've been saying. You'd be doing me a favour, if you tried it out.'

Andrèz is not an easy man to refuse, once his mind is made up, so we accepted, praying that it would not break down on us.

A few days later, we enjoyed a bit of culture, Stanley style, going to the Town Hall to watch the amateur dramatic society put on Gilbert and Sullivan's *Pirates of Penzance*. Apart from a very slow Major General, it was a super performance with wonderful policemen, one or two of them the genuine article! Dianne was on the door and Devina was also there, kindly driving us home, which we appreciated, with it being a very cold night.

A French boat was towed in by the Fisheries Protection ship and we saw it at FIPAS. There appeared to be nothing wrong with it and we gathered that the crew had been frightened by the heavy weather that they were experiencing and, while the skipper was steering in the cockpit, had called for assistance on the VHF. The tow had cost the Islands several thousand pounds and, astonishingly, the forty-four pound entry `fine' had been waived in their case, because they had been in distress! It was an upsetting incident, because it is the type of irresponsible behaviour that gives yachtsmen a bad name and inspires governments with ideas about controlling our movements. One of the drawbacks of the increased number of yachts sailing in high latitudes, is that completely inexperienced people are tempted by the accounts they read, with no idea of what they might have to put up with and lacking the necessary skills to deal with situations that they encounter. We led up to our more adventurous voyages very gradually and have frequently been appalled by people who have done only a little, local sailing and with blithe confidence, announce their intentions of sailing off to the Antarctic. It would not matter if these people truly had the desire to experience this more arduous type of cruising, but most of them are actually looking for `no-risk adventure' and the first thing that they do is to provide themselves with radios so that they can call for help should it all become too much for them. They like the idea of following in the steps of Tilman, the Smeetons and the Poncets, but do not have the same independent spirit which gave these sailors their true greatness.

Pete was working out how to get our engine on board and gathering bits together for its installation. He came back one day, looking pleased and announced:

`I've got a surprise for you, Annie.'

`Oh? Good news, obviously.'

`You'll think so. The engine isn't nine horsepower, after all. In fact it's eighteen!'

`Eighteen! Are you sure? But Andrèz was convinced that it was nine.'

`Well I found a plaque on it which says "1S15/18". I suppose in fact that means it's really fifteen horsepower. Anyway, I remembered the other one we looked at had "20/22" on it, so popped in to see Zack — you know, the chap who originally owned it — and asked him about it. "Oh yes," he said, "it's certainly fifteen horsepower."'

`Well, that *is* good news, but I hope Andrèz won't be upset when he finds out.'

If he was, he certainly did not show it.

`You'll be pleased about that,' he said, `but I really wanted thirty horsepower and besides, I wouldn't want an air-cooled engine. Too noisy.' And, of course, he refused to listen to any suggestion of our offering more money. Indeed, just before we left, he tore up the cheque that we had given him saying that he was happy with what we had traded. It is not every

*Panoramic view of **Curlew's** anchorage at Port Stanley.*

Badger's new engine in Andrèz's container.

day that people effectively give you an engine and throw in a generous measure of friendship, to boot. Meeting Andrèz was one of our luckiest encounters.

The clocks had gone back, Sally and Jérôme were asking if we would be at Beaver in time for our first stint of island sitting, we were stocked up and when we walked the long road into Stanley in the mornings, the puddles had a film of ice on them. It was time to be leaving, but we had one curious piece of business to complete before we set off for winter quarters. We had received a letter from Customs and Immigration requesting that we `tell them our intentions'. When we saw them, they told us that our visitors' permits must have run out, as we had been in the Falklands for more than four months, but that they could find no record of them. That was easily explained: we had not been given any. This caused a certain amount of embarrassed consternation, as it meant that Someone Had Blundered.

`Didn't you ask why your passport wasn't stamped?' we were asked.

`Of course not. We're in a British Colony. We're British citizens and taxpayers. Falkland Islanders can go to Britain as and when they wish and, not unnaturally, we assumed that there was a *quid quo pro*.'

In truth, this was said a little tongue in cheek as we knew that there were immigration controls, but had chosen to assume that being on our own boat and able to leave whenever we wished, they might not apply to us. Needless to say, we had not enquired, for when asked, the instinctive response of the bureaucrat is to play as safe as possible and if you do not ask you can often get away with doing things that otherwise they might veto. Least said, soonest mended is our motto.

`How long do you intend to stay?' the officer asked.

`We're intending to spend the winter here. Indeed, we plan on leaving Stanley in a couple of days for our winter quarters.'

`But you need permission to stay so long.'

`But it's too late in the season to leave now — I don't think it would be very wise.'

Pete was teasing him a little; had we been told to leave, it was not far back up to Uruguay. Then, he tried our other successful ploy: ask for help and make them feel both benevolent and important.

`What do you suggest we do? All our plans are made — we're hoping to go further south next year — it would really be a disaster for us if we had to leave the Islands.'

`The rule for people staying longer than four months is to apply to the Governor for residency.'

`But what if we don't get it? We've never met him. He may not approve.'

`It's just a formality really. He listens to our recommendation.'

`Oh, in that case ...'

`Well, not *quite* a formality, but I don't think there should be any problems.'

I bet there won't, we thought to ourselves, you don't want to be admitting to the Governor that you never stamped our passports!

The officer perhaps read our thoughts and made a final effort to reassert his authority.

`Of course, on no account must you undertake paid employment — we know all about the squid work, you know,' he said sternly to Pete.

`I'm sure you do, but in fact I was asked to work as a favour because no-one else could be found. I don't need a job — we have independent means,' he concluded grandly, if somewhat misleadingly. I felt sure that if the extent of our `independent means' was investigated, we would be asked to leave forthwith, as they would appear hopelessly inadequate to most land-based people. We filled in the appropriate forms and in due course, our request for Residency was granted. It was rather nice to feel that there was somewhere in the world that we had a right to live.

Before we left, we hoped to join in the celebrations for Queen Elizabeth's birthday and anchor off Victory Green, dressed overall to watch the band march by. Instead, we found ourselves cowering at the end of the harbour in Force 10 squalls, while the birthday parade ended up in the Town Hall and the fly past was cancelled. It was a shame; everyone enjoys the pageantry of the soldiers in their best uniforms, but the day could not have been worse, with hail, rain and sleet as well as the storm force winds. Nothing daunted, the Queens' Lancers beat their drums and tootled their flutes under cover and everyone made the best of a bad job. We heard the following day that there were gusts of seventy-four knots at Stanley airport.

Saturday, St George's day, was the day scheduled for us to sail to FIPAS and pick up the engine. Pete started getting in the CQR, which had held us during the storm and was so well dug in that the shaft in the windlass sheared. We started the Seagull to assist in breaking out the anchor and for some inexplicable reason, the float chamber cracked and petrol started pouring out. It was obviously going to be one of those days. We did a bodge job using masking tape, polythene and a jubilee clip for a repair, then motored out the anchors with difficulty, the Seagull stalling whenever I throttled down. By now it was getting late and Andrèz would be waiting for us, so we motorsailed up to FIPAS. We had to turn at right angles to go alongside a short length of quay and as I reduced speed to turn in, the engine conked out. We continued to sail in, a straightforward manoeuvre, but I was flustered, did not let out enough sheet for the sails to feather properly and made a bit of a hash of it. Still, at least we were there. A few minutes later, Andrèz brought the engine and we lowered it into the lazarette, where I was relieved to see that it was not quite such a monster as it had appeared on land. The ever-helpful Andrèz ran me to Stanley Growers for the seven or eight kilos of cabbages that I wanted and then I went into town to buy some bits and pieces to take along for the Poncets. Coming back, I was given a lift by some Spanish sailors from a trawler at FIPAS. They asked me if I was one of the 'distressed yachtsmen', probably referring to the French yacht that had been towed in. I denied it indignantly, adding, 'I'm from a *British* yacht!'

Sunday evening saw us paying our last visit to Carl and Dianne and we found that Dianne had arranged quite a dinner party, with both Ian and Marcel, the 'distressed French yachtsman', there. She had put on a lovely spread and we had a very pleasant evening. It was with real regret that we said good-bye to them for what was to be several months.

At last, on April 26th, we managed to get away. Pete went to say goodbye to Andrèz and Carl and I to the Harbourmaster, who gave me a copy of the latest weather chart. We had been concerned about the cost of staying alongside, but the FIPAS boss waived any

charges and was very kind and helpful. All the people at FIPAS seemed to be very friendly.

We made everything as shipshape as possible, not easy with the engine sitting in the lazarette. I hoped that we had wedged it in well enough and with all its struts and braces, the companionway was like an obstacle course. With the inevitable last-minute chores, it was a great rush, but we managed to be underway at 1620, by which time it was nearly dark. My excitements were not yet over, however, because the skipper nearly frightened me to death, by going out past Billy Rock, on which at least five ships are known to have foundered. He then chose to go through the narrow gap between Seal Rocks and Cape Pembroke. The latter was the only danger lit and with having to tack in a nasty jobble, *I* was just about a wreck by the time we could turn west. After that, things calmed down and we actually had a rather pleasant night's sail, with a big, fat moon and the winds a lot lighter than forecast.

The road into Stanley from Curlew's anchorage, looking west.

After all the rush of our previous twenty days in Stanley, I slept like a log and in the morning, woke to find us sailing up Choiseul Sound.

'There's hardly any wind now,' Pete told me, 'and the forecast is for rather too much wind later this afternoon, so I thought we might as well put into Lively. I know you wanted to see Elly and Alec again and if we don't go now, we won't see them until spring.'

I was delighted and it was with real pleasure that we rowed ashore after lunch to find Alec and Elly just finishing their own meal. I took them a jar of pickled fish, because last time we had visited, Alec had mentioned that he was fond of fish and never had time to catch any. They welcomed us like long-lost friends and we spent a wonderful afternoon there. Elly

A Stanley street.

'It's a cold day,' Alec commented, 'how would you like a hot bath?'

'That would be wonderful.' And so it was, with gallons of scalding hot water. The season being well advanced, they were happy to take the day off and Elly simply assumed that we would stay for supper and quietly went about getting it. We had a lovely evening, listening to Alec's yarns with a warm feeling of belonging, almost as though we were family. We had only met Alec and Elly a couple of times, but had become really fond of them.

Jubilee Terrace, Stanley.

obviously missed her own children and treated me like a daughter and Pete was taken away by Alec to get a load of firewood, coming back with about ten pounds of potatoes while Alec apologized that they were rather small and not as good a crop as usual.

'*You* might think that, Alec,' I told him, 'but they're ten times as good as the ones we bought in Stanley. You're used to having good, fresh food, but it's a real treat for us since being down here. The spuds they sell in Stanley are the ones the Chileans up north reject and send down to Punta. We reckon they sell the ones nobody in Punta will buy, to the Falklands!'

I was barely exaggerating and we really appreciated the gift. The breeze was getting up, so we had regretfully to decline tea and row back, where I consoled myself by making stuffed cabbage leaves *à la provençale*, which we ate with some of Alec's delicious potatoes.

It was only blowing a strong breeze when we came to turn in, but the wind really picked up in the small hours and in spite of our precaution of sleeping in the saloon, we did not get much repose. After a late start, I made bread and a cake and used some of the plums we had bought for jam, thinking that we might appreciate that more in the depths of winter than the pound of plums now. By this time the wind had decreased enough that we could row ashore. Elly was pleased with the little jar of jam that I took with me and Alec told me that he had really enjoyed the pickled fish.

'I don't think it'll last long, Annie,' Elly smilingly told me and I was sorry that we did not have more to give .

Elly bustled round making us welcome with tea and cake.

Their friendship filled the need that we sometimes have for our own family: they enjoyed having someone to look after for a while, missing their own children and we enjoyed the feeling of being accepted and at home. When we eventually went back to *Badger*, it was with strict instructions to return for eggs and mutton in the morning.

Going ashore for a last cup of coffee and piece of cake with Elly, we found that Alec had got up at the crack of dawn to quarter our mutton, before going off fencing. Elly had twenty-one eggs for us.

'All these! I scoured Stanley for weeks and didn't manage to buy so many. Are you sure you can spare them? Surely your hens have stopped laying, too.'

'Oh no, Annie, we have eggs all the year round. I feed my hens properly in the winter. Why, they're just like us really, they feel the cold, too. They get a hot supper in cold weather just like we do — and need it as much.'

Dear Elly. I do believe that she loves and cherishes all creatures. Before we left, she showed us round the small house that they had recently re-decorated. Alec had told us that one day they hoped to pay off their mortgage and employ another person on the farm, who would live there. One of his brothers was keen to get back on the land. It was a lovely little place and I am sure that had we asked, it would have been ours for the winter and we would have been spoilt to death! But we had made other arrangements, so picking up our enormous mutton that Alec had butchered so neatly, I gave Elly a big hug. We were sorry to have missed Alec.

`We'll come and visit you in the spring,' I promised.

`Stay a bit longer, next time,' Elly told us.

The wind had not yet arrived and we had wonderful sailing, in mild sunny conditions. Gale warnings were out, but there were sufficient boltholes along the way to warrant us carrying on. The weather continued unseasonably fine, with a fair, whole sail wind and the night was beautiful with the moon and stars shining.

By morning, it had become windy and rough. In a half awake and half asleep state, my mind was haunted with the fear that the monster engine would get adrift, but when I checked it had not budged. We had a true Falkland Islands breakfast of mutton chops and fried eggs, by which time the sun had come out. Having to beat from Cape Meredith towards Rodney Cove, we were lucky to reach the latter before dark, but we had had a good day and were quite happy where we were, with only twenty-one miles to go. One advantage of the long nights was that we had a relaxing evening and after savouring a rum and orange, I cooked Pete his favourite steak and chips for supper, which, it being Saturday, we washed down with a glass or two of wine.

Sunday, 1st May turned out to be what one might term a full day. We were underway by 0630 with a wind which slowly backed during the morning bringing showers and a lurid dawn appeared to confirm the forecast of strong south-westerly gales later. We made pretty good time going through the Governor Channel where I saw my first all-white giant petrel and arrived at Stick-in-the-Mud a quarter of an hour after Pete reckoned slack water to be, fortunately finding no current against us, which was just as well, as the wind was not only dying, but had backed so far that we had to beat through. I spared what time I could from the helm to watch the sea lions and pups on the little island in the middle and we just cleared the passage as the tide turned against us, so Pete's calculations had not been too far out. From there we had a lovely sunny sail to Beaver, making the best of what was to be our last for several months. It was nearly lunchtime when we anchored off the pier and after tidying up, we went ashore. Jérôme was in his workshop; he had not seen

Hulks at Stanley.

us come in and we gave him quite a shock; Diti was away in Stanley, which explained how we had been able to arrive unannounced. We were invited for lunch and stayed for a while, catching up on the news, but with the wind getting up, we thought it prudent to return to *Badger*. The glass was going up like a rocket and we were not surprised when the wind did the same, so hauled *Skip* back aboard, while it was still easy. It was bitterly cold, but when we tried to light the fire, it smoked terribly what with the gusts and, probably, a partly blocked chimney. Almost choking, we opened the forehatch a crack to make a through draught and a few moments later, a solid wave came over the foredeck, down the hatch and onto the bunk, duvet and pillows. Such a thing had never happened before at anchor and it was much worse than the previous two douches, as everything was thoroughly soaked. I could not bear even to contemplate the thought of getting it all dry again. It was very rough and I was seasick; it was a miserable start to our winter sojourn and a bad omen for the future. Pete tried to cheer me up and when, as we expected, the wind decreased to about Force 7, I distracted myself by cooking a pot roast with some of Alec's mutton. The pusser served out an extra stiff pre-prandial snorter and the hot food plus a couple of glasses of wine made life seem less awful. With the quilt unusable, there was not enough bedding to keep us warm on the settees and no chance of keeping a fire in, that needed stoking up every twenty minutes, so we donned our warmest thermal underwear and turned in, both worn out from the day's events.

Chapter Seventeen

View across Beaver Island towards settlement (at centre).

We woke to a glassy calm, cold morning, more than happy to wrap ourselves around a substantial breakfast after which we went up to join Sally and meet the 'plane which was bringing Diti back to Beaver. This was not a straightforward operation; the mail had to be put into a bag, entailing last minute scribblings and a frantic search for stamps and the radio had to be collected and plugged into the Rover. Then all hands climbed aboard and we jolted off over the rough track towards the airstrip, opening gates on the way as required. Arriving at the airstrip, late as usual, we rushed frantically to prepare for the landing: hoisting the windsock, unwrapping the fire extinguisher on its sled and attaching this to the tow bar of the Rover, while Sally searched desperately for its pin. At the end of the strip was an area of tussac that Sally was trying to regenerate, protected from the sheep by an electric fence, which had to be dismantled, to obviate the risk of the aeroplane catching its wheels in the wires. Taking it down was not a problem, but putting it back up was a tedious task and we came to discover that it was far preferable to go with Sally rather than Jérôme, because while Sally took out the fence posts neatly, laying them down flat near their holes, Jérôme simply hauled them out and flung them aside, necessitating a lot more work to reassemble the whole thing. Today everything went smoothly and we even had time for Sally to work out the wind direction, look at the airstrip and shoo away the grazing upland geese, before the little red dot appeared in the sky.

After it had taxied to a halt, we went over to meet it. Along with Diti, was an Agriculture Inspector called Mandy, two hens, four drakes and a duck, and Ray, the boys' dog. When the family had gone off in the summer there was no-one to look after the island so Ray had been left at another settlement. She came home about to have puppies and when she had difficulties whelping, Sally had sent her in to Stanley, for the vet to sort the problem out: apparently, one of the puppies was enormous and too big for her. Sally had asked the vet to dispose of all the puppies and now the poor little bitch seemed very miserable. It took her a long time to recover and her unhappiness was increased by the addition of a new dog to the farm, Lady. After her friendly overtures were rebuffed, Lady simply ignored Ray's existence, which nearly drove the latter to distraction, but she was so jealous of Lady that there was never a chance for them even to establish a working relationship. It was fascinating to watch how they reacted to each other.

The 'plane flew off, we put back the fence, wrapped up the fire extinguisher, hauled down the wind sock and bounced and jolted back to the settlement. After coffee, I took our wet bedding up to the Other House, to rinse out the saltwater in the bath. The sheet and quilt cover would soon dry, but the duvet had acted like a sponge and would be wet for ages; at least it was not down-filled. The range had been lit, as Mandy was sleeping there and we were allowed to use the hot water, if no-one else wanted it. After I had rinsed everything out, I put it on the line to dry.

We had decided to go alongside the jetty as soon as possible, lying behind *Damien II* until Jérôme moved her round to the 'marina' as he called it. This was an area in a small, superbly protected bight off Fish Creek, where Jérôme had built a wall of gabions where *Damien II* could lie, dried out most of the time, in soft mud. It was close to the Iron Shed, Jérôme's workshop and once the boat was secured with extra lines to a couple of buoys that had been laid, she was a safe as

houses. After lunch, we moved *Badger* and put out her legs, then we unloaded the engine, using the main halliard to haul it up through the hatch and swing it ashore onto the jetty. Jérôme came to look at it and we were gratified when it received his seal of approval. That afternoon, he brought round the tractor so that the engine could be taken into the Iron Shed where it would live until we were ready to install it.

By now, it was getting dark, so I went and took in the washing before starting dinner. In spite of keeping

Islander landing at Beaver Island airstrip.

hot water bottles on it all day, the bunk was still sodden, so we turned in on the settees again, but were both rather cold during the night.

'Tonight,' Pete declared as he got up, 'we sleep in the forecabin, regardless.'

'I know we don't have enough spare bedding to keep warm in separate beds, but I don't think that the bed will be dry by tonight.'

'It'll still be a damn' sight warmer than in the saloon. It'll take ages to dry properly anyway, but if we move the hot water bottles around before we go to bed, at least it will be warm and we won't really notice if it's a bit damp. With two blankets and the sleeping bag, we should be warm enough.'

That afternoon I went and cleaned out the meat house. In the cool, fresh climate of the Falklands, meat does not require refrigeration, but it needs to be hung up where air can circulate around it, away from bluebottles, whose eggs hatch into maggots in short order, as we had discovered. Sally and Jérôme's meathouse was one of the best that we had seen, but no-one seemed to have time to keep it clean, so I felt that this was a task that I could take on. It took the whole afternoon, a lot of débris having to be scraped off the floor, but I fetched hot water from the Other House, which made life a lot easier and when it was finished, it seemed almost a shame to use it!

We were starting to settle in. Jérôme shifted *Damien II* round to the marina, and as the tides grew

Badger's engine in the Iron Shed at Beaver Island.

bigger, we moved *Badger* further and further up the beach in an effort to neap her. Apart from making it easier to work on the engine installation, when the gales came, *Badger* would be high and dry rather than snatching at her lines. With ropes to the masts and the wide wing on her keel, she was really very secure, dried out and the jetty provided a good lee from the south west, the direction from where the worst gales were supposed to come.

Jérôme was in the throes of tidying up the Iron Shed and Pete helped him by building some shelves to organise things. They had tried to hand start the engine, but although Andrèz had done it without apparent effort, neither Jérôme nor Pete seemed to have the knack. There were two systems: a hand crank and a rope pulley. The former was abandoned after Jérôme bent the handle

and he eventually managed to start it with the rope, as Andrèz had done, but as Pete only succeeded once, they concluded that some sort of electric start was needed. This was a disappointment, one of the main attractions of the engine being its hand-starting capability and Pete was reluctant to have to rely on electricity, feeling that it was bound to fail in an emergency.

`Nevair mind, Pete,' Jérôme reassured him. `If ze rocks air only a few feet away, you will find ze strength to pull ze rope, I can promise you! 'Owevair, we must do somezing else for when ze rocks air not thair, I believe.'

Jérôme was nothing if not resourceful and eventually designed a device that utilised an old electric motor that he had found. This was to be attached to a bracket which would move it up and down against a belt which ran from the rope-pulley wheel to an alternator, also second-hand, that Jérôme bolted to the engine. The idea was that when one wanted to start the engine, the starter motor would be tensioned against the belt and switched on, the belt would turn the pulley and this in turn would start the engine, which was fitted with a decompression lever. Once the engine was running, the starter motor would swing out of the way and the pulley wheel would continue to charge the battery. When Jérôme had got the old motor to work, Pete cleaned it up using a compressor to sand blast it, it was fitted to the bracket and the whole assembly put together with a temporary fan belt. I was

Badger high and dry for the winter at the Beaver Island jetty.

fortunate enough to be around at The Moment of Truth and it was most gratifying to see the engine start when the belt was tensioned and electricity put into the system. A starter button was required and it needed finishing off, but we now felt that there was a real chance of having a reliable engine.

All this involved metal work and electrics, neither of which are Pete's *forte*. On the other hand, *Damien II* needed a new wooden self-steering rudder, which was something that Pete could do very well. When Jérôme decided to build *Damien II*, knowing exactly what he wanted he gave the specification to a French naval architect whose job was to refine the design using his skills and training. Unfortunately, he failed in his task and *Damien II* sails poorly in certain conditions. Jérôme had to make radical changes to the stern, lengthening it, adding an outboard rudder and further modifying it with a sort of dagger board that sticks down underneath the cockpit. This had been lost on the last voyage and Pete made a new one at the same time as the paddle for the self-steering gear. It seemed a fair *quid pro quo* that while Jérôme worked on our engine, Pete worked on his boat and they were both doing something that they enjoyed. Keeping them supplied with hot drinks, morning and afternoon I apprised myself of the progress.

On the day that Mandy left, we went up to take a bath at the Other House, while there was still some hot water. It started to pour while we were there and I suggested to Pete that I wait for him as we only had one torch and it was very dark outside.

`No, no. You go ahead and get supper ready, Annie. I'll be able to see O.K.'

`But it's absolutely Stygian out there.'

`I'll be all right. Once I'm down on the jetty, I'll be able to see the boat and work out where to go. You go on down.'

I left him to it and went back aboard. About ten minutes later, I heard footsteps on the gang plank and Pete came down below. He was sopping wet.

`Look at you! It's really tippling down, isn't it?'

`I fell in — that's why I'm so wet!'

`What do you mean? How on earth did you manage to fall in?'

`Well you were right about it being dark, It was so bad I couldn't see a blind thing. I only found my way

Beaver Island settlement. "Their House" is to the right.

back by following the hedge and then the fence and touching them. Then I could see *Badger*, so walked along the jetty, to where the gangplank was, but can't have been parallel with the boat and just walked right off.'

`Are you all right? Did you land on all those stones?'

`I fell on my feet, but one of them seems quite bruised. And the tide's in so I'm all salty and so are your clothes too, which were in the bag.'

`Oh well, I suppose I'll have to wash them again. It was rather a waste of your bath though!'

I found Pete a dry towel and he got changed, throwing all the wet things into the cockpit until daylight.

We were soon introduced to farming and I found out how to kill and butcher the mutton that we ate. Sally and Jérôme offered to keep us provided with meat during our stay and while we appreciated the gesture, it was a mixed blessing because we can soon have too much meat and even Pete, who enjoys meat much more than I do, prefers our usual vegetarian diet. On the other hand, it would have been churlish to refuse and with Sally and Jérôme both being rabid anti-vegetarians, I was too cowardly to mention my preferences in the matter. Jérôme killed a sheep by wrestling it on its side and cutting its throat, but I had neither the strength nor the confidence to do this quickly and cleanly and could never bring myself to try. I would have been prepared to shoot it, but Sally said, quite rightly, that it was `rather stupid to kill a sheep twice,' and as its throat had to be cut to drain the blood, I appreciated her point, but as Sally never killed any sheep either, I felt that my refusal was supported by precedent. On the other hand, as we were eating the meat, the least we could do was help in the butchering of it and while Pete had too many other tasks on his hands, I learnt to skin, gut and cut up the mutton. I never became very good at it, particularly the skinning, which was very hard work, the sheep being hung up by its back legs and the skin removed by punching between it and the flesh. It was very inefficient because half one's energy was converted into thrusting away the carcass, like a punchbag while the rest went into separating the skin. Removing the skin with a knife, the easier option, made a much more messy piece of meat although left to my own devices, I should probably have done it that way, but Jérôme's comments, when I suggested it, were so scathing that I never dared. I was always surprised how small the carcass looked compared with the live, woolly sheep. Due to the presence of hydatic disease in the Islands, the eating of sheep offal is expressly forbidden, but Jérôme, partly to shock and partly from a genuine liking for it, would occasionally take mouthfuls of the still-warm, raw liver as we butchered the sheep. I tried some, at his suggestion and found it neither revolting nor delicious.

One of Jérôme's latest projects was smoking meat and as anything to do with food interests me, I volunteered to help him with the preparation. Suitable pieces of meat were trimmed of their surplus fat, rolled into tight bundles and secured with string, tied with a special slip knot, which was then locked with another knot. The bundles were then immersed in brine for several days before being hung up to dry for a day or so, after which they were ready for smoking. The preparation took quite some time and Jérôme was a hard

taskmaster, accepting only perfection and condemning out of hand, those bundles tied up too loosely, but it was interesting work and the little bundles looked wonderful when they were completed.

One afternoon, Sally wanted to move a ram from the wool shed to a pen, so I offered to help.

`The battery's flat in the Rover,' Sally told me, `so we need to connect the spare one to start it.' This done, we drove down to Iron Shed for Jérôme, who was required to handle the ram. After waiting for him for a while, Sally decided that it might be better to put the ram in the back of the tractor, instead of the Rover, so we went into the Big Shed to empty out what was already in the tractor. Then Jérôme came to start it, only to find that its battery was flat, too. We opened the shed doors and Sally drove the Rover in to use jump leads to start the tractor, but there was not enough life in the battery. Then it was back to the house for another battery, which we took back to the Big Shed, only to find that Jérôme had managed to get the tractor going. The Rover was now in the way and had to be moved, after which the tractor was driven out and the doors were shut. At the wool shed, ready to deal with the ram, Sally had a word with Jérôme.

`It's OK, Annie. We're doing it another way now and only need the two of us.'

By that time, most of the afternoon had disappeared.

Another day we went gathering and fencing. Firstly, we had to get the fencing materials, so Jérôme and I went to the stable for those, but the Rover had a flat battery again. We tried another, which was also flat and then a third. This was fine, but the terminals were the wrong way round, so I left Jérôme to get on with it and went to fetch Pete who had suggested that he carry on with the self-steering paddle until we were ready to go. Sally packed lunch and at about eleven o'clock, two hours later than planned, we set off. Some rams had escaped and had to be pushed back from where they had come. Unfortunately, one of them got away by jumping the fence and getting mixed in with Sally's stud ewes. There followed much running about and Jérôme got extremely annoyed with Lady who apparently refused to obey him. Personally, I felt that like most Falkland Islanders, she simply did not understand what he was

Meat tied and ready for smoking.

saying and in the end she ran off and did what she thought was right. It seemed to produce results, but there was a continual stream of *merdes* from Jérôme, which I found more than amusing because Jérôme has an absolute loathing of any strong language in Anglo-Saxon, so much so, that in times of stress, Sally's strongest oath was a ladylike `Drat!' At least, when Jérôme is in earshot. Swearing in French was apparently acceptable.

Once the other rams were where they should have been, we drove on to North End. Jérôme jumped out to go and rescue the motor bike that he had abandoned some days previously, when it had broken down, and we carried on to fence. Diti, who was nobody's fool, went `exploring,' while the three of us settled down to stretching wires and burying cables for the electricity. The motor bike was still refusing to work and when we had finished fencing, we picked it up and squeezed it into the back of the Rover, with the rest of us. It was leaking petrol, but Jérôme, quite unperturbed, started rolling a cigarette. Sally had her work cut out, driving the Rover over the rough track and arguing with Jérôme, but eventually managed to dissuade him from lighting up. Pete and I were heartily relieved.

Gathering sheep was often quite physical and on a day of sunshine and showers, we went to catch the `Jumping Ram' that had got in with Sally's stud ewes. Due to start at eight o'clock, Pete and I had got up early and finished breakfast, in good time, but obviously things had gone less smoothly at Their House, because it was well after nine before we heard the sound of the Rover. Pete, whose foot was still giving him trouble, was told off to drive. Jérôme bailed out at one point and Sally and I climbed out at the bottom of a hill, which I was dismayed to learn, we had to climb in order to head off the sheep that Jérôme was to drive towards us. Worse still, I discovered that we were to do it at the double. I have never pretended to be fit, but I have my pride, so to the accompaniment of lots of puffing and panting, I gritted my teeth and went at it, sighing with relief each time Sally stopped to say, `Where are they?' or, `Jérôme's over there,' or `Go that way!' I have to confess that I took advantage of Sally's short-sightedness to get my breath back while she searched the landscape. On top of the hill there was lots of wind and icy showers added to my discomfort, but at last we managed to gather the sheep and drive them back to the pens, without their eluding us. Sally thought that we would have to push the whole flock through the `race,' which is a narrow chute through which only one sheep at a time can pass. At the end of it there are two gates which can be moved to direct the sheep into either of two pens thus separating out an individual as

required. On this occasion, Sally spotted the ram and separated him without needing to use the race. It all seemed an awful lot of effort for one sheep and I was becoming convinced by the arguments of George at Johnson's Harbour, in favour of horses. They could have run up and down the hills with no problem, would not have frightened the sheep and seemed no more work to look after than the motorbikes. At that time, all three of them were out of order, while the two ponies who lived at Beaver waxed fat, happy and idle.

The boys were due a holiday and we would be left on our own on the Island while the family went off sailing. Before that happened, Sally thought it would be worth our while becoming qualified fire fighters up at the airstrip. It turned out to be quite straightforward and in due course we were sent our certificates. The most alarming aspect was the thought that the foam only lasted for about a minute, so that if you had not controlled the fire in that time, there would be no chance. Fortunately, accidents are extremely rare in the Falklands and even though Beaver was regarded as a particularly tricky strip, it seemed highly unlikely that our newly-acquired skills would be required.

The meat was ready for smoking and Jérôme had decided to turn the old meathouse into a smokehouse. Great and detailed were the alterations to the erstwhile meathouse to ready it for its new rôle. In the end, Pete clad the whole of the inside with plywood, while I taped up all the seams, sealed the door frame with rubber and dug a pit, lined with bricks for the old galvanized tank that Jérôme had converted into a fire box. Sally wanted to go and check on her tussac plants at The Bluff and so we were told off to make a wooding party of it. The beach was covered in wood and Leiv and Diti threw themselves wholeheartedly into the operation. We brought a load back in the Rover and Pete sawed it up later with Jérôme's chainsaw. Only large pieces of hardwood were to be used for smoking, which meant that there was a lot left over for our fire, too.

The first day's smoking seemed to be a great success and the job of tending the fire was delegated to me, but a couple of days later, when I lit it, the smoke would not go up the chimney. After investigating the matter, we concluded that the fire needed to be on the other side of the smokehouse in order for the draught to work properly in the prevailing winds. In due course, I dug a pit on that side and moved the firebox round, but in truth the site was really too windy and smoking could only successfully be carried out on calm days. This was not as much of a drawback as it seems, because it used less wood and the whole process is better carried out in the low temperatures of winter, when there are more calms, but Jérôme, liking to work on impulse, was very irritated and found it more than annoying not to be able to use it as and when he wanted to. In spite of this, we smoked a fair amount of meat over the winter, and it was generally a success.

I was helping Sally get *Damien II* ready for their holiday and we took out the carpets to scrub. Unfortunately for us, Jérôme, who was a great believer in using technology to save effort, heard of this and suggested that we use the pressure washer, rather than simply scrubbing them in the yard of the Other House, as we had planned.

`It will be a lot quickair, you know and zey will be much more clean at ze end.'

Sally tried to dodge the issue, but Jérôme was determined. We *would* use the pressure washer: that was what it was for, so Sally and I took the Rover down to the Big Shed and spent about twenty minutes finding all its components. Then we noticed that someone had got water in the plug at one time, so a new one was required. We found one, surplus to requirements in the Other House, and my Swiss Army Knife was to hand, but an electrical screwdriver was required and when I asked Sally where I could find one, she looked blank. I discovered that she had never changed a plug

The beef being butchered.

in her life and had no idea of what was needed. I walked to Their House, where Leiv and Diti searched with enthusiasm, but without success, so I had to go to the Iron Shed to find one. I returned and fitted the plug, we switched the machine on and then we discovered another slight hitch: the hose was too small to fit it. Having found a smaller fitting, we then needed a spanner to replace it.

`I *knew* it would be like this!' Sally exclaimed. `Jérôme always wants me to use this dratted thing and it never works! We could have had the carpets cleaned by now!'

`I'll go and fetch a spanner,' said I, hiking off once more to the Iron Shed, where Jérôme, obviously thinking that we were not really trying, decided to come back with me. The fitting could not be changed and although we managed to force the hose on and got the pressure washer working, by now it was dark, so Sally and I gave up until the next day. I spent all morning on the job, with the hose coming off each time I turned my back and although the carpets came up very clean, I do not think that we saved much time.

Before they left for their holiday, Jérôme killed a beef, not only for themselves, but also to ensure that there was plenty of meat for the dogs and us. The herd was gathered into the corral and the victim selected. In this instance, it was considered acceptable to waste a bullet and once the animal was shot, the other cows were driven out and Jérôme cut its throat to drain the blood, before hitching the carcase to the back of the tractor and driving down to the gallows. Here it was decapitated and gutted to the delight of the gulls and Johnny rooks, who squabbled over the choicer parts as they were flung into the creek, although we saved the kidneys to make a first class steak and kidney pudding. Then the corpse had to be skinned, but this time knives were used as only a Hercules could `punch' the skin from a cow. It was a far less grisly business than one might have supposed, because, with the blood drained from the animal, taking the skin off was more like peeling back a turf than anything else. It seemed a shame to have to throw it away, but we did not have the wherewithal to tan it. Before being butchered, the carcase had to hang for twenty-four hours, which made it easier to handle and with some difficulty and a certain amount of trepidation, the gallows looking `precarious and none too permanent', the beast was hoisted up by its hind legs and covered with a net, to keep off the Johnny rooks. This latter activity was easier said that done, the net appearing to have been used on the Ark and tearing asunder at the slightest tug. It was not unlike trying to wrap a package in damp brown paper.

The following day, after the carcase had `set,' it was butchered. Jérôme did this with his usual efficiency, but was somewhat lacking in finesse, the implement of choice being a chain saw. It was undoubtedly effective, but we felt that he would not win any prizes for his style at Smithfield. With cigarette dangling from the lower lip, hat rakishly over one eye and the chainsaw whining away, it was an unforgettable sight. Bits of bone, flesh and fat scattered in all directions to the hysterical delight of the kelp gulls and in a remarkably short space of time, the beef swung from the chains in two parts. Quartering it was more difficult and it took the combined efforts of several people to load each piece into the back of the tractor and up to the meat house. It did not seem the most hygienic process, but it was all good clean dirt.

Damien II was just about ready; Pete fitted a teak box that he had made for Jérôme's new Autohelm and repaired the window in the cockpit dodger. In between tides, we helped him weld end plates on his rudder: an idea that Pete had suggested to help with the boat's steering and it was a somewhat disconcerting experience, with the welding set in the damp mud, water round our feet and the tide rising. I was shown how much food to give the poultry and the dogs and we were instructed in turning off the water and one or two other things, so that we could look after the place properly, At last, they got away, heading towards Staten Island, with half a beef lashed to the guardrails, handy to the helm, so that Jérôme could carve off a piece when he felt peckish. It was six o'clock and going dark, but nobody seemed unduly concerned. They had not bothered with a forecast and I was more than a little impressed at people whose idea of a family holiday was a jaunt across the Southern Ocean in the middle of winter.

I tended the animals, which meant feeding the fowl and dogs and letting the latter out for exercise. Sally had told me how much to feed the poultry, but half a cup did not seem a lot for twelve birds, so I supplemented it with fat from the meathouse. They obviously needed it, racing to the pieces and fighting and squabbling. The ducks seemed to be near the bottom of the pecking order and as their ability to lay eggs made them near the top in importance, I took to cutting the fat into small pieces and scattering them about under the bushes so that all the birds had a chance. The Johnny rooks would hang around, sitting on the hen house roof and perching on the fence in the hope of dashing down and grabbing a piece. One of the roosters, a little red fellow, was very tame and let me pick him up and stroke his soft feathers. He was very brave and would rush at the Johnny rooks leaping into the air at them as they flew down. The other rooster, a huge grey, showy bird, cowered under the bush when they came near and they were becoming increasingly bold and numerous as the freezing weather took hold and their food sources dried up. It was a lot easier scavenging hen food than searching for hibernating beetles.

The ducks and drakes were rather disreputable, their only water supply being a large enamel dish, which was refilled every morning. There was a hose coming down from the stream which gave a constant supply of running water and I made them a bit of a pond from an old oil drum, leading the hose into it. I had first to dig a trench from the hen run to the stream to drain away the excess water as the running hose would obviously cause the pond to overflow, but it was not a difficult job and I rather enjoyed my civil engineering. I put chicken wire, weighted down with sods, over the trench where it led into the hen run and later used the rest of the turves to put round the run in places where the defences against hungry foxes looked rather weak. As well as being too heavy for these dainty animals to move, I hoped that they would grow together and make the run more fox proof on a permanent basis. I set the drum into the ground with some bricks round it and secured the hose to the rim. It took quite a while to fill and the ducks did not at first notice it, but after about an hour, a black one, with a beautiful green sheen to her feathers noticed the sound of the water and waddled over to investigate. At first she just drank a little. Then she dipped her head in and started flinging the water over her back. After a little while she leant further and further over the `pond' until eventually she jumped in and began to swim round and round, flapping and splashing, quacking happily and throwing water everywhere. The other birds came to see what the fuss was about and even the hens seemed to appreciate having the fresh, clean water to drink, instead of having to make do with a bowl of rather muddy water, changed once a day. The other duck soon got the idea, but the young drakes never seemed to cotton on and although they would dip their heads under, I never saw one swimming.

Five sheep were badly affected by worms, which Sally suspected had been introduced by a stud ram, imported from Tasmania. She had been upset to realise that the infestation was in the field that she used when her stud ewes were lambing and even after treatment, these five were very poor when they left. One of them died the day after and we had to carry it down to the pier and throw it over and another one, which had been put in the garden of the Other House was obviously on its way out. Next morning, I noticed Johnny rooks hanging around and, frightened that they might attack it before it was dead, I asked Pete to fetch Jérôme's .22 rifle and put it out of its misery. It was not a pleasant job and we then had to carry that one down to the jetty, too.

The dogs responded quite differently to the family's departure. Ray would come and lie down near the workshop or the Big Shed, but it was Lady who wanted affection. This was curious, because Diti had

Beaver Island picnic with Ray and Lady.

Ray with him all the time he was outside, apart from the odd occasion when Sally wanted her to work sheep. Lady, on the other hand, was regarded purely as a working dog, but she followed me round like a shadow and would sneak onto *Badger* and lie down in the cockpit when I was on board. I became very fond of her and although I tried to discourage her from coming aboard, I did not really have the heart to scold her when I found her curled up in the lee of the cabin. Walking up to the hen run to release and feed the poultry and then to the dog pens to let them out and, in the afternoon putting the ducks and hens to bed, walking to the meathouse for the dogs' dinner and then putting them away, seemed to use up half the day and as they

were so short, there did not seem much daylight left over for anything else. I also found that cutting up our own meat seemed to take an unconscionable amount of time. The Islanders simply put a joint in the oven, but not having one on *Badger*, I had to cut all the meat up into pieces that could be stewed or, at best, pot roasted and I never did get the hang of filleting a shoulder. I was also keeping the fire in for smoking Jérôme's *charcutérie* and Pete spent quite a lot of time sorting out and sawing up wood. The large pieces of hardwood went to the smokehouse, whose fire seemed insatiable and the small pieces and softwood came to us.

One morning I saw a large white bird in the creek and going back for the binoculars, identified it as a great egret, which must have been blown from South America. They are not common visitors to the Islands, but it stayed around for quite a while and I often saw it wading and fishing, apparently successfully.

We tried to take the day off on Sunday, go for a good walk with the dogs and have a picnic. The first Sunday was cold, but sunny and the wind having at last died down, we went to Split Creek in the hope of catching some mullet. I cut a couple of steaks off the beef and we set off about mid morning. It was about an hour's walk and was a pleasant outing, which the dogs also seemed to enjoy. We had no luck with the fishing, but lit a fire and had a splendid barbecue, in spite of the steaks soon going cold, a situation that was not helped by its snowing while we were eating. Ray, who really seemed to have some mental problems, went demented with the flames, leaping about and snapping at them, while Lady, not realising the focus of Rays's obsession became convinced that Ray was snapping at *her* and it was with some difficulty that I prevented her from making a counter attack. She was just as peculiar, in her own way, because she could not resist our empty beer tins, and was not happy until she had bitten holes in them and squashed them flat.

On the way back, we had further snow showers, but I really enjoyed it, for it was a long time since I had seen snow and the boat seemed all the cosier, once we had the fire going and the oil lamps lit.

In the winter, the Patagonian foxes came into the settlement and Sally had asked us to set the traps for them. These were of the humane variety, consisting of a small cage whose door shut when the fox grabbed the bait hanging up inside. I hated catching them and let one or two out because they were so fearless and beautiful, but I remembered my duty on most occasions and Pete nobly took the .22 and shot them. It seemed such a pity.

Pete had decided to make a stairway into the door at the back of the Big Shed, which was the closest door to Jérôme's workshop, but difficult to use because it was about eight feet up and could only be opened by climbing up a ladder and then balancing precariously on top. He constructed a stout platform at the top so that several things could be put down when taking them either to or from the shed and used some six by threes of softwood from the wood pile round the back of the Iron Shed, for the framework and steps. It made a tremendous difference and was very effective and he also made some steps for the side door of the wool shed, which was also frequently used. It had been a nuisance going in and out after meat had been butchered and was being taken up to the meathouse. Such little things can make a large difference in one's day-to-day life.

During this time, I took the chance to catch up with my letter writing and what with looking after the animals and domestic chores, I seemed to have plenty to do. I had always `baked' my bread by steaming it in the pressure cooker at five pounds pressure, but although this resulted in a satisfactory loaf as far as the crumb was concerned, it had no crust and being very moist, tended to go mouldy very quickly. I knew that many people used a pressure cooker as an oven, removing the gasket and safety valve and putting it over the flame, so decided to experiment with making bread in this way. Although it took a little longer the resulting loaf was greatly superior, with a lovely hard crust. I gave it forty-five minutes and then turned it over and cooked it upside down for another quarter of an hour, which gave the top a crisp crust, too. It was voted a great success and it was with difficulty that we restrained ourselves from eating the whole thing as it came out of the `oven'!

In early June the sun only rose at ten to eight and Pete found it difficult to motivate himself when he woke up to a cold dark morning and a cabin temperature in the low forties Fahrenheit, with the prospect of a day spent working in the unheated and draughty Iron Shed. I attempted to alleviate his lot by making hot and filling lunches: thick soups, pizza and occasionally, a pile of mussels. The one advantage of eating meat was that it made a rich and tasty stock for soup and enabled me to ring the changes on pea, lentil, minestrone or potato. Scotch broth appeared regularly on the menu, but such recipes as french onion soup were rejected on grounds of insubstantiality. Consumed with large quantities of fresh bread, and followed often by cold cuts for Pete and cheese for me, they would normally have been sufficient for the main meal of the day, but did not prevent us from eating huge dinners in the evening. There were frequent snow flurries and hard frosts and the cold weather and time spent out of doors demanded a large calorie input. Cutting off the evening's ration of meat, with the icy wind howling through the fly screens in the meathouse was wicked work. Our usual mutton was supplemented by beef from the unfortunate bullock that had met its end before *Damien II* left; Pete reckoned quite highly to it, but I found the mutton less strong and preferred it. Certainly it made a much better curry.

Winter was hardening its grip and at times it was bitterly cold. One morning, as I went up to let the dogs out and feed the fowl, I saw a big fox next to the wool shed; they were getting very bold. Pete seemed half frozen when he came in from the Iron Shed: everything seemed to take a long time and I suspect that the short days and the cold do actually slow one down. He had plenty to do on the engine and was getting on well with alterations to our self-steering gear. Fed-up with kelp wrapping around the servo-pendulum rudder, Pete had designed a trim-tab to attach to our rudder.

Originally, we had fitted *Badger* with a trim tab, but the rudder had been wrongly designed and the boat had been almost uncontrollable in winds over Force 5. After a couple of months of struggling, we took off the rudder and fitted a completely new one which Pete designed, but we did not have time to experiment with a home-made gear before we went south, so had bought a commercially-made Aries self-steering gear. This had worked fine and we had only replaced it with the Hasler, because we bought the latter for a tenth of what the Aries would fetch. Now, we had decided to go back to the original idea, which was one of the reasons for having an outboard rudder in the first place. Pete's ultimate ambition was to have an entirely home-made gear, made largely out of wood.

In due course, *Damien II* returned, bringing great piles of stores for Beaver and a huge stack of mail for us, so once the boat was settled, Pete and I returned to *Badger* to look at all that we'd received.

`I'll make a pot of coffee, first, shall I?' suggested Pete. I gave an affirmative while opening the packages and parcels and slitting envelopes. There was a whole heap of stuff from Steve, who had been concerned about my getting cold and had sent some thermal gear, which included a wonderful pile jacket, with a nylon outer `shell' (as the label described it) which made it both wind and waterproof. I saved it until we went sailing again, not wanting it to be mauled by dogs and covered in dead animal while we were at Beaver. Steve wrote that he was in touch with Sally about helping Falklands Conservation buy some islands to be used as wildlife sanctuaries. It all took a long time, but eventually, with his assistance, several islands were purchased and we were delighted that one of these was

Motley Island, on which I had done the survey. I was also somewhat worried about it, because no-one else had been there and as I am not a trained naturalist, I was concerned that I had been in error. Some months after we had left the Falklands, Steve sent me a report of a survey that had been carried out on Motley after it had been bought, which confirmed my findings.

After we had opened all our packages and drunk the coffee, I read out the letters, but it was thirsty work and we had to open some beer to help me. When we had finished, Pete went back to work in a more buoyant mood than he had been in for a while.

On one of our Sundays off, a beautifully sunny one, we walked to the Bluff to have a barbecue. After a morning of sheep drenching and changing over a propane cylinder, I had everything ready for our picnic by coffee time. Fully insulated against the piercing cold, we had a delightful walk and a delicious barbecue. Coming back, I saw the great egret again and pointed it out to Pete.

`Isn't it like those birds we saw in Brazil?' he asked me.

`Yes. I told you it had probably been blown here from South America, if you remember.'

`Well, I couldn't think what a "great egret" looked like until I actually saw it. Have you told Sally about it?'

`No. I forgot, but I'll mention it when we get back.'

Jérôme had been up to the meathouse and announced that our first batch of charcutérie should be ready to eat. We had some that evening and were delighted with it.

`Jérôme's giving us quite a lot for ourselves,' I told Pete. `He told me to take half, but of course I won't. I only helped him so he would have plenty for when he goes chartering. He says they can get through a whole piece once it's started, and Jérôme is the last man to start rationing things out.'

I had mentioned to Pete that the meat had been getting spoilt because snow could blow in through the flyscreen on the south side of the meathouse; the north side had a louvre, to keep off the sun, but it also kept out the weather. When Jérôme returned, Pete offered to make a louvred framework to fit in the other side of the building. Jérôme thought it a good idea and Pete set to work making one, after which I painted it. The end result looked very well and did a first class job of keeping out snow and rain, so we felt that the joint effort had been more than worth while. Pete also asked Sally about some rather tired-looking gates that he had noticed and these were soon re-hung and opening properly.

With the winter solstice came a gale from the north-northeast, and in combination with the big tides, there was enough water for us to float. It was very worrying and although the lines were sufficiently tight to keep us away from the rock wall under the jetty, we were both relieved when she settled down again until the next time. Four days later, there was another wild night when we hardly slept, with *Badger* shaking and bashing up and down as the tide came in and then again, when it left her. It was horrible and we wondered if her designer had ever expected her to take such a severe pounding; had we realised the frequency and strength of northeasterly gales during the winter months, I doubt that we would have risked staying in that spot.

The wind continued blowing the next day, the woollies lifting water off the creek and at lunchtime, *Badger* started crashing about again. I was nearly blown off the jetty in one gust and the great sheets of water swirling down the harbour made an impressive sight. As Pete pointed out, we should have photographed them, but at the time, we were too worried to think about such things. *Badger* floated again that night, but the wind died away and we settled back quietly, gratefully aware that the tides were taking off.

Sally and Jérôme went back to Stanley again, intending to stay at least a month, to take part in Farmers' Week and see more of Dion and Leiv, who would be able to stay on *Damien II*, if they wanted to. Before they left, Pete spent several more cold evenings up at the Other House, repairing the genoa, which had blown out yet again. It was interesting to see the difference between a boat in constant use and one that is used only occasionally. To get *Badger* ready for sea, all that is required is a tidy up and off we go, but with *Damien II* it was quite another matter. Gear that had made its way up to Their House had to be found and returned, sails bent on, food brought down and lists drawn up of Items Required on Board. Tools had found their way into the Iron Shed and had to be located and returned and the boat appeared less and less ready for sea, the closer the time came, with boxes and bits all over the place. She was moved to the jetty astern of us, to make it easier to load everything aboard, but eventually managed to get away only a couple of days behind schedule.

We were on our own again; it was a wonderful feeling. The snow-covered islands looked incredibly beautiful in the brief periods of sunshine, almost as though it were all for our benefit. The wind had picked up again and there were gale-force snow squalls all day. Veritable little blizzards, but we stoked up the fire and had a celebratory dinner: smoked meat followed by stir-fried beef (from the eternal bullock) in sweet-and-sour sauce, and marmalade sponge and custard for Pete.

I have already mentioned my fondness for celebrating events and in the cold and dark days of winter, we found plenty of excuses: the Fourth of July, Bastille Day and other dates marked on the calendar provided sufficient excuse to spend time in the galley and see what was left in the rather bare treats locker. We still had plenty of wine on board, and on one such evening, feeling warm, replete and mellow, I listened to Pete's plans for the following summer with more enthusiasm and less trepidation than was usually the case.

`I never thought I'd live to see the day when we'd be planning to go to the Antarctic!'

`But we're not,' Pete reminded me. `You can't really call South Georgia the Antarctic.'

`Well, you know what I mean. It's a pity really, to be so close and *not* to go there. Is there any near by?' I went up forward and brought back the inflatable globe, passing it to Pete.

`This would be the place to go,' he said, `the South Orkney Islands. Look, they're almost on the way.' As I studied the globe, he slyly topped up my glass.

`The South Orkney Islands. I don't think I've ever heard of them.'

`Yes you have. That's where David Lewis went in *Ice Bird*.'

`Oh, but that sounded dreadful! He had tons of ice to contend with! We don't want to go there.'

`Don't forget he was taking a completely different route, from the one we'd take,' Pete swiftly countered. `We'd be going from the north, down to them and then back north again and would hardly see any ice until we got there. He was actually travelling *with* the ice.'

`In that case, we might as well go. It would be a shame to go all that way and not visit the Antarctic proper!'

It was the wine talking and it is not always true that *in vino veritas*, but I am sorry to say that Pete took advantage of the situation and continued ungallantly to remind me that I had suggested we go to the Antarctic, so that I could not back out of it. Just *thinking* about South Georgia scared me silly, but in the end I accepted the inevitable on the principle that I might as well be

Beaver Island in winter, looking towards Staats across Fish Creek. **Badger** *is visible just right of centre, with the settlement at right.*

hung for a sheep as a lamb. If I had to be terrified, at least I would have plenty to show for it!

After breakfast, I went up to herd three cows and a bull from the Stable Paddock up to North End head, the dogs full of enthusiasm for the task, bouncing into snow drifts and thoroughly enjoying themselves. The Paddock is only about an acre or so and although there were several extensive patches of gorse in it, I did not anticipate any difficulties in locating four large animals. Imagine therefore, my consternation when I could discover no sign of the bull: he had vanished off the face of the earth. Although the snow revealed a multitude of fox tracks, there was nothing to indicate that the bull had jumped a fence and got out, but there seemed no other explanation, so I made do with pushing through the three cows on their own. Docile and tractable, in spite of being half wild, they made little fuss about the business.

Sally had asked Pete to repair some of the windows and the wool shed, one of the few buildings that was in a generally good state of repair, had one that had been leaking for some time, starting wet rot in one of the main beams. The building was fronted with wriggly tin and the old and well-proportioned window was to be replaced with corrugated plastic. This should have been a fairly straightforward job, but like so many on Beaver, turned out to be rather more than we had bargained for. The plastic of course, was of a different vintage from the wriggly tin and either the metric system or an urge to 'improve' had intervened so that the two were of different wave lengths, so to speak. It turned out to be a real struggle to fit it properly. The old wriggly tin was well-secured and strong and the plastic, in such cold weather, horribly brittle and in less than plentiful supply, but eventually the job was done. Less than elegant, at least it kept out the weather. I had another fruitless search for the bull. It was definitely not there and I concluded that there was no evidence of it for the simple reason that it had escaped before Sally left the island.

We slipped back into our routines, Pete working in the Iron Shed on various projects for us and the farm while I helped when I could or carried on with other jobs and tended the animals. We saw foxes most days and eventually caught several, although the Johnny rooks, also hungry, occasionally set off the traps. When I let them out, they were absolutely furious and flew away, spitting curses.

Ray was obviously missing Diti, but tolerated us and often spent the day curled up on a pile of sacks in the Iron Shed out of the weather, while Pete worked. Lady was revelling in the attention that I gave her, following me everywhere, a very affectionate animal.

Usually she spent the day somewhere near the boat, if I was on board, but one day she must have thought that I was out of doors because I saw her at the top of the green near the houses, as I walked up the hill. I called to her and she came bounding down to me, sliding to a halt in a sheepdog crouch, ears flattened and tail thumping with delight as I bent down to stroke her. She took to escaping from her pen at night and coming down to lie in the cold, windswept cockpit, huddling in the slight lee provided by the backrest. Lady was a lovely dog and I was very fond of her; it seemed a shame to have to lock her up in her pen when she obviously enjoyed our proximity, but she was supposed to be a working dog, so it had to be done. In the end I blocked off under her door so that she could no longer escape.

Going up to feed the hens one morning, I noticed a fountain coming up from the hosepipe. When I went to investigate, I discovered that a small trout, about four inches long, was jammed in a connection. The poor thing was quite dead, drowned, no doubt from the water running into its gills. I had not realised that there were trout in Beaver's streams.

I prepared more meat for salting and smoking and Pete suggested that I do a couple of legs like they do in Norway, one for us and one for Jérôme. Until then, I had been doing the work under Jérôme's supervision, but he was a great one for working by intuition, while I am of the opposite nature. I read up about salting meat in one of my books and in the end followed its suggestions, rather than doing it the same way as we had to date. We saved ours until after we had left the Falklands and it turned out to be the best of them all, keeping better and absorbing less of the bitterness from the smoke and I regretted not having done more at the time, when we were having to eat up the mutton that had been left. It was bitterly cold in the meathouse, with the howling wind blowing through and on one occasion, my hands clumsy with cold, the knife slipped cutting my finger to the bone. It did not hurt at the time, but after it had thawed out, it throbbed sickeningly and was painful for a long time after the flesh had healed.

It was dark by tea time and Pete spent the time before dinner up at The Other House, mending our sails. He eventually worked out what the problem was with the machine, after which progress speeded up, but it was never quite satisfactory.

'Can't you use our machine?' I asked him.

'But Jérôme's does a zig-zag stitch,' he told me 'and as I can't heat-seal the acrylic, it stops the edges from fraying.'

'We'll have to find a hand-cranked machine that does zig-zag stitches one day,' I said 'and then we can be totally independent.'

Sally had also asked me to dig up her potatoes and I thought that I had better get the job done. There were several garden forks available, but when I came to dig, I found that the meagre crop was of tiny potatoes which slipped between the tines of most of the forks. The only one suitable was very heavy, of all-steel construction and as each forkful had to be shaken several times in an effort to dislodge the worst of the mud, the labour required for the pitiful result seemed somewhat excessive. When I had completed the job, however, I was sure that not a solitary spud remained in the patch. Sally had told me to help myself to a share of them, but had I taken so much as a bucketful of the puny things, it would have appeared greedy. I took enough for a couple of meals and put the others in the kitchen of The Other House, in the hope that they would escape the frost there. The following day my right elbow was stiff and sore. I was neither unduly surprised nor concerned: sailors use different muscles from gardeners. It stayed sore and tender, but with having to be butcher not only for ourselves but also for the dogs, which was heavy work, I still did not worry. I should have. The soreness turned out to be a badly damaged ligament, which still gives me trouble from time to time.

A further batch of meat was ready for smoking, so we sorted through the woodpiles and Pete sawed up another great pile of big pieces. The fire in the pit seemed to use a huge amount of fuel, so on windy days, I lit a very small fire in the smokehouse itself, which I kept damped down with sawdust from the pile produced by the chain saw. In fact, this small fire used hardly any wood and seemed to do an equally good job, but there was only a limited supply of sawdust.

Our fire aboard was doing sterling work, and Pete built another woodbox, clad in pitch pine that had once been part of the *Afterglow*. It looked very attractive and we were pleased to have part of one of Stanley's famous wrecks on board. The forward cabin did not benefit much from the saloon's heat and the bunk cushions had become very damp. We were forced to sleep in the saloon again, while I took the cushions into the wool shed to dry out once more. They never really recovered from getting soaked in salt water.

On another sunny Sunday, we went for a picnic, walking with the dogs over to Shell Point, near the airstrip. Ray disappeared early on chasing a fox, but Lady stayed with us, while we found a lee and ate lunch, watching seals and penguins on the beach below. Then she saw a fox on the beach and tore off after it,

nearly catching it before I called her off, when she ran back to me seeming almost relieved. She seemed disobedient, on occasion, ignoring me when called, but after watching the way that she would turn her head to listen, I concluded that she was deaf in one ear. This did not help her on the occasions that she was called upon to work, but neither Ray nor Lady would have put up much of a show on *One Man and his Dog*, I fear.

It seemed to be getting colder and colder. Whenever I came to do the washing, I thought longingly of Sally's machine and to make the chore more acceptable, I heated up some water and did the washing and rinsing below. Rubber gloves helped lessen the shock of the rinsing water and kept the wind off my hands while I pegged clothes out, but it was still a horrible job. One morning it was quite windy and a real tussle to get the sheet pegged out. I was in tears when I came down below and felt the life returning to my numbed fingers, chiding myself for being such a wimp. I felt a little less feeble when I went to peg out the next load and saw that the sheet had frozen as stiff as a board. In fact the clothes dried very quickly in those conditions: the wind soon shook out the ice crystals. Our water, during this time, was fetched from containers which we had filled and stored in the Wool Shed before *Damien II* left.

The next Sunday was bitterly cold and the seawater in our deck bucket had frozen overnight. Even the dogs were finding the weather a bit much; they were still in their kennel when I arrived to let them out, but the sun came out and we had a good walk over to the gentoo rookery. The dogs cornered two foxes on this walk and we had the devil of a job keeping them off. We had taken a flask of tea with us and drank it while we watched the penguins, which seemed much more tame at this time of the year and it was a shame that we had the dogs with us, because they were not so well disciplined that they would lie still when the birds approached us. We also noticed about half a dozen foxes around the rookery, scavenging what they could, no doubt.

The next spring tide was once again accompanied by a north-easterly gale and another night was spent bouncing up and down and worrying. The gale brought a heavy fall of snow and Pete and I had a great time throwing snowballs at each other. *Damien II* returned with just Jérôme on board and we were soon helping him unload the boat: quite a job. The back of the Rover was filled and there were two tractor loads for the Big Shed and the Iron Shed. One of the things that Jérôme brought from Stanley was a huge sewing machine, but it would only do straight stitch and was not in working order. Pete had paid special attention to it, knowing that there would be more repairs for him to do on *Damien II*'s sails before Jérôme left for his first charter. There was lots of mail for us, including a box of books from Steve and we had a treat for our breakfast: Dianne had sent us half a dozen oranges with *Damien II*. We eked them out over the next couple of weeks and they tasted wonderful.

Pete was clearing out the lazarette to start fitting the engine and it was really quite exciting, but it was rather disconcerting how much stuff we took out for temporary storage in the Big Shed. The wood supply for our needs was beginning to look limited, so Pete spent a couple of days sorting out the huge heap of timber at the back of the Iron Shed. Although a lot of it looked fine, it had been piled in a higgledy-piggledy fashion and much of it had suffered from the damp and started to rot. Pete separated out the decent stuff and stacked it carefully, with spacers between each piece. The rest he divided into softwood and hardwood. The former went to *Badger* and much of the latter was consumed by the voracious smokehouse.

The next spring tide was accompanied by yet another northeasterly gale which blew all day, but mercifully had disappeared almost completely by the time we went to bed.

Work on our engine was slow, but sure. We had to do jobs such as boring a hole through the hull for the propeller shaft, or cutting out the propeller aperture in the skeg, between tides, but there was plenty of other work to do, with the engine beds to make and the lockers in the lazarette to modify, Jérôme helping with advice and any welding that needed doing.

For a few days, our lives were ruled by the tides, while we fitted the cutlass bearing and shaft. Holding the bits outside, while Pete fiddled about inside was a horribly cold job and every day, we had to cover up the hole in the hull while the water lapped about the boat.

By the 1st September, with neap tides and the water only just touching the keel, Pete could finish fibreglassing the cutlass bearing on to the skeg, a job that took far less time than we had expected. The next day we were ready to put the engine back into the boat, for fitting to the beds. Pete asked Jérôme if he would carry the engine with the tractor and after lunch, he went off to get the gearbox and sort out other bits and pieces, while I let off the ropes from the starboard side to the shore, so that the tractor could get through. With the tractor alongside, we attached the main halliard to a rope secured around the engine and hauled away. There was no problem lifting the engine up, but getting it down proved more difficult: a knot was in the way and then the bolts for the gearbox needed to be removed. Uncharacteristically, Pete had not thought

ahead, but we eventually lowered the monster into place only to find that the alternator prevented it from going onto the engine bed. We put it on a cushion on the starboard side of the lazarette, while Pete thought about it and Jérôme and Dion went off to their own jobs. A locker that Pete had fitted back and I had been carefully varnishing was still in the way: Pete had not done his sums properly, but considering the shape of the engine and the limited space available for it, it was not that surprising.

`Let's sleep on it,' Pete finally suggested, `it won't seem so difficult in the morning. It'll soon be dark, anyway — I might as well carry on with the sails.'

In the end, he altered the locker that interfered with the alternator, but now we were waiting for decent weather so that we could fit the propeller shaft. The delay gave Pete time to consider other matters and he devised a way of fitting one of the five gallon petrol tanks from the Seagull under the after deck, where it would make a perfect gravity supply diesel tank. We were very pleased with the result.

Winter was coming to an end and we also were kept busy helping prepare *Damien II* for charter, Pete once again sewing away at the weary sails. Crew were arriving and the island was very different from the one we had known on our own. About a week into September, Pete told me some bad news.

`I've just been checking the paraffin situation.'

`And?'

`And I've discovered that the spare five gallon container has diesel in it, not paraffin.'

`Oh no! You've got to be joking! How much have we got left?'

We carefully measured what we had and even diluted one third with diesel, there was only just about enough for a month, assuming that we had enough juice to use electric lights all the time.

`Well,' I said, trying to be positive, `we can cook quite a lot of things on the fire, but we no longer have much wood and the fire needs to be in all day, if I'm going to cook on it.'

`I think we can probably find enough wood on the beach and so on. We'll manage.'

`We'll have to!' But it was easier said than done, because although the fire would soon boil a kettle when it was drawing well and burning hardwood, it needed to be stoked every twenty minutes and our various jobs often took us off the boat.

There was, on the other hand, genuine cause for celebration, that evening: we succeeded in fitting the prop shaft. This was more than a mere step along the way. Now that it was in, the hole in the bottom was filled and we no longer needed to be dried out for the other jobs on the engine.

The next job was to put the engine on its beds, so that the holes could be drilled for it and the engine aligned. It took the best part of one day to get it more or less right, but Pete had a hellish time the next day, lining up the engine. By the end of the day, it was *nearly* there, but not yet down to plus or minus three thousandths of an inch, the maximum permissible misalignment. I found it hard to credit that any great lump of metal could be fitted to such a fine tolerance.

Spring was on its way and we put the clocks forward. After a period of frantic activity, *Damien II* was at last ready to leave. The morning was absolutely perfect for sailing and poor Sally looked a bit upset at the thought that they were going off and leaving her to all the problems of running the farm, for having done most of the hard work of organising it, she must have felt that Jérôme was almost off for a paid holiday.

With *Damien II* gone, we could really get on with *Badger* and Pete could at last finish aligning the engine. It was a dreadful job, the only consolation being that it needed thin pieces of aluminium to shim it and the only way we could obtain them was from beer cans. Pete's temper got shorter and shorter as the day progressed and I tiptoed around, hardly daring to breathe. The situation was not improved when he badly gashed his right forefinger while cutting up a beer tin. It bled copiously and I made a finger stall for it, after which he left the engine for the rest of the day, having run out of patience.

The next day was the equinox and cause for a celebration and if Pete finished the engine, there would be even more justification. He had to file out several of the holes, which was a long, hard and tedious job, but he finished about seven o'clock, declaring himself satisfied.

`And it's to the nearest three thou?' I asked, incredulously.

`Less than that,' he replied with justifiable smugness. `Come and look.'

There sat the engine, finally installed, rock steady and looking as though it belonged.

The fire had been burning well and during the day I had cooked chick-pea curry, rice and pudding on it, to say nothing of a huge pan of soup for lunch. I even managed to crisp the poppadums over the fire, but had to resort to the primus for the cabbage and washing up water.

We opened a carton of white wine, as it was an Occasion and had a very pleasant evening, the boat warm and cosy for a change.

The engine had come with a gear lever on its side, which we decided to keep `for the moment' when we discovered that we could reach it with our feet. The throttle was more of a problem, but Pete solved it by leading a length of string to a little throttle control that Andrèz had given us. Turned one way, it increased the throttle and if it was pushed right over the other way, it turned the engine off. It was an extremely simple system, but worked very effectively.

The next day we tried out the engine. Jérôme had taken back the original starter motor, wanting to pair it with the one on his anchor windlass, to increase the power, but had found another one for us. Pete finished wiring up the engine and invited me to witness the results.

`I'm not sure that I've got it all the right way round,' he commented, pressing the button, but the starter motor whizzed round.

`Whoopee! Does that mean we have an engine now?'

`Not quite, but we're nearly there.' He looked quite pleased with himself, as well he might.

Although it was officially spring, it still felt like winter and we were a little surprised to hear that the shearers were due. It seemed a strange time of year to shear the sheep, before the lambs were even born, but Sally explained that when the mothers could feel the cold, they looked after the lambs much better than when they had their full fleece on. Indeed, when the lambs were born, I could see why she was concerned that the mothers would do a good job. Unlike in the UK, where sheep are generally brought indoors to lamb, or at least are put in a small enclosure and supervised, the sheep in the Falklands just have to get on with it, wherever they happen to be. I could see what Antoinette at Port Salvador had meant about `ranching' sheep. Sally's stud ewes were brought into a nearby field, where she could check up on them every day, but even they had to get on with giving birth on their own.

We had expected to help with the shearing, but there seemed to be plenty of people around and Sally didn't really need us. However, Kenn, who was staying at Beaver doing odd jobs around the farm, as well as cooking for everyone, was run off his feet at times, so I went up and did the washing up, enjoying having masses of hot soapy water. I also found a new way of butchering mutton: the young shearer, Critter, showed Pete and me how he prepared the carcase. He made life a lot easier for himself by punching the skin off on the cradle instead of hanging the sheep up, taking a lot of care to keep it clean. The end result would have graced any butchers' shop.

`You do a really professional job,' I complimented him.

Badger painted and ready to float.

`I used to do all the meat when we lived at Port Howard and learnt how to do it properly. The way you've been taught, punching it hanging up, that's how all the older people do it, but it's a lot easier on the cradle.'

Pete had now finished all the preparations and we at last tried starting the engine, but could not get it to go. All our efforts were in vain and we concluded that the `new' starter motor did not have enough power. It was a real disappointment after Pete had worked so hard. There were one or two other things he could try and if they failed, we could buy a new and powerful starter motor, but it would have been nice to have had it running before we left and Pete deserved some reward for his efforts.

September came to an end, the shearing was finished and everyone had left the island, bar Critter, who was staying behind to do some fencing. We were no longer needed and *Badger* was nearly ready. We had to do some painting and finish the antifouling and, of course, there were a thousand and one small jobs to do, but the end was in sight. When the next big tide came and the boat started floating, Pete went and moved us back a lot further along the jetty.

All afternoon we worked hard in the hope of getting out to anchor the next day and after dinner, when *Badger* floated, we moved her even further along the jetty.

We awoke to a glorious morning, which we spent scurrying round, I sorting out down below while Pete brought stuff back from the Big Shed and finished the self-steering gear. Nothing like leaving things until the last minute! When we floated before lunch, we sailed off the dock to go and anchor, sailing up the creek a little way to give the self-steering gear a brief trial. It was over-steering, but Pete knew what the problem was. The day continued sunny, with light winds and we could hardly believe our luck. In the afternoon, we ferried stuff aboard and tested our new echo sounder, which to our surprised delight seemed to function perfectly. I sadly said goodbye to Lady, upset at the thought of her dashing down to come aboard and see me as she so often had, only to find no-one there.

While I cooked supper, Pete sorted out as much as he could, but had to leave quite a lot of stuff on deck. We prayed that the winds would stay light overnight.

Sunday 9th October saw us up with the sun. We tidied up, had breakfast, made everything shipshape and at last, at half past eleven, we could get under way. The wind was blowing fresh from the north-west and as *Badger* turned on her heel to reach up the harbour, I looked back at the settlement whose affairs had dominated our lives for so long. If it had not always been easy, we had enjoyed some wonderful times there and I felt anew the privilege of having had the island entirely to ourselves through some of the most beautiful days of the winter. But as *Badger* heeled gently, her tiller pulled my thoughts back to the present and a feeling of sheer delight swept over me as I realised that once again we were sailing.

Pete came back to the cockpit. `It's good to be off again.'

`Isn't it?'

Chapter Eighteen

The tide through Stick-in-the-Mud was fair, as planned, the water really boiling in places and at Tea Island Passage the overfalls were quite impressive as the tide swept us out, but by keeping the boat speed down, they were fun rather than frightening. For the rest of the day we had a fresh westerly breeze which brought us to Kit's Creek, near Port Stephens, for six o'clock.

As soon as it was feasible, we tried out our new trim-tab self-steering gear and were very pleased with it. Pete seemed to have stopped it oversteering and we were surprised and gratified to note that it appeared to be as powerful as the servo-gear. And, of course it did not pick up kelp. The trim tab made the helm more heavy, but that seemed a small price to pay.

In compensation for the extravagance of cutting out the fillet of mutton to eat as steaks, I always used the breast, for another meal, almost unheard of in the Islands. Tonight it was stuffed, rolled and well under way when the cooker started playing up. I managed to finish cooking on the fire, but we realised that our Primus burners were seriously objecting to having thirty per cent diesel in their fuel. After dinner, Pete tried to get it working again, but what it really wanted was clean fuel and what it probably required, was a complete overhaul. We needed to get to Stanley as soon as possible.

Pete got me up at five-thirty just as a northwest breeze was starting to fill in and we got under way immediately, the anchorage being exposed to this direction. We had a longish beat out while Pete made breakfast, the cooker still playing up. At the entrance to the bay, a most unpleasant popple caused us to miss stays, so that we had to wear round, with little room to spare. Never having been able to get used to this aspect of `sporting' sailing, I found it a bit hard on the nerves.

Outside we found a bonny breeze and bright sunshine and bowled merrily on our way, but on this point of sailing, the trim tab was oversteering again, so I held the tiller as a human shock cord for about five hours, while Pete struggled with the stove. He was paying dearly for not checking his containers properly. I was frozen, by this time and after spending some time fiddling with a length of shock cord, went below to warm up, only to discover that the skipper had let the fire go out; he had felt pleasantly warm. Fed-up with the cooker anyway, Pete went out to help the self-steering, while I turned in, partially-clothed, in an effort to get warm.

I got up to make a rather inadequate lunch of sandwiches and a cup of tea made from a flask of hot water. Pete had rigged tiller lines and his paltry meal gave him either the energy or the incentive to have another go at the cooker.

`The outboard burner's working fine now, Annie,' he eventually announced, `but the pipe to the other seems blocked.'

`You may as well leave it as it is — I'm only usually using one burner anyway, with being so short of paraffin. I can cook now, that's the main thing.'

The day became even colder and the wind was very fresh, making for quite a beat to Swan Cove, which did not look as pretty as I remembered, under a leaden sky, but it gave as good shelter as we had anticipated and we were glad to get the hook down. Sailing can be a life of extremes: in thirty-six hours I had moved from euphoria through fear to near misery and was now relaxed and made happy by the simple pleasure of being securely anchored and having one burner working like a little blast furnace.

Waking to a lovely morning, we got under way after breakfast, the wind gradually taking off to a glassy calm, which was accompanied by a large and ominous swell. It was delightful to be able to loaf around in the sun, with no list of jobs hanging over us and we treated ourselves to a glass of beer in the afternoon.

With such slow progress, we decided to press on for Stanley and although I was a bit worried that we would be swept on to the Shag Rocks, a breeze filled in later, to send us on our way once more. The swell had been a warning, for the wind increased and became quite ferocious not long after I took over the second watch. Around dawn, it died right away and I shook the reefs out, but it soon returned, the reefs went back in and were followed by more as it picked up, with gale force squalls.

We were concerned that we had slipped to lee-ward of Cape Pembroke, but were lucky and had the tide with us. I turned in, but did not get much sleep as it was extremely rough, coming on deck again to find that we had just made Port William. We tacked and although the wind was really howling, we could lay up, so I started making breakfast.

Badger anchored once more at Stanley by the Government dock.

Pete called down the hatch. `We're making too much leeway and can't weather the Tussac Islands. I'm going to gybe round.'

Looking out I saw that we were very close to them and we seemed to miss by a matter of yards. My hands were shaking when I went back to the cooker. It was vile weather, but as so often happened, it eased off a bit as we got further up Port William and we could shake out a reef; by the time we were in Stanley Harbour, the wind had eased right down. We came to anchor and while I heated up soup for lunch, Pete put out a second anchor. It was good to be in. The wind returned, so we had a lazy afternoon and a good

dinner, treating ourselves to a bottle of wine and turning in early.

One thing that can be said about the Falklands is that the weather is never boring and the next day was one of sunshine and light winds. After breakfast, Pete went ashore for some wood, and then we sailed up to the moorings, to be closer to town. The wind was so light that we experimented with putting out a stern anchor and mooring bows on to the Government Dock, which was in a dire state of repair. All went according to plan and once we were comfortably secured, we went to collect our mail and then waited for Dianne to leave the bank on her lunch break so that we could invite them round for dinner on Sunday.

In the afternoon, we paid a visit to Craig, the Assistant Commissioner for South Georgia, whom we had met once or twice when he visited Beaver. We needed to apply for permission to go to South Georgia, which we hoped would be simply a formality and, while we were there, invited him round for supper that evening, knowing that in his position, it was difficult for him to make many friends. Foreign Office staff are distrusted by the Islanders, who consider them, not without reason, to be spies for the FO and Craig, a single man, did not really have a lot in common with the ex-pat community.

Having unfinished business with Customs and Immigration, we went to get our passports stamped, which should have been done in May, then went to the shops to see what bargains were available.

After tea, I had a frantic tidying up session, while Pete went and sawed wood. I cooked spinach koftas, mutton curry, rice, carrots with turmeric and coconut and egg custard for supper. Craig brought two good bottles of wine with him and a Good Time was Had By All. He was one of the `other sort' in the Foreign Office, having joined it in order to have the opportunity of living in foreign parts. Unlike his career-minded colleagues, his idea of a good posting was some obscure backwater in a country that most people had hardly heard of. Although the Falklands would not normally be described as exotic, he was relishing the wonderful scenery, the chances for walking and the completely different way of life. We thoroughly enjoyed his company and, as he did not leave until well after midnight, we trusted that he felt the same.

In two months' time, we planned to be off to the South Orkneys, South Georgia and thence to South Africa. We would need to provision carefully and might need to order some items. On the other hand, we still wanted to see more of the Falklands, so decided to organise the bulk of our provisions now, which would leave us free to go cruising again. Before we did anything else, however, Pete had to get some paraffin for our poor, suffering cooker.

Awaking to another perfect day, we settled down to business. Pete went off with his fuel containers, while I checked our supplies and made a list of what we needed to buy. After lunch, we visited the FIC warehouse to buy flour, potatoes and wine. We had asked about buying duty-free alcohol, the previous day and the obliging Customs officer had told us that not only would it be no problem, but that they would waive the £38 charge, a courtesy that we much appreciated. The cheap wine that we had bought the previous January was back in stock and we wanted to buy some cases while the going was good, but if we bought it duty free, we could not collect it until we were ready to leave. We explained this to the charming young lady at the office, who dealt with the bulk orders.

Oh, that's no problem,' she smilingly told us, `we'll keep it in store until you want it.'

`We also want a "case" of wholemeal flour — what does that weigh, do you know? — and a sack of potatoes.'

`Hmm. A bulk order of flour is eighteen kilos, is that OK? But I think they've sent all the sacks of potatoes up to the West Store. Let me check.'

She went to the telephone and after a few moments' conversation came back to the counter.

`They didn't have any left, but I've asked them to weigh out a sack for you.'

`How kind of you. You've gone to a lot of trouble for us.'

`Not at all. That's what I'm paid to do.'

We left wishing that all employees who deal with the public had the same attitude.

At the place that sold automotive spares, we arranged to pick up a new battery the following Monday, having decided to fit one solely for the engine and separate from the battery we used for lighting, etc.

Later on, Pete at last managed to fix the cooker and I was able to indulge in the unwonted luxury of two roaring burners and as much paraffin as I wanted.

Our berth by the Government Dock was open to the north and very exposed to the east, so when we woke up to a fresh northerly that seemed to be thinking of swinging to the east, we were rather concerned. Being a Saturday, we had been unable to catch a forecast, which seemed to be put out at random at the weekend, so I went to telephone the Met people. The post office being closed, I went to the Upland Goose to see if they had a payphone. Vera was at Reception.

`Hello, there! We saw that you were back. How are you?'

We chatted for a while, catching up on the news and then I mentioned my reason for being there.

`Oh, that's only a local call. Use this 'phone,' Vera offered, finding the number. The man at the Met office was really very helpful.

`I'm not a forecaster, but I can read it out for you.' This he did, but it was not very clear.

`What I'm concerned about,' I told him, `is whether the wind is going to increase out of the north or east, but I can't make that out from the official bulletin.'

`Well, I'll tell you what the present situation is. The weather we have at the moment is caused by a low coming right over the islands and we're unsure if the wind is going to back or veer. Whichever, it will go west before increasing any further. Does that help?'

`That's great. Thank you. I can relax now.'

I had a few more words with Vera, who asked us to call by some evening, and then went back to *Badger*, telling Pete the good news.

It came onto rain, so we spent the rest of the day aboard. In the afternoon, we heard a hail from the dock and looking out, saw Andrèz so Pete jumped into *Skip* and went and fetched him. It was great to see him again and to catch up on the gossip over a glass or two of wine.

`We got that house in Pioneer Row, you know, the one that was in my family when it was first built, and we've moved in now. There's tons of work to do, of course, but we're hoping to restore it like the original.'

`That's great! We must come up and see it.'

`Are you going to join the sail in company to Port Louis and back?'

`What's this? We've heard nothing about it.'

`Haven't you? We're celebrating the removal of the capital from Port Louis to Stanley, during December, and it's one of the events. The sail's planned over the weekend of the tenth of December. I'm sure you'll be invited to join. All the visiting and local boats will be. We're hoping to be ready by then — not finished, of course, but at least able to join in.'

`I hope we can come. It should be fun.'

We told Andrèz that his echo sounder had worked perfectly and he then asked us about the engine. We explained about the starter motor, but I think he was a bit surprised that we could not start it by hand.

The following afternoon, the rain having turned to showers, we took the cart and walked to FIPAS, intending to collect wood on the way back and hoping to see how our friends were getting on with their several projects. Neither Carl and Dianne nor Andrèz and Alison were around, but Larry and Maxine seemed pleased to see us, plying us with tea and biscuits. By the time we left, Carl and Dianne had arrived and we could have a look at *Pale Maiden*, which was really coming along. Andrèz's boat had the mast in, so everyone seemed to be making progress. Having confirmed the evening's arrangements, we walked back to *Badger*, collecting plenty of driftwood and, with difficulty, refraining from salvaging some more of the *Afterglow's* pitch pine from the beach. We would not have dreamt of burning it, but wished that we had some project planned for which we could use it.

The family Freeman arrived in due course, approving our new and more convenient berth. It was splendid to see them again and the evening passed all too quickly.

Pete collected our new battery, the following morning, but even that was not enough to get the engine going: the starter motor was just not powerful enough. We had seen Ian Bury a few days back, and he thought that he might have a better one, so the next day we went to see him. The one that Jérôme had given us came from a petrol Rover, so we really wanted the same model so that it would fit.

`I always have diesel Rovers,' Ian told us, `but I think I have one somewhere.' He rummaged around the bits and pieces in his garage. `Here it is!' He looked at it. `It's the only one I've got, I'm afraid, but there's a brush missing. You're very welcome to have it if you want it. It's no use to me.'

`I'm sure I can use it,' Pete told him. `Our motor just doesn't seem to be developing the power, but I can probably cannibalise what we now have to make one good one.'

We felt a little more hopeful as we made our goodbyes and walked up to Carl and Dianne's for dinner.

The engine was beginning to take on all the aspects of a saga and after a morning spent up to his ears in starter motors, Pete was still getting no joy from it. Larry and Maxine came for lunch and after they had left, Pete carried on trying to get the engine going, finally giving up in disgust when both starter motors packed in.

Our social life, on the other hand, was going at full steam and the early evening saw Andrèz and Alison arriving for dinner, bringing Andrèz's son, Marc, a pleasant boy. Andrèz, who regarded our non-starting engine as both a challenge and an insult, had brought another starter motor. He and Pete were soon ensconced in the lazarette, but after a certain amount of fruitless effort, retired defeated.

`I think, Pete, that you should just get the knack of starting it by hand.'

`Well, perhaps you could do it and then I can see where I'm going wrong.'

`Sure, is this the rope?'

Andrèz wrapped it round the pulley wheel and, standing over the companionway, bent down and gave the rope a lusty tug. He was more than surprised when nothing happened. After trying again without success, he came back below and pondered for a few moments.

`You know what, Pete, it may be something to do with the gearbox or I reckon we could try thinning the oil to see how that works.'

We had all had enough of engines by that time and settled down, glass in hand, to talk of other matters.

After another fruitless morning, Pete was ready to throw the engine overboard, so at lunch time, we went up to see Andrèz and Alison to discuss the matter and also to have a look at their house. It was an interesting old place, small, but with quite a bit of land. We could see the potential in it and as it had not been much modernised, could also envisage what it would look like when they had finished the work, of which there would be plenty.

Talking about the engine, Andrèz and Pete wondered if the friction of the belt going to the alternator as well as the starter motor, was too much. The latest idea was to link the starter motor to the rope pulley, while the alternator was driven by the flywheel.

Larry and Maxine must have thought our lunch invitation a good idea, because we had been invited back. We arrived at FIPAS a bit early so that we could see Andrèz, who gave us three different fan belts.

`One of these should do the trick, Pete. I've also found this,' he said, picking up another starter motor. If all else fails, we could try taking the engine out and fitting another flywheel'.

Pete looked as if he would sooner die than do that and remembering the agony of lining up the engine, I did not blame him. We truly appreciated Andrèz's efforts, however and were grateful for his encouragement.

We arrived at *Shingebiss II* and ended up having quite a party, being joined by one of the FIGAS pilots, Anthony, Dianne, who managed the IMAX film budgets and Simon Worsley. We all had a bit to drink and a jolly good time. With being alongside and in Stanley for so long, as well as being very convivial, Larry and Maxine always seemed to have company. They intended to see a bit more of the Islands and part of the reason for our being there was to discuss places to go, but we did not get very far: Larry was easily sidetracked into other topics of conversation and none of us was concentrating too well anyway.

A couple of days previously, we had been delighted to bump into Kenn, who was staying with an old friend Mrs Biggs, in Stanley doing a bit of gardening. We had met him at Beaver. Kenn, middle-aged, lean, always ready to laugh and with the kindest face of anyone I have ever met, was the most extraordinary man. Having left University with a Classics degree he, more or less by accident, got a job with the British Antarctic Survey and spent no fewer than seven winters in the Antarctic, a BAS record. He would cheerfully have spent another seven winters there, but his employers were worried that he had done too many and was becoming somewhat maverick. They gave him a job at their headquarters in Cambridge, but he had soon had enough of office work and all the in-fighting, so he left and went to see some of his relatives in Chile. He found that he rather enjoyed that, so he carried on.

Kenn never looked back. He had been travelling ever since: Australia, China, Canada, South America. Friends all over the world gave him food and lodging and in return he painted or gardened or cooked for them. We assumed that Kenn must have been like us and put money aside to give him a small income, but we were quite wrong. When we met him in Stanley, we discovered that he was a trifle concerned about the fact that he did not have enough money to pay for an air fare from the Falklands.

`I used about the last of my money getting here,' he told us.

`But what are you going to do?'

`Oh, something will turn up.' And, of course it did. He had planned his retirement; he would go and live with his sister in Essex and pay his way by looking after the garden and decorating. Kenn never worried about the future. He made his plans: a little work here, a visit to England, grape-picking in Bordeaux, back to friends in Chile. Despite having no `marketable skills' nor private means, he lived a pleasant life and always managed to have the wherewithal to buy a round of drinks for his friends and, being one of the most likable people I know, his friends are manifold.

He was due to fly back to Beaver soon, and we had booked him in for dinner. It was a delight to have him on board again; we had not known him long, but it was like having an old friend around. We had a wonderful evening, Kenn making us laugh with his stories of places he had worked and we were touched by the two bottles of wine and chocolate that he brought with him, which he could ill afford.

We saw Kenn again the next day. He was laden down with cold beers and a bunch of daffodils, rhubarb and some swedes from Mrs Biggs' garden. I instantly found a container for the daffodils, overjoyed to have some flowers on the boat again. He had only just left when Craig came round for an hour or so, with an invitation for dinner and a hot bath the next day. Our social life seemed to be getting out of hand when Andrèz rolled up, while Pete was taking Craig ashore,

but he had only stopped by to see if we had got the engine going.

The next morning at breakfast, Pete announced that today was the last day he was going to spend trying to get the engine going.

`If it won't start, I'm taking it out and we're going back to the Seagull,' he declared. I said nothing.

The first thing we tried was taking out some of the oil and replacing it with diesel, as Andrèz had suggested. Then we tried starting the engine. Nothing. Pete muttered curses and we sat and looked at the engine.

`If we try too often,' said Pete morosely, `the new battery is going to be flat.' Silence.

`Andrèz said that drag in the gear box may have something to do with the problem. Why don't you disconnect the shaft and try once more, with that fanbelt that fits round the rope pulley and the starter motor pulley? At least we'll know whether or not it works,' I suggested.

`We could try that, but the starter motor can't swing enough so that the belt can come off. Still, if it does start, I can stop it straight away.'

A few minutes later, everything was ready and Pete pressed the button. *Chunter-chunter-chunter — thump-thump-thump*. Pete was so astonished that he almost forgot to stop it!

`Hooray! We've cracked it!' I cried. `And what's more, I've worked out how we can get the fan belt off the starter motor!'

`Go on,' Pete encouraged me.

`Look, if we put the fan belt onto the *edge* of the pulley on the starter motor, which is the same diameter as the inside of the pulley itself, it'll allow the belt to slip off.'

`You know, this might work.' After several adjustments to ensure it did not slip off until we wanted it to, we tried again and off the engine roared. After re-connecting the shaft, we tried again and to our jubilation, it started without hesitation and when we shifted the gear stick, the prop shaft went round and round. Pete was over the moon.

`Good Little Engine', he said, as he turned it off and patted it.

`That's not what you called it an hour ago!' but Pete just grinned.

In the best of good spirits, we got changed and wandered up to Craig's house. I had the decadent delight of a boiling hot bath *and* a glass of gin and tonic, but was slightly inhibited by the incredibly pristine bathroom, which I was more than a little worried about messing up. While I was wallowing, I heard Kenn's voice, which made the evening perfect; Craig had invited him after seeing us the previous day. He had done us proud, persuading the Government House cook to make chicken and mushroom pie followed by a summer pudding. He did not know much about cooking, himself, but Kenn and I had been encouraging him to make bread and he showed off his latest loaf, which was duly sampled and declared first rate. It was a happy party.

The following morning, we started the engine again, just to be sure that it was not a fluke and spent the rest of the day involved in provisioning.

Andrèz came by — we had left a note at his house — delighted with our success and tried hand starting the engine again. This time there was no problem and even Pete managed, although he has never really got the knack of it. After trying once or twice, I ceded victory to the engine. Andrèz had brought a different grade of oil, so they emptied out the old stuff and changed it.

`That alternator you've got, Pete. It's no good, you know, without a regulator.'

`It's not perfect, I know. But they're a hell of a price and Annie's uncle is going to make a box so that we can control the output.'

`Well, that might be better, but I found this and you may as well have it at least to be going on with. I checked it — it works OK.' He handed Pete an alternator, `and you'd better give me that fan belt. I'll find you another one for a spare.'

We were overwhelmed. Andrèz had already done so much for us and there was little we could do in return. We had our old solar panel, but it might stop working any day, and some spare rope, but they could not even be considered a token payment. As ever, Andrèz waved away our thanks and the only request that he made of us was to have a look at his sails and see if we could make any suggestions

This we duly did, going round to FIPAS, where we could spread them out. Unfortunately, the mainsail was in a really poor state and the best advice we could

*The well-preserved wreck of the iron barque **Garland.***

give him was to buy another one. Not surprisingly, he was quite cast down about this, but cheered up a little when we told him about the places that advertised in the yachting press and sold nearly new sails at very low prices. In an effort to be positive, we pointed out that as the old one did not fit the mast and boom properly, he could take the opportunity to think about his rig and choose the correct sail for it.

The end of October it might have been, but the weather went bitterly cold. All the wood we could find seemed damp, so we resorted to buying coal, which at least did not need topping up every twenty minutes. My elbow was still giving me problems, so I went along to the hospital, where a doctor diagnosed it as tennis elbow.

`What should I do about it?'

`Well, it won't get better on its own. You can try a course of pills, which will take some time, or an injection, which should work within a few days.

`I don't fancy either, to tell the truth, but I'd better get it over with, I suppose. I'll have the injection.'

The actual injection was quite excruciating and later on my elbow swelled up like an egg, becoming horribly painful.

That evening, we went ashore in a veritable blizzard, to see a performance of `No Sex Please, We're British', by the amateur dramatic company, who put on a wonderful performance. I felt rather sorry for them running around in their nightwear, the heating being very inadequate. We had a drink with Simon and Devina in the interval and Craig invited us back to his place after the play for a Scotch or two. It was all very civilized. Craig kindly drove us back and it was so cold that we really appreciated it; we also appreciated the fact that the fire was still in because I had left the kettle on it for the hot water bottle.

We were hoping to be off again soon, as it was nearly November, but the injection on my arm seemed to have done more harm than good because it was more painful than ever. I was keeping my fingers crossed that it was just tenderness from the injection itself, but it was a worry. I was cheered up by our friends, however. It was great being by the Government Dock, because if anyone wanted to see us, they could easily attract our attention. Craig popped along for a cup of tea several times after work, occasionally staying for supper and Andrèz and Ali dropped by once or twice.

Sunday, 30th October saw us underway once again and although the day was cloudy, the wind was never more than Force 4, which more than compensated. We had hoped to get to Island Harbour, but with wind and tide against us, only made the lagoon off Bold Point, a run of twenty-two miles, spending a lot of the time below, keeping warm. Although the sound of the surf was disconcerting, the anchorage was only slightly rolly and better than I had anticipated.

Amazingly, the wind was still light and still out of the east when we got up and the conditions were perfect for trying out the engine. The trim tab had to be locked, or else the helm was unmanageable and there was a very strong bias to starboard, but we had expected that. Otherwise, we were really quite delighted with it and there seemed to be plenty of power there.

The historic but less well-preserved **Vicar of Bray.**

As sailing up Choiseul Sound would usually entail a stiff beat, we took advantage of the east wind to head up towards Darwin Harbour, somewhere I had been longing to visit because of the wreck of the *Vicar of Bray*, being there. We ran up Choiseul Sound, fortifying ourselves against the cold with coffee and a hot lunch and just before we arrived at Goose Green, we had the opportunity of a fairly close look at a really well-preserved wreck, the *Garland*, an iron barque. We came to anchor about tea time and after we had tidied up, went ashore.

Tom and June McMullen, who manage Goose Green, made us very welcome and we settled down with a cup of tea. Goose Green, of course, became notorious during the Falklands Conflict and not surprisingly the subject came up. Tom's most interesting comment, however, was that throughout the whole period, the *Garland* had been used by a member of the SAS as a shelter from which he could keep watch on all that was happening. Having heard about some of their exploits during this period, one begins to understand why these soldiers are every bloodthirsty little boy's (and girl's?) heroes.

`I was hoping to have a look at the *Vicar of Bray*, if that would be all right,' I mentioned to Tom, while we were on the subject of ships.

`Of course. Go anywhere you want, but I think you'll find the old *Vicar* a bit disappointing. She belongs to some Museum in America and they came down a few years ago measuring her all up and everything. Then they took off the stern to take back with them and we haven't seen them since. I don't know what's going on with her now.'

Sure enough, when we went to see her, she really was a wreck. I was very upset to see what state she was in because I could remember seeing photographs of her in *WoodenBoat* magazine, about fifteen years previously. Now, in the thin drizzle that was falling, she was a melancholy sight, haunt of night herons and sheathbills, the tides washing in and out, planks sagging away from the stern where the transom had been removed. Although all the timbers were labelled, no effort had been made even to stabilise them. It was very sad: she is the only surviving ship of the more than 700 that sailed to San Francisco in 1849-50, in the days of the California Gold Rush. In the article that I had read, she had looked to be in really very good order, but like so many of the wrecks in the Falklands now, she is no more than a pile of timber. It is impossible to restore or even to preserve every old wreck, but I felt that one of such historic significance deserved a better end.

Having looked over the rest of the settlement, which had the most enormous wool shed that we had seen, we went back to the beach on which we had landed, collecting a good pile of firewood before starting to row back in the now pouring rain. As Pete pulled away, a Rover stopped and an elderly man climbed out, so we turned back to talk to him. He told us that he had been concerned that we would land on the mined part of the beach, but we reassured him that we had noticed the markers. After a few more pleasantries we got back into *Skip* and returned to *Badger*.

Our plans were to head west again, to cruise around Weddell Island, Port Philomel and other areas in northwest Falkland. With luck we might even make it to the Jason Islands. For once, we were *pleased* to find that the wind had gone back into northwest next morning, because it made for a wonderful run down the sound, the bright sunshine making the little tussac islands that we passed look particularly attractive. The breeze died away and was barely enough to keep the sails asleep, so still charmed by the novelty of it, we started the engine so that we could make it to Pyramid Cove in time for the tide and a spot of fishing. We had to admit that it was an excessively noisy form of locomotion, but then, one of the many advantages of an air-cooled engine is that the racket it makes does discourage one from using it.

The fishing was not quite up to standard, but we caught two mullet, one of which was huge. Back on board, I pickled some and fried the rest in batter with chips, for dinner.

Pyramid Cove being one of our favourite spots and the wind still light, we stayed at anchor the next day to get on with some jobs and try fishing again. We had better luck, this time, catching seven mullet, which gave me nine jars plus a litre one to give to Alec, the night's supper (my specialty of fish in a white sauce flavoured with mushrooms, tarragon and green peppercorns, eaten with pasta) and enough for the next day.

We awoke to another morning of light winds, but the breeze filled in after lunch and sailing past Pyramid Island, we saw the remarkable sight of a sea lion in the kelp, flaying and eating a penguin. It was a lovely sunny afternoon, and as the wind seemed set to continue, we did the same.

With a whole sail breeze, we made fine progress through the night, but we must have had some current against us because at a time when we should have been past Speedwell Island, I discovered that we were on the edge of the kelp bank, to the east of it. It was only when it became light enough to see clearly, that I could identify Speedwell and be absolutely certain of where we were. I had to alter course to the southwest to dodge round another bank of kelp, after which I had a cup of cocoa, although I could have done with something stronger.

The wind died away mid morning and missing our tide to pass Cape Orford, with it went our hopes of catching the tide through the Smylie Channel. We made it to Rodney Cove by late afternoon, grateful for the rapidly lengthening days. With the wind in the north, we found a peaceful anchorage right at the head of the bay, finally back out west.

We could have a leisurely start the next morning, due to the time of the tides and, once again in moderate winds, had a pleasant sail up to Smylie Channel, passing inside Seadog Island. To our astonishment, there was really quite a popple, which would have been dangerous on a windy day and far from being bang on slack water, as we had calculated, the tide did not appear to change until about three hours later.

As we approached Dyke Island, we saw a shimmering mass in the air ahead which proved to be literally thousands of slender-biller prions, an amazing sight. Once they start breeding, they stay in their burrows during the daylight hours, so we had rarely seen any before and to come across them in such quantities was an unforgettable experience.

We were heading for Anthony Creek, the best anchorage for South Harbour settlement, and were preparing to drop the hook when the echo sounder went haywire, confused by the kelp. Cursing it roundly, Pete scrabbled for the lead and finding only six feet of water, we gybed round and ran back a little before anchoring. Once we were at rest, the echo sounder started working again and smugly confirmed the leadline.

'Bloody thing,' I said to Pete, 'these digital things are as nervy as racehorses!'

After a cup of tea, we went ashore to South Harbour, where Mike and Linda had spotted us and come out to greet us. We had met Mike at Port Stephens the previous summer and they made us very welcome with tea and biscuits. We found them a lively and attractive couple and were all happily chewing the fat when Peter and Anne Robertson turned up for dinner. Tea things were cleared away and something stronger was offered round. When we had emptied our glasses, we got up to leave.

'You're not going, surely?' Mike protested.

'Well, time's getting on ...'

'But aren't you going to eat with us?' asked Linda, 'there's plenty of food for everyone and you don't want to have to go back and start cooking. Come on, sit down and have another drink.'

So we stayed to enjoy a very typical Falklands party. There was an abundance of food and although no-one drank wine or beer, rum, gin and whisky were in plentiful supply and everyone helped themselves. Peter sank a good few, while telling us fascinating stories of life in the Islands when he was a young man, and how dramatically the gentoos and sea lions have declined since then, and the skuas, too. We teased him about breathalysers and how he would be in trouble 'once the road comes'.

'You're right, of course. It will all be different then. Even now the "two nighters" aren't the same as they used to be.'

'"Two nighters"? I don't think we've heard about them.'

'Haven't you?' said Anne, 'why, they were one of the best things when we had the big settlements. You must tell them about those Peter.'

He poured himself another stiff drink and settled back in his chair. '"Two nighters" are what we used to call the parties that were given, especially in the winter, in the old days. Everyone drove to a settlement, and stayed there for a couple of nights, meeting up with the other campers and catching up on all the gossip and scandal.' He chuckled. 'And it wasn't that uncommon for there to be a change or two of partners, either. The parties were good, but so was getting there. We always travelled in company so as to help each other if somebody got bogged down. There weren't so many Rovers then, of course, and quite a lot of people used horses, but as we got closer and closer to where the party was being held, the cars and carts would increase in number. Well, as we got to each gate, it was a good time to get out and talk to people, so we'd all have a drink.

And the gates were also where we'd meet another party from another settlement, so then we might have a couple of drinks. Then we'd have to stop for smoko, or dinner — of course there was plenty of food — and then we needed another drop to keep out the cold. I tell you, by the time we got to the party, we were all in the right mood.'

Anne laughed at the memory. 'They were wonderful those trips. You know, twenty years ago, it was a real adventure going to visit someone, but when the road comes, all that fun will be gone. I used to think that the journey to the "two nighters" was actually the best bit. It didn't matter how drunk people got, no-one ever came to any harm — the cars couldn't move fast enough, and there was always someone else to help you if you got into trouble. We don't have the good times that we used to,' she concluded wistfully.

Around midnight, the party broke up and Peter made his less-than-sober way to the Rover.

'Don't drive through any of my gates, now,' Mike called after him and we stood laughing as the car made its unsteady way along the track.

'Will they be all right?'

The settlement at South Harbour.

`Oh sure. Peter knows the track blindfold, and if anything happened, they've got blankets and things in the Rover. They'll 'phone tomorrow, just to tell us they got home OK. Here, hop into the car and I'll take you back to the creek.'

His Range Rover seemed to have an exceptionally noisy and powerful engine and when we commented on it, Mike told us that he had fitted it with an old diesel engine from a tractor. Like the rest of us, he had not been particularly abstemious and I was impressed at the way he handled the car over the rough country and almost invisible track, a task that would have challenged most drivers in daylight and stone-cold sober. He dropped us off and we scrambled down to the dinghy to find that it had got caught under a rock and was nearly full of water with one of the oars lying alongside, but fortunately, nothing had been lost.

We stayed a further day at Anthony Creek and after a lazy morning, walked up to the house. Linda showed us round the garden and after having a cup of tea, we invited them round for supper. It was a lovely evening with light winds when they arrived, and as they were interested in boats, I suggested that we go for a sail, cooking the meal as we went along, an idea that met with general approval. Over dinner, Linda and I started talking about books; although the library will send books on the 'plane, she was often short of something to read and as we had a shelf full of swops, I gave them to her. With it being almost summer they had a lot of work to do and had not intended to stay late, but it was almost midnight when we rowed them ashore.

We were underway after coffee, having been up to the settlement to collect a big bag of wood that Mike had kindly put out for us. After investigating another anchorage, we sailed round to Double Creek. It was what we called `a typical Falklands day', sunny with a very fresh breeze and the first arm of Double Creek did not look too inviting, but we had a look at an anchorage

there before returning to the other arm, where a Rover stopped to watch us. Sadly, the wind would have made the anchorage in the creek nearest to the settlement very uncomfortable: it was gusting like fury down some of the valleys, but we managed to find a comfortable spot elsewhere, anchoring at about six o'clock.

The previous day had been the first anniversary of our arrival in the Falklands, an event that surely needed celebrating. Having found ourselves a good berth, I could get down to preparing the appropriate blow-out meal. The wind obligingly died away and we had a quiet evening to enjoy rum and pineapple juice with nibbles; fish paté and water biscuits; chickpea fritters in sweet and sour sauce, stir-fried carrots, bean sprouts, `spring' onions and rice, and pudding, all washed down with a litre of wine. Talking about all we had seen and done over the previous twelve months, it seemed incredible that we could ever have considered coming for only a few weeks.

The morning forecast was dreadful, but as neither the barograph nor the sky seemed to agree with it, we got underway for Shallow Harbour, in Philomel Road. We found a shoal off one of the islands at Double Creek, which was not marked on the chart and made us feel that our efforts were worth while. A couple of reefs were dropped as we entered Queen Charlotte Harbour and as we sailed across this large stretch of water, we were again surrounded by prions, swooping across our bows and soaring round the sails.

We were at anchor in time for lunch and bearing in mind the forecast, put down two anchors and were just about to eat when I noticed a Rover driving down.

We donned oilskins and launched the dinghy, rowing ashore to find that most of the population of Shallow Harbour had come down to invite us to visit. Here were Ali(stair) and Marlene Marsh, their daughter Tanya and Marlene's Mum and Dad, George and Joan Porter; the other two children, Kevin and Michelle were at school in Stanley. Needless to say, we accepted the invitation.

`We couldn't believe it when we saw you sailing in,' Marlene said. `I'm just sorry that Kevin isn't here — he's boat mad and will be broken-hearted to have missed you.'

`Oh, what a shame! But we'll be back in Stanley early in December — get him to look us up. We'll probably tie up to the Government Dock again and if he gives us a call, we'll show him over the boat.'

As we came to the settlement they pointed it out, with justifiable pride. It was a very pretty spot, clean and tidy.

'We only have 4,000 sheep,' Ali told us, 'but it's good camp and we don't need to employ anybody, so we can look after the place properly.'

Their house was either new or completely modernised, with a huge verandah, in which grapes and other exotic plants were growing.

'In the summer, it gets almost too hot in here,' Marlene remarked, 'but it's a lovely place to sit on a sunny day in the winter, when it's cold outside.'

Marlene did a lot of knitting, using a machine. She had just bought a new one, and I was amazed at its virtuosity; like so many things nowadays, it was controlled by a computer chip and could be set up to do very complicated and colourful designs.

Joan and George had gone to their own house and after spending an hour or so with Ali and Marlene, chatting and drinking tea, we went over to the other house. George was another natural storyteller and as he recounted tales about the old days and of the boats that used to serve the Islands, I thought what a shame it was that there was no-one to record all the yarns of the older people who grew up without radios, electricity and airstrips, collect them together and ensure that they were there to be passed on to future generations. Already the way of life has changed enormously; should oil exploitation become a reality, the Falklands are likely to alter out of all recognition and a unique way of life will be lost forever.

We could have stayed there all day, but time was getting on and we needed to be making tracks. Joan, like Linda, loved books and gave us some before we left; surprisingly, the campers by and large, are not great readers and we often wondered how they spent the long winter days. As we walked out of the garden, Marlene was there with the gift of a dozen eggs and the offer of a lift, but as she stopped on the way to check something, we got out so that we could admire the views as we walked back.

From such an elevation, they were well worth looking at and we enjoyed the best walk we had had for a long time. It was low water when we got back and a long way to carry the dinghy, but checking the echo sounder, we found well over seven feet, so although the harbour is shallow, there is plenty of water for even quite a large yacht.

The predicted gale arrived in the small hours of the morning and I abandoned the forward cabin, settling down with sleeping bag, hot water bottle and rug in the saloon, after which I got some sleep, although I was only just warm enough. The wind was forecast to moderate slowly and even by the time we had finished breakfast, it seemed to be doing so, but we decided to spend a day at anchor so that Pete could update his Falklands notes and sketch charts while I worked away on my word processor. By mid afternoon, the wind had died right away, and although the forecast had been amended to a gale warning, we guessed it was over.

The following morning we walked over to a nearby gentoo colony and then on to another beach, where we collected some driftwood, of which there appeared to be an endless supply. Back on board, Pete did his sums about the tides, which are very strong in this area and we got underway after lunch, the sun shining and a moderate breeze sending us merrily on our way to Philomel Pass. Having been swept through the first narrows, we jilled around for a while in Halfway Harbour, trying to decided whether to carry on or to wait for slack water; there is only a narrow pass between two shoals which block the entrance into Port Philomel and with the strong tides, the kelp, which can usually be relied upon to mark such dangers, runs under. The thought of the reported fourteen knot currents was not reassuring, either, but we gave it a try and had no problems. The tide was with us for a way in Port Philomel, too, and we sailed along in fine style with a following breeze, sharing a can of beer to celebrate.

Anchoring in East Bay, we went ashore and had quite a hike over to the settlement, tripping over diddle-dee and plunging our feet into deep holes full of

Port Philomel, West Falkland.

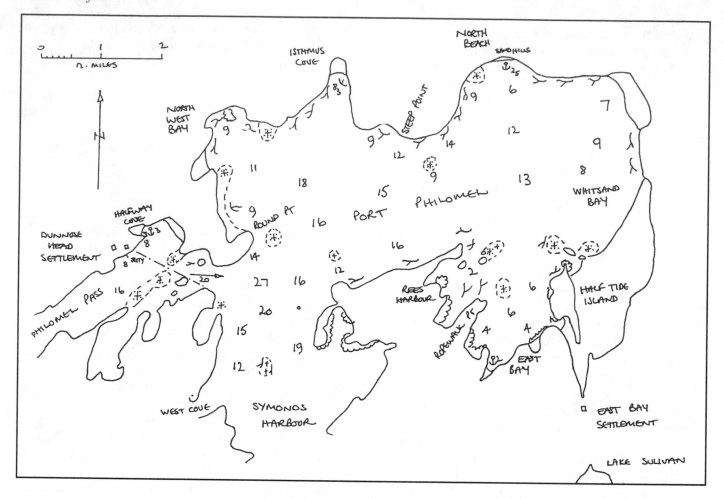

water. The settlement looked a bit run down, but when we met the owner, Ian, we understood why. Inviting us in, with all hospitality, he explained that he was a widower, living with his son and had obviously had quite a struggle, managing more or less on his own. He was busy making cakes and seemed pleased at our compliments and obviously enjoyed having somebody to talk to. We felt sorry for him; his was a remote settlement and he must often have been very lonely.

It was another hard trek back to the boat and late in the evening before we were back on board.

Our anchorage was open to the north, from which direction it was still blowing. It had not gone calm when we came to turn in, and this realisation, together with the jobble that the wind was sending in, prevented me from sleeping properly. At about half past three, Pete woke up.

'D'you think we should move into the saloon, Annie?'

'I think we should move completely, to be honest.'

'OK — you're probably right, but let's wait until it's light.'

About an hour later, we got up, hauled *Skip* aboard and commenced sailing out the anchor.

'Go head to wind,' Pete called to me, 'We're overrunning the anchor!'

By now, it was quite rough and I knew that if I went head to wind, we would instantly fall off on one tack or the other, so I let the sheet fly, at which moment, Pete told me that the anchor was up. With insufficient way on to tack, I had to gybe round and as I already had the foresheet in hand and wanted the sail in hard so that she would turn quickly, I could not let off the mainsail. Hauling in with both hands, my right foot pushing the tiller up and with visions of running the boat hard ashore, I shouted: 'For God's sake, come and let out the bloody mainsheet!'

It was one of those situations that made me wonder just what I was doing there.

'I don't understand why you get so ratty,' Pete complained as he close-hauled the mainsail and we started to beat up the bay.

'I'm not ratty,' I said between clenched teeth, 'I'm frightened! I'd have thought you could tell the difference by now!'

Trauma over, we sailed up to North Beach and dropped the hook off a strip of golden sand, had breakfast and turned in. An increase in the wind woke me later and I realised that we were in for one of those strange Falkland gales that come out of the north and seem to accompany a high glass in the summer months.

Getting up about coffee time, Pete took out the Ventimeter and announced, to my profound relief, that we would stay put. It seemed a good opportunity to make Christmas puddings and there was plenty to keep us occupied.

It blew throughout the day, but by the middle of the next morning, we reckoned that it had eased off enough to go exploring again and with well-reefed sails we set out. About half an hour later, the wind died right away, so shaking out the reefs and feeling pleased with ourselves, we sailed happily along in the bright sunshine. We anchored for lunch, looked at another spot and then, hoping that we had timed the tides correctly, set off for the pass. Slack water should have been somewhere between five and half past, but by seven o'clock we were still struggling to get through, sailing close-hauled in a dying breeze, having concluded that the stand was at a different time from high water. We wound up the engine, trying it out in earnest for the first time and it pushed us splendidly against the current so that before long we were at anchor in Halfway Cove.

A gloriously sunny day followed a wonderfully calm night and we went ashore to Dunnose Head settlement to visit Marla and Raymond McBeth, who greeted us kindly. We discovered that Marla came from Texas and she was just like my picture of a lady from the southern states: very warm, kind in her comments about people, her strongest exclamation a decorous `Mercy!'. As we settled down to talk, we were surprised at their excellent knowledge of geography, not most people's strong point.

`Oh, but we enjoy looking at maps,' Marla explained in her delightful, slow drawl, `and one day, we hope to get a tad of money together to go travel.'

They asked us about different countries that we had visited and we enjoyed describing our experiences to people who were so genuinely interested. We had collected some yachting magazines together and asked them to pass them on to Kevin in Shallow Harbour, in case we missed him in Stanley. Marla and Raymond were yet another couple that we should have liked to get to know better, but it was their busy season and our time was short so, reluctantly, we took our leave.

Although strong winds were forecast, it was only blowing about a Force 3 and by the time we had beat up to Dunnose Head, the tide had long turned against us. It seemed to take forever to round it and we wondered if we would have time to make Roy Cove, where we hoped to spend the night. However, no other anchorage looked suitable if there was a blow from the northwest, and if we failed to get to Roy Cove, we would have lost another day. Convincing ourselves that the breeze was filling in a little, we pressed on, soon having our beliefs vindicated as the wind picked up to about Force 5. I covered myself in glory (at least in my estimation) when the skipper mistook the entrance and I put him right on it. Roy Cove being a very narrow creek with barely room to anchor, Pete fouled the Luke as he let it go, something that had not happened before, but I managed to hold *Badger* in position while he had a second — and successful — attempt. Once settled, we realised that there was complete shelter, which with the increasing wind, we much appreciated.

Roy Cove settlement nestled against the hillside.

Roy Cove settlement belongs to Susie and Simon Bonner, son of Don and we were looking forward to meeting them. The morning saw us rowing across the creek, pulling the dinghy up on the rocky shore and climbing the steep slope towards the settlement. As we reached the top, we looked across on the most delightful scene. The neat farm buildings, with their brightly-painted red roofs, nestled against a stand of firs and were situated among pretty creeks, and hills where great splashes of yellow gorse glowed in the sunshine, filling the air with the scent of coconut.

The buildings actually represent two settlements, Roy Cove and Pickthorne Farm. Unsure as to which was which and feeling that as we more or less had an introduction to Simon Bonner, we should go to his, we hoped to choose correctly and found that we had. They seemed pleased to see us and had obviously heard about us from Don and Carol. Over coffee and biscuits we talked about their life and were intrigued to hear

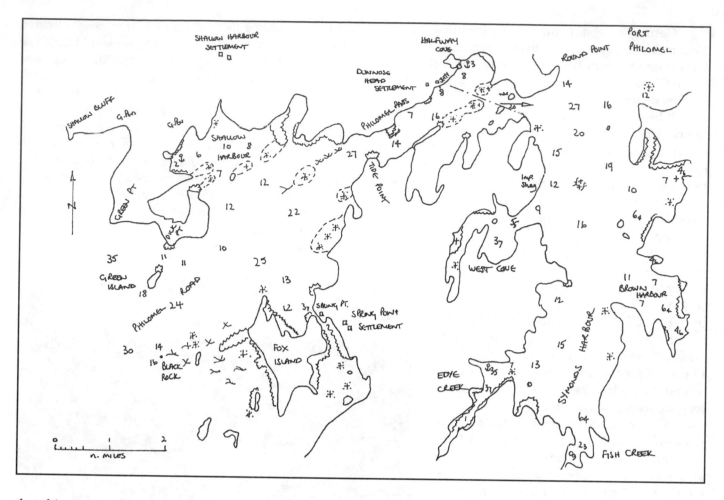

that this was another very small settlement, which nevertheless provided a reasonable standard of living. In fact the Bonners owned quite a lot of land, but a lot of it consisted of islands, which needed good boats if they were to be used properly and neither Susie nor Simon were happy on the water. On the other hand, they confirmed something that we had already heard: on good camp, it paid to run fewer sheep as the better grazing made for finer wool. It also made it perfectly feasible for them to shear their own sheep, although Simon admitted to being a far-from-champion shearer. As we left, Susie suggested that I bring along my washing later.

Like most of the settlements out west, Roy Cove was on camp time, which was one hour before Stanley time. Susie had told me that the generator went on at six o'clock, so at that time I went ashore, taking a mullet that Pete had caught that afternoon. We put my washing in the machine and while it ran through its cycle, I talked with Susie and fussed over an ill lamb in the kitchen, which had been abandoned by its mother and had insufficient wool to keep it warm. Simon came in, most of the day's work completed.

`Just one job left to do,' he said, `we have to feed the hens and geese. Would you like to come?'

It was a beautiful, mild evening as we visited the first hen house.

`Good heavens!' I exclaimed. `What sort of hens are those?'

Simon smiled. `These are Silkies,' he told me. `They're the first ones we've reared. Everyone keeps telling us to diversify, so Susie and I thought we'd try with exotic birds. There's a good market for them, if we get known.'

`But how do you export birds from the Falklands?'

`It's not the hens you send, but the eggs. A lot of the exotics don't make very good mothers — although the Silkies do — so you have to make sure the eggs go under a nice, broody hen who'll look after the chicks properly. We started off with some eggs, which we hatched out and now we're hoping they'll lay.'

The hens were the most charming and quaint birds, with soft, shiny feathers that gave them their name, topknots on their heads and feathery ruffs around their legs.

`I remember seeing these at County Shows,' I commented, `they're really rather amazing, aren't they?'

Simon laughed. `I've got some different ones, too — come and see.'

There were several cabins and in each the hens scratched contentedly in the clean straw, their water clean and feeding troughs immaculate.

`Come and see the geese, Annie,' Susie suggested, and we walked down the green to a little dell where several geese, with swan-like necks and colouring similar to Canada geese, were grazing.

`Oh! Aren't they lovely! What are they?'

`Chinese geese — we like them too.'

We ushered them into their shed for the night and then went back to the house, so that I could pick up my washing.

`By the way,' said Simon as I was leaving, `I heard on the radio that a yacht's on the beach, but didn't catch where.'

`Oh no, how awful! It has to be Larry and Maxine — they're the only other yacht cruising. D'you know if they're all right.'

`I didn't really hear it. I suppose you know them, do you?'

`Yes, they're a couple of Americans. If I dash back now, we should catch the next news. I hope they're OK.'

`I'll take you back on the four-wheel drive,' Susie offered, so she, Katie, their little girl and I climbed on and bounced back to where I had left the dinghy. I scrambled off.

`Will you come round to *Badger* for lunch tomorrow?'

Susie hesitated. `I'm sorry. But really, we don't like boats. I mean your big boat would be all right, but we're a bit frightened in dinghies and things,' she confessed. `You come up and see us again, instead.'

`We'll do that. Thanks for the lift, but I must hurry back!'

I rowed back like a Cambridge Blue, rushing on board and giving a garbled account to Pete, while I switched on the radio, just in time. Sure enough, *Shingebiss II* had dragged her anchor at Port Edgar, but fortunately, the farmers happened to be there on their tractor and managed to pull them off. Apparently, when they started their engine, they discovered gear box trouble and were on the beach before they could get sailing.

`Poor Larry — he was sure the engine was sorted,' Pete commented as he switched the radio off, `but I wonder why they dragged — it's not been blowing that hard.'

`I knew they weren't really listening when we warned them about kelp,' I said. `We told them we'd dragged our Bruce and they needed a fisherman if they were near kelp, but I don't think they believed us.'

`Still, at least there's no real damage done. They got away with it this time.'

`I feel sorry for Maxine, though. First the Drake Passage and now this. And still problems with that damn' engine.'

The wind had picked up to a near gale overnight and after coffee, we went up to the settlement. Having climbed up the side of the creek, we realised how strongly it was blowing, but *Badger* was hardly affected where she lay, tugging at one anchor and then the other. Walking towards the settlement, we were overhauled by Simon in the tractor, who stopped to give us a lift.

`This is a fine machine,' Pete commented, as indeed it was, nearly new and relatively quiet.'

`Yes, it is, isn't it? Daniel — from Pickthorne — and I share it.'

`Really? That's unusual.'

`You're right, it is. I can't understand it. We share quite a few things and help each other out, but most of the campers don't seem to want to co-operate like that. We got a grant for the tractor and so did Daniel, which just about paid for it, but neither of us would have been able to afford one on our own.' He pulled up outside the house. `Go on in — I'll be round in a minute.'

Susie and Katie were busy with lessons, but were happy to stop for a while. The poor little lamb, looking very weak and poorly, died while we were there.

`I don't think these sheep are tough enough for the Falklands,' Simon remarked ruefully, carrying the little body outside, `but the "experts" have been telling us to use them. We're going to get some decent rams, I think, and breed something a bit stronger.'

After staying for an hour or so, we left Susie and Katie to their work. Simon drove us back in the tractor.

`It seems very rough,' he commented, looking concerned, `I'll watch you getting back to make sure

Badger snug at anchor in Roy Cove.

you're OK. Will you come up again this evening, if you're going off tomorrow?'

Remembering they were on camp time, we had an early supper and spent a pleasant couple of hours in their warm kitchen. In all our years of wandering, we have never found it so easy to get to know people as we did in the Falkland Islands and the pleasure that this gave us more than compensated for the worry and physical effort that was so often involved in exploring the archipelago.

Some of the gusts had set our anchors very firmly and when we came to leave the next day, it was a bit tricky ensuring that we got off on the right tack. Susie and Simon were there to see us leave and there was barely room to go about in the narrow creek, but with our reputation to consider, we persevered and succeeded with no real problems. It was good practice.

With a fresh breeze and a forecast of strong westerly winds, we regretfully decided against Chartres, but consoled ourselves with exploring Crooked Inlet. This was great fun, although when we got underway after anchoring for lunch, we put ourselves aground. We got off without too much difficulty, but had our share of problems beating out. It was very tricky, with strong, fluky winds and in the end we were defeated and had to resort to the Ducati.

Whaler Bay sounded a romantic spot, but it was quite a long sail there because the wind shifted, forcing us to beat. It was worth the effort, for it was a pretty spot and we anchored in good time to cook supper.

It was past the middle of November and still we had not visited the Jason Islands. A bright and breezy morning seemed to offer a good opportunity, but after working out the tides, we found that it was not a particularly sound scheme as they were at springs, which

Pete and the unruffled young elephant seal on Little Bense Island.

sounded unpleasantly exciting around the Jasons. Instead, we sailed to the Bense Islands, which were part of Roy Cove and sounded very attractive. After clearing the bottom of Rabbit Island, where a nasty tidal jobble and islands to leeward, shaped exactly like fangs, made it somewhat hairy, we came to anchor in a charming spot between the two islands.

So inviting was it ashore, that I put together a barbecue and as we sat eating our veggie-burgers and sipping our beer, we admired our surroundings. It was incredibly pretty with white sandy beaches and lots of lovely tussac about.

`Simon and Susie don't need these islands any more, you know, Pete. I thought Blind Island was lovely, but these are just marvellous. Let's buy them.'

`Why not? They really are special, aren't they. It's a good anchorage and we could do up the shanty. And we could be sure that no-one would ever put sheep or cattle on them again.'

`Could we afford them, d'you think?'

`I suppose we probably could, really. Though it would take a big chunk from the money we use to reinvest every year.'

I sighed. `It'd be nice, all the same.'

After lunch, we went across to Little Bense, crossing a tidal causeway between the two islands. We had seen some sea lions, as we sailed in and now counted no fewer than forty-eight, lying on the white sand, grunting, scratching and dozing in the sunshine. Thinking that we might be cut off by the tide, we did not linger, but could have stayed a lot longer because the causeway was still uncovered when we went back aboard a considerable while later. We returned to the dinghy, collecting driftwood, which Pete sawed up while I wandered round Bense Island. To my surprise, there was a multitude of rabbits, not your usual brown bunny, but black, grey, brown and pied, which must have bred from some domestic ones; I wondered how they had ended up on the island. When Pete finished sawing up wood, we walked to the old shanty which was, as Simon suspected, in a very poor state of repair. Noticing a sea lion on the shingle beach and wanting to take a photograph of the anchorage, I suggested to Pete that he walk towards it.

`The photo will be better with a figure in it, and if the sea lion sees you, it'll probably sit up and add a bit more interest.'

But it refused to co-operate, totally ignoring Pete, who was by now almost on top of it. Then he waved vigorously at me, obviously wanting me to join him and as I approached, I realised that it was a young sea elephant, placid and lazy as most of its species. It did deign to raise its head and look at us, and we were thrilled to have seen it. Walking along the beach, we saw birds galore; kelp geese, Magellanic and black oyster catchers and some jackasses, back from sea, once more.

'There are no tussac birds or Cobb's wren, Pete.' I commented. 'I'm afraid there must be rats. What a shame. Perhaps we won't buy the islands, after all!'

'I think we should have a go at Weddell, today,' Pete announced, shaking me awake at six o'clock. 'It'll be a beat all the way, but it's a lovely, sunny morning, with a nice breeze.'

Reluctantly I crawled out of bed, but had to admit that he was right. It was a perfect day. We sailed along and after breakfast, I did some of my chores. The wind shifted from time to time, and we tacked accordingly. Pete came below to look at the chart.

'You know, Annie, the wind seems to have settled down and I think we could probably lay up to the Jasons.'

'But I thought we'd decided not to go on spring tides.'

'They're probably not as bad as they sound and we can't lose anything by trying. Come neap tides, the weather might be too bad to go there.'

'OK then. You've talked me into it.'

I was more reluctant than I sounded, my fears having been aroused by reading Ewen Southby-Tailyour's notes on the islands. They had not been surveyed since the middle of the last century and Ewen advised waiting 'until the wind and tides are suitable', which I read as meaning neap tides. Then he went on to say: 'The worst part of the passage is the comparative short section ... to South Jason past the notorious Gibraltar Reef', which is the route we were taking, adding 'The exact positions of some of the islands are not as charted. The passage between North Fur Island and the rocks to the north-west (Seal Rocks), for instance, is charted as being approximately 4 cables where it is nearer 9 cables. North Fur Island is further east than charted, and the Gibraltar Reef extends to at least 9.5 [miles] from Cape Terrible.

'There are a number of areas where the tide overfalls and rips may be dangerous to a yacht. The Gibraltar Reef, across which the tides have been reported to run at up to 15 knots, extends a possible two miles further than charted. It was reported to me that many wrecks exist on the reef, and once the full flood is seen crossing it it is easy to see why.' And as if that was not enough, he cheerfully points out that 'There are no safe havens or bolt holes along the Jason Islands' coastline.' It made me a little apprehensive.

The breeze started dying away after lunch and we felt the effect of the tides.

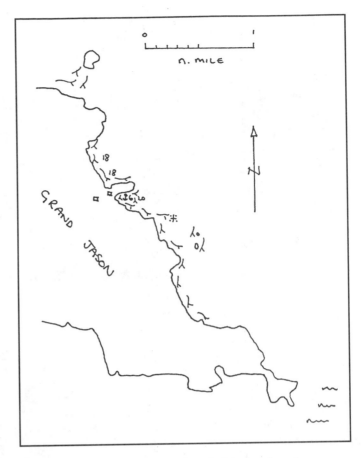

'Well, I suppose we fitted this engine for something,' Pete said reluctantly. 'At this rate, I'm not sure that we'll clear Gibraltar Reef and South Jason, so we'd better start it.'

Willing as ever, the motor sprang into life and although a little breeze allowed us to sail for a while, after tea we started the engine again because the wind had once more died away and we were worried about missing our tide.

Rounding the southeast end of Grand Jason at about half past six, we could switch off the engine again and a light, uncertain breeze came and went as we sailed along the coast with the last of the tide. Only one anchorage was mentioned in *Falkland Island Shores*, but as we approached it, there seemed to be an awful lot of kelp. Even right at the edge of the weed we had over sixty feet and in desperation, we went into it for a short way, but found deep water even horribly close to the shore, still in very thick kelp. We both felt appallingly disappointed, having actually succeeded in getting to the islands, only to find that there was nowhere to anchor. Determined not to give in so easily, we sailed back along the shore a little way finding a very small cove to the southeast of the usual anchorage.

'What d'you think, Annie. Shall we give it a try?'

'Well, we can't lose anything,' and so we went forward. The wind was on the nose and the kelp was

The snug but kelp-filled anchorage at Grand Jason.

*Pete (just visible left of center) looks at the gentoo colony, while **Badger** rests in the background.*

`But surely we can go ashore!'

`Too right! Come on, let's get the dinghy over.'

With some difficulty, we found a landing place, and on a nearby ledge, a rock shag gazed at us with intense curiosity. Astonishingly, considering their remoteness and difficulty of access, the Jasons were once actively farmed. The boats that carried men — and sheep — to and fro did not have any engines and one can only wonder at the ability and endurance of those farmhands-turned-sailors. When the tussac was eaten out, the islands

too thick to tack through, so we dropped the sails, resorting to motor. I called off the depths.

`Ten metres . . . nine . . . eight . . . seven . . . six and a half . . . '

Pete signalled for me to stop and started lowering the anchor over the bow. Then he looked back at me and called something, but I could not hear him over the noise of the engine, so pointed at it and shrugged. He nodded in comprehension and continued to lower the anchor, then signalled to me to stop the motor.

Coming back to the cockpit, Pete asked, `Did you notice the depth when I dropped the hook?'

`Yes, it was six metres — twenty feet. What were you trying to tell me?'

`It didn't really matter, it was just if we had gone a few feet further forward, we could have anchored in a patch of sand and with luck, the anchor would have come up clean.'

`What do you think of this as an anchorage?'

`It's a really snug little spot and probably secure in anything from the west, although it might be affected by katabatics. It seems protected from the north, too.'

`Well that's what they're forecasting. Do you want to stay?'

`I'd love to, but I think it's a bit of a risk. They're talking of gale force winds and that might send down a big swell. There's a chance we might be trapped — by waves, if nothing else.'

were abandoned and had not seen sheep for years; now they are a nature reserve. The old shearing shed still stood, in surprisingly good condition and there was a shanty, too, but this looked as though it was about to fall down. In the wool shed were some cages marked `Birdland' and the shanty had been visited by *HMS Bedford*, whose crew had been unable to leave without recording the names of their ship and of the football and rugby clubs they supported. A 1967 calendar hung on one wall and the pantry still contained a few tins and some pots and pans, but the roof was rotting and thrushes had got in, so it was a bit of a mess.

The island did not feel lonely, in spite of the empty buildings and its isolation because there was so much wildlife. We saw upland geese with well-advanced goslings, tussac birds abounded and Magellanic penguins were everywhere, much tamer than usual, letting us approach to within a couple of feet before they popped down their holes, instantly peeping out again to examine these strange beings. We walked over to a gentoo rookery, the birds sitting on very elegant pebble nests, much more elaborate than the ones we had seen before. We took several photos, I suppose to prove that we had actually got there and been ashore, but it did seem rather a `tick'. Even our brief visit was quite unforgettable though, because the island was such a magical place.

Walking back, we had to detour round a kelp goose, spread over her eggs in the grass and then found ourselves unintentionally herding a family of upland geese who insisted on heading directly towards the dinghy. They made a lot of noise about it and another kelp goose came down to see what all the fuss was about. Everything was so unafraid. The rock shag, was still there, incredibly tame and peering at me with as much interest as I looked at him. We could have stayed forever, but with the bad forecast, it seemed wiser to leave.

There was no room to turn around in the harbour, so we started the engine, Pete got the anchor, I put her in astern and then, as the bow fell off, pulled up a little foresail. It went very well. The wind was light and fluky and as we drifted back down the coast, we had a drink to celebrate our landing. Off the end of Grand Jason, there were the most tremendous tide rips and overfalls, which made me wonder just what it would be like in any wind. At last we got through it, turned our bows towards New Island and settled down to watches.

The winds stayed very light overnight, but picked up a little in the morning and after an uneventful sail, that had us regretting our maybe overhasty departure from Grand Jason, we anchored in North Harbour at about ten o'clock. Although the wind picked up in the afternoon, it never got above Force 5 and we could probably have stayed another day. On the other hand, I would have been extremely worried and should have hated to have gone through those overfalls in much breeze. `Prudence', as the Sage says,

`quenches that ardour of enterprise by which everything is done that can claim praise or admiration, and represses that generous temerity which often fails and often succeeds.' We consoled ourselves with the recollection that not only had we achieved our aim, we had `discovered' a new harbour.

After a good night's sleep, we woke up to a bright and breezy day, which turned to rain by mid morning. It was so unappealing that we postponed our departure for South Harbour and for once our prudence was vindicated, for by lunchtime it had really started blowing and Pete put out the CQR, in case. The wind increased to a strong gale, with impressive woollies running across the anchorage, but the glass was going up like a rocket, so the blow did not last long, By the time we turned in, the stars were out and it was relatively calm.

In the morning, Pete went up the foremast to put up a new windsock and also made a new burgee stick; a Johnny rook had landed on it, breaking it, when we arrived at North Harbour. Both anchor cables were fouled with kelp, but at last we got underway, having a wonderful sail in light breezes and bright sunshine.

We were pleased to find that Ian was on the island, although with it being term time, he was on his own. He greeted us kindly, giving us carte blanche to walk around and asking us to join him for a cup of tea later. The skuas were not yet nesting, so we had a pleasant walk to the fur seal colony. They were a delight to watch, playing in the water, chasing one another about and slithering through the fronds of kelp with effortless grace. We had brought a picnic and sitting in the sunshine on the rocks above, could watch them in comfort while we ate our

The rock shag looks back with curiosity.

Grand Jason Island.

Above: Blue-eyed shag and black-browed albatross nest side by side on New Island.

Right: the settlement at New Island.

It was time to move on and despite the forecast, we reckoned it looked set fine, so after breakfast, we went to say goodbye to Ian, who courteously thanked Pete for his help.

It was almost calm when we sailed out, but once clear of the harbour, there was a little more wind and we were pleased to see that Pete had timed his tides for the Grey Channel correctly. The intention was to visit Split Creek on Beaver Island, do a bit of a survey, anchor there and maybe do some fishing. The

lunch. Eventually we tore ourselves away and went to see the rockhoppers, mollyhawks and shags, enjoying the sublime views, one of the qualities that made New Island our favourite. Back at the settlement, we stayed a while with Ian, talking about wildlife and his conservation work.

In the morning, Pete went to help Ian pull out old fence posts and as I could do nothing to assist, I went off to the gentoo colony, which we had missed on our last visit, seeing cottontails everywhere as I passed the old whaling station. The gentoos were very quiet, letting me approach quite closely and I watched one of them, who should probably have been at sea, picking up stones and adding them to its mate's nest. The other birds did not reckon much to its activities.

When I got back, Pete was loading water containers into the dinghy.

`Hello! Ian gave us some water, as you can see and he's asked us to join him for some soup for lunch.'

`How kind! That sounds good.'

The soup and home-made bread were delicious and after we had eaten, Ian offered me a bath, which luxury I gladly accepted, soaking in the hot water while Ian and Pete went and pulled more posts.

`Will you come and have supper with us tonight,' I asked Ian, when they came back to the house.

`That would be nice, but I'll have to refuse, I'm afraid. I can't really bend my knees and I suspect that I couldn't even get into your dinghy, let alone on to the boat.'

We were disappointed; quite apart from the fact that it would have been gratifying to be able to repay his hospitality, we enjoyed his company and conversation.

bottom end of the creek, where we had hoped to anchor, proved too shallow, so we tried anchoring at another spot, which was also unsatisfactory.

`Let's try off Split Island,' Pete suggested, and this we did, counting no fewer than seventeen sea lions sunning themselves there. There was no point fishing here, so after making notes on our interesting and somewhat unexpected findings, we sailed off for Fish Creek. In the light breeze, we progressed in a leisurely fashion down towards Governor Channel and decided to try the pass between Green and Governor Islands. It was nearly slack water, but while the thick kelp hindered progress, it marked any dangers and we succeeded in barging through and could even tack when we had to.

The following morning, it was calm first thing and we missed our tide through Stick-in-the-Mud, so went again through Green Island passage, finding that with the tide running, the kelp had all but disappeared, swept under by the current. Although light, it was a leading wind and we sailed out without undue difficulty.

Our plan to visit Albermarle was foiled by the wind being too light, so I suggested that we should pay a visit to Bird Island. After checking the chart, Pete reckoned that in the present conditions, it was worth the risk even though we really had no information beyond the small-scale chart. As we approached, we

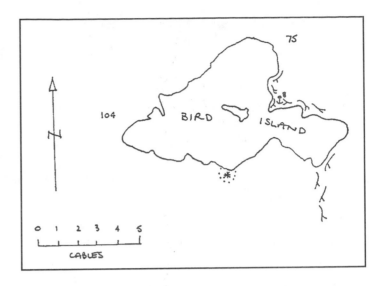

noticed a little beach and sailed towards that, but with the fluky wind and thick kelp, we needed the engine to get in. A raft of rockhoppers porpoised away as we drew near and finding thirty feet, we dropped the anchor and rowed ashore. It was not easy to locate a landing place, but it was more than worth the effort. The hillside was covered in black-browed mollyhawks and rockhoppers sitting on their nests, who were so completely unafraid that they did not move, even when we had to brush right past, the mollyhawks merely leaning away from us, while the rockies glared at us from their little red eyes. They were packed so closely that it was difficult to thread our way among them, so soon we simply settled ourselves comfortably and observed them until we had to leave.

It took us some time to extricate ourselves from the kelp and when we left the island, the wind had shifted to the southeast, right on the nose for our intended anchorage at Sweeney Creek, but a favourable tide made our progress much less slow than we had envisaged. We anchored with plenty of time to have a drink before dinner, to celebrate our visit to wonderful Bird Island.

It had been a poor forecast and for once it was correct, the wind reaching the predicted Force 6 by the time we got up. Finding ourselves in a comfortable harbour, we had a lay day, remarking that such enforced stops were far less frequent than they had been the previous year. Indeed, had we really felt we ought to, we could have pressed on, but as well as being windy it was bitterly cold.

Although we had no difficulties leaving the creek the following day, as we drew abreast Cross Island, I could see the spray going right up the cliffs and even breaking over. Pete was making breakfast and I called to him that it looked horrid, but he told me that it would be all right. In the narrows, the lop was really tremendous and I found it extremely nerve-racking.

Pete looked out again. `Don't worry, we'll be OK.'

`God, Pete,' I lamented, `I hate this', but I stuck grimly to the helm, while he passed me my favourite fried-egg sandwiches, which were as dust and ashes. By the time my first cup of coffee was drunk, the passage perilous was

*Below: **Badger** sits at anchor off Bird Island while Annie goes bird-watching. Bottom: Black-browed mollyhawks (albatross) guard their nests.*

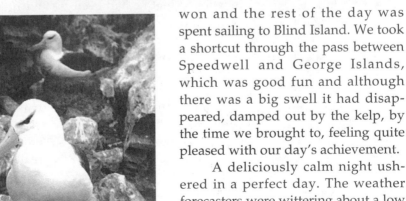

won and the rest of the day was spent sailing to Blind Island. We took a shortcut through the pass between Speedwell and George Islands, which was good fun and although there was a big swell it had disappeared, damped out by the kelp, by the time we brought to, feeling quite pleased with our day's achievement.

A deliciously calm night ushered in a perfect day. The weather forecasters were wittering about a low coming in, but any fool could see that it was set for near calms for the day, despite which we managed to sail about thirty-five miles, taking full advantage of any fair breeze. Pete occupied himself in the afternoon with fitting a brown-stick to the self-steering. This device, allows one to disconnect the vane and move the trim tab manually but remotely, in order to alter course temporarily, in order, for example, to avoid a floating hazard. Upon letting it go, the self-steering resets itself and the vessel resumes her course. We both had a play with it and I was surprised how effective it was.

There was just enough breeze to force a passage through Bleaker Jump and, deciding to anchor up in Adventure Harbour, making use of our own notes, we brought to off Urchin Island where we spent a tranquil night.

We wanted to pay one last visit to Lively Island before we left the Falklands, so left early determined to keep going until we got there. In spite of having to beat nearly all the way we saved our daylight into Shallow Harbour, but it was too late to go visiting.

In the morning, we rowed ashore where Elly greeted us with open arms.

`We saw you out there! Come in, come in. We're just having smoko!'

`How's your winter been?'

`Oh, not too bad, but my pet cow had to be put down — she fell off one of the clay cliffs. It was so sad, she'd been there a while when we found her and she'd broken her leg and must have been in pain. Alec had to shoot her and she was such a nice little thing.'

Poor Elly had tears in her eyes as she remembered. I quickly changed the subject.

`Have your geese come back?'

`Oh yes,' she brightened up. `They've quite taken over the green again!'

There was a stranger in the living room, who was introduced to us as Howie Peck, an old friend who had come for a few days to work on their various machines. As we got talking, Howie mentioned that he had been in South Georgia as engineer and had met Tilman.

`Are you the man who helped him do some repairs?' asked Pete, in something like awe.

`I did give him a hand with one or two things, yes.'

`He mentions you in one of his books.' Howie looked pleased. `What did you think of him?'

`I liked him. He seemed to know what he was talking about — though not much about engines!'

Our conversation was interrupted by the entrance of another two men. In an effort to improve the quality of the sheep in the Falklands, a stud flock had been set up and when a place for a flock of young rams was required, Alec had offered to look after them. From the start, he had been less than impressed with their condition and over the winter a lot of them had died. The two men were there to take blood samples, photograph and shear them and then kill four of them so that they

could have autopsies and try to find out what was wrong. A little later Alec came in with Ian, the vet and Jay who was going to do the shearing. It was a full house, but when they had gone their separate ways, we had time to chat with Elly.

Later in the afternoon, we went into the wool shed to see what was going on. Elly had said that the rams were small and she was right. Although a year older, they were not much bigger than her pet lambs. Alec had had a lot of work and worry with these sheep and in payment, he was to have their fleeces when they were shorn, but these sorry little rams were only giving about three pounds of wool.

`They look a bit small,' I commented to Robert, one of the stud flock people.

`They've had a hard winter', he replied.

Knowing that they had been given extra food, which is more than Alec's own sheep received, I was puzzled as to why they should have deteriorated while the Lively sheep lived up to their names.

We had afternoon smoko with Howie and Elly.

`I'd have invited you for supper,' she apologised, `but there are too many in the house as it is. Everyone's leaving tomorrow — well, not Howie — so you must come tomorrow.'

`We'd love to Elly. You must be feeling overrun at the moment. Is there anything I can do to help?'

`Yes, you could finish up that cake I've cut up!' Elly retorted, smiling at us both.

The first of December came in wet and windy. For the past five days, the weathermen had been promising winds from northwest, but it was still northeast which made our berth a bit bouncy and today it had picked up again so that we could not get ashore.

We had been looking forward to our evening with Alec and Elly and although it was still quite rough, we girded up our loins and rowed to the beach next to the pier.

Elly met us in the porch.

`I wasn't expecting you to come, it's so wild out there. I didn't make a hot meal, I'm afraid. I was sure you'd stay on board.'

`It doesn't matter. But we wanted to see you. We have to leave in a couple of weeks and although we'd really love to stay longer, we must get back to Stanley soon to get ready.'

`Well come on in. Howie and Alec are still outside, but they'll soon be here.'

We took off our oilskins and boots and followed her indoors, settling ourselves in the cosy living room that felt almost like home.

`You've got rid of the stud people, then?'

`Yes, they left this morning, but would you believe it — they sheared all those little rams!'

`What — in weather like this and pouring rain?'

Strange to say, it is not the snow that is a danger to newly shorn sheep, but rain. It soaks through the little bit of wool that is left on them in a very short time and a strong wind makes it even worse. Within a few days of shearing, the natural grease starts to protect them again.

`Alec's really upset about it. He's sure some of them will die if they go out.'

Alec came in a few minutes later with Howie.

`How's it going?'

`I can't believe it. Those so-called "experts" have told me I've got to put those poor little beggars out. Do you know what they're forecasting for windchill? Ninety-three! And in the rain, too. I'm going to phone up Sea Lion Island and see if they've changed their minds. I'll ask them if I can bring them in for the night.'

He made the call and, from our end, sounded less than pleased. At last he slammed the 'phone down and turned round to us.

`They insist that I leave them out. I tell you, if they all survive the night, I'm a Dutchman.'

Poor Alec felt very bad about it; it went against the grain to do something that he felt was wrong.

`Come on!' he said, `we'll forget about them for the moment. I've done my best. Now who's for a beer'

We had a lovely evening and although Elly apologised for the meal, we dined royally on soup and cold mutton, with heaps of potatoes and tomatoes and cake for anyone who still had room. Elly and Alec were pleased that Falklands Conservation were going to buy up their islands in Lively Sound and unlike several of the Islanders to whom we spoke later, who regretted the loss of good grazing, were quite happy that they would be used as wildlife reserves. We stayed late, it was midnight our time by the time we left and poor Elly had to get up at five o'clock.

With the thought of our preparations for departure, we reluctantly concluded that we had to leave and rowed ashore to see Elly and Alec one last time.

`Are you sure you won't stay longer?' Elly asked.

`We'd love to, but we must get away. You know how short the summers are and we've set our hearts on going to South Georgia.'

`And you're not coming back for the winter? You'd be very welcome to stay here, you know.'

`Thank you. But we plan to go on to South Africa. But we'll be back one day. And in the meantime, we'll keep in touch.'

`Well, at least you managed a couple of days — it's a shame the weather's been so bad. Before you go, come and get some rhubarb.'

Dinner with friends on Lively Island.
Left to right: Pete, Alec, Elly, Howie.

So Elly led us off into the garden, picking a huge pile of rhubarb and several large sprigs of mint, which I later dried. We went back in to wait for Alec, who was away to the airport to fetch the vet. Before long, they breezed into the living room.

`How are the rams, Alec?'

`Three of them died last night, but Ian's going to give glucose injections to the rest — they might just pull round then. I told them not to put them out and we'll be lucky if more of them don't die, yet,' he added angrily.

`Aye, it's no' good weather for the wee beasts to be out, Alec. Don't be asking yon people what to do. If it carries on drizzling and raw like this, let's fetch them in under cover until it improves.'

`Anyway,' Alec said, the twinkle returning to his eye, `with having to kill those four yesterday, we've no shortage of mutton. You may as well take one with you. And make sure you enjoy it,' he added, wickedly. `Those rams have been fetching a hundred pounds a piece!'

It was time to make our good-byes and they were not easy; Elly was in tears and I was chewing hard on my lower lip. They loaded us with bags containing cream and milk, the rhubarb and mint, the mutton and a pile of empty jars, which turned out to include half a dozen packets of soup and a jar of chutney. I gave Alec the big jar of pickled fish I had made for him, and his eyes lit up. Howie stopped us from getting too maudlin, wanting to take our photographs with his new camera and making us laugh as he tried to find out which button to press so that it would have `Season's Greetings' written across it.

We rowed back aboard and as they were standing to watch us leave, got underway immediately, waving until they were out of sight. I felt really sad at the thought that we might never see them again.

Leaving Lively Island. Photo by Howie Peck.

`We'll have to come back sometime, Pete.'

`And next time, we'll keep sailing in the winter. It's often less windy and people have more time, so we're not interfering with their work.'

We were able to lay our course most of the way, but it was a miserable day, with a thin, cold rain falling all the time. A large swell crashed against the shore and entering Pleasant Harbour was hair-raising, with great breakers over the rocks and foam everywhere. It seemed to get colder and colder as we sailed along and we were heartily glad to get in, although the anchorage did not look anywhere near as interesting as it had on the chart. As we had cream and mutton, I cooked steak *au poivre vert* for dinner and we had some wine with it, all of which helped to cheer us up.

We were underway before six o'clock the next morning, in the hope of reaching Stanley. The winds were light and as we came out of Pleasant Harbour, we were confronted with the sight of huge breakers once more, the sea covered with acres of foam, which we later discovered were a form of algae. There was enough wind to get through and once clear, we had breakfast: porridge, made with fresh milk and topped with cream.

With the wind so light, I bottled most of Elly's rhubarb and despite leaving some back for stewing and some more for jam, ran out of preserving jars, so used some of the jam jars that she had given me.

The swell was enormous and in spite of a light breeze, the sails had a job to stay asleep, but we had the tide with us and managed surprisingly well. As we came into Port William, we had the wind and swell behind us at last and were now certain of getting in before dark. The Billy Rock was showing in the bottom of the swells, looking very sinister and I felt a chill as I thought of all the ships it had claimed. The wind was dying away all the time and we came in through the narrows after a splendid tea of scones, Rolo's raspberry

jam and Elly's cream. Sailing more and more slowly down the harbour, we eventually resorted to engine and brought to by the Government Dock, once more. Pete sorted out all the lines while I started supper.

`Who were you talking to on the dock?' I asked as he came back below.

`They're a couple of chaps from a Forces group who are going out to Smith Island, to have a go at climbing the mountain.'

`Good for them. How are they getting there?'

`They're going down in a ship and are to be landed by helicopter.'

`*Helicopter*! Why don't they just fly straight up to the top. I thought the whole point was that the landing and so on is as difficult as the climb. Tilman wouldn't have approved.'

Pete laughed. `I said that, too and the bloke did look a bit embarrassed about it.'

`Well, I hope they don't make it,' I declared uncharitably. And I am pleased to say that they did not, but that several years later an amateur expedition climbed Mount Foster for the first time, from a yacht, in a truly sporting manner that Tilman would have appreciated.

After supper we went up to Carl and Dianne's, who made us welcome as ever and it was late before we were home.

Pete had just started breakfast when he heard a hail ashore. Craig had come to see if we wanted to go with him to the ceremony at Port Louis, to commemorate moving the capital to Stanley.

`We'll be with you in ten minutes,' Pete called. We gulped down a glass of orange juice and gobbled a slice of bread and marmalade, scrambled into jackets and went ashore. To our delight, Tim Carr of *Curlew* fame was there. When they had lived in the Falklands,

Arriving at Stanley Harbour for the last time. Photo by Howie Peck.

Tim had restored the Whalebone Arch near the Cathedral and was now on a visit in order to maintain it. Dianne from the IMAX film company was also in Craig's Rover and we were a jolly crew as we drove through the wonderful Falklands landscape.

A tremendous number of people had gathered at Port Louis, to watch the ceremony and many of them were going to ride back to Stanley across country, either on horseback or by four-wheel drive. The ceremony of lowering the flag from the newly erected flagpole (complete with cannon

who then raised it again, while the Governor and a visiting Royal Engineers colonel, both in full regalia, saluted and the bugler bugled. It was all very charming.

Having met Larry, Maxine and Gary, we suggested that they come back aboard for a cream tea and warm up by the fire before starting their long walk back to FIPAS.

alongside) was very correctly done with a bugler accompanying. Then everyone set off on the ride and drive and having exchanged pleasantries with the Governor, Don Bonner and Ian Bury, we followed Craig and Tim to the manager's house, Di itching to see inside the old building. Mike and Sue Morrison invited us in making us very welcome with coffee and wads, in spite of having already been inundated by visitors. When we left, they found a camera, my sweater, a pair of shoes and Craig's bag all left behind!

Craig dropped us off just in time for lunch and in the afternoon, we went to Government House to observe the flag raising ceremony. We had arrived far too early, but Don Bonner saw us and invited us in to his house. We were talking about the sail round, the following weekend and Don asked if he could sail with us. Needless to say, we were delighted to be able to take him.

The first Rovers were arriving, so we wandered round to the lawn standing for quite a long time in a rather cool breeze until the horsemen arrived. The flag was handed to the granddaughter of young Biggs, who first raised the flag in Stanley, a hundred and fifty years previously and she passed it to her great-grandson,

The ceremonies to commemorate moving the capital from Port Louis to Stanley.

I spent some time the next day making Christmas cards and then boned a leg of mutton to pot-roast for the evening; Tim and Craig were coming for dinner. We enjoyed the evening, fascinated by Tim's accounts of their adventures in the Antarctic and their life in South Georgia. I was even beginning to look forward to seeing it all, especially as Tim was so understated as to make it all sound quite straightforward. I knew better, of course. Anyone who sails an engineless, wooden gaff cutter in those places, for so long, without accident has to be an incomparable seaman, but it was reassuring all the same. Craig had brought two good bottles of wine and in combination with the food, warm cabin and, I suspect, the `boaty' conversation, they seemed to make him sleepy because he kept nodding off, but I felt very pleased that he felt sufficiently at home to do so.

We collected our mail and some new sailcloth that we had ordered from the UK. We did not have time to make the sails now, but at least if our ten-year old ones proved inadequate, we could either repair or replace them. Then of course, there was the shopping to do, which occupied a fair bit of our time; once it was on board, we then had to stow it all away. The lockers were bursting by the time we left because we had to be completely self-sufficient from the middle of December until we arrived in South Africa, probably some time in April. There are no supermarkets in the Antarctic.

We were being very lucky with the weather, the light winds continuing day after day. Our berth by the Government Dock was infinitely more convenient than *Curlew's* anchorage and we had put out a second anchor, so that when the wind shifted to the north, we could lie more head to wind.

Lugging back thirty-six kilos of potatoes, and eighteen each of carrots and onions, one day, we were more than pleased when Don Bonner offered to take them back for us in his Rover.

`That was great, Don. Thanks a lot. Will you come and have a cup of coffee?'

`I won't, thanks, I've got to get home to cook lunch for the wife and daughter.'

We filled up with paraffin and coal.

Dianne, `Dimax' as we called her, to save confusion, came one afternoon, curious to look over the boat. She had kindly brought us some cakes, so we invited her to come and eat them and have a cup of tea.

`You're going on this sail round, aren't you?' she asked us.

`We certainly are, if the weather's OK; we're looking forward to it. Apparently there's a barbecue afterwards, so it should be a good party.'

`You don't have a spare bed, do you?'

`Would you like to come? You'd be very welcome. Don Bonner's joining us, but you can have the other settee if you don't mind. Would you be able to get hold of a sleeping bag, do you think? I never thought to ask Don and we only have the one.'

`I'm sure I could.'

We were pleased that she had asked; the more the merrier.

I was peeling all the brown skins off the onions when another voice hailed us and looking out, I saw Craig.

`I'm in desperate need of recuperation and a cup of tea!' so Pete went and brought him off.

I had been making jam and gave him a jar.

`That marmalade you gave me was absolutely delicious,' he said `and I've brought the empty jar back for you.'

I laughed. `Is that a subtle hint?' and found him another full jar. Craig was somebody else whose company we were going to miss.

Carl, Dianne and the girls were going to join Larry and Maxine, for the sail round and like us, they were looking forward to it. We had of course, asked them if they wanted to come with us, but Larry and Maxine had got in first, and as *Shingebiss II*'s design had many similarities to *Pale Maiden*, Carl and Dianne were interested to examine it more closely and see how it worked under way. An evening that they spent on *Badger* was devoted to the endlessly fascinating topic of fitting out boats.

When Ali and Andrèz came to dinner, he was beaming from ear to ear because the Governor was to join *Alpha Carinae* for the sail round. They brought a bottle of *Pisco* with them, a sort of Chilean brandy which we had never had before. We tried it with pineapple juice and even Ali, who normally never drank, had some. We ended up having a riotous evening, demolishing most of the pisco and a fair amount of wine. Ali and I were discussing dinghy names.

`You know what you must call yours,' I said.

`No, what's that?'

`Cream cake.'

`Why on earth would we call her that?'

`'Cos your boat's called "Have a cream cake"!' At which we both erupted into gales of laughter to the bemusement of our menfolk. With tears rolling down our cheeks, we explained the joke. At the time we thought it killingly funny, which just shows what alcohol can do!

On Battle Day, the eighth of December, we went to watch the wreath-laying ceremony at the Battle of the Falklands memorial and the Beating of the Retreat. The weather could not have been better for either. When we heard the band of the Royal Marines, we went ashore and a fine sight they were too. We walked on ahead and found ourselves a good site to watch them marching along Ross Road, before walking on to watch the ceremony, which was conducted by Canon Stephen Palmer, a couple of Forces chaplains and the Catholic priest, who all said their bit. The Governor was there in full fig, chauffeured in the old London taxi by Don Bonner, out of retirement for the day and as pleased as punch. C-BFFI (pronounced Sea Biffy and the commander of the British force in the Falklands) was also there along with the top army and navy brass inspecting the troops. Then there was a fly past, with two wonderful Hercules accompanied by three jet fighters, who came back somewhat more noisily and climbed into the sun. The best was a RN *Lynx* helicopter, which came past with a huge white ensign. It was all good fun, full of pageantry and enough to make a jingoist out of anyone!

When we gathered on the playing fields in front of the school to watch the beating of the retreat, it was still beautifully sunny. The Royal Marines put on an excellent show, playing such patriotic `come-all-yez' as *Rule Britannia*, *Land of Hope and Glory* and, of course *A Life on the Ocean Waves*. Walking back, we stopped to pass the time of day with Canon Palmer, a huge man whose voice beguiled me when he introduced his classical music programme on a Sunday night.

`How did you like the Royal Machines?' he asked and indeed, their co-ordination had been so perfect as to seem almost mechanical.

As we walked back to *Badger*, Pete said, `I saw Craig, earlier and asked him to come for a drink, but I think you ought to offer him dinner.'

`Why's that?'

`He reckons he has no food in the house!' Pete laughed, so we fed him on hot-pot and in return, he offered to drive us back to his house to do the laundry and have baths; a perfectly satisfactory arrangement for all parties. As we were leaving, we confirmed our arrangements for meeting Craig on Sunday; he was busy on the Saturday, but was to join us for the sail back to Stanley, driving round to Port Louis with the Governor.

The next day I went to see the quack once again and to my relief, he did not suggest an injection, but instead gave me some pills to take, which I suppose did some good.

Saturday morning saw us up bright and early, a prudent move because it took quite a while to get in the anchors. With the wind in the west, we were happy just to hang off the Dock, ready for a quick getaway. Don turned up with a suitcase, survival suit, camera, flash, radio receiver and binoculars, along with a bottle of rum for the ship, a real kindness from a non-drinker. He seemed tickled to death to be along and delighted with *Badger*. Don has his own boat, a lovely little wooden yacht that Tim and Pauline had helped him restore, but she was out of commission and it would have been a shame for him to

have missed out. Dimax came along ten minutes later with little more than her shoulder bag and we set off almost immediately. The weather was kind, for which I was profoundly grateful and we had a lovely sail out of the harbour and down Port William, with the rare experience of being able to catch the odd glimpse of sails in the distance. Don was a great raconteur and kept us entertained with his wonderful tales of days in Government House, as well as giving us a first-hand account of the defence of that building during the opening hours of the Conflict, where he and Rex Hunt sheltered under a desk as the bullets whistled overhead.

After lunch, both Di and Don had a snooze and by the time they reappeared, the wind had become pretty fresh and we had quite a hard beat up Berkeley Sound, which they both seemed really to enjoy. We were catching up with Andrèz, but he resorted to motor, confiding later that he felt he ought to get in as his Mum, Maud, was not feeling too chipper. It was blowing about Force 6 by the time we came up with the other boats, who had anchored of Port Louis and not at the head of the bay as had originally been suggested. It looked rather exposed at the edge of the fleet, so we beat in among the other yachts and closer inshore found pretty flat water and a little less wind, so dropped the hook there.

An afternoon sail with Di and Don.

There had been talk of a barbecue, but as nothing seemed to be happening, I made a dish of spaghetti, which we washed down with a bottle of wine, courtesy of Dimax. Larry and Maxine had asked us to call round, so we rowed over and joined them in a glass or two.

`I see that someone has lit a bonfire on the beach, after all,' I observed, looking out. We really ought to go and join them.'

`Oh heck, Annie, I'm too old to be sitting on beaches in the dark,' said Larry. `Stay here and have another glass.'

`OK, we'll stay a bit longer, but I really feel we should join the others. What do the rest of you think?'

Di was happy to stay, but agreed that it looked a bit stand-offish, as did Pete. Don obviously felt a bit like Larry, but very co-operatively said that he would go along with the majority.

We went ashore and somebody gave us a beer and we chatted to some other people, hardly any of whom we knew. Later, we discovered that there had been a barbecue and a bit of bad feeling about the yachts that did not join in, so we were pleased that we had not upset anybody.

We were all up, somewhat blearily, at half past five to find a flat calm. Pete made breakfast and we were ready in good time, the RFA *Grey Rover* standing by to accompany us. Unfortunately, she sent up the flares to start before the Governor and therefore Craig, were even aboard. We got our anchor and waited for Di who had gone to fetch Craig off the beach. We were in hysterics, watching their efforts to return, Craig apparently finding that *Skip* handled rather differently from one of the sculls at Oxford. By the time the dinghy was on board, everyone else was off in a cloud of diesel smoke and, far from keeping together, they seemed to treat it as a race. Bearing in mind that it was meant to be a *sail* round, we eschewed the motor, pulling up the sails to drift gently along. As none of our crew seemed to be in a hurry, we ghosted down the sound waiting for the breeze, which filled in as usual a little after eight o'clock. For most of the way, we were convinced that we would not arrive in time and I was chagrined as I had looked forward to sailing in company and also to a party with our friends. Don, Dimax and Craig, their lives full of socialising and parties could not have cared less, although I guessed that Pete had been looking forward to the barbecue. But as usual, I was shouting before I was hurt, the breeze picked up and in spite of giving Di a sailing lesson, which she took to like a duck to water, we concentrated on getting everything we could from *Badger* and rejoiced to find we could almost lay up Port William. By half past two, we were coming in to anchor off the Public Jetty, an hour and a half late. Our three friends were all saying how much they had enjoyed it — the peace, the silence when there was hardly any wind and the boat had been gliding through the tranquil water, the excitement of the final sail up Port William — and I was delighted that they had all had such a memorable time.

Pete ferried people ashore while I made all shipshape and we found the party in *The Globe's* garden, in full swing when we arrived. Andrèz waved to us and we joined him.

`I was really annoyed the way everyone left you behind,' he remarked. `I'd hoped to sail, too, but the Governor had to be back for one o'clock, so I couldn't, but I don't know why everyone else was in such a hurry.'

`It doesn't matter. We had a nice sail and all our guests really enjoyed themselves, which was the main thing.'

Then Jon Clarke, the harbourmaster came to reassure us that someone had been keeping an eye on us by radar all the way. It was kind of him, but I suspect that he probably had felt that we could look after ourselves.

We were ravenous and attacked the chicken, sausages, chops, burgers et al with gusto. It was a wonderful party and we were astonished to find that everything was free. When it came on to rain, we all went into *The Globe* and continued eating, drinking and talking.

Larry was funny. Everyone had been making complimentary noises about our sailing all the way, and he perhaps felt that we had upstaged him in some way. He kept telling everyone that he had only used a tenth of a litre of diesel to motor round until Maxine said, `who cares, Larry?' and I, trying to stifle my giggles while smoothing his ruffled feathers, mendaciously declared that it was because the engine was so noisy that we used it so little. The bar extension ran out at four o'clock, which was a bit of a shame, as everyone was ready to carry on with the party, but we had to move *Badger* anyway. We were given a load of fish, left over from the barbecue, before we left. `It will only go to waste,' they said, but as it was, their generosity had been almost overwhelming.

The last evening in Stanley.

We returned to our spot off the Government Dock and sorted ourselves out. Still full, we took a walk, a final one, down to Moody Brook and came back home to listen to the Folk Show, have a sandwich and turn in.

Craig came round one last time to stay for supper and say good-bye, Andrèz and Ali gave us a calendar as a farewell gift and Dimax came to wish us well. We went to FIPAS to say good-bye to Larry, Maxine and Gary and to ask the *James Clark Ross* for an ice report. The mate told us that it seemed a bad year for ice: in November it was further north than he had ever known it, but had started to recede. It did not sound too promising, but Pete said that we could at least give it a try. Knowing that would be his reaction, I privately wondered why he had bothered to ask. The mate obviously thought that we were a little insane, but was too polite to say so.

We paid a final visit to Carl and Dianne. We talked about the sail round, of our plans and their plans, of places to go to and places we had been. Dianne had baked us a wonderful, rich fruit cake to take with us. It was late when we finally tore ourselves away, and the night was unbearably clear and lovely as we walked home.

We were almost ready to leave. There were some jobs to do, some last-minute provisions to get in, diesel and coal containers to fill to the brim. Worn out, our final evening was spent alone and we relaxed, listening to Stephen Palmer's *Variations*, in which he included several carols sung by the choristers in the chapel of King's College, Cambridge.

It was the fifteenth of December. Howie came round with the photographs he had taken at Lively and when we told him that we could not find the right fuel filter, went off to find us one, while the Customs man checked that we had not sold off our duty-free booze, so that I could then put it all away. Howie returned triumphantly waving the fuel filter and reluctantly allowed us to give him a cheque for it, which was never cashed. He gave us three Falkland Islands tea towels, to remind us of them.

We got in the big Luke anchor and took it apart: we should not need it until South Georgia, there would

Leaving the Falklands.

be no kelp in the South Orkneys, the pack ice would see to that. It was midday, everything had been found a home for, we had no deck cargo, all we needed to do was cast off. The wind had picked up to Force 6 and was still increasing. Should we go? But staying meant setting the big Luke again and anyway, had we not always reckoned on a `Stanley Harbour effect'? If it was too bad, we could go and anchor somewhere else.

It was heart-breaking to be leaving. We hoisted a few panels of each sail and I could hardly see for tears as we sped down the harbour. On the FIC jetty, several people were waving like fury; we waved back and, knowing they would be at home for lunch and watching, we waved at Carl and Dianne's house, too. As we sailed through the Narrows and bore away down Port William, Stanley disappeared from view. I looked back towards the Two Sisters, the gale and the whitecaps the same as they had been when I first viewed them with such apprehension over a year ago; now, I saw only beauty in the bleak, treeless and windswept scene. Pete squeezed my hand. Smiling, I wiped away my tears and looked out to sea, and as we sailed between Mengeary Point and Cape Pembroke, a pale beam of sunlight danced over the green sails and *Badger* turned her bows to the southern horizon.

Index